THE FUTURE OF THE PERSON

This book rigorously debates the notion of the person, a fundamental concept which underpins national private law orders worldwide.

In the 20th century, the unity of the person came under pressure – firstly through the rise of labour law and then secondly (post-World War II) through consumer law. The book moves this debate on, exploring the ongoing fragmentation of the concept of the person and the unique challenges that this gives rise to, and suggesting how this might impact on the future of private law. The book asks three questions:

- are the 'subject' of the 19th-century Codes or the 'person' of 20th-century constitutions useful categories of reference for the person?
- could fundamental rights, currently central to the notion of the person, be replaced by forms of the 'impersonal'?
- how, and why, should subjectivities be rethought in the age of infocracy and autocracies?

Thought-provoking and paradigm-shifting, this is a fascinating examination of the bedrock of private law.

The Future of Private Law

Series Editors
Marija Bartl, Anna Beckers, Simon Deakin, Daniel Markovits, and Hans-W. Micklitz

A new wave of scholarship is remaking and invigorating private law. Legal regimes that were long understood as invisible systems of technical rules governing purely private relations are being reconsidered in their social, economic, and political context. This scholarly trend interacts with three major developments in 20th century private law. First, private law itself has undergone a series of fundamental transformation. Openly public and political values were inserted into private law regimes both before and immediately after 1945, only to be rejected in favour of a purported re-privatisation of law and society alike in the heyday of neoliberalism. Neoliberalism itself is now subject to increasingly intense critique, under the mounting pressure of multiple social and environmental crises. Second, private law has had to respond to fundamental transformations in the global economy, which have simultaneously placed inherited legal orders under economic and political pressure, and denaturalized previously unquestioned doctrinal arrangements. And, third, private law has been challenged by the call for and recognition of legal pluralism as a constitutive feature of legal systems.

Legislatures and courts, responding to these forces, have relied on private law to achieve openly moral ends, such as social justice, gender and ethnic equality, and more recently, sustainability, climate change and intergenerational justice, as well as adaptation to a digitalized economy and society. Scholars have similarly begun to observe the regulatory character of private law, its connection to public values, and even its 'constitutionalisation'. These developments blur the boundaries between what has been perceived as the 'classical' private law of the nineteenth century and the new regulatory private law of the twentieth. Along the way, they are redefining the relation between private law, societal values, and political objectives. Even 'classical', formal, or, as it is sometimes labelled, 'neutral' private law, is becoming inflected with political objectives. The possibility that the basic concepts that traditional private law scholarship deploys could themselves be related to hegemonies based on race, gender, or class, or the outcome of colonial imaginaries and interests, only reinforces the importance of unmasking the supposedly neutral or technical quality of private law. All these developments suggest that private law will in the future become even more clearly interwoven with normative objectives and societal claims. The question of which values will infuse private law therefore becomes unavoidable.

Changes in the economic regime that private law governs – both domestically and at a global scale – are reinforcing the need for new approaches. Within countries, private actors (including civil society organisations, trade and industry groups, and even individual firms) have gained the power to influence law-making and legal enforcement, and to create their own regulatory orders. Private forms of rule-making and administration have therefore become a part of private law, both by constraining the state from making effective law, and by empowering non-state actors to use law as a tool for promoting private interests. Moreover, across countries, a liberal commercial order that once purported to separate international economic law from domestic private law has been displaced by a transnational commercial regime that openly confers on private law a central role in global economic arrangements. Digital technologies, and the new forms of regulation that they enable – including in particular data- and code-driven regimes that fuse legal regulation with technical infrastructure and interfaces – further reinforce these trends. These new forms of digital governance threaten the state's traditional monopoly over legal regulation, while breaking down the legal categories through which private law has traditionally constrained state over-reach. In short: non-state actors have increasingly used private law for their own increasingly political ends, and states have sought to shape nominally private economic arrangements in order to promote national economic and geopolitical interests. Critical legal scholarship is beginning to expose the ways in which these developments within private law are not simply failing to address inequalities of resources and power, but actively perpetuating them.

Such developments are not entirely new, but they were previously confined to the borders of private law. Now, under new conditions, they appear in a vivid and insistent light. Together, these developments demand a new orientation from private law and place private law scholarship at the centre of the broader development of legal thought. The objective of this series is to publish books that answer this call.

This objective requires the series to embrace a broad understanding of private law, which combines the traditional core of private law with regulatory private law and its interaction with international economic law and legal pluralism. Substantively, the series stresses the need to think through the future of private law and to understand anew its pillars, modules, and institutions, including its most fundamental conceptions of the person, contract, tort, and property. The series will also pay close regard to legal process, by attending to interactions among the several national private law orders and between domestic and transnational law. To this end it will aim to analyse the relationships among different levels of legislation and between law, private regulation and technology. It will also pay close attention to the way private law is made to work in practice through a variety of public and private enforcement mechanisms, on the part not just of the executive and judiciary, but via non-state actors.

Methodologically, the series is committed to exploring the breadth and depth of the challenges private law is facing from the perspective of multiple disciplines. We expect the series to reflect the growing debate about exactly what doctrinal method consists of, as part of which a comparison of legal methods with those of other disciplines is becoming increasingly necessary. Thus not just the paradigms of other disciplines in the human and social sciences, but the methods they typically employ, ranging from statistical and other quantitative approaches to the ethnographies used in fieldwork and the hermeneutic techniques employed in the analysis of texts, will be of interest. Contributions from scholars engaged in critical analysis of inequalities and power relations, associated with race, gender and class among other categories, are among those we particularly welcome, as are contributions from legal researchers engaging with the data sciences across a broad range of applications, including but not limited to those associated with artificial intelligence. Our hope for the series is that it will expand the boundaries of private law scholarship as conventionally understood, while retaining the coherence necessary for private law as both discipline and practice.

The Future of the Person

Edited by
Hans-W. Micklitz
and
Giuseppe Vettori

•HART•
OXFORD • LONDON • NEW YORK • NEW DELHI • SYDNEY

HART PUBLISHING

Bloomsbury Publishing Plc

Kemp House, Chawley Park, Cumnor Hill, Oxford, OX2 9PH, UK

1385 Broadway, New York, NY 10018, USA

Bloomsbury Publishing Ireland Limited, 29 Earlsfort Terrace, Dublin 2, D02 AY28, Ireland

HART PUBLISHING, the Hart/Stag logo, BLOOMSBURY and the Diana logo are trademarks of Bloomsbury Publishing Plc

First published in Great Britain 2025

A catalogue record for this book is available from the British Library.

A catalogue record for this book is available from the Library of Congress.

Library of Congress Control Number: 2024949370

ISBN: HB: 978-1-50998-272-1
ePDF: 978-1-50998-274-5
ePub: 978-1-50998-273-8

Typeset by Compuscript Ltd, Shannon

For product safety related questions contact productsafety@bloomsbury.com

To find out more about our authors and books visit www.hartpublishing.co.uk. Here you will find extracts, author information, details of forthcoming events and the option to sign up for our newsletters.

Contents

PART III
TECHNOLOGY

PART IV
SOCIETY, ECONOMY AND NATURE

List of Contributors

Guido Alpa, Professor of Private Law, Università La Sapienza, Rome

Anna Beckers, Professor of Private Law and Social Theory, Faculty of Law, Maastricht University, Maastricht University, Faculty of Law

Roger Brownsword, Professor of Law at King's College London and at Bournemouth University

Valentina Calderai, Professor of Comparative Private Law, Jean Monnet Chair 'Health Law and Development in the European Union, Università di Pisa Dipartimento di Giurisprudenza

Hanoch Dagan, Elizabeth J. Boalt Distinguished Professor of Law and Founding Director, Berkeley Center for Private Law Theory, University of California, Berkeley, School of Law

Avihay Dorfman Professor of Law, Tel Aviv University Faculty of Law

Muriel Fabre-Magnan, Professor of law at the University of Paris 1 (Panthéon-Sorbonne), Member of the Institut Universitaire de France

Pasquale Femia, Professor of Private Law, University of Salerno, Dipartimento di Scienze giuridiche

Martijn Hesselink, Professor of Transnational Law and Theory, European University Institute, Department of Law

Pia Letto-Vanamo, Professor emerita, Faculty of Law, University of Helsinki

Vanessa Mak, Professor of Civil Law, Leiden University, Leiden Law School

Mariasaria Maugeri, Professor of Private law, Department of Law, University of Catania

Hans-W. Micklitz, Part-time Professor of Economic Law, European University Institute, Florence

Giovanni Passagnoli, Rrofessor of Civil Law, Department of Law, University of Florence

Giorgio Resta, Professor of Comparative Law, Università di Roma 3

Antonio Punzi, Professor of Legal Theory, Department of Law, Luiss University, Rome

Vibe Ulfbek, Professor in Private Law, Faculty of Law, Centre of Private Governance (CEPRI), University of Copenhagen, Det Juridiske Fakultet

Michael Veale, Professor, Faculty of Laws, University College London and Fellow, Institute for Information Law, University of Amsterdam

Giuseppe Vettori, Professor (emeritus) of Private Law, University of Florence

Thomas Wilhelmsson, Chancellor (emeritus), Professor (emeritus) of civil and commercial law, University of Helsinki

1

Introduction

HANS-W. MICKLITZ AND GIUSEPPE VETTORI[1]

I. CONTEXT AND FOCUS OF THIS BOOK

ALL CONTRIBUTIONS TO this volume are based on a conference organised by the University of Florence in October 2022. The purpose of the conference was to initiate an intellectual debate on the notion and the concept of the person, which in turn underpins national private law orders around the world. In the twentieth century, the unity of the person came under pressure – first through the rise of labour law, then after the Second World War through consumer law. This twofold development has led to a never-ending debate on the concept of the worker and the consumer, with changing patterns and a growing diversity of the respective 'Leitbild', or image.

The conference sought to push the debate further, combining the fragmentation of the person already visible with a whole range of current challenges which must be put centre stage as a basis for opening new perspectives for the future of private law. Outside and beyond labour and consumer law, we identified the following issues to be discussed, though stress that these are certainly far from being complete:

- impact of constitutionalisation on private law and the potential constitutional constraints on redesigning the person;
- impact of private law beyond the state and the 'global citizen person';
- the impact of non-discrimination on private law as well as sex and gender as a societal construct;
- the impact of digitalisation of the economy and potential clash between the person as an individual and their alter ego in the net;
- human dignity and red lines;
- the impact of sustainability (UN Sustainable Development Goals) and the responsibilisation of private parties;

[1] Florence (June 2024). We would like to thank the head of department of University of Florence, Andrea Simoncini, for his support, Caterina Bresci for helping us in the formatting of the chapters and Christopher Goddard for transforming our European English into true English.

- the problematique of designing a new person and a new Leitbild (image) – the experience and lessons from fascism and communism;
- philosophical foundations of private law and a revised concept of the person;
- the autonomy of private law as a self-standing discipline';
- interpersonal justice as well as rights and duties/responsibilities;
- the impersonal and the status of the body;
- whether the person, power and law are three sides of the same coin;
- equality in the new millennium.

After the conference, and after having heard and read the contributions of our colleagues, we believe it is necessary to dwell on three aspects, or rather on three questions that have inspired our discussion:

(1) whether after the 'subject' of the nineteenth-century Codes and the 'person' of twentieth-century constitutions, is a social figure or figures, or do other categories of reference emerge that is/are useful for our work;
(2) whether the centrality of fundamental rights can be replaced by forms of the 'impersonal'; and
(3) how and why subjectivities must be rethought in the age of infocracy and autocracies.

II. THE ABSTRACT SUBJECT OF THE NINETEENTH CENTURY AND THE *HOMO DIGNUS* OF THE TWENTIETH CENTURY

The path from the subject to the person is well marked out at the beginning of this, the twenty-first century, following the constitutional system, reform of codes and the Charter of Fundamental Rights of the European Union, where diversity and self-determination come to the fore as values that complete the structure of the legal order.

The stages are well known. Dignity broadens the dialectic between formal and substantive equality, and brings out 'the material conditions of concrete persons'. Article 2 of the Italian Constitution incorporates rights and duties in the bond of inviolability and the bond of solidarity, while Article 32 of the same text ensures that 'the democratic sovereign renews the promise of intangibility of the individual sphere'. In 2010, the well-known Italian scholar Stefano Rodotà theorised a new social figure constructed by law. This is *homo dignus*, holder of inviolable rights and recipient of the promise of a life worth living thanks to the inviolability of the fundamental rights and subjective situations of every individual. It is difficult to say whether a different anthropological model has taken hold since the mid-2010s. Indeed, some observe that the story and the traditional function of the subject of law seem to have come to an end just when a category of great persuasive force would be of help to us in tackling today's problems: from protection against Big Data and AI, to guaranteeing the rights of future generations, to the issue of the environment and sustainability.

And so, we return to the question whether a foundation can still be found in the universal vocation of the person, which of course requires a global dimension, rendered ever more demanding in light of the critique raised against the foundational concepts of private law from scholars of the Global South. Duncan Kennedy breaks down legal thought into three historical phases: classical thought between the mid-nineteenth and early twentieth century, followed by social thought around the 1970s, and lastly contemporary thought. The shattering of the subject is largely the result of the sharp decline of the welfare state and is confirmed by the exponential growth of inequality in its various forms, which has reached intolerable levels. From here, three possible 'deconstructive' projects may be identified: the relaunching of distributive justice through new instruments; credible status on common goods in contrast to the subject–object dichotomy; and reflection on the non-subject in the various declinations of the philosophy of the impersonal. Since around the start of the new millennium, this is the path most frequently followed in part of philosophy and the history of ideas.

III. THE NON-SUBJECT

Personalism in the twentieth century affirmed the value of the human being in opposition to the various doctrines of the time (idealism, positivism, Marxism and existentialism), and must be conjugated in the plural because it has both a religious root (in patristics, scholasticism and humanism) and a secular root (renaissance, enlightenment, romantic) with a common trait throughout the century. Personalism affirms itself, in a recurring manner, whenever the person is at risk and flows, in the 1960s and 1970s, into a strong criticism of nihilism and relativism. For a clear reason: The person is more than the egocentric individual, is more than the totalitarian state, and is more than the massified consumer society: the person is a subject committed to the 'conquest of freedom'.

With radical adhesions and criticisms, Maritain's reflection occupies over 40 years of the twentieth century (1920s–1960s) with a vision aimed at enabling a reconciliation of pre-modern and modern, in what the one and the other have in common for a concrete defence of the human person in the different fields of knowing, acting and doing. Roberto Esposito in Italy and many others in Europe, between the end of the twentieth century and the current century, indicate a different path. Just a hint. The philosophy of the impersonal opposes both demolition of the concept of the person and restoration of its sacredness, with a clear vision. In all its expressions, modern personalism on the one hand distinguishes in the person a higher part 'of the rational or spiritual type' and a lower part 'driven into the regime of the object'. On the other, modern personalism considers the concept of the person capable of filling the gap between men/women and citizen, soul and body. However, with a strong contradiction, because such a concept is unable to recompose a gap that it produces, separating a rational zone and a biological dimension. Starting from the body instead of the person can (in certain cases) help to challenge the status of both and can favour a vision capable of affirming the unity of the living being – a unity expressed by the impersonal, precisely as a 'non-oppositional' theory, which does not annihilate the person but pushes the person out of its logical boundaries, the abstract and the ontological.

This is what is discussed in this volume on themes of identity and gender, on the incidence and role of AI, the consumer and the citizen, the legal person and the company – with one question: should we abandon the concept of the person that dominated the second half of the twentieth century, and are identification and guarantee of rights still a primary task of our work? Common to all authors is a rejection of rights proclaimed and denied in practice, promised but not implemented. For some, strong words still have a role to play. This is a masquerade, but it is also an ordering structure that supports and accompanies the value and legal relevance of the fundamental principles of equality, identity and dignity of every human being by bringing them to life. Established and guaranteed in history by the long march of rights. These issues are examined in depth in this volume. Just a nod to the present.

IV. THE SUBJECT AND THE PERSON IN THE TIME OF INFO-CRACY AND SELF-CRACIES

The history of domination has been described with different metaphors: Plato's Cave, Orwell's television set, the *homo videns*. Today, the surveillance of power takes place through data. The human being is a prisoner of information, but the digital prison is untransparent. The visibility of power is realised not through isolation but through connection. Humans, though, do not feel under surveillance but free. Freedom and equality coincide, even if our lives are subjected to psycho-political control of behaviour, through new means: Big Data and AI operate on the 'unconscious hidden behind the space of conscious action'. There is more: our emotions, captured by facial expressions, words and eye movements, are collected and a digital unconsciousness is formed, not yet ours, but anticipated and created by intelligent machines and capable of conditioning our desires and behaviour at a level below the threshold of consciousness. Rules exist at European level, as we shall see, but the remedies largely remain to be constructed.

What happens today in the face of the crisis of representation and the emergence of forms of autocracy can be described with a recent example. On 5 June 2023, a communiqué was issued on the publication of the ruling of the Court of Justice of the European Union against Poland, in a case brought by the European Commission. The Polish law of 2019 introduced two innovations:

- giving the Disciplinary Chamber of the Supreme Court, 'whose independence and impartiality are not guaranteed' the competence to decide on the status and functions of judges; and
- requiring judges to disclose information about their private activities, which is then published.

The CJEU confirmed its competence to assess the Member States' respect for the values and principles of the rule of law and ruled that the powers conferred on the

Polish Supreme Court are such that they limit the independence of judges and weaken the fundamental right to effective judicial protection, as provided for by the Treaties,

The consequences are clear. If power and law are two sides of the same coin, if law is politics but politics by other means, then protection of the individual and pluralism are closely connected, if not inseparable. The constitutional state rests on two pillars: solidarity as the political side of legislative power, committed to the realisation of a more just society; and the inviolability of rights, guaranteed by the Courts. This strong balance has ensured well-considered choices on some key problems of the subject. But much remains to be done, and requires a clear method. Pluralism and the structure of powers must be preserved and strengthened in the search for a polyphonic truth that is subject to constant revision and contamination, to find the most suitable solution appropriate to provide an answer to every problem of life. It is up to legal science, philosophy and the history of thought to watch over the maintenance of this operational value, which is always at risk because, as Norberto Bobbio observes, 'wherever power has been established, sooner or later it will show its demonic face'. A reflection on the future of the person, we believe, must above all take this into account.

Part I

Conceptual

2

Private Law and the Embedded Person

HANOCH DAGAN AND AVIHAY DORFMAN*

I. INTRODUCTION

PRIVATE LAW IS the law that governs our horizontal interactions in a variety of social settings – the market, the workplace, the neighbourhood, the road – where we encounter other persons in our capacity as persons rather than as citizens or co-citizens. Identifying the conception of the person that underlies or should underlie its prescriptions, therefore, is key to any viable account – explanatory, justificatory, or reformist – of private law. The conveners of our conference remind us that this is a challenging task for several reasons and, in what follows, we focus on the three that seem to us fundamental. The first and the one they most emphasise is the emergence of two robust bodies of law, one dealing with employment/labour contracts and the other with consumer contracts. The significance of these legal corpora, so they claim, is that the subject or the image of the person presumed in them differs from the canonical subject of private law. The two other reasons reflect the increasing impact of human rights law – notably, the idea that human dignity sets private law's 'red lines' as well as the prescription of non-discrimination – and the growth of private law interactions across borders, which purportedly put pressure on private law's 'unity of the person' idea.

Our conveners have apparently chosen to address these developments as a series of disparate challenges increasingly fragmenting the person of private law. Thus, in this view, the worker, the consumer, or the 'global citizen person' are the offspring of the traditional person of private law, and our task in this conference is to anticipate further variations likely to be added to this increasingly split and disharmonious field. And yet, against this trajectory of fragmentation that we consider briefly in section II, our conveners also hint – or at least this is how we read their synopsis – at an alternate way of facing these challenges, resting on the 'philosophical foundations of private

* Berkeley Law School and Tel-Aviv University Buchmann Faculty of Law, respectively, daganh@berkeley.edu; dorfman@tauex.tau.ac.il.

law' as 'a self-standing discipline', which implies a 'revised concept of the person' from within and offers a solid premise for 'interpersonal justice.'

According to the latter approach, the new developments may highlight previously discerned flaws in what conventional wisdom regards as the image of the person in private law, which triggered its rethinking. But although the role of these flaws in prompting the re-examination of private law may be causally important, this view argues it was normatively – and maybe also descriptively – required in any event, since the accepted view was neither conceptually/descriptively necessary nor normatively defensible. This is the approach we take in this chapter. Private law, we argue, is the law governing (and at times, indeed more often than usually appreciated, constructing) our horizontal, personal interactions in a variety of social settings. This means that private law is the law of the embedded person.[1]

This claim, which we present in section IV, needs to be contrasted first with three competing – and more familiar – views that identify 'private' with, respectively, the *dissociated person*, the *executive agent* and the *civic person*. The first view, which probably reflects the traditional account of private law's subjects, is associated with the strict (Kantian) division of institutional and moral labour between private law and public law. The second, antithetical view, underlies the – otherwise very different – positions of the economic analysis of law and the left-leaning critics of liberalism and legalism. Finally, the third approach to private law smooths the rough edges of the first view by insisting that, in a democracy, citizens cannot relinquish their civic duties even when interacting in their private capacity and, therefore, they must respect the human rights of others.

The critical examination of these three prevalent approaches in section III creates the normative space needed for elucidating our own competing understanding. Private law governs people who are embedded in their various interaction settings, implying they must not be approached as dissociated individuals. Moreover, private law neither reduces individuals to the role of executive agents of the state nor derives their mutual obligations from any civic duties they might (or not) owe to their compatriots.

The consumer and the worker may be the heroes of momentous developments in recent decades but they are not particularly special; they are no different, for example, from the neighbour or the pedestrian. The market, the workplace, the neighbourhood, the road – like many other social loci – are all partly constituted by the law governing our horizontal interactions, namely, private law. Private law is the law of the embedded person because it necessarily addresses the human condition of interdependence and the fact of personal differences that, as they should, affect the basic rules of human interaction. Moreover, many private law conceptions and doctrines not only respond to the social settings that their subject is embedded in, but proactively participate in the constitution of these settings. In the many settings where private law's doctrines are (at least partly) power-conferring rather than merely duty-imposing, the function of private law is both constructive and prospective.

[1] As we hint above and elaborate below, the embeddedness of the embedded person is by no means natural, inescapable, or deterministic. *Contra* MA Fineman, 'The Vulnerable Subject: Anchoring Equality in the Human Condition' (2008) 20 *Yale Journal of Law and Feminism* 1. Quite the contrary: it takes people's agency seriously and, at its best, enhances their autonomy and equal standing in relation to others.

Subjects of private law, then, act in a legally structured universe that turns them into embedded persons. The implication, we argue, is that a legitimate – let alone an appealing – private law should proactively seek to empower people's self-determination. Furthermore, it should construct these settings in compliance with the rule fitting the embedded person: reciprocal respect for self-determination and substantive equality, which we have termed relational justice.[2]

II. A FRAGMENTED PERSON?

But now we are getting ahead of ourselves, so let us retract and start with the possibility of a private law's fragmented person. This trajectory, writes Hans-W. Micklitz, emerges from the legislation of 'status-related rights', which 'introduces the distinction between the normal person and persons with particular rights', who, as noted, are the employee and the consumer: 'Labour law and consumer law are linked to the status of the employee and the status of the consumer and both legal fields put great emphasis on state interventions.'[3]

The employee is the beneficiary of the legal course followed in the first half of the twentieth century, when 'the social question' was confronted by legislating 'special private law rules and regulations' that 'were "outsourced" from the grand codifications' of Germany and France. They thus left intact the 'theoretical and ideological structure of the two civil codes,' so that 'Contract not status continued to govern private law relations.' A similar development took place in Europe regarding consumers after World War II when, 'Based on the experience in the shaping of labour law, urgent problems were delegated to special consumer protection legislation' typified by 'reversal of rule and exception [and] a rediscovery of the political in civil law'. Initially, consumer law remained 'an autonomous subject' that exists 'independently of the civil code', so that 'The basic structure of private law, based on contract instead of status, remained untouched.' But gradually, and in some cases (notably Germany's) quite grudgingly, consumer law was integrated into private law. To be sure, 'the concretization of the consumer as a legal subject [still] faces conceptual and theoretical difficulties', but 'What was at the time a rather revolutionary trisection of a status-based private law has become to a large extent reality.'[4]

Although this description is probably commonplace, we find it problematic. Consider first its implicit conceptions of status and contract. If this dichotomy rests on Henry Maine's famous discussion re the 'uniform' movement of 'progressive societies' towards contract, status is strictly understood as innate, comprehensive and inalienable,[5] a definition fitting neither employees nor consumers.[6] Even more

[2] See H Dagan and A Dorfman, 'Just Relationships' (2016) 116 *Columbia Law Review* 1395.

[3] HW Micklitz, 'Person, Civil Status and Private Law' in S Grundmann, HW Micklitz and M Renner (eds), *New Private Law Theory: A Pluralist Approach* (Cambridge, Cambridge University Press, 2021) 341, 354.

[4] ibid, 345–46, 355–57.

[5] HS Maine, *Ancient Law: Its Connection with the Early History of Society, and its Relation to Modern Ideas* (London, J.M. Dent & Sons Ltd, 1917) 99–100. See also CK Allen, 'Status and Capacity' (1930) 46 *LQR* 277, 286.

[6] See H Dagan and ES Scott, 'Reinterpreting the Status-Contract Divide: The Case of Fiduciaries' in PB Miller and AS Gold (eds), *Contract, Status, and Fiduciary* (Oxford, Oxford University Press, 2016) 51,

significant for our purposes is the understanding of contract that is implicit in this familiar account – a wholly open-ended, empty framework, indifferent to substantive inequality between the parties as well as to the identitarian nature of their relationships. This understanding may fit conceptions of contract grounded in the corrective justice view of private law as the bastion of reciprocal respect for independence (or negative liberty) and formal equality. Historically, it is associated with the will theory of contract and, in current scholarship, with the transfer theory of contract.[7] But as we show elsewhere in some detail, it hardly fits contemporary contract law.

Briefly, for contract to be an empty framework, *all* contractual obligations must be strictly grounded in explicit or implicit undertakings by the parties, but this picture is incompatible with the extensive default rules apparatus that typifies modern contract law. Similarly, strict adherence to corrective justice casts doubt on a significant subset of the canon of contract's justice-oriented rules, which go well beyond the demands of reciprocal respect for independence and formal equality. Consider, for example, law's deviations from the laissez-faire mode of regulating the parties' bargaining process, as in the expansion of the law of fraud beyond the traditional categories of misrepresentation and concealment to include affirmative duties of disclosure. Or modern rules dealing with unilateral mistakes, duress, anti-price-gouging, and unconscionability. Or key rules in the life of a contract epitomised by the duty of good faith and fair dealing, which shield the parties from the heightened interpersonal vulnerability engendered by contract performance and solidify a conception of contract as a cooperative venture.[8]

Therefore, the conventional description of work law or consumer law as exercises of 'state intervention' is deeply misleading. True, these doctrines set up the rules of the game in a specific social setting. But so do the specific rules that govern, for example, the tort responsibilities incumbent on owners of lands or cars, on sellers of goods, or providers of services. Both contract law and tort law prescribe, together with the residual rules applicable outside our familiar social categories, more particularised sets of rules that apply, and indeed regulate, these categories. Especially in liberal polities, these residual rules are critical as means for law to develop new categories and also as freestanding and thus not necessarily conventional interaction frameworks. But *both* the socially familiar and the more idiosyncratic settings do rely on a robust legal infrastructure[9] and, in both, law prescribes rules that do not merely abide by the parties' will or preserve their independence.

52–60; KI Schmidt, 'Henry Maine's 'Modern Law': From Status to Contract and Back Again?' (2017) 65 *American Journal of Comparative Law* 145, 166–67.

[7] See respectively, eg, D Ibbetson, *A Historical Introduction to the Law of Obligations* (Oxford, Oxford University Press, 2001) ch 12; P Benson, *Justice in Transactions: A Theory of Contract Law* (Cambridge MA, Harvard University Press, 2019).

[8] See H Dagan, 'Two Visions of Contract' (2021) 119 *Michigan Law Review* 1247; H Dagan, 'The Liberal Promise of Contract' in H Psarras and S Steel (eds), *Private Law and Practical Reason: Essays on John Gardner's Private Law Theory* (Oxford, Oxford University Press, 2023) 311, 315; H Dagan and A Dorfman, 'Justice in Contract' (2022) 67 *American Journal of Jurisprudence* 1; H Dagan and A Dorfman, 'Precontractual Justice' (2022) 28 *Legal Theory* 89.

[9] See H Dagan et al, 'The Law of the Market' (2020) 83 *Law and Contemporary Problems* 1.

This continuity between work law and consumer law on the one hand and residual (more typically called 'general') contract law[10] on the other implies not only that the story of gradual fragmentation misrepresents the role of law. It also suggests that this narrative relies on an inadequate image of the person – the 'normal person' – who is the main character of private law. This image, we suspect, is that of the 'dissociated' person at the focus of private law's traditional account. That traditional account is the particularly dominant view of private law, which resists the fragmentation of the image of the person at its center although, as noted, it is not the only one. In section III, we discuss three views of private law that reflect different conceptions of the person. While each one captures a major truth about private law, all are deeply problematic. Studying both the insights and pitfalls of these accounts of private law is intrinsically valuable and consequential for developing our own – the law of the embedded person.

III. THREE DISAPPOINTING ALTERNATIVES

A. Private Law and Dissociated Persons

The traditional account of private law, which Micklitz's narrative about the fragmentation of the person of private law presupposes, is most forcefully elaborated by the Kantian (and corrective justice) theories of the Toronto School of Private Law. This school deserves great credit for resisting the tendency of previous theorists to perceive private law as the continuation of public law by other means, an aim that was attained by highlighting the normative significance of private law's relational form. On this front, we join forces. What matters to us at this stage, however, is the substantive aspect of the Toronto School, which offers a clear articulation of the dissociated person as private law's main character. On that front, we part ways.

For Kantians, the interpersonal respect we owe one another as free and equal persons means respecting each other's *abstract* personalities. The 'particular features – desires, endowments, circumstances, and so on – that might distinguish one agent from another' are, as Ernest Weinrib claims, 'irrelevan[t]'.[11] By virtue of their capacity to set and pursue ends, private individuals are free to deploy their person and property without subordination to the choices of others. Private individuals, moreover, are equal by virtue of having this capacity. They are thus 'purposive beings who are not under duties to act for any purposes in particular, no matter how meritorious'; as such, they are subject to 'a system of negative duties of non-interference with the rights of others' – namely, private law.[12]

[10] On work law, see H Dagan and M Heller, 'Can Contract Emancipate? Contract Theory and the Law of Work' (2022) 23 *Theoretical Inquiries in Law*; on consumer law, see Dagan and Dorfman (n 8).
[11] EJ Weinrib, *The Idea of Private Law* (Cambridge MA, Harvard University Press, 1995) 82.
[12] EJ Weinrib, *Corrective Justice* (Oxford, Oxford University Press, 2012) 11.

Indeed, Kant's theory of private law builds exclusively on one underlying ideal: freedom cast in terms of 'independence from being constrained by another's choice'.[13] As Arthur Ripstein clarifies, independence implies that 'each person is entitled to be his or her own master … in the contrastive sense of not being subordinated to the choice of any other particular person.' Accordingly, independence requires that no one gets to tell you what purposes to pursue and, therefore, is 'not compromised if others decline to accommodate you'.[14] Quite the contrary: 'Because the fair terms of a bilateral interaction cannot be set on a unilateral basis, considerations whose justificatory force extends only to one party are inadmissible.'[15]

The principle of independence and, accordingly, the requirement that the terms of people's interactions manifest the formal equal independence of each interacting party, underlie modern Kantian accounts of private law's three building blocks: property, contracts and torts.[16] Yet, it is not solely Kantian. Alan Brudner, a modern Hegelian, refers to private law as the 'law for persons regarded as ends outside of human association – as morally self-sufficient atoms'.[17]

Similarly, a recent major book on private law by a Toronto School scholar – Peter Benson's *Justice in Transactions: A Theory of Contract Law* – celebrates a conception of 'juridical autonomy' which 'presupposes particular notions of freedom and equality specified in terms of the innate mutual independence of all persons in relation to others'. This conception emphatically excludes any reference to the parties' self-determination, namely, their 'forming and rationally pursuing a conception of their substantive good'. It likewise rejects any consideration of substantive equality, subscribing instead to a formal equality wherein 'the claims parties make in relation to each other must be absolutely the same'. In this view, then, contractual fairness has no business protecting particular categories of individuals, be they 'the economically or cognitively disadvantaged, the commercially inexperienced or the emotionally vulnerable', nor should it 'aim to redress differences in bargaining power per se or unfair and unequal starting points' or 'ensure the satisfaction of needs, however urgent'.[18]

This view of private law and its person is to be rejected on three types of grounds: descriptive, jurisprudential and normative. Descriptively, as we hope to have shown across a wide range of private law doctrines, *pace* the Toronto School, private law is committed to enhancing a capacious vision of autonomy rather than merely safeguarding independence. Indeed, it is not content with formal equality but aims at positively establishing substantive equality. Numerous doctrines of private law – including long-established common law rules that require potential tortfeasors to

[13] I Kant, *The Metaphysics of Morals* (Cambridge, Cambridge University Press, 1991) 63. See also A Ripstein, *Force and Freedom: Kant's Legal and Political Theory* (Cambridge MA, Harvard University Press, 2009) 35.

[14] Ripstein (n 13) 4, 14–45.

[15] Weinrib (n 12) 36.

[16] See Dagan and Dorfman (n 2) 1404–05.

[17] A Brudner, *The Unity of the Common Law*, 2nd edn (Oxford, Oxford University Press, 2013) 353. *cf* R Dworkin, *Law's Empire* (Cambridge MA, Harvard University Press, 1986) 296, 299 (claiming that, insofar as the conduct of private individuals is concerned, the liberal-egalitarian and libertarian conceptions of equality are similar).

[18] Benson (n 7) 188, 373, 388, 468–69. See also ibid 8, 24, 26–27, 186, 188, 352, 364, 367–69, 371–72, 377–78, 385, 387–88, 393–94, 396, 470.

accommodate the relevant constitutive features of their victims, help solve collective action problems, or oblige recipients of mistaken payments to reverse mistakes they are not responsible for – follow directly from the injunction of reciprocal respect for self-determination and substantive equality.[19] Excluding these rules from private law and renaming them as public law or regulatory interventions entails a vast excision, leaving little of what usually passes for private law as deserving this title.

But the problems with the traditional view are even deeper. Not only does modern private law have little in common with its imaginary counterpart and with the dissociated self at its centre. One profound difficulty relates to the role of law, which the Toronto School marginalises and indeed obscures. This jurisprudential point is crucial for our account of the embedded person and is discussed in section IV below. As for the normative pitfall of private law's traditional view, we deal with it here because of its embrace of the dissociated person.

A law of dissociated persons may be well-fitted to a world of (to use Brudner's words) morally self-sufficient atoms, but this only means it is ill-fitted to the social world as we know it. Consider two facts about our human condition – our interdependence and our differences. Both these facts indicate that the law governing our interpersonal relationships has profound implications for our ability to lead a successful life. They suggest that a law that authorises people to ignore others' right to self-determination and substantive equality dramatically – and indeed tragically – undervalues the significance of interpersonal relationships to our conceptions of the good life. They thus explain and indeed justify the expulsion of the dissociated person from modern private law.

Our practical affairs are deeply interdependent. They are replete with interactions with others that range from fairly trivial transactions to the most crucial relationships in our lives related to family, friends, work and positions we occupy in society. These interactions can be voluntary or involuntary. Thus, we invite others or are invited by others to join projects, be it because social interaction is critical to the project or because enlisting others is instrumentally helpful. Our projects could also affect the legitimate interests of others, including those beyond the privity of such joint endeavours. Indeed, the ability to lead one's life, and certainly to do so successfully, is influenced at almost every turn by both of these forms of interaction. Our conception of private law cannot renounce the responsibility of private law to facilitate these interactions lest it compromises the significance of interpersonal relationships in people's lives.

The significance of our standing vis-à-vis others also implies that the terms of interactions arising under conditions of interdependence should be assessed as just or unjust. Given that we all constitute our distinctive personhoods against the background of our peculiar circumstances, public law cannot be charged with sole responsibility for addressing our personal differences since private law cannot contend with the

[19] See Dagan and Dorfman (n 2) 1430–59. For contract, torts, property, and restitution, see respectively n 9 and accompanying text; A Dorfman, 'Relational Justice and Torts' in H Dagan and B Zipursky (eds), *Research Handbook on Private Law Theory* (Cheltenham Massachusetts, Edward Elgar Publishing, 2020) 321; H Dagan, *A Liberal Theory of Property* (Cambridge, Cambridge University Press, 2021) 131–46; H Dagan, 'Autonomy, Relational Justice, And Restitution' in E Banet et al (eds), *Research Handbook on Unjust Enrichment and Restitution* (Cheltenham-Massachusetts, Edward Elgar Publishing, 2020) 219.

requirement that people respect each other as independent and formally equal individuals. Indeed, quite the contrary. Given personal differences and the significance of interdependence, private law must not specify the terms of interpersonal interactions in complete disregard of people's circumstances and their constitutive choices. As opposed to brute preferences, these choices pertain to their ground projects insofar as they are crucial for the interacting parties' ability to act as self-determining agents.

Therefore, any polity that pays heed to people's rights to individual self-determination and substantive equality cannot approach these rights as irrelevant to our interpersonal relationships. These rights are crucial to both our horizontal and our vertical interactions, although they entail different implications for each of them. Since a just interpersonal relationship requires reciprocal respect for each party's claim to self-determination, a credible conception of interpersonal justice cannot be exhausted by the duty of non-interference. At times it may require law to proactively facilitate people's cooperative efforts and furthermore, it may impose certain affirmative duties of accommodation founded on such a robust notion of interpersonal respect.

B. Private Law and the State's Executive Agents

If the dissociated person is expected to see others merely as sources of normative constraints over her freedom to set and pursue ends, the executive agent is required to incorporate others' needs, preferences and interests into her ends as if they were her own. The executive agent is the hero of those who see private law as simply one possible form of public allocation and regulation –'public law in disguise'.[20] The person of private law in this view is thus no different from the duty-bearer in public law. Like the public official, the executive agent should act to further the public interest writ large.

Typically, the executive agent is implicit in views that perceive the division of labour between private and public law as purely conventional. Many of these views are espoused by critics of the traditional conception of private law, who perceive it as a sheer delegation of public power, a legitimating device that only serves to obscure law's many injustices.[21] But a similar – and in a sense clearer – approach characterises the economic analysis of law that, in many other contexts, is viewed as the nemesis of critical theory. As Alon Harel notes, law and economics theorists tend to be indifferent toward – if not impatient with – any effort to differentiate between private and public law. Their basic approach is that 'There is work to be done and it ought to be done in the best possible way', with the choice between private or public agents a 'pragmatic' one that 'depends on a comparison between the expected efficacy' of these possible agents 'in performing the job'.[22]

[20] L Green, 'Tort Law Public Law in Disguise' (1959) 38 *Texas Law Review* 1, 1–2.

[21] MJ Horwitz, 'The History of the Public/Private Distinction' (1982) 130 *University of Pennsylvania Law Review* 1423; D Kennedy, 'The Stages of the Decline of the Public/Private Distinction' (1982) 130 *University of Pennsylvania Law Review* 1349; A Freeman and E Mensch, 'The Public–Private Distinction in American Law and Life' (1987) 36 *Buffalo Law Review* 237.

[22] A Harel, 'Public and Private Law' in M Dubber and T Hörnle (eds), *The Oxford Handbook of Criminal Law* (Oxford, Oxford University Press, 2014) 1040, 1050–51.

On its face, presenting *homo economicus* as an executive agent seems confusing, if not ironic. Rather than pursuing everyone's interests, *homo economicus* is said to choose and behave *without* regard for anyone else's interests. But the *reason* for sanctioning (at times even valorising) this attitude, as Adam Smith and its other supporters tell us, is that people's rational pursuit of their subjective self-interest, narrowly defined, would yield the greatest good for the greatest number. The invisible hand is understood as a superior *social* mechanism of allocation given the expected failings of central planning, which faces unsurmountable difficulties in obtaining and processing pertinent information. The implication, however, is that all private law rights are necessarily contingent on a comparative institutional analysis. For lawyer economists, a market failure is often a valid reason for eliminating such rights. Similarly, new technologies that might eventually solve the epistemological and computational difficulties the market is supposed to overcome, could justify obliterating both property rights and freedom of contract.[23]

The resulting despotic world is reminiscent of familiar liberal lessons. Lawyer economists are right when joining critical thinkers who repudiate the dissociated person of traditional private law theory. But the idea that society should 'maximize the net balance of satisfaction taken over all of its members' conflates, as John Rawls famously argued, 'all persons into one through the imaginative acts of the impartial sympathetic spectator', and thus fails to 'take seriously the distinction between persons'.[24] People are not passive consumers or carriers of well-being, and their choices and interactions matter because they are part of their individual lives. Bundling people's property rights and their freedom of contract into one collective welfare package could lead to the nullification of their autonomy and dignity. The subjects of the canonical economic analysis of law are definitely executives, but not so definitely individual persons.[25]

This may explain why some versions of the economic analyses of private law can be read as grounded in a commitment to people's self-determination (although in most of them, this commitment is at best implicit[26]). A similar concern about effacing individuals while promoting the common good may likewise explain why some critics of the traditional conception of private law (at least those opposed to its sharp disjunction between the fundamental normative principles that apply to people and those that apply to institutions) do not dispute the distinction between our private and our collective responsibilities.[27]

[23] See H Dagan, 'Why Markets? Welfare, Autonomy, and The Just Society' (2019) 117 *Michigan Law Review* 1289, 1295–97.

[24] J Rawls, *A Theory of Justice*, revised edn, (Cambridge MA, Harvard University Press, 1999) 23–24.

[25] As the text implies, more modest versions of the economic analysis are not vulnerable to this critique and can, and indeed should, play an important role in legal theory. See H Dagan and R Kreitner, 'Economic Analysis *in* Law' (2021) 38 *Yale Journal on Regulation* 566.

[26] For an example where this commitment is explicit, see RE Scott, 'A Joint Maximization Theory of Contract and Regulation' in H Dagan and B Zipursky (eds), *Research Handbook on Private Law Theory* (Cheltenham Massachusetts, Edward Elgar Publishing, 2020) 22.

[27] See LB Murphy, 'Institutions and the Demands of Justice' (1998) 27 *Philosophy and Public Affairs* 251; GA Cohen, *Rescuing Justice & Equality* (London-Cambridge MA, Harvard University Press, 2008) 10, 375.

C. Private Law and the Good Citizen

This last observation brings us to the good citizens of private law who take these collective responsibilities seriously, as indeed they should according to Elizabeth Anderson, whose influential work on 'democratic equality' is often referred to as relational egalitarianism.[28] Egalitarianism, argues Anderson, requires private individuals to bear direct responsibility for realising the demands of justice given that they are citizens of a polity, and the democratic ideal covers not only political engagement (such as voting and protesting against the government) but also requires social relations of equality in and around the institutions of civil society (such as public accommodation and the workplace).[29] Thus, in her thorough analysis of racial segregation (including in the housing context), Anderson articulates a vision of social integration comprising the citizens of a democratic state, including its permanent residents.[30]

This shift, from the dissociated person of traditional private law to the civic person required to take responsibility for the justness of the polity she belongs to, closely aligns with the 'materialisation' path of European (especially German) private law, famously theorised by Jürgen Habermas. While traditional private law sought to guarantee the negative freedom of legal subjects, its application, according to Habermas, requires a more fundamental right – 'equal treatment according to norms that guarantee substantive legal equality'. It thus introduces 'a new category of basic rights grounding claims to a more just distribution of social wealth (and a more effective protection from socially produced dangers)'. But these basic rights also have a 'radiating effect' or 'third-party effect': they prompt changes 'in the classical areas of property law and contract law'. Thus, materialisation represents a 'paradigm shift' from a facilitative 'framework for private activity' that is 'limited only by the contingencies of the quasi-natural social situation' to 'the paternalistic provisions of a superior political will that, attempting to influence and shape these social contingencies, intervenes with the intention of enhancing the opportunities for an equal use of legal freedoms'.[31]

Like the two other approaches surveyed above, this civic understanding of the person of private law offers a noteworthy insight. Because all citizens, as Rawls argued, are duty-bound to support just institutions,[32] they may not always be exempted from this obligation even in their capacity as individuals.[33] This plausibly

[28] ES Anderson, 'What Is the Point of Equality?' (1999) 109 *Ethics* 287, 289. Another seminal piece is S Scheffler, 'What Is Egalitarianism?' (2003) 31 *Philosophy and Public Affairs* 5. See also K Lippert-Rasmussen, *Relational Egalitarianism: Living as Equals* (Cambridge, Cambridge University Press, 2018).

[29] Anderson (n 28) 317.

[30] See E Anderson, *The Imperative of Integration* (Princeton, Princeton University Press, 2010) 89, 94–95.

[31] J Habermas, *Between Facts and Norms: Contributions to a Discourse Theory of Law and Democracy* (Cambridge MA, The MIT Press, 1996) 391, 396–97, 400–03, 405–06. Habermas, to be sure, is critical of materialisation per se and suggests democracy as a redeeming approach,. ibid 398, 407–09, 426–28. But as we hint below (text accompanying n 35) we do not think that democracy alone can be the solution.

[32] See Rawls (n 25) 293–94.

[33] The republican ideal of law further demands from all members of the political community a measure of 'civic virtue' or 'good citizenship'. The republican tradition, according to Pettit, is 'primarily distinguished, not by its distinctive conception of liberty, and not by its image of the form that constitutionalism and democracy and regulation should take, but by its insistence on the need for civic virtue.' P Pettit, *Republicanism: A Theory of Freedom and Government* (Oxford, Oxford University Press, 1997) 245.

means that our vertical rights – the fundamental rights we hold vis-à-vis the state – may, legitimately, be slightly somewhat extended to the private sphere and invoked against private actors as well. But the civic person, though certainly to be welcomed into the drama of private law, cannot be its central figure.

One reason is that, although all citizens are subject to civic duties, introducing material justice into private law seems to impose the *disproportionate* burden of a *social* problem on a private actor whose negative (or republican) liberty is now constrained. The post-materialisation of private law, therefore, even if democratically prescribed,[34] directly confronts the core justificatory query of the law of our interpersonal relations: 'Why me?' Why should *I* incur a significantly higher burden than all others in the name of *social* justice?[35] The familiar answers are not always adequate since – barring a few exceptions – the duty-ower is not a public (or even a 'quasi' public) official and, in many cases, does not enjoy disproportionate market power or provide some essential good.[36]

Moreover, something is fundamentally troubling in the grounding of private law responsibilities in our civic capacity. A citizen-based duty owed to one's fellow citizens creates the false impression that the wrong done by private discrimination, for example, is fundamentally that of disrespecting another's privileged status of national citizenship (or, more broadly, membership in a political community). But the thought that this wrong is mediated by people's affiliation with a given polity or nation-state is counterintuitive. The persons of private law do not interact as citizens in (or permanent residents of) the state but as private individuals *simpliciter*.[37] A worker is not necessarily a member of the same polity as her employer, nor do consumer and producer/service-provider or, for that matter, pedestrian and driver, share membership in the same political community. These observations are not merely statistical or empirical but make a normative point: private law rights and duties are not grounded in citizenship or membership in a political community.

The difference between the civic person and the executive agent implies that supporters of the former do acknowledge that the rights and obligations of private law are neither dependent nor founded on the common good of the pertinent collective as such. Rather than rethinking the persons of private law from the exogenous perspective of the constitutional order to which they belong, then, we need to reimagine them within the most charitable interpretation of private law as a domain of interpersonal justice. This brings us – finally – to the embedded person: the hero of a

[34] The text should not be interpreted as degrading democratic prescriptions. Quite the contrary: it follows a happy conception of democracy that addresses people's right to justification – *cf* R Forst, *The Right to Justification: Elements of a Constructivist Theory of Justice* (New York, Columbia University Press, 2012) 188–228 – and thus refines its specific content in the pertinent (private law) context.

[35] See H Collins, 'The Challenge Presented by Fundamental Rights to Private Law' in K Barker et al (eds), *Private Law in the 21st Century* (London, Bloomsbury Publishing, 2017) 213, 223, 234–35.

[36] Compare T Khaitan, *A Theory of Discrimination Law* (Oxford, Oxford University Press, 2015) 201. For a more promising route, see J Thomas, *Public Rights, Private Relations* (Oxford, Oxford University Press, 2015). But the crucial step of Thomas's analysis implies that she ends up reinventing the embedded person of private law. See H Dagan and A Dorfman, 'Interpersonal Human Rights' (2018) 51 *Cornell International Law Journal* 361, 367–68 and fn 29.

[37] See H Dagan and A Dorfman, 'Justice in Private: Beyond the Rawlsian Framework' (2018) 37 *Law and Philosophy* 171, 185–86.

liberal (properly understood) private law, grounded in the relational justice maxim of reciprocal respect for self-determination and substantive equality.

IV. PRIVATE LAW'S EMBEDDED PERSON

We hope we have established that the three conceptions of the person of private law considered so far – the dissociated person, the executive agent and the civic person – are all unacceptable. Our critical analysis of these alternatives, however, yields important lessons. The major pitfall in viewing the person of private law as an executive agent or a citizen is that both these views discard a core insight of the traditional approach – private law deals with quotidian interpersonal interactions that neither need to implicate nor are tied to our capacities as citizens or to the normative (or other) well-being of the polity as a whole. The reverse side, of course, is that these approaches are correct in rejecting the indefensible account of private law's normative foundations endorsed by the traditional view. The moderate voices supporting the executive agent approach sensibly look for a middle ground between the unappealing ideal of formal freedom and equality and the despotic vision of full collectivisation. The civic person approach correctly insists that it is not enough for the state to respect its constituents as genuinely free and equal persons. A properly liberal polity must not abdicate its responsibility for ensuring people's substantive freedom and equality in civil society as well.

Is there a way out from this tragic choice between the traditional Scylla of a normatively objectionable private law and the Charybdis unacceptable alternative of fully subordinating the justice of private law to domestic constitutions or the public good? We think that the focus of private law on social (not civic) interactions can be preserved while discarding the disappointing normative commitments of the traditionalists' dissociated person. The key to the elucidation of this happy alternative lies in refining the continuity between the jurisprudential underpinnings of private law before and after the development of work law and consumer law as robust legal fields.

This continuity thesis, as noted, is by no means conventional. Indeed, quite the contrary. Recall, for example, Habermas's discussion of the materialisation process. Private law pre-materialisation, in his narrative, was a 'quasi-natural' bastion of negative liberty inhabited – exactly as imagined by traditionalists – by dissociated persons. Its normative rehabilitation, so the argument goes, was a 'paradigm shift', effectuated only thanks to the intervention of the state superimposing its paternalistic provisions.[38] Similar views on the workings of private law are widely shared among theorists. Thus, John Gardner claims that, like all law, private law's 'main point' is to help 'people to do what they ought to be doing anyway, quite apart from the law'. Tort law in this view is about enforcing such *pre-existing* norms of appropriate behaviour, even though law can improve things 'by rendering [them] more determinate'. Gardner argues the same applies to contracts, which 'exist apart from the law and are merely recognised and upheld (under limited circumstances) by the law'.[39]

[38] See text accompanying n 31.

[39] J Gardner, 'Dagan and Dorfman on the Value of Private Law' (2017) 117 *Columbia Law Review* 179, 193–94, 197–98. The exceptional case for Gardner is trust law, for it is a genuine creature of law (equity included).

But the radical understatement of private law's role in people's practical affairs advocated by Habermas, Gardner and like-minded theorists clashes with its particularly conspicuous role in its power-conferring sections. A good starting point when considering this issue, then, is HLA Hart's famous definition of power-conferring rules and institutions. As Hart notes, beside laws that 'impose duties or obligations' requiring 'persons to act in certain ways whether they wish to or not', other laws – Hart discussed contracts, wills and marriages – 'provide individuals with *facilities* for realizing their wishes, by conferring legal powers upon them to create, by certain specified procedures and subject to certain conditions, structures of rights and duties within the coercive framework of the law'.[40]

Thus, instantiating contract as a legal institution empowers people to solicit the commitments of other people, including total strangers, and insist on their performance even absent any detrimental reliance. Promisees enjoy this authority over promisors because once law renders certain types of promises enforceable, promisors are legally obligated to respect their contractual obligations and are subject to the coercive power of the law if they do not. As Hart implies, law's function here is both constructive and prospective. Contract law constructs promisees' authority: it prospectively sets up the rules of the contractual game wherein this authority is created and applied, and prescribes its proper scope as well as the limits of its power. This authority is not – at least should not be – obvious (recall that it applies even absent detrimental reliance). Rather, as one of us argues elsewhere, it is premised upon, and thus circumscribed by, contract's service to people's self-determination.[41] Property roughly shares, we think, the same conceptual structure.[42]

The significance of these power-conferring institutions for people's right to self-determination implies that any humanist polity has a compelling reason to instantiate them.[43] But both contract and property can take many forms, and an essential part of law's task in instantiating them is prescribing their constitutive *terms of interaction*. These terms are not limited to the ex-post response of private law to what parties in a particular interaction have done independently of it, nor do they replicate some 'quasi-natural' analogue. While people in both contract and property are vested with private normative powers, law not only prescribes what types of promises and what categories of resources are, respectively, proper objects of contracts and property. It also – and necessarily – sets up the rules that circumscribe the scope of promisees' and owners' authority and thus its limitations and qualifications.

The ambition of private law's terms of interaction, then, is both constructive and prospective. Terms of interaction construct edifices of human relationships and

[40] HLA Hart, *The Concept of Law* (Oxford, Oxford University Press, 1961) 27–28.

[41] See H Dagan and M Heller, 'Autonomy for Contract, Refined' (2021) 40 *Law and Philosophy* 213; H Dagan and M Heller, 'Choice Theory: A Restatement' in H Dagan and B Zipursky (eds), *Research Handbook on Private Law Theory* (Cheltenham Massachusetts, Edward Elgar Publishing, 2020) 112.

[42] See H Dagan, 'Liberal Property and the Power of Law. Response to a Critical Notice by James Penner' (2023) 36 *Canadian Journal of Law and Jurisprudence* 281; A Dorfman, 'When, and How, Does Property Matter?' (2022) 72 *University of Toronto Law Journal* 81.

[43] *cf* SV Shiffrin, 'Promising, Intimate Relationships, and Conventionalism' (2008) 117 *Philosophical Review* 481, 520. Put differently, the (properly liberal) ideas of private property and freedom of contract should be included in Rawls's list of social primary goods: goods that are supposed to be desired by every human being. *cf* Rawls (n 24) 92.

are not merely ad hoc encounters between, for example, this or that employer and employee, or seller and buyer. A constructive ambition of this sort entails a prospective one as well: private law's terms of interaction function as stage-setters, establishing preconditions for interpersonal transactions by dismantling certain entry and exit barriers, outlawing some forms of impermissible behaviour, and empowering parties to design their social and economic arrangements by forming rights and obligations.

In the vast areas of private law that, above all, are empowering, law *structures* our interpersonal interactions. This means that insisting that these structures should be just cannot plausibly be termed 'intervention'. The language of intervention is appropriate for law's work in *re*distributing wealth, resources or entitlements in order to correct deviations from distributive justice. By contrast, our private law rights *precede* any such intervention. If tax is law's primary *locus* of *redistribution*, private law is its main scene of *predistribution*.[44]

What about the duty-imposing sections of private law? Are not at least these sections shaped by 'the contingencies of the quasi-natural social situation', as Habermas and Gardner suggest? Some sections of tort law obviously are not since the aim of their duty-imposing rules is to vindicate people's contract and property rights, which means that they either piggyback on or participate in the construction of the pertinent terms of interaction.[45] But even the other (core) sections of tort law, which vindicate people's innate rights – say to their bodily integrity and good name – do not simply follow morality's pre-existing norms of appropriate behaviour. One key role of any tort duty is to delineate an arena of permissibility so that even risk-creators, who owe a duty of care, are *entitled* to place others in harm's way insofar as they are discharging the duty. More importantly, tort duties are often used to facilitate valuable activities, including by encouraging risky behaviour (say in the case of investigative journalism or the case of the business judgement rule).[46]

We all certainly share Gardner's intuition that what he calls 'raw morality' and 'raw moral rights and duties'[47] often provides a secure starting point. A critical contribution of law to morality, then, is to render an 'already-constitutive (set of) norms' more determinate.[48] Given that all private persons have basic rights to a good name and bodily integrity, core aspects of the rights protected by such torts as battery, defamation or negligence can be identified quite apart from the law, and yet they often require legal specification. But even regarding these rules, Gardner understates law's significance by eliding a vital distinction touching on the epistemic role of law in giving effect to moral duties. To say that law's added value applies only at the margins as if tort law were merely reporting what counts as wrongdoing is quite different from saying that law turns crude moral prescriptions into fully fleshed norms of respectful interactions. The distance between the moral requirement to refrain from punching

[44] *cf* E Jacobs, 'Everywhere and Nowhere: Politics in Capital in the Twenty-First Century' in H Boushey et al (eds), *After Piketty: The Agenda for Economics and Inequality* (Cambridge MA, Harvard University Press, 2017) 512, 515–18, 24–31.

[45] *cf* A Dorfman, *Conflict between Equals: Tort Law for a Liberal Society* (unpublished manuscript).

[46] ibid ch 5.

[47] J Gardner, 'What Is Tort Law For? Part II: The Place of Distributive Justice' in J Oberdiek (ed), *Philosophical Foundations of the Law of Torts* (Oxford, Oxford University Press, 2014) 335, 338–39.

[48] Gardner (n 39) 183.

someone's nose and the mature tort of battery, with all its doctrinal complexities, comes closer to the latter pole. And so does much of tort law. Tort law is often needed to decide what behaviour counts as appropriate interpersonal respect as well as whether victims have legal rights (and injurers correlated duties) to begin with.

Notice where we end up: private law, even in its most conventional rendition, is in the business of structuring our interpersonal interactions in the various settings where we encounter one another as private individuals. It sets the rules of the various games that constitute our social life. Although these rules can, they certainly need not follow the traditionalist-cum-Kantian mold of non-interference and, as noted, many of them do not. Indeed, given that the person of private law is embedded in *legally* structured frameworks, it seems incumbent upon the law to structure these frameworks by reference to a more normatively appealing lodestar.

As we hope to have clarified by now, we think that the maxim of relational justice, meaning reciprocal respect for self-determination and substantive equality, is the proper lodestar, and existing private law already responds to its prescriptions to a significant degree. We will not rehearse our normative defence of this maxim or elaborate on its interpretive credentials and reformist implications here. Three propositions, however, are central to our current attempt to elucidate private law's conception of the person and its significance.

First, the relational justice theory of private law offers a coherent framework that seamlessly integrates employment law, consumer law, and the like (eg, products liability law) into the fabric of private law, beside their long-established correlates. As we have recurrently emphasised, there is no principled distinction between the rules that prescribe the floor of legitimate interaction in these contexts and those that apply regarding car accidents or the sale of goods and services. In all these contexts, modern private law follows – and should where it does not – the implications of the maxim of relational justice for the typical interpersonal interaction in the social category at hand. Thus, to return to a challenge noted at the outset, the prohibition of private discrimination in the housing or employment markets relies on the very same normative infrastructure that guides the disclosure doctrine typical of modern private law.[49]

Second, this coherence of normative foundations of private law and of the image of the person it anticipates emerges from a proper appreciation of the role of law across these various subfields of private law. The person of private law is the embedded person because private law plays a significant role in structuring our horizontal interactions. This role implies that private law must not abdicate its responsibility for shaping the terms of these interactions in compliance with the most fundamental humanist commitment: to respect everyone's self-determination and substantive equality. Hence, before private law reaches out to public law for normative guidance based on some parties' civic obligations (or, in Habermas's words, before relying on the 'radiating effect' of the constitution and of human rights law) private law can, and should, rely on its indigenous normative resources: the normative commitments underlying private law as the law of the embedded person.

Therefore – and this is our final proposition – anti-discrimination rules and similar affirmative duties and burdens typical of the new chapters of modern private

[49] See respectively Dagan and Dorfman (n 2) 1438–42; Dagan and Dorfman (n 8) 112–15.

law can now be seen for what they are. Rather than external impositions or interventions, they are necessary developments of private law that bring it closer to its (implicit) normative DNA. These, then, are manifestations of the obligation of reasonable accommodation *integral* to the terms of interaction between, say, owners and promisees (eg, employers) and non-owners and promisors (eg, employees) simply as *private* individuals.[50] While the specific content of this obligation may depend on the background (public law) regime surrounding the parties' interactions, its normative underpinning is freestanding. These duties derive from the type of interaction at hand and, consequently, the identification of duty-owers is not arbitrary. In other words, our theory dismisses the difficulty posed by the 'Why me?' question in the civic-person account. Moreover, because duty-owers do not act as executive agents of the state or as its good citizens, their interpersonal responsibilities remain intact even if the parties do not belong to the same political community.

V. THE ROAD AHEAD

We conclude by alluding to two challenges confronting a private law determined to serve the embedded person. One challenge is institutional. Conventional approaches to private law – especially in common law jurisdictions – perceive adjudication as its essential home and, at times this is a duly hospitable setting for the complex task of fashioning the legal infrastructure of interpersonal relationships. In increasingly complex and interconnected social environments, however, adjudication often encounters significant limitations when handling private law's relational task of developing and enforcing a juridical infrastructure for the embedded person. The courts' *modus operandi* is *re*active and their perspective and information on key categories of relationships involving employers, landlords, banks and the like are framed by the specific disputes they encounter. In this light, expecting them to face these challenges on their own becomes an increasingly difficult task that may require private law to recruit an administrative apparatus, supplementing or even supplanting courts. Regulatory underpinning may be necessary to ensure the generality of legal prescription, maintain the required technological expertise for legal decision-making, and target systemic market failures. It may also be necessary to establish effective tools for proactive (as opposed to reactive) *ex ante* guarantees of just interpersonal relationships in various social settings and to ensure that they are sufficiently predictable to effectively guide people's behaviour as required by the rule of law. It is thus not surprising that significant parts of private law (properly understood) are already administered through regulatory agencies, which only emphasizes the need for private law theory to follow suit.[51]

[50] As the text implies, relational justice also offers an internal guide as to the scope of private responsibility: it must be consistent with the self-determination and equal standing of the person responsible. See Dagan and Dorfman (n 1) 1445.

[51] See H Dagan and R Kreitner, 'The Other Half of Regulatory Theory' (2020) 52 *Connecticut Law Review* 605. Needless to say, the institutional challenge is significantly magnified in transnational contexts. See Dagan and Dorfman (n 36) 382.

The second challenge also relates to the gap between law-in-action and legal theory. While most private law theories envision an actual person as their hero – the embedded person in this respect is no different from its dissociated, executive and civic counterparts – many parties to private law interactions are artificial persons, notably corporations. At times, this reality need not lead to many changes. For example, our relational justice theory of private law captures corporations inasmuch as they are duty-bound to interact respectfully with natural persons (eg, as sellers or employers). But cases involving corporations on both sides of the interaction as well as those involving duties of natural persons to corporations are more complicated. Indeed, a theory of incorporated persons that transcend their economic function is urgently required in private law theory. This truly awesome task, however, will wait for another day.

3

'Discourses Survive, Humans Die': Trans-subjective Rights

PASQUALE FEMIA

I. FROM 'SOMETHING' TO 'SOMEONE': NAMING AND WATCHING

THE GREEKS, NOT unlike other old religions (and modern), subjectified their gods. Although being a god-person in ancient Greece did not mean (nor does it still mean) having a personal life, a psyche and perhaps an unconscious,[1] divine anthropomorphism enabled the deification – better, the denaturalisation of Greek man.[2] Bringing gods closer to humans makes humans feel distinct from the reality surrounding them. The aspiration to the divine in human legitimises his position of dominance over reality; the subjectification of the divine constitutes the reification of the non-human, of Nature.

Naming has its pitfalls.[3] The named god speaks to us in a new way. And if this god is a goddess, her fundamental unknowability[4] slips from mystery to anguish. There was Gaea, the divine personification of Mother Earth; and there were the Greek normative deities, all female: Metis, Nemesis, Themis, Dike.[5] The feminine accentuates an original character of Greek religion: the Non-Human, the god who has a name and subjectivity, is a verb, is nothing but acting.[6]

[1] JP Vernant, 'Some Aspects of Personal Identity in Greek Religion' in JP Vernant, *Myth and Thought among the Greeks* (English trans) (New York, Zone Books, 2006) 353.

[2] WF Otto, *Theophania. Der Geist der altgriechischen Religion* (Hamburg, Rowohlt, 1959) 76–77.

[3] Parmenides, *Fragments*, 8, 50: 'Therewith I put a stop for you to my reliable discourse and thought about reality; from this point learn human beliefs, hearing the deceptive composition of my verse. For they resolved to name two Forms (of which it is wrong to name only one, wherein men have gone astray)' in AH Coxon and RD McKirahan (eds), *The Fragments of Parmenides: A Critical Text with Introduction, Translation, the Ancient Testimonia and a Commentary* (Las Vegas-Zurich-Athens, Parmenides Publishing, 2009) 80.

[4] N Loraux, 'What is a Goddess?' in P Schmitt Pantel (ed), *History of Women in the West*, vol I: *From Ancient Goddesses to Christian Saints* (English trans) (Cambridge Mass, Belknap Press, 1994) 11.

[5] G Scalera McClintok, 'Dalle personificazioni di Esiodo alla Thea di Parmenide. Considerazioni sul rapporto tra femminile e astratto' (2006) 28 *A.I.O.N.: Annali dell'Istituto Universitario Orientale di Napoli. Dipartimento di studi del mondo classico e del Mediterraneo antico: sezione filologico-letteraria* 25.

[6] C Kérényi, *Eleusis: Archetypal Image of Mother and Daughter* (Ralph Manheim tr) (Princeton, Princeton University Press, 2020) 27–28.

Naming 'God' a matrix of action transforms a verb in an *act-that-sees*: now God is watching you. In front of the climate crisis, Nature looks at you, not unlike the eye of the Law. Is this gaze its norm or its right? Does this gaze, the gaze of Someone, of a subject, compel us?

II. BECOMING A SUBJECT IN A COURTROOM

If a river becomes a person in a courtroom,[7] if a Constitution discusses (subjective) rights of nature, we must ask what are the political reasons for this linguistic turn.

The political purpose – which becomes legal *rationale* – of this conceptual game is merely to circumvent the insufficiency of public protection, hegemonised by global capitalist myopia. The subjective rights of non-human natural entities are thus merely a strategy to ground *someone's* claim that someone *else's* environmental behaviour conforms to.

Although we will shortly present an alternative proposal to the subjectivation method, two elements can be drawn from its path. First: subjectification of nature has a strictly remedial genealogy.[8] Second: subjectification implies a reaction to the inadequacies of public law in the forms of private law.

The subject of the claim, however, is not the claimant: nature is a subject who does not speak in judgement except through the mouth of someone else.[9] A natural person or group of natural persons, therefore, acts so that in the same trial their representative status, the subjectivity of the represented ecosystem (which should be the plaintiff in the judgement), and the wrongful act committed by the defendants are recognised.

So, a typical public law proceeding (establishment/recognition of an exponential body of a collective interest) has taken place in the forms of a private law damages trial.

III. STRUCTURAL WEAKNESS OF LONG-TERM INTERESTS IN ELECTORAL DEMOCRATIC SYSTEMS

The private law climate change litigation is a sign of the dissolution of the public–private paradigm, yet, even before that, of the need to provoke a structural change in the production forms of collective deliberation within democratic systems.

[7] R Míguez Núñez, *Le avventure del soggetto. Contributo teorico-comparativo sulle nuove forme di soggettività giuridica*, The Cardozo Electronic Law Bulletin Monograph Series (Milan-Udine, Mimesis, 2018) 111; Monterossi, *L'orizzonte intergenerazionale del diritto civile. Tutela, soggettività, azione*, Jura. Temi e problemi del diritto (Edizioni ETS, Pisa, 2020) 263; M Kramm 'When a River Becomes a Person' (2020) 21 *Journal of Human Development and Capabilities* 307; F Caroccia, 'Una personalità giuridica per le risorse naturali?' in F Politi and F Marinelli (eds), *Domini collettivi e risorse idriche* (Pacini, Pisa, 2022) 45.

[8] EL O'Donnell and J Talbot-Jones, 'Creating legal rights for rivers: lessons from Australia, New Zealand, and India' (2018) 23 *Ecology and Society* 7.

[9] CD Stone, *Should the Trees Have Standing? Law, Morality, and the Environment*, 3rd edn (New York, Oxford University Press, 2010) 70 (arguing that 'No litigation, of any sort, is going to have a major impact on climate policy – certainly not any suit on behalf of the "climate"' – Stone prefers diplomatic efforts).

Political representation mediated by elections – understood as an instrument that ensures the formation of the popular will in the form of parliamentary legislation – is a function that depends on the temporal structure of interest, on its measurability and, most of all, on the media visibility of the results achieved through the actions taken by the political decision-maker. Every political decision-maker (political party, institution, individual) is induced to direct the results of his initiative in order to achieve the highest possible consensus: he wants to win the next election, and he will do anything (anything that is lawful, hopefully) to win it. One can reply – and with very good reasons – that from an ethical-political point of view this is not only wrong, but also irrational, since it does not take into account the level of benefit of future populations;[10] however, it does remain empirically observable that political decisions are biased by the electoral cycle.[11]

Ensuring the effectiveness of fundamental rights prohibits settling for consolatory formulas (such as: 'it is exclusively up to parliament to make collective decisions'): a realist analysis of the functioning of legal systems reveals the slowness and difficulty of the penetration of the climate change discourses within political-governmental systems; and this governmental inertia reproduced itself on all levels, from the local to the global, from the regulatory choices of a small city council to the big decisions of international organisations, where unending obstacles and strategies of covert resistance by industrial and domestic lobbies are interposed. All this makes it necessary to distinguish between *electorally strong* and *weak* representativeness of collective interests. Long-term collective interests are each discursive aggregation of goals, values, reasons and strategies for which appreciable satisfaction can only be obtained over a period of time that is *not short* – such surely is the interest in climate justice, the observability of which crosses far more than the time scale of a generation. When the policymaker has to choose between increasing the distribution of wealth within the time leading up to the next electoral contest (short-term interest) or supporting a long-term collective justice interest, he or she will – in the vast majority of cases – give short-term interests far greater weight than they would have, if they were considered under an intergenerational veil of ignorance. The structural weakness of long-term collective interests is a consistent problem in contemporary democracies, exacerbated by the molecularisation of consensus formation through communication on social platforms. That structural deficiency in constitutional law is not easily overcome, but is remedied by enhancing the protection of electorally weak interests with the instruments of private law. The move towards forms of mass-tort litigation in climate change issues has thus gradually gathered strength as the instruments of politics and international law have missed their goal.

Any counter argument, aimed at preserving the monopoly of public power in climate protection (as of any other electorally weak collective interest), is based on an misleading image of how political-legal systems work. To deny the private subjective right to protect the climate would mean taking away from the community the direct power to act against ineffective legislative choices.

[10] D Parfit, 'Future People, the Non-Identity Problem, and Person-Affecting Principles' (2017) 45 *Philosophy & Public Affairs* 118.

[11] WD Nordhaus, 'The Political Business Cycle' (1975) 42 *The Review of Economic Studies* 169; E Dubois, 'Political business cycles 40 years after Nordhaus' (2016) 166 *Public Choice* 235.

But if there is a legal-political need to uphold private counter-rights in order to make the political process of enforcing fundamental rights effective, we must ask: what is the better strategy? Subjectifying natural resources, subjectifying future generations, or *trans-subjectifying* ourselves through our rights?

IV. AGENCY FOR MOTHER EARTH: CONTRASTING REPRESENTATIVE HEGEMONIES OVER SOCIAL DISCOURSES

The greater difficulty of the subjectification of the non-human is that it occasionally ends up attributing to plaintiffs victorious in court a full representative role, which very quickly occupies the entire discursive field, drying up democratic debate.

Subjectification of the non-human implies necessary representation. The judgement recognising/constituting the non-human subject works together with the constitutive proceeding of the power of representation.[12] In this way the 'violence of representation' is perpetuated.[13] In reality, to represent a non-human is to *assume control of a discursive center*, to increase one's personal power ('*I* (and not *you*!) speak for Mother Earth'), endangering the democratic composition of discursive forces. The representative by *res iudicata* of the Common Good could be now in a position to hand out patents of goodness, single out enemies, brand all dissent as betrayal of just cause. That is the fear: a closed class of Nature's professionals, like the '*antimafia*' professionals who disgusted the Italian writer Leonardo Sciascia, who saw in such a law-upholding agency more attachment to professional career than a desire to eliminate social evil, if not outright open hypocrisy:[14] '*We, the people* – but *it's me*, only I represent you all, that *We* is *my agency*, *your salvation is my representation*.' A Foucaultian pastoral power.[15]

Thus, the problem with non-human subjectivation is that it exacerbates the problem it would like to solve, ie the problem of human relationality with the environment, calling this relation trans-individuality or ego-altruism. Étienne Balibar proposed his 'trans-individual' as the intersection of imagination and reason.[16] The trans-individual is conceived as the continuous exchange of identity between individuals during the process of individuation. Individualising oneself, being singular, does not mean being closed objects against the outside; on the contrary: it means having a necessarily unstable balance, consisting of continuous exchanges with the outside. Individual is the one who exists because he continuously exchanges parts of himself with the outside; he loses them and receives them.

[12] The point is further explored, from the perspective of subjectification, by A Fischer-Lescano, 'Nature as a Legal Person: Proxy Constellations in Law' (2020) 32 *Law & Literature* 237 (but better understood from the original German: A Fischer-Lescano, 'Natur als Rechtsperson. Konstellationen der Stellvertretung im Recht' (2018) 29 *Zeitschrift für Umweltrecht* 205; Fischer-Lescano, 'Subjektlose Rechte' (2017) 50 *Kritische Justiz* 475.

[13] Fischer-Lescano, *Nature as a Legal* (n 12) 244–45.

[14] L Sciascia, 'I professionisti dell'antimafia' (1987) in L Sciascia, *Opere*, III *Inquisizioni, memorie, saggi*, vol 2: *Saggi letterari, storici, civili* (Adelphi, Milan, 2019) 1285.

[15] M Foucault, *Security, Territory, Population. Lectures at the Collège de France 1977–78* (English trans) (Michel Senellart, François Ewald, Alessandro Fontana, ed, Graham Burchell ed, New York, Palgrave MacMillan, 2007) 265–66.

[16] E Balibar, *Spinoza, the Transindividual* (Edinburgh, Edinburgh University Press, 2020) 137.

This theory is original, but its concept remains within the boundary of intersubjectivity: the exchange takes place between homogeneous entities, human beings. And with non-humans? Can one (if not exchange fragments of the Self with each other) come to a form of sharing with them? If we follow Alexandre Matheron's formula, *ego-altruism*, it makes it possible to think of hybridisation in the form of an agreement: ego-altruism reveals itself, when 'the desire to be is at the same time desire of agreement'.[17] What if, then, when the desire of being an agreement among humanity comes to be a desire for agreement with the whole world, even the non-human one? Here trans-subjectivity comes out of the inner traps of Husserlian intersubjectivity.

However, we need to go a step further, beyond the fiction of equalisation: man and non-human do not have to be fictitiously placed on the same plane of subjectivity, without any common point, without any element that acts as a channel for decoding regulatory needs: neither heritage nor psyche. To speak of a plant or mineral or cosmic psyche is, at least for now, a nonsense. An animal psyche is sensible, but inaccessible. What will be the point of contact between category and world?

That is why it is easier to leave humans not with the pride of domination, but with the burden of 'Nature's rights' discourse. Nature has no rights, but is a matrix of regulatory discourses. The subjectification of Nature is thus a discursive metaphor, a product of the human symbiosis between imagination and reason; a social discursive metaphor, not a legal technique, which that discourse must operationalise, that is, translate into repeatable and measurable procedures. The rules that humans produce by exchanging their identity, by metaphorically identifying Nature, are rules that produce for humans trans-subjective rights and obligations.

V. TRANS-SUBJECTIVE RIGHT: A RIGHT TO ACT *THROUGH HERSELF*

The key word is trans-subjectivity. The term is not quite original: it belongs to a vast constellation, from Gustav Radbruch's transpersonalism[18] to Gilbert Simodon's and Étienne Balibar's transindividualism.[19]

It is no coincidence that this word emerged in response to a very strong intellectual provocation, Christoph Menke's *Kritik der Rechte*. In a mightily dialectical framework, according to which the subjective rights legalised the vital moment by dissolving law from within, Menke's theory conjures up the concept of 'counter-rights', but does not elaborate them into operationalisable categories in applied law.[20] In the Bremen seminar devoted to the discussion of the book,[21] it occurred to both Gunther Teubner

[17] A Matheron, *Individu et communauté chez Spinoza* (1966) (Paris, Editions de Minuit, 1988) 266: 'Le désir d'être est en même temps désir d'accord.' .

[18] G Radbruch, *Rechtsphilosophie*, 4th edn (Erik Wolf ed, Stuttgart, Koehler, 1950) 151.

[19] G Simondon, *L'individuation psychique et collective: A la lumière des notions de forme, information, potentiel et métastabilité* (Paris, Aubier, 1989) 173.

[20] C Menke, *Critique of Right* (Christopher Turner tr, Cambridge, Polity Press, 2020) 276.

[21] A Fischer-Lescano, H Franzki and J Horst (eds), *Gegenrechte. Rechte jenseits des Subjekts* (Tübingen, Mohr Siebeck, 2018).

and myself (and without prior agreement),[22] to respond to the fruitful provocation of counter-rights with the assertion of trans-subjectivity.[23]

To understand what a trans-subjective right is, it is sufficient to ask this simple question: if 'commons' exist, what kind of *rights* are people *entitled to* when they act out a right *on their own behalf* but *for the benefit of all*?[24]

It is the subjective right of those who never act for themselves, but only for the benefit of a collective of which they are a part, within a collective regulatory discourse, without the place of a state public agency that expropriates citizens of the power to act for the collective. *The subject's action, the exercise of its right, does not return to the subject itself, but is inscribed in the common space of collective actions among which it blends*. It transits, moves from the subject to the common.

The subjectivity of the right-holder, according to private law, is historically linked to the subject's attribution of a patrimony: subjectivity and patrimoniality emerge in the same context. Man has a patrimony; the legal person (if does not resolve itself into a patrimony) also has a patrimony. But what do Nature, rivers, animals have? Facing nature each of us is provided with trans-subjective rights to activate protection discourses and active litigation.[25]

In this individual acting for the collective good, where does patrimony fit in? To whose benefit do the consequences of exercising a trans-subjective right fall? Before concluding that since trans-subjective rights are rights without patrimony, they would only be false rights (and, therefore, behind the appearance of private law, would only be the continuation of politics by other means), it is good to take a closer look at the relationship between patrimony and subject. We will conclude that the relation of those rights to the legal system is patrimonially incommensurable.

VI. NON-APPROPRIABILITY OF TRANS-SUBJECTIVE RIGHTS

Patrimony has been the measure of private subjectivity: every private law remedy has historically been legitimised to the extent that both the consequences of suing and, more importantly, the consequences of exercising the right (before and outside of trial) were consequences that can be appropriated by the person who is entitled. To *have a right* means to *have a right in one's patrimony*. But this consequence has

[22] Gunther Teubner did not take part, due to contingent personal difficulties, in the Bremen conference and unfortunately, unlike on other occasions, a preliminary dialogue among us on Menke was not possible. A dialogue that I missed very much.

[23] P Femia, 'Transsubjektive (Gegen)Rechte, oder die Notwendigkeit die Wolken in einen Sack zu fangen' and G Teubner, 'Zum transsubjektiven Potential subjektiver Rechte' in Fischer-Lescano et al (n 21) 343 and 357.

[24] P Femia, 'Il civile senso dell'autonomia' (2019) 25 *The Cardozo Electronic Law Bulletin* 1, 8–10; PL Portaluri, *La cambiale di Forsthoff. Creazionismo giurisprudenziale e diritto al giudice amministrativo* (Napoli, Edizioni Scientifiche Italiane, 2021) 159.

[25] V Conte, 'Per una teoria civilistica del danno climatico. Interessi non appropriativi, tecniche processuali per diritti trans-soggettivi, dimensione intergenerazionale dei diritti fondamentali' (2023) 58 *DPCE Online*, www.dpceonline.it/index.php/dpceonline/article/view/1912, §§ 4–5; M Zarro, *Danno da cambiamento climatico e funzione sociale della responsabilità civile* (Napoli, Edizioni Scientifiche Italiane, 2022) 206–30.

induced the patrimonial confinement of private law remedies and now thwarts the effectiveness of any right altruistically grounded in collective benefit. This does not imply the need to recognise rights without patrimony (since every social action – and the exercise of a right is always a socially relevant action – always has an economic-patrimonial structure), but rights in which *patrimony is solely and only an instrument of altruistic consumption* and therefore configures the trans-subjective right as a right that is not reducible to patrimony (*incommensurable*) and by definition unsuitable for increasing an individual patrimony (*non-appropriatable*).[26]

What transits through the subject to go beyond it is not merely movement, circulation, transfer of rights; it is essentially *non-appropriation.* Non-appropriability is not guaranteed by exclusion from commerce (technically: through rules of inalienability),[27] but through the inclusion of the protected good (environmental or natural or cultural) in a circuit of trans-subjective counter-rights operating in the market, in order to defend *within the* market and *from the* market the good being protected.

The novelty introduced by the trans-subjectivation of rights is that it is *within* the patrimonial system in order to *contrast it.* Patrimony (*das Vermögen*) has been the only universal communicative code of the operations of private law. Every tort results, when a specific form of reparation lacks, in the compensation of damages by means of monetary equivalent, albeit with a punitive function.[28]

This difference between infra- and trans-subjectivation must be closely analysed. The overcoming of subjective self-reference in the collective reference of individual action requires us to distinguish between the operation of subjectivation of the individual, of the legal person and trans-subjectivation. Subjectifying as a natural person, subjectifying as a legal person, trans-subjectifying are different operations: with the physical person, we recognise the naturalness of a human being's position in the legal system; with the legal person, we establish a collective action oriented to a purpose and patrimony as a single centre of imputation of rights and obligations; with trans-subjectivity, we shift the boundary of the right-holder's action from himself to the collectivity and the space of objectifications within which the regulatory discourse (which he articulates as one of multiple speakers within a discursive system) defines his operations as part of an environment.

These three such different forms cannot be understood under the same concept. Between human subject (natural person) and patrimonial aggregate subject (legal person) the differences are intuitively posited: anything that is not organic to the function of patrimonial subjectification is legally impossible (the legal person cannot marry, for example, but can have a patrimonial form of personality rights). The

[26] I owe this concept to P Napoli, 'Indisponibilité, service public, usage. Trois concepts fondamentaux pour le 'commun' et les 'biens communs' (2014) 27 *Tracés. Revue de sciences humaines* 211.

[27] MJ Radin, 'Market-Inalienability' (1987) 100 *Harvard Law Review* 1849.

[28] The antagonistic nature of trans-subjectivity, as the movement of the public into the private, is our major debt to the brilliant theory of Christoph Menke, who first posed the question of the dialectic within the legal form. His analysis moves strictly on a philosophical stage. However, transposing counter-right to legal theory and, above all, on a concrete trial before a judge, implies hard interactions with the (traditionally, but very well protected) opponent's rights, which, in a trial, nobody could simply philosophically 'overcome'.

qualitative difference between human subjectivation and trans-subjectivation, on the other hand, tends towards infinity, and the analogy that 'saves' the understanding of the operations of the legal person through similarity/dissimilarity with those of the natural person does not apply. A man has assets; a legal person (if it is not itself an asset) also has assets. But what about nature, rivers, animals? Their relationship with the legal system is patrimonially incommensurable.

VII. FROM RIGHTS WITHOUT SUBJECT TO RIGHTS '*THROUGH BUT BEYOND*' SUBJECT

And here is a story. Considering subjective right as interest, according to the 'infra-systemic revolution' conducted within the dogmatics of private law by Rudolf von Jhering,[29] had an important consequence: subjective right would become a form of social rationalisation of individual action. And as always happens when humans, once they have been personified, are reduced to discourses of legitimation (the *subject* becomes the *holder of* subjective rights): *discourses survive, humans die*.

At this point arises the problem of subjectless right. This is a creation of the patrimony as a set of potentialities attributed by objective law to those who can occupy them (patrimony, or *das Vermögen*, in German: and *mögen* (modal verb) – 'to will', 'power', 'desire', 'pleasure', 'have the desire to'). The shift from interest to purpose and to patrimony facing the problem of subjectivity and permanence of the right, when the subject is missing, becomes vividly evident in the *Notes* that two influential Italian jurists, Fadda and Bensa, wrote in the early twentieth century, commenting on Windscheid's *Pandects*:

> The law protects certain interests in view of a certain purpose [in Italian '*scopo*', in German: '*Zweck*']. Jhering's doctrine of the teleology of law is fertile with important results and is valuable in explaining many legal phenomena to us. Sometimes the interest is of the individual, sometimes it is collective with a more or less extensive character. But in either hypothesis decisive is the purpose. As long as this endures, the right cannot fail. When the quality of the holder is not intrinsically connected with the essence of the right, as in the rights that *personae cohaerent*, the purpose in the right does not fail merely because the subject fails. As a consequence there is the transmissibility of rights both in universal and in particular title. As long as the subject does not cast the right this subsists. *The individuality of the subject is indifferent*: the objective element is not changed by the mutation of the subject. Now if by law or by legal transaction ['*negozio giuridico*', '*Rechtsgeschäft*'] the right should revert to the benefit of a definite or determinable subject, who does not subsist or is not known at present, shall it be said, for that reason alone, that the right has ceased to exist? *The purpose has not ceased, the relation to a subject is there*: why should the existence of the right be truncated without waiting, that this subject exists and is known? It is a matter of expediency, to be decided by the lawmaker, to determine whether and to what extent the right can exert efficacy in spite of the present absence of the subject. Doctrine cannot in such cases, in order to save the wrong principle of the necessity of the subject,

[29] R von Jhering, *Geist des römischen Rechts auf den verschiedenen Stufen seiner Entwicklung*, III, 1 (Leipzig, Breitkopf und Härtel, 1865) 316–27.

> create fictional subjects. *We must take reality for what it is*, and recognize, that pending the subject the right can explicate its efficacy, albeit in a limited way.[30]

Jhering solved the problem in 1871 by postulating a 'passive side of the right': that side which remains, until the new incumbent takes over.[31] But soon the question enlarges itself, investing collective human actions, collective forms of association or enterprise. Is a corporation a *subject* or is *an asset*, through which individuals acted in a rationalised form, mediated by the patrimonial function? We know how the story turned out: the legal personality theory won out. Its great opponent was Alois von Brinz, who devoted immense energy to proving that we could not speak of legal personhood, but should speak of assets without subjects, of purpose assets (*Zweckvermögen*).[32]

Despite tenacity and some consensus, the subjectless patrimony theory lost and the legal person theory won. But here as never before *Graecia capta victorem cepit*: patrimonial rationalisation by means of a scope became the focus of all subsequent discussions on the relationship between contract and organisation in business corporations and in associational phenomena in general.[33]

Ernst Immanuel Bekker, linking to Brinz's theories, emphasised, as early as 1873, that the theory of purpose asset allowed for a *positive* understanding of *res extra commercium* (and not only a *negative* one, as things that cannot be exchanged).[34] The purpose became the qualifying element of the *res*, constituting its legal status. At this point, *res communes omnium* – we might add according to the current legal sensibility – became purpose assets, ie *non-appropriable purpose patrimonies*.

It would be simple, at this point, to draw the moral of the story. In the same way as the theory of subjectless assets, the theory of trans-subjectivity has value (at least so we hope) not only and not always if it succeeds in supplanting the theory of the subjectification of Nature, but only and only if it succeeds in imposing in the conduct referred to non-human entities the principles of democracy and non-appropriation: *This will be possible if the objectified appropriative patrimonial discursiveness is countered* – within the legal system – *by a dissemination of non-appropriative trans-subjective rights*. The pointillistic plurality of acts of their exercise will, in the long run, be the only remedy against hegemonies and in favour of democracy.

[30] C Fadda and PE Bensa, 'Note a Windscheid' in BJH Windscheid, *Diritto delle Pandette*, IV (Carlo Fadda Paolo and Emilio Bensa tr, Padua, UTET, 1925–1926), 238 (italics added). On this passage see the fine analysis of V Conte, 'Servitù su *res nullius* e a vantaggio di collettività indeterminate' (2022) 12 *Quaderni Lupiensi* 134–138.

[31] R von Jhering, 'Passive Wirkungen der Rechte. Ein Beitrag zur Theorie der Rechte' in CF von Gerber and R von Jhering (eds), *Jahrbücher für die Dogmatik des heutigen römischen und deutschen Privatrechts. Band 10* (Jena, Mauke, 1871) 387, 444–45.

[32] The definitive version of his thought (which runs in parallel with Jhering's investigations) is found in the second edition of his *Lehrbuch*, published posthumously: A von Brinz, *Lehrbuch der Pandekten*, III, 2, 1, *Das Zweckvermögen* (Erlangen et al, Deichert,1888) 453, 453–74.

[33] SJ Stoljar, *Groups and Entities. An Inquiry into Corporate Theory* (Canberra, Australian National University Press, 1973) 113 (sharing the concept of *Zweckvermögen*, but criticising the radical desubjectivation).

[34] EI Bekker, 'Zur Lehre von Rechtssubjekt: Genuss und Verfügung; Zwecksatzungen, Zweckvermögen und juristische Personen' in CF von Gerber and R von Jhering (eds), *Jahrbücher für die Dogmatik des heutigen römischen und deutschen Privatrechts. Band 12* (Jena, Mauke, 1873) 1, 132.

Economics has produced rights without the subject: ecology produces rights that go beyond it. Trans-subjective rights are the counter-rights against collective hypocrisy. As was said by Paolo Napoli in a different discussion, one has to go beyond the subject-person and, I would add, beyond the institution itself.[35]

VIII. RIGHTS THROUGH THEIR SUBJECTS BRUNS/JHERING

The exercise of the right does not return, to exhaustion, to the sphere of its holder's domain: this is the fundamental characteristic of the trans-subjective right.

However, this is not an absolute novelty.

In 1852 Jhering, in the first volume of the *Geist des römischen Rechts*, reasoned on the subject of *actio popularis*. Popular action enforces an individual subjective right that belongs to all, because it relates to a thing of all. *Res publica* thus does not mean 'owned by the State', but a common good, a 'particular relation of an undivided common right' (*eigenthümliches Verhältnis des ungetheilt-gemeinsamen Rechts*),[36] a *common undivided right secured by popular police.*

Here is what can be produced with this formula by Carl Georg Bruns in Holtzendorff's *Enzyklopädiae* (first edition, 1870):

> Individuals are thus in themselves the true bearers and organs of the ideal totality; their common will is certainly not the will of the individual, but it is valid as such insofar as it is only within the collective purpose and also insofar as no special representation is ordained. The totality and individuals are thus distinct persons, even though the former legally consists only of the latter. The relationship does not allow to be reduced to the usual legal categories of agency, community, power, etc., which are possible between individuals. The personification of the totality is thus not the formation of a new fictitious person alongside the physical person, but the unification of physical persons into a higher ideal personality, which, however, has its peculiar foundation precisely and only in the rights and interests of individual men.[37]

Acting for the totality without representation (agency): trans-subjective right is nothing more than the revival of ancient issues that now arise on a very different terrain of organisational experiences of public power.

But the last and profound word, in 1865, once again is from Jhering, in the very final pages of the third volume of his *Geist*, at the conclusion of a course of intellectual maturation. Subjective right opens to future generations who are protected by the individual initiative of living citizens:

> Just as the state, in guardianship, takes care of people who are unable to safeguard their rights on their own, just as the unborn are assured their share of their inheritance, so the state must take care of future generations and be vigilant that a selfish present does not

[35] P Napoli, 'L'istituzione oltre il soggetto-persona' (2017) 35 *Rivista critica del diritto privato* 451; X Chiaramonte, 'Instituting: A Legal Practice' (2022) 41 *HUMANA.MENTE Journal of Philosophical Studies* 1.

[36] R von Jhering, *Geist des römischen Rechts auf den verschiedenen Stufen seiner Entwicklung*, I (Leipzig, Breitkopf und Härtel, 1852) 187.

[37] CG Bruns, 'Das heutige Römische Recht' in F von Holtzendorff (ed), *Encyclopädie der Rechtswissenschaft*, Erster Theil: *Systematische Darstellung* (Leipzig, Dunker & Humblot, 1870) 247, 273.

> commit theft against them by alienating what is intended even for them from its purpose and consuming it only for its own ends. But on the other hand, if the living kind has a higher right than the unborn, if the necessity of the day raises a more urgent claim than having regard for the future, there may be cases in which that consumption or that change of purpose determination is entirely justified. This mediation between the interests and rights of generations: between the settled will of the past, the necessity of the present, and the expectancy of the future is a matter of higher historical justice, for which not the legal rule, but consciousness and free intuition shall put a stop – on this point the right passes to administration.[38]

A close reading of this passage (and its variants in later editions)[39] does not allow us to say that Jhering asserted the existence of a full and autonomous private subjective right of future generations, rather, he argues that the interests of the future must be protected against the selfishness of the present. Yet, we can think with Jhering beyond Jhering: if future generations have a protected interest against the present, one must postulate present remedy to protect the future. Future generations are protected by the subjective right thus devised against the present's stealing from them, but in so doing – and here Jhering's insight is more brilliant than ever – the law passes into administration. This does not mean that the protection of the future is reserved for administrative (public) law; but it does mean that the private activity of trans-subjective governance of the subjective rights of present private subjects, for the protection of *future* private subjects, cannot be carried out according to the winner-take-all logic of traditional appropriative private law.

Taking action to prevent the selfish present from stealing the future: trans-subjective rights are a collective law remedy activated in individual form, since and as long as no other better remedy realistically exists in the current legal system. Trans-subjective counter-rights are thus merely a reflex of the existing structural weakness of long-term interests in the political system hegemonised by electoral cycles. Trans-subjective rights therefore do not express a sovereign unity of political decision-making about the future of collectivities or generations; but constitute the present defence of a radical pluralism that cannot be dominated by anyone (and therefore cannot be planned from the top). Private old subjectification marked the expansion of the domain; trans-subjectification now signifies its dissemination.

IX. NO TRANS-SUBJECTIVITY WITHOUT CONFINEMENT. THE HETERO-DESTINATION OF COMPENSATION

Viewed from the perspective of the object of right the question is even more complex. *The object of the trans-subjective right is the application of a discursive fragment.* It is therefore not a right to the common good, but a right to apply a discursive fragment to the good. The trans-subjective right arises as an effect of the communicative circularity of regulatory discourses on the conservation of ecosystems. The right arises as a claim to the application of discourse confined to a clearly identifiable sphere of action.

[38] Jhering, *Geist*, III, 1 (n 29), s 338 (our translation).

[39] P Femia, *Sentimento e moltitudine* (Bologna, Il Mulino, 2024) § 52.

This point deserves further consideration: there is no trans-subjectivity without confinement. It is impossible to constitute a right to an exercise that goes through and beyond the subject (as trans-subjective rights do), if at the same time we do not define where this action intends to direct itself. Thus, compensation for violation of the trans-subjective right will always in favour of third parts (environmental associations, restorative activities, possibly established in the form of a trust) – *trans-subjectivity requires the hetero-destination of compensation for damages* – no private citizen can be allowed to enrich himself through the exercise of a judicial action aimed at the protection of a trans-subjective right. We could never sustain a legal system in which a *quisque de populo*, a private citizen, could act to demand the healthiness of the air for all and against all, or the preservation of all living species *uno actu*, with a single super-court's judgement, with a maxi-trial against Humanity in the name of Nature. Dissemination, non-appropriation of power, a pluralistic and even chaotic constellation of judicial remedies without individual enrichment, is private law's best contribution to the future of humanity.

X. THE DISCURSIVE MULTIVERSE OF TRANS-SUBJECTIVITY

We can conclude by situating the theory advanced here within a broader political view on the role of private law in the transnational context.[40]

A transnational theory of (trans)subjective right must deconstruct its appropriative power and construct its non-appropriative side. Subjective right is not the attribute of the power of the subject (instituted by Nature or Norm), but the power of the socialisation movement. Subjective right is not claim of domination asserted in court, but subjective precipitation (subjectification) of a universe within a discursive multiverse.

The legal system's response to this regulatory crisis through the entrusting of a deliberately unorganised myriad of micro-powers of intervention in the form of individual trans-subjective rights, aimed at counteracting the degradation of common goods, is a response that returns private law to its function as the 'school of political education of a people' – to borrow again a statement, taken this time from Rudolf von Jhering's *Struggle for Law*.[41] Even with all the historical distance between Jhering's model and current discourses on social (and societal) justice in private law, the trans-subjective position fits in with the awareness that 'private law plays an eminently societal role in the building of a legal order and a civil society beyond the nation-state'.[42]

With a quip – which has its own kernel of truth – one could, however, look to a less juridical authority, but one closer to the complexity of our time: to Gilles Deleuze's

[40] A Fischer-Lescano and G Teubner, 'Regime-Collisions: The Vain Search for Legal Unity in the Fragmentation of Global Law' (2004) 25 *Michigan Journal of International Law* 999; PS Berman, *Global Legal Pluralism: A Jurisprudence of Law beyond Borders* (Cambridge, Cambridge University Press, 2012) 25–57.

[41] R von Jhering, *The Struggle for Law* (John J Lalor tr, Chicago, Callaghan and Company, 1879) 93.

[42] HW Micklitz, *The Politics of Justice in European Private Law* (Cambridge, Cambridge University Press, 2018) 358.

great companion, Félix Guattari. He envisioned a molecular revolution,[43] a series of practices each of which, individually taken, does not reverse the cycle of hegemonies, but their flow, their aggregation in ever new ways, producing sensible and surprising results. Here, we could say that trans-subjective private law is a *droit privé guattari-enne*, a law in which subjective rights are multiple, unpredictable, changeable and even incoherent, so that no one can appropriate the regulatory discourse on the constitutive conditions of the reproduction of life.

A law that is not afraid to be imperfect and to fail – a law that works as an anti-paranoia of order and non-order, these obsessions of all Kelsenian producers of valid norms – is a condition that only genuinely democratic regimes can afford. Only in democracy can no value adopt the same appropriative attitude as the self-ish subject towards others; only in democracy can no value become an absolute principle (except, one likes to say, dignity: but dignity is the dream of the common good). Trans-subjective counter-rights lead us to travel freely in the infinite possibilities of social knowledge, to fractious hegemonies: a complex multiverse in which, 'with regard to the non-simplicity of the good there is a truth that we know but that we do not understand'.[44] The law, enlightened by knowledge, exists even against itself: 'Whoever says law (*das Gesetz*) says positing (*das Gesetzte*), and whoever says positing says "stop" and "decree," a thetic blow and a tragic denial.'[45] Law – the legal system – can never permanently deny tragedy. Reality and its painful becoming sooner or later reasserts their rights over law. Active human participation in the tragic course of becoming takes no other form than the assertion of subjective rights beyond the subject. The subject dies; its rights, transfigured and operating in trans-subjective discourses, never.

To love becoming is to love its constitutive unpredictability: we can only strive for becoming to be; not for it to have just the content we like. To act by oneself yet only for others, to act for all without claiming to have the power to be all, without claiming to be the sole voice of all, in a word, to act trans-subjectively: this is the only way, above all, not to transit through the nightmares of totalitarian reason.

[43] F Guattari, *Molecular Revolution: Psychiatry and Politics* (English trans) (Harmondsworth, Penguin Books, 1984) 268–72; but it is also possible to find the same sets of needs in very different contexts: see eg RH Weaver and DA Kysar, 'Courting Disaster: Climate Change and the Adjudication of Catastrophe' (2017) 93 *Notre Dame Law Review* 295; RB Siegel, 'Constitutional Culture, Social Movement Conflict and Constitutional Change: The Case of the de facto ERA. 2005–06 Brennan Center Symposium Lecture' (2006) 94 *California Law Review* 1323.

[44] R Schürmann, *Broken Hegemonies* (Reginald Lilly tr, Bloomington, Indiana University Press) 625.

[45] ibid.

4

Private Law Subjects in European Mini-publics

MARTIJN W HESSELINK*

I. INTRODUCTION

IN THIS CHAPTER, I explore viable roads towards a more radically democratic European private law.[1] In particular, I argue that European private law should 'catch the deliberative wave'.[2] To this end, I propose the introduction of deliberative citizens' assemblies and citizens' panels in the context of EU private law making, especially its reform.[3] My argument is grounded in the dialectic relationship between the private autonomy of persons as legal subjects (individual self-determination), and their public autonomy as citizens (collective self-determination). However, on the same grounds, I also caution against possible exclusionary effects of setting up mini-publics constituted through sortition, which could end up undermining both individual and collective self-determination.

The chapter is organised as follows: section II grounds the argument normatively in the moral status of each person as a justificatory equal. Then, it critically examines the current state of affairs of private law making in the EU (section III). Subsequently, it makes the core case for a radically democratic European private law more concrete by arguing that various recent democratic innovations, such as deliberative mini-publics, could and should be introduced also in the context of EU private law-making and – especially – its reform (section IV). Then, it goes on to caution against the possible exclusionary effects of deliberative assemblies constituted through sortition (section V). Finally, it undertakes a brief reality check (section VI).

* European University Institute, Florence. This chapter was previously published as an article in 22(4) *International Journal of Constitutional Law*.

[1] In the following, I will use 'EU private law', 'European private law', and 'EPL' interchangeably to refer to the private law of the European Union.

[2] OECD, 'Innovative citizen participation and new democratic institutions: catching the deliberative wave' (Paris, OECD Publishing, 2020).

[3] This chapter understands citizens in the wide non-formal sense of including residents, except when indicated otherwise.

II. THE PERSON AS A JUSTIFICATORY EQUAL

A. The Dialectics of Individual and Collective Self-determination

Private and public autonomy, individual and collective self-determination, stand in a dialectic relationship to one another. They mutually presuppose each other, are interdependent and give each other meaning. True private autonomy can exist only in a true democracy. The scope of private autonomy can legitimately be determined only through a properly democratic procedure. No one ought to be subject to a normative order of which they cannot meaningfully understand themselves to be a co-author, and this applies just as much to an order of private law as to any other legal order. Individual self-determination through autonomous private acts presupposes collective self-determination through autonomous public acts. There is no room for private law exceptionalism: private law, properly understood, is democratic at root.

To be sure, this is not an empirical or doctrinal claim. Not only does private law exist, are contracts enforced, and are property rights protected in authoritarian and other pre-, post- and sub-democratic regimes; so, too is the democratic grounding of private law systems in democratic societies often – perhaps even typically – little more than nominal. The claim is normative – in other words, partly counter-factual. The normative claim that individual and collective self-determination, properly understood, stand in a dialectic relationship has a long pedigree, running from Rousseau and Kant to Habermas and Forst. In the following, I will rely mostly on Rainer Forst's understanding of the dialectics of self-determination.[4]

On this neo-Kantian view, private autonomy and political autonomy have the same normative source: they co-originate in the moral right to justification, which entails for the legal-political context a right for each person not to be subjected to a legal-political order whose basic structure they can reasonably reject. The right to justification is grounded in a conception of persons as equal justificatory authorities. In other words, on this neo-Kantian view, the co-originality of private and public autonomy derives from the moral status of each person as a justificatory equal. Or, to put it differently, from the point of view of the moral conception the person as a justificatory equal, individual and collective self-determination (private and public autonomy) are two sides of the same coin.

The principle of justification reflexively demands the creation of practices of justification; and democracy in *the* political practice of justification.[5] It is not good enough merely to be provided with proper justifications. For, crucially, the right to

[4] See R Forst, 'The justification of basic rights: a discourse-theoretical approach' (2016) 45 *Netherlands Journal of Legal Philosophy* 7. Jürgen Habermas proposes the co-originality thesis in his reconstruction of the self-understanding of modern legal orders. This means that in his account the co-originality of private and public autonomy is not grounded – morally – in a moral conception of the person, but – between facts and norms – in a reconstructive conception of modern law (and hence of modernity). See J Habermas, *Between facts and norms: contributions to a discourse theory of law and democracy* (Cambridge MA, MIT Press, 1996) ch 3.

[5] R Forst, 'Legitimacy, democracy, and justice: on the reflexivity of normative orders' in R Forst, *Normativity and power: analyzing social orders of justification* (Oxford, Oxford University Press, 2017) 131–40, 135.

justification includes the right to be an agent of justification through democratic participation.[6]

B. Progress as Emancipation from Domination

In the following, I will refer to cases where a person is subjected to a normative order – in our case the European private law order – which cannot be justified towards them with reasonably non-rejectable reasons as instances of domination by (or through) that order – in our case European private law.[7] Thus, the conception of the person as a justificatory equal provides the basis for a conception of justice as non-domination (and of injustice as domination), where 'domination' refers to a normative order that cannot be justified with reasonably non-rejectable reasons, to be understood as reasons that are both reciprocal and general. 'Reciprocity' means that no one is allowed to claim privileges for themselves that they are not prepared to grant others as well (reciprocity of content) and that no one should project their own higher truths onto others (reciprocity of reasons). 'Generality' denotes that the point of view of no one subject to the normative order should be excluded from the justificatory discourse.[8]

The conception of justice as non-domination (and of domination as injustice) is fundamentally a relational conception. It is relational in the discourse-theoretical sense of justice as justifiability with reasonably non-rejectable reasons. To be justifiable, a normative order – including the order of European private law – must be justified dialogically, that is *horizontally*, by and towards those subject to it to one another. Moreover, as said, the approach is grounded in a moral conception of the person as a justificatory equal, which is already relational. The standing of equal justificatory authority is obtained through justification rather than postulated prior to justification.[9] The conception of justice as non-domination, in its turn, grounds an understanding of progress as emancipation from domination (and of emancipation from domination as progress).[10]

[6] R Forst, 'Justice, democracy and the right to justification: reflections on Jürgen Neyer's normative theory of the European Union' in D Kochenov, G de Búrca and A Williams (eds), *Europe's justice deficit?* (Oxford, Hart Publishing, 2015) ch 15, 229 (emphasis in original).

[7] See further, MW Hesselink, 'EU private law injustices' (2022) 41 *Yearbook of European Law* 1.

[8] See R Forst, *The Right to Justification: Elements of a Constructivist Theory of Justice* (New York, Columbia University Press, 2012).

[9] As such, the conception is more relational than 'relational' views grounded in *a priori* conceptions of the person, such as Ripstein's (Kantian metaphysical) innate right to freedom as independence and Dagan's and Dorfman's thick, ethical conception of the autonomous person. See, respectively, A Ripstein, *Force and freedom: Kant's Legal and Political Philosophy* (Cambridge MA, Harvard University Press, 2009) Appendix: 'A postulate incapable of further proof'; and H Dagan and A Dorfman, 'Just relationships' (2016) 116 *Columbia Law Review* 1395. *cf* R Forst, 'The constitution of justification: replies and comments' in E Herlin-Karnell, M Klatt and HA Morales-Zúñiga (eds), *Constitutionalism justified: Rainer Forst in discourse* (New York, Oxford University Press, 2020) 295, esp 296–302, with specific reference to Ripstein.

[10] On progress in European contract law, see MW Hesselink, 'Progress in EU contract law' (2022) 18 *European Review of Contract Law* 281. More generally, see R Forst, 'The Justification of Progress and the Progress of Justification' in A Allen and E Mendieta (eds), *Justification and emancipation: the critical theory of Rainer Forst* (University Park, Pennsylvania State University Press, 2019) 17.

C. Responsibility for Democratic Exclusion

Autonomy comes with responsibility. Indeed, autonomy means taking responsibility. Thus, political autonomy implies political responsibility. And collective self-determination comes with collective responsibility, first and foremost collective political responsibility for non-domination. Those who set up a normative order, or exercise power within an existing one, are collectively responsible for ensuring that this order is a non-dominating order. For a legal order, including the order of European private law, this means that those who exclude certain social groups from having equal influence on law-making are responsible for the democratic exclusion. That is, they are responsible for undermining or removing the political autonomy and the right to collective self-determination from individuals belonging to groups whose social subordination is produced, reproduced, and reinforced through legislative, judicial or expert domination.[11]

D. Moral and Epistemic Authority

The argument for a radically democratic European private law proposed here is, thus, grounded in the moral conception of the individual person as an equal justificatory authority and in each person's moral right not to be subjected to a normative order of which they cannot reasonably consider themselves a co-author. This argument is distinct from another argument for democratic law-making which is grounded in citizens' collective epistemic authority. That argument is based on an understanding of democratic law that is both instrumentalist and collectivist. On that view, the aim of democratic deliberation is to achieve better outcomes,[12] or to get closer to the correct answer to political questions.[13] Thus, the significance of human persons is reduced to their statistical representativeness. To put it in Kantian terms, epistemic democrats see citizens merely as means, not also as ends in themselves. Or, to adapt Rawls's phrase, epistemic democrats neglect the separateness of persons.[14] As we will see, this point is crucial, especially when it comes to the justification and proper role of deliberative assemblies based on sortition (lottery). In short, on the view defended here even full representativeness of such a lottery-based assembly is neither a sufficient nor a necessary condition for democratic legitimacy. The practical upshot is that even an ideal mini-public, ie a perfect statistical sample of the general public, can never replace representative democracy, only improve its functioning and complement it.[15] Radical democracy must remain rooted in the political

[11] For a critique of judicial and expert domination in European private law, see Hesselink (n 7) esp sections III.B and III.C.

[12] See eg OECD (n 2) 16.

[13] See H Landemore, *Democratic Reason: Politics, Collective Intelligence, and the Rule of the Many* (Princeton, Princeton University Press, 2013).

[14] See J Rawls, *A Theory of Justice* (Cambridge, Massachusetts, Belknap, 1999) 24 (with reference to utilitarianism).

[15] For eight models for institutionalising deliberative bodies, such as citizens' assemblies, juries, and panels, see OECD, 'Eight ways to institutionalise deliberative democracy' OECD Public Governance Policy Papers 12 (Paris, OECD Publishing, 2021).

autonomy and agency of the person. No one should be subject to laws – in our case European private laws – made by others.

III. COLLECTIVE PRIVATE LAW SELF-DETERMINATION IN THE EU TODAY

After having discussed how the right to a radically democratic private law is morally grounded, it is now time to turn to what this means in practice. Before considering possible avenues for change, I will start from the here and now, with a brief diagnosis of real existing EPL democracy. What is the state of play when it comes to the person as a co-author of EU private law?

A. Representative Democracy

Most of EU private law consists of directives and regulations. These come about nowadays through the ordinary legislative procedure, which means that they are adopted by the European Parliament and the Council jointly on a proposal from the Commission.[16] In other words, just like the Union in general so too is the EU private law *acquis* grounded in the principle of representative democracy.[17] Citizens are represented both directly, as EU citizens, in the European Parliament, and indirectly, as national citizens, in the Council by their national governments which are accountable to their national parliaments.[18] This means that EU citizens get to express their views once every five years in European Parliament elections,[19] and with a similar frequency in national elections. European elections have the well-known and often criticised democratic flaw of lacking pan-European electoral lists of candidates and EU-wide campaigns, which has had a distinctly depoliticising effect. So far, European private law has never played any role as a theme in European Parliament election campaigns.[20] In national elections, the responsibilities of national governments as European co-legislators are usually not considered at all, let alone specifically for European private law.

Thus, in practice the democratic legitimacy of European private law through representative democracy is formal (ie nominal) at best. At best, because much of EU private law making de facto does not even occur through representative democracy at all, not even nominally. This is because a significant part of EU private law is made de facto by the Court of Justice of the European Union, which has taken a rather active role in shaping the private law of the EU, which frequently turns into outright activism (as opposed to deference towards elected legislatures).

[16] See Consolidated Version of the Treaty on the Functioning of the European Union [2012] OJ C 326, Art 289.

[17] See Consolidated Version of the Treaty on European Union [2008] OJ C115/13, Art 10(1).

[18] See EU Treaty, Art 10(2).

[19] EU Treaty Art 14(3).

[20] For a failed attempt to introduce the subject into the debates preceding the 2004 European Parliament elections, see MW Hesselink, 'Europese verkiezingen moeten over Europees Burgerlijk Wetboek gaan' (2004) *Nederlands Juristenblad* 1769.

B. The Public Sphere

i. Public Autonomy and Public Sphere

Another institution crucial for ensuring the political autonomy of the person understood as political agency through collective self-determination, and in a deliberative understanding of democracy at least as important as the formal law-making process, is the informal public sphere, where individuals and groups can make a substantive impact on the opinion and will formation that both precedes and follows formal law making.[21] Through the confrontation of different information claims, opinions and ideas in the public sphere citizens collectively gain clarity about their (respective or shared) interests, needs, preferences and rights, as well as about the likely consequences and risks of different political decisions. A functioning public sphere is equally open to everyone, and enables for each citizen, including those at the periphery of society, an equal possibility to influence the political decision- and law-making at its centre.

Of course, this is a highly idealised – ie largely counterfactual – image of the public sphere. As Nancy Fraser has pointed out, 'deliberation can serve as a mask for domination'.[22] In reality, deliberation in the public sphere is often dominated by illegitimate power, which frequently is structural. Think only of the illegitimate hierarchies following from economic, gender, racial and class oppression. Indeed, the actual public sphere is constituted for an important part by what cannot be said,[23] and by what is arbitrarily granted a lower authority.[24] In other words, the real existing public sphere often remains largely a forum of privilege. For this reason, at least in a non-ideal society (such as the European one), where structural social inequalities not only exist but are on the rise, counter-publics are not merely acceptable but also necessary.[25]

Yet, the idea of a healthy public sphere serves as a crucial indicator in a substantive diagnosis of the state of our democracies and can serve in pointing to specific pathologies, in particular exclusions and inequalities. For, the more there exists a realistic opportunity for the unforced force of arguments from the periphery to prevail in political debates and have a decisive impact on law-making at the political centre, the more political autonomy is ensured, and the less citizens are dominated by laws made by others. And vice versa: the more deliberation in the public sphere serves as a mask of domination and exclusion, the less do citizens respect each other as equal normative authorities. What is the state of the European public sphere?

[21] See Habermas (n 4) ch 8; N Fraser, 'Transnationalizing the Public Sphere: on the Legitimacy and Efficacy of Public Opinion in a Postwestphalian World' in N Fraser, *Scales of Justice: Reimagining Political Space in a Globalizing World* (New York, Columbia University Press, 2009) 76; R Forst, 'The Rule of Reasons: Three Models of Deliberative Democracy' (2001) 14 *Ratio Juris* 345. On public sphere and private law, see also MW Hesselink, *Justifying Contract in Europe: Political Philosophies of European Contract Law* (Oxford, Oxford University Press, 2021) 128–32.

[22] N Fraser, 'Rethinking the Public Sphere: A Contribution to the Critique of Actually Existing Democracy' (1990) *Social Text* 56, 64.

[23] J Butler, *Precarious Life: The Powers of Mourning and Violence* (London, Verso, 2004) xvii.

[24] M Fricker, *Epistemic Injustice: Power and the Ethics of Knowing* (Oxford, Oxford University Press, 2007).

[25] Fraser (n 22) 67.

ii. The State of the European Public Sphere

Notoriously, the public sphere in the EU has been fragmented and compartmentalised along national (or at least linguistic) lines to the point that it has been questioned whether we can properly speak of a truly transnational European public sphere. In particular, it seems implausible to speak of any existing EU-wide political opinion- and will-formation on most issues, including European private law. Things could be changing today because of the increasing transnationalisation of communication through social media and the Internet, where especially the younger generation and the elite engage in transnational exchanges – increasingly in English – of information, ideas and opinions.

However, the transnationalisation of the public sphere through social media does not seem to make the public sphere become any less fragmented, indeed rather more so, albeit along different lines. This is so because exchanges on social media, even when transnational, tend to take place in bubbles, which often serve as echo chambers. And when impervious to views that the members of groups do not already share, then, even though formally accessible to anyone, in practice they often remain at best half-public opinions in a half-public sphere.[26] Another reason for concern about the transnational public sphere derives from the ever further reaching commodification of information. To be sure, newspapers have always been sold on a commercial basis. However, much of the information available on the Internet today is produced with the exclusive motivation of profit. As Habermas points out, this has made online information (as well as offline sources that try to compete) subject to product quality standards (entertainment) rather than to the epistemic standards prevailing in journalism (verifiability).[27] The commodification of information means a shift in the news media's understanding of their public from citizens to consumers.[28] Finally, the anarchic and emancipatory promises of the Internet, where the unforced force of the better argument could prevail, is rapidly being replaced by domination through algorithms. These developments seem particularly worrying for the transnational public sphere, which, even more than the local ones, depends on digital information and communication rather than on face-to-face encounters.

iii. Domination in the Specialised EPL Sphere

In addition to the general public sphere, there exist also functionally differentiated specialised public spheres. While specialised public spheres are not problematic per se, from the point of view of political autonomy as collective self-determination it is crucial that they remain easily accessible to members of the general public. Specialised public spheres should not turn into gated communities of experts.

For European private law, Micklitz and Svetiev have shown the existence of hyper-specialised publics composed exclusively of sectoral technical experts in specific

[26] See the recent diagnosis by J Habermas, *Ein neuer Strukturwandel der Öffentlichkeit und die deliberative Politik* (Berlin, Suhrkamp, 2022) 61.

[27] bid 63, 66.

[28] ibid 57.

economic sectors, such as finance, energy, transport or food, which deliberate and set regulatory standards – usually a mix of private and public – with a varying regulatory impact on private relationships.[29] These 'regulatory silos', as Micklitz and Svetiev call them, have played a crucial role in shaping European regulatory private law. They also recall almost literally the 'discursive enclaves', which Nancy Fraser denounced, where a very limited set of persons and their concerns are admitted to the deliberation, and where there is no room for public contestation.[30]

In addition to the general democratic problem of expert government, there is also the specific one of unequal access to these specialised public spheres, and unequal voice within them, for different experts. When expert debates take place among a socially homogenous group, then, again, influential expert discourses amount to the government of some over others.[31] The specialised discourse in the specialised public sphere of European private law stands out by its whiteness. As I have argued elsewhere, so far, the building and shaping of the field of European private law has been nearly exclusively a white privilege.[32] Insofar as the European private law discourse, especially the agenda-setting, is shaped by the experiences, concerns and needs of white Europeans, and this dominant discourse has an impact on European private law making – as it certainly does – Europeans of colour are dominated by European private law.

C. Citizens' Initiatives

One already existing possible way to increase citizens' participation in EU private law making is through the institution of European Citizens' Initiatives (ECIs).

In most democracies, the government has a right of initiative. This right is sometimes shared with parliament, but not always. In the EU the right of initiative rests exclusively with the executive, the European Commission.[33] Neither the European Parliament nor the Council can initiate legislation, which typically goes through the ordinary legislative procedure discussed above. However, both the Parliament and the Council can request the Commission to submit a legislative proposal if the proposed legislative act is deemed necessary for attaining the objectives set by the Treaties.[34] Any (constitutional) reforms of primary EU law, through treaty change, on the other hand, can be proposed only to the Council by the governments of the

[29] See HW Micklitz and Y Svetiev, 'The transformation(s) of private law' in HW Micklitz, Y Svetiev and G Comparato (eds), *European Regulatory Private Law – The Paradigms Tested*, EUI Working papers, LAW 2014/04, 69, 78, cadmus.eui.eu/handle/1814/31137.

[30] Fraser (n 22) 71.

[31] The exclusion of specialists belonging to marginalised social groups from the dominant discourse may lead to the creation of specialised counter public spheres. A striking example is given by GU Charles and L Fuentes-Rohwer, 'Habermas, the Public Sphere, and the Creation of a Racial Counterpublic' (2015) 21 *Michigan Journal of Race and Law* 1, who recount how the *Michigan Journal of Race and Law* was founded by students of colour as a response to the structural whiteness of the flagship law journal of their university.

[32] Hesselink (n 7) section III.E.

[33] See Art 17(2) TEU, and for the ordinary legislative procedure, Art 289(1) TFEU.

[34] See Arts 225 and 241 TFEU.

Member States, the European Parliament, or the Commission (ordinary revision procedure).[35]

The ECI was introduced in 2012 as an outcome of the Convention on the Future of Europe (2002–2003).[36] Prima facie, the ECI could increase citizens' political autonomy and agency. For example, on its website the European Commission presents the ECI as follows:[37] 'Get a greater say in the policies that affect your live [*sic!*]. The European Citizens' Initiative is a unique way for you to help shape the EU by calling on the European Commission to propose new laws.' However, while ECIs introduce an element of participatory democracy,[38] they otherwise rely fully on representative democracy. Organised citizens can now submit a proposal for a legislative initiative, but the legislative decision-making fully remains the prerogative of the legislature. When an initiative meets the requirements (first and foremost, one million signatures from citizens from one quarter of the Member States),[39] then the organisers are invited to present their initiative at a public hearing in the European Parliament, following which the Parliament assesses political support,[40] and the Commission receives the organisers to allow them to explain the objective of the initiative in detail, after which the Commission decides whether or not to propose legislation.[41]

So far, there have been six successful ECIs. None of them was in the area of private law or on subjects with an obvious private law dimension (for example, private law remedies, such as civil liability), but in principle this should be perfectly possible. At least there is nothing in the legal setup to exclude an EPL-ECI. Sceptics of participatory democracy – or of a more democratic private law – will argue that the lack of private law initiatives reflects private law apathy among citizens who may consider it just too technical. Citizens seem more interested in the right to water,[42] phasing out animal experiments[43] and improving minority protection.[44] However, critics of private law expert government may reply that private law discourse is unduly doctrinal and hence exclusionary.[45] Doubtlessly, any ECI on what legal scholars would consider to be a private law question would have to be presented in very different terms to interest, let alone mobilise, one million citizens from one quarter of the Member States. Perhaps civil liability and injunctions as remedies for various public policy concern would be the most likely private law aspect of an ECI.

[35] See Art 48 TEU.

[36] See Art 11(4) TEU and Art 24(1) TFEU, and Regulation (EU) 2019/788 of the European Parliament and of the Council of 17 April 2019 on the European citizens' initiative [2019] OJ L 130/55 (ECI Regulation). For a recent (self-)assessment by the European Commission, see Report from the Commission to the European Parliament and the Council on the application of Regulation (EU) 2019/788 on the European citizens' initiative, Brussels, 6.12.2023 COM(2023) 787 final.

[37] See europa.eu/citizens-initiative/en.

[38] The first preliminary recital of the original regulation, ie Regulation (EU) No 211/2011 of the European Parliament and of the Council of 16 February 2011 on the citizens' initiative [2011] OJ L 65/1, refers to Art 10(3) TEU, which proclaims that every citizen has 'the right to participate in the democratic life of the Union', while its 14th recital explicitly refers to 'participatory democracy'.

[39] Art 3 ECI Regulation (n 36).

[40] ibid Art 14.

[41] ibid Art 15.

[42] *cf* europa.eu/citizens-initiative/initiatives/details/2012/000003_en.

[43] *cf* europa.eu/citizens-initiative/initiatives/details/2012/000007_en.

[44] *cf* europa.eu/citizens-initiative/initiatives/details/2017/000004_en.

[45] I will come back to this in the final section.

An important limitation is the fact that the possibility to propose ECIs is reserved to EU citizens resident in the EU.[46] This excludes both non-resident EU citizens and resident non-EU citizens. The latter limitation may perhaps be seen as logical because the European Parliament can be elected also only by EU citizens. On the other hand, however, the right to address a petition to the European Parliament 'on a matter which comes within the Union's fields of activity, and which affects him, her or it directly' is granted also to non-citizen residents (even to legal persons).[47] Moreover, and most relevant here, in their application private law rules do not distinguish between citizen and non-citizen residents. Indeed, via private international law, they may even come to apply to non-citizen non-residents too.[48] In other words, the ECI regulation excludes an important section of EU private law addressees from possible EPL co-authorship. Arguably, at least, the ECI could and should be opened to resident non-citizens and become a (citizens' and other) residents' initiative (EC&RI).

IV. TOWARDS A MORE RADICALLY DEMOCRATIC EUROPEAN PRIVATE LAW

The previous section showed how addressees of European private law have reason to understand themselves as its co-authors only in a rather formal sense. When it comes to European private law, their public autonomy and agency, through representative democracy, the public sphere and even the recent democratic innovation of the citizens' initiative, is rather thin. Moreover, EPL addressees who are not citizens are excluded entirely, while the impact on EU law-making through deliberation in the public sphere is very unevenly distributed.

It is now time to discuss how European private law making could become more democratic in a more capacious, substantive sense. To that end, I will discuss whether a recent democratic innovation – deliberative mini-publics – could and should also be introduced in the context of EU private law-making, with a view to moving beyond the formal political equality of EU citizens, enhancing their substantive political autonomy understood as participatory agency.[49]

A. European Private Law (Re)constitution and Ordinary EPL-making

In this regard, it may be helpful to distinguish between ordinary EPL-making and a more fundamental EPL reform.

[46] See Art 5(2) ECI Regulation (n 36).

[47] Art 227 TFEU.

[48] Whether they do will depend in large part on party autonomy. Which legal system comes to apply is determined by the choice of the parties. See, in particular, Regulation 593/2008 of the European Parliament and of the Council of 17 June 2008 on the law applicable to contractual obligations (Rome I) [2008] OJ L 177/6. The choice may be either active, by 'choice of law' (see Art 3 Rome I), or passive when parties accept the applicable law determined by conflict rules (see Art 4 Rome I). There exist well-known structural risks of domination in cases of formal party autonomy under unequal bargaining conditions, where the joint 'choice' of law is de facto made unilaterally by the stronger party.

[49] *cf* A Alemanno and K Nicolaïdis, 'Citizen power Europe: the making of a European Citizens' Assembly' in A Alemanno and P Sellal (eds), *The Groundwork of European Power* (2021) *Revue Européenne du Droit* 7: 'move beyond a formal understanding of the principle of political equality'.

Systemic injustices require systemic reform. Katharina Pistor has demonstrated how contemporary financial capitalism crucially depends on general private law for securing legal privileges.[50] And Aditi Bagchi has argued convincingly that the fact that power asymmetries resulting from a lack of background distributive justice are reproduced and exacerbated in (horizontal) interpersonal relationships through the application of general private law, raises the fundamental question of which structural role private law must play in non-ideal societies like our own.[51] Elsewhere, I have argued for the introduction of a progressive code of European private law as a response to the social inequalities and the democratic disempowerment resulting from contemporary capitalism.[52]

Similar systemic responses may be needed to fight other structural social injustices than economic inequalities (which are interconnected at least in part), for example the oppressions following from structural racism, patriarchy and ableism. Each of these types of oppression constitute social injustices, which are however reproduced as structural power asymmetries in relationships governed by private law. Again, under non-ideal circumstances, like our own, private law may have to play a corrective role in preventing such structural social injustices from being reproduced and exacerbated in relationships governed by private law, for example in oppressive, exploitative, dominating or alienating contracts.[53]

Apart from the fight against structural social and interpersonal injustice there may also exist other reasons for systemic private law reform. For example, it may be necessary from time to time to 'modernise' a civil code to bring it up to speed with various developments (technological or other), as happened, for example, in the Netherlands in 1992 (*Nieuw Burgerlijk Wetboek*), in Germany in 2002 (*Schuldrechtsmodernisierung*) and in France in 2016 (*Réforme du droit des contrats*).

A fundamental reconsideration may even go as far as questioning whether subjective private rights and corresponding obligations, as we know them, are still the right way to deal with entitlements. This fundamental question, which has been on the table at least since Marx, was recently reintroduced, in a novel way, by Christoph Menke in his radical critique of subjective rights.[54] Similarly, and relatedly at least in part, the need for a general private law (with its core pillars of property,

[50] K Pistor, *The Code of Capital: How the Law Creates Wealth and Inequality* (Princeton, Princeton University Press, 2019).

[51] A Bagchi, 'Distributive Injustice and Private Law' (2008) 60 *Hastings Law Journal* (2008) 105; A Bagchi, 'Distributive Justice and Contract' in G Klass, G Letsas and P Saprai (eds), *Philosophical Foundations of Contract Law* (Oxford, Oxford University Press, 2014) 193.

[52] See MW Hesselink, 'Reconstituting the code of capital: could a progressive European code of private law help us reduce inequality and regain democratic control?' (2022) 1 *European Law Open* 316.

[53] See CW Mills, *Black Rights/White Wrongs: The Critique of Racial Liberalism* (Oxford, Oxford University Press, 2017). With specific reference to EPL, see LKL Tjon Soei Len, 'Justifying Racial and Gendered Contract in Europe' (2022) 51 *Netherlands Journal of Legal Philosophy*25; MW Hesselink, 'The power of reasons in European private law' (2022) 51 *Netherlands Journal of Legal Philosophy* 58, section 4.

[54] See C Menke, *Critique of rights* (Cambridge, Polity, 2020), arguing for counter-rights (*Gegenrechte*) to remain passive (as distinct from liberal freedom). See also G Teubner, 'Zum transsubjektiven Potential subjektiver Rechte: Gegenrechte in ihrer kommunikativen, kollektiven und institutionellen Dimension' in A Fischer-Lescano, H Franzki and J Horst (eds), *Gegenrechte: Recht jenseits des Subjekts*, (Tübingen, Mohr Siebeck, 2018) 357, arguing that such counter-rights should be thought and ensured not only for individuals but also – trans-subjectively – for collective actors.

contract and tort) may be questioned, either because it is somehow obsolete (understood as 'classical' or 'traditional', the action being elsewhere), or because the idea of a general private law (indeed the very idea and practice of singling out private law) entrenches one political philosophy, ie liberalism, by being centred around private autonomy.[55] This question has been raised with particular force for EU private law whose basic structure is not based on an idea of general private law (or a general idea of private law) or even only of general contract law (or a general idea of contract law), as was reaffirmed by the failure of the European Civil Code / Common Frame of Reference / Common European Sales law project (even though some nostalgics may still be in denial).[56]

We may refer to such instances of fundamental rethinking and structural reform as constitutional private law moments, where a society reconstitutes the basic structure of its private law. These can be contrasted with deliberation on and drafting and enacting of more specific and detailed rules, which may be referred to as ordinary private law- making. (Note that this distinction is not the same as the one between technical (non-political) and non-technical (political) private law questions. To the extent that such a distinction can meaningfully be made,[57] it clearly is not a bright line analytical one; it is itself political.) The distinction between private law reconstitution and ordinary private law making may be worth keeping in mind when considering various possible types of involvement of the democratic public and what can reasonably be expected from them in this regard.

B. EPL Catching the Deliberative Wave

i. Deliberative Mini-publics

Let's now turn to deliberative mini-publics. These are bodies of citizens who have been selected randomly in such a way that they are statistically representative of the general public, and who deliberate on public policy questions for a significant amount of time with a view to making joint recommendations to public authorities.[58] The random selection ('sortition') may be 'stratified' with a view to ensuring proper representation of various demographic groups. There exist various procedural tools and techniques to ensure quality of deliberation (that is, for the unforced force of the better argument to prevail) and to prevent distortions (eg from social inequalities or group psychology), which may include professional discussion moderation, and the availability of diverse information materials prepared

[55] For the argument that contract law and property law ought to be understood as essentially liberal, see H Dagan and M Heller, *The Choice Theory of Contracts* (Cambridge, Cambridge University Press, 2017) and H Dagan, *A Liberal Theory of Property* (Cambridge, Cambridge University Press, 2021), respectively.

[56] See C Leone, 'Searching For Contract (Law) in Europe' (2022) 51 *Netherlands Journal of Legal Philosophy* 48.

[57] *Contra*, D Kennedy, 'The Political Stakes in "Merely Technical" Issues of Contract law' (2002) 10 *European Review of Private Law* 7.

[58] *cf* G Smith and M Setälä, 'Mini-Publics and Deliberative Democracy' in A Bächtiger, JS Dryzek, J Mansbridge and M Warren (eds), *The Oxford Handbook of Deliberative Democracy* (Oxford, Oxford University Press, 2018) 300.

by experts, etc.[59] Deliberative mini-publics can be set up ad hoc, for one specific political question, or run for a longer time with a (more) open agenda. Examples of the former include constitutional conventions.

A striking example is provided by Iceland.[60] After the meltdown of its banking system during the financial crisis of 2008, a constitutional assembly of 25 members was elected, which drafted a new constitution in four months in 2011,[61] not behind closed doors but through active crowdsourcing through social media. The new constitution was accepted by a large majority (67 per cent) in a consultative national referendum in 2012, but Parliament turned against it and never brought the constitutional bill to a vote.[62] With reference to the Icelandic experience, Landemore asks the question: 'If a constitutional process can be reinvented in such innovate and inclusive ways, why couldn't processes for ordinary law- and policy making?'[63] For our present purposes, we could specify: and why not for European private law- making? Strikingly (for legal scholars), in the Icelandic process neither the agenda-setting for the deliberation nor the actual writing of the document, which was meant to have (constitutional) legal force, was delegated to experts, but remained firmly in the hands of the 'assembly of amateurs', ie non-specialist citizens.[64] Yet, interestingly, the result was internationally acclaimed by constitutional law experts. In particular, it was commended for the many possibilities the new constitution meant to introduce for citizens to participate in the law-making process (albeit that this was meant to occur mostly through referendums).[65]

Another example, perhaps even more relevant, is the Conference on the Future of Europe, which took place across the EU in 2021–2022.[66] The Conference's final

[59] See eg OECD (n 2) 36 ff.

[60] Think also of Ireland's Constitutional Convention on same-sex marriage and its Citizens' Assembly on abortion and climate change, as well as the French Citizens' Convention for Climate (2019–2020). G de Búrca, 'An EU Citizens' Assembly on Refugee Law and Policy' (2020) 21 *German Law Journal* 23, proposes the Irish experience as a model for citizens' deliberation on the EU's refugee law and policy. The recent Chilean Constitutional Convention (2021–2022), whose radical proposal was rejected in a referendum in 2022, was constituted through popular vote, not sortition.

[61] The first paragraph of the Preamble reads as follows: 'We, the people of Iceland, wish to create a just society with equal opportunities for everyone. Our different origins enrich the whole, and together we are responsible for the heritage of the generations, the land and history, nature, language and culture.'

[62] See T Gylfason, 'Putsch: Iceland's crowd-sourced constitution killed by parliament' Verfassungsblog.de (30 March 2013), verfassungsblog.de/putsch-icelands-crowd-sourced-constitution-killed-by-parliament; H Landemore, *Open Democracy: Reinventing Popular Rule for the Twenty-First Century* (Princeton, Princeton University Press, 2020) ch 7. Recently, the Government opted for a more piecemeal and more classical approach towards constitutional reform, setting the original aside. On this choice, the Venice Commission expressed its concern: 'the Commission considers that the Icelandic people should be given transparent, clear and convincing explanations for the government's choices, and the underlying reasons for any substantive departure from the previous 2012 draft should be explained to the public' (European Commission For Democracy Through Law (Venice Commission), 'Opinion on Four Constitutional Draft Bills on the protection of the environment, on natural resources, on referendums and on the President of Iceland, the Government, the functions of the Executive and Other Institutional Matters' (Opinion No 997/2020) 28, www.venice.coe.int/webforms/documents/default.aspx?pdffile=CDL-AD(2020)020-e.

[63] Landemore (n 62) 153–54, 178.

[64] ibid 157, 160.

[65] European Commission for Democracy Through Law (Venice Commission), 'Opinion on the Draft New Constitution of Iceland' (Opinion No 702/2013) 183.

[66] For an earlier experimental Europe-wide deliberative poll ('Europolis'), involving 348 participants, on two questions – climate change and immigration – conducted around the European Parliament

report refers to itself – in rather self-congratulatory fashion – as 'an unprecedented experience of transnational deliberative democracy'.[67] As part of the Conference, several thousand events were organised across Europe involving around 650,000 participants.[68] Moreover, through a multilingual digital platform more than 17,000 ideas were fed into the conference.[69] A core element of the Conference was the European Citizens' Panels, which included 800 randomly selected European citizens in total, divided over four panels which met in different European cities,[70] as well as the National Citizens' Panels in six Member States,[71] which deliberated with a view to making recommendations. These recommendations were then discussed by the Conference Plenary in Strasbourg, which consisted of representatives from EU institutions (European Parliament, Council and European Commission), from national parliaments and from the European Citizens' Panel as well as from the National Citizens' Panels (or from connected national events). The Plenary worked in nine thematic working groups, after which 49 proposals were adopted. Each proposal consists of a title (for example, proposal 5: 'sustainable consumption, packaging and production'), a stated objective and a set of measures (in the case of proposal 5, 13 measures). The Conference on the Future of Europe differed considerably from the Islandic process, in its scale, working method and output. Striking features of the Conference were its sheer size, the fact that in the final stage the EU institutions took the overhand, and the fact that the result was not a draft legal text (a proposed treaty reform, for example).

In its Report on the final outcome, published in May 2022, the Conference on the Future of Europe made a proposal (under the heading of 'European democracy') to 'increase citizens' participation and youth involvement in the democracy at the European Union level', and as a specific appropriate form of participation they proposed:[72]

> Holding Citizens' assemblies periodically, on the basis of legally binding EU law. Participants must be selected randomly, with representativeness criteria, and participation should be incentivized. If needed, there will be support of experts so that assembly members have enough information for deliberation. If the outcomes are not taken on board by the institutions, this should be duly justified.

elections of 2009, whose main finding was that 'it is indeed possible for the people of Europe to deliberate together across the many barriers of language and nationality, to weigh competing arguments, become more informed, and arrive at considered judgments both about policy issues and voting intention', see JS Fishkin, *Democracy when the people are thinking: revitalizing our politics* (Oxford, Oxford University Press, 2019) 111–36, 124.

[67] Conference on the Future of Europe, 'Report on the Final Outcome' (May 2022) 5, www.europarl.europa.eu/resources/library/media/20220509RES29121/20220509RES29121.pdf.

[68] ibid 8.

[69] ibid 9.

[70] ibid 15. The citizens were randomly selected, however with the aim of the panels being 'representative of the EU's diversity on the basis of five criteria: gender, age, geographic origin (nationality as well as urban/rural), socio-economic background and level of education' (ibid). Note that race, ethnicity, religion and ableness, among others, were not among the criteria.

[71] ibid 22. Member States had the choice whether to organise national panels. Only Belgium, Germany, France, Italy, Lithuania and the Netherlands decided to do so.

[72] ibid 79 (Proposal 36, measure 7).

Arguably, such citizens' assemblies, under certain conditions, could also contribute to making EU law-making more democratic. In this regard, the recent announcement by Commission President Von der Leyen, that, 'the Citizens' Panels that were central to the Conference will now become a regular feature of our democratic life,' is to be welcomed.[73]

Turning now to the subject of EU private law, there is no reason why citizens could not meaningfully deliberate also about horizontal questions, principles and rules – no ground for private law exceptionalism.[74] The main difficulty may be with agenda-setting, because citizens may not know the status quo (ie the private law *acquis*) very well if at all, nor its main possible alternatives. But that may also turn out to be their main strength. Doctrinal legal reasoning (going back to Roman law) has been one of the most path-dependent and conservative sectors of European cultures. And some thinking outside the box (eg questioning the very idea of subjective rights, the legal personhood of corporations, property as the most absolute right, and the sanctity of contract) may be exactly what society needs. Consider now two concrete possible ways to make EPL become more democratic.

ii. A Citizens' Assembly on the Future of European Private Law

In 2010, the European Commission set up an expert group with the task of assisting the Commission in preparing a proposal for a Common Frame of Reference in the area of European contract law.[75] The eventual outcome was called (by the Commission) a 'feasibility study',[76] which the Commission then turned into a proposal (with only a small amount of changes) for a regulation on a Common European Sales Law.[77] That proposal met with strong opposition, both from Member States and from consumer protection groups. And although it was adopted eventually by the European Parliament by a large majority, the proposal was ultimately withdrawn by the Commission.

Now imagine that the European Commission had not created a relatively homogeneous expert group (most academic members, who were the majority, had already known and worked with each other for a long time),[78] that deliberated behind closed doors, but instead had set up a deliberative assembly: a citizens' assembly on the

[73] 2022 State of the Union Address by President von der Leyen (Strasbourg, 14 September 2022), ec.europa.eu/commission/presscorner/detail/en/speech_22_5493.

[74] For the idea that private law is morally-ontologically different, see EJ Weinrib, *The Idea of Private Law* (Cambridge MA, Harvard University Press, 1995).

[75] European Commission, 'Decision of 26 April 2010 setting up the Expert Group on a Common Frame of Reference in the area of European contract law (2010/233/EU)', [2010] OJ L 105/109, Art 2.

[76] Commission Expert Group on European Contract Law, 'Feasibility study for a future instrument in European Contract Law' (3 May 2011), eusoco.eu/wp-content/uploads/2011/05/paper_expertgroup_feasibility_study_may_2011_en.pdf.

[77] European Commission, 'Proposal for a regulation of the European Parliament and of the Council on a Common European Sales Law' COM(2011) 635 final.

[78] Several expert group members (including myself) had been involved in the Draft Common Frame of Reference (Study Group on a European Civil Code and the Research Group on EC Private Law (Acquis Group), *Principles, Definitions and Model Rules of European Private Law. Draft Common Frame of Reference (DCFR). Outline edition* (München, Sellier, 2009).

future of European private law (CAFEPL). It seems likely that the outcome would have been quite different. By definition, the content would have been difficult to predict. Yet, in all likelihood the citizens' assembly would not have been burdened by strong (personal) commitments to the Draft Common Frame of Reference (DCFR) or its main sources of inspiration, the Principles of European Contract Law (PECL) and the United Nations Convention on Contracts for the International Sale of Goods (CISG).[79] Nor would they necessarily have made the choice, natural to all doctrinal legal scholar but also strongly determinative for the outcome, to focus on general rules of contract law (cloaked very late in the day as slightly less general rules of sales law).

The expert group worked for around a year, meeting once a month for two–three days each time on complex questions, with strong value implications, at least some of them arguable of a constitutional nature. Now note that these characteristics correspond exactly to the main factors for the OECD to recommend deliberative assemblies.[80] According to the OECD, representative deliberative processes (mini-publics) are generally well-suited for addressing values-driven dilemmas, complex problems that require trade-offs, and long-term issues going beyond the short-term incentives of electoral cycles.[81] In its empirical study (based on 289 case studies) the OECD found more specifically that 'citizens' assemblies' typically consist of around 80 persons, meet two days a month during a year, and are particularly useful for considered and detailed collective recommendations on complex policy problems that involve many trade-offs. Private law addresses value-based dilemmas (that is the one thing on which private law theorists agree; they quarrel about which is private law's essential value); every private-law rule-choice implies a trade-off (between autonomy and solidarity, between formal and substantive equality, between weaker party protection and freedom of contract, etc); private law problems are complex because of the (perceived) strongly systematic nature of private law, where all rule choices seem to hang together; private law questions are long-term (in some cases perennial) while even an excellent private law reform will never get a politician re-elected; and, finally, in order to make a real impact (and to interest potential assembly members in the first place) the outcome of the deliberation would have to be a draft reform with a form of prior political commitment, for example to comply or explain.[82]

I think that with hindsight a citizens' assembly on the future of European private law would have been the much better option. More importantly, the Commission

[79] Several members of the Study Group on a European Civil Code, responsible for the bulk of the drafting of the DCFR, were also members of the Lando Commission, who drafted the Principles of European Contract Law (PECL) (for further reference, see O Lando and HG Beale (eds), *Principles of European Contract Law: Parts I, II and III*, Student edn (Alphen a/d Rijn, Wolters Kluwer, 2019)); several of them were involved also in the drafting of – and negotiations in Vienna about – UN Convention on Contracts for the International Sale of Goods (CISG) (Vienna, 1980), uncitral.un.org/en/texts/salegoods/conventions/sale_of_goods/cisg.

[80] OECD (n 3).

[81] ibid 27.

[82] At the time, with regard to a 'political' CFR a political commitment, in an inter-institutional agreement between Commission, European Parliament and Council to 'comply or explain', was considered. Such a commitment would have been much more legitimate for a citizens' draft than for an experts' draft.

could still choose to convene such an EPL citizens' assembly today. Agenda-setting is crucial in deliberative democracy – indeed, its practical core. Therefore, ideally such an EPL citizens' assembly would set its own agenda. However, the scope of the deliberation is likely to be determined in advance at least in part. Coming back to the distinction between a fundamental reconstitution of European private law and ordinary EPL-making, obviously the former should not be constrained *ex ante* by the current limited set of competences; it should rather explicitly address the issue. In this regard, it would be similar to the Icelandic assembly and to the Conference on the Future of Europe. As to the latter, ordinary European private law making is of course strongly constrained by the current constitutional set-up laid down in primary EU law, as well as, for each specific topic, by the surrounding acquis of secondary EU law. In either case, it would be for the citizens on the panel themselves to decide whether and how they would like to be informed by any expert advice,[83] although perhaps in the case of ordinary EPL-making unsolicited evidence on constraints following from the EU's constitutional framework (legal basis and other) should be provided.[84]

iii. A Citizens' Panel on Digital Fairness

The European Commission is currently undertaking a 'Fitness Check of EU consumer law on digital fairness'.[85] The check will examine the UCTD,[86] UCPD[87] and CRD[88] 'to determine whether they ensure a high level of protection in the digital environment'. To this end, the Commission launched a public consultation in the fourth quarter of 2022, which consisted, as usual, in the publication of a questionnaire on its webpage 'Have your say'.[89]

Instead – or better, in addition – the Commission could have opted for a citizens' panel on digital fairness. According to the OECD report, citizens' panels are the most-often used form of deliberative mini-publics.[90] They are like citizens' assemblies,

[83] The assembly, or its individual members, could turn to experts for advice on answers as well as on questions. In the past, I suggested that a set of political questions should be submitted to the European Parliament for political guidance in expert drafting, thus rendering the role of experts more technical, more concerned with means than with ends. Even better, now mini-publics could decide to seek lists of salient political private law questions from several experts for inspiration. *cf* MW Hesselink, 'The Politics of a European Civil Code' (2004) 10 *European Law Journal* 675.

[84] *cf* A Michels and H Binnema, 'Deepening and connecting democratic processes. The opportunities and pitfalls of mini-publics in renewing democracy' 7 *Social Sciences* (2018) 236, 8.

[85] See ec.europa.eu/info/law/better-regulation/have-your-say/initiatives/13413-Digital-fairness-fitness-check-on-EU-consumer-law_en.

[86] Council Directive 93/13/EEC of 5 April 1993 on unfair terms in consumer contracts [1993] OJ L 95/29.

[87] Directive 2005/29/EC of the European Parliament and of the Council of 11 May 2005 concerning unfair business-to-consumer commercial practices in the internal market and amending Council Directive 84/450/EEC, Directives 97/7/EC, 98/27/EC and 2002/65/EC of the European Parliament and of the Council and Regulation (EC) No 2006/2004 of the European Parliament and of the Council ('Unfair Commercial Practices Directive') [2005] OJ L149/22.

[88] Directive 2011/83/EU of the European Parliament and of the Council of 25 October 2011 on consumer rights, amending Council Directive 93/13/EEC and Directive 1999/44/EC of the European Parliament and of the Council and repealing Council Directive 85/577/EEC and Directive 97/7/EC of the European Parliament and of the Council [2011] OJ L 304/64.

[89] See ec.europa.eu/info/law/better-regulation/have-your-say_en.

[90] See OECD (n 3) 39ff.

but on a smaller scale: deliberation by a smaller group (around 30), for a shorter time (around four days), on a more specific question. In light of the Commission President's recent announcement that the citizens' panels will become a regular feature of the EU's democratic life, cited above, a citizens' panel digital fairness might have been a good first candidate.

Other possible candidates for Commission citizens' panels in the area of European private law could have included the consumer right to repair (with a view to circular economy),[91] and corporate liability for human rights violations in value chains.[92]

Alternatively, the citizens panels could be coupled to the European Parliament, for example by their formal integration into the relevant legislative committees, such as Internal Market and Consumer Protection (IMCO) and Legal Affairs (JURI), thus empowering mini-public of ordinary citizens to feed their deliberative inputs into the European legislature.[93]

C. Citizens' Judicial Committees

Much of private law making is done by courts. As said, some courts are particularly activistic, which raises serious legitimacy concerns. However, it is a well-known fact that a degree of law-making is inevitable when it comes to the application of abstract rules to concrete cases. Whether a new fact pattern is within the scope of an established rule, for example, is a matter of judgement, which involves both positive and normative considerations. Yet, the scope of judicial law-making in private law could be reduced by letting citizens' committees decide over legal interpretation on questions with obvious important policy implications beyond the case at hand that should not be left to the judiciary. This was recently proposed by Katharina Pistor.[94] She gives the example of the question whether Uber Eats couriers should be considered employees or entrepreneurs. In civil litigation, such a question could be submitted to an ad hoc committee, which could be selected through sortition, in a way quite similar to juries, or to a more permanent committee, with changing membership. These preliminary references to a citizens' judicial committee could be either optional, for example at the request of one of the litigating parties, or mandatory for courts for a defined set of cases (for example, uncertainty

[91] *cf* European Commission, 'Proposal for a Directive of the European Parliament and of the Council on common rules promoting the repair of goods and amending Regulation (EU) 2017/2394, Directives (EU) 2019/771 and (EU) 2020/1828' COM(2023) 155 final; European Parliament resolution of 7 April 2022 on the right to repair (2022/2515(RSP)) [2022] C 434/81.

[92] *cf* European Commission, 'Proposal for a Directive of the European Parliament and of the Council on Corporate Sustainability Due Diligence and amending Directive (EU) 2019/1937' COM(2022) 71 final, which however proposes no direct liability, Art 22.

[93] For a study of the case where a mini-public was formally integrated into a legislative committee of the New South Wales Parliament in Australia, see CM Hendriks, 'Coupling citizens and elites in deliberative systems: the role of institutional design' (2016) 55 *European Journal of Political Research* 43.

[94] K Pistor, 'Legal coding beyond capital?' (2022) 1 *European Law Open* 344. The idea reminds of the *référé législatif*, introduced in France after the Revolution in response to the judicial activism of the courts under the *ancien régime*.

about the implication of a private law rule for a certain type of cases with important social, economic or political implications). Note that the idea would not be that these citizens' judicial committees should write new abstract rules. Rather, they would always respond to a specific question arisen in a concrete case.[95]

D. Wiki Codes

Finally, if the aim is deliberation on principles, without any concrete expected follow-up in terms of political decision-making, then other types of options could be considered too. These include a wiki code of EU private law and various other forms of open-sources drafting.[96] The idea would be to develop a set of principles or a common frame of reference through an open and non-hierarchical process of drafting. This would be a fully anarchic mode of private law drafting. As such, it could correspond well to the Habermasian ideal of a vibrant public sphere.[97]

From both an epistemic and a legitimacy point of view, if done right, such an open-source private law code would seem superior at least to sets of principles drafted by experts, such as the PECL, the DCFR and the various model laws drafted by the European Law Institute.[98] To be clear, the point here is not that publicly enacted and enforced private law could be replaced by a private code made through an open method. The point is rather that such a wiki EPL code seems superior, both in terms of legitimacy and in epistemic terms, because of its inclusiveness and transparency, to various soft law texts drafted by expert committees behind closed doors. This means, that for whichever role an expert text is going to be used, be it as a soft law device or eventually as a draft for formal legislation, as was the (unilateral) aspiration of both the Lando Commission and the Study Group on a European Civil Code, an open-source code would seem the preferred option.

Finally, such an open-source code could also become the counter-discourse of a counter-public in a counter public sphere, where members of marginalised groups (and their allies) come together to discuss and develop concrete alternatives. This could prove particularly relevant and even necessary when not only representative democracy, but also deliberative min-publics, turned out to be too demographically homogeneous and socially exclusionary, leading to the political alienation of

[95] The general improvement of working conditions in platform work was the object of a recent legislative proposal from the European Commission: European Commission, 'Proposal for a Directive of the European Parliament and of the Council on improving working conditions in platform work' COM(2021) 762 final. For a response from the European social partners, see Opinion of the European Economic and Social Committee on the Communication from the Commission to the European Parliament, the Council, the European Economic and Social Committee and the Committee of the Regions – Better working conditions for a stronger social Europe: harnessing the full benefits of digitalisation for the future of work (COM(2021) 761 final) and the Proposal for a Directive of the European Parliament and of the Council on improving working conditions in platform work (COM(2021) 762 final) (2022/C 290/16).

[96] For the idea of a 'WikiCFR', see MW Hesselink, 'The Common Frame of Reference as a Source of European Private Law' (2009) 83 *Tulane Law Review* 919, 960–61.

[97] Habermas (n 4) 185, 307.

[98] Think also of the various law reform proposals made in the UK by the English and Scottish Law Commissions.

members of marginalised social groups following from their (correct) impression of being subject to European private laws made by others, without any realistic sense of ownership of these laws for them.

V. DEMOCRATIC EXCLUSION THROUGH SORTITION

Mini-publics are at the heart of Hélène Landemore's argument for what she calls 'open democracy'.[99] In her argument, she strongly relies on the epistemic role of democratic deliberation. Indeed, for Landemore, the epistemic role of democratic deliberation (what she calls 'democratic reason') is the core normative foundation of democratic law.[100] She is committed to political cognitivism, which is the proposition that for all political questions there are correct and incorrect answers, or at least ones that are better or worse.[101] And she argues – contrary to the long anti-democratic tradition in political cognitivism going back to Plato's philosopher king – that inclusive democratic deliberation is the best tracker of 'smart' political decisions, always (!) better than policy- and law-making by experts. This point is crucial, because if the main purpose of democracy were indeed epistemic, ie correctly figuring out what's in the public interest, then representative democracy could become wholly dispensable. All we would have to do is to ensure that mini-publics meet the requirements for optimal (or at least sufficient) epistemic functioning. The aim would be to ensure that all relevant considerations are on the table, every point of view being properly (re)presented and considered. And to achieve that we would not need the full public; a mini-public would suffice, both for deliberation and for decision-making.

However, from the normative point of view of collective self-determination grounded in a conception of the person as an equal normative authority, as defended here, it is not good enough if a mini-public correctly represents the wider public. If deliberative assemblies adequately reproduce the democratic exclusions and the democratic domination existing in the wider public, then mini-publics remain as unjustifiable as the status quo. This is not merely a hypothetical possibility. It is exactly what happened, for example, in the case of the Conference on the Future of Europe, where citizens were 'randomly selected' for the panels, however with the explicit aim of the Panels being 'representative of the EU's diversity on the basis of five criteria: gender, age, geographic origin (nationality as well as urban/rural), socio-economic background and level of education'.[102] Strikingly, race, ethnicity,

[99] Landemore (n 62).

[100] On democratic reason, see earlier Landemore (n 13). By contrast, Jürgen Habermas, while emphasising the epistemic dimension of the public sphere (see J Habermas, 'Political Communication in Media Society: Does Democracy Still Have an Epistemic Dimension? The Impact of Normative Theory on Empirical Research' in J Habermas, *Europe: The Faltering Project* (Cambridge, Polity, 2009) 138, does not ground deliberatively democracy epistemically, in its superior truth-tracking capacity, but, as we saw, in the presuppositions of communicative action (deriving from his version of discourse theory) combined with the (historically contingent) reality of the medium of positive law.

[101] See Landemore (n 13) ch 8.

[102] Conference on the Future of Europe (n 67) 15.

religion and ableness, among others, were not among the criteria.[103] So, first of all, criteria like race and ethnicity were not deemed necessary even to ensure that that the panels were 'representative of the EU's diversity'. But most importantly, given that marginalised groups do not have an equal voice in deliberative spaces dominated by dominant discourses, mere representation would still in all likelihood have made the deliberation colour-blind.[104] It is, therefore, not at all surprising that the 338-page report mentions 'racism' only once, under proposal 46 on 'Education', measure 2, item 8: 'Combating bullying and racism',[105] and 'ethnicity' also once, but only in the Annex.[106]

So, while organisers of mini-publics generally seem happy to refer to stratified sortition for the composition of mini-publics, even stratified random sampling along the lines of established demographic categories raises difficult practical and normative questions about how to split up a pluralist society, where individuals tend to have multiple and instable identities,[107] into different sections for the purpose of group representation. In addition, it would be naïve to think that newly established mini-publics would have a clean slate when it comes to power dynamics in deliberations grounded in structural power asymmetries present in the general public they represent. Finally, political deliberation (as opposed to moral deliberation) is always deliberation within a specific political community, with its specific citizens, and its specific legal order, which inevitably raises questions of inclusion and exclusion. For private law these questions of territorial scope are dealt with chiefly by the rules of private international law, which does not mean that they have already been solved satisfactorily.[108]

I am not arguing here that 'smart' practical solutions cannot be found. Stratified sortition could be made less blind towards marginalised groups; deliberation rules and practices could explicitly address (perhaps through training) deliberative biases; and mini-publics for private law could include resident non-citizens and maybe also some non-resident non-citizens. The point is rather that the risk of democratic exclusion – even beyond statistical representation – should be a core concern from the point of any understanding of democracy grounded in a conception of the person as a justificatory equal. Therefore, any 'smart' solutions must also be able to

[103] See also the criticism by Alemanno and Nicolaïdis (n 49) 7: 'the panels failed to be as inclusive as one would have hoped of marginalised groups across Europe, from residents without EU passports to racial and ethnic communities'.

[104] On colour-blindness in law-making and elsewhere, see K Williams Crenshaw, LC Harris, D Martinez HoSang and G Lipsitz (eds), *Seeing Race Again: Countering Colorblindness Across the Disciplines* (Oakland, University of California Press, 2019).

[105] ibid 89.

[106] ibid 102.

[107] See A Sen, *Identity and Violence: The illusion of Destiny* (London, Penguin Books, 2006).

[108] What about temporal scope and the inclusion of future generations? While their various points of view seem difficult to guess, especially if we image their societies as pluralist, with regard to at least some of their interests (notably their survival) we may be more confident. Perhaps future generations should be represented in the mini-publics by trustees? However, this immediately raises new questions, eg about the possible representation of nature as such (or specific items like a river) and of various impersonal interests. In each of these cases, there is also a clear risk (indeed, inevitability in the case of statistic representation) of the representation becoming fictitious, or paternalistic. Although clearly relevant, I will not further pursue these important questions and their implications here.

pass the further test of meeting the threshold of generally reciprocally non-rejectable reasons,[109] which excludes any sortition- and deliberative rules and practices privileging the members of some social groups, their concerns, interests and views, over those of others.

VI. REALISTIC?

In this chapter, I have sketched a few concrete ways in which a more radically democratic private law could come about. My discussion of specifics was in terms of possibility rather than in more normative terms of desirability, let alone moral rightness. The reason is that which option(s) are to be preferred, be it in terms of legitimacy or for epistemic reasons, will depend a lot on context and implementation. While the most abstract principles of legitimacy and justifiability can be formulated, in the abstract, as the right to collective self-determination or public autonomy or a universal human right to democracy, the concrete implications will depend on many facts on the ground and will therefore differ from one polity to another. There is not one size which fits all.[110] Rather, concrete solutions will have to be found deliberatively between facts and norms, to use Habermas's phrase. And in any case, the moral bottom line is also that ultimately the democratic procedures to be legitimate will have to be decided upon by the people themselves.

If indeed mini-publics cannot legitimately replace representative democracy and only supplement it (no democratic shortcuts), this raises questions about the link between mini-publics and political institutions of representative democracy. There exists a sizeable political science literature on this question of the macro-political uptake of the outcomes of mini-publics, some of it quite sobering.[111] Clearly, when it comes to the institutional design for fruitful deliberation of private law subjects in mini-publics available insights from political science should be taken on board. While more legitimacy-oriented strands in the literature are concerned with the risk of disempowerment of the wider public, the more impact-oriented contributions

[109] On this demand, see above, section II.

[110] For a much more universalist (and metaphysical) understanding of detailed private law justice, see Dagan and Dorfman (n 9).

[111] See eg RE Goodin and JS Dryzek, 'Deliberative impacts: the macro-political uptake of mini-publics'(2006) 34 *Politics & Society* 219 (introducing the problem of linking the micro-publics to the macro political system and highlighting cases of successful political uptake); S Chambers, 'Rhetoric and the public sphere: has deliberative democracy abandoned mass democracy?' (2009) 37 *Political Theory* 323 (arguing that the focus on bounded deliberation in mini-publics moves attention toward democratic deliberation and away from deliberative democracy, and that mini-publics to be democratic must convince the general public of the merits of their recommendations); EDH Olsen and H-J Trenz, 'From Citizens' Deliberation to Popular Will Formation? Generating Democratic Legitimacy in Transnational Deliberative Polling' (2014) 62 *Politics Studies* 117 (on the difference between the scientific validity derived from a statistically perfect sample and democratic validity grounded in the inclusion of everyone affected); Michels and Binnema (n 84) 236 (pointing to contingent design problems as well as the structural tension between deliberative quality and political impact); M Jäske and M Setälä, 'A Functionalist Approach to Democratic Innovations' (2020) 56 *Representation* 467 (evaluating recent democratic innovations in terms of their contribution to functions attributed to democratic institutions, ie inclusion, collective will-formation and decision-making).

wonder how mini-publics can be of any political consequence at all. Empirical studies on the (dis)connection between deliberation in mini-publics and collective will-formation by the mass public show that deliberative outcomes are often ignored or explicitly rejected by elected politicians or in referenda. Possible ways to improve the political uptake – and thus to give citizens reason to spend time on deliberating in mini-publics in the first place – include *ex ante* commitments by political institutions, either to accept the proposals made by mini-publics or at least to respond to them and explain why they will not be taken up (as suggested above).[112]

A second more general consideration regarding different deliberative models also has to do with realism but in a different sense. Can we really entrust ordinary citizens with the task of making private law? A first response to this sceptical remark is that private lawmaking through deliberation in mini-publics, etc is not different *in this regard* from representative democracy. A law degree, let alone a specialisation in private law, is not a requirement to be elected as an MP or MEP, or to become a Minister of or EU Commissioner for Justice. Secondly, while private law may be a technical subject (in the sense that it is a field of expertise), that is hardly different for any other subject that legislators legislate on. Thirdly, while members of the public may not know much about the technicalities of, say, contract law, contract law experts may have no idea about the various types of contracts governed by contract law or of the contractual relationships and disputes they may give rise to (apart from the very few that end up in law reports). And if they do, eg because they are both a law professor and a practicing lawyer (or do legal consultancy work), then most likely they will be most familiar with the interests and perspectives of certain types of contracting parties, ie the economically stronger or otherwise more powerful ones. This may still be compatible with a form of realism, ie political realism, but clearly such a view of politics is at direct odds with a conception of democracy grounded in a moral understanding of the person as a justificatory equal. Finally, arguably contract law scholars have made contract law much more technical-doctrinal than necessary or desirable. In any case, that latter question is not for them to decide; it is the addressees of the law who, as co-authors, should determine politically how doctrinal, conceptual, and otherwise technical private law should be.

A third possible objection grounded in a form of 'realism' is public apathy. If much of the public already does not turn out once every four or five years to cast their votes, what reason is there to think that they would be willing to deliberate in a mini-public on private law? In response, as a general matter it is not clear that current attitudes of citizens towards the current institutions and practices of representative democracy provide a proper basis for determining the realism of proposals to change these very practices and institutions in the future. Indeed, insofar as such proposals can be seen as plausible improvements in terms of political autonomy and political agency (or of the epistemic virtue of getting the public interest right),

[112] It should be noted that this latter much more limited commitment would not go any further than the European Commission's current duties with regard to the European Citizens' initiative, that was discussed above (n 8ff).

these proposed new practices would be more meaningful (in terms of legitimacy and epistemology). And insofar it would be rational (as well as reasonable) at least for citizens who care about their political agency and about the public interest, to engage in these new democratic practices, while it is equally rational (even though perhaps not in all cases fully reasonable) for them to remain passive and apathetic under the current democratic institutions and practices.

Moreover, the response to this third realism objection is related to the other two. To the extent, first, that more democratic practices present a better fit in various respects with the current public (especially their understanding of political agency) than the institutions and practices that were designed for another age; and, second, that the democratic deliberation about private law becomes less technical, doctrinal and abstract (eg by moving beyond general private law) and more political, partly as a result of the fact that the deliberation is now among the general (mini-)public rather than among experts, citizens may be more interested and willing to participate. For example, if the debate was more about the merits and implications of Pistor's diagnosis in *The code of capital* than, say, about the usefulness as a model for European private law of the German or French reforms of the law of obligations, then the wider public would seem more likely to be interested. And as Landemore points out, successful, enthusiastic and engaged deliberation in conventions have taken place on what otherwise would have seemed rather technical questions on which specialists (legal or other) would claim expertise. Finally, both the OECD report and the Conference conclusions suggest that panel membership should perhaps come with financial compensation or a statutory right to be absent from work, based on an understanding of mini-public membership as a civic duty akin to jury service.[113] In sum, public deliberation in mini-publics even on private law questions would not necessarily suffer from the problem of taking too many evenings.[114]

While liberals of various stripes are known for their distrust of the public, progressives may also be hesitant about giving reform – in this case private law reform – into the hands of a mini-public. Is it realistic to expect, for example, that a progressive EU private law code, aimed at making progress towards a more just society where there is less inequality and where we have more democratic control over our future, as I have proposed elsewhere,[115] could ever be the outcome deliberation by a mini-public? Aditi Bagchi is sceptical. She believes that 'radical democracy is unlikely to realise a radically progressive vision of private law'.[116] The reason is, she argues, that the general public tends to be risk-averse, in particular when

[113] In the same sense, Michels and Binnema (n 84) 9.

[114] *cf* the saying, widely attributed to Oscar Wilde, that 'the trouble with socialism is that it takes too many evenings'. As Landemore (n 13) 10, 205, points out, deliberation in mini publics established through sortition does not involve all citizens at the same time and, therefore, avoids taking too many evenings. Indeed, except for the very local level, it will be unlikely that anyone will be called upon more than once if at all.

[115] Hesselink (n 52) 316.

[116] A Bagchi, 'The Challenge of Radical Reform in Pluralist Democracies' (2022) 1 *European Law Open* 374.

it comes to the material consequences of reform and the demands of egalitarian private law justice to be made on them. Katharina Pistor is more optimistic. She is sympathetic to the idea of a radically democratic EPL code consisting of broad principles (not detailed rules) with constitutional status, but argues that in order to succeed such a code should be complemented by structural reforms in mechanisms for legal change and law enforcement.[117] Whether radical private law reform through radical democracy is possible and desirable is a radically open question, as it should be in any society where every person is respected as an justificatory equal.

Perhaps the most important democratic promise of deliberative mini-publics has been their capacity to ensure the kind of face-to-face deliberation, where citizens actively engage with each other's views and arguments, in a way that is not possible on the scale of mass democracies today, and most certainly not of the size of the EU. However, this may give rise to yet another risk, the opposite of public apathy. What if deliberation in mini-publics goes too easily? What, that is, if the members of mini-public become carried away by their civic enthusiasm and reach consensus on issues where the wider public has been deadlocked and polarised perhaps for decades, or, conversely, on matters in which citizens have never shown any interest whatsoever? Indeed, what if the mini-public came up with a truly innovative and progressive EPL code? Could the wider public, which was not privy to the transformative deliberations bringing about new microcosmic public opinions, but has remained stuck with its pre-deliberative radically divergent opinions, ever accept or even understand such a proposal? Perhaps democratic law-making through mini-publics is too good to be true, a fundamentally flawed attempt to bypass the hard work of convincing political opponents – an impermissible shortcut. As Cristina Lafont has pointed out, in the case of empowered mini-publics (ie ones that have decision-making power rather than merely making recommendations), apart from unjustifiable political heteronomy (ie being subject to laws made by others), there would be the additional risk of political alienation, where addressees of the law do not even understand the reasons for the laws to which they are subjected, experiencing these reasons as alien, with the result that they become estranged from the legal order.[118]

Clearly, political alienation would be highly problematic from the point of view of any understanding of democracy grounded in the equal respect owed to every person as justificatory equals. However, it must be said that, at least for now, that risk seems rather slim (especially when compared to the much more acute risk of political alienation through the use doctrinal jargon), not least because it seems neither likely (given the constitutional entrenchment in the treaties of the ordinary legislative procedure) nor desirable that mini-publics in the EU would be empowered with actual decision-making powers. What seems much more likely and

[117] Pistor (n 94).

[118] C Lafont, *Democracy Without Shortcuts: A Participatory Conception of Deliberative Democracy* (Oxford, Oxford University Press, 2019).

desirable is a dialectic, mutually transformative relationship between the European mini-public, and its perhaps more radical proposals, on the one hand, and the general European public with its indeed maybe more cautious anticipated response, on the other. While perhaps modest, such a political transformation of European private law without political alienation, through the involvement of mini-publics and the gradual creation of a Europe-wide private law public sphere, could mean real democratic progress in European private law making.

5

The Person of the Future: The Dialogue of Intelligences between Humanism and Technoscience

ANTONIO PUNZI

IN RECENT YEARS, in the debate following the rise of neuroscience and the advent of artificial intelligence, scholars have focused more on the intelligence rather than on the concept of the person. This chapter reflects on the possibility of restoring a central role for the concept of person, neither before nor outside, but within, the reflection on intelligence that characterises our time.

I. THE UNCERTAINTIES OF TIME AND THE TASK OF BECOMING WHAT WE ARE

Reflecting on our 'being person' today is extremely problematic.[1] We are entering a new era, afflicted by doubts and uncertainties. We are orphans of the certitudes of classical and medieval thought, which assumed that the ontological question could be approached and solved, and stated that man was both an individual and a person (think of Boethius or St Thomas). Today, we do not have confidence in one ontology. It is therefore worth asking if it is possible to reconsider the concept of person in the absence of an ontology.

In order to provide an answer to this question, some steps need to be taken in the area either of philosophy or of the analysis of language, which, in line with the Heideggerian teaching so often mentioned by Giuseppe Benedetti, can be considered 'the house of Being'.[2] A starting point could be the ancient debate on the etymological roots of the word 'person'. As we know, this origin is not clear: this word may derive from the Greek πρόσωπον, the Etruscan *phersu* or the Sanskrit *phersuna*: in

[1] Among the many philosophical essays on this subject, see R Spaemann, *Personen. Versuche über den Unterschied zwischen 'etwas' und 'jemand'* (Stuttgart, Klett-Cotta, 1996) and S Cotta, *Diritto persona mondo umano* (Torino, Giappichelli, 1989).

[2] M Heidegger, 'Letter on Humanism' in M Heidegger, *Pathmarks* (Cambridge, Cambridge University Press, 1998) 254.

any case, it evokes the world of the theatre. However, there is another interpretation according to which the Latin word *persona* would be related to the verb *per-sonare* (to re-sonate).[3] Whether this interpretation is correct or not, it suggests an interesting route when connected with the first one. Our concern is not only the difference between the face and the mask covering it, but rather the idea that the mask makes the voice of the actor resonate. We could say that the being-person makes the individual's voice resound, giving depth to its *flatus vocis*.[4] It is certainly no coincidence, after all, that, as Carlo Sini writes, our being comes into the world through a vocal gesture.[5]

This evocative insight coming from the etymological research is especially helpful in today's context where, as mentioned, thinking philosophically about the person carries with it several problems. Today we also feel the lack of the certitudes of modern thought, which put not the person, but the philosophical subject at the centre of the stage (to follow the theatre metaphor). The modern subject no longer turns its gaze to being, as a metaphysical entity (or however to the question of being). Once it has gained certainty of itself as a self-conscious entity (think of Descartes), it concentrates on the observation of nature to identify its laws, to measure and transform it. This modern transition from the person to the subject has a dual nature. On the one hand it expresses Francis Bacon's belief in the '*ipsa scientia potestas est*',[6] in knowledge removing pain, disorder and injustice; on the other hand, it initiates a scientific and technical project of domination over the world.

This project – of which the Industrial Revolution is the first major exemplification – began to be perceived as a source of unease during the nineteenth century. Humanity suspects being trapped in what Max Weber called the 'iron cage'.[7] And it is precisely here that the concept of person and the role it has played not only in philosophical debate, but in social life and the development of democratic institutions come into play. This notion is now used – by philosophy and social doctrines referring to the

[3] Starting with the *De origine vocabulorum* of Gavio Basso (1st century BC), an etymological origin of *persona* has been supposed from *personare*, ie 'to make resound', a characteristic ascribed to the masks of ancient theatre. Aulus Gellius reported on this hypothesis: 'Gustosa davvero, e dotta, l'interpretazione della parola persona «maschera da teatro», data da Gavio Basso nei libri da lui composti 'Sull'origine dei nomi'; egli congettura che la parola derivi dal verbo *personare* "risuonare". Testa e volto, coperti da ogni lato dall'involucro della maschera e accessibili solo per l'unica via – non instabile né dispersiva – che consente l'emissione della voce, raccolgono e costringono la voce dirigendola verso un unico sbocco e così rendono il suono più squillante e armonioso. Quell'indumento del volto, dunque, fa diventare la voce chiara e risonante: perciò è detto persona, con allungamento della vocale o provocato dalla forma della parola' (Aulo Gellio, *Le notti attiche*, (Torino, UTET, 2007) 487). On the etymological question, see the renowned investigation by A Trendelenburg, 'Zur Geschichte des Wortes Person' (1908) 13 *Kant Studien* 1. See now R Brouwer 'One Funerals, Faces, and Hellenistic Philosophers: On the Origins of the Concept of Person in Rome' in A LoLordo (ed), *Person. A History* (Oxford, Oxford University Press, 2019), which also acknowledges that 'nowadays Gavius Bassus's etymology of the word persona is generally rejected' (27).

[4] C Bologna, *Flatus vocis. Metafisica e antropologia della voce* (Bologna, Il Mulino, 1992) 23: 'Prima ancora che il linguaggio abbia inizio e si articoli in parole per trasmettere messaggi in forma di enunciati, la voce ha già da sempre origine, c'è come potenzialità di significazione e vibra quale indistinto flusso di vitalità'.

[5] C Sini, *Il silenzio e la parola. Luoghi e confini del sapere per l'uomo planetario* (Milano, IPOC, 2012) 46.

[6] F Bacon, 'Meditationes sacrae' [1597] in F Bacon, *The Works of Francis Bacon* (London, Rivington, 1826) 308.

[7] M Weber, *Protestant Ethic and the Spirit of Capitalism* (London-New York, Routledge Classics, 2001) 123–24.

personalist perspective – as a limitation on the arbitrary use of the political and technological power, in the name of that dignity every human being carries.

It is not by chance that, throughout the twentieth century, philosophical thought – reinterpreting Hegel's dialectic of recognition – discovered the concept of intersubjectivity: the gaze of the modern subject resting on nature in order to dominate it, is now flanked by the gaze of the person meeting with its fellow-person (Husserl, Merleau-Ponty, Buber) and recognises it as being part of its own world, of its own path in search of freedom and happiness. By addressing the other-person, its gaze also meets the poor, the sick, the migrant, the victim of inequalities. Consistent with this 'turn' in social philosophy arises the personalist and solidaristic vocation of the Constitutions of the twentieth century, which, taking care of the person, distance themselves from both possessive individualism and totalitarian collectivism.

However, more recent times have called into question this theoretical, ethical and political development. Throughout the twentieth century, the value of the person was increasingly recognised and protected: by national and European legislators and by the courts of justice themselves, which have gone beyond the formalist approach, interpreting the law by looking at the principles, using general clauses, and accepting the responsibility to guarantee effective remedies.[8] Nevertheless, at the dawn of the new millennium, we find ourselves on a horizon characterised by many uncertainties and some pitfalls. Consider the digital revolution, where the relationship between man and technology shows its new and even more frightening face: technology is no longer just the iron cage that threatens but remains external to human beings. Instead, it presents itself as a combination of material and immaterial devices that interface with humans' organic constitution and impact their cognitive and decision-making processes. It is now difficult, if not impossible, to even distinguish what is natural from what is artificial. The uncertainty about the future of the person is

[8] See HW Micklitz, 'Constitutionalization, Regulation and Private Law' in S Grundmann, HW Micklitz and M Renner, *New Private Law. A Pluralistic Approach* (Cambridge, Cambridge University Press, 2021). In the broad chapter opening *New Private Law* we read: 'In law, the challenge is to create and reason through a result which, given the value judgments of the legal community, can claim acceptance in that community even though interpretation is a creative act, influenced by the personality and the preconception(s) of the interpreter. In this act, written law, precedent, etc., but also convictions of what is legally justified, as embedded in society, are integrated and gradually merged. In this respect, a reformulation of what other social or behavioural sciences opine about a legal rule or issue – positions that often offer a more precise reformulation of important value judgments in society at large – can also be integrated into the process, "reformulated" and indeed "reconstructed". Through this reconstruction, adequacy to the domain of law and to the legal community is to be positively created and looked for, taking the core parameters of legal evaluation as the guiding framework – fundamental rights for example, or the fundamental principles of whatever field of (private) law is at stake – particularly when national law is to be applied. In private law beyond the state, human rights are a necessary point of reference, but also customary principles that guide private ordering in the transnational arena' (Grundmann, Micklitz and Renner (ibid) 1, 13). Within the context of rethinking the forms of contemporary private law, special attention must be given to Giuseppe Vettori's investigation (*Effettività tra legge e diritto* (Milano, Giuffrè Francis Lefebvre, 2020)), which sees in those forms 'una dinamica giuridica fondata sulle acquisizioni maturate in un ordine costituzionale ove le regole vengono scritte da soggetti diversi: il legislatore, la giurisprudenza, le Autorità indipendenti, la scienza giuridica. Tutti alla ricerca di una verità parziale e della soluzione più giusta in un sistema complesso e plurale. Ricerca che deve, sempre più spesso, abbandonare visioni generali e astratte. Perché la verità si manifesta dal basso, fissando i fatti vivi con una flessibilità cognitiva che non è assenza di certezza, ma attitudine a comprendere e affrontare situazioni difficili e complesse'.

increased by the awareness that the gaze resting on man today is not only that of the other-man calling him to responsibility (Lévinas[9]), but is the gaze of the information society collecting data, monitoring movements, building digital profiles to influence economic and political choices.

Yet, as will be emphasised throughout this chapter, despite the concerns of many scholars who see the growing dominance of technocracy in recent history, the *nòmos* has not bowed before the overbearing force of *techné*. Keeping in mind the lesson of personalism, law has and continues to fulfil a social and civil role, in order to prevent digital civilisation from opening the door to surveillance capitalism.[10] From the perspective of legal philosophy, regulations – both *hard law* and *soft law* – such as those on personal data protection, consumer protection, countering disinformation and hate speech, seem to be aimed not only at protecting the abstract rights of the individual, but at safeguarding that being-person whose voice – as in its unclear, and perhaps dual, etymological root mentioned at the beginning of this chapter – resounds through the mask.

Nevertheless, we cannot deny that many pitfalls are hidden on the horizon. For example, the ever-increasing intertwining of man and machine could lead to the dissolution of the person in the information flow of collective intelligence. Think of the new horizon of the metaverse, in which the user's gaze is no longer focused on nature nor on the other man, but will be entirely enclosed by a world resembling a video game. The person even risks having the connection to its physical dimension dissolved, to the point of being identified or at least confused with an avatar.

In this delicate transition, philosophical reflection is called to an effort of thinking, to the questioning of some of its comforting clichés and to an assumption of responsibility in trying to think of technique in a new way. In this sense, it may be useful to wonder if the philosopher Heidegger is right when, drawing from the poet Hölderlin, he asserts 'Wo aber Gefahr ist, wächst / Das Rettende auch' ('Where the danger lies, also grows the saving power').[11] At the very moment when the boundaries between the natural and the artificial dimensions seem to be blurring, grounds for a revival of the person could be glimpsed. For this to happen, intellectual and civil bravery are required: first of all, the bravery to leave behind the (comforting but misleading) dichotomy between natural and artificial, and to become aware of the intrinsic technical constitution of human nature (think of social scientists or anthropologists like Gehlen and Plessner). Then, the bravery to rethink our philosophical

[9] 'Il faut aussi penser l'homme à partir de la responsabilité plus ancienne que le conatus de la substance ou que l'identification intérieure; à partir de la responsabilité qui, appelant toujours au-dehors dérange précisément cette intériorité; il faut penser l'homme à partir du soi se mettant malgré soi à la place de tous, substitué à tous de par sa non-interchangeabilité même; il faut penser l'homme à partir de la condition ou de l'incondition d'otage – d'otage de tous les autres qui précisément, autres, n'appartiennent pas au même genre que moi, puisque je suis responsable d'eux, sans me reposer sur leur responsabilité à mon égard qui leur permettrait de se substituer à moi, car même de leur responsabilité je suis, en fin de compte, et de l'abord, responsable. C'est par cette responsabilité supplémentaire que la subjectivité n'est pas le Moi, mais moi' (E Lévinas, *Humanisme de l'autre homme* (Montpellier, Fata Morgana, 1972) 110–11).

[10] S Zuboff, *The Age of Surveillance Capitalism. The Fight for a Human Future at the New Frontier of Power* (New York, Public affairs-Hachette, 2019) esp ch 18.

[11] M Heidegger, 'Die Frage nach der Technik' in M Heidegger, *Vorträge und Aufsätze*, Gesamtausgabe, Band 7, (Frankfurt a.M., Klostermann, 2000) 29.

and anthropological dictionary and to start considering our being-person not as something that belongs to us, as an ontological quality, but rather as something that we have to create daily through our free and responsible action.

To consider our being-person as a task rather than an ontological quality, does not mean, of course, that we should compete with machines or pursue the dream of technologically enhancing our defective nature.[12] The scenario proposed by transhumanist theories does indeed look like a disturbing dream, whose danger has been repeatedly emphasised not only by this or that moral philosopher, but by national bioethics committees, even standing on different ideological positions. After all, these perspectives end up eliminating the strength of the human race. Setting us exactly in the opposite direction, it is precisely our incompleteness, our being-defective that is the ineradicable root of our being human, and at the same time the reason for its non-reproducibility. What is missing from the intelligence of machines and their extraordinary computational speed is precisely that inner universe of man that has taken on different names over time – from soul to spirit, to the deep self as enlightened by psychoanalysis – and still resonates in us through the mask of our being-person.

In this sense, the age of techno-humanism invites us to take up a double challenge. First, *to become different from what we've always been*, to explore new horizons of intelligence through a fundamental process of emotional and cognitive education and training in co-determination between human and artificial intelligence. Secondly, our task is *to really become who we are*, to reconcile with our own incompleteness, to rediscover in it the root of our dignity and the reason why we are not artificially reproducible.

II. THE DIGITAL REVOLUTION: PROMISES, DOUBTS, RIGHTS

But what does it mean to become different from what we are? How should we understand the co-determination between human and artificial intelligence? Should we perhaps hybridise our intelligence? Isn't there a risk of distorting it to the point of endangering our human being? Do the potential benefits really justify the assumption of risks? And, if we want to set limits, who will be empowered to do so?

These are issues that appeal to jurists, sociologists and all citizens who are entering the third phase of the information society. The widespread use of PCs in the 1980s began to change work methods, particularly the way we handle, organise and store documents. The explosion of the Internet at the turn of the millennium then impacted the processes of acquiring knowledge, social interaction and self-representation. Today, the stakes are higher: the advent of artificial intelligence seems to affect the very use of human intelligence.[13]

[12] In critical terms on the mythology of enhancement, see, eg, M Hauskeller, *Mythologies of Transhumanism* (Cham, Palgrave Macmillan, 2016). With specific reference to bioethical implications see, eg, L d'Avack, *Il dominio delle biotecnologie. L'opportunità e i limiti dell'intervento del diritto*, vol I (Torino, Giappichelli, 2018) and L Palazzani, *Dalla bio-etica alla tecno-etica: nuove sfide al diritto* (Torino, Giappichelli, 2017).

[13] See L Floridi, *The Fourth Revolution. How the Infosphere is Reshaping Human Reality* (Oxford, Oxford University Press, 2014).

This entry into a new era of intelligence is taking place at a time when humans, at least in the Global North, are experiencing a state of disorientation. The second stage of the information society has had a strong impact: we barely had time to become fully familiar with the new status of being navigators of the infospace, such that we immediately felt as if we ended up in a big videogame over which we had no control.[14]

While sailing in an immaterial space full of information, services and entertainment initially gave the impression of renewed freedom, doubts arose during the journey. Suddenly, contemporary humans felt subjected to a sort of permanent control: they realised that information, services and entertainment, despite the promise of being free, were paid for with their personal data; that these data were used to profile their interests, preferences and purchasing decisions; that traces of their telematic navigation – processed and indexed by algorithms – allow their mosaic of identity to be exposed to the public by simply entering their identifying data into search engines; that a part of their past life has become a sort of common good because, as humans unlearn the use of memory, the network remembers everything and resists the idea of forgetting, even very distant events.[15]

The reasons for concern increased when contemporary humans, looking at the management and control processes of their data, realised that these are governed by private actors, and that public institutions, at the national and supranational levels, find it difficult to regulate the strategic choices of owners of digital capital. The hope that institutions can influence the governance of the digital world is further weakened by the crisis affecting today's democracies and by citizens' distrust in being able to effectively participate in decision-making processes.

Thus, in the transition from the second to the third stage of the information society, the promise of a renewed freedom, announced by the open sea of telematic navigation, seems to turn into its opposite: the spectre of a new and more insidious form of domination. It is no coincidence that, in such a bleak scenario, the theories of surveillance capitalism[16] are eagerly embraced (while data continues to be given away with the same flippancy).

Yet, today's feeling of disorientation, and the very theoretical positions that justify it, raise some questions. It is worthwhile focusing on this point in order to clarify in what terms, in this chapter, a deconstruction of the most radical critical positions of digital society is proposed.

The primary objection that must be made relates to the capacity of such stances to fully understand the present times and especially to grasp the ambivalent potentiality provided by the digital revolution. First, there is a serious lack of awareness of the rights and related protections afforded by national and supranational legal systems.[17]

[14] One of the clearest reconstructions is provided by D Cardon, *À quoi rêvent les algorithmes. Nos vies à l'heure des big data* (Paris, Éditions du Seuil et La République des Idées, 2015) esp ch 3.

[15] An interesting reconstruction of the Internet evolution, based on an analysis of empirical evidence, can be read in J Curran, N Fenton and D Freedman, *Misunderstanding the Internet*, 2nd edn (New York, Routledge, 2016) esp ch 1, 1, ch 3, and ch 5, 145.

[16] See Zuboff (n 10). Indeed, some of the critical issues of the information society had been identified well in advance and with a much different balance by Stefano Rodotà, see eg *Tecnopolitica. La democrazia e le nuove tecnologie della comunicazione* (Roma-Bari, Laterza, 1997).

[17] See L DeNardis, DL Cogburn, NS Levinson and F Musiani, *Researching Internet Governance. Methods, Frameworks, Futures* (Cambridge MA, The MIT Press, 2020) esp ch 5, 105ff.

In order to clarify this objection, a few examples can be given. It is complained that data are being used abusively, consumer decisions (and perhaps also political decisions, as in the case of Cambridge Analytica) are influenced by extensive profiling or hidden influencer marketing, algorithms induce desires for readily available products, search engine result indexing distorts knowledge of facts, the Internet is controlled by a few private players driven solely by profit, etc. All of this is part of a critical assessment of the alleged inefficiency of countermeasures taken by public institutions. However, this critique, despite being rooted in valid concerns, seems to overlook the fact that precise regulations exist for each of these phenomena (such as the European General Data Protection Regulation or coordinated consumer laws at the European level), as well as codes of conduct, guidelines and best practices (including legal tools for influencer marketing implemented by regulatory authorities and self-regulatory bodies), which are inspired by the recognition of the intrinsic worth of human beings and can serve as a basis for imposing sanctions and demanding adequate protection of their rights (eg, data deletion or de-indexing of web pages).

This is not the place to identify the many causes of this insufficient culture of rights and the inadequate theoretical appreciation of existing regulations which protect our personality. In the Italian tradition, for instance, a latent anti-juridical sentiment has its roots not only in a certain strand of idealistic philosophy but also in some currents of Catholic culture, particularly those who consider that positive law, if not in accordance with natural law, is reduced to a mere technique at the service of whatever purpose. It is interesting to observe how this anti-juridical sentiment has often been accompanied by a strong politicisation, with the axiom that the state, especially parliament, should provide the solution to every problem.[18]

The harmful effects of this ideologisation which has long dominated public discourse, creating sharp divisions and conferring a distinct identity-based significance to political engagement, are even more evident nowadays as the digital revolution demands open-mindedness and solutions to previously unknown problems. Prior to adopting an approach to problem management, ideologism[19] is a disposition of mind characterising individuals or social groups who believe they possess the *correct answers* rather than recognising the need to pose the *right questions*. It becomes secondary whether the answers are derived from a dogmatic system from which the worldview of a political party or religious denomination church is derived, or rather from a doctrine derived from tradition: these are in any case answers believed to be

[18] Some useful suggestions can be found in the 'Dialogo sulla filosofia a venire' between JL Nancy and R Esposito, opening the Italian translation of JL Nancy, *Être singulier pluriel* (*Essere singolare plurale* (Torino, Einaudi, 2001) esp ch 16.

[19] Of course, the defence of ideology woven by Natalino Irti (*La tenaglia. In difesa dell'ideologia politica* (Roma-Bari, Laterza, 2008)) escapes such ideologism. It is no coincidence that he contrasts the approach of the ideologue with that of the doctrinaire. 'L'ideologo muove da una filosofia o concezione della vita verso la realtà, e ad essa la applica e commisura; il dottrinario ripudia la realtà, e, dove le cose siano diverse e discordi, le dice erronee e le rifiuta nella loro effettualità. Il dottrinario giudica la realtà dall'esterno, come conforme o difforme; l'ideologo sta all'interno della realtà, e vi esprime il proprio pensiero e la propria azione'. In Irti's perspective, therefore, while the doctrinaire has no need to question the real, and rejects reality that does not allow itself to be shaped by the ideal form, the ideologue, on the other hand, aspires to shape the reality, but, being inside it, is induced to subject his ideas to a constant practice of proof and refutation, verifying their feasibility and appropriateness with respect to the object (16).

exact by definition, and it is argued that public institutions should merely take them on board as premises for solving any problem.

Such remarks suggest a provisional conclusion about the excess of ideology and the lack of realism that characterise some critics of the current age. Indeed, there are scholars who, while warning against the apocalyptic outcomes of algorithmic governance, yearn for an era when public space was a battleground of opposing life visions. Well, it is worth remembering that the ideological use of human intelligence has significantly hindered its evolution.

III. THINKING ABOUT TECHNOLOGY AND THE TEACHINGS OF SCIENCE

The analysis so far can be furthered by reflecting on the methodological approach that should shape the investigation of the phenomena brought by technological innovation. What is lacking in the face of the digital revolution is a genuine inclination to engage in research and formulate the right questions. The internal debate within the humanities is emblematic in this regard: after the era of ideology with its unshakable certainties, the philosophical and literary postmodernism that followed, in the wake of Lyotard's outstanding investigation into the legitimation of science,[20] filled universities and scientific journals with fine discussions on the deconstruction of grand narratives, but ultimately only replaced collective illusions with a sad and somewhat complacent disenchantment. Certainly, globalisation and the advent of the information society have brought forth new issues. However, the aforementioned sense of disorientation persists, stemming from the difficulty of recognising phenomena, especially those related to the latest technological innovations, and deciding how to classify them.

In this context, the encounter with artificial intelligence can provide an opportunity to embrace a renewed research mindset and ask us what it means to be human in a world increasingly inhabited by non-human yet thinking and speaking entities. This requires a shift in perspective, moving beyond mere criticism of ideology and seeking to understand what still makes reflection on the fate of technology problematic. It is no longer sufficient to point out the inadequacy of the dichotomy – brilliantly conceived by Umberto Eco,[21] but now deceptive – between the apocalyptic and the integrated. Rather, it is about identifying the factors that continue to hinder the development of a new knowledge, a culture that combines both technical and genuinely humanistic aspects.

One of these factors is the separation between STEM disciplines and humanistic thought. This separation has a long history (although it is absent, not by chance, in both the Renaissance and the Enlightenment) and has had devastating effects, leaving us with the enduring dichotomy between humanism and technoscience. Therefore, an essential condition for a reflection on technology that meets the challenges ahead is

[20] JF Lyotard, *La condition postmoderne. Rapport sur le savoir* (Paris, Les Editions de Minuit, 1979).

[21] U Eco, *Apocalittici e integrati. Comunicazione di massa e teorie della cultura di massa* [1964] (Milano, Bompiani, 2008).

the education of young generations in the dialogue between hard and technological sciences on one hand, and humanities on the other.[22] Some universities have recognised this and have started to design interdisciplinary programmes or to include, for example, the study of machine learning as well as literature, sustainable technologies, philosophy or art history in the education of future managers, jurists or public administrators.

It is not appropriate to discuss here the factors that have caused, particularly in continental Europe, the divorce between quantitative and qualitative methods, between hard and social sciences, between laboratory-based experimentation and speculative intellectualism.[23] However, we can contemplate their effects. Today, there is considerable support for a reflection on technology that, in the name of defending human dignity and centrality, adopts a backward stance towards technological innovation. These positions seem to be motivated by a resistance, once again ideological, to understanding innovation and examining its potential and risks. It is a retreat from the unknown that, by relying on familiar and reassuring answers, relieves us from the task of asking new questions and, thus, from the weight of doubt.

Yet, the lesson of history was clear: the art of doubt is a prerequisite for genuine knowledge (and indeed, for civilised coexistence). This lesson is connected to the scientific method,[24] but has not always been valued by the humanities, whose interpreters have often assumed a militant role, reading history through ideologically distorted lenses and observing reality in terms of *how it should be* rather than *as it actually is*. In doing so, they have forgotten the epistemic and civil message of the best scientific method, which trains humility, transforms convictions into hypotheses, tests them against facts, repeats experiments, and shares results with the scientific community. It is a message that immunises against prejudice, educates in doubt before constructing theories, fosters listening to others and weighing their arguments, especially if they express dissent or refutation.

To put it simply: the correcting of Newtonian physics by Einstein's relativity serves as a lesson of ethics because it reminds us that no outcome of research can claim indisputable certainty. Similarly, Popper's falsificationism, challenged by Kuhn's paradigms, urges vigilance towards the scientific method itself, avoiding any form of absolutism.

[22] Interesting suggestions can be found in A de la Garza and C Travis, *The STEAM Revolution. Transdisciplinary Approach to Science, Technology, Engineering, Arts, Humanities and Mathematics* (Cham, Springer, 2019). See also H Vaziri an NM Bradburn, 'Flourishing Effects of Integrating the Arts and Humanities in STEM Education. A Review of Past Studies and an Agenda for Future Research' in L Tay and JO Pawelsky (eds), *The Oxford Handbook of the Positive Humanities* (New York, Oxford University Press, 2021) 71.

[23] An interesting proposal in order to reactivate the dialogue between the hard sciences and philosophy had been earlier formulated by P Frank in *Philosophy of Science. The Link Between Science and Philosophy* [1957] (Mineola NY, Dover, 2004).

[24] 'I think that when we know that we actually do live in uncertainty, then we ought to admit it; it is of great value to realize that we do not know the answers to different questions. This attitude of mind – this attitude of uncertainty – is vital to the scientist, and it is this attitude of mind which the student must first acquire. It becomes a habit of thought. Once acquired, one cannot retreat from it any more' (RP Feynman, *The Relation of Science and Religion* [1956] in RP Feynman *The Pleasure of Findings Things Out. The best short works of Richard P. Feynman* (New York, Basic Books, 1999) 248).

What seems to sometimes be lacking in certain contemporary reflections on the digital revolution is the courage to confront unknown phenomena, freeing oneself from prejudices and searching for the right questions. A humanistic culture devoid of doubt risks to erode the foundations on which it rests and to jeopardise its contribution to the development of a more intelligent and just civilisation. Moreover, today's criticism of the digital society seems to forget that the formidable computational power of artificial intelligence is one of the ways in which human creative action manifests itself – a manifestation that objectifies itself in the present and continually transcends its own concretions, opening up to the further production of reality and meaning, thus continuing the mysterious work of creation and/or evolution, regardless of how they occurred.[25]

So, we go back to the initial questions: what role does our human existence play in the horizon of techno-humanism? In what terms and with what limitations can we consider a co-determination between human intelligence and artificial intelligence?

IV. THE TECHNICAL CONSTITUTION OF THE INDIVIDUAL

To evaluate possible answers, we must first become aware that – according to the principles of hermeneutic philosophy, from Gadamer onwards[26] – these questions can be formulated from a temporal horizon in which our cognitive and decision-making processes are already hybridised through daily interaction with intelligent machines. We must then come to terms with our intrinsic technical constitution, freeing ourselves from the natural/artificial dichotomy and rediscovering in artifice the expression of our inventive nature. After all, humans are technical beings no less than they are social beings: they transcend the limitations of their organic apparatus through technical action on themselves and the surrounding environment.[27] If it is true, as psychoanalysis teaches, that human existence is marked by an original lack,[28] this is expressed both in the demand for sense[29] and in the search for technical solutions that impact one's life. In this perspective, the creation of intelligent machines should be understood as a response to our constitutive incompleteness. Consider the fact that our world is filling up with speaking machines: while it is true that human speech is primarily expressed through voice and only later through writing, it can be said that humans are devising technical devices that present themselves in the way most congenial to them: by becoming audible speech.

[25] An original and well-balanced reading of the technical constitution of man can be read in M Magatti, *Oltre l'infinito. Storia della potenza dal sacro alla tecnica* (Milano, Feltrinelli, 2018).

[26] HG Gadamer, *Wahrheit und Methode. Grundzüge einer philosophischen Hermeneutik* (Tübingen, JCB Mohr, 1960).

[27] See A Gehlen, *Der Mensch. Seine Natur und seine Stellung in der Welt* [1940–1959] (Frankfurt a.M., Klostermann, 2016) and H Plessner, *Die Stufen des Organischen und der Mensch: Einleitung in die philosophische Anthropologie* [1928], 3rd edn (Berlin-Boston, De Gruyter, 1975).

[28] J Lacan, *Le Séminaire de Jacques Lacan. Livre XI. Les quatre concepts fondamentaux de la psychanalyse* [1964] (Paris, Éditions du Seuil, 1973) Leçons 2 and 3, 21.

[29] A fine investigation from a legal-philosophical perspective on the demand for sense is offered by B Romano, *Forma del senso. Legalità e giustizia* (Torino, Giappichelli, 2012).

It is almost superfluous to emphasise, however, that this does not mean that a voicebot can be confused with a human voice, and above all, it does not eliminate the many problems that contaminating it with artificial intelligence may bring. For example, consider the theorists of transhumanism who hope that humans can achieve performance similar to that of thinking machines by artificially enhancing their biological constitution.[30] Such projects of biotechnological hybridisation are not convincing on theoretical grounds, before even considering ethical concerns. They measure intelligence by the standard of computational capacity, thus reducing our ontological incompleteness to a defect, to a performative deficit of a human machine that is too natural and too poorly implemented technically. In doing so, they seem to underestimate certain typical characteristics of the human person that artificial intelligence lacks. Consider emotional intelligence, which is not a secondary expression of our ontological incompleteness: we know that a machine programmed to exhibit emotional states is simply executing a program without grasping its meaning because its *logos* is disembodied.[31]

It is precisely the perfect and disembodied functionality of the intelligent machine that emphasises the value of human incompleteness, leading us to unafraid consideration of the contamination between natural and artificial intelligence.

V. THE EMBODIED PERSON, THE HISTORICAL HORIZON AND THE COMPASS OF PRINCIPLES

Embracing the idea of such contamination certainly does not guarantee prudent and appropriate choices. As always, in the face of new and mostly unknown phenomena, rules, limits and sanctions are invoked. However, in this regard, the legal experience of our time provides a useful suggestion: before discussing the content of rules, we may need to learn a new way of regulating.

Two examples can illustrate this point. The first can already be found in the Italian Constitution of 1948, which has been previously mentioned for its personalistic inspiration. Consider the role played by principles in it: unlike the modern legislator, convinced of being able to eliminate the uncertainty of the future through a body of laws ready to provide solutions for every case, the founding fathers of the Italian Republic professed realism, acknowledging the variety and never definitive foreseeability of experience. In a sense, they reconciled with the idea of uncertainty that modern law had rejected.[32] In a complex society, the new ultimately eludes any predictive capacity, to the point of blurring the very line of demarcation between the abstract and the concrete on which the classical logical order of law rests. Hence, the lesson from those founding fathers: principles offer a compass to protect the dignity of the individual, guiding them through the sea of uncertainty.

[30] See, eg, R Kurzweil, *The Singularity is Near. When Humans transcend Biology* (New York, Penguin Books, 2005), as well as the earlier *The Age of Spiritual Machines. When Computers exceed Human Intelligence* (New York, Penguin Books, 2000).

[31] On the being-body understood as a properly human experience, subtle considerations can be read in JL Nancy, *Corpus* (Paris, Métailié, 2000) eg 97ff.

[32] Masterful, on this theme, the reading by P Grossi, *Oltre la legalità* (Roma-Bari, Laterza, 2020) 14ff.

The second example can be found in the AI Act that came into force on 1 August 2024. In much of the text, the legislator prefers to identify compliance objectives, leaving operators discretion in choosing the most suitable methods to achieve them. Thus, a flexible and collaborative legislative approach is adopted, involving all relevant actors in finding the most appropriate technological solutions, considering the evolution of knowledge and best practices in achieving those objectives. In this way, the law itself assumes a realistic attitude, allowing the opportunity and time to observe phenomena, record changes and constantly adjust regulations, while keeping its gaze oriented toward principles. This preference for flexible and dynamic regulation is particularly evident in the provision for *regulatory sandboxes*, allowing the development and testing of new artificial intelligence systems in a protected environment where regulatory authorities can monitor the impact of innovations on deserving interests.[33]

The lesson delivered by contemporary law can be useful for those who are currently pondering the potential and the risks for our being-person in the prospect of co-determination between our intelligence and artificial intelligence. Adopting an ideological stance of resistance towards innovation means to deny our own technical constitution. Merely setting off the alarm about the alleged fate of algorithmic governance means to ignore the tools available to demand the protection of our rights. We are instead called upon, especially as scholars in human and social sciences, to recover the best lesson from modern science, that is to set aside our prejudices, to transform our certainties into hypotheses, and to have the humility to test them – without ever forgetting, of course, that the scientist also has a responsibility and that the fate of the technical animal that we are is at stake in every experiment. In this sense, it is precisely the task of contemporary law to establish principles and rules for these 'new times', always taking care of our intrinsic and ingenious weakness: in regulating artificial intelligence as in guaranteeing proper living conditions, in preventing human beings from being subject to algorithmic decisions as in taking on the misery of those suffering and lacking even the strength to make their voices *per-sonare* (resound) through the mask.

While keeping its gaze open to the future, law must first and foremost lend its ear to that *flatus vocis* if, even in times of outstanding technological innovation, it really wants to continue taking the person seriously.

[33] See, eg, S Ranchordas, 'Experimental Regulations for AI: Sandboxes for Morals and Mores' (2021) *Morals + Machines* 86.

6

Person and Future

GIUSEPPE VETTORI

I. A PREMISE. THE HISTORICITY OF THE 'PERSON'

THE CORE IDEA of this chapter is the following. The individual subject of law is a distant memory. Philosophers and historians who speak of the impersonal evoke 'a society turned to the common' against the sanctity of rights. But the jurist 'is not yet ready to give up the language of the Person',[1] for two reasons. Firstly, jurists have always been accustomed to filling their tools with new content. And secondly, they are bound, in the European Union, by a system of sources where the person is central. Not only that: in the time of digital innovation and the epochal crisis of politics, civil law must know how to build a general theory capable of ordering the needs and expectations of this century. With a clear objective: the person must be 'historicised' and conjugated with the many variables of the human and those who are not yet there. Sustainability demands that we give order to new ways of living and thinking. The environment and climate demand activity with ever-tightening deadlines. The market must know how to value the 'common' within the framework of a plural and democratic order all to be built. Without falling into the myth of unitary and authoritarian recomposition, but with a new juridicity expressed today by a plurality of sources and actors.

Let us begin with the past.

II. FLORENCE, *GENIUS LOCI* OF HUMANISM AND SOCIAL PERSONALISM

During the Lent of 1491, Pico della Mirandola and Agnolo Poliziano, together with Marsilio Ficino and members of the Platonic Academy, met at the Badia Fiesolana, now the seat of the European University Institute. They came with a strong mission: they attempted 'to combine the evangelical message and the *paideia* of the ancients',

[1] B Sordi, 'Pubblico e privato: ancora su confini, identità, intersezioni' in F Pistelli (ed), *Diritto pubblico e diritto privato. La grande "dicotomia" ieri e oggi*, Persona e Mercato, Dialoghi sul nostro tempo (Bologna, 2020) 27, 32–35. M Spanò, *Fare il molteplice. Il diritto privato alla prova del comune* (Turin, Rosenberg & Sellier, 2022) 9; N Lipari, '*Un problema di confini*? (A *proposito di due libri recenti*)' (2022) 76 *Rivista trimestrale di diritto e procedura civile* 195.

to forge 'the vision in which humanism has always identified with':[2] human beings, so says Pico's Oration, are capable of obtaining and possessing 'everything according to (their) desire and (their) will' to take on any aspect, 'free from any constraint' to establish their nature based on a '[free] will', assigned by God to each one. A human being placed 'at the center of the world', 'neither heavenly nor earthly, neither mortal nor immortal', 'invested with the honour of freely deciding' and 'moulding themselves as they prefer'.[3] Many centuries later, in 1944, Giorgio La Pira left Florence to evade an arrest order by the fascist police and, in the loneliness of his escape, began a reflection[4] on the condition of the human being at that time, moving from a point of view, a *Weltanschauung*, capable of providing answers to questions on the essential problems of reality and history. His critique of the thought of Hegel and later Marx and Engels, 'is measured by the yardstick of the person',[5] whom Hegel considers 'as a derived value; a moment over time; a moment in the flow of reality'. To La Pira's criticism, even Kant's construction appears limpid in its proclamation of a 'starry sky' and a 'moral law', but full of contradictions when one wonders 'what is hidden behind this thick veil that prevents, without remedy, knowledge of the self, of things, of others'. Nor is he convinced by Rousseau's reduction of the human being 'to the order of nature and reason', which attempts to 'explain the whole of the human being by remaining on the level of the human being' with an impossible task.[6] According to our author, the crisis of the person begins with the Reformation,[7] strengthens in the modern age[8] and is accentuated in 'bourgeois-capitalist civilisation' with 'the emergence of that minority of oppressors and that immense majority of oppressed that characterises the capitalist economy' of the time. Against this crisis, 'the socialist and communist reaction' does not appear groundless to La Pira: 'the pendulum that had swung violently to the right could not but swing, with equal violence, to the left: the individualism of Hobbes, Locke, Rousseau and Kant, could not but be

[2] E Balducci, *The Land of Sunset. Saggio sulla transizione* ([1992] Florence, Giunti, 2005) 6–7.

[3] G Pico della Mirandola, *La dignità dell'uomo*, (ed R Ebgi, transl F Padovani) (Turin, Einaudi, 2021) 7, 9.

[4] G La Pira, *Premesse della Politica e Architettura di uno Stato democratico* (Florence, Libreria Editrice Fiorentina, 1945) XV (reprinted 1978): 'Bourgeois society and capitalism are based on precise metaphysical causes that originate "from the individualist practice and politics that flourished between the end of the 18th century and the first decades of the 19th century"'. The genesis of Marxism also has ideal causes based on 'a collectivist and materialist view of the world, of man and of history' as elaborated with great rigour by Marx, Engels and Feuerbach. In both cases, 'when research is conducted down to its elementary nuclei, the metaphysical root is ineluctably manifested' and the conclusion is clear: the roots of the crisis of time, before being a 'political and economic crisis, is a crisis of ideas' and social problems must be examined by moving from a point of view that dominates them, a metaphysical background, a *Weltanschauung* that provides answers to questions on the essential problems of 'reality': God, the universe, man, society and history.

[5] ibid 23.

[6] ibid 28.

[7] ibid 28: 'Destroying a hierarchical system of human and divine values on which Christian history and civilisation had been built'.

[8] ibid 32: '[It] will be the age of nature without grace, of man without Christ, of philosophy without theology, of art without religion, of law, economics and politics without morality, of the state without the church, of the earth without heaven.' 'One thinks of the bourgeois-capitalist civilisation that flourished on the metaphysical foundations of the Reformation, of the English and French Enlightenment and of Kant's own meditation.'

replaced by Hegel's idealist statolatry or Marx's materialist statolatry'. Hence the need to overcome the human being's annihilating 'collectivism' and enlightenment 'without mystery and without warmth'[9] to return to St Thomas and the 'skeletal and coldly exact' structure of the *Summa Theologica*.[10] All this leads him to state that society is a means and the human being an end: the destiny of the human being '*is not closed in time, but is outside time*', so that 'no temporal reality – family, state, class, race – can claim to "totalise" him'.[11] La Pira's subsequent intense political activity is well known. Elected to the Constituent Assembly, he wrote some fundamental articles of the Constitution. He was part of the De Gasperi Government and was Mayor of Florence three times, aiming to protect the poor, and being in dialogue with the world.

III. FROM THE SUBJECT TO THE PERSON

In Italy, the path from the subject to the person[12] is well marked at the beginning of this century, following the constitutional framework, reform of the codes and the Charter of Fundamental Rights of the European Union. Where diversity and self-determination come to the fore is as values that complete the structure of the legal order. The stages are well known: dignity (Articles 3, 32, 36, 41 Const) that broadens the dialectic between formal and substantive equality and brings out 'the material conditions of concrete persons' of flesh; Article 2, which incorporates rights and duties in the bond of inviolability and the bond of solidarity; and Article 32 where 'the democratic sovereign renews the promise of intangibility of the individual sphere'.[13] In the early years of the new century, a new social figure constructed by law is theorised. The *homo dignus*, the holder of inviolable rights and recipient of the promise of a life worth living thanks to the inviolability of fundamental rights and subjective situations of every human. In the mid-2010s to the mid-2020s, it is difficult to say whether a different anthropological model has asserted itself.[14] Indeed, some observe that the story and the traditional function of the subject of law seem to have come to an end just when a category of great persuasive force would help us in tackling today's problems: from protection against Big Data and AI, to guaranteeing the rights of future generations, to the issue of the environment and sustainability. And we return to the question whether a foundation can still be found in the universal vocation of the person – which requires, of course, a global dimension, articulated, according to Duncan Kennedy, in three historical phases:[15] classical thought, between the mid-nineteenth and early twentieth centuries, social

[9] ibid 35–36.
[10] ibid 37.
[11] ibid 40.
[12] S Rodotà, *Dal Soggetto alla Persona* (Napoli, Editoriale scientifica, 2007).
[13] ibid 15ff, 44ff.
[14] S Rodotà, *Antropologia dell'homo dignus* (Lectio Magistralis, Università di Macerata, 2010) 57ff.
[15] MR Marella, 'Antropologia del soggetto di diritto. Note sulla trasformazione di una categoria giuridica' in F Bilotta and F Raimondi, (eds), *Il soggetto di diritto. Storia ed evoluzione di un concetto nel diritto privato* (Napoli, Jovene, 2020) 47ff; and the reference to D Kennedy, 'Tree Globalisations of Law and Legal Thought: 1850–2000' in DM Trubek and A Santos (eds), *The New Law and Economic Development*.

thought, around the 1970s, and contemporary thought. Where the shattering of the subject is largely the result of the sharp decline of the welfare state and is confirmed by the exponential growth of inequalities, which have reached an intolerable level. From here three possible 'deconstructive' projects are articulated: the relaunching of a strong idea of distributive justice, through new instruments; a credible statute on common goods in contrast to the subject–object dichotomy; and reflection on the non-subject in the various declinations of the philosophy of the impersonal. This is the path most followed by philosophy and the history of ideas in recent decades.

IV. PERSONALISM AND THE PHILOSOPHY OF THE IMPERSONAL

As is well known, during the twentieth century, the value of the human being was affirmed by personalism in opposition to the various doctrines of the time (idealism, positivism, Marxism and existentialism), and had to be conjugated in the plural because of its roots: religious (in patristics, scholasticism and humanism) and secular (Renaissance, Enlightenment, Romantic). A common trait marks personalism throughout the century:[16] 'It [personalism] comes into play, in a recurring manner, whenever the person is at stake[17] and, during the 1960s and 1970s, gives rise to a strong criticism of nihilism and relativism',[18] for a clear reason: 'the person is more than the egocentric individual, it is more than the totalitarian state, it is more than the massified consumer society: the person is a subject engaged in the conquest of freedom'.[19] With radical adhesions and criticisms, Maritain's reflection occupies more than 40 years of the twentieth century, aiming at 'making possible a reconciliation of pre-modern and modern, for a concrete defence of the human person in the various fields of knowing, acting and doing'.[20] Roberto Esposito in Italy, and many other scholars in Europe,[21] indicate a different path between the end of the

A Critical Appraisal (Cambridge, Cambridge University Press, 2006) 19ff; R Míguez Núñez, *Le avventure del soggetto. Contributo teorico comparativo sulle nuove forme di soggettività giuridica* (Milan, Mimesis, 2018); E Resta, *Potere e diritti* (Turin, Giappichelli, 1996) 170. G Teubner, *Ibridi e Attanti. Attori collettivi e enti non umani nella società e nel diritto* (trans Ludovica Zampino) (Milan-Udine, Mimesis, 2015).

[16] G Fornero and S Tassinari, *Le filosofie del Novecento* (Milan, Bruno Mondadori, 2002) 901.

[17] J Maritain, *Umanesimo integrale* (Giampietro Dore tr) ([1936] Rome, Studium, 1946), followed by the same author, among other works, *La Persona e il bene comune* ([1947] Brescia, Morcelliana, 1948 and 1973); *L'uomo e lo Stato* ([1951] Milan, Vita e Pensiero, 1982 and 1992). See also L Grassi, *Jacques Maritain* (S Domenico di Fiesole, Edizioni Cultura della Pace, 1993), in particular in the Introduction, where the debate of the 1990s and the criticism of Maritain, indicated as a 'sign of contradiction' at an ecclesial and political level (at 9), are reported; see B Ventavoli, 'Esplode la bomba Maritain. I cattolici di fronte all'Umanesimo "nefasto"', *La Stampa* (Turin, 7 September 1992) 1, E Balducci, *Il cerchio che si chiude* (Genoa, Marietti, 1986) speaks of 'his farewell to Maritain' as early as 1963 with the book *Cristianesimo e cristianità* (Brescia, Morcelliana, 1963), going so far as to say, shortly afterwards, that 'Maritainism functions as integrism': see Grassi (ibid) 15 fn 4.

[18] Fornero and Tassinari (n 16) 877.

[19] ibid 878; see the references to Maritain, 'La conquista della libertà' in J Maritain, *Per una politica più umana* (Brescia, Morcelliana, 1968) 7; 'Una filosofia della libertà' in *Strutture politiche e libertà* (Brescia, Morcelliana, 1968) 9; *Cultura e libertà: alcune riflessioni* (Bologna, Boni, 1986).

[20] Fornero and Tassinari (n 16) 878.

[21] S. 'Lexicon of the 21st Century', Treccani, impersonal entry: 'The personalist paradigm is opposed by that of the impersonal which, starting from Bichat's biology, Nietzsche's philosophy, passes through

twentieth century and the new century. Let me give just a hint – in the early years of the nineteenth century, anthropology outlined the process of what we nowadays call 'biopolitics': 'This challenges the notion of the person as the centre of imputation and the rational subject of political action. It theorises a double biological stratum within every living being: one of a vegetative and unconscious type and another of a cerebral and relational character.' A process has started and is aimed at changing the framework of modern political conception based on a precise conclusion: the organisation of society does not mainly rely 'upon the free will of citizens and the sovereignty instituted by it', but rather upon a 'biological aspect that is both pre-existent and unchangeable in its overall structure'. This biopolitical strand 'will first cross paths with the hierarchical anthropology of the late 20th century and then with the decidedly racist anthropology of the early 20th century' and, subsequently, the picture will rapidly change.[22] The influence of biology on politics is first 'charged with an aggressive meaning' and in the 1930s Nazism 'crushes the person to the point of denying any transcendence of human life'.[23]

In the following years, after the tragedy of the war, a transcendent and ontological character of the person was re-established and entered modern culture[24] and all contemporary philosophy,[25] with two main sticking points: bioethics and fundamental rights. The Christian thesis on the sanctity of life and the secular thesis on the quality of life diverge,[26] but they meet on one point: it is sacred and 'appreciable only what is capable of being understood within the idea of person', which overcomes the hiatus between man[27] and citizen,[28] 'right and life'.[29] The philosophy of impersonality opposes both demolition of the concept of the person and restoration of its sanctity,[30] with a clear vision. According to this thinking,

Simone Weil's rejection of the sacredness of the person, arriving at Foucault's biopolitics or Deleuze's critique, up to the point of posing the question of a third-personal elaboration of politics in which life and law converge.' (www.treccani.it/enciclopedia/impersonale_(Lessico-del-XXI-Secolo).

[22] Esposito (n 21) 10.

[23] ibid.

[24] P Ricoeur, 'Meurt le personnalisme, revient la personne ...' (1983) *Esprit* 113, then published in Italian as P Ricoeur, *La Persona* (trans Ilario Bertoletti) ([1997] Brescia, Morcelliana, 2002) 21ff.

[25] R De Monticelli, *La conoscenza personale. Introduzione alla fenomenologia* (Milan, Guerini, 1998); R De Monticelli (ed), *La persona apparenza e realtà. Testi fenomenologici (1911–1933)* (Milan, Raffaello Cortina Editore, 2000); Di Francesco, *L'io e i suoi sé. Personal identity* (Milan, Raffaello Cortina Editore, 1998); R Bodei, *Personal destinies. L'età della colonizzazione delle coscienze* (Milan, Feltrinelli, 2002).

[26] Now Fornero and Tassinari (n 16) 876ff.

[27] The reference for this summary and the following pages quoted in the text is the volume by R Esposito, *Terza Persona. Politica della vita e filosofia dell'impersonale* (Turin, Einaudi, 200) 3–24; *Le persone e le cose* (Turin, Einaudi, 2014), and again, *Bìos. Biopolitica e filosofia* (Turin, Einaudi, 2004) and already *Immunitas. Protezione e negazione della vita* (Turin, Einaudi, 2002). All writings on the relationship that binds, from Nazi theory onwards, life and politics, technology, and economics in the new ascertainment of the body as something 'programmable and manipulable'. This issue involves the role of law in regulating the *bios* in a huge struggle among 'religious faiths, creedal claims to happiness, rejection of pain, myths of technical progress', with an unknown outcome. Thus, N Irti, 'Il diritto oltre la vita' *Corriere della sera* (14 June 2005).

[28] M Nussbaum, *Social Justice and Human Dignity. Da individui a persone* (Bologna, Il Mulino, 2002); L Ferrajoli, *Diritti fondamentali: un dibattito teorico* (Ermanno Vitale ed) (Rome-Bari, Laterza, 2001); S Rodotà, *La vita e le regole. Tra diritto e non diritto* (Milan, Feltrinelli, 2006); Rodotà (n 12).

[29] Esposito (n 27) 7ff.

[30] ibid 15: the thought of Roman Law, to which we owe the 'device of the person', is confronted with the *status of* the slave 'situated in the middle or in transit, from person to thing', 'the visible tip of an order

modern personalism, within all its expressions, considers the concept of the person capable of filling the gaps 'between human being and citizen, soul and body'. With a strong contradiction: that is, this concept is not able, it is observed, 'to recompose the gaps' that it produces itself, separating 'a rational area and a biological dimension'.[31] On the contrary, 'starting from the body or from things, rather than from the person, can help to discuss (in certain cases) the status of both' and can favour a different viewpoint, capable of affirming 'the unity of the living being'.[32] Unity is expressed by the impersonal, precisely as a 'non-oppositional' theory, which does not annihilate the person but 'pushes it out of its logical boundaries',[33] abstract and ontological.

Viewpoints on that point are wide-ranging. Simone Weil[34] rejects the sanctity of the person.[35] Foucault speaks of a life 'that never coincides with subjectivity and is rather a space that power invests without ever managing to occupy it in its entirety'.[36] Deleuze writes of a reality 'outside the contours of the person and the thing, capable of "reuniting form and substance"'.[37] In all these cases, the 'device of the person' is criticised for being unable to grasp every aspect of a human as a natural being.[38] At the same time, 'contemporary moral philosophy and ethics' does not deal with a person, but rather with "persons"', expressed by a plurality of cultures without any unifying claim, that places itself above 'the concrete and multiple individuals and the concrete ways' in which people live in the world.[39] I believe that this reflection should be developed within the context of contemporary legal dynamics, oriented by new words and old words.

where the categorical thresholds of all living beings are continually shifting'. The Roman Law division between person and man 'penetrates like a deep wedge into modern legal and political philosophy' until the theory of law from natural law progressively erases the Roman tradition, even if a deep trace remains in legal scholars. With 'the individualistic subjectivism of modern law, the Roman separation seems to give way along with the distance between mask and face' because 'the mask adheres intrinsically to the human face. The notion of person is extended to every subject 'but only as far as its rational and moral part is concerned.' Thus, the original gap implicit in the concept elaborated by Christian dogmatics and subsequently reconverted into a juridical key return. R Esposito, *La persona e le cose* (Turin, Einaudi, 2014), back cover: 'neither person nor thing, the human body becomes a diriment element in the rethinking of the concepts and values that govern our lexicon, philosophical, legal and political'.

[31] Esposito (ibid) 17ff: 'If Nazism entrusts ownership of the body to state sovereignty, the liberal conception assigns it to the Person and in both cases a productivist vision of life dominates, in one expressed by the chosen race, in the other by maximum individual freedom'.

[32] ibid 18.

[33] E Benveniste 'Structure des relations de personne dans le verbe' in *Problèmes de linguistique générale* (Paris, Gallimard, 1966); Italian trans: 'Struttura delle relazioni di persona nel verbo' in *Problemi di linguistica generale* (Maria Vittoria Giuliani tr) (Milan, Il Saggiatore, 1971) 273, quoted by Esposito (n 27) 130.

[34] S Weil, 'La personne e le sacré' in *Écrits de Londres et dernières lettres* (Paris, Gallimard, 1957); Italian trans: 'La persona e il sacro' in R Esposito (ed), *Oltre la politica. Antologia del pensiero impolitico* (Milan, Mondadori Bruno, 1996) 76: 'What is sacred is not the person but what is not covered by his mask. Only it can succeed in reconstructing the relationship … between humanity and the law.'

[35] Esposito (n 27) 21.

[36] The sentence is taken from Esposito (n 27) 24; *cf* M Foucault, 'Le penseé du dehors' in *Dits et écrits I. 1954–1969* (Paris, Gallimard, 1994) 521; Italian trans: 'Il pensiero del di fuori, in *Scritti letterari* (Cesare Milanese ed) (Milan, Feltrinelli, 1984).

[37] Esposito (n 27) 24; see, however, G Deleuze, *Pourparler* (Paris, Gallimard, 1990); Italian trans: *Pourparler* (Stefano Verdicchio tr) (Macerata, Quodlibet, 2000) 154.

[38] Y Thomas, 'Le sujet de droit, la personne et la nature' (1998) 100 *Le debat* 85, quoted by Esposito (n 27) 13 fn 12.

[39] Thus in Lexicon of the 21st century, Treccani (n 21).

V. THE PREAMBLE TO THE EU CHARTER OF FUNDAMENTAL RIGHTS – THE PERSON AND THE PRINCIPLES OF DEMOCRACY AND THE RULE OF LAW

The Preamble to the Charter recalls that the peoples of Europe have decided to share a peaceful future founded on 'common values' (dignity, freedom, equality, solidarity) and on the principles of democracy and the rule of law. It is said that the Union also places the individual at the centre of its action to strengthen protection of fundamental rights and duties towards future generations. So that reference is not a concept elaborated on other concepts. It is an instrument to make a legal form effective. Because the European Charter does not proclaim an abstract, ontological entity. But it calls for action to protect life (Article 2), and physical and psychic integrity (Article 3). It prohibits eugenic practices, cloning and other ways of 'making the body a source of profit' (Article 3). It guarantees freedom (Title II), equality and non-discrimination (Title III). It protects minors (Article 24), the elderly (Article 25) and the disabled (Article 26). It affirms the importance of the body (Article 3), of Solidarity (Title IV), of Citizenship (Title V) and of Justice (Title VI). And, finally, it gives every person whose rights and freedoms have been violated a claim 'to an effective remedy before a judge'. In short, the text does not merely proclaim subjectivity or abstract rights, but endows every human being with protection capable of fully realising their life, with adequate instruments that it is up to political, administrative and judicial action to implement in practice.

The text does not abandon the legal form of the person but articulates it, following new needs and new protections. Not only that; the preamble states that the Union is based on the 'principle of democracy and the principle of the rule of law'. Let us begin here. The times we live in tell us of the crisis of democracies and the emergence of forms of autocracy in Europe and throughout the world.[40] All this demands a strong role in place for legal science, once again, for defence of the rights of the individual and democratic institutional foundations as a priority – for several very clear reasons. If power and law are sides of the same coin, if law is politics, but politics by other means, then protection of the individual and pluralism are closely connected – I would say inseparable for protection of civil, political and social-political rights. For over 75 years, the constitutional state in Europe has rested on two pillars: legislative power committed to achieving a more just society, and the inviolability of rights, guaranteed by the Constitutional Court and, in their respective functions, by every other constitutional body.[41] This strong balance

[40] On 5 June 2023, a statement was issued on the publication of the Court of Justice ruling against Poland in the case brought by the European Commission (Case C-204/21 R *Commission v Poland (Independence and private life of judges* ECLI:EU:C:2023:442 [2023]). This is the fact. The 2019 Polish law contains two innovations. First, it gives the Supreme Court Disciplinary Chamber, 'whose independence and impartiality are not guaranteed', the power to decide on the status and functions of judges, and secondly, it requires judges to disclose information about their private activities, which is then published. The Court upheld the appeal and first confirmed its jurisdiction to assess Member States' respect for the values and principles of the rule of law and decided that the powers conferred on the Supreme Court are such as to limit the independence of judges and weaken the fundamental right to effective judicial protection, as provided for in the Treaties.

[41] M Fioravanti, *Il cerchio e l'ellisse. I fondamenti dello Stato costituzionale* (Rome-Bari, Laterza, 2020) 29ff.

has ensured well-considered choices on some absolute problems of the subject. But much remains to be done. Pluralism and the structure of powers must be preserved and strengthened in the search for a polyphonic truth that is subject to constant revision and contamination, to find the most suitable solution, appropriate to offering an answer to every problem of life. It is up to legal science, philosophy and the history of thought to watch over the maintenance of this operational value, always at risk, because, as Bobbio observes, 'wherever power has been established, sooner or later it will show its demonic face'.[42] In this context, civil dogmatics, ever since Roman law, assumes a precise role and purpose as part of politics. A reflection on the person, I believe, must also – but above all – take this into account.

VI. THE CONSUMER AS A PERSON

In its most recent case law, the Court of Justice does not attribute to the consumer the status of a passive market participant, but the status of a person. This is to extend their rights, based on an evolutionary interpretation of directives and the principles of the Charter. To ensure full protection for a consumer purchaser of a property subject to a mortgage, in enforcement proceedings brought by the bank, the Court[43] decided to go beyond the limit of the civil judgement, allowing the judge of the opposition to raise – *ex officio* for the first time – the vexatiousness of contractual clauses, even though the objection had not been raised during the enforcement proceedings. This is because national legislators, it is observed, may not undermine the actual substance of the right guaranteed by Articles 38 and 47 EUCFR, even for the procedural modalities of legal proceedings.

The Italian Court of Cassation,[44] in Plenary Session, recently intervened on this point, in line with the case law of the Court of Justice. The judgment reaffirms the complementary relationship between the Court of Justice of the European Union and the national court.[45] It expressly cites Articles 11 and 117(1) of the Italian Constitution, Constitutional Court Ruling No 263 of 2022,[46] the principles established in the *Banca Desio* case[47] ([50]ff) on the civil judgment, and on the 'principle of effectiveness' ([66]). It clarifies that, given the primacy of the supranational system,

[42] N Bobbio, *Il problema del potere. Introduzione al corso di scienza della politica* with an Introduction by T Greco (Tommaso Greco ed) (Turin, Giappichelli, 2020) VIIff.

[43] Joined Cases C-693/19 and C-831/19, *SPV Project 1503* and *Banco di Desio e della Brianza*, ECLI:EU:C:2022:395 [2022].

[44] Court of Cassation. Plenary Session, decision of 6 April 2023 No 9479 ECLI:IT:CASS:2023:9479CIV. The Italian court held that it was pronouncing a judgment 'in the interest of the law' under the new Art 363-bis cpc, in line with the case law of the Court of Justice.

[45] This question arose following four consecutive CJEU rulings, issued by the Grand Chamber on 17 May 2022 (Case C-600/19, *Ibercaja Banco* ECLI:EU:C:2022:394 [2022]; Joined Cases C-693/19 *SPV Project 1503* and C-831/19 *Banco di Desio e della Brianza* (n 43); Case C-725/19, *Impuls Leasing Romania* ECLI:EU:C:2022:396 [2022]; Case C-869/19, *Unicaja Banco* ECLI:EU:C:2022:397 [2022]). In particular, the question emerged in Joined Cases 693/19 and 831/19, in a preliminary ruling ordered by the Tribunal of Milan (orders of 10 August 2019 and 31 October 2019).

[46] Constitutional Court, decision of 22 December 2022, No 263 ECLI:IT:COST:2022:263.

[47] Case C-831/19 (n 45).

'a functional complementarity of national procedural rules has taken shape with respect to European substantive law which, guided by the principles of equivalence and effectiveness, finds development in a dynamic and complex process of integration'. This is in line

> with the advent of the Charter of Fundamental Rights of the European Union (EUCFR) and, therefore, of the Treaty of Lisbon [which] aim at an ever deeper integration, whose horizons open up to a wider territory than the traditional one, in which market efficiency had an absorbing centrality, in order to annex to it, not only in a mediated way, the needs of protection of the individual and, therefore, to build a "community of rights."[48]

With an important consequence: the declination 'of the figure of the consumer also in personalistic terms, to whom the Treaties assign a central role in the definition and implementation of other Union policies or activities' (Article 12 TFEU), such as to guarantee a high level of protection that goes beyond strictly economic interests (albeit present and relevant), to extend to health and safety (Article 169 TFEU), in a perspective that the Nice Charter ascribes as a whole to the principle of solidarity (Article 38 EUCFR). That is to say, 'to that paradigm common to the constitutional traditions of the Member States that binds together the rights and duties of the individual within a community'. This is a perspective 'to the concreteness of which the objectives and the general economy of Directive 93/13/EEC also contribute', which, in harmony with the provisions of the Treaties and the EUCFR, 'as a whole, constitutes an indispensable measure for the fulfilment of the tasks entrusted to the Union and, in particular, for the raising of the level and quality of life within it'.[49]

VII. THE RIGHTS OF FUTURE GENERATIONS

Since 2015, authoritative documents have highlighted a clear passage of epoch that demands 'the care of the common home' because 'the human environment and the natural environment are deteriorating together', affecting 'especially the weakest on the planet'. Hence the need to build knowledge capable of innovating traditional legal instruments. From the subject to subjective situations, from the juridical good to the notion of property, concerning a 'common home', in fact, 'for which everyone must take responsibility 'by seeking new techniques and new tools for interpreting the world surrounding juridical knowledge'. In September of the same year, 193 countries expressed the will to rethink the global model of development, in Agenda 2030, under the aegis of the United Nations. In December, an Agreement was signed in Paris to drastically reduce harmful emissions within a set timeframe. In 2020 the new encyclical called for a new open and welcoming culture and an integral approach, based on an interdisciplinary dialogue capable of reforming institutions and equipping them

[48] Court of Cassation, decision 9479/2023 (n 44), section 5.2.

[49] Case C-168/05 *Mostaza Claro* ECLI:EU:C:2006:675 [2006] ECR I-10421; Case C-243/08, *Pannon GSM* ECLI:EU:C:2009:350 [2009] ECR I-4713; Case C-40/08, *Asturcom Telecomunicaciones* ECLI:EU:C:2009:615 [2009] ECR I-9579; Case C-618/10, *Banco Español de Crédito* ECLI:EU:C:2012:349 [2012].

with good practices, thinking of the common good in the long term and subsequent generations.[50]

Hence, the call for a strong role for law in responding to absolute problems in the face of great perplexity: can we say that we have harmed someone who has no identity and does not yet exist? How and why can our choices be morally wrong? Can we assume compensation for an indeterminate loss? Is it possible to speak of rights and obligations in the future? As we shall see, these perplexities are by no means invincible. Suffice it to say that fundamental subjective situations of a collective nature are in question, 'part of a public interest' that goes beyond the rigid nineteenth-century schemes of the subject of law, the theory of goods and tort. In short, good arguments are surfacing in studies and legislation. Let us take a closer look at some of them.

Constitutions play a central role due to their nature as charters written to last for a long time with a character of reciprocity between generations, unlike politics which is, all too often, only concerned with the present. Even more central is the role of international and supranational law, and of the Declarations and Reports where, for decades, sustainability has been referred to as a transversal, revolutionary theme, a reflection of an authentic ideal of social justice, affirmed in the Treaties of the European Union (Article 3 TEU and Article 11 TFEU) and in the Italian Constitution, in a plurality of norms (Articles 9, 41, 47, 52, 67). And it is precisely to this system of sources, in profound evolution, that we must look rather than to the categories and ideas of codifications based on values and assumptions of an individualistic and exclusively proprietary nature. Furthermore, the preamble to the EUCFR speaks of duties towards future generations while the Italian Constitution (Articles 9 and 41) regulates new interests. So it can be said that future generations have, in the system of sources of European law, a new primary claim on things (such as the environment, biodiversity, the ecosystem and health) included in the discipline of fundamental principles, guaranteed and implemented not only by political action, but by a new form of protection concerning goods to which the legislator, the public administration and the courts must guarantee full effectiveness.

The question is how. EU regulation follows an effective approach to the environment with the Aarhus Convention[51] and the 2017 Commission Communication.[52] The Convention affirms the right to a healthy environment and the duty to protect this good, individually and in the interest of future generations. It obliges nation-states to allow access to information, participation in decision-making processes,

[50] Holy Father Francis, The Encyclical Letter 'Laudato si'' on Care of Our Common Home (Vatican City, Libreria Editrice Vaticana, 2015), https://www.vatican.va/content/francesco/en/encyclicals/documents/papa-francesco_20150524_enciclica-laudato-si.html; and S Grassi, 'Sul a cura della casa comune: il ruolo del diritto' (2017) 17 *Incontri* 51.

[51] Convention on Access to Information, Public Participation in Decision-Making and Access to Justice in Environmental Matters done at Århus, Denmark, 25 June 1998. The system is enhanced by the European Commission, 'Commission Notice on Access to Justice in Environmental Matters' (2017/C 275/01) of 18 August 2017.

[52] Regulation (EC) No 1367/2006 of the European Parliament and of the Council of 6 September 2006 on the application of the provisions of the Aarhus Convention on Access to Information, Public Participation in Decision-making and Access to Justice in Environmental Matters to Community institutions and bodies [2006] OJ L264/13.

and effective judicial protection. It recognises political and civil rights for individuals and associations in the interest of future generations, and identifies duties for public parties. The 2017 Communication systematises existing EU and secondary legislation as a necessary framework for access to environmental justice with effective remedies. It examines and compiles the judgments of the Court of Justice, enhances the role of national courts, as a means to ensure the effectiveness of EU law, including through the preliminary reference procedure (Article 267 TFEU), and facilitates access to justice by explaining and interpreting existing provisions to help improve the application of rules and principles. It ensures that the Commission will follow the development of case law and consider updating the text. All of this takes place with great attention to Member States, judges, legal practitioners and the general public.

And all this requires a new task for legal science – just one example. Niklas Luhmann,[53] in a critical stance against the then-prevailing positivism, observed that justice is not a superior norm, but only an obligation to increase the complexity of the decision. Therefore, dogmatics must reduce this complexity so that 'that turning one's gaze now to norms and now to facts does not remain unguided but knows that it is bound to the legal system'. At the end of the last century, Luigi Mengoni[54] went further: the norm is not the text, but its meaning understood about the case to be decided. Analysis of language must also be supplemented with data outside the text, and dogmatics has a precise task. It must provide a stable framework of evaluative reference, also using already known decision models. Open the way for analogy. Allow the use of a critical syllogism that permits solutions that can be justified *ex ante* and checked ex post.

If we update these warnings, a precise task emerges today. It is necessary to construct rules and remedies contextually, taking into account a plurality of subjects producing law based on a plurality of surces. Let us see how. In extreme synthesis. In the early 2000s, the expansion of markets and the increasing complexity of systems produced similar phenomena in every legal system. The role and usefulness of traditional categories wanes, the importance of sectoral disciplines waxes, and what happens in EU law is well known. The fervour of studies and the flourishing of commissions and texts for creation of a common law of obligations and contracts ended with the abandonment of any organic project. On the other hand, Community action as indicated in the Preamble to the Charter of Fundamental Rights of the European Union – namely to create a nucleus of uniform principles at the supranational level – has not ceased. In the field of the environment and beyond, the Commission and the Court of Justice are playing a fundamental role. Without generalisations. And with a clear method. There is a need to rethink abstract concepts and instead identify effective remedies. This poses an initial problem: clarifying the meaning of 'remedy' and 'effective'.[55]

Let us start with the first, the substantive profile. Repeating things known to all. In continental systems, unlike common law, the subjective right precedes the remedy

[53] N Luhmann, *Sistema giuridico e dogmatica giuridica* ([1974] Bologna, Il Mulino, 1978) 48–49, 58 ff.
[54] L Mengoni, 'Problema e sistema nella controversia sul metodo giuridico' (1976) *Jus* 3, 24–25.
[55] G Vettori, *Effettività fra legge e diritto* (Milan, Giuffrè, 2020) 11ff.

with a precise consequence. Analysis of the forms of protection presupposes the existence of a protected interest, so that the remedial approach does not affect the object of the protection, but only the mode of seeking and implementing the most efficient protection. This means that the remedy does not replace the substantive right or obligation, but rather aims to provide adequate protection against violations of interests that are already protected. The method thus rejects formalism, and further clarification is needed on this point. Rejection of formalism means attributing a role to the principles in recognising the legal significance of an interest. In the absence of a precise provision, there is no vacuum if there is a principle. This is clear from the supranational nature of the European law of the Treaties and from Article 117 of the Italian Constitution, which subjects legislative power to respect for the Constitution and the constraints deriving from the Community system and international obligations. The clear attribution of pre-eminence to forms hierarchically superordinate to the law, gives superior principles the value of indices of a juridical nature, which exists even in the absence of precise and complete provision. And this is what happens with the Charter of Fundamental Rights of the European Union and with reform of Article 9 of the Italian Constitution.

What is needed, therefore, is a rethinking of language and conceptual tools, still relying on the 'creative power of law' and the most brilliant insights of the past. According to which rights and protected interests are 'constraints for the action of powers'. They are defended through collective behaviour, in certain cases overcoming the very idea of capacity and ownership to focus their identity on the representation of those who can enforce them. Hence, the reference to future generations and their interests is the most pressing opportunity to rethink the language of law and rights. Based on a synthesis with the duties of solidarity expressed by the Nice Charter and the principle of effectiveness of actions and protections that must incorporate the demands of time and responsibility towards others.

As has been recalled, ample regulatory material accompanies and exceeds civil codification, and we need to start again from solicitation of legislative activity and a sapiential construction that knows how to build new categories and new protections to give a voice to those who are not yet there and to provide answers to the sceptics in the face of a change that is now impressive. We are not starting from scratch. One example is enough: the German Constitutional Tribunal ruled on the fulfilment of obligations to protect fundamental rights in an action brought by someone exercising a fundamental right to a decent future (Article 1 1 German Constitution). This is infringed by insufficient measures on climate change. This is because the principle of human dignity cannot be violated by institutions obliged to guarantee 'the basis of self-development and the preservation of the conditions of existence of future generations'. The Court admitted appeals against German law but not the constitutional complaint against omission by the legislature, which had nevertheless enacted a measure based on its discretionary power. But there are now more than 1,500 disputes worldwide. The Court in Strasbourg recently ruled against Switzerland.[56]

[56] I draw these data and the many suggestions from the essay by M Graziadei and F Di Micco, 'The Italian Way to the Rights of Nature' in M Graziadei and M Torsello (eds), Rapports Nationaux

A very extensive literature indicates that civil law doctrine is being called upon to rethink fundamental categories in depth: from the structure of private law to subjectivity, to subjective situations. On the procedural level, the words of Giuseppe Chiovenda are still paradigmatic.[57] The basic theoretical premise of his discourse is clear: the absolute atypicality of the right of action because: 'in modern law, there are as many actions as there are rules that can be implemented'. So 'in civil proceedings, one can ask for implementation of any will of the law that guarantees a good'. In short, 'every concrete will of law whose formation is possible according to substantive law must find suitable means of implementation in procedural law'. Hence the famous conclusion:

> The will of the law tends to be implemented in the field of facts up to extreme consequences that are practically and legally possible. Consequently, the process must, as far as practically possible, give the person who has a right to everything and precisely what he is entitled to achieve. The process as a public body for implementation of the law is in itself the source of all practically possible actions that tend towards implementation of a will of the law. And therefore every mode of implementation of the law (and every means of enforcement) that is practically possible and not contrary to a general or special rule of law must be considered admissible.

And the task of doctrine is clear. Remedies will have to be rethought, but not only that. The role of the constitutional courts, the public administration and the ordinary and administrative judges, in strengthening the instruments of control against the inactivity or abuse of power and the abuse of authority, will change. With action that understands the human experience in this historical moment and is capable of providing answers to everyone's expectations and responsibilities towards the future.

VIII. THE POLITICAL VALUE OF THE SUBJECT AND THE HISTORICITY OF THE PERSON

The subject of law – one of the great inventions of legal modernity[58] – has become a fluid notion encompassing plural articulations,[59] difficult to ascribe to unitary parameters.[60] Hence, it is difficult to evoke new ordering categories based on the qualities of the subject. In this sense, the legal prominence of any situation assessed by an unequal right in accordance with the constitutional and supranational principles of the European Union is decisive. In turn, this reinforces a more general notation. Both the subject and the contract, in every market and in every place of expression of their prominence, cannot be enclosed in abstract and rigid legal

Italiens au XXIe Congrès International de Droit Comparé – Asunción 2022 Italian National Reports to the XXIst International Congress of Comparative Law – Asunción 2022 (Naples, Edizioni Scientifiche Italiane, 2022), which I was able to examine before publication through the courtesy of Michele Graziadei.

[57] A Proto Pisani, 'Principi e valori ancora attuali del sistema di Giuseppe Chiovenda' (2023) *Rivista di diritto processuale* 526.

[58] V Roppo, *Il racconto della legge*, (Milano, Baldini-Castoldi, 2019) 338.

[59] P Zatti, *Maschere del diritto volti della vita* (Milan, Giuffrè, 2009) XI–XXIII.

[60] P Stanzione, *Dal Soggetto alle persone*, in V Scalisi (ed), *Scienza e insegnamento del diritto civile in Italia* (Milan, Giuffrè, 2004) 385.

categories. Conversely, there is a need to rethink the autonomy of private individuals, to support it if vulnerable, to control it in its purposes, in its applications, in its protection of rights and freedoms of other individuals, and to conform it with the market and the legal sources of the *environment* in which it is called on to operate. With special attention to the current digital world, that is very clear about this. The first article of the DSA purports to set the rules 'for a safe, predictable and trusted online environment … in which the fundamental rights enshrined in the Charter, including the principle of consumer protection, are effectively protected':[61] no subjective abstraction but a broad appeal to rights and principles capable of fully and differently protecting every human being.

The space opened up for legal science is evident. The Italian Constitution, as well as the German and Spanish Constitutions, considers the person the recipient of certain fundamental political rights such as personal freedom, freedom of domicile, freedom of movement but also 'other forms of freedom, of assembly, of association, that typically embody political values'. The common feature is clear. The inviolability of these subjective situations is neither a call to nature nor a 'fallen form'.[62] It is much more: Articles 2 and 139 of our Charter prevent any parliamentary majority from eliminating, or correcting in substance, the current legal form, which could be eliminated only by an event that overturns the constitutional political order. This means an act that overturns a given order but not an internal fact of an institutional political order. Only a revolution can establish a new order and erode constitutional rights, fundamental duties and freedoms.[63] Only violence or a de facto power can alter in substance the legal realm that a norm declares inviolable. For a specific reason: fundamental rights do not have a spiritual nature, but they are certainly the results of legitimation of political and normative action that the constituent power in Europe has recognised. This means that the person and their rights are not outside time but live in the present time and affect it on the basis of a historically determined legal form set in a precise system of legal sources.

Not only that: 'the expansion of the notion of humanity', the problem of future generations as well as new problems of equality and identity do not distance the reference to the person, because that word 'has its roots' in a realistic dimension of rights and duties, capable of overcoming the abstraction of new realities. These are not justified by thinking about 'new rights for new subjects', but 'the emergence of rights and goods that challenge the very way in which the subject has been historically constructed'. Juxtaposed to the abstract and ideological schema of the wealth and owner male of the modern age, it is the person who has 'an intimate … aptitude to act as an intermediary of the complexity of existence and of the evaluation

[61] Regulation (EU) 2022/2065 of the European Parliament and of the Council of 19 October 2022 on a Single Market For Digital Services and amending Directive 2000/31/EC (Digital Services Act) [2022] OJ L277/1, Art 1.

[62] N Irti, 'L'ultima transizione' (2022) 64 *Rivista di diritto civile* 269.

[63] S Romano, 'Rivoluzione e diritto' in *Frammenti di un dizionario giuridico* (Milan, Giuffré, 1947) 220ff: 'the revolution cannot be, by definition, other than a state of fact, unlawful, even when it is just' (222). 'However, it is necessary to specify the meaning, entirely relative of such unlawfulness … when then a new order is established, the possibility that the revolution will be qualified again by positive law, which will be the one that will have replaced the older one, rises again' (223).

yardsticks' of the human.[64] With it, the subject is not abandoned in order to constitute a similar abstraction. If only because 'the ways of constructing the person [are] different from those which, in modernity, founded the subject'.[65] Hence, 'the obsession with discontinuity' cannot elude the relevance of legal forms, that can grasp the essence of 'change for what it actually is', with an awareness that the 'hypertrophy'[66] of a concept such as its placement outside of history can lead to its rejection.

But with the conviction that our sources express with the person a tool for overcoming particularism, comes case-by-case decision-making and the negative shattering of the human that needs appropriate and thoughtful responses. In every historical moment. All this is not an imagery of natural law, but rather a technique of reduction of complexity, based on 'an ideal and legal objectivity' expressed by two factors: pluralism (social and political); and the person as the 'impulse to an action' ordering the ever-new dimension of existence. In short, an intangible theoretical and operational pair, from Magna Carta[67] to the Treaties of the European Union.[68]

If it is difficult today to identify the traits of the person, it is necessary to start with language. The usual reference is to the term 'mask' in a theatrical dimension to be taken, not so much in the meaning of something that stands between the face and the subject, but in the sense of 'that which makes the voice of the actor resonate (to-sound)'.[69] So a subject who soon discovers that they live within a 'steel cage'[70] from which they are freed, precisely, from reference to the person in the various ethical and solidaristic meanings developed in the twentieth century. In the new millennium, technology takes on a new form of oppression with which we are familiar, and our task is complex. But if the boundaries between the natural and the artificial seem to blur, we must rediscover a concept of the human that is different from the past.[71] We need to revise the conviction that it is up to the state and parliament alone 'to provide the solution to every problem' because what is needed, today, is a 'renewed research disposition, to ask what it means to be a person in a world increasingly inhabited by non-human but thinking and speaking entities'.[72] Not only that: beyond the sharp separation between 'hard sciences and humanistic thought', one must humbly resume the courage to face unknown phenomena 'that impact our lives'.

[64] S Rodotà, *Il diritto di avere diritti* (Rome-Bari, Laterza, 2013) 177ff.

[65] ibid 178.

[66] ibid 178.

[67] G Zanon, *Magna Charta Libertatum*, in A Mariani Marini and U Vincenti (eds), *Le carte storiche dei diritti* (Pisa, Pisa University Press, 2013) 17.

[68] M Fioravanti, *Appunti di storia delle costituzioni moderne, I: Le libertà: presupposti culturali e modelli storici*, 2nd edn (Turin, Giappichelli, 1995).

[69] A Punzi, 'Il dialogo delle intelligenze tra umanesimo e tecnoscienza' (2023) *Persona e mercato* 160; and ch 5 in this volume.

[70] M Weber, *Protestant Ethic and the Spirit of Capitalism* ([1930] London-New York, Routledge, 2001) 123–24, quoted by Punzi (n 69) 162ff.

[71] ibid 160ff.

[72] ibid 160ff.

In all this, 'law is called on to play an essential function' by building 'protections, limits, sanctions' based on a 'new way of regulating', with an approach that is 'flexible and open to sharing' in order to forge instruments 'more suitable to achieve the objectives set'. All according to the lesson of our time that demands 'codetermination between our intelligence and artificial intelligence'. Without excessive alarmism and without fatalism, but by reflecting on new rules and new principles suited to an idea of the person not abstract and static, but as an ordering tool aimed at the future.[73] Today in a time of technological innovations and the epochal crisis of politics, civil law must once again become, 'with its ordering plot', the basis of a new general theory capable of representing the needs and expectations of this century. With a goal set by new words. The person has to be 'historicised' and conjugated with the variables of existing human beings and those who have yet to come into existence. Sustainability evokes a bridge to a new way of living and thinking. The environment and climate dictate an agenda with ever-tightening deadlines. The market must know how to value the 'common', within the framework of a plural and democratic order all to be built. All this without falling into the myth of unitary and authoritarian recomposition, but with a new juridicity expressed today by a plurality of sources and actors.

In this context, civil law, in its theoretical and general vocation, must be able to deconstruct every mythology of power and the sacred, and debunk every universal fantasy to ensure the full effectiveness of rights, duties and every material and immaterial interest of the person. Constructing remedies against inequalities and new forms to regulate the fluid identities of the present in balance with the needs for certainty and stability. With conviction. The complexity of the present cannot be reduced by political choice alone but by respecting and implementing the existing system of sources: the Constitution, national, EU and supranational law (Article 117 Constitution), national, European and EU courts, independent and sovereign, and legal science.

IX. TOWARDS THE FUTURE. THE ROLE OF RIGHTS AND LAW

If power and law are sides of the same coin,[74] person and (social, political and legal) pluralism share the same bipolar morphology. Personalism is the synthesis of all the interests of human beings developing within their real history, while power recognises, uses and sometimes distorts the attributes and concepts of the human being in a totalitarian or autocratic ideological dimension. Only the proclamation and implementation of rights have transformed human consciousness through a non-violent revolution on 'three distinct levels': the legal relevance of the Charters of the twentieth century; their international dimension; and the ethical legal significance they express. Only a plural order of sovereignty that excludes and denies the absoluteness of power and articulates it in a dialogical dimension between different organs can ensure a view where the equality, identity and dignity of each person are respected.

[73] ibid 161ff, esp fn 20.
[74] Bobbio (n 42) IX.

The reason is clear: power not only has the task to guarantee the full relevance of rights and duties, but rather to give them full implementation. However, the constitutional order that continental Europe delivered to us in the second half of the twentieth century is clear: we do not need just a finalist system that can predetermine the future 'by choosing the only one deemed to be right',[75] but rather an order that leaves up to politics the aim of identifying the direction that best suits the current times. With a limit: rights and inviolable principles must be respected and are unchangeable even by a constitutional revision process. Legal science must take these limits and these rights 'seriously', overcoming old patterns such as the worn-out alternative between natural law and legal positivism towards 'a new legality that is at once formal, content-based and rational'.[76] This is to build and use subjective forms and situations, new and different, but indispensable to guarantee the full development of everyone's personality.

Legal science must be capable of deconstructing any mythology of power and the sacred, debunking every universal fantasy to ensure the full effectiveness of rights, duties and every material and immaterial interest of the person. This purpose can be achieved by constructing remedies against inequalities and poverty, and forms aimed to regulate the fluid identities of the present, as balanced with the needs for certainty and stability, or by making life and law converge. The tools are clear: national, European and supranational law; analogy; general clauses; norms establishing rights and duties; and principles and rules. Logic and dogmatics meet in this function because they do not deny the wealth of knowledge and tools experienced by the *ius civile*. Quite the contrary: having abandoned the illusion of axiological neutrality, dogmatics must contribute to implementing the complex system of the sources of the national states and the European order, but with new means and remedies. Thus, it must fulfil an ordering and political function 'in the broad sense', combining legality and effectiveness in an order dictated by time and expressed by a connected set of facts and rules that produce law; the tired dialectic between law and judges should be overcome at this time of constructing a new order, as a result of strong collective commitment.

[75] M Fioravanti, '*Alle radici della democrazia costituzionale*' (2007) 453–454 *Testimonianze* 57.
[76] G Zaccaria, *Postdiritto* (Bologna, Il Mulino, 2022).

Part II

Reconstruction

7

Persons, Identities and the 'Right to be Oneself'

GUIDO ALPA

WHILE OTHER SCIENCES ask whether we can get rid of identity, this question makes no sense for law. The answer on a legal level is negative. As long as a society is built on roles – and it could not be any other way – the human is destined to be the *person* Gaius spoke of, and to be identified in the three forms that have been described: by what they feel they are; by what they want to appear to be; and by what society requires them to be. The relationship between these forms of identity is measured by the ways in which identity is constructed, by the extent of the spaces from which a person has to construct an identity, and by the greater or lesser coercive force with which identity is imposed on each subject.

Hence the need to defend fundamental rights. In the imagination of jurists, identity crosses the centuries in a continuum of rules, theories and concepts.

This is a laboratory for jurists, who use it from time to time, depending on the finality pursued, either to discriminate or to protect the individual. At the end of the day, identity is neither a photograph nor a point of arrival: identity is an instrument, which from time to time can fulfil a liberating or persecutory function. And the level of civilisation of a society is measured by the extent to which it is able to guarantee everyone the *right to be oneself*.

I. 'IDENTITY': A MULTIFACETED SELF

Common language knows different types of identity: individual identity is flanked by group identity, and – gradually widening the circle – collective identity, social identity and national identity. Each identity is defined in its role and has its own history. The law does not normally offer a literal definition: it uses synonyms; it refers to identity factors; and is concerned – today – with defending everyone from harmful treatment related to those identity components. On the one hand, the law defends those factors as if they were offshoots of the person, from appropriation or alteration, elevating them to inviolable subjective rights, such as the right to one's name, the right to physical integrity, the right to one's image, or the right to proper processing of personal data;

on the other hand, the law defends the person from discrimination based on those identity factors, such as gender, sex, sexual orientation, ethnicity, social origin, and so on.

Over time, some previously ignored aspects have become relevant to the law; others, at first meticulously regulated, have lost their legal relevance; the law has become the medium of social and economic instances, shaping the person from time to time. It has done so by delimiting their freedom of action, delineating their social position, and establishing power relations with other citizens. In most cases, the law has compressed the development of the person; only recently has it taken protection of the person in all their dimensions as its primary purpose.

When one specifies that identity is to be considered in a (minimum) threefold dimension, considering what a person believes they are (who am I?) and how they want to be represented (how am I?) and how others represent them (how do they see me?), one grasps a psychological dimension of identity, which in turn is accompanied by a social dimension, an anthropological dimension, a political dimension and a cultural dimension. And this both considering the person as *self* and considering the person in relation to the *other*.[1]

These aspects constitute the substrate on which the law builds its identity dimension.

As can be seen, identity means, on the one hand, the uniqueness of a human being who, seen from the outside, is an unrepeatable being and different from others, and on the other hand *hypseity*, that is, the way the person perceives themselves and wants to appear. Identity also means identity of treatment, insofar as it wants to preach *equality* between human beings.

Law catalogues the criteria for identifying individuals. These criteria have been formed over time, and occasionally changing in order, importance and consistency; and they are connected with the characteristics that the person wants to exhibit, sometimes choosing between unmasking or concealing.

In everyday language, identity refers indifferently to living beings, to human beings, to men and women, to individuals, to *persons*. In legal language, the human being is translated into concepts that by their nature are abstract. By linguistic convention today, the terms 'person' and 'man' or 'woman' allude to the same meaning, that is, to a living being endowed with certain identifying characteristics. But in Roman law, *personae* were related to their *role*: of father of the family; of married woman; of unmarried woman; of adult child; of minor child; of slave; of freed slave; of citizen; of foreigner, and so on. And it was debated whether slaves were in a proper sense *personae* rather than things. In the medieval period, social roles multiplied, and stratifications became fixed and immutable: humans were distinguished as peasants, merchants, warriors, nobles, ecclesiastics.[2] Law has always been an instrument of these classifications.

[1] S Rodotà, *Dal soggetto alla persona* (Napoli, Edizioni scientifiche italiane, 2007); V Possenti, *Il nuovo principio persona* (Roma, Armando Editore, 2013).

[2] J Le Goff, *Uomini e donne nel Medioevo* (Roma-Bari, Laterza, 2016); J Le Goff, *Tempo della Chiesa e tempo del mercante* (Torino, Einaudi, 1983).

If only those who had power, a 'status', could consider themselves well-rounded people, what were all the others? They were anonymous individuals.

Nobles, ecclesiastics and the military had their own individuality, and therefore a political and social identity, a rank, a *dignitas*, to which the law provided terminology, categories and rules. Other individuals, who were not identifiable through their *dignitas*, belonged to groups from time to time qualified as artisan, mercantile, intellectual, technical or manual, or belonged generically to the common people, to the serfs: they were peasants,[3] labourers, soldiers, and remained so throughout their lives. No one remembered them except family and friends; the short parable of their lives was consumed in anonymity.

Those to whom it was reserved by birth or who had exceptionally succeeded in earning a higher lineage also had a name, often accompanied by a title. Lineage was associated with immunities and privileges, offices, emoluments, pensions. And guarantees offered by law, such as the right to be judged by one's peers, the right to royal protection, the right to wear arms, to bear distinguishing marks, and others.

For everyone else, identity was marked by geographical origin, the places where they were born and lived their lives, language, religion, social status.

This first age, which we could call the age of *privilege*, which lasted until the eighteenth-century revolutions, is succeeded by a second period in which the individual is configured by jurists in a neutral and abstract way; terminology and categories are refined, rules reflect political and economic needs; most jurists and legislators resort to technical formulas, 'magic' as Wiethölter put it, and we could therefore call this age the age of *indifference*. However, this is not a harmless difference: it is an indifference that legitimises the actual state of affairs.

It lasts until the constitutional 'revolutions' after the Second World War, through which *the individual becomes a person*, no longer an abstract concept, but is considered as a man or woman in the flesh, in their 'carnality', with their needs, aspirations, dignity and inviolable rights. This age has been defined by Norberto Bobbio as the *age of rights*.[4]

Of course, it was a crescendo of positions in which the person was first granted civil rights, then political rights, then social rights. It has been a long and complicated path, with advances and retreats; each position could never be considered conquered for ever.

This difficult past has left its marks in language, behaviour, relationships and, of course, in regulatory texts. More. Acquired rights are often contested. New dangers are appearing, brought about by the development of science and technology. Today, conquered rights are threatened: a few years ago, Stefano Rodotà wondered whether rights were in their twilight years.[5]

Every age has obeyed the classificatory categories of jurists: the archaeology of knowledge applied to law shows us that each individual is qualified by criteria that carve out their identity.[6]

[3] M Bloch, *La servitù nella società medievale* (Firenze, La Nuova Italia, 1975).
[4] N Bobbio, *L'età dei diritti*, (Torino, Einaudi, 2007).
[5] S Rodotà, *Il diritto di avere diritti* (Roma-Bari, Laterza, 2013).
[6] M Foucault, *L'archeologia del sapere* (Milano, Biblioteca Universale Rizzoli, 1998).

How should we define the age we are going through? With the overlapping in each of us of the different identities that we will try to qualify, we could call it the '*age of conquest*', because we have to take into account the arduous path that each of us has to take in order to be able to make the real identity prevail over the artificial one, constructed by the media, the desired identity over the fragmented and untruthful one emerging from networks, the desired identity over that imposed by law.

So as we have seen, in each age law has isolated identifying criteria, which may vary in number, relevance and meaning.

Biological identity was confined to sex; the body, the parts of the body, the corpse, depending on the era and social status were subject to the most varied religious, moral and legal rules.

Social identity has always followed the ordering categories of power. For a long time, the tripartition of statuses has been preserved: 'status accipitur tripliciter', recited the Roman adage, referring to freedom, citizenship and family, that is, an individual's relations with other individuals, with the city or state, and with one's family members.[7]

The history of statuses is a history of *liberation and equality*:[8] petrified in the social structure of the Ancien Régime, in the nineteenth century they are transformed into classes, and a certain social mobility begins to take place. *Homo hierarchicus* is being transformed into *homo aequalis*. Overcoming the statuses delivered by tradition only takes place fully in the contemporary age, in which the statuses of the past are replaced by the statuses (or roles) of the postmodern, that is, the consumer, the saver, the cybernaut, and so on.

Registry identity is the bearer of a more complex history. With the Council of Trent and the establishment of *parish registers*, rules were codified that assigned the individual a *surname* next to a *first name*, for tax and military conscription reasons. In countries where religions other than Catholic were practised, *civil registers* were also established. The surname extended to all individuals was consolidated after the sixteenth century. Jurists carefully study the history of the surname. The most authoritative among them is Bartolo da Sassoferrato, the first to study, and to prescribe rules of conduct concerning the attachment of 'arms', shields, mottos and heraldic coats of arms to the family name.[9] The surname underwent meticulous regulation from time to time dictated by political, religious and social reasons. Name and surname are linked to the family, and their legal regime varies according to the legal regime of the family, the status of legitimate and natural children, marriages and divorces, adoptions, abjurations, conversions, persecutions. Other distinctive elements are then added to the surname, coming from baptism, body features, nicknames, visible natural or imprinted marks as *stigma*.[10]

[7] P Cappellini, '"Status" accipitur tripliciter: postilla breve per un'anamnesi di "capacità giuridica" e "sistema del diritto" romano attuale' in (1987) 1 *Annali dell'Università di Ferrara – Scienze Giuridiche. Nuova Serie* 29.

[8] G Alpa, *Status e capacità. La costruzione giuridica delle differenze individuali* (Roma-Bari, Laterza, 1993).

[9] Bartolus, Tractatus de Insignis et Armis (reprinted by F Hauptmann, Bonn, 1883).

[10] J Waldron, *Dignity, Rank and Rights: The Berkeley Tanner Lectures* (M Dein-Cohen ed) (New York, Oxford University Press, 2013).

Religious identity is linked to belief and worship; it is the reason for wars, upheavals, reforms and counter-reforms; it is closely linked to politics, and it is an engine of human history. Religious identity first stands in opposition to power, because believers refuse to recognise the emperor as a deity, and then, with the conversion of Constantine the Great, a Christian religious identity takes shape that prevails over the others, and marginalises them.[11]

The division of the Roman Empire creates another fracture in identity, linked to the opposition between East and West. The liberation of the Holy Sepulchre becomes the focus of the Crusades, and with the Crusades, noble identity is consolidated;[12] the end of the fifteenth century marks an unbridgeable furrow between the Latin Christians and the Muslim people, and perpetuates the Jewish diaspora.[13]

The conquest of America discovers another identity, that of the 'savage', from whom humanity, freedom and property are taken away.[14]

The slow disappearance of feudalism added to urbanisation create new identities.

Citizenship also has a long history, as demonstrated by the meanings that gradually stratify in the term *civis, civitas* in the ancient sense and in the modern sense.[15] With the rise of nation-states, the ideas of sovereignty and citizenship became stronger, and the identity of the individual became both a registry notion, a social notion and a legal notion, with which rights and remedies were associated.

The works of the jurists reflect the philosophical trends of Humanism, the Renaissance and, above all, Natural Law and the Enlightenment.

The first Constitutions and Declarations of Rights, at the end of the eighteenth century, as well as the Civil Codes of the early nineteenth century, take upon themselves the definition of *human* rights and duties. Not all individuals are represented in the Charters: the American Constitution of 1787 ignores women, but not slaves; the 13th Amendment, intended to abolish slavery, ends up shattering a Union born of independence; it will take almost a century to recompose it; the descendants of slaves will take two centuries to gain full freedom. In France, the 1789 Declaration of the Rights of Man and of the Citizen cancels social distinctions not based on common utility and proclaims the primary rights, liberty, property, security and resistance to oppression, but the codes that will follow – the Civil Code of 1804 and the Commercial Code of 1807 supervised by Napoleon – will inevitably be the bulwark of the bourgeoisie. Slavery was tolerated outside France, and Jews, even after equalisations, were subjected to other limitations.[16]

In the nineteenth century, personal identity is shaped according to the needs of the economy. The movement began for the liberation of women, workers, the lower

[11] F Guizzi, *La città di Augusto. Amministrazione e ordine pubblico a Roma agli inizi del Principato* (Milano, Giuffrè, 2015).

[12] F Cardini, *Alle origini della cavalleria medievale* (Bologna, Il Mulino, 2014).

[13] PG Donini, *Le comunità ebraiche nel mondo. Storia della diaspora dalle origini ad oggi* (Roma, Editori Riuniti, 1988).

[14] This is the famous discussion about the nature of Indios: B de Las Casas and JG de Sepúlveda, *La controversia sugli indios* (Bari, Edizioni di pagina, 2006).

[15] P Costa, *Civitas, storia della cittadinanza in Europa.IV. L'età dei totalitarismi* (Roma-Bari, Laterza, 2002).

[16] R Anchel, *Napoléon et les Juifs* (Paris, Presses Universitaires de France, 1931).

classes, and participation of the disenfranchised and illiterate in public life through the right to vote. Gender, social status, cultural level together with property constitute as many fences – petrified identities – that regulate society.[17]

But colonialism adds other identities. Colonialism exalts the difference of 'races', of skin colour, classifies colonists, 'natives' and individuals of 'mixed blood'.

In the nineteenth century, nationalisms explode, leading to the First World War. Identities changed again: the affirmation of women's rights strengthened sexual identity, but at the same time differences took root stemming from sexual orientation, 'racial' origins, religious beliefs and social conditions.

The twentieth century witnessed two world wars: the First World War changed the social condition of individuals, reinforcing economic differences, dissolving the aristocratic class, in some respects emancipating women from a condition of subservience to men. The Second World War confronts the abyss of degradation, the annihilation of the individual in extermination and prison camps, and lays the foundations for a catharsis, for redemption, *for elevation of the individual to a person.*

Even from these first lines, it is understood that 'identity' means not only the identification of a human being but much more: it connotes the individual and builds its destiny around them.

We have to reach back to the constitutions of the second half of the twentieth century, to the new declarations of human and fundamental rights, to discover that the role of law is not to discriminate but to offer tools to fight discrimination, it is not to persecute but to recognise and guarantee – to all – a liberating identity. However, law must overcome the abstract categories it is a prisoner of in order to make identity a choice and an opportunity.

Personal identity today is associated with recognition, guarantee, and exercise of human and fundamental rights; in other words, the *fight against discrimination.*[18]

But it is a struggle for 'mobile' identities, so to speak.

Sexual identity comes into crisis. *Gender* is affirmed, according to which sex is identified on the basis of will, culture and environment rather than biological data.

Racial identity is banished. Ethnic identity is affirmed, associated with linguistic identity and cultural identity.

Novelties multiply, along with identities.

But not all identities of the past can be considered to have definitively disappeared.

[17] We have documents for any legal order: for the US see L Friedman, *A History of American Law*, 3rd edn (New York, Simon and Schuster, 2005); for France, J Brasseul, 'L'industrialisation dans le monde au XIXe siècle' in J Brasseul, *Petite histoire des faits économiques et sociaux. Des origines à nos jours*, Collections 'U' (Armand Colin, Makaloff, 2013) 121; for Germany, R Schroeder, 'Lessons from the Past: Legal Transformation in Germany of the 19th Century' (2000) 156 *Journal of Institutional and Theoretical Economics (JITE) / Zeitschrift für die gesamte Staatswissenschaft* 180; for Austria, V Mataja, *Das Recht des Schadensersatzes vom Standpunkt der Nationalökonomie* (Leipzig, Dunker & Humblot, 1888) and N Jansen, 'Duties and Rights in Negligence: A Comparative and Historical Perspective on the European Law of Extracontractual Liability' (2004) 24 *Oxford Journal of Legal Studies* 443; for Italy, G Alpa, *Diritto civile. Due secoli di storia* (Bologna, Il Mulino, 2018).

[18] J Marshall, *Personal Identity and the European Court of Human Rights* (Abingdon-New York, Routledge, 2016).

For example, slavery, which had been suppressed, has been replaced by other forms of appropriation and exploitation: these are the new forms of slavery we hear about in the daily news.

The question arises whether citizenship should only be linked to birth from citizen parents, but can be connected to *ius soli* or to *ius scholae*.

The biological revolution and the telematic revolution transform identity.

Biology makes it possible to ascertain real family relationships, and thus recognition of paternity and maternity, and to discover the lineage that transmits identity traits as well as forms of heredity that can affect an individual's health.

The digital revolution transforms identity, constructs a virtual identity obtained through the composition of personal data, which from time to time are offered, collected, processed, manipulated, sold, exported.

'Identity' therefore traverses the centuries carrying with it the onerous baggage of the past, is reflected in the present and projected into the future.

Identity is singular and plural. When plural, it becomes a group identity; it embraces all those who live in a given historical memento in a given era, it becomes a *collective identity* that can be coloured, according to culture, language, religion, traditions, by nationality. The progressive abstraction from reality ends up by constructing a law consigned to law and technology: the masks of law hide the faces of life, as Paolo Zatti has emblematically written.[19] Here, to ensure that everyone can be themselves, a system of guarantees must be put in place to overcome the identity imposed by law.

Article 21 of the Charter of Fundamental Rights of the European Union prohibits discrimination based, in particular, 'on sex, race, colour, ethnic or racial origin, genetic features, language, religion or belief, political or any other opinion, membership of a national minority, property, birth, disability, age or sexual orientation.' Furthermore, the Union respects cultural, religious, linguistic diversity (Article 22), ensures equality between men and women (Article 23), and protects minors (Article 24) and the elderly (Article 25).

Article 21 outlines some of the distinguishing characteristics of persons: the term 'person' is repeated almost obsessively in the Charter. In order to fully understand the meaning and normative scope of these provisions, one cannot ignore how distinctions and discrimination arose, and why in turn an urgent need arose to place them at the heart of the Bill of Rights, as indeed of many modern constitutions.

Identification of the person proceeds hand in hand with *its differentiation and thus with its distinction*.[20] This process directly affects the social sciences, especially sociology and anthropology, as well as psychology and medicine, but also economics and politics. What role has law played in this process? In order to understand it, one has to break down the provisions, deconstruct the legal form to highlight its components, go to the root of the terms and rules.

[19] P Zatti, *Maschere del diritto volti della via* (Milano, Giuffré, 2009).

[20] P Bourdieu, *La Distinction: Critique sociale du jugement* (Paris, Les Editions de Minuit, 1996).

II. THE HISTORICISATION OF THE DISTINCTIVE CRITERIA AND ATTRIBUTES OF THE INDIVIDUAL

Whether reading the provisions of the civil code and reformulating the catalogue of personality rights as resulting from direct application of constitutional provisions, or reading the provisions of the supranational charters of rights on fundamental rights and on discrimination, one might get the impression that individual rights – which correspond to as many distinctive criteria – have been recognised as a unitary whole over time, as 'monolithic blocks'. In reality, history teaches us that they do not drag on from age to age, or shape each other by expanding or shrinking, but are constructed on the basis of political upheavals, social achievements, doctrinal elaborations and jurisprudential solutions.

In order to fully understand individual rights, it is therefore necessary to trace their course, indicating which of them date back and have come down to us with an onerous burden of events, of manipulations, of daring hermeneutic operations, and those which are the product of new techniques, digital and biological. But it is precisely new techniques that, besides being the occasion for creation of new rights, allow the jurist to re-examine previously formulated rights, enriching their contents with new aspects. Two examples are striking, among the many that will be examined. The right to know one's biological origins brings family law closer to the laws of nature; the right to oblivion erases from computer or paper records the past of a person who is the subject of journalistic investigations and data collection for inquisitorial and sensationalist purposes, and shields them from speculation and discrimination. The first did not exist until it was possible to ascertain an individual's ancestry through DNA; however, the right to ascertain paternity did exist, as it was considered unnecessary to ascertain maternity because the mother's identity is always certain (*mater semper certa est*), needless to say, before the spread of assisted procreation and surrogate motherhood practices, where permitted. The right to oblivion also did not exist, because a person's past could be defended, to a limited extent, by recourse to protection of honour and reputation.

If we look at the factors of discrimination, we immediately see that they have come down to us via very different routes: Discrimination against women goes back to primordial times; discrimination of those different on account of their sexual habits to the Middle Ages, if their classification derived from religious reasons, or to the late nineteenth century, if linked to medical, biological and psychological reasons; discrimination against the Jews is also linked to political reasons – think of the laws of the Roman emperors aimed at stifling the impulses for freedom of the Jewish people of Palestine – or to religious reasons, in Catholic and Muslim countries, or even to reasons of affirmation of the Aryan 'race', according to the Nazi and Fascist laws of the twentieth century; discrimination on the grounds of social and economic status is linked to the fight against vagrancy, to repression of poverty, but also to the statuses established from the Middle Ages onwards and that run throughout the modern age.

Historical analysis also warns us that certain distinguishing criteria considered to have disappeared are reappearing in other guises: think of the new slavery, which in fact re-proposes the establishment of a right of one human over another human; think of the condition of immigrants and stateless persons; think of the elderly, of patients, of the disabled. Think again of the marginalisation of the mentally ill. All human conditions to which contemporary philosophy – the works of Michel Foucault immediately come to mind – has devoted extensive studies to investigate: the evolution of social classes, forms of power, the metamorphosis of the ego.

In these paths, the law has played its part. Hence the need to distinguish rights and criteria of recognition and discrimination, going down to the origins of distinction and classification and then going back to its modes of expression in the world of legal forms, in an investigation that must then necessarily be carried out *diachronically for each* criterion of discrimination, for each right linked to it, for each sector in which it operates.

A close link can thus be made between the criteria for identifying a subject and in turn its identity, the rights assigned to that subject, and the political, social, cultural and legal structure of the community in which that subject lives and operates. Distinctive signs are at the same time external signs, because they are used to 'recognise', to 'be recognised' and to 'recognise' – almost as if they were a mirror in which the individual's outward appearance is reflected, but also their status and rank – and the role that individual plays in society. The distinctive signs that make up the individual are not random, nor are they free, but are ordered by law because they place the individual precisely in the social order. The same could be said of the rites, or symbols, that accompany the statuses and ranks associated with the individual.

Rights and duties are attached to the criteria of identification, by which signs of distinction are imposed or displayed.

Some constants run through the historical phases and enable large geographical areas to be standardised according to ordering factors, rights and duties, identification criteria and distinctive signs.

But, as we have seen, the identification criteria, the distinguishing marks, do not change *en bloc*; they take root in the constituent meanderings of the individual's 'mask', they perpetuate, they take root, perhaps they even evolve while keeping their roots intact, crossing the centuries.

In contrast to the image of the individual seen from the outside stands the image that the individual sees from within and decides to expose – if able to do so – freely and consciously. Political history, literary and theatrical history all tell us of the self, of its double, of falsified identities, of constructed identities, of exchanged identities: all hypotheses opposed by law, which aims to make the real identity coincide with the imposed identity.

When does this correspondence erode; when does erosion become fracture?

Erosion begins with the spread of the mass media: the history of the right to privacy is the most overt example of this; fracture begins with affirmation of information technology, in which more than one identity manifests itself: real identity, understood as the registry identity, is flanked by digital identity, which splits into identity constructed by data collectors and manipulators, and identity constructed by the person concerned who disseminates data on themselves through the network and 'social'.

And another identification process linked to biological technology is has a consolidating effect: the comparison between registry and biological identity, which do not always correspond. The law tends to privilege the anagraphic identity, but cracks have appeared in this established direction, because the individual may want to know their biological origins. In this case, the evolution of law has meant that a link can be made between biological identity and the claim to know one's origins.

As can be seen, now law plays a conservative and constricting role, a liberating and guaranteeing role.

III. COMBINATIONS AND INTERSECTIONS OF IDENTIFICATION AND DISCRIMINATION CRITERIA

Within a society, forms of discrimination affect both the individual *qua* individual and the individual *qua* member of a community; but individual discrimination can also affect the individual within their own community.

Combinations are almost compulsory, as it is difficult for a discrete criterion to stand alone and not be combined with others. As an individual's way of being, sex is always combined with another criterion: with 'race', skin colour, ethnic or social origin, genetic characteristics, and so on. Being a white or black woman in a class society changes her legal situation a great deal; so does being a rich or poor woman, or a woman belonging to a high or low social status history teaches us that queens and mistresses of kings were placed in a situation not of minority but quite equal to that of men; indeed, it was the men who, if lovers of the queen, or of the king, placed themselves in a situation of power and wealth that was only temporary and mocked by the other courtiers. The history of the kings, queens and mistresses of France and England bears an innumerable list of such situations. Each of them can be catalogued on the basis of its characteristics in the light of the conventions and beliefs of the time in question. However, according to the rules of nobility, the noble woman who united herself in marriage to a commoner lost her noble title, but if the man was a servant, she became free, whereas the noble man who united himself to a commoner made her noble: 'la verge anoblist, le ventre afranchist', according to the French and English Dictionary.[21]

In contrast, being female can become a further form of discrimination insofar as it is coupled with another discretionary criterion: from a religious point of view, women can be treated less well than men, as happens in the religions of the Book, in which women assume an ancillary position. Therefore, to be a 'woman' and a 'Jew' is to be in a weaker position within the Jewish community, not being able to exercise the same powers over herself and her family as a man, not being able to profess her beliefs in the same ways as a man does, not being able to acquire religious offices as a man does. And so, to be Jewish and dark-skinned is to have a marginal position within the community; to be Jewish and homosexual is to place oneself in a difficult position within the community; and again with regard to cultural traditions, think of the great divisions of Jews into Ashkenazi and Sephardim, Orthodox and Reformed, assimilated and non-assimilated.

[21] Which in the title states: 'A French and English dictionary composed by Mr Randle Cotgrave: With another, in English and French' (London, printed for Anthony Doll, 1673).

And so it is with regard to individual discrimination versus collective discrimination, as is the case for minorities within a community, or an entire community within a state, or a state within an empire, confederation or federation.

Again, the principle of relativity prevails in any research conditioned by time and place.

IV. IDENTITY, HUMAN RIGHTS, DISCRIMINATION

In the extraordinarily acute writing of Hanna Arendt, one finds the fiercest critique of the traditional conception of human rights, as she states in *The Origins of Totalitarianism*:[22]

> The conception of human rights foundered the moment individuals appeared who had lost all other specific qualities and relations except their human quality. ... If an individual loses his political status, he should find himself, according to the implications of innate and inalienable human rights, in the situation contemplated by the declarations proclaiming them. Exactly the opposite happens: a man who is no more than a man seems to have lost the qualities that prompted others to treat him as one of their own kind.

And again:

> [F]or the confirmation of my identity I depend entirely on others; and it is the great grace of companionship that makes the loner a 'whole again', rescuing him from the dialogue of reflection in which one always remains equivocal, and giving him back the identity that allows him to speak with the unique voice of a non-exchangeable person.

In Arendt's thought, these assertions are fully justified and are consistent with the consideration of those who – as Jews – were deprived of the very essence of humanity, being considered *Untermenschen*, being assimilated to things, the object of property and therefore of appropriation and exploitation. The Jewish identity becomes a burden that shifts the past into the future (*a future behind it*) and condemns those who bear it to suffer harassment, persecution, torture and murder. The proclamation of human rights has not prevented genocide, the Shoah, oppression of all kinds perpetrated against individuals or entire communities.

Human rights have been the subject of much scrutiny but also much criticism, which means, on the one hand, that their vitality has been strengthened by their normative elaboration, that is, their transformation from principles of philosophical and political significance to precepts that impose their observance. On the other hand, however, they retain their fragility and charge of abstraction, because they are violated everywhere and every time, as the jurisprudence of the European Court of Human rights testifies in its annual reports, even in 'civilized' Nations.[23]

Studies of international law document the history and force of human rights, at the conventional level. Constitutional law studies indicate their limits, within the

[22] H Arendt, *The Origins of Totalitarianism* (1951) (New York, Mariner Books, 1973); H Arendt, *Between Past and Future: Six Exercises in Political Thought*, 4th edn ([1954] New York, The Viking Press, 1961).

[23] Council of Europe – European Court of Human Rights, 'Annual Report, 20023' (2024).

framework of national legal systems. Studies of domestic law explain how they can be applied, by way of interpretation, and whether they can be filtered in order not to comply with them if they ever conflict with national constitutional law or public order.

The fact that their substance almost coincides with that of the fundamental rights of the European Union and national constitutional principles makes this eventuality entirely marginal, if not impossible in practice.

So the proclamation of human rights is in itself no guarantee of their implementation.

It is on their origin and their connection with the right to property and with the entrenchment of the idea of race (well before it was reduced to a biological belonging) that the criticism is levelled at human rights in the present hour, a historical phase in which they are redeemed from their origin and positivised so that they can be recognised and guaranteed as fundamental rights.

Their enucleation from the *ius gentium* referred to by Ulpian allows Vitoria to isolate the freedom to move from one land to another (*ius peregrinandi*), the freedom to trade, the right to acquire property (including appropriation of *res nullius*), freedom of establishment and to become citizens of provinces other than that of one's origin. Therefore, the legitimisation of dominium is their primary function, dominium that is also exercised over one's own person. Hence, the *regime of differences* becomes the foundation of society, of the order within the categories of individuals, of the hierarchy existing between them. If humans organise themselves into a rationally upright society, they can also exercise dominium. And so we distinguish barbarians – capable of reasoning – from Aborigines, natives, 'savages', who have a weak capacity for reasoning – and therefore must be guided – and are unable to take full advantage of property. They are included in the human category, they are not *others*, but they cannot claim the same rights as their conquerors because they are placed at the bottom of the hierarchy that governs the *societas christiana*.[24] Locke perfects the transition from human rights to property rights, and sees in the lands used by the *Indios* an infinite expanse of *res nullius*. In other words, everyone is equal, but the subject is a historical, social and cultural construction, so that at its birth the subject already finds its place within the hierarchy. Next to the hierarchy, therefore, stands race, with which gender – with discrimination against women – and age are then associated. Property, gender, race and age radicalise this hierarchy, which overlaps with the equality of human rights.

Human rights, associated with property and status from a philosophical conception and which qualifies them as 'moral rights', is transformed into a matrix of rights concretised in norms: these are the norms of the Declarations of Rights of the late nineteenth century. Clearly, those who consider this a falsification are fighting the privileges of the ruling classes, be they aristocrats or ecclesiastics; but at the level of the bourgeoisie, proponents of private property and advocates of equality identified with citizenship still clash.

[24] P Costa, 'Dai diritti naturali ai diritti umani: episodi di retorica universalistica' in M Meccarelli, P Palchetti and C Sotis, *Il lato oscuro dei diritti umani. Esigenze emancipatorie e logiche di dominio nella tutela giuridica dell'individuo* (Madrid, Carlos III University of Madrid, 2014) 27, esp 33–35.

The parable of human rights runs through the nineteenth century and develops together with the cult of the right to property, legitimising colonialism, which resorts, in a certain direction,[25] to the same arguments as Spanish jurists and theologians to legitimise the conquest of the Indies, so that the critique of human rights ends up being confused with a critique of the right to property.[26]

A novelty – that is, a different conception of human rights – begins to emerge at the time of the new constitutions, in which equality is understood as protection of differences and the fight against discrimination. In order to overcome the rhetoric of human rights, it is therefore necessary to move beyond the abstract identity of the rights of the individual and enter into the differences that each person *wishes to bear*: not the differences with which they are echoed; but the differences that nourish their yearning for freedom and that are a sign – insofar as they are respected, not simply 'tolerated' – of their security and independence in society.

V. DOCTRINAL, LEGISLATIVE, JURISPRUDENTIAL CREATION OF HUMAN RIGHTS

A well-known aspect of fundamental rights, and before them, human rights and natural rights, is that they have been elaborated doctrinally, eminently by scholars of moral philosophy and philosophy of politics, and have gradually multiplied, moving from the first elementary claims – the right to life, the right to personal freedom, the right to resist unjust order or law, the right to property – to more or less longer lists of rights in which moral imperatives and the conditions for living in a civilised society coagulate, as conditioned by culture, socio-economic conditions, and contingent contacts between proponents of this normative process. From the works of philosophers to texts prepared by jurists, accepted by legislators, applied by judges, the step was not a short one, as we learn from their history.

Much discussion has revolved around the circular 'itinerary' of the rights contained in the Bill of Rights and the first Declarations of the late eighteenth century, and whether human rights could be recognised as having effects in the context of relations between private individuals, thus overcoming the private law/public law dichotomy.

With the codification of these rights – that is, with their transposition from doctrinal text to normative text – the work of doctrine, from being a source of inspiration and elaboration, is transformed into a predominantly exegetical work of normative texts, but some legislators – using different formulas and alluding to different techniques – leave the field open to the novelties created by the interpreter.

Among the various models that can be considered, some seem emblematic.

In historical progression, one of the most interesting is offered by the Ninth Amendment of the US Constitution, which specifies that the rights protected in the text do not exclude other rights from being protected even if not explicitly mentioned.

[25] An address that goes along with, rather than *against*, the justification given by the need to acquire uncultivated or under-cultivated land to feed overpopulated nations: see AA.VV. (2004/2005) 33 *Quaderni fiorentini. L'Europa e gli «altri». Il diritto coloniale fra Otto e Novecento*.

[25] As Marx lucidly argued, 'On the Jewish Question' (1843) in R Tucker (ed), *The Marx-Engels Reader* (Norton & Company, New York, 1978) 26.

The amendment, proposed by James Madison in 1791 reads: 'The enumeration in the Constitution, of certain rights, shall not be construed to deny or disparage others retained by the people.' The amendment was introduced by the Anti-Federalists, who wanted to limit federal power, which was seen as a threat to individual liberties. In truth, the text is somewhat obscure because, while the first part is reasonable in suggesting that the rights enumerated in the text do not constitute a closed list, the second part is much less so: What are the 'other rights' held by the people? Does 'the people' mean every individual? And who assigns the rights not mentioned? Is this a blank bill of exchange?

In fact, the Ninth Amendment was not applied for more than a century and a half. But, in connection with other Amendments, it was mentioned in the first US Constitutional Court ruling that created the right to privacy, with the 1965 case *Griswold v Connecticut*. The issue was whether a Connecticut law prohibiting the sale of contraceptives complied with the Constitution. In that case, Justice Douglas pointed out that 'the specific guarantees of the Bill of Rights have a penumbra, formed by the radiations of those guarantees that support the protected rights by giving them life and substance'.[27] And the Court held that the law violated a constitutionally guaranteed right, namely the right to privacy. The Court had thus created a right that doctrine had long elaborated: witness the essay by Senator Warren and Justice Brandeis published in 1890 in the *Harvard Law Review*, the first and most important American legal journal.[28]

The Ninth Amendment, along with other provisions of the Constitution, was also referred to by the constitutional judges when they drafted the right to abortion. Also in that case, in a landmark judgment, *Roe v Wade*,[29] the judges held that state legislation could not intrude into the secret sphere of the individual and that it was therefore legitimate not only to provide medical intervention to bring a pregnancy to term but also to terminate it.

Today, the Ninth Amendment is under challenge by tradition-bound jurists, qualified as 'conservatives', who, with the expedient of the original meaning of the constitutional text (the so-called originalist interpretation) would like to circumscribe the scope of constitutionally guaranteed rights. But this is an entirely marginal direction.

A different model can be found in Austrian law, where human rights are codified.

Indeed, the Austrian Civil Code of 1811 (ABGB), which came into force in the Italian-speaking provinces of the Empire in 1816, contains a provision denouncing its natural law origin. It states in §16: 'Every person has rights that are evidently the result of reason alone and must therefore be considered as a person. Slavery and personal servitude, and the exercise of relative power, are not permitted in these states.' The distinction between *Mensch* and *Person* should be noted: man as such is a *person*. From personhood, that is, the essence of humanity, derive rights that only *civil society* recognises and guarantees.

[27] *Griswold v Connecticut*, 381 US 479 (1965) at 484. The opinion was concurred in by Chief Justice Warren and Justices Clark, Goldberg and Brennan.

[28] SD Warren and LD Brandeis, 'The Right to Privacy' (1890) 4 *Harvard Law Review* 193.

[29] *Roe v Wade*, 410 US 113 (1973).

Originally, the commentators did not question that we were talking about natural rights, rather about *a right* consisting of the 'power to undertake all those actions (but only those) that can be undertaken with a social state of being independent.' The resulting rights are either natural or acquired. As for natural rights, these derive 'from the character of the personality'. Slavery occurs when someone is the object of someone else's property; servitude when someone is considered to be the appurtenance of a property.[30] It is therefore a matter of freedom that the status of *libertatis* was handed down over the centuries and which the Empire guaranteed to its subjects.

Remaining virtually ignored for more than a century, this provision has once again provided working material for jurists in constructing the category of personality rights. Austrian doctrine has long disputed whether innate rights included other rights besides those ordinarily included in the category of natural rights and concluded that although the list was originally reduced to the essentials (life, personal liberty, resistance, honour, property), the evolutionary interpretation allowed protection of life, liberty, health, privacy and dignity to be based on this provision.[31]

In other systems, as will be seen, protection of human rights derives from the application of constitutional norms that regulate relations between the individual and the state, but also regulate, through their indirect application (*Drittwirkung*), relations between private individuals. Among the rights granted to the individual is the right not to be discriminated against.

VI. HUMAN RIGHTS BEYOND RHETORIC: THE ACCEPTANCE OF IDENTITIES

In identifying discrimination to which the individual may be subjected, the normative texts set out the identifying criteria; but in applying them, the courts extend them. This is a consideration that concerns all courts dealing with human rights and fundamental rights.[32] This consideration unites jurists who come from very different normative and cultural backgrounds. The common denominator: the *right to personal identity*, understood in an even broader sense than that recognised by our jurisprudence under this terminology, namely the right to be '*re-acknowledged*', that is, the right to have the identity that a subject has constructed for themselves and the *right to be accepted as one is*.[33]

According to some scholars, this opportunity is offered to the individual by protection of the right to privacy, which is transformed into the right to personal identity.[34]

The Italian system has already arrived at this solution, not only by recognising the right to privacy, but also by assigning citizenship to the right to *personal identity*,

[30] F de Zeiller (ed), *Commentario sopra il Codice civile Universale Austriaco per tutti gli Stati ereditari tedeschi della Monarchia austriaca*, vol 1 (Milano, AF Stella Sonzogno F Baret G Silvestri, 1815) 108.

[31] E Ondresova, 'Personality Rights in Different European Legal Systems: Privacy, Dignity, Honour and Reputation' in K Oliphant, Z Pinghua and C Lei, *The Legal Protection of Privacy Rights: Chinese and European Perspectives* (Leiden, Brill, 2017) 32.

[32] J Marshall, *Human Rights Law and Personal Identity* (Abingdon, Routledge, 2014) 33.

[33] P Leuprecht, 'The Difficult Acceptance of Diversity' (2006) 30 *Vermont Law Review* 552.

[34] Marshall (n 32) 35.

understood as the right to be portrayed or described correctly with regard to shared cultural, political and religious orientations, thus widening the range of codified personality rights. This has been a long road, dogmatically difficult, and in practice exhausting, as will be discussed in pages devoted to construction of the legal category of personality rights. Now we are discussing whether we can go a step further, recognising and guaranteeing the right to *be oneself*, which means the right to control techniques of identification, the external image constructed by the person and the information circulating about the person.

Each system has its own sources and uses supranational sources non-uniformly. Needless to say, this is the lowest common denominator, because every court – like every jurist – has its own interpretative direction and every jurist their own opinions. However, further progress in the construction of personal rights stems from the fact that (almost) every legal system has proclaimed the right to privacy and the right to personal identity, understood as the right to be identified in the way one's own identity has been constructed, or that the tendency is towards this recognition.

VII. RECENT TEXTUAL MODELS OF HUMAN RIGHTS PROTECTION

The Universal Declaration of Human Rights was approved by the United Nations in 1948; two years later the European Convention on Human Rights was approved.

Comparison of the texts reveals how the sensibilities of the drafters, who also came from different cultures – those who converged on the universal text were more varied, those who converged on the European text were more cohesive – found themselves in the same position.

The general opening clause and the distinguishing criteria are almost the same:

Universal Declaration:

> Article 1 All human beings are born free and equal in dignity and rights. They are endowed with reason and conscience and must act towards one another in a spirit of brotherhood.
>
> Article 2 Everyone is entitled to all the rights and freedoms set forth in this Declaration, without distinction of any kind, such as race, colour, sex, language, religion, political or other opinion, national or social origin, property, birth or other status. Furthermore, no distinction shall be made on the basis of the political, legal or international status of the country or territory to which a person belongs, whether independent, under trusteeship or otherwise, or subject to any limitation of sovereignty.

European Convention:

> Article 1 Obligation to respect human rights. The High Contracting Parties recognise the rights and freedoms set forth in Title I of this Convention to every person under their jurisdiction.
>
> Article 14 Prohibition of discrimination. The enjoyment of the rights and freedoms set forth in this Convention shall be secured without discrimination on any ground such as sex, race, colour, language, religion, political or other opinion, national or social origin, membership of a national minority, property, birth or other status.

What is striking is the way the text is written.

The Universal Declaration recalls the Rousseauvian definition of human rights, and uses the expression 'dignity', on which we shall dwell at the end of this discourse, specifying in any case that the textual absence of this word in the European Declaration does not imply its absence among the value parameters that the Strasbourg Court uses to scrutinise the conduct of states. 'Brotherhood' recalls the opening words of the American Constitution and the French Declaration of Rights.

The enumerations of the distinguishing criteria are equivalent, and both have a closing clause that allows them to be extended.

On the closure clauses, no debate has taken place that continues to fuel American literature on the subject. This is because the two politically conflicting conceptions of the constitution between 'evolutionists' and 'originalists' did not clash. In fact, the closing formula legitimised in the United States the jurisprudential creation of new rights, not contemplated in the original text, such as the right to privacy with its subsequent elaborations concerning the right to use contraceptives, the right to abortion, the right to have sexual relations between consenting adults of the same sex, and gay marriage.

The distinguishing criteria listed in the two texts correspond to each other, and also correspond to the lists in post-Second World War constitutions, as well as to the list included in the European Charter of Fundamental Rights half a century later. A sign of the persistence of distinctions and discrimination. A sign that certain traits – psychological, somatic, apparent or hidden but 'unveiled' – form a part of archetypes that are transmitted over time and become such ingrained prejudices that they are considered 'natural'.

VIII. 'NATURE' AND SEX DISCRIMINATION

The expression 'nature' referring to humans can be read in different ways: as a force that distinguishes humans from animals and things, through rationality, conscience, expression of feelings, or on the contrary as an instrument of oppression. Sex, sexual orientation, blood and skin colour are data connected to the individual and derive from the co-essentiality of the human being and nature; in short, they portray humans' 'natural' way of being. Alongside individual data, collective data are constructed: women constitute a category 'disabled' by '*imbecillitas sexus*'; Jews and homosexuals constitute a minority to be marginalised, black-skinned people a race to be subjugated or colonised. Not to forget socially constructed minorities, such as heretics, subversives, the poor.

However, a difference exists between the first and second groups of distinctive traits, because the first group is the result of an old classification based on persistent data that originates from birth and marks the individual for ever, as if it were an indelible mark against which one cannot fight – indeed, one *should* not fight against it because nature demands it. The second group results first from Christianisation and then of secularisation, so are more recent and mainly concern the individual immersed in their environment, in the social formations in which they develop their personality.

The idea of *nature* that penetrates legal culture is the result of the thinking of Western history. The semantic and historical analysis of the Latin word, which corresponds exactly, in its phoneme, to the Italian one, is a path that winds its way from the Greek *fusis*, indicating human nature, the nature of things, poetic nature, to the Latin *natura*, which in Lucretius indicates not only things, animals and humans, but also physical force, cosmic force, the life-giving power, as the generator of life itself in its various phases, from conception to birth.

Scholars decline different meanings of nature, linked to the 'laws' that govern the universe, and then descend through the branches to medieval theology and philosophy, in which nature is related directly to God (natura *naturans*) who created the world (*natura naturata*), to the science of the Renaissance and the seventeenth century; according to the Spinozan conception, nature is confused with God, up to the so-to-speak ideological and secular revisitation carried out by the Enlightenment[35] and then by the powerful analyses of its transfigurations by Hegel and Marx.

André Pellicer demonstrated the unification of *fusis* and *nature* in the first century BC and the consolidation of its semantic value: nature as a mode of being, encompassing humans' innate character, their physical and psychic aspects, and thus spontaneity, naturalness, but also necessity; nature as property, quality, and thus power; nature as universality and as cause.[36]

Behind this evocative and polysemous term lie the orders of society: its physicality, but above all its moral order, laws and law. Nature is already placed by the Latin rhetoricians and philosophers as the basis of the family, it is considered as the foundation of friendship and of society itself, which is 'good' if it conforms to nature: Socrates and Plato unite nature with justice; the Romans dubbed the law of nature as the law of all peoples, *ius gentium*, and civil law as the law of the *cives*: according to Gaius in the opening of his *Institutions*, in that 'what is *according to nature is the rule of law*' (Leg.I,44).

In legal thought, the 'nature of things' becomes a real source of law.

IX. NATURE AND RELIGIONS OF THE BOOK

Consider the idea of nature that emerges from the religions of the Book.[37]

In its conception, nature is the fruit of God's creation; it is identified with the world, and the world is God's creation *ex nihilo*: before creation there was nothing; after creation God placed himself at the helm of the world: 'In Judaism, the material

[35] J Ehrard, *L'idée de nature en France dans la moitié du XVIIIe siècle*, reprinted edn (Paris, Albin Michel, 1994).

[36] A Pellicer, *Natura. Etude sémantique et historique du mot latin* (Paris, Presses Universitaires de France, 1966): *fusis* is a mode of being, which appears at birth, and, in a translated sense, is innate; while *natura*, according to Ciceronian usage, is the proper and external character of things and persons. This is a semantic analysis, while for the philosophical analysis see G Naddaf, *The Greek Concept of Nature* (New York, State University of New York, 2005).

[37] The Jewish religious idea of nature is much debated: see R Di Segni, 'Il concetto di natura nel pensiero Greco e nella Bibbia' (1974) 40 *La Rassegna mensile di Israel* 252 and E Lévinas, *Totalità e infinito: saggio sull'esteriorità* (Milano, Jaca Books, 1990).

nature of the world has never been inferior or subordinate to the spiritual: all reality is the fruit of divine creation and, by virtue of this, its goodness and positivity must be preached and appreciated'.[38] Many passages in the Bible ground this tradition, in which soul and body support each other – in a synergy that leads to realisation of the person – with the man–woman relationship, aimed not only at procreation but also at exalting the importance of eros and physical pleasure.[39] And again, the passages in which humans – Abraham representing them universally – comes to know God through nature. That is, they come to God through observation of nature and its laws. Behind this representation lies the idea of 'a design and order of reality as creation'[40]

So it follows naturally that women are submissive to men and that their relationship cannot be approached as one between persons of the same sex. But figures of extraordinary women emerge from the Bible, such as Ruth, Deborah, Judith and Esther.

The interpretation of God's word is reserved for men. In the synagogue, women are separated and placed in the women's gallery. And woman is created from Adam's rib, so she is the result of a derivation rather than an independent creation.

And yet man is born of woman, which proves that the two sexes are inseparable.

In the Gospel, the woman possesses greater prominence, potentially equal to that of the man: Jesus entertains women, imparts teachings to them, not caring about the rabbinical prescriptions that forbade it (Luke 10:39).

Jesus recognises the equal dignity of man and woman (*cf* Luke 13:16) and it is to a woman, and a foreign one at that, that he addresses the highest praise for faith (Matthew 15:28). Man and woman are complementary: the two 'shall be one flesh' (Mark 10:6; Genesis 18–20).

But the Christian tradition accepts the subaltern status of women. It is Paul who writes in the *First Letter to the Corinthians* (1 Cor 14:34–35):

> Let the women in the meetings be silent, for it has not been entrusted to them to speak, but let them be submissive, as the law says. If they wish to be instructed in anything, let them question their husbands at home, for it is unseemly for a woman to speak in an assembly.

And in the *First Epistle to Timothy* (1 Tim 2:9–15):

> I also want women to be dressed with decorum, adorned with modesty and truthfulness, not with braids of gold, pearls, and luxurious garments, but with good works, as befits women who make profession of piety.

The Koran is no exception. In Sura II, the heifer, verse 228 reads:

> Let the divorced women observe a three-cycle retreat, and they are not allowed to hide what Allah has created in their wombs, if they believe in Allah and the Last Day. And their spouses will have priority if, wishing to reconcile, they take them back during this period. They have rights equivalent to their duties, according to good custom, but men are superior. Allah is Mighty, He is Wise.

[38] G Laras, *Natura e pensiero ebraico* (Milano, Jaca Books, 2015) 27.
[39] ibid 28.
[40] ibid 37.

Interpretation of the Koran also leads to the subordination of women to men. In Sura IV, on women, verse 34 states:

> Men are preeminent over women because of the preference Allah grants to one over the other and because they spend [on them] their wealth. Virtuous [women] are the pious ones, who protect in secret that which Allah has preserved. Admonish those whose insubordination ye fear, leave them alone in their beds, beat them. If they then obey you, do nothing more against them. Allah is Most High, Most Great.[41]

And with regard to same-sex relationships – ordinarily between men, those between women being ignored – Genesis 19 and Leviticus 18 and 20 condemn this practice, striking it with the death penalty. The Gospels contain no mention of the matter, while Paul interprets the episode of the destruction of Sodom and Gomorrah – not as the effect of violation of the principle of hospitality,[42] but as condemnation of an abominable practice (Romans I, 24–27; Corinthians I, 6, 9; I Timothy I, 1, 10).

In Greek history, which begins with the myth of Pandora, woman is the cause of all evil.[43] She is an ambiguous character, reflected in all female versions of divinity, from Juno, mother of the gods, to Venus, repository of pleasure, to Athena, symbol of intelligence. Moreover, all virtues are feminine. In classical works, woman reflects all these aspects, positive and negative, from the capricious Helen to the hard-working and patient Penelope. And in the Roman world, woman is seen as a necessary complement to man, always in an ancillary position.[44]

X. THE IDEOLOGICAL USE OF NATURE AND SEX DISCRIMINATION

In short, the man–woman contraposition is a constant in human history, at any latitude and at any time in history. From the point of view of identity, it is found in the conception of nature, in the narrative of each person's life, and in the organisation of the family, which has its own history, and again in the organisation of society with its distribution of power. The position of women until the middle of the twentieth century, and beyond, is considered inferior and complementary to that of men: beyond the pages of the Scriptures, the natural physical weakness of women compared to the strength of men (*imbecillitas sexus*) has repercussions on the allocation of work within and outside the family, and the marginal role of women even within the social aggregate. Law reflects this condition, not only because legal rules are written by men, but because law is precisely the mirror of society, of social conventions, of a common mentality. But Pothier in the *Treatise on Persons* points out that, in addition to the weakness of sex, the role of women in the family must

[41] M Riber, *La donna nella Bibbia* (Alba, Edizioni Paoline, 1971); E Bosetti, *Donne della Bibbia. Bellezza, intrighi, fede, passione* (Assisi, Cittadella, 2010).

[42] JW Donald, *Out of Order: Homosexuality in the Bible and the Ancient Near East* (Grand Rapids, Baker Books, 1998); in general see T Römer and L Bonjour, *L'omosessualità nella Bibbia e nell'Antico Vicino Oriente* (Roma, Claudiana, 2007) 65ff, 120ff.

[43] E Cantarella, *Gli inganni di Pandora. L'origine delle discriminazioni di genere nella Grecia antica* (Milano, Feltrinelli, 2019).

[44] E Cantarella, *L'ambiguo malanno. Condizione e immagine della donna nell'antichità greca e romana* (Milano, Feltrinelli, 2010).

also be taken into account: women are expected to behave discreetly, away from the public eye, and for this reason they cannot be assigned public office, which would require them to expose themselves to the outside world, removing themselves from the protection of domestic walls.

Already at the moment of her birth, woman's destiny is sealed: sublime is the novel within the novel, the story of the Nun of Monza with which Alessandro Manzoni depicts the legal status of Gertrude, who was brought up in such a way that entry into the convent and the monastic choice were expressions of free will, while in the contrary reality they were an expedient to avoid dispersion of the ancestral heritage. The rules of status have persecuted women for centuries and centuries, while male culture gradually constructs them as the object of feelings, desire, faithful cooperation and the pious conduct of a life dedicated to hearth and family.

Hence redemption, emancipation, freedom, the fight against discrimination, the demand for equal opportunities, the more-than-justified antagonism destined to support individual acculturation and careers, family formation, child-rearing, the sharing of work and power. A long time will be needed to realise that *imbecillitas sexus* is a mystification, that law supports discrimination, oppression, marginalisation as an instrument of preservation; change will be achieved at the price of grave sacrifices and difficult struggles.

The complex history that the law of the past gives us is a valuable document for understanding this path, which is both a path of civilisation and morality. And it should be noted that even today the tendency is to see a woman's legal status more in relation to the environment in which she lives – the family, associations, the world of work and the professions – than in terms of the individual path she takes.

XI. THE ROLE OF 'NATURE' IN DISCRIMINATION BASED ON SEXUAL ORIENTATION

Nature and acts 'against nature' dominate the moral, religious and legal conceptions by which those who are attracted to persons of the same sex are evaluated.

Dealing with forms of discrimination due to sexual orientation is highly complex. Unlike other figures of diversity, dating back in time, this has only recently been defined in terms of 'homosexuality'. We must therefore beware of anachronistic projections, because the very identification of diversity in the affective and sexual sphere is inextricably linked to culture, social practices and, in this case, the state of science. And it must be borne in mind that for many centuries it was individual acts, rather than affections, that were taken into consideration, no matter how performed, hence even if they occurred between persons of different sexes and even between spouses. Legally relevant was the act, qualified as 'against nature', therefore morally reprehensible and criminally relevant; the act was penalised by corporal punishment, sometimes with imprisonment and burning. The behaviour was not taken into account, nor was it thought that the subject had been induced to perform the act because of a mental illness.

It is rare to find in classical sources characters – historical or fictional – who present a constant propensity for their own sex. Usually, reference is made to single acts, or single relationships; the propensity for one's own sex coexists with bisexuality; it is not a definitive election.

In Greece, however, this practice was not matched by moral judgement. The fact that on Olympus love affairs or encounters of this kind frequently occurred, that Jupiter, the father of the gods, had abducted and loved Ganymede, that in *The Iliad* Achilles placed Patroclus at the top of the pyramid of his affections, that in the Athenian chronicles it was claimed that Alcibiades nurtured a particular affection for Socrates, that in historical sources it was reported that Alexander the Great had loved Hephaistion, indicates that in the collective imagination, in the figurative arts, in lyric poetry, in comedy, same-sex love was not an object of scandal. One of the best known and most studied of the Platonic dialogues is precisely the *Symposium*, which tradition has handed down to us as the text in which *Platonic love* is codified.[45]

In Rome, mentality and customs were different, propensity for the same sex barely tolerated, more often blamed. Nevertheless, valour, prestige and *auctoritas* were a safe screen for any criticism or aggression. Thus, Caesar was jokingly mocked by his soldiers, but appreciated as a valiant commander, Nero feared and hated for his bloodthirsty despotism, not because he had contracted three marriages with men with impunity, Hadrian respected for his wit, not despised for the love that had bound him to Antinous.

Pagan culture was indifferent or at most tolerant. Rather, moral evaluation of same-sex love is linked to more solid and authoritative religious traditions.

Precisely for this reason, one cannot read ancient history with the eyes of the present: the most appropriate terminology and table of values must be found for each era.

From the biblical episode of the destruction of Sodom and Gomorrah we derive the reasons for condemning sodomy, a behaviour that is morally reprehensible as a *sin*.[46]

The religions of the Book are opposed to any behaviour that is not functional to the preservation and development of society, that is not functional to protection of the family, that can disrupt the social order; the non-procreative sexual act is contrary to the divine will, is immoral and therefore illegal.

Indeed, some passages in Leviticus sound like curses, at least on literal interpretation:[22]

> You shall not lie down with a man as you do with a woman: it is an abominable thing. Do not make yourself unclean with any of these practices, for with all these things the nations I am about to drive out before you have made themselves unclean. Every one who practices any of these abominations, everyone who commits them, shall be cut off from his people. (Leviticus 18:22, 24, 29)

[45] KJ Dover, *Homosexualité grecque* (Grenoble, Pensée sauvage, 1980); M Foucault, *Histoire de la sexualité, Tome I. La volonté de savoir* (Paris, Gallimard, 1976), and *Tome II. L'usage des plaisirs* (Paris, Gallimard, 1984); DM Halperin, *Cent ans d'homosexualité et autres essais sur l'amour grec* (Paris, EPEL Editions, 2000); JJ Winkler, *The Constraints of Desire: The Anthropology of Sex and Gender in Ancient Greece* (New York, Routledge, 1989).

[46] DS Bailey, *Homosexuality and the Western Christian Tradition* (London, Longmans, Green, 1955) 73–74; M Brinkschröde, '*Christian Homophobia: Four Central Discourses*' in M Groneberg and C Funke (eds), *Combatting Homophobia* (Münster, LIT, 2011) 166; Römer and Bonjour (n 42).

No explicit condemnations of same-sex sexual practices are found in the Gospels, whereas they are found in the letters of Paul of Tarsus:

> Or do you not know that the unjust will not inherit the kingdom of God? Be not deceived: neither the immoral, nor idolaters, nor adulterers, nor effeminate, nor sodomites, nor thieves, nor misers, nor drunkards, nor revilers, nor rapacious shall inherit the kingdom of God. (1 Corinthians 6: 9, 10).
>
> We also know that the law is made not for the righteous but for the unrighteous and rebellious, for the wicked and sinners, for the sacrilegious and the irreligious, for those who kill father and mother, for murderers, for fornicators, for sodomites, for slave traders, for liars, for perjurers, and for anything else contrary to sound doctrine. (1 Timothy 1:10)

Christian thought is fuelled by sentiments and words of condemnation because acts with persons of the same sex imply social 'disorder', conflict with the sanctity of the family, and violate the rules of Creation.

Augustine writes: 'Crimes that go against nature, such as those committed by sodomites, must be condemned and punished everywhere and always' (*Confessions*, c.III, p.8). John Chrysostom reiterates: 'Not only are the passions of homosexuals satanic, but their lives are diabolic' (*Homilia IV in Epistola Pauli ad Romanos*). Thomas Aquinas asserts: 'In sins against nature in which the natural order is violated, God himself is offended as the orderer of Nature' (*Summa Theologica*, II-II, q.154, a.12.).[47]

Nevertheless, attitudes towards same-sex sexual acts have had a sinusoidal pattern over time, showing long periods of persecution alongside short periods of tolerance.

However, social status was an excuse, as was the case in the England of Edward II in the early thirteenth–fourteenth centuries, or in the France of Henry III in the second half of the sixteenth century, in Venice in the eighteenth century, and in Prussia with Frederick II, in Bavaria in the reign of Ludwig II, in Berlin in the 1920s and 1930s. Even Popes such as Sixtus IV della Rovere and Julius II della Rovere, together with extraordinary masters of the arts, such as Michelangelo, Leonardo, Cellini, Caravaggio, Canova and Winckelmann for so many intuitable reasons were not the object of aversion or retaliation.

In the second half of the nineteenth century, medicine was the laboratory in which an attempt was made to settle this phenomenon scientifically, starting with the coining of a new name: *homosexuality*.[48]

But placing the phenomenon within a scientific framework does not exclude it from continuing to be discriminated against and persecuted.

[47] J Boswell, *Alla scoperta dell'amore. Critianesimo e omosessualità* (Roma, Castelvecchi, 2015). Only recently has there been more openness since the Dutch Catechism, although the official position is in the sense of defending the individual from aggression but deploring the practice as immoral because it is an expression of disorder: *Il nuovo catechismo olandese: Annuncio della fede agli uomini di oggi: Con la "dichiarazione della commissione cardinalizia" del 15 ottobre 1968 e il "supplemento al nuovo catechismo"* (Torino, Elle Di Ci-Leumann, 1969).

[48] M Foucault, *History of Sexuality. 1. The Will to Knowledge*, (London, Penguin Books, 1998) / *Storia della sessualità. 1. La volontò di sapere* (Milano, Feltrinelli, 1978).

XII. THE QUALIFICATION OF THE 'DIFFERENT'. MEDICINE AND PSYCHOLOGY

It was not until 1990 that the World Health Organization delisted homosexuality as a mental disease.

However, psychologists are divided. Some see homosexuality as a *natural* tendency, that is, a condition dictated by the psyche, or biological inheritance; the different cannot escape it; others see it as the result of social conditioning, family life and social life. For a long time, it was believed that these behaviours could be corrected through therapeutic or psychiatric treatment.

The peculiarity of this human condition is that over two millennia and possibly more it has been the subject of repressive measures:

> Throughout history, homosexuals have encountered very different modes of tolerance or intolerance, but the great novelty at the end of the last century was their becoming a public feature and acquiring a dimension of claiming rights and equality in difference. This led to the homosexual person becoming a citizen or citizen, thanks to the laws enacted to make possible the recognition of the affective bond between persons of the same sex and the possibility of creating a family.[49]

The path to decriminalising homosexuality in history has been long and tortuous. Italy was among the first states to decriminalise homosexuality, with the Zanardelli code of 1889; the United Kingdom did so only in 1967, Germany in 1969, Spain in 1979, France in 1982, Ireland in 1993.

Particularly heated was the press campaign organised by the jurist Ulrichs in the years preceding the founding of the Prussian Empire for recognition of the rights of homosexuals (of whom psychologists and anthropologists had claimed to identify specific distinctive traits of psychophysical origin) and following the founding by other scholars for the repeal of § 175 of the penal code then in force, which criminalised fornication and lust between men or of persons with animals.[50] At the same time, a well-known physician, Hirschfeld, had theorised the naturalness of love for persons of the same sex (believing, moreover, that an intermediate sex, the third sex, could be identified between men and women), created a vast cultural movement in favour of homosexuality and activated the first civil rights movements.[51] The collapse of the Empire and the advent of the Weimar Republic introduced forms of extended freedom that favoured the spread of a tolerant attitude towards homosexuals, which was to be seen especially in Berlin in the 1920s.

For a long time, law affected the practice of diversity, not the condition of, or way of being, homosexual. Only with the advent of Nazism did the homosexual condition become a crime in and of itself, and, in addition to the extensive application

[49] V Lingiardi, *Citizen Gay. Affetti e diritti* (Milano, Il Saggiatore, 2013).

[50] In the literature on the subject see IV Hull, *Sexuality, State and Civil Society in Germany, 1700–1815* (Ithaca,NY-London, Cornell University Press, 1997); H Puff, *Sodomy in Reformation Germany and Switzerland* (Chicago, The University of Chicago Press, 2003).

[51] The Zanardelli code of 1889 had ignored homosexuality: see G Dall' Orto, 'La "tolleranza repressiva" dell'omosessualità. Quando un atteggiamento legale diviene tradizione' in Arci GAY (ed), *Omosessuali e Stato* (Cassero, Bologna, 1988) 37.

of § 175 of the penal code, special minute legislation was introduced providing for systems of 'prevention' and medical treatment of homosexuality, and for punishment, this being considered a crime against the purity of the race. From here to internment and annihilation in extermination camps was but a short step.

The history of these events has been investigated by an extensive literature, especially abroad.

With the approval of new constitutions, the hostile attitude towards homosexuality has gradually eased, thanks also to the action of civil rights and diversity movements and initiatives of LGBT associations.

It was not until 2000, with the Nice Charter, that discrimination on the grounds of sexual orientation was explicitly stigmatised (Article 21), even though at the level of interpretation the principle of formal equality and the prohibition of discrimination on the grounds of sex have founded tolerant orientations in almost all systems of Western countries.

The paradox of protection is that it presupposes 'disclosure': a person is protected if they announce their diversity. But how is diversity defined? By their acts, their behaviour, their feelings, their 'nature'?

According to Michel Foucault, in *The Will to Knowledge*, the text with which his history of sexuality begins:

> Sodomy – that of ancient civil and canon law – was a particular type of prohibited act; its perpetrator was merely its legal subject. The nineteenth century homosexual, on the other hand, has become a character: a past, a history, and a childhood, a character, a form of life; a morphology too, with an indiscreet anatomy and perhaps a mysterious physiology. Nothing of what he altogether is escapes his sexuality.

One could discuss this conviction at length: reading this passage, it seems that homosexuality was only relevant because it legally configured a case under canon law or criminal law. In reality, a study of the phenomenon convinces one of the opposite: law has never formulated definitions and solutions *autonomous* from the religious moral or political and social conceptions that existed at the time when it intervened to repress homosexuality. On the contrary, it has made itself the bearer of legal forms to prevent, prohibit, punish acts and behaviour 'against nature'.

Foucault also argues that it was only at the end of the eighteenth century that sexual relations 'against nature' were legally penalised because, like incest, rape and adultery, homosexuality was considered one of the crimes that disrupted the family. The prohibition of incest is based on biological, religious and moral arguments; the prohibition of rape is placed to safeguard consent of the betrothed and, where appropriate, seals class endogamy; repression of adultery reinforces the husband's power over his wife and prevents uncertainties over the paternity of children; homosexuality is opposed to procreation and constitutes a brake on propagation of the species.

Family historians accredit this perspective and place repression of sodomy in the context of the cultural and religious climate of the Reformation and Counter-Reformation.

In other words, sodomy presupposes that marriage (understood as the legal institutionalisation of sexual union) must be directed towards procreation; sodomy does not entail procreation and is therefore a threat to the survival of society.

However, this historical progression must be corrected.

As mentioned above, the notion of homosexuality constructed at the end of the nineteenth century marks a break with the past and favours a transition from the atomistic conception founded on single acts to a syncretic conception founded on quality, that is, on *identity*, which is a permanent way of being of the individual. From the physical dimension, the focus shifts to the psyche, which becomes the working ground for understanding the individual's identity and correcting their nature. But also to mock it.[52]

The social reaction is expressed in a stigma that persecutes the individual throughout their life.[53] Even the lexicon with all its variants, including dialect and slang, becomes an instrument of discrimination: the homosexual becomes the *different person* par excellence.[54]

On the website of the World Health Organization (WHO), studies, statistics and recommendations are collected on the health situation of the 'different' in different areas of the world. The results of these reports indicate, in a 2019 publication, that homosexual behaviour is one of the causes of the spread of HIV, which is found above all in the poorer classes, since the poorest are unable or hindered by their economic conditions to provide themselves with preventive tools, are poorly informed, and are often unaware of the risks to which they expose themselves.[55] Children are the most affected.[56]

The WHO thus attests to a link between *gender-related* sexual behaviour and the spread of socially dangerous diseases (at 25) and emphasises the need to make each individual responsible so that the misuse of gender can result in harm to society.

Clearly, these considerations must be measured, because they tend, if taken to extremes, to criminalise those who appeal to gender in order to affirm their identity. And at the same time to provoke reactions against anything that brings uncertainty about sexual identification or sexual orientation.

A vicious circle then arises: those who are different are criminalised, so they are forced to act covertly; this prompts them not to avail themselves of medical aids to treat themselves if they are infected, with the consequence that those who come into contact with them risk putting their health at risk. Identity is correlated with social exclusion, poverty, social conditions and health. WHO studies highlight the correlation between the status of the 'different' and social marginalisation. Sex is seen only in its physical-biological aspect, gender in its cultural and social aspect. Gender identity also implies role awareness and is the result of inner experience with respect to

[52] M Barbagli and A Colombo, *Omosessuali moderni. Gay e lesbiche in Italia* (Bologna, Il Mulino, 2007).

[53] I Goffman and Bontempi, *Stigma. Notes on the Management of Spoiled Identity* (Harmondsworth, Penguin Books, 1973).

[54] GA Stella, *Negri, froci, giudei & co.: L'eterna guerra contro l'altro* (Milano, BURbig Rizzoli, 2018).

[55] WHO, 'Breaking Barriers Towards more gender-responsive and equitable health systems' (18 October 2019), www.who.int/publications/m/item/breaking-barriers-towards-more-gender-responsive-and-equitable-health-systems.

[56] ibid 11. Countries must consider inequities and disparities within and across groups and geographic areas in accessing health care, learn how gender norms and unequal power relations impede access and identify the key barriers to access for women, men, and lesbian, gay, bisexual, transgender and intersex populations.

the sex assigned by the community.[57] The conclusion of these studies is that gender should not be used to discriminate against individuals even in the field of health.[58] The WHO recently denounced the situation of the 'different' in the world. Violence and discrimination are common in countries in Africa and Asia.[59]

XIII. HUMAN RIGHTS AND GENDER

The most complicated cases concern the *gender of* an individual. Identity plays an essential role here, right from birth; it can affect the individual throughout life.

The judges of the European Court of Human Rights are aware of this, both when they deny the individual the right to change their identity and when they accept it.

Two examples apply in this context.

In 1986, deciding the case of *Rees v UK*,[60] a woman who had undergone sex reassignment surgery had asked for her documents to be amended on the basis of her sex at birth. The European Court of Human Rights balanced the interests at stake and, noting that in the United Kingdom and most European countries, rectification of civil status documents was not permitted even if the person concerned had biologically and physically changed sex, and quoting Article 8 of the ECHR (which protects the right to privacy) and Article 14 (which protects the right to start a family) stated that 'it cannot be said, for the time being, that there is a unity of views in this matter, and that on the whole, it seems to be going through a transitional phase, in which states have a large margin of appreciation'.

In contrast, in the last few years, as the orientations of legislators and judges in most states have changed, the Court has found violation of these rights. This is the

[57] 'Sex' refers to biological and physiological characteristics, such as chromosomes, hormones and anatomy that distinguish males and females. While sex is often referred to as a binary category – male or female – other categories do not fall under either of these characteristics, such as intersex. 'Gender' encompasses socially constructed norms, roles, behaviours, activities and attributes that a given society considers appropriate for individuals based on the sex assigned to them at birth. Individuals are socialised into a gender and are taught behaviours considered appropriate for women and men, including how to interact with others of the same or opposite sex. Gender roles are also affected by age, class, race, ethnicity and religion, as well as by geographic, economic and political environments. Gender identity is a person's deeply felt internal and individual experience of gender (as male, female, a blend of both or neither), which may or may not correspond with the sex assigned at birth or the gender attributed to them by society. Gender identity includes the personal sense of the body (which may involve, if freely chosen, modification of appearance or function by medical, surgical or other means) and expressions of gender, including dress, speech and mannerisms. 'Gender equality' means equal opportunities for women and men to access and control social, economic and political resources, including equal and fair protection under the law. It means that the different behaviours, aspirations and needs of women and men are considered, valued and favoured equally and that there is no discrimination on the grounds of gender in the allocation of resources or benefits.

[58] B Ki-Moon, 'Message to Human Rights Council meeting on Violence and Discrimination based on Sexual Orientation or Gender Identity' 30 (7 March 2012), www.who.int/hiv/pub/toolkits/kppmonitoring-tools/en; United Nations Women. Joint UN statement on Ending violence and discrimination against Lesbian, gay, bisexual, transgender and intersex people (1 October 2015), www.ohchr.org/Documents/Issues/Discrimination/Joint_LGBTI_Statement_ENG.PDF.

[59] UN Human Rights Council, 'Report of the Independent Expert on protection against violence and discrimination based on sexual orientation and gender identity' (6–23 June 2017), ap.ohchr.org/documents/dpage_e.aspx?si=A/HRC/35/36.

[60] *Rees v UK*, Case No 47159/08 (ECtHR, 10 October 1986).

case for rectification of the first name (*SV v Italy* 55216/08 11 October 2018); for rectification of civil status documents in the case of sex change (a case concerning Ukraine, 40296/16), though the case was deemed inadmissible because the three levels of proceedings required for access to the Court had not been completed; but in *AP, Garçon and Nicot v France* the Court completely changed its direction, noting that sexual identity is a relevant aspect of a person's identity and therefore – if obstacles are placed in the way of its exact registration – Articles 8 and 14 ECHR are violated.[61]

In the constitutional court's creative process of rights, many personal rights have been coined, including, most recently, the right to *gender*, that is, the right to have one's sexual gender recognised without the expectation that it conforms to the person's physical nature. This implies the person's freedom to express belongingness to a sex other than the one that their physical conformation would claim to give them; a freedom that is expressed in not being forced to undergo surgical intervention to ensure identity between sexual awareness and sexual appearance.

In two subsequent rulings, the Italian Constitutional Court affirmed this right; the first, No 30 of 2021, through the words of the judge rapporteur, Giuliano Amato, explained:

> A rigorous judicial ascertainment of the manner in which the change has taken place and of its definitive character is unavoidable. With respect to this, surgical treatment constitutes a potential instrument that helps to guarantee, by means of a tendency for somatic features to correspond to those of the sex to which one belongs, achievement of the person's full psychological and physical well-being.[62]

It is in this perspective that the reference, contained in Article 31 of Legislative Decree no 150 of 2011, to the possibility ('When it is necessary') of medical-surgical treatment for adjustment of sexual characteristics should also be read. Indeed, in that provision the legislature itself reiterates, almost 30 years after the introduction of Law No 164 of 1982, that it wishes to leave it to the judge's appreciation, within the scope of authorisation for surgery, the actual necessity of the surgery in relation to the specifics of the case.

Recourse to surgical modification of sexual characteristics is therefore authorised as a guarantee of the right to health, that is, where it is intended to allow the person to achieve a stable psycho-physical balance, particularly in those cases in which divergence between the anatomical sex and psychosexuality is such as to determine a conflictual attitude and a rejection of one's anatomical morphology.

The prevalence of protection of the health of the individual over correspondence between anatomical sex and registry sex leads to the conclusion that surgical treatment is not a prerequisite for access to the rectification procedure – as suggested by the referring party – but a possible means of achieving full psycho-physical well-being.

Thus, the hermeneutic path highlighted above recognises the role of the provision in question as a guarantee of the right to gender identity, as an expression of the right to personal identity (Article 2 of the Constitution and Article 8 of the ECHR) and, at

[61] *AP, Garçon et Nicot v France*, Cases No 79885/12, 52471/13 and 52596/13 (ECtHR, 6 April 2017).
[62] The translation is mine.

the same time, as an instrument for full realisation of the right to health, which also has constitutional coverage (Constitutional Court no 221 of 2015).

The second (No 31 of 2021), in the words of President Giancarlo Coraggio:

> In the light of the principles affirmed in Judgment No. 221 of 2015, it must be reiterated that the constitutionally adequate interpretation of Law No. 164 of 1982 allows the requirement of normally correct surgery to be excluded. And yet this in no way excludes, but rather corroborates, the need for a rigorous assessment not only of the seriousness and unambiguousness of the intent, but also of the objective transition of gender identity that has taken place, which has emerged in the path followed by the person concerned; a path that corroborates and strengthens the intent thus manifested. Therefore, in line with the principles set out in the aforementioned judgment, it must be ruled out that the voluntarist element alone can have priority or exclusive importance in ascertaining the transition.

Consistent with what was stated in this judgment, it should be noted once again that the individual's aspiration to have the sex attributed to them in the civil registers at the time of birth correspond to their subjectively perceived and experienced sex is undoubtedly an expression of the individual's desire to have their sex correspond to the subjectively perceived and experienced sex'.[63] (Constitutional Court, no 180, 2017.)

The right to *gender* goes beyond the right to personal identity (that is, the ideal identity) because it demystifies the idea of nature that jurists have codified for millennia and considers the person to be a unicum made up of body and psyche, giving prevalence to the act of self-determination of the individual who, following their natural inclinations, manifests the will to change their body sex into the other, more psychologically appropriate, sex.

XIV. THE DIGITAL IDENTITY

Technological innovations have led to creation of a new type of identity which emerges from collection of data about a person. Purchases, travel, use of houses and hotels, performance of economic transactions, and countless acts of daily, family and working life are recorded using digital technologies. This data, carefully collected and manipulated (or 'processed') shapes a person's way of being. However, digital identity reflects neither the real identity nor the identity that the person would like to give themselves in public, but only the identity that emerges from the manipulation of data collected in individual acts and thus lacking the requirement of totality. In order to enable the individual to control the collection, processing and dissemination of data concerning them, the European Charter of Fundamental Rights has incorporated an ad hoc provision related to the right to privacy:

> Article 7 Respect for private and family life
>
> Everyone has the right to respect for his or her private and family life, home and communications.

[63] The translation is mine.

Article 8 Protection of personal data

1. Everyone has the right to the protection of personal data concerning him or her.
2. Such data must be processed fairly, for specified purposes and with the consent of the person concerned or on another legitimate basis laid down by law. Everyone shall have the right of access to the data collected concerning him or her and the right to have them rectified.
3. Compliance with these rules shall be subject to control by an independent authority.

Information technology has transformed the individual, adding a virtual dimension to their corporeal dimension, the former known within the circle in which they live, the latter projected into the infinite world of information technology. Free circulation of data of the person concerned, the possibility of these being commercialised without limits (and provided that a legal barrier is not erected, dictated by respect for the dignity of the individual), balanced by addition of the right to be forgotten and strengthening of control with multiplication of responsible parties, appears more like a regression with a mercantilist flavour than progress in guarantees of individual rights.

After regulating this matter in the shape of a directive, the European Union introduced a regulation for protection of personal data (Regulation No 2016/679, GDPR). Hence the many rules concerning construction of the market in data, which are an essential component of the digital market, their circulation and thus authorisation, or consent by the person concerned, to their acquisition, processing and use, and also the ownership of databases created by economic operators.[64] Another Regulation relates to contracts with digital content, among which data of a personal nature may be found.[65] Of course, other lines of development are under way, intertwined with the world of information technology, cybernetics and artificial intelligence. But for the time being, literature, case law, acts of independent

[64] European Commission, 'Communication to the European Parliament, the Council, the European Economic and Social Committee and the Committee of the Regions. A Digital Single Market Strategy for Europe' COM(2015) 192 final; G Simeone, 'Mercato unico digitale' in *Enciclopedia Treccani online* (2016), www.treccani.it/enciclopedia/mercato-unico-digitale_%28Diritto-on-line%29; C Prins, C Cuipers, PL Lindseth and M Rosina (eds), *Digital Democracy in a Globalized World* (Cheltenham, Edward Elgar Publishing, 2017); OECD, 'Key Issues for Digital Transformation in the G20. Report prepared for a joint G20 German Presidency/ OECD Conference' Berlin (12 January 2017), www.de.digital/DIGITAL/Redaktion/EN/Publikation/key-issues-for-digital-transformation-g20.pdf?__blob=publicationFile&v=1; European Commission, Directorate-General for Communications Networks, Content and Technology, P Foley, D Sutton, I Wiseman et al, 'International Digital Economy and Society Index 2018, Final Report' (Publication Office of the European Union, Luxembourg, 2018).

[65] Briefing disseminated by the European Parliament in May 2007, R Mańko and S Monteleone 'Contracts for the supply of digital content and personal data protection', PE 603.929, www.europarl.europa.eu/thinktank/en/document/EPRS_BRI(2017)603929; Works of the General Secretariat of the Council ('Proposal for a directive on certain aspects concerning contracts for the supply of digital content – Compilation of Member States' replies concerning Articles 3(6) and 16' of 11th April 2017'), n 8229/17; note of the Presidency of the Council of 1st June 2017, 'Proposal for a directive on certain aspects concerning contracts for the supply of digital content (First Reading) – General Approach' n 9901/17, data.consilium.europa.eu/doc/document/ST-9901-2017-ADD-1/en/pdf, and within the wide scholarly literature, the contributions gathered in A De Franceschi, *European Contract Law and the Digital Single Market. The Implication of the Digital Revolution* (Cambridge, Cambridge University Press, 2017).

authorities, resolutions of European and international socio-economic bodies, and codes of conduct focus mainly on personal data and their relationship with the market.[66]

XV. THE RIGHT TO BE ONESELF

So can we get rid of identity, since over the centuries it has served to suffocate the person rather than to enhance their qualities and value?

Divergent answers from different cultural backgrounds point in a negative direction.

On the moral level, Kwame Anthony Appiah states that it is not necessary to adopt a stance either in favour of or against identity: what is important is to understand how it is constructed, so to speak, on the fixed level. If shortcomings there be, it will be up to others to identify the cure. Following the teaching of John Stuart Mill, Appiah points out that what is important is to leave each individual free to realise their own life programme, since it is not the status one acquires that is important, but the life model one wishes to pursue.[67] The ethics of identity in this view becomes the *ethics of individuality*. Identity – and individuality – are thus closely connected with *freedom*: what matters is not to be different from others, but rather to enjoy the freedom to construct oneself. But, Appiah emphasises, we have to take into account three factors: the inventive capacity of each of us who wants to design our lives according to our own aspirations, our own ideals; the authenticity of this image, which corresponds to what we actually achieve; and the collective dimension of individual identity.

The collective dimension, we might add, is particularly important for jurists, because for its part the law, which is the result of decisions of the community, constructs the identity of each of us, from the moment of birth to life's end, with the identity constructed by the individual a continuous duel between the identity one would like to have and the identity that society imposes on us.

In ethical terms, individuality, namely individual identity, implies that we have duties towards ourselves, whereas social identity implies that we have duties towards others. Solidarity is triggered towards those who are similar to us, so that it is a unifying factor for many individualities. In order to guarantee this opportunity for all, it is necessary to achieve global human rights, safeguarding individualities and thus differences, because 'in a single society there is no wisdom'.[68]

Clearly, then, it is not enough to demand more freedom for everyone, but rather that everyone must be put in a position to make free life choices. And here, of course, radical liberalism clashes with factual reality, which today is made even more difficult to govern due to the current economic crisis.

[66] A Mantelero, *Il costo della privacy tra valore della persona e ragioni dell'impresa* (Milano, Giuffrè, 2007); S Rodotà, *Il mondo nella rete. Quali diritti, quali vincoli* (Roma-Bari, Laterza, 2014).

[67] KA Appiah, *The Ethics of Identity* (Princeton, Princeton University Press, 2005) 5.

[68] ibid 252.

The problem of identity thus merges with analysis of human nature throughout the entire course of philosophical thought: every philosopher poses the problem 'Who are we?' and strives to answer this question with the methodological choices proper to their system of thought. The nature of the person becomes an interpretative key to the entire history of philosophy.[69]

The *person* is a central notion in the world of law, and so is identity. But as mentioned above, it is only recently that *individual* identity has been valued.

On the basis of historical and analytical research of normative texts, we can therefore consider that the right to be oneself has now been accredited after a long and bumpy ride: transition from the neutral concept of the subject of law to the composite and comprehensive concept of the person is now complete.

[69] W Bourgeois, *Persons – What Philosophers Say About You* (Waterloo Ont, Wilfrid Laurier University Press, 1995); PL Pojman, *Who are we? Theories of Human Nature* (Oxford, Oxford University Press, 2006).

8

Intersectionality and Law: Right or Method?

MARISARIA MAUGERI AND PASQUALE FEMIA*

I. INTRODUCTION

UNLIKE ELSEWHERE,[1] THE topic of intersectionality and the law is not at the centre of the debate of Italian civil law scholars dealing with contract law. Indeed, with the exception of a few authors, whom I shall cite below, I believe it can be said that the notion is not contemplated by them at all.

I will therefore try, here, first of all, to give an account of the origins of the term 'intersectionality' and the type of problem it signals. However, it seems appropriate to point out that the notion, from the point of view of sociological studies, is evolving and that it indicates more a possible tension towards overcoming current patterns than a defined strategy.[2]

Below, I will represent some of the positions taken by supranational bodies.

Finally, I will ask how intersectionality can affect contract law and, if and to what extent, the attribution of relevance to intersectionality in that specific context can lead to social equalisation.

II. INTERSECTIONALITY

The legal notion of intersectionality was first theorised by Kimberlé Crenshaw in 1989[3] concerning the intersection of race and gender in the discriminatory experiences of black women.

* Sections I–IV are by Marisaria Maugeri; sections V–XII are by Pasquale Femia.

[1] See eg MJ Hesselink, 'EU Private Law Injustices' (2022) 41 *Yearbook of European Law* 83.

[2] See BG Bello, *Intersezionalità. Teorie e pratiche tra diritto e società* (Milano, Franco Angeli, 2020) 31ff. The quotations herein refer to those in the eBook. See also G Marini, 'Intersezionalità. Genealogia di un metodo giuridico' (2021) 39 *Rivista critica di diritto privato* 475.

[3] K Crenshaw, 'Demarginalizing the Intersection of Race and Sex: A Black Feminist Critique of Antidiscrimination Doctrine, Feminist Theory and Antiracist Politics' (1989) *University of Chicago Legal Forum* 139. The relationship between intersectionality and Critical Race Theory is described by D Kennedy, 'Intersezionalità e Critical Race Theory: una genealogia dal punto di vista dei Critical Legal Studies' (2021) 39 *Rivista critica di diritto privato* 9.

Kimberlé Crenshaw pointed out how the law against discrimination against women had the white woman as its reference and the law against racial discrimination had the black man as its reference, thus leaving black women unseen.

One of the cases analysed by the author was *DeGraffenreid v General*, concerning five Black women dismissed by General Motors. The recession of 1970 had forced General Motors to make job cuts and it had decided to fire the workers with the least seniority first. This choice, however, abstractly neutral, had resulted in the dismissal of Black women. This was because, until 1964, the latter had not been hired by General Motors. Judge Wangelin had dismissed the action. This was because formally both Black men and white women (hired before 1964) had remained in service.

Crenshaw highlights how the different form of discrimination has not been 'considered' (or seen) by the legal system.[4]

Intersectional discrimination is characterised, as stated in a recent study, as

> different from other types of single, multiple or compound discrimination because of the cause of the discrimination (two or more factors that cannot be separated from each other) and the effects of the discrimination (more serious violation than discrimination produced by a single factor).

In this perspective, in her study on intersectionality in the European Union, Sandra Fredman proposed the following definition of intersectional discrimination: 'Intersectional discrimination happens when two or multiple grounds operate simultaneously and interact in an inseparable manner, producing distinct and specific forms of discrimination.'[5]

What one part of the doctrine wishes to emphasise, however, is that this is not a new identity to be protected, but a different approach to the relevance of marginality.

Some go so far as to claim that anti-discrimination policies that consider people's identity on the basis of only one factor at a time risk reinforcing marginality.[6]

For example, as Giovanni Marini writes in a very recent essay,

> At the heart of the problem, for black women, is not just the fact that they are not 'represented' and remain invisible in the process of categorisation, but rather the social and material consequences that this combination of identities causes and which relegates them to the margins of social geography: in a position in which the instruments of social

[4] For more on the cases considered by Kimberlé Crenshaw, see Marini (n 2) 478ff; Bello (n 2) 35.

[5] D Ferrari, I Valenzi and N Palazzo, 'L'intersezionalità come approccio giuridico: una prospettiva multilivello tra diritto internazionale, diritto europeo, diritto italiano e prospettive di comparazione', Report 'INtersecting GRounds of Discrimination in Italy' (2022) 12, www.projectingrid.eu/wp-content/uploads/2022/03/D2.1-Lintersezionalita%CC%80-come-approccio-giuridico-ITA.pdf. Sandra Fredman's definition, quoted in the text, is taken from European Commission, Directorate-General for Justice and Consumers and S Fredman, *Intersectional discrimination in EU gender equality and non-discrimination law* (Publications Office, Brussels, 2016).

[6] With reference to Italy, she considers that the PNRR, in addition to declining the principle of non-discrimination in a manner inferior to the protection offered by EU law, is further weakened by the 'failure to consider intersectionality, which risks significantly compromising the PNRR's ability to meet the challenges that also in the field of gender equality arise in an increasingly composite society such as Italy'; M Evola, 'La parità di genere nel Piano nazionale di ripresa e resilienza. Brevi considerazioni in chiave UE' (2022) *La Magistratura* 95, lamagistratura.it/diritto-europeo-e-sovranazionale/la-parita-di-genere-nel-piano-nazionale-di-ripresa-e-resilienza.

> justice no longer work and the strategies of resistance adopted within the framework of the various identity politics may even prove harmful, causing a boomerang effect that replicates and reinforces marginality.[7]

The idea of the intersectionality theorists is to leave room for intersection and not addition between discriminating factors.[8]

III. REFERENCES TO INTERSECTIONALITY IN UNITED NATIONS DOCUMENTS AND EUROPEAN LAW

The United Nations has referred in some documents to gender identity or sexual orientation as vectors of specific forms of vulnerability when intersected with other characteristics of the person, such as professed religion or membership of a specific community.

Article 6 of the UN Convention on the Rights of Persons with Disabilities, which came into force with Law 18/2009, for example, recognises that 'women and children with disabilities are subject to multiple discrimination' and requires states to take 'measures to ensure the full and equal enjoyment of all human rights and fundamental freedoms by women and children with disabilities'.[9]

Non-linear in terms of the recognition of intersectionality seems to be EU law.

While, on the one hand, some recitals (*cf* recital 14 of Directive 2000/43/EC and recital 3 of Directive 2000/78/EC) give relevance to intersections or, at the very least, multiple discrimination, on the other hand, some anti-discrimination directives make no mention of this notion.[10]

The Court of Justice, moreover, is essentially stuck to single-factor discrimination.

Very interesting in this respect is the *Parris* decision (Case C-443/15).[11] The Court questioned the legal possibility of adopting an intersectional approach. The Court, in fact, referred to a new category of discrimination that would have arisen from the combination of several personal characteristics to conclude, however, that 'no new category of discrimination resulting from the combination of more than one … ground … may be found where discrimination on the basis of those grounds taken in isolation has not been established'.[12]

[7] Marini (n 2) 476.

[8] Marella points out how intersectional criticism, unlike queer criticism, has nevertheless remained linked to the ontology of real identities: see MR Marella, 'Teoria queer e analisi giuridica' in M Pellissero and A Vercellone (eds), *Diritto e persone LGBTQI+* (Turin, Giappichelli, 2022) 45.

[9] On intersectionality in the United Nations system, see Bello (n 2) 139ff; Ferrari, Valenzi and Palazzo (n 5).

[10] *cf* the analysis of Bello (n 2) 441ff.

[11] Case C-443/15 *Parris*, ECLI:EU:C:2016:897 [2017] ICR 313 (CJEU): 'Mr. Parris had a same-sex partner who, due to discriminatory legal requirements – according to the applicant – could not obtain a survivor's pension unlike opposite-sex partners. The contested legislative requirement, in fact, was that the two spouses must marry before reaching the age of 60. However, and therein lay the discrimination, Parris and her partner could not have done so because same-sex unions in Ireland were introduced when the two partners had already reached the age of 60. In this case, the discrimination was peculiar as it did not affect same-sex couples tout court, but a specific group.'

[12] ibid [80].

In particular, the Court held that

> Articles 2 and 6(2) of Directive 2000/78 must be interpreted as meaning that national rule such as that at issue in the main proceedings is not capable of creating discrimination as a result of the combined effect of sexual orientation and age where that rule does not constitute discrimination either on the ground of sexual orientation or on the ground of age taken in isolation.[13]

Advocate General Kokott had taken a different view, which was not followed by the Court: 'the Court's judgment will reflect real life only if it duly analyses the combination of these two factors, rather than considering each of the factors of age and sexual orientation in isolation' because[14] 'The combination of two or more different grounds … is a feature that lends a new dimension to a case.'[15]

Most recently, the Parliament issued a Resolution on 'Intersectional discrimination in the EU: the socio-economic situation of women of African, Middle Eastern, Latin American and Asian descent',[16] which seems to want to give relevance to the notion.[17]

The invitation to collect data appears interesting.

Parliament, has stated that:

> [W]hereas applying an intersectional analysis allows us to address and understand social inequalities, exclusion and discrimination from a comprehensive, systemic and structural perspective, while overcoming a single-axis approach to discrimination; whereas EU policies have not involved an intersectional approach thus far, whereas they have focused only on the individual dimensions of discrimination, which downplays from the institutional, structural and historical dimensions,

it calls, inter alia, on the Commission and the Member States, on the basis of 'voluntary participation, confidentiality, anonymity, self-identification and informed consent, [to] *take steps toward the collection of reliable and comparable equality data*',[18] including data disaggregated by gender, racial and ethnic origin (as defined by the EU Racial Equality Directive), sexual orientation and sexual identity, in accordance with key EU data protection and fundamental rights principles and standards, with the aim of identifying root causes, combating racism and discrimination and measuring their extent in accordance with relevant national legal frameworks, and to work towards using these data to inform policy-making notes that equality data is an essential tool for understanding, uncovering and combating all types and forms of discrimination, particularly intersectional, structural and institutional discrimination; urges the EU to encourage the collection of such data and to provide technical support to implement the Commission's existing guidelines on the subject and to promote the participation of affected communities in the process.

[13] ibid [82].

[14] Opinion of Advocate General Kokott in ibid [4].

[15] Opinion of Advocate General Kokott in ibid [153].

[16] European Parliament, Resolution of 6 July 2022 P9TA(2022)0289 in OJ, 7.2.2023.

[17] Previous Resolutions of 29 November 2018 on the situation of women with disabilities and 26 March 2019 on the fundamental rights of persons of African descent in Europe already referred to the intersection.

[18] n 16, para 5; emphasis added.

Such a measure had been strongly advocated because it was considered suitable to counter discriminatory phenomena and capable of producing empirical evidence on the marginalisation of groups of people.[19]

The European Convention on Human Rights opted for an open list of discriminatory factors, ending with the formula 'and any other conditions' (Article 14), and this allowed a wider margin to sanction intersectional discrimination.

Consider, in this regard, the case of *BS v Spain* in the European Court of Human Rights in 2012, which considered the vulnerability of an African woman working as a prostitute.[20]

IV. THE INTERSECTIONALITY PERSPECTIVE: INCREASING SOCIAL EQUALISATION OR WEAKENING THE DISCRIMINATED?

The developments in the area of intersectionality have not directly affected contract law, except employment contracts, which have long had their own characteristics and disciplines.

In truth, there is also discrimination in the field of tenancy. I cannot say whether it is mono-factorial, multi-factorial or intersectional.

It should be emphasised that utility exchange today is highly standardised. Discrimination in the given context is fundamentally linked to the economic possibility of accessing goods.[21] The poor who cannot buy goods are discriminated against, more so than those who, like me, are women and from the South.

This does not mean that the intersection of two or more fragilities should not be seen and resolved by the legal system.

A distinction must be made, however, between intersectionality resulting in a describable and identifiable sub-category, also through the collection of data mentioned earlier, and intersectionality understood as referring to the specific situation of a given subject.

Concerning the first hypothesis, there seems to me to be no doubt that the new social category can and must be included, if necessary also by using the evolutionary interpretation where the anti-discrimination discipline does not contain general closing clauses, within the categories protected by the various anti-discrimination disciplines.[22]

Concerning the second hypothesis, on the other hand, it seems to me that the attribution of relevance to the 'shattered' subject runs the risk of thwarting the strength of social battles.

In other words, struggles have historically been identity-based because they also reflect the exploitation of one class or personal or social condition over another.

[19] Bello (n 2) 449.

[20] *BS v Spain* (Application No 47159/08) ECtHR, 24 July 2012.

[21] In other words, one thing is to discuss domination of an institutional model (eg one that has wealth and contract as its cornerstones for access to goods); quite another thing is to discuss domination that is realised through a private act. Hesselink (n 1) 14 correctly points out this distinction.

[22] See P Femia, 'Discriminazione (divieto di)' *Enciclopedia del diritto – I Tematici – Contratto* (2021) 499.

The risk that the overcoming of identity, even characterised by a combination of 'weaknesses', may lead to a loss of reactionary force exists. Identity aggregation, in fact, creates shock mass.

Identity, of course, can also be plural. One thinks of the LGBTQIA+ movement. Once we understand how structures of power and domination can be interlinked, it becomes possible to also imagine a connection between groups fighting and resisting against identical forms of discrimination, marginalisation and privilege.

Identity evolves and the law must be able to read this evolution, but to do this it is sufficient to use evolutionary and/or analogical interpretation.

V. A LOOK FROM THE RIGHT DISTANCE. INTERSECTIONALITY: TO WHAT END?

Intersectionality is a widespread term, and in some contexts, it has become a kind of symbol of radical and sometimes elitist thinking, especially in feminist thought.[23] Its success is undoubtedly due to its simplicity: simple to intuit (each person can carry the weight of multiple discriminating factors on him or her: race, gender, religion, education, language, mental weakness, etc), and simple to construct critical essays (essays generally seek to convince that intersectionality of discrimination is a multiplication, not a sum).[24] Simple, then, in *descriptive* use; not simple at all, however, in *normative* use.

Let us imagine that we are faced with a person who claims to be a victim: she is discriminated against, and she is seeking protection in a courtroom. But against whom? Indeed, it is clear what is meant by 'intersectionality' when describing a victim's condition: she is a woman, Black, poor, immigrant, Islamic in a Western country, fat, lesbian, sex worker. Those who talk about intersectionality call for these factors of discrimination to be considered in their overall interaction, not one at a time. But from their unitary consideration in *describing* a specific person, how does one transition to *prescription*? How are rights claimed for this person? Under what conditions and, more importantly, *against whom*?

It is indeed difficult to meet anyone who opposes intersectionality (as indeed it is impossible to read someone who openly declares himself an enemy of equality, unless uncultured), but the fact remains of the resistance of the judiciary to assimilate it into its argumentative procedures. This is not a matter of ill will; on the contrary, the causes of this resistance are structural, and it would be superficial to reply that this happens because of the sexism of judges (including women) or because of an alleged assimilation of patriarchal culture by the judiciary, even if it is composed of women. On the contrary, by studying the reasons for this 'resistance' we will encounter the problems that discourses on intersectionality do not grasp because of their own internal epistemic limitation, and we will find, at the same time, reasons for a legal

[23] VM May, 'Speaking into the Void? Intersectionality Critiques and Epistemic Backlash' (2014) 29 *Hypatia* 94.

[24] K Davis, 'Intersectionality as buzzword: A sociology of science perspective on what makes a feminist theory successful' (2008) 9 *Feminist Theory* 67.

assimilation of intersectionality that finally makes it not a political ideology aimed at the descriptive sociology of inequality, but an internal tool of legal methodology.

VI. INTERSECTIONS OF CATEGORIES AND CRITIQUE OF CATEGORICAL ABSTRACTION

The essay by Kimberlé Crenshaw mentioned above,[25] with which the term intersectionality became part of the public debate, appears in the 1989 *University of Chicago Legal Forum* and is followed by another in the 1991 *Stanford Law Review*,[26] which is devoted primarily to critiquing court decisions in trials on discrimination against Black women in the workplace. The immense success of this writing has distorted its reception: it is renowned for using the metaphor of discrimination intersecting, much like being at a crossroads and for the firm belief that discourses on racial discrimination have been all too much oriented to certain stereotypes, primarily the Black male (as far as criticism of racial segregation is concerned) and the white woman (as far as criticism of female subjugation is concerned). These observations are incontrovertible, and in this respect Crenshaw's success is richly deserved.

Almost simultaneously Angela Harris published, and again in the *Stanford Law Review*, a tight critique of 'white' feminism.[27] This is a fascinating and arguably more profound essay (but to each his preference): Harris moves primarily from the accusation of 'essentialism': the discourses on women in American feminism (the criticisms are aimed particularly at the theories of Catharine MacKinnon and Robin West) would, she argues, celebrate a white woman's rights-oriented point of view. In practice, Angela Harris invites us to be wary of abstraction: general categories would not be general at all, but sub-inclusive abstractions. 'Woman' ('women's rights') would like to represent the whole gender of women, but in reality, it is a category constructed to facilitate the claim of only some women, white women, leaving Black women voiceless, whose specific needs would be underrepresented. This is what Harris calls 'gender essentialism', which:

> [I]s dangerous to feminist legal theory because in the attempt to extract an essential female self and voice from the diversity of women's experience, the experiences of women perceived as 'different' are ignored or treated as variations on the (white) norm. Now I want to return to an earlier point: that legal theory, including feminist legal theory, has been entranced for too long and to too great an extent by the voice of 'We the People.' In order to energize legal theory, we need to subvert it with narratives and stories, accounts of the particular, the different, and the hitherto silenced.[28]

It could not be said, the author continues, that the loss of specificity is inevitable in any categorisation, for it is precisely the socially disadvantaged categories whose

[25] See section II above.

[26] Crenshaw (n 3) 141; K Crenshaw, 'Mapping the Margins: Intersectionality, Identity Politics, and Violence against Women of Color' (1991) 43 *Stanford Law Review* 1241.

[27] AP Harris, 'Race and Essentialism in Feminist Legal Theory' (1990) 42 *Stanford Law Review* 581.

[28] ibid 615.

voices are, once again, suppressed by dominant anti-discriminatory thinking.[29] The individual personality is unrepeatable multiplicity of voices in each of us: in Harris's words, 'a multiple consciousness'.[30]

The theories of Crenshaw and Harris have sometimes been assimilated,[31] are sometimes distinct.[32] The question is open; however, both move from what an old *civil lawyer* would call the critique of the subsumption of the norm to the fact: that illusion that the application of the law is a logical operation that the followers of the free law movement (the *Freirechtslehre* of the early twentieth century) would point to as the defect of the formalist judge, oblivious to social needs, the deprecated judge who became a *Subsumptionsautomat*.[33] Common the inspiration, divergent the terminologies and points of attack of the discourse: Harris foregrounds a political critique of abstraction but seems far more aware of the impossibility of operating without constructing concepts and therefore risking with each operation the oppression of someone for the benefit of someone else. Undoubtedly – and this is a point that has been a target of several Marxist-oriented critiques – intersectionality, as argued by some, tends to overshadow the significance of class differences. It's noteworthy that this perspective contrasts a comprehensive abstraction, 'class', with others focused on differentiation. In challenging dominant classifications, this mode of thinking seems to offer nothing beyond substituting alternative 'emancipatory' classifications. *What*, what social object, intersects in *what* person, in Crenshaw's theory? The lack of precision undermines the efficacy of the theory, potentially confining it to the realm of profound insights that are challenging to translate into legal procedures.

VII. THE EPISTEMIC LIMIT OF INTERSECTIONALITY. AXIOMATIC GROUPINGS, CLAIM ACTION, REACTIVE AGGRESSION

The epistemic limitation of intersectional theory is that it falls into the very contradictions it intends to remove. The parameters by which differences are produced are assumed to be axioms derived from social-political preferences. Sex and skin colour are factors in discrimination: but what sexuality and what colour? A binary or multifaceted sexuality, transgender or deliberately undefined, assumed as a biological datum or a psychic orientation? The same could be said for skin colour: the same skin colour (same? Any 'colour' would itself be further differentiable) can define groups

[29] ibid 585: 'I argue, is not only that some voices are silenced in order to privilege others (for this is an inevitable result of categorization, which is necessary both for human communication and political movement), but that the voices that are silenced turn out to be the same voices silenced by the mainstream legal voice of "We the People"-among them, the voices of black women.'

[30] ibid 584, following MJ Matsuda, 'When the First Quail Calls: Multiple Consciousness as Jurisprudential Method' (1989) 11 *Women's Rights Law Reporter* 9.

[31] NE Dowd, 'The "F" Factor: Fineman as Method and Substance' (2010) 59 *Emory Law Journal* 1199; Angela Harris herself seems to believe in the possible convergence of viewpoints: JM Culp Jr, AP Harris and F Valdes, 'Subject Unrest' (2003) 55 *Stanford Law Review* 2435, 2447.

[32] DW Carbado and CI Harris, 'Intersectionality at 30: Mapping the Margins of Anti-Essentialism, Intersectionality, and Dominance Theory' (2019) 132 *Harvard Law Review* 2193.

[33] S Meder, *Rechtsmaschinen: Von Subsumtionsautomaten, Künstlicher Intelligenz und der Suche nach dem 'richtigen' Urteil* (Köln, Böhlau, 2020) 127ff.

and cultures profoundly different and even incapable of any real communication.[34] A Black New York woman has, perhaps, far more in common with a white Parisian or Berlin woman than she may share with an Islamic African woman living in a small village community and tenaciously attached to her traditionalist identity. Above all – and here socialist criticism returns[35] – how much does social class, or more trivially the heritage, the wealth of the subject matter in the intersection?

The categories of intersectionality are not fixed (the shift from binary to multiple sexuality is a good example of variation) and especially not natural.[36] They are the product of the categorical selection of a style of thinking, convinced that society must improve and can only do so by intervening in certain distinguishing factors, removing them even and especially when they act in combination with one another. In doing so, intersectionality simply ends up creating subsets resulting from the starting axiomatics, which could be employed in ways as rigid as those practiced with the non-intersectional categories they are intended to remove. Do all black women have the same aspirations? All white males have the same duties of reparation to all of these women? All Muslims, Catholics, agnostics (male, female, third sex; poor, rich, impoverished but educated, enriched but uncultured) have the same tolerance?

Individual personalities, given by the combination of preferences in which a single evolutionary path is mirrored;[37] narrative identities, those of 'I am my own story', for whom the turning points of one's life are far more important than straight paths; inwardly shattered subjectivities, for whom the subject is a disgusting imperialist metaphor, to deconstruct which all the antihegemonic resources of heterogeneous cultures are employed: what can the language of intersectionality say to these people, open to every event or (depending on one's point of view) locked in narcissistic contemplation of a self as adored as it is empty? Mono-categorical sets ('woman') are from the point of view of social time unchangeable at least over a few generations: and, while the great abstractions remain stationary, each woman can write the biography of her own liberation (provided that society has *truly* assimilated equality); intersectional multi-categorical sets, on the other hand, change much more rapidly: today Black woman, tomorrow Black immigrant woman, the day after tomorrow Black immigrant woman and lesbian, tomorrow the next Black immigrant woman lesbian and obese – but in each of these manifestations, she will be in danger of meeting someone who will tell her even more stringently what she must do to be a good intersectional woman. What if tomorrow I were a Black woman, Ivy League-full professor of political philosophy, affirmed for my studies on intersectionality? What would I have in common, really, with the experience of previous

[34] An invitation to consider more carefully methodological issues is included in JC Nash, 'Re-thinking Intersectionality' (2008) 89 *Feminist Review* 1.

[35] B Foley, 'Intersectionality: A Marxist Critique' (2019) 28 *New Labor Forum* 10.

[36] On the power structures inherent in such proceedings, IM Young, 'Structural injustice and the politics of difference' in E Grabham et al (eds), *Intersectionality and Beyond* (Abingdon, Routledge-Cavendish, 2008) 273.

[37] G Moon, 'Justice for the Whole Person: The UK's Partial Success Story' in D Schiek and A Lawson (eds), *European Union Non-Discrimination: Investigating The Triangle of Racial, Gender and Disability Discrimination* (Farnham, Ashgate, 2011) 157.

Black women? And how much would they have in common with their white work colleague, especially after they were both fired from their cleaning company?

A mathematician will know better than I how many subcategories can be created by combining all the individual intersecting elements and how continuously variable, therefore, is the subset to which the person must fall.[38] In Crenshaw's view – or at least in the unfolding of intersectional theories – it seems that the subject is always *either* satisfied with the parameters that, by defining his or her condition as a victim, allow him or her a peculiar claim to rights, *or* free to dispose of them, because if intersectionality did not suit him or her, he or she would still be free not to invoke it, since (let us explicate a fact often implicit in these theories) the intersectional condition is conceived as a matrix of rights, not also of duties to society. And so, I invoke a parameter of discrimination from which I am affected only if it suits me. But (anticipating a problem that we will develop in the next section) can the judge know intersectional parameters other than those invoked by the plaintiff in the trial? Is intersectionality objective or subjective? Is it a right available to the person who invokes it or a quality of fact to which all applicable rules (principles included) must be objectively applied?

Certainly, intersectionality is a powerful form of descriptive simplification.[39] Instead of delving into intricate analyses that delineate the unique interweaving of each identity, considering both social-psychological and historical aspects, and addressing the inherent challenges tied to an identity inseparable from one's life story (interpreted as a journey from one historical context to another), intersectionality opts for a more straightforward approach. This approach sidesteps the complexities involved in distributing resources and understanding the interplay between societal constraints and individual aspirations: positing the thesis that everything depends on how sufficiently narrow and apparently intuitive collective categories intersect in an entity (the intersected individual) and defining it as intersectionality and nothing else. Sociological research is simplified, and trivialised to the repetition of the existing; until the next 'discovery' of a discriminating factor (ie, the emergence of some other claim in social communication), which occurs outside of adequate historical awareness. Yesterday, intersections were primarily defined by factors such as religion, sexual gender and skin colour. Although there was some oversight in acknowledging the influence of wealth and social power, these intersections operated within specific groups and extended to a broader territorial scope, eventually reaching a global scale. Today, the focus has shifted towards considerations like transgender identity, body weight, limited linguistic-cultural competence, and potentially other factors in the future. Unfortunately, the significance of these evolving intersections seems to be given insufficient attention.

The *epistemic limitation* of intersectionality is its historical opacity, its categorical axiomatics, which render opaque the social determinants of category formation and dissolution, the presumed shared evidence of every discriminating factor introduced by the speaker (ie, by an academic authority that claims

[38] P Hill Collins, 'Intersectionality's Definitional Dilemmas' (2015) 41 *Annual Review of Sociology* 1.

[39] However, there is no lack of attention to relationships with economic dynamics: D Cooper, 'Intersectional Travel Through Everyday Utopias: The Difference Sexual and Economic Dynamics Make' in E Grabham et al (eds), *Intersectionality and Beyond* (Abingdon, Routledge-Cavendish, 2008) 299.

to possess the right social vision) and the consequent claim to diversity based on evidence imposed by the speaker himself.[40] Its *political limitation* is the increase in opposition between imaginary communities, for which rights are claimed, the freezing of the dialectic in the opposition between (micro)collective identities that are increasingly rigid, increasingly less negotiable, and increasingly conflictual, since they are constituted on the terrain of claims, of oppositions, not on that of grand emancipatory narratives.

It is precisely this position of axiomatic naturalism of vindication that generates (or at least facilitates) the reactive waves of a certain widespread course of traditionalist views. While we hold a supreme disdain for the assertive victimhood evident in the resurgence of political conservatism today – wherein symbolic violence is wielded to portray present suffering as a consequence of past oppressions – it is essential to acknowledge that this conservative victimhood gains traction, in part, due to the simplification of intersectional claims. The focus on demanding recognition as a victim and subsequent compensation aligns with reactive victimhood seen in significant portions of the populist population. This group feels under attack and legitimises their resistance to self-reflection by multiplying claims for rights, seemingly oblivious to the societal costs associated with such demands. If political discourse continues to revolve around group dynamics, clashes between these groups become an inevitable outcome.

VIII. INTERSECTING IN COURT

If we step outside of the discussions of critical theory – which all repeat that one must consider the overall condition of a person as belonging to a given subset, that it is erroneous to evaluate discriminating factors one at a time, that the social and legislative policies of states and the European Union are insufficient and perpetuate varied inequalities[41] – and face a courtroom, what would we find? We would find mostly accounts in which jurisprudential decisions are challenged, ignoring the combination of discriminating factors, purporting to consider them one at a time. The trials mostly involve cases in which the plaintiff complaining of discrimination is a female worker, to which an additional discriminating factor is added: predominantly sexual orientation, religion, language, sometimes all together.[42] Other cases involve foreign women seeking access to welfare state benefits.[43]

[40] A careful methodological analysis distinguishes among three levels of complexity (anticategorical, intercategorical and intracategorical): L McCall, 'The Complexity of Intersectionality' (2005) 30 *Signs* 1171, 1173–74.

[41] S Carnovali, 'Profili delle politiche nazionali ed europee di contrasto alle discriminazioni multiple' (2016) *Gruppo di Pisa – La rivista*, 1; MV Onufrio, 'Intersectional discrimination in the European legal systems: Toward a common solution?' (2014) 14 *International Journal of Discrimination and the Law* 126.

[42] Extensive analysis in BL Graham, *Social Identity and the Law: Race, Sexuality, and Intersectionality* (New York, Routledge, 2019).

[43] M Hugentobler and B von Rütte, 'Die sogenannte "intersektionelle" Diskriminierung. Der Umgang Schweizer Gerichte mit dem Konzept der Intersektionalität am Beispiel des Einbürgerungsrechts' (2022) *cognitio – studentisches Forum für Recht und Gesellschaft* 1; CO'Cinneide, 'The Potential and Pitfalls of Intersectionality in the Context of Social Rights Adjudication' in S Atrey and P Dunne (eds), *Intersectionality and Human Rights Law* (Oxford, Hart, 2020) 59.

Let us try to offer a more accurate reconstruction. Invoking intersectionality in a courtroom implies two possibilities:

(1) *Distributional conflicts* – invoking its entitlement to receive a good, since its denial would be discriminatory, proving discrimination through the multiplication of discriminatory factors in a single person: this happens when the plaintiff in the suit believes that the proof of only one discriminatory factor would be insufficient to ensure her a favourable judgment, since for each factor, individually considered, the defendant could put up substantial defences: therefore, if each individual factor was insufficient to substantiate the claim in the suit, their synthesis would be.

(2) *Appropriative conflicts* – invoking their own entitlement to receive certain goods, identified as goods bearing the claimed intersectional identity, goods pertaining exclusively to the (sub)group thus identified: in such a case, the judicial claim takes on a real claiming character, a kind of *ius excludendi alios*.

Appropriative conflicts are the most problematic, both because they claim exclusivity for a group, the boundaries of which may change with each new intersection, and because they ultimately consist of claims for the group, a kind of fractional *actio popularis*, an 'intersectional' class action: only Black women can decide on the working conditions of Black women; only homosexuals can decide on the parental rights of homosexuals; only victims of terrorism can decide on the parole granted to a terrorist even though long incarcerated and later rehabilitated, and so on. Thus, rights involving relationships with non-member individuals would be decided solely by the members. And furthermore, once a normative status of the rights of the group's members against other groups is defined by the group's internal hierarchies (each group has its own hierarchies), thinking otherwise, internal dissent, would imply the risk of expulsion for the dissident, 'disavowed' as a traitor to the 'just cause' of the group's legal warfare. This is the experience Baruch Spinoza had when expelled from his Dutch community.

If all this rush to appropriate the – literal – *juris-dictio*, the exclusive power to *say the subjective rights* for oneself, to which the holders of the corresponding duties must be subjected, even, and especially, if outside the group: if all this seems intuitively reasonable to us, the constituent social dialogue is dead. Each person locks himself (or is locked by socially emergent discourse) in his own identity enclosure as if it were his own private dwelling, and from that dwelling declares war on the rest of the world.

Appropriative conflicts are but a contingency at present. Preferable then is to focus on the problems generated by distributive conflicts.

IX. RIGHT TO ASSERT INTERSECTION OR JUDICIAL DUTY TO CONSIDER IT?

Each definition includes something on the inside and excludes others on the outside. Each definition admits further differentiation: the inside splits into many subgroups, infinitesimally. Assume that in a concrete context of appropriative conflict, a term is assumed to be a suitable definer of an intersectional class, and that it makes no practical sense in that context to further discuss its further 'intersectionality'.

We have finally reached a courtroom. The plaintiff seeks recognition of a right to something and bases her claim on intersectional discrimination. She therefore asks the judge to offer a unique test: she will not have to prove that she is discriminated against because either of sex or skin colour, but because of the intersection of the two elements. How will the defendant respond?

It depends first of all on whether the plaintiff's claim is based on an individual act of discrimination or whether it is instead claiming recognition of a collective one. In the former case, invoking intersectionality does not change the course of the judgment: the plaintiff must show that she is discriminated against as an individual (and thus for whatever individual reasons attributable to those who allegedly discriminated against her). However complex the reasons for the individual guilty of discrimination, he has discriminated against her (if he has discriminated against her, this is for the judge to decide) as a person. The judgment is individual and all-encompassing of the whole matter asserted in court.

In the second case (collective discrimination) things change. The plaintiff will invoke statistical evidence; and intersectionality serves to avoid incurring the defendant's counterevidence. For example, the plaintiff, a Black woman, will complain that she is discriminated against in job promotions. The defendant will not be able to defend herself by showing statistical data proving the promotion of Black males because women and Black males for this purpose belong to two different sets. The Black woman has a higher discrimination index than a Black male colleague.

All of this is fully agreeable.

But the reasonable evidence ends there. What if the defendant's lawyer retorts, invoking the existence of additional and conflicting discriminatory indices that would this time benefit his client? Imagine: the Black woman sues her employer, alleging that he granted a better job position to a male colleague. But the woman is the adopted daughter of a very wealthy Milanese family, studied in one of the academic cathedrals of global economic thought, lives in a mansion she owns, and has no children; the man is white, a second-generation immigrant, studied in night schools, graduated from college while he was working, has a disabled son, is divorced, and lives in rent. Nevertheless, he has always worked diligently and assiduously; the woman has added up multiple absences for study. Who is worse off? What if the employer preferred the male because he was in an inferior condition to the woman?

To respond without unleashing intergroup wars, without dissolving civil society in court into a dusting of warring classes, we need to deconstruct intersectionality:

(1) *Intersectionality is not a subjective right, but a hermeneutical category of inequality*. For this reason, intersectionality is not a power at the disposal of the subject who invokes it. It belongs to the world of facts to be evaluated in court, not to the stock of rights that the holder can choose to exercise or not. The individual raising a discrimination claim cannot selectively emphasise only certain indicators of discrimination that they find convenient to support their case. The entire factual reality will be the subject of judicial assessment, taking into account all potential factors of discrimination that the judge deems relevant.

(2) Intersectionality must be substantiated by narrating the specifics of the case, rather than relying on abstract subsumptions of the individual into a judicially constructed social category. Instead, being part of a category serves as concrete

evidence demonstrating discrimination suffered by the plaintiff in court. *Membership in a category is not a claim to entitlement but rather an indicator of discrimination.*

(3) Intersectionality must distinguish the different impacts of individual intersectional factors: whether social or biological or both, whether visible (gender) or invisible (sexual orientation).[44] True, it seems impossible – nor do I think anyone has ever sensibly attempted to propose it – to establish a hierarchy among the factors of discrimination (is it better to prefer women or the poor?), because that is exactly what the theory of intersectionality disputes. However, one cannot consider a harm event as a whole (the harm is being discriminated against; the event is the set of conduct that produced the harm) without asking the question of what the incidence of each element is in determining the harm. Asserting that everything intersecting has the same causal efficiency is possible only after trying, and failing, to differentiate the 'weight' of the multiple causes of the event. *The fact of intersection does not negate the different social potency of each discriminatory practice, even when it is composed of multiple injuries.*

All this converges into one thesis: the issue of intersectionality must be addressed on the general normative level, not on the level of group claims. The social dialectic between groups (and within groups) must be a dialectic focused on the just distribution of goods, not on the claim of exclusive rights of one group against another. Conflicting pluralism is good, inter-group dialectics is good, and division in representing different visions of the common good is still good; however, it is not good to do this by thinking of securing one group's exclusive dominance of a resource. The struggle for rights is a struggle to assert the just distribution of rights, not to appropriate them.

Put simply: the *terrain of intersectionality is that of normative equality*. And this must now be arrived at.

X. INTERSECTING MULTIPLE ANTI-DISCRIMINATION NORMS

The logic of intersectionality studies, we have said, is claimative. It is the rhetoric of the judicial claim: claiming a right against someone else. If we shift to the perspective of the recipient of anti-discrimination norms, the issue will appear in a very different light.

How does one obey a plurality of anti-discrimination norms? Obviously by considering them all in the particular case. True intersectionality is not in the claim construction but in the logic of contextual application of a plurality of norms, of a normative whole. Obeying anti-discrimination norms means intersecting them in the activity of the decision-maker. The intersectionality of the victim is contrasted

[44] On visible and invisible minorities, BA Ackerman, 'Beyond "Carolene Products"' (1985) 98 *Harvard Law Review* 713.

with that of the perpetrator. And to both, that of the decision-maker, also the result of intersectionality: subject to the duty to apply multiple rules and especially corresponding principles.

Let us get to the root of the problem: *intersectionality is a problem to remedy the defective application of a concurrence of anti-discrimination rules*. Defective, because it is under the illusion that it is possible to administer the concurrence of rules without their systematic coordination, that is, ignoring that resolving questions of application of rules (which are not elementary) necessarily implies consideration of normative principles of those rules are mere partial applications. There is no need to decline the entire continental legal methodology, from Josef Esser to Robert Alexy and beyond. Suffice it to say that no rule is *truly* understandable without reference to at least one principle. It is no accident that intersectionality was born in the legal context of the United States, in which there is no room for a *Drittwirkung* of constitutional principles in private law. It could never have happened in Europe, except (and this is no accident either) in discussions of European Union law,[45] where the question of constitutionalisation was first and foremost promoted by the doctrine.[46] It was a serious mistake, a political naiveté, to develop a European anti-discrimination law by producing a forest of directives and regulatory provisions, however detailed. Oblivion of principles, reluctance to discuss direct application of the principle of equality openly and simply, perhaps in the belief, inspired by only superficial pragmatism, that it was more efficient and immediate to promulgate one anti-discrimination rule after another.[47] This is reflected in the consistent dissatisfaction of intersectionality theorists with the missed opportunities for full affirmation of the theory in jurisprudential practice.[48]

And now the patchwork of rules ends up engulfing itself, where the stage has been set for a battle of one discrimination against another, to the point of regulatory aphasia that preludes the replacement of law by political force.

But no set of anti-discrimination rules can be applied without coming to terms with the constitutional (and, I would say without hesitation, constitutionally transnational) principle of equality. We all know the retort to this objection: to still evoke the generalising myth of equality would mean – our imaginary contradictor would say – to be left behind, stuck in the myth of unique identity, in the essentialist myth of the liberated and well-socialised man, an oppressive myth behind which there would be nothing but patriarchy, colonialism, Occidentalism. Invoking the *principle of equality* (perhaps *universal*) in our postcolonial, post-hegemonic, post-whatever-you-want-to-call-it societies would now be sheer naivety.

[45] J Kantola and K Nousiainen, 'Institutionalizing Intersectionality in Europe' (2009) 11 *International Feminist Journal of Politics* 459.

[46] HW Micklitz, 'Introduction' in HW Micklitz (ed), *Constitutionalization of European Private Law* XXII/2, Collected Courses of the Academy of European Law (Oxford, Oxford University Press, 2014) 1.

[47] See, however, D Schiek and J Mulder, 'Intersectionality in EU Law: A Critical Re-appraisal' in D Schiek and A Lawson (eds), *European Union Non-Discrimination: Investigating The Triangle of Racial, Gender and Disability Discrimination* (Farnham, Ashgate, 2011) 259.

[48] D Schiek, 'Intersektionelle Diskriminierung vor dem Europäischen Gerichtshof – Ein erster verfehlter Versuch? Urteil des Europäischen Gerichtshofs vom 24.11.2016 – Rechtssache Parris' (2017) 10 *Europäische Zeitschrift für Arbeitsrecht (EuZA)* 407; D Schiek, 'On uses, mis-uses and non-uses of intersectionality before the Court of Justice (EU)' (2018) 18 *International Journal of Discrimination and the Law* 82.

Difference *from what*? And where, in what contexts, and in what areas of coexistence?

XI. VERY SHORT TREATISE OF EQUALITY AND DIFFERENCE

Equality is the normative suppression of diversity. If two entities were collectively perceived as equal, the problem of equalising them would not arise. Two ants are equal to a man; two men are equal to a shark or a virus. Yet to ants, not all ants are equal, and so are sharks and viruses. A social practice of distinction underlies the normative claim to equality, to making different people equal: we are different, but we are not allowed to be unequal. Differences need not count for the allocation of a good, as long as there is enough of that good for everyone, otherwise the conflict returns in another form, eg origin, birth, merit (merit, a capitalist fairy tale), and, often, at that point claims to equality become intergroup claims: *we* are equal, *they* … make do.

Entities susceptible to equality are agentive entities, for simplicity's sake we would say: agents. As a normative constraint on diversity, equality assumes a causal connection between the qualities of one individual and the behaviour of another. This connection relies on either a natural regularity, such as the instinctual fear a child may experience when encountering something unfamiliar or weird, which necessitates the establishment of social norms to mitigate these fears and encourage the acceptance of differences. Alternatively, and notably, it presupposes the existence of a discriminatory social norm.

Equality is therefore a social and then legal norm (principles are norms) that counteracts other biological and social norms (surmountable by education, that is, by the introjection of equalising norms). The starting point is the social perception of difference that has been normatively established as inequality. Equality is the normative principle by which inequalities are disestablished, either by dismissing discriminatory social rules from relevance (by declaration of the unlawfulness of legal acts that reverse them) or by dismissing the normativity of discriminatory legal norms (by declaration of the unconstitutionality of laws that violate the principle of equality).

The right to difference emerges – in a more complex systemic framework that has yet introjected the effectiveness of the principle of equality, that is, the need to deconstruct the normativity of discriminatory practices – whenever, *on the other hand, the difference is not perceived as a discriminating factor, but as a resource of one's identity, when the claim for the recognition of difference takes the form of a fundamental right*. Very often, what is now claimed as a matter for the exercise of a right to difference (eg, sexual orientation) was in the past a stigma, a sign of discrimination, a criterion for the suppression of equality. This means that it is only possible to postulate a right to difference when socially the content of the right (sexual orientation in our example) to which corresponded a previous discriminatory social (and possibly also legal) norm has been legally and constitutionally deconstructed in its potential for inequality. Only after something has been deactivated as a criterion for legitimising deterrent treatment will it be possible to overturn its normative value and claim it as a right. Paradoxical as it may seem, *it is legally meaningful to assert the right to difference only after it becomes evident that the norm of equality has been established and internalised by all.*

XII. GOOD INTERSECTIONS IN THE COURT. HERMENEUTICS OF NORMATIVE EFFECTIVENESS

Intersectionality seeks to subvert from within the logic of equality: there would be no set of rights defining what it is to be a … man (indeed!), or a citizen ('*cittadino*', in Italian, still a generic masculine) or a civilised human being (colonialism!), but a set of groups formed by different socio-normative codes of differentiation.

The lack of historical consciousness and the tendency towards the aggressive adoption of 'groupification' were first identified as dangers in the context of individualistic-vindictive, rather than normative-evaluative, use of facts to be judged. This occurs within the real context of conflict between subjects. These trends shift the focus of legal-political reflection on the equal dignity of historically discriminated categories and the need for their recognition, particularly in areas where inequality has not yet been fully dismantled. However, this reflection narrows the scope to a new and more confined space: micro-group identity, leaving in the shadows the hegemonic practices within each group, as well as the rise of isolationist cultures and narcissistic subcultures.

But intersectionality also has an indisputable merit, a clear contribution to the effectiveness of fundamental rights.[49] It has called into question the regulatory policy of anti-discrimination law as a law composed of rules without principles; it has revealed the inadequacies of policy oriented toward short-term results. Intersectionality, therefore, served to challenge the false neutrality of the abstraction of the emancipated subject of law through the claim of fundamental rights (in short: white male; or Black male).

It has been argued that all of this does not constitute a set of powers over which the possessor can freely decide whether to utilise or not. There is no subjective right to intersectionality; rather, there exists a hermeneutic legal duty to interpret the law by considering all norms, including principles such as the principle of equality, and all the specifics of the case at hand. This includes recognising that a multitude of discriminatory profiles intersect within that particular case. Intersectionality is, in essence, nothing more than complexity.[50]

The hermeneutic question, then. What is to be done? How should a judge decide, so that nothing of the destructive potential of an inequality escapes him? So that in his judgment he does not just write the act of war of one group against another, the act of imposing compensation in which one member of a group is favoured while

[49] E Roig, 'Wird Gleichberechtigung noch … intersektional?' (2019) 2 *Zeitschrift des Deutschen Juristinnenbundes (djbZ)* 71; S Atrey, 'Beyond Universality: An Intersectional Justification of Human Rights' in S Atrey and P Dunne (eds), *Intersectionality and Human Rights Law* (Oxford, Hart, 2020) 17.

[50] McCall (n 40); on the hermeneutical role of complexity, P Perlingieri, 'Complessità e unitarietà dell'ordinamento giuridico vigente' (2005) 26 *Rassegna di diritto civile* 188.

another is disadvantaged solely because the advantaged individual belongs to a group that faced historical discrimination, and the disadvantaged individual belongs to a group that historically oppressed the former. Are we rewarding and punishing based on the present circumstances or the past actions of their ancestors? The question revolves around whether a judge can mandate compensation or other remedies solely based on an individual's affiliation with a historically oppressive group.

The intersections do not only concern the plaintiff and defendant in court. They also concern the judge, who is no less characterised by multiple factors of cultural difference. Gadamerian hermeneutics has taught us to distinguish between prejudice (*Vorurteil*) and pre-judgement (*Vorverständnis*).[51] The judge must bring before himself the danger of being partial, and recognise that his own cognitive horizon is historically conditioned. This hermeneutic school harbours an excessive, fideistic confidence in the reconciliation of all points of view in a nice reasonable argument that pacifies all. It is only an ideal, dangerous if the judge really believes that what he is doing is drawing the best of all possible worlds through his ruling. Nevertheless, even when relinquishing the belief that a single method can rescue us, the judge has no alternative: they must consider everything, all discriminatory factors at play in the case, the involved parties, and even their own role.[52]

While intersectionality as a method might leave certain ideologues discontented with the ease of conducting too simple battles, it can ensure more honest argumentative procedures, suitable for navigating the intricate landscape of growing differences within a framework of equalities.

[51] T Gizbert-Studnicki, 'Der Vorverständnisbegriff in der juristischen Hermeneutik' (1987) 73 *Archiv für Rechts- und Sozialphilosophie* 476.

[52] T Collins and L Moyer, 'Gender, Race, and Intersectionality on the Federal Appellate Bench' (2008) 61 *Political Research Quarterly* 219.

9

The Many Persons of Law – History of Ideas and Practices

PIA LETTO-VANAMO

I. PERSONS vs THINGS

BOTH LEGAL HISTORY and legal theory scholars refer to Roman law when the origin of the person/thing division is discussed.[1] In particular, the Roman division (*ius in rem – ius in personam*) has inspired the modern understanding of legal personhood. However, in his *Institutiones* (*c* 170 AD), Gaius, the founding father of the division, does not specify exactly what it implies for an entity to be a person (*persona*) or a thing (*res*).[2] Furthermore, it is not at all obvious that the Roman jurists applied the distinction in any abstract or systematic way: Ancient Roman law is characterised as unsystematic, casuistic and practically oriented. At the same time, as discussed later in this chapter, the substantive and procedural rights of a human being were closely intertwined.[3] In the Rome of the republican and early imperial period, substantive and procedural law were closely interconnected, and restrictions on access to justice many. For instance, non-citizens were excluded from the *ius civile* and the *legis actio* procedure.[4]

Scholars usually agree on the etymology of the word *persona*. The term is a translation of the Greek *prosopon* (πρόσωπον, in Etruscan *phersu*, in Sanskrit *phersuna)* meaning 'face' or 'appearance'. In Latin, the term was used to announce the mask

[1] See, eg, C Hattenhauer, '"Der Mensch als Solcher Rechtsfähig" – Von der Person zur Rechtsperson' in F Klein and C Menke (eds), *Der Mensch als Person und Rechtsperson* (Berlin, Berliner Wissenschaftsverlag, 2011) 44–46, and V Kurki, *A Theory of legal Personhood* (Oxford, Oxford University Press, 2019).

[2] In English: *The Institutes of Gaius*, translated with an introduction by WM Gordon and OF Robinson (London, Duckworth, 1988).

[3] The whole of the fourth book of Gaius deals with *ius quod ad actiones pertinent*; on actions, see F Schulz, *Classical Roman Law* (Oxford, Clarendon Press 1951) 11–27; classical law might be called action-related law or law of actions since it appears in the shape of statements about judicial remedies.

[4] Roman private law applied to Roman citizens wherever they lived within the Roman Empire. If they appeared before a Roman court, its rules applied to them. In accordance with the principle of personality, Roman private law did not apply to foreigners, but there was a special magistrate, the *praetor peregrinus*, for foreigners.

worn by actors and their characters.[5] This usage, again, was extended to refer to the roles or qualities of human beings. For instance, Cicero (*De Officiis*) is known for his theory of the four *personae* in every human being: rationality, personal attributes, status and profession. Nevertheless, *persona* also acquired another meaning, which begins to look like our everyday concept of the person, namely that of the individual human being stripped of their roles. It has been argued that the origins of this semantic change lie in Stoic philosophy (eg, Seneca). Man became both an individual and a person.[6]

Developments towards a modern understanding of 'person' can also be seen in debates around the natures of the Trinity and Christ within the early Christian church, where the notion of *persona* became important. In 362, the Council of Alexandria declared that the Father, the Son and the Holy Spirit were all distinguishable *hypostases* (substances) but shared a single divine nature. *Hypostasis* (ὑπόστασις) was translated into Latin as *persona*. In the sixth century, the Roman philosopher Boetius, an expert (also) in Greek philosophy and Christian theology, tried to resolve dilemmas arising from the traditional description of Christ as both human and divine, by bringing up precise definitions of 'substance', 'nature' and 'person'. Thus, he defined *persona* as 'the individual substance of rational nature', a definition that became highly influential.[7]

During the same century, *persona* was used by Emperor Justinian's (527–565) compilation, later known as *Corpus iuris civilis*, both in the sense of 'role' and in the sense of 'individual', but not in the technical sense in which a contemporary jurist uses the phrase 'legal person'. In this context, however, the term *caput* ('head') ought to be mentioned. The term was used to refer to human individuals, the closest translation being 'legal standing'; maybe also 'legal condition'. As discussed later in this chapter, *caput* was used in Roman law texts and their commentaries, for instance when the legal status of slaves was defined. Anyhow, the idea of *caput* might be the closest the Roman jurists got to a concept resembling the current understanding of legal personhood.

Nevertheless, it must be noted that, rather than defining who were persons in the eyes of the law, the 'law of persons' of the first book of Justinian's Institutes *(Institutiones*,[8] a part of the *Corpus iuris civilis)* addresses the different roles (statuses) of human beings in Ancient Roman society. There were three primary groups of statuses, all having also some legal implications: *status libertatis* (whether one was

[5] Punzi refers in ch 5 of this book also to another interpretation according to which the Latin word *persona* should be related to the form *per-sonare* (to re-sonate) or to 'to make resound', a characteristic ascribed to the masks of ancient theatre. Today, however, this etymology of the word is generally rejected. Still, it can be said that the being-person makes the individual's voice resound.

[6] According to Schermaier, as part of the reception of Greek culture, Stoic ethics found great favour among Rome's educated classes. This was probably the driving force behind acceptance of the concept of the equality of all human beings endorsed in learned discourses. M Schermaier, 'Without Rights? Social Theories Meet Roman Law Texts' in M Schermaier (ed), *The Position of Roman Slaves. Social Reality and Legal Differences* (Berlin/Boston, De Gruyter, 2022) 1–24, 5.

[7] Boethius, 'Liber de persona et duabus naturis contra Eutychen et Nestorium' in J Migne, *Patrologiae. Cursus completes* (Paris, Vrayet de Surcy, 1847) PL 64, PL, 64, 1344 A.

[8] Mostly based on the *Institutiones* of Gaius; *Justinian's Institutes*. Translated with an Introduction by P Birks and G McLeod. With the Latin text of P Krueger (Ithaka NY, Cornell University Press, 1987).

free or a slave); *status civitatis* (whether one was a Roman citizen or a foreigner or belonged to one of the less privileged groups); and *status familiae* (whether one was legally independent or under the power of one's *paterfamilias*, the head of the household). The law of things, on the other hand, pertained to how certain human beings – if they possessed the requisite status under the law of persons – could achieve rights pertaining to things that have value, such as material objects and slaves. In contrast to the current understanding, the category of things also included obligations and 'rights' (*iura*), which the Romans took to be incorporeal / non-material things (see Inst Tit II *de rebus incorporalis*). Yet the Romans did not have the abstract notion of subjective rights that today's jurists employ. As noted, classical Roman law did not separate substantive claims from procedural remedies.

In the Middle Ages, many scholars addressed the question of corporations, as the legal statuses of guilds, towns, and particularly universities and monasteries, became important. The phrase *persona ficta* was coined by Pope Innocent IV (Sinibaldo Fieschi; as Pope 1243–1254) to refer to such corporations in Canon law. The fictitiousness of corporations implied first and foremost that they could not be excommunicated. Hence, the term *persona* was applied to corporations, which Roman jurists most likely would not have done – although the idea of a corporation (such as *societas*) can easily be found in Roman law sources.[9]

Additionally, steps were taken towards the idea of abstract, subjective rights, separated from legal remedies, and from *ius* as objective law / right. However, there is no consensus on when exactly scholars started using *ius* (also) in the sense of subjective right. Nonetheless, some legal historians see steps towards this in the works of some medieval scholars, such as William of Ockham (an opponent of Thomas Aquinas). Still, the concept of right, and its relation to personhood, would become important, first among legal humanists,[10] then in systems of natural law.

II. PERSON OF RIGHTS AND DUTIES

A. Free Will

The French legal humanist Hugo Donellus (Hugues Doneau, 1527–1591) took the first steps in developing a technical legal concept of personhood; he uses the word *persona* in a new, technical sense in his work, *Commentarii in iure civili*. *Persona* is now the point of departure of legal analysis, and any individual that has a positive

[9] Classical law knows only one type of so-called (fictional) legal person, namely the corporation. However, as the legal term 'corporation' was entirely unknown, nor was *universitas* a technical term to designate a corporation, the words *collegium* and *corpus* were used to specify a certain kind of corporation, but to classical lawyers the corporation was simply a body of human persons with variable number of persons – as opposed to the *societas*, partnership, as an organised body of persons with a fixed number of members, each partner having a disposable share of the common property. It is the members and not the fictitious 'legal person' who are the owners of property though not as single persons but rather as joint tenants. Schulz (n 3) 87.

[10] In contrast to their predecessors of the 12th–15th centuries, the legal humanists were interested in classical Roman law – not to build up practical law based on the *Corpus Iuris Civilis*.

status libertatis, *civitatis* and *familiae* is a person.[11] Thus there is an analogy to ancient Roman law, while one's legal personhood refers to one's roles in society. However, Donellus did not yet clearly distinguish between *homo* and *persona*. This was done by the German jurist Hermann Vultejus (1555–1634), according to whom *homo* refers to a human being, whereas *persona* is a *homo habens caput civile* – a human being with (civil) standing.[12] He uses the word *caput*, which the Romans occasionally used, to refer to the standing that free men had, and slaves lacked. Thus, Vultejus seems to be the one of the first to have defined the terms clearly, and who claimed that slaves lacked legal personhood, that they were not *personae*.[13]

The natural law scholar Hugo Grotius (1583–1645) associated personhood and right-holding in a new way:

> In order to understand rights of persons to things, since law exists between persons, to whom the right belongs, and between things, over which the right extends, we must treat first of the legal condition of persons, secondly of the legal condition of things.[14]

This is already quite close to the modern understanding of legal personhood as right-holding. Thomas Hobbes (1588–1679) goes even further when distinguishing 'man' and 'person' – and writing also on representation: A 'man' is 'a living body with the capacity to reason'. This is different from 'person' and whose 'words or actions are considered, either as his own, or as representing the words or actions of another man, or of any other thing to whom they are attributed, whether truly or by fiction'. Thus, Hobbesian persons are authors of actions. Some men are not persons (like children), but they can be 'personated' by guardians.[15]

Samuel Pufendorf (1632–1694) belongs to those who distinguish between 'moral person' and 'human being' (man), linking moral to will.[16] The concept of 'moral' is also important for Gottfried Leibnitz (1646–1716). The holding of a right means that a person has the moral power to execute their will while a right imposes a duty on some other person and the moral necessity to forebear from exercise of some right, which is in Leibniz's terms an obligation (*obligatio*).[17] This means that Leibniz might be the first who associated (legal) personhood with both right-holding and duty-bearing. In turn, prominent German philosopher Christian Wolff (1679–1754) distinguished *homo moralis* and *persona moralis*: the former is the subject of rights and duties, being a potential right-holder and duty-bearer, whereas the latter refers to a concrete human being who holds specific rights and / or duties.[18] Indeed, the Prussian Civil Code of 1794 (ALR), the first of the so-called natural law codes, seems to reflect Wolff's approach. According to the Code (1.Tit. §1), '*Der Mensch wird,*

[11] Vol I (Frankfurt am Main 1589); see also Hattenhauer (n 1) 42–47.

[12] H Vultejus, *In Institutiones Juris Civilis a Justiniano Compositas Commentarius* (Marburg 1598) 40.

[13] See more in section IV of this chapter.

[14] H de Groot, *Inleidning tot de hollandsche Rechts-Gelerdheid*, 2nd edn (1910) 8, in English: H Grotius, *The Jurisprudence of Holland* (trans TW Lee) (Oxford, The Clarendon Press, 1926) 15.

[15] T Hobbes, *Leviathan* (ed WGP Smith, repr edn 1651 (Oxford, Clarendon Press, 1929).

[16] S Pufendorf, *De Iure Naturae et Gentium* (Londini Scanorum, 1672) lib 1 cap 1 § 12.

[17] See in more detail C Johns, *The Science of Right in Leibniz's Moral and Political Philosophy* (London, Bloomsbury, 2013).

[18] C Wolff, *Institutiones iuris natreae et gentium* (1750; Reproduction 2015, Arkose Press) § 96.

in so fern er gewisse Rechte in der bürgerlichen Gesellschaft genießt, eine Person genannt': a human being was referred to as a person insofar as they enjoyed specific rights in civil society.

The other two definitions – still influential today – that explain legal personhood in terms of the capacity to hold rights and duties and of being part of legal relations were formulated towards the end of the eighteenth century, when Immanuel Kant (1724–1804) overtook Wolff. For Kant, too, a person is a rational agent. Furthermore, Kant's (ethical) thought is concerned with internal freedom, that is, a rational agent's ability to determine their will independently of outside influences. In contrast to Wolff, Kant's political and legal philosophy is founded on the idea of external or negative freedom – a rational agent's ability to set and pursue ends for themselves without being subject to the choices of others.[19] Every person's right to external freedom is, according to Kant, the only natural right. Furthermore, state power is justified only insofar as it protects this freedom. A person would be granted a sphere of external freedom where their will would reign supreme, and this sphere would be as large as is commensurate with similar spheres of other persons.[20] At the same time, the phrase 'legal relationship' (*rechtliches Verhältnis/ Rechtsverhältnis*) is used to describe the relationship between a right and its correlative duty: not only are persons the only possible holders of rights and duties, but they are also the only possible parties in legal relationships.

Georg Wilhelm Friederich Hegel (1770–1831), arguing inter alia about the roles of family and state, identifies the key words 'freedom', 'will' and 'morality' (*sittlichkeit*). For Hegel, 'personhood' refers to an individual willing subject.[21] Thus freedom and will of persons are of fundamental value. Persons have *Rechtsfähigkeit*, the 'capacity for rights', as a foundation of the abstract, and then of the formal, right (*Recht*).[22] Furthermore, the command of law (*Rechtsgebot*) insists: be a person and respect other persons. Persons are also taken to have rights pertaining to things; in contrast to the distinctions of Roman Law (*personae – res – actiones*) and to Kant, Hegel maintains that personality can simply be understood as the abstract basis for the right to things. Thus, the 'personal right' (*Personenrecht*) is the capacity to hold rights to things, while things are anything external to persons. This is related to the idea of a 'sphere of freedom' that persons hold in relation to things that are external to them – and of contracts not about personal rights but rights to things. Persons can 'place' their will in 'any thing' whereby the thing becomes mine and acquires my will as its substantial end (since it has no such end within itself), its determination, and its soul.

[19] See in more detail LP Hodgson, 'Kant on the Right to Freedom: a Defence' (2010) *Ethics* 791–819.

[20] Kant also refers to children as persons. They do not meet Kant's criteria for personhood but are endowed with freedom. I Kant, *Die Metaphysik der* Sitten. 2. Teil: Metaphysische Anfangsgründe der Rechtslehre (1797); see also G Mohr, 'Person, Recht und Menschenrecht bei Kant' in E Klein and C Menke (eds), *Der Mensch als Person und Rechtsperson* (Berlin, Berliner Wissenschaftsverlag, 2011) 17–37.

[21] GWF Hegel, *Grundlinien der Philosophie des Rechts* (Berlin, Duncker und Humblot, 1833) § 35–40, 73–78; § 35: 'Individuen und Völker haben noch keine Persönlichkeit, insofern sie noch nicht zu diesem reinen Denken und Wissen von sich gekommen sind'. See also § 57 on slavery, 94–96.

[22] See esp § 36: 'Die Persönlichkeit enthält überhaupt die Rechtsfähigkeit und macht den Begriff und die selbst abstrakte Grudlage des abstrakten und daher formellen Rechtes aus. Das Rechtsgebot ist daher: sei eine Person und respektiere die anderen Personen'.

B. Subjective and Objective Right/s

In legal scholarship of the European Continent, the construction of 'personal right' (*Personenrecht*) derives mainly from the influence of German legal doctrine of the second half of the nineteenth century. Essential here were works of the so-called Pandectists, scholars interested in 'new use of Roman law' (*usus modernus pandectarum*) in which the theme of 'rights over one's own person' is embedded within the doctrine of subjective law (*subjektives Recht*). In addition to the contribution of Bernhard Windscheid,[23] the ideas of Friedrich Carl von Savigny and Rudolf von Jhering ought to be mentioned. Savigny (1779–1861), the most influential scholar of the German Historical School, operates with the concepts of the human being and the person. Persons (natural or artificial) enjoy their own legal capacity, *Rechtsfähigkeit*, which is the capacity to hold rights and bear obligations. Savigny also introduces a synonym for (legal) person, that is, *Rechtssubjekt* (subject of law, legal subject, or subject of right/s). At the same time, the origin of the person is characterised by stating that 'the original concept of the person or of the legal subject coincides with the concept of man'.[24] In other words, all law exists for the sake of the innate moral freedom that resides in every human being. This is why the original concept of person or legal subject must coincide with the concept of a human being. The original identity of both concepts can be expressed as follows: every individual human being, and only the individual human being, possesses legal capacity.

That said, in the spirit of Kant and Hegel, Savigny distinguishes the law or objective right (*objektives Recht*) from (subjective) right (*subjektives Recht*). Hence, the law determines the boundaries of persons' external freedom, whereas a right is the power of a person to affect other persons' choices (the will-theory right). The 'potentiality of reason and freedom' may explain why Savigny takes even children to have innate moral freedom. Indeed, he recognises that newborn children are unable to reign over their spheres of freedom provided by the law, which is why he separates legal capacity and legal competence. Human beings become legal persons at birth and thus receive the legal capacity to hold private-law rights.

Jhering (1818–1892), a representative of the Historical School who later became a critic of the School and a founding father of the so-called *Interessenjurisprudenz*, considered a subjective right as an interest.[25] Consequently, a subjective right (*subjektives Recht*) became a form of social rationalisation of individual action while

[23] Especially interesting is B Windscheid, *Lehrbuch des Pandektenrechts*, 8th edn, vol 1, commenting on the new German Civil Code (BGB) (Frankfurt am Main, Literarische Anstalt Rütten & Boening, 1906) 231–96.

[24] FC von Savigny, *System des heutigen Römischen Rechts*, vol 2 (Berlin, Veit, 1840) 1–2; see also S Kirste, 'The Theory and Ethics of the Person in Law: The German Perspective' in P Collin and A Casagrande (eds), *Law and Diversity: European and Latin American Experiences from a Legal Historical Perspective* Vol 1: Fundamental Questions (Frankfurt am Main, Max-Planck-Institut für Rechtsgeschichte und Rechtstheorie, 2023) 625–39, esp 632–33. On the influence of Savigny's personhood theory on Nordic legal scholarship, see L Björne, *Brytningstiden: den nordiska rättsvetenskapens historia. Del II, 1815–1870* (Stockholm, Institutet för rättshistorisk forskning, 1998) 349–65.

[25] R von Jhering, 'Rechte sind rechtlich geschützte Interessen' in R von Jhering, *Geist des römischen Recht auf den verschiedenen Stufen seiner Entwicklung* III.1 (Leipzig, Druck und Verlag von Breitkopf und Härtel, 1865) 316–27; see also ch 3 by Femia in this book.

the subject was the holder of subjective right/s. This again caused discussion, for instance among Italian scholars of the subjectless right, as noted by Pasquale Femia in chapter three[26] of this book. Jhering, however, resolved the problem in 1871 by postulating a 'passive side of the right': the side which remains, while the new incumbent is missing.[27] Still, the problem remained about collective forms of association or enterprise. Is a corporation a subject or is it an asset through which individuals act in a rationalised form, mediated by the patrimonial function? The opponent of the legal personality rights, Alois von Brinz, argued that we could not speak of legal personhood, but should speak of assets without subjects, of so-called purpose assets (*Zweckvermögen*).[28] Nonetheless, the subjectless patrimony theory lost and the legal person theory won.

Finally, Hans Kelsen (1881–1973), one of the most powerful legal theorists of our time, also combined legal persons with rights and obligations.[29] To him, however, the physical or legal person was characterised as a complex of legal rights and obligations whose totality is expressed figuratively in the concept of 'person'. Thus, the person is the personification of this totality (*ein personifizierender Einheitsausdruck für ein Bündel von Rechtspfichten und Berechtigungen*).[30] At the same time, the legal subject is a creation of legal language, and a legal order regulates only certain human acts. According to Kelsen, it is also possible for a human being to belong to more than one legal community each separate from the other, while their behaviour is regulated by various legal orders.[31]

III. TOWARDS NEW LEGAL PERSONS

As we have seen above, theories of legal personhood developed in symbiosis with theories of rights. Indeed, modern theories of personhood have not changed much. However, the contemporary understanding of rights is changing, which in turn challenges our understanding and the concept/s of legal personhood.

In current legal practice, the idea of legal personhood, grounded on the concept of human autonomy, is changing. Apart from animals, jurisprudence has favoured granting rights to rivers. For instance, in 1999 the New Zealand Waitangi Tribunal and in 2017 the New Zealand Parliament accorded legal personhood to the river Whanganui.[32] In India, the High Court of Uttarakhand declared in March 2017,

[26] Femia is referring to Carlo Fadda and Paolo Emilio Bensa commenting on Windscheid's *Pandektenrecht*.

[27] R von Jhering, 'Passive Wirkungen der Rechte. Ein Beitrag zur Theorie der Rechte' in R von Jhering, *Gesammelte Aufsätze aus Jahrbüchern für die Dogmatik des heutigen römischen und deutschen Privatrechts*, 2 vol (Jena, Verlag von Gustav Fischer, 1882) 179–351.

[28] Femia in ch 3 of this book.

[29] Kelsen also refers to the concept of freedom, citing Georg Friedrich Puchta, according to whom it is 'Möglichkeit, sich zu etwas zu bestimmen'. Thus, a human being is 'Subjekt des Rechts darum, dass ihm jene Möglichkeit, sich zu bestimmen, zukommt, dass er einen Willen hat' H Kelsen *Reine Rechtslehre*. Studiensausgabe der 1. Auflage 1934, edited by Matthias Jestaedt (Tübingen, Mohr Siebeck, 2008) 54.

[30] ibid 64.

[31] ibid 64–68.

[32] 'Whanganui River Report' forms.justice.govt.nz/search/Documents/WT/wt_DOC_68450539/Whanganui%20River%20Report%201999.pdf and www.legislation.govt.nz/act/public/2017/0007/latest/whole.html.

only a few weeks after the Whanganui Bill, that the rivers Ganges and Yamuna are 'living entities', that is, 'legal persons', and appointed a trustee to 'protect the rights of the rivers against the pollution caused by the humans'.[33] In addition, in 2016 the Colombian Constitutional Court recognised the river Atrato as a legal subject and equipped it with comprehensive rights. According to the press release from the Court:

> [F]ollowing an ecocentric apporoach, the Court started from a basic premise: the earth does not belong to man but, on the contrary, man and all other species belong to the earth. Thus, the river Atrato, including its basins and contributors, was recognised as a public corporation with a right to protection, conservation, and recovery by the state and the ethnic communities. In order to institutionalise its protection, the Court established a proxy structure and stated, 'that the Colombian state together with the ethnic communities living in the basin of the river Atrato in Choc takes on the custodianship and the statutory representation of the rights of the river …[34]

In codifications of fundamental and human rights, animals and the nature / environment are not explicitly listed as rights-bearers, nor are they afforded explicit procedural rights.[35] Still, legislators have shown themselves to be open to interpretation for endowing non-human legal persons with rights to take legal action. This is not just a matter of turning nature and animals into quasi-human persons. The recognition of legal personhood for non-human persons does not entitle them in the same way as humans, but rather allows a distinction between the personal rights of humans and non-humans. Generally speaking, the legal concept of personhood tries to free itself from its constitutive link to the human individual, understood as a rational subject. In the legal sphere, the person no longer represents humans as individuals (natural persons) or as the social substrate of organisations (legal persons). The equivalence doctrine (all humans are legal persons) is no longer an exclusive doctrine but has given way to a principle of complementarity: being human or having a human substrate is a sufficient, but not a necessary condition for legal personhood.[36]

As asserted by Kelsen, modern law generates its own forms of personhood. And this personhood differs from the personhood of the political system, from the economic system, and so on. Furthermore, the legal person never involves an entire (human) being. The legal person can never incorporate into law the human being as such, never nature as such, never the animal as such. Rather, the legal person is only able to establish legal points of recognition. In fact, as argued by Andreas Fischer-Lescano, the legal person could be understood as the legal representative of an extra-legal

[33] See in more detail, www.ielrc.org/content/e1704.pdf.

[34] Constitutional Court of Colombia, judgment of 10 November 2016, no T-622/ 2016; English summary of the decision: www.corteconstitucional.gov.co/english/Decision.php?IdPublicacion=9336.

[35] According to Art 20a of Germany's Fundamental Law (*Grundgesetz*), the state protects animals, taking responsibility for future generations: 'Der Staat schützt auch in Verantwortung für die künftigen Generationen die natürlichen Lebensgrundlagen und die Tiere im Rahmen der verfassungsmäßigen Ordnung durch die Gesetzgebung und nach Maßgabe von Gesetz und Recht durch die vollziehende Gewalt und die Rechtsprechung.'

[36] A Fischer-Lescano, 'Nature as a Legal Person: Proxy Constellations in Law' (2020) *Law & Literature* 237–62, 241; See also A Fischer-Lescano, 'Subjektloses Recht' (2017) *Kritische Justiz* 475–96.

entity, while legal reality is representation.[37] Nonetheless, the legal person, as a legal representative, and its extra-legal point of reference, the party represented (humans, ecosystems, animals), are not identical. This holds for human legal persons as well as non-human ones. Derrida goes even further by emphasising legal personhood as a matter of interconnected speech acts. Thus, the legal tie is never between the one that gives something and the one to whom it is given, but rather between two texts.[38]

However, in contrast to classical theories, the criteria for the limits of representation cannot be exclusively determined by the free will of legal subjects. By presupposing a free will, the law of representation would assume a unitary, rational subject who interacts with other subjects voluntarily. However, this unitary subject does not exist. This is already suggested by such cases as unborn children, disabled people, etc, where the capacity for absolute binding declarations of intent might be obvious legal fictions. But even outside of such cases, the relationship between the legal person and the individual, volitional subject is more complex than traditional theories would like it to be. Indeed, the individual or collective legal subject is nothing but a juridical 'character mask' while the mask does not concern the entire non-legal entity.

As Fischer-Lescano proposes, the putative free will of supposedly rational, unitary subjects cannot form the normative limit of legal representation. Rather, we must develop new standards for successful representation without referring to the putative nature of subjects.[39] This makes it necessary to reflect on the difference between a representative and the party whom it represents, and, on that basis, to draw conclusions regarding the most appropriate architecture of representation for non-human legal persons. How the law adapts to this challenge is inter alia a matter of 'ecological justice' as argued by the Colombian Constitutional Court.[40] In any case, the challenge is to minimise the distance between law and non-law and to enable a more suitable way of dealing with social, human and ecological conflicts, understood as trans-subjective conflicts (ecological, human, institutional) in legal questions.

Quite similarly, Bruno Latour defines the legal personhood of non-humans – of animals or ecosystems – as hybrid. According to his idea of the 'Parliament of Things', articulating an idea with respect to the legal construction of non-human persons, these are acting in the sphere of law and politics as hybrids, as associations of non-human and human legal persons. In law, these hybrid persons constitute legal

[37] Fischer-Lescano (2020) (ibid) 243–44 referring to C Menke, 'Genealogie, Paradoxie, Transformation' in A Fischer-Lescano, H Franski and J Horst (eds), *Gegenrechte. Recht jenseits des Subjekts* (Tübingen, Mohr Siebeck, 2018) 13–31.

[38] J Derrida, 'Des tours de Babel' in P Kamul and E Rottenberg (eds), *Psyche. Invention of the Other*, vol 1 (Stanford, Stanford University Press, 1995) 195–225.

[39] Fischer-Lescano 2020 (n 36) 248.

[40] According to Fischer-Lescano, the decision of the Colombian Constitutional Court in 2016 seems to point in the right direction, requiring procedural and organisational mechanisms to prevent abuse of representative power. It poses a potential model for proceduralisation in the area of statutory custody, in which the ability of the represented party to verbally articulate itself is precarious – eg, through implementing such measures as the inclusion of experts and stakeholders, a demand for a judicial warrant, informational requirements, and establishing a mix of official and societal actors. Fischer-Lescano (2020) (n 36) 249.

persons *sui generis*. Should legal action become necessary, the non-human person (river, animal, etc) is complemented by the natural person (individual claimant) or a juridical one (collective claimant), forming a juridical association with it, and thereby a new legal person.[41]

As seen in chapter three of this book, Femia is also interested in legal developments enabling a river to become a person in the courtroom and the constitution, and discusses (subjective) rights of nature.[42] According to him, in the cases concerned, the subject of the claim is not the claimant: nature is a subject who only speaks in judgment through the mouth of someone else. Therefore, a natural person or group of natural persons acts so that in the same trial their representative status, the subjectivity of the represented ecosystem (as 'the plaintiff' in the judgment) and the wrongful act committed by the defendants are recognised. As a result, subjectification of the non-human implies necessary representation, as Fischer-Lescano also argues. A judgment recognising or constituting a non-human subject works together with the constitutive proceeding of the power of representation. Consequently, Femia's key word is 'trans-subjectivity'.

The fundamental characteristic of the trans-subjective right is that its exercise does not return fully to the sphere of its holder's domain. Indeed, trans-subjectivity can, for instance, be found in past and present concepts of so-called *actio popularis*. In Ancient Rome, when a freeman had been killed, the action was treated as an *actio popularis*, which meant that everybody was entitled to claim the penalty for themselves.[43] Similarly, the *habitator* of a house, a man who rented the whole block, letting different flats or rooms to other tenants, was made strictly liable for damage caused by things thrown out of the building. Thus, the prime purpose of this praetorian *actio de deiectis vel effusis* was a public policy one – not fair compensation but to fight the dangerous practice of throwing waste out of the upper floor windows. The *habitator* was made liable independently of any personal fault because he was the only person who could possibly proceed against the bad habits of his tenants. Furthermore, Rudolf von Jhering reasoned in his book *Geist des römischen Rechts* (1852) on *actio popularis*, with a subject acting for the totality without representation (agency).[44] A popular action – that is currently used for instance in discrimination cases[45] – enforces an individual subjective right that belongs to all, because it relates to a thing of all, to a common good. As asserted by Femia, a trans-subjective right could be seen as the revival of ancient issues that now arises on a very different terrain of organisational experiences of public power.[46]

[41] B Latour, *Politics of Nature. How to Bring the Science into Democracy* (Cambridge, Harvard University Press 1993) 82–87.

[42] Femia in ch 3 of this book.

[43] N Jansen and R Michaels, 'Private Law and The State. Comparative Perceptions and Historical Observations' (2007) *Rabels Zeitschrift* 345–97, 363.

[44] R von Jhering, *Geist des römischen Rechts auf den verschiedenen Stufen seiner Entwicklung* I (Leipzig, Druck und Verlag von Breitkopf und Härtel, 1852) 187.

[45] See further: 'Use of actio popularis in Cases of Discrimination' (2022 Helsinki Committee of Human Rights), www.osce.org/files/f/documents/3/1/337191.pdf.

[46] Femia in ch 3 of this book.

IV. LEGAL PERSONHOOD AS A 'CLUSTER PROPERTY'

A. Incidents of Legal Personhood

Changes to the concept of legal personhood are challenging the system of rights and obligations to be differentiated. Furthermore, legal persons need to be shaped in various ways (eg, rivers do not need free will), and the 'bundle of rights and obligations' granted to persons adjusted accordingly. Nonetheless, this is not (only) a matter of distinguishing between legal persons with full legal capacity and those only partially capable of bearing rights and being held legally accountable. Instead, it is a matter inter alia of developing a bundle or package of rights and obligations specific to each person/subject in question. From this perspective, no legal person could be denied full legal capacity if it cannot bear all legal rights and duties within its own person. Yet full legal persons do not exist: being a legal person means having only a specific bundle of rights and duties. This, again, varies according to the legal order – and in both time and space.[47]

According to legal philosopher and animal law scholar Visa Kurki,[48] legal personhood[49] cannot be dependent on any single characteristic. To Kurki, legal personhood is a 'cluster property', in contrast to the traditional view according to which one is a legal person if and only if one holds legal rights and bears legal duties. As a cluster property, legal personhood consists of interconnected but divisible 'incidents', while no exact border between legal personhood and non-personhood exists. Unlike many other researchers, Kurki does not understand legal personhood only as an umbrella that encompasses separate issues, nor does he address each of the different legal incidents separately. At the same time, he opposes the idea of 'anything goes'. Not all (human and non-human) entities can be labelled as legal persons. What constitutes one's legal personhood is the holding of entitlements and burdens that constitute the incidents of legal personhood. In other words, 'legal person' refers to an entity that holds entitlements and burdens constituting their holder's legal personhood. At the same time, one's being a legal person is an attribute of a non-legal entity, granted by a legal system.[50] Furthermore, one is always a subject of law (legal subject) within some area/s of law and/or with regard to legal institutions.

Except for the idea of the cluster, the concept of 'legal platform' plays a central role in Kurki's analysis. A legal platform is a specific kind of bundle of legal entitlements and burdens. Legal platforms exist only in law and can attach (only) to certain

[47] As asserted by Fischer-Lescano, this does not change personal status, only the content of each person's respective rights and duties. Understood in this way, being a legal person therefore always means being a 'full person', even if the respective rights and duties of each person vary. Fischer-Lescano (2020) (n 36) 146.

[48] Kurki (n 1) and Kurki, *Legal Personhood. Cambridge Elements. Philosophy of Law* (Cambridge, Cambridge University Press, 2023).

[49] According to Kurki, a necessary condition for the legal personhood of any entity is that the entity is treated as a legal person by the prevailing legal system. Whether or not one is a legal person is thus an institutional fact. Kurki (n 1) 92.

[50] According to the main rule in European jurisdictions, only legal persons are recognised as parties to lawsuits.

kinds of entities.[51] It is a bundle of legal positions with three main features: it is named; it is integrated; and it is separate from other similar bundles.[52] Hence, an important aspect of being a legal person is that the entity concerned corresponds to at least one legal platform, meaning that one holds the entitlements and burdens which pertain to that platform. Indeed, the person/platform distinction shows how both the traditional senses of *persona* (individual and mask or role) are relevant with regard to Kurki's approach to legal personhood. An individual's natural legal platform exemplifies the idea of a continuous whole: whatever roles that individual has, any special rights and duties as well as assets and liabilities that they acquire will be assimilated into the same legal platform.[53]

Incidents can be grouped in various ways. Neil Mac Cormick has written of passive and active elements of personhood. He is first and foremost interested in the capacities of a legal person and classifies them into four categories:

(1) pure passive capacity;
(2) passive transactional capacity;
(3) capacity responsibility; and
(4) transactional capacity.[54]

Kurki seeks to develop MacCormick's ideas further.[55] To him, the main groups of incidents of legal personhood are the passive and active incidents.[56] In both groups, Kurki addresses legal subjecthood separating substantive incidents from procedural (remedy) ones.

Incidents of passive legal personhood (incidents that infants are usually endowed with) fall into two groups: substantive passive incidents; and remedy incidents. Substantive passive legal personhood, determining one's primary rights in relation to others and the state, consists of:

(1) fundamental protections (protection of life, liberty, and bodily integrity);
(2) the capacity to be the beneficiary of special rights – referring for example to the fact that contracts can be made in one's name;
(3) the capacity to own property;[57] and
(4) non-susceptibility to being owned.[58]

[51] He calls it 'attachment': legal platforms attach to legal persons. Kurki (2019) (n 1) 135; in addition, he is merely expounding what is necessary and sufficient for the attachment of a legal platform to an individual or a creature (139).

[52] A legislator/lawmaker can create a virtually infinite number of legal platforms – each of which comprises an array of legal positions – but it does not follow that absolutely anything could be a legal person. Rather, the incidence of legal personhood can only be attributed to entities that can hold claim-rights or perform acts.

[53] Kurki (2019) (n 1) 136.

[54] N MacCormick, *Institutions of Law: An Essay in Legal Theory* (Oxford, Oxford University Press, 2007) 77–99.

[55] Kurki (2019) (n 1) 95; See also Kurki's criticism on MacCormick, ibid 101.

[56] ibid 95–118 and Kurki (n 48) 14–15; Kurki also distinguishes independent, dependent and purely passive legal personhood; Kurki (n 1) 119.

[57] Owning property is a central hallmark of legal personhood; even passive legal persons (eg children) may own property.

[58] This incident is mentioned only in Kurki (2023) (n 48) 14.

Passive incidents include three more incidents, called remedy incidents. They concern the enforceability of one's substantive incidents, as well as sanctions that may be applied if the duties pertaining to the substantive incidents are not fulfilled. They determine what legal means one (or rather one's representative) can resort to if the substantive incidents are not respected. Hence, the remedy incidents are:

(1) standing;
(2) victim status in criminal law; and
(3) capacity to suffer harms; thus, harms are recognised and ought to be compensated.

So-called active incidents of legal personhood belong to active legal persons, such as adults of sound mind. Kurki divides them into:

(1) legal competences and elements of
(2) 'onerous legal personhood'.

'Competences' refers to one's capacity to administer other incidents (ie rights and duties) without a representative, for instance to the capacity to enter into contracts. In other words, 'capacity' means one's ability to perform acts-in-the-law; acts that effect changes in legal relations in virtue of the fact that they have been performed with the intention to effect the change in question. 'Onerous legal personhood' again consists of criminal law responsibility, tort law responsibility and other types of legal responsibility. Here, entities that can hold duties are the only candidates for onerous legal personhood.

According to Kurki, passive legal personhood functions primarily through the award of benefits in the form of claim-rights,[59] whereas the key elements of active legal personhood are centred on legal responsibility and legal competences. Legal responsibility is connected to the capacity to bear duties. Legal competences are primarily exercised through acts-in-the-law. It is possible to have different combinations of the three relevant dimensions of legal personhood: benefits, responsibilities and capacity for legal acts. Each of these dimensions can also be realised to various degrees. For instance, one's capacity for acts-in-the-law can be dependent or independent. Similarly, one can be held responsible in some respects and not in others, and enjoy some benefits of passive legal personhood without others.[60]

In terms of platforms, a platform confers benefits through claim-rights, imposes responsibilities and grants competences that are primarily exercised through acts-in-the-law. Indeed, a lawmaker can create a virtually infinite number of legal platforms – each of which comprises an array of legal positions. Nonetheless, it does not follow that absolutely anything could be a legal person. Rather, the incidents of legal personhood can only be attributed to entities that can hold claim-rights or perform acts, which are the crucial incidents of legal personhood.

As a result, not only are incidents important, but also identification of the entities that can hold the relevant types of legal positions. For instance, the scope of passive

[59] Thus, X can be a passive legal person if and only if X can hold claim-rights. Claim-rights involve the directedness of duties; they are held by beings to whom duties are owed.

[60] The historical cases of animal trials were examples of purely onerous legal personhood, where only criminal responsibility was extended to these beings (eg pigs).

legal personhood can be determined by asking who or what can hold claim-rights. The capacity to perform acts-in-the-law presupposes a certain degree of understanding of the institutional reality and in particular of 'the ways in which one can avail oneself of the institutions through the use of symbols'.[61] Furthermore, an entity must meet three criteria in order to be a potential duty-bearer:

(1) it must be able to perform acts;
(2) it must be able to benefit and suffer harm from states of affairs; and
(3) there must be a way of communicating legal requirements to the entity.

According to Kurki, adults, children and many animals meet these criteria, which is why they can be granted so-called onerous legal personhood. They are also candidates for an arrangement where one is endowed with passive incidents of legal personhood and onerous active incidents. This means that animals can be passive legal persons, but bodies of water cannot because animals can hold claim-rights whereas bodies of water cannot. In other words, animals can be passive legal persons because the duties pertaining to a legal platform could be borne towards an animal.[62] According to Kurki's classification, the passive incidents of personhood, victim status and capacity to undergo harms concern animals as well. In short, a legal platform can attach to human beings and non-human animals.[63]

As a legal historian, I see Kurki's grouping into passive and active elements (incidents) of personhood as well as the classifications within the two categories as highly innovative. They may open new possibilities towards understanding developments of legal ideas and practices connected to personhood before modern times. Undoubtedly, they enable analysis and reconceptualising of the new trends and practices discussed in section III of this chapter, which seems to be one of the main purposes of Kurki's approach as a legal philosopher with an interest in animal law. Indeed, Kurki proposes, that 'subject' and 'person' should be distinguished, instead of using them synonymously inter alia by the legislator/lawmaker.[64] For instance, animals are already subjects of animal welfare law, but not legal persons in the modern sense.

B. (New) Histories of Legal Personhood?

i. Legal Personhood of Slaves

Inspired by Kurki's approach, I will discuss ideas of personhood in Ancient Roman law, which has been a continuously self-evident basis or starting point of studies of legal personhood. The focus will be on the legal status of Roman slaves. Thereafter, some later developments of women's legal personhood will be dealt with. In general,

[61] Kurki (2019) (n 1) 138.
[62] ibid 143–51.
[63] This also concerns certain collectivities and artificial intelligences (AI), Kurki (2019) (n 1) 150–52.
[64] Kurki is referring to a former suggestion by Tomasz Pietrzykowski: T Pietrzykowski, 'The Idea of Non-personal Subjects of Law' in V Kurki and T Pietrzykowski (eds), *Legal Personhood: Animals, Artificial Intelligence and the Unborn* (Heidelberg, Springer, 2017) 49–67.

Kurki's approach could make the nearly tautological and unproblematised references to Roman law more nuanced. This especially concerns (re-)analysis of the legal position of slaves. As legal personhood is not treated as a strictly binary concept, we can at least account for the fact that slaves held some claim-rights, but were not legal persons in the modern sense.[65] Simultaneously, developments of the legal position of women could be better clarified by approaching legal personhood as a 'cluster property', whereby women gradually – and in various ways – were gaining personhood-related benefits and burdens.

Indeed, in empirical, socio-legal studies of history, Kurki's 'remedy incidents' of legal personhood play a central role. Very often, access to justice – in the sense of access to the court – is the (only) key concept of historical studies of the legal status or right/s of a person. Hence, it is quite well known that both in classical Athens and Rome access to the court depended on a combination of social, cultural and procedural law factors. For instance, in Athens only people of a certain status could have access to justice.[66] Slaves did not have any access to the courts, except in some few maritime law cases in the fourth century, while foreigners (*metokoi*) living in Athens could bring their cases to some procedures. Women – both citizens and foreigners – did not have access to the court, but in inheritance cases they were represented by their guardians (*kyrioi*). As discussed later, in Rome slaves but also others under the power of their *pater familias* lacked 'independent' access to the court. Women and minors who were not under a *pater familias* needed a guardian/tutor. In the Middle Ages, access to the court depended on personal and substantive factors.[67] In general, women and minors needed a guardian. However, there existed a spectrum of legal orders and dispute resolution systems; indeed, quite often town laws recognised the legal and procedural competence of (unmarried) women. In certain cases, this also concerns Canon law and the courts of the Catholic Church.[68]

That said, according to Roman law sources of the so-called classical period (from the first century BC to *c* 250 AD), the term *persona* was used as an equivalent to a human being.[69] Thus, all human beings including slaves were persons. Gaius makes

[65] Also the fact that slaves were 'legal nonpersons' in the modern sense but could nevertheless in the European colonies of the 17th–19th centuries be sentenced in criminal trials, is problematic to explain with the dichotomy person-thing and/or if legal personhood is defined by holding rights and bearing duties.

[66] B Kelly, 'Access to justice: Die soziale Reichweite gerichtlicher Konfliktregulierung' in N Grotkamp and A Seelentag (eds), *Konfliktlösung in der Antike*. Handbuch zur Geschichte der Konfliktlösung in Europa 1 (Heidelberg, Springer, 2021) 13–25; see also A Lanni, *Law and justice in the courts of classical Athens* (Cambridge/New York, Cambridge University Press, 2006).

[67] D von Mayenburg, 'Einführung' in D von Mayenburg (ed), *Geschichte der Konfliktlösung im europäischen Mittelalter*. Handbuch zur Gescichte der Konfliktlösung in Europa 2 (Heidelberg, Springer, 2021) 1–12.

[68] The medieval legal system was a combination or a multi-layered network of several normative orders, based on different sources of domination. People were subject to different legal orders and 'members' of different/ several jurisdictions (the local statutes of their city or to the customs and laws of the place where they lived). In addition, noblemen were subject to feudal law and privileges, and peasants could be subject to manorial law. Many artisans had to obey the local statutes and customs of their gilds. Merchants did their business according to a supposedly universal *lex mercatoria*. At the same time, everybody was subject to the universal Canon law.

[69] Schulz (n 3) 71.

that quite clear by dealing with the law of slavery in his exposition *ius quod ad personas pertinent* (the law relating to persons) and speaking without hesitation of *persona servilis* (*quod personae serviles et liberae*, Inst. 1.121) and a *persona servi* (Inst. III 189).[70] Nonetheless, it is not in conflict with this usage that he also denotes slaves as *res corporales*. Thus, a slave is both *persona* and *res*. However, Roman lawyers never regarded a slave as an animal, nor could they legally do so since they could not deny the slave's capacity for legal acts. Human beings alone are styled *personae* while the concept and term 'legal person' was absent. In post-classical times slaves were excluded from the class of *personae*, but only in the Middle Ages did the idea of legal person become current in legal scholarship.

Nevertheless, the parallel to the 'Roman model' was repeatedly invoked in the era of the transatlantic slave trade.[71] Even if, in the seventeenth or eighteenth centuries, people thought that their own regulations on slavery would follow Roman law, this was not a historical claim. At that time, as in the *usus modernus iuris romani* in general, the ancient texts were mainly used to resolve current legal questions. Quite often, they have but little or nothing to do with the historical Roman law that we know today.[72] Indeed, in Ancient Roman sources, we are well informed about the much smaller number of more advantaged domestic slaves,[73] which in turn may mispresent the view of ancient slavery. Even so, comparisons with transatlantic slavery are misleading. For instance, one essential difference is clear: Roman slavery, unlike its transatlantic counterpart, had no racist basis.

Generally speaking, Roman slaves were of many types.[74] Persons captured in war became slaves. In addition, a slave born to a female slave became a slave, and a free woman who persisted in cohabitation with a slave in spite of a warning from the master became his slave. Sometimes, conviction and sentencing in criminal proceedings entailed so-called penal slavery. Nonetheless, all slaves were 'unfree', and as such unable to enter into valid marriages, to acquire property, or to undertake political tasks. In addition, they were the 'property' of their masters. Thus, the meanings of 'unfreedom' and the 'property' of another person need a closer look – and from the 'cluster' perspective proposed by Kurki.

Regardless of their social positions, the legal status of all slaves was the same. *Servile caput nullum ius habet*: a slave's *caput* is possessed of 'no right', as the Roman

[70] *The Institutes of Gaius* (n 2).

[71] eg, in Brazil: S Barbosa, 'Masks of Legal Subjectivity: Equality and Differences within Personal Regimes in Brazil (1824–1988)' in P Collin and A Casagrande (eds), *Law and Diversity: European and Latin American Experiences from a Legal Historical Perspective* Vol 1: Fundamental Questions (Frankfurt am Main, Max-Planck-Institut für Rechtsgeschichte und Rechtstheorie, 2023) 601–23. See also MI Finley, *Ancient Slavery and Modern Ideology* (New York, The Viking Press, 1980).

[72] As asserted by Schermaier, the study of Roman slavery must begin *ab ovo*: we must first understand the role of the *servi* in the small-scale structures of early Rome; Schermaier (n 6) 24.

[73] Such slaves, whose occupation, training or special talents ensured their higher rank, as a rule were able to have their own families, to count on later *manumission*, and to accumulate wealth of their own. These privileges, however, were not legally protected; see further M Schermaier, 'Neither Fish nor Fowl: Some Grey Areas of Roman Slave Law' in M Schermaier (ed), *The Position of Roman Slaves. Social Reality and Legal Differences* (Berlin/Boston, De Gruyter, 2022) 237–68.

[74] See, eg, A Watson, *The Law of Persons in the Later Roman Republic* (Oxford, Clarendon Press, 1967); on the condition of slaves, see WW Buckland, *The Roman Law of Slavery. The Condition of the Slave in Private Law from Augustus to Justinian* (Cambridge, Cambridge University Press, 1908, reprinted 1970).

jurist Paul (Paulus; second and third century AD) wrote.[75] But this sentence is easily misunderstood if the context is neglected: the fragment is about changes in the legal status of a person. As noted earlier, there were three statuses: *status libertatis*, *status civitatis*, and *status familiae*. Since the time of Cicero, a loss of status was called *capitis deminutio*. But because there could be not only loss but also gain, Gaius noted, *capitis minutio est status permutatio* – *capitis minutio* is a change of status.[76] In fact, Paul considers the question whether *manumission* (release from slavery) of a slave is also a *capitis minutio*. He rejects this because a slave, who has no status, cannot change it. Hence, Justinian added a clarification with a reference to Modestinus (*c* 250 AD): *Hodie enim incipit statum habere*.[77] Thus, status could only be discussed where it existed. From a strictly conceptual point of view, the acquisition of *status libertatis* therefore cannot be described as a change of status. In any case, Paul did not mean that a slave had no rights.

But how else, apart from their status, could the legal position of slaves be defined? As we have seen, in legal texts they are also treated as *res*. At the same time, slaves' ability to establish rights and obligations through their own actions is taken into account.[78] Actually, the fact that slaves were human beings who thought and acted is never generally addressed in legal sources. According to Roman law scholars, this only implies that it has been taken for granted.[79] This was also probably why Gaius, when he distinguished things (*res*) and persons (*personae*), counts slaves among the *personae*.[80] At the same time, classification as *personae* clearly did not mean that slaves were always treated as subjects. Similarly, even when a jurist counted slaves as a part in their master's estate, they were not completely dehumanised.[81] Thus, the modern division between persons and things, or the modern concepts of person and thing understood as legal subject and object of law, are rather poorly suited for clarifying the legal position of Roman slaves.

To say that slaves were the 'property' of their masters also inadequately describes the legal position of slaves. Certainly, it is true that in Roman thinking slaves were property: they were *in persona servi dominium*, as Paul described the power relationship between masters and slaves.[82] Even if other jurists employed similar terms,

[75] D (=Digesta/Digest) 4.5.3.1(Paulus 11 ad ed).

[76] D 4.5.1 (Gai ad ed prov).

[77] D 4.5.4 (Mod. 1 pandect.): 'For now he begins to have status', McCormack's translation in A Watson, *The Digest of Justinian*, vol 1–4 (Pennsylvania, University of Pennsylvania Press, 1985).

[78] See eg. Buckland (n 74) 1–38.

[79] See eg. ibid and Shermaier (n 6) 8.

[80] Furthermore, that Gaius describes 'man' (*homo*) as things (*res*) does not prevent him from classifying slaves as *personae*. See Inst. II 13: *(Corporales) hae, quae tangi possunt, velut fundus, homo, vestis, aurum argentum et denique aliae res innumerabiles* 'Corporeal things can be touched – land, a slave, clothes, gold, silver and of course countless others'. In English: *The Institutes of Gaius* (n 2).

[81] Yet, as asserted by Schermaier, it is difficult to define the 'rights' of slaves in specific terms or case groups. What frequently happened in social practice was that slaves were granted favours. Such concessions created grey areas in legal terms because, while slaves could expect their masters to grant them certain privileges, there was no legal means of enforcing those privileges. Schermaier (n 73).

[82] D. 50.16.215 (Paul. 1 ad legem Fufiam et Caniniam*): 'Potestatis' verbo plura significantur: in persona magistratuum imperium: in persona liberorum patria potestas: in persona servi dominium …*: – 'The word "potestas" has many meanings; in the person of magistrates it means imperium; in the person of children it means parental power; in the person of a slave it means ownership'. In English: Crawford in Watson (n 77).

it was not the fact of being the property of their master that made the slave a slave. Moreover, the connection between slave status and property is quite obvious: being a slave usually entailed belonging to the *dominium* of another. Therefore, the Roman concept of *dominium* ought to be explored. Paul describes it as a form of *potestas* which pertains to slaves and objects. The children of the family, however, were under comparable *potestas*, as was the wife[83] in a so-called *manus* marriage. *Dominium*, *patria potestas* and *manus* were forms of being under the domestic power of the *pater familias* – as was the Swedish *målsmanskap*, discussed later in this chapter. In fact, *dominium* included all objects or persons of which or whom the head of the household could say, *mea sunt*: they belong to me. This, however, in no way implies that he was able to exercise unlimited power over the persons in question.

At the same time, Roman property was conceptualised from the possibility to bring an action, especially from *ius vindicandi*.[84] Whoever was able to demand the return of the thing (or person) in question from another was considered its owner. Thus, property was understood from the potential to bring a lawsuit, in contrast to the current material definition, according to which children are not the 'property' of their parents. In fact, the *dominus* gets his name from the *domus*, the house or household he heads. It has been assumed that the terms *dominus* and *dominium* were derived from 'domestic property', that property which in contrast to so-called gentile property, was held exclusively by the *pater familias*, the master of all persons and objects in the household. Even this classification says quite little about the legal position of slaves. In any case, it would be overstated to think of *dominium* as an 'absolute' concept of property.[85] Only in late medieval law (since the fourteenth century) did property as *dominium* become a concept in which the right was founded on the owner's authority or power in dealing with the thing in question.

It is not only *dominium* that has induced jurists to re-project later conditions back onto Roman slavery, and even define slaves as things. A popular example has been Ulpian's statement that slaves counted *pro nullis*, as nothing, under civil law. This sounds quite clear: slaves do not legally exist. But that is probably not what Ulpian wanted to express. When reading the fragment to the end, we see that the position is different according to natural law: 'As far as concerns the civil law, slaves are regarded as not existing, not, however, in natural law, because as far as concerns natural law all men are equal.'[86] Thus, according to natural law, all men were equal, both slaves and free men. And again, we must put Ulpian's statement that *ius civile* regards slaves 'as nothing' into context. Namely, Roman jurists regarded *ius civile* as only one part of positive law. There were also *ius gentium* (international law) and

[83] The wife, however, is not mentioned in D. 50.16.2.

[84] The concept might also be understood as the owner's ability to demand the return of the object or the person from anyone less entitled to possess it, as Celsus wrote (D. 6.1.49 1 Cels. 18 dig): *Meum est, quod ex re mea superest, cuius vindicandi ius habeo*. – 'Whatever remains from my property which I have a right to vindicate is itself mine'. In English: Stein's translation in Watson (n 77).

[85] See, eg, Buckland (n 74) 86–88. However, it is a different matter that the classification of Roman slaves into their master's *dominium* resulted in social discrimination, which occurred at the time of Rome's expansion.

[86] D. 50.17.32 (Ulp. 43 ad Sab.): *Quod attinet ad ius civile, servi pro nullis habentur: non tamen et iure naturali, quia, quod ad ius naturale attinet, omnes homines aequales sunt*.

ius honorarium, made up by decisions and edicts of the magistrates (praetors). Thus, when Ulpian refers to *ius civile*, he means only a certain part of the legal order. Under *ius civile*, for instance, a slave could be neither a creditor nor a debtor. This was because slaves were not entitled to take legal action, that is, they could not assert claims in court or be sued for debt.[87] Nonetheless, the *servile* lack of entitlement did not exclude slaves from being able to establish debts or claims, as the text continues: Their master could claim what they were owed, while, if a slave owed a debt to another person, their master would be liable for it from the slave's *peculium*.[88] Although the *peculium* belonged to the *dominus*, who alone as the person in authority was able to be owner and proprietor, it enabled slaves to make their own economic dispositions, which legally were treated as if they had been transacted by the *dominus*. Formally, slaves remained without property: de facto they were regarded as proprietors.[89]

Thus, the procedural (remedy) view was that no claim could be brought for the debts of slaves. They could, however, be effectively settled;[90] from the 'natural' (law) perspective they were still owed, and this is the reason why Roman jurists called them *obligationes naturales*. If the two fragments[91] were closely associated, *servi pro nullis habentur* merely means that from the point of view of procedural law, slaves were treated as non-existent – just as, incidentally, women were.[92] So, this does not mean that slaves were without rights. It only means that slaves could not bring effective procedural actions – in a legal system where procedural capacity determined substantive law. In this respect, it could be argued that slaves possessed no rights merely because they were denied access to the courts. But this conclusion may also be incorrect. According to studies of Roman social history, the conclusion fails to recognise the legal reality, which could diverge from formal law: the principle that slaves could not appeal to the *praetor* and the courts was broken several times.[93]

However, we should note that *pro nullo habere* should not be taken literally. At least, it says but little or nothing about the substantive entitlements and burdens of slaves. One excellent option would be to argue, similarly to Okko Behrends or

[87] *Cum servo nulla actio est*. – 'There is no action with a slave', as Gaius noted D. 50.17.107 (Gai. 1 ad ed prov). In English: Crawford in Watson (n 77).

[88] D. 15.1.41 (Ulp. 43 ad Sab.): *Nec servus quicquam debere potest nec servo potest deberi, sed cum eo verbo abutimur, factum magis demonstramus quam ad ius civile referimus obligationem. itaque quod servo debetur, ab extraneis dominus recte petet, quod servus ipse debet, eo nomine in peculium et si quidinde in rem domini versum est in dominum actio datur*. – 'A slave cannot really owe or be owed anything, but we use the word loosely to indicate the facts rather than with reference to obligations at civil law. Thus, a master may sue third parties for what they owe the slave, and he may be sued for what the slave owes them up to the amount of the peculium, and for any benefit thereby accruing to him'. In English: Gordon in Watson (n 77).

[89] On *peculium* see A Watson (n 75) 178–84, and R Gamauf, '*Peculium*. Paradoxes of Slaves with Property' in M Schermaier (ed), *The Position of Roman Slaves. Social Reality and Legal Differences* (Berlin/Boston, De Gruyter, 2022) 87–127.

[90] See n 88.

[91] D. 50.17.32 and D. 15.1.41.

[92] D. 28.1.20.7 (Ulp. 1 ad Sab.): *Servus quoque merito ad sollemnia adhiberi non potest, cum iuris civilis communionem non habeat in totum, ne praetoris quidem edicti*. 'It is also right that a slave cannot be used in solemn acts as he is totally excluded from participation in the civil law, and even in the praetor's edict.' Gordon in Watson (n 77).

[93] Schermaier (n 73) 249–51.

Martin Avenarius, for the 'partial legal capacity' of slaves.[94] Rather than linking that to the notion of a (legal) person, they base it on the ability of slaves to litigate certain matters themselves. As far as Kurki's proposal is concerned, the legal position of Roman slaves consists of at least some passive incidents of legal personhood or subjecthood. In addition, there were also some elements of so-called onerous legal personhood (criminal responsibility).[95] The conclusion, however, requires understanding that one is always a subject of law within some sectors of the legal order (or areas of law) and/or regarding one or several legal institutions. At the same time, Kurki's division into dependent, independent and pure passive personhood should be accepted. Similar conclusions can be drawn about – much later – developments of modern legal personhood of women, discussed briefly in the following.

ii. Women as Legal Persons

In European pre-modern societies, birth and marriage were the most significant factors defining a woman's social and legal status. In Sweden and Finland, an institution called *målsmansakap*, or household mastership, was a collective institution of guardianship. At the same time, it was an institution to uphold the structures linked both with kin and society. It was tied to the hierarchical structure and the moral codes of the so-called estate society. Thus, abolishing the institution and making all individuals responsible for themselves became necessary only later, in the industrialising societies of the nineteenth and twentieth centuries.[96] Nevertheless, the power of the household master was not the power of the Roman *pater familas* or of the owner of property in the modern sense.

A central feature of the power of the household master was household discipline. He could chastise his wife, children and servants.[97] The institution also had a specific meaning in marriage. According to the Code of Marriage of Swedish Law (*Sveriges Rikes lag*, 1734, applied also in Finland), the husband was the guardian, a *målsman*, of his wife. It was his right and duty to represent her in public and administer her property. The wife followed the estate of the husband, which meant that she shared the social status and legal privileges of her husband and his estate. However, the wife did not completely lose her earlier legal status or her legal competences by

[94] That is what they had from imperial times onwards. Okko Behrends, 'Prinzipat und Sklavenrecht. Zu den geistigen Grundlagen der augusteischen Verfassungsschöpfung' in U Immenga (ed), *Rechtswissenschaft und Rechtsentwicklung* (Göttingen, Schwartz, 1980) 56–62 and M Avenarius, 'Einleitung' in Avenarius, *Stellung des Sklaven im Privatrecht*, vol 3, Erbrecht. Aktive Stellung: Personeneigenschaft und Ansätze zur Anerkennung von Rechten, Corpus der römischen Rechtsquellen zur Sklaverei 4 (Stuttgart, Franz Steiner Verlag, 2017) 1–5; see also R Knütel, 'Freikauf mit eigenem Geld' in H Heinen et al (eds), *Handwörterbuch der antiken Sklaverei*, (Stuttgart, Franz Steiner Verlag, 2012) 1095–97.

[95] Slaves were also liable for crimes. However, the rule that slaves cannot take part in judicial proceedings was applied even where they were the accused. Their master or any other could defend him, and the defender was the real party, but it was necessary to say that, after the trial, it was the slave, not the defender, who was condemned. See in more detail Buckland (n 74) 91–93.

[96] A Pylkkänen, *Trapped in Equality. Women as Legal Persons in the Modernisation of Finnish Law* (Helsinki, Finnish Literature Society, 2009) 38–39. According to her, the system of household mastership signifies economic, social, and religious subordination to a large majority of people as well as stability of the hierarchical social order, which was enforced with several criminal sanctions.

[97] Abolished mainly in the second half of the 19th century.

marriage. Indeed, she became a leading member of the household, as its mistress, with both husband and wife fulfilling their authoritative roles in maintaining the hierarchy and discipline. They both enjoyed inheritance rights derived from their kin and had a marital portion. In exceptional situations, the wife also could represent the household, but usually it was a gender division of tasks – hers in the inner household, his in the administration of the household and its property. In contrast, a widow was allowed to act independently.

In the society concerned, social stability and the hierarchal social order were the two utmost values controlled by the leading males, whereas wives had very little if anything to do with matters of economic value, such as land ownership. The husband administered all property, but he was not allowed to alienate his wife's land without her permission. Nor could her private property be used to cover debts that had accrued to cover his specific personal expenditure. A wife could not contest a husband's legal acts other than alienations of property, even if in most cases they also made her portion liable for debts.[98]

When this model started dissolving, giving way to a society of free individuals, it was a matter of abolishing the social and economic binds based on the quite widespread legal powers of the household master. The institution of *målsmanskap* as the combined power over household and kin property, representation of household members, and household discipline, was gradually dissolved through the process of individualisation of the household members. First, the family emerged out of the larger household. The family unit consisting of man, wife and children became the new basic measure – not the household or the individual. Even though individual guilt had already been established during early modern times, universal economic and legal individualisation took place only from the late nineteenth century onwards.[99]

Maintenance was one of the first issues to be tackled. First, unmarried women were freed from the guardianship of their father, while so-called marriage guardianship (*målsmanskap*) was later also abolished. The second issue to be dealt with was to make people in service positions independent workers. Forced labour and subordination to the household master were finally abolished in Finland in the 1880s. Another aspect of individualisation was related to the property rights of individuals. In 1864, Finnish unmarried women over 25 gained full control over their property and income. In 1889, married women were allowed to administer their income.

According to Anu Pylkkänen, legislative steps in the nineteenth century did little, if anything, to the institution of marriage as the locus of gender hierarchy: As married women were gradually given some rights that in some sense could be called individual, these rights were carefully designed not to shatter the husband's authority or to go against his interests or those of the family. A married woman was not regarded

[98] Actually, the Swedish/Finnish system differed considerably from the Danish, where wives were regarded as minors and all property of the spouses became a community that the husband controlled. I Dübeck, *Kvinder, familie og formue* (Copenhagen, Museum Tusculanum Foerlag, 2003) 218.

[99] A Pylkkänen, 'The Responsible Self. Relational Gender Construction in the History of Finnish Law' in K Nousiainen, Å Gunnarsson, K Lundström and J Niemi-Kielsiläinen (eds), *Responsible Selves. Women in the Nordic Legal Culture* (Aldershot, Ashgate, 2001).

as an economic actor with her own rights even though it was often stressed that she was not subjugated to the husband. However, according to contemporary interpretations, married women had since time immemorial reached majority and had never been equated to minors. They enjoyed the right of the matron, *husfrudöme*. Nor was *målsmanskap* comparable to the guardianship of minors; it was only a restriction of the wife's legal capacity during marriage. Nonetheless, the motives behind the nineteenth-century reforms were not connected to emancipation as such, but focused on economic incentives, to loosen the kin-related ties of hereditary land to the extent that it could be used as capital. For instance, in Finland, until the Marriage Act of 1929, it was assumed that there was only one economic actor in the family, the husband, who would act in the interest of the whole family.

With Kurki's idea of personhood as a cluster property in mind, it is possible to conclude, that for a long time – and instead of the *målsmanskap* of the husband – the wife's legal standing (as an incident of passive personhood) was recognised. Not always, however, was she enabled to take legal action (active personhood) independently. The institution of *målsmanskap* did not exempt women from owning property altogether but provided that most legal competences pertaining to property had to be exercised by the husband or some other male, or could only be exercised by the wife with the man's permission. In such cases, the property was acknowledged as belonging to the wife, giving her standing in any lawsuits over the property. However, she was denied the competence to decide whether to pursue any such lawsuits.

V. CONCLUSIONS

As discussed above, the Roman law division *persona–res* was a self-evident starting point for theoretical and historical analysis of the concept of legal personhood. Later, a more technical concept of legal personhood was developed, and 'person' referred to a human being's civil/legal standing. With natural law, legal personhood became linked to a person's rights and obligations. In the twentieth century, Hans Kelsen also combined legal personhood with rights and obligations, but to him the person was the personification of a totality of rights and obligations. At the same time, a person – as a legal subject – was only a creation of legal language, of the legal system concerned.

In current legal practice, the modern (nineteenth- and twentieth-century) concept of legal personhood, grounded on the idea of human autonomy, is being challenged. Not only animals, but rivers or nature as such are being granted rights. Hence, legal scholars see legal persons as legal representatives of extra-legal entities but pointing out that the legal representative and the party represented cannot be one and the same. At the same time, free will as the only limit of representation is denied, and new standards are being called for. In this context, in particular the idea of trans-subjectivity, inter alia with reference to historical and current institutions of *actio popularis* about the common good, have been taken up.

Not only is the current concept of legal personhood changing: the traditional system of rights and duties is also being questioned. There is a need for a new 'bundle' of rights and obligations – not a universal one but specific to each person or entity in question. Thus, being a person means having only a specific bundle of rights and obligations, which varies according to the legal order – in both time and space. In this context, especially the idea of legal personhood as a cluster concept as proposed by Visa Kurki was addressed. As a 'cluster property' legal personhood consists of interconnected but divisible 'incidents', while no exact border between legal personhood and non-personhood exists. Incidents, again, can be classified as passive and active, the first being substantive and remedy incidents. Active incidents refer to legal competences and to so-called onerous legal personhood consisting of different legal responsibilities.

The proposal of a cluster of different incidents was found to be an innovative option to analyse and reconceptualise new trends and practices connected to person, or better said to legal subjects, and their legal position. The idea of incidents was also applied or tested in historical analysis. First, issues of personhood in Roman law, mainly connected to slaves, were dealt with. In the analysis, the strict binary classification of *persona–res* was rejected. Furthermore, textual and social history studies reveal that neither modern concepts of person and thing nor the idea of the legal subject and legal object could sufficiently describe the legal position of Roman slaves. Moreover, to say that slaves were the 'property' (*dominium*) of their masters inadequately describes their legal position. Although the terms *dominus* and *dominium* probably refer to 'domestic property' that was exclusively held by the *pater familias* – having the children and wife also under his power – it would be overstated to think of *dominium* as 'absolute' property in the modern sense.

Finally, the meaning of the statement that slaves counted *pro nullis*, as nothing, under Ancient Roman civil law, was discussed, pointing out that this concerned only a certain part of the Roman legal order, the so-called *ius civile*. Under this, for instance, a slave could be neither a creditor nor a debtor. This was because slaves were not entitled to take legal action, meaning that no claim could be brought to the court for the debts of slaves. They could, however, be effectively settled, at least from the slave's *peculium*. Indeed, scholars of Roman law agree that there existed a 'partial legal capacity', or slaves' ability to litigate certain matters themselves. Thus, in the terms of Kurki, legal personhood consisted of at least incidents of so-called passive legal personhood or subjecthood, even some of active (onerous) legal personhood. However, this conclusion requires that one is always seen as a subject of law within some sectors of the legal order or regarding certain legal institutions.

Similar conclusions could be drawn when much later developments of legal personhood of women were discussed. The focus was on the Swedish–Finnish institution of guardianship called the husband's *målsmansakap* (household mastership), and its slow abolition towards the end of the nineteenth century. According to the idea of legal personhood as a cluster property, it was possible to conclude that, despite the *målsmanskap* of the husband, the wife's passive personhood was recognised. Furthermore, the institution of *målsmanskap* did not exempt women from owning property altogether, but provided that most legal competences pertaining to property had to be exercised by the husband, or could only be exercised by the wife with the man's permission. In such cases, the property was acknowledged as belonging to the wife, giving her standing in any lawsuits over the property. At the same time, a wife's legal personhood included incidents of active personhood when her criminal law and other responsibilities were concerned.

Yet, releasing ourselves from the traditional dichotomy of persons and things, and looking more closely at the different dimensions (incidents) of legal personhood, have opened new, more nuanced, horizons to studies of the history of the concept and practices of legal personhood. The same, however, could be said of the future of the person.

10

From Abstract Legal Subjects to Real Life

THOMAS WILHELMSSON

I. RETURNING TO PAST SINS

AS AN ILLUSTRATION of my theme I will start by presenting two practical cases: one decided by the Finnish Supreme Court; the other constructed to reflect the wording of a Finnish enactment.

The concrete case is from 1981.[1] A had been driving while drunk and without a driver's licence, and thereby caused a collision with another car. His traffic insurance company had paid compensation both for personal injury and for damage to the other car. In the resulting criminal case, in which A was sentenced to five months' imprisonment, the insurance company, referring to its right of subrogation, claimed from A the 11,572,77 FIM[2] that it had paid. It won its case in the lower courts, but the Finnish Supreme Court adjusted the amount A had to pay to a little more than a third of the claim (4,000 FIM), with reference to A's low income and lack of property. The adjustment was made on the basis of a general clause in the Finnish Act on Torts,[3] according to which the amount of damages may be adjusted, if the liability is deemed unreasonably onerous in view of the financial status of the person causing the injury or damage and the person suffering it, and of other circumstances. Similar general clauses are also included in the legislation on torts in the other Nordic countries.[4]

The second example concerns a consumer who has not paid his or her debt in time and is therefore liable to pay interest for late payment. According to the Finnish Act on Interest, however, the court is not obliged to award the full legal amount of interest in such a case. It can adjust the interest if the payment is delayed due to financial difficulties that the debtor has suffered because of illness, unemployment

[1] Finnish Supreme Court 1981 II 102.

[2] The present value being about €5,400 (ie, not an exceptionally high amount).

[3] Finnish Tort Liability Act (as it is called in the translation of the Ministry of Justice; in Finnish Vahingonkorvauslaki, in Swedish Skadeståndslag), Ch 2, Sec 1(2).

[4] See the Swedish Skadeståndslag, Ch 6, Sec 2, the Norwegian Lov om skadeserstatning, Ch 5, Sec 2 and the Danish Lov om erstatningsansvar, Sec 24(1).

or other special reason which is primarily not attributable to the debtor himself or herself. Nowadays another broader general clause is added to this provision: adjustment may also take place if there are weighty reasons for the adjustment when the amount of the interest for late payment in relation to the financial status of the debtor is taken into consideration.[5]

In both cases a well-established private law principle is overridden by an argument related to the personal features of one of the parties. The principle of full compensation in tort law has given way to a reference to the poor financial situation of the tortfeasor. The obligation to pay interest on late payment has been balanced by properties of the debtor that relate to his or her personal financial situation. More generally, both cases are in conflict with a general starting point of the law of obligations according to which the financial situation of the party lacks legal relevance: 'you've got to have money'.[6]

The examples illustrate how a person hit by poverty or financial distress may be expressly supported in private law decision-making. This, however, is not the only context in which personal properties and the financial situation of a party may be relevant. One may also find examples from other, very different, contexts.[7] However, I will not discuss such other examples further in this paper.

Cases and laws such as those mentioned above inspired me in the 1980s to write a book on need-rationality in private law.[8] My goal was to see, whether and to what extent one could take into account the financial and social position of a party as a legal fact in private law, as a welfarism-based intra-legal critique of the prevailing narrative that emphasises the abstract description of private law subjects. Various weaker party roles in use in private law are analysed from this perspective. Based on a conceptual analysis of concrete legal materials (predominantly, but not only from Finnish law) I have discussed the possibility of using private law concepts like a 'debtor with limited means', a 'debtor in need of housing', a 'low income debtor', an 'unemployed debtor', an 'ill debtor', a 'debtor burdened with considerable maintenance liabilities' and a 'small-enterprise debtor of limited financial strength'.[9] The result is an acknowledgement that such person-related arguments are used and at least to some extent fall within the boundaries of the 'legally possible'.

[5] Act on Interest (Korkolaki, Räntelag), Sec 11 (by Act 340/2002).

[6] D Medicus, '"Geld muß man haben". Unvermögen und Schuldnerverzug bei Geldmangel' (1988) 188 *Archiv für die civilistische Praxis* 489.

[7] An extreme example from a completely different context is the sanctions directed towards Russian oligarchs as a consequence of the war in Ukraine (and, earlier on, named people classified as terrorists). They seem to question many basic private law principles, related to ownership and validity of contracts. I want to underline that I do not mention this as a criticism of the sanctions, as all efforts to support Ukraine in this tragic situation are important. It is just theoretically interesting to see how private law principles can be set aside by extremely personalised sanctions, when this is needed – and, astonishingly, that private law analysis, as well as legal-theoretical analysis of these measures, is hard to find. *Inter arma silent leges*? On the implementation of the sanctions, see eg Case T-720/14 *Arkady Romanovich Rotenberg v Council of the European Union*, ECLI:EU:T:2016:689.

[8] T Wilhelmsson, *Critical Studies in Private Law: A Treatise on Need-Rational Principles in Modern Law*, Law and Philosophy Library 16 (Dordrecht, Kluwer Academic Publishers, 1992).

[9] ibid 151–52.

Having written the book, are there any reasons for me to return to the issue (other than my friend Hans-W. Micklitz inviting me to the interesting conference on legal subjectivity)? I think there is. Even though welfarism might be on the decline, there are other societal, technological and legal developments that may affect the possible use of person-related concepts like those mentioned above. I am thinking in particular of three kinds of changes. First, there seems to be a general tendency towards the fragmentation of private law in the globalised, digitalised and individualised[10] late modern society that pushes private law discourse to focus more on concrete situations, described in real-life language. One may ask whether this tendency may support and even strengthen the development of a person-related conceptuality, as one way of looking at real life behind abstract legal concepts. Secondly, digitalisation has produced interesting debates on the possible development of a 'personalised law', in which person-related features would expressly or impliedly be introduced as relevant elements in the detailed normative structures. The discourse concerning a personalised law clearly relate to the issue, whether and to what extent concrete descriptions of the legal subject can be legally relevant and what legal consequences that may have. Thirdly, in the legal sphere the position of fundamental rights and their influence on private law have undergone considerable change, both in Europe and nationally. Fundamental rights reasoning has become increasingly important in the private law setting. For example, when discussing person-related concepts in private law, the right of equality certainly has a role to play.

I will in the following focus in particular on these new perspectives. Before looking at them, however, I will introduce the chapter's key question, and explain why I consider the question important.

II. QUESTION: HOW BLINDFOLDED SHOULD THE GODDESS OF JUSTICE BE?

So why do I find it interesting to look at these dispersed examples on how the abstract legal subject, without empirical properties (other than being a physical person who is not under guardianship), is replaced by somebody who is for example poor, unemployed or ill? It is because they in a particularly obvious way bring to the fore the issue to what extent legal discourse is and should be relatively autonomous in relation to other societal discourses.

The abstract way of defining the relevant legal subjects is an important tool for keeping legal discourse isolated from societal, moral and political discourses. The discussion on what one can expect from 'a debtor' and 'a creditor' or 'a seller' and 'a buyer' is different from what it were, if one would describe the subjects concretely; eg 'a poor person', 'a multimillionaire' (let's call him 'Elon'), 'a large firm' or 'a financial institution'. The blindfolded Goddess of Justice – being neutral and unattached as to whom she deals with – is forced to reason and act differently if she is confronted by the real 'other', a person with real qualities: parties A, B and C invite different reasoning than Elon, the poor Alice and the unemployed John.

[10] See A Reckwitz, *Die Gesellschaft der Singularitäten: Zum Strukturwandel der Moderne* (Berlin, Suhrkamp, 2017).

As we all know, private law has not been completely blind with regard to the concrete needs of disadvantaged persons. What is sometimes called 'welfarism in private law'[11] or 'social private law'[12] comprises rules that are particularly designed to take into account the interests of so-called 'weaker parties'. In our context it is essential to note, however, that this development has usually not required abandoning of the abstract way of defining the legal subject. The traditional way of taking into account the particular needs of a private law party has been a mandatory regulation of contract types in which one party is typically regarded as weaker, such as hire-purchase contracts or lease agreements concerning housing. The next step has been to consider particular roles as deserving protection, such as the role of a consumer. Both steps can be taken without giving express relevance to the concrete properties of the parties. Both Alice, John and Elon can act as tenants and consumers and are (formally) protected by the same rules (even though Elon hardly needs the protection).

The attempts to define a consumer image (*Leitbild*)[13] reinforces this approach. The use of such an image is a refined way of safeguarding the abstract approach to the legal subject. The European consumer is understood as being 'reasonably well-informed and reasonably observant and circumspect',[14] irrespective of whether he or she is able to act like this in real life. Only the introduction of the 'vulnerable consumer' may refer to more concrete properties of the actual subject,[15] but this concept is mostly used in collective measures like the Unfair Commercial Practices Directive and the collective supervision of unfair terms,[16] and does not necessarily affect the individual private law rights of the consumer. In so far as vulnerability is used as a criterion in individual disputes, it tends to relate more to the abilities than the financial needs of the consumer. The Unfair Commercial Practices Directive speaks about 'consumers who are particularly vulnerable … because of their mental or physical infirmity, age or credulity'[17] and does not include the low-income

[11] R Brownsword et al (eds), *Welfarism in Contract Law* (Aldershot, Dartmouth, 1994).

[12] eg B Lurger, 'The "social" Side of Contract Law and the New Principle of Regard and Fairness' in A Hartkamp et al (eds), *Towards a European Civil Code*, 4th edn (Alpheen aan den Rijn-Nijmegen, Kluwer, 2011) 353.

[13] See eg D Leczykiewicz and S Weatherill (eds), *The Images of the Consumer in EU Law: Legislation, Free Movement and Competition Law* (Oxford, Hart Publishing, 2015).

[14] As first defined in Case C-210/96 *Gut Springenheide GmbH and Rudolf Tusky v Oberkreisdirektor des Kreises Steinfurt* [1998] ECR I-04657.

[15] If used as a suggested new consumer image (see I Domurath, 'The Case for Vulnerability as the Normative Standard in European Credit and Mortgage Law – An Inquiry into the Paradigms of Consumer Law' (2013) 2 *Journal of European Consumer and Market Law* 124), it still functions as a description of an abstract legal subject. If vulnerability, however, is referred to in a more flexible way, taking into account the individual vulnerability of the consumer, the vulnerability concept challenges the abstract legal subjectivity. See eg the interesting analysis of three types of vulnerability, including for example 'low-net-worth consumers' (116) as an example of lack of resilience, by I Domurath, *Consumer Vulnerability and Welfare in Mortgage Contracts* (Oxford, Hart Publishing, 2017). Domurath here also speaks about the 'real-life mortgagor' (125).

[16] See the interesting analysis by F Esposito and M Grochowski, 'The Consumer Benchmark, Vulnerability, and the Contract Terms Transparency: A Plea for Reconsideration' (2022) 18 *European Review of Contract Law* 1.

[17] Art 5(3).

consumer in the interpretation of 'vulnerability'.[18] 'Vulnerability' is also in many cases understood as a dynamic concept that has a situational content.[19]

Furthermore, other areas of private law, and in particular tort law, have traditionally included ability-oriented arguments in their toolkit. For example, the ability of the tortfeasor can be taken into account as an argument in the assessment of negligence. One expects more diligence from professionals than from non-professionals. Ability-oriented roles are to some extent a part of the concrete cast of private law. The pressure from real life, however, seems to require more. As illustrated by my examples, the acknowledgement of the financial situation of a party as a relevant legal argument brings the different needs of Elon, John and Alice more expressly on the legal table. In a way such need-rational interventions are the most pronounced examples of a kind of welfarist private law, as they introduce into private law the person-oriented reasoning typical for welfarist social security law. The Goddess of social security justice has never been blindfolded as to the financial situation of her clients.

I will in this chapter focus on such an express welfarist conceptuality in private law, discussing the possibility of need-rational descriptions of legal subjects and what the discourses on personalised law, fragmentation of private law and fundamental rights may add to the analysis of this issue. Without taking a stand on personalisation of law in general – it may be useful as a means to include party preferences and informational needs in the decision-making (as long as privacy rules can be respected) – I will in the following continue the discussion on the relevance of the financial situation and needs of the individual party in private law decision-making. How far should one go in acknowledging the different financial needs of Elon, Alice and John?

I want to make it clear that I am discussing only the financial properties of physical persons. Other aspects may be relevant with regard to legal persons. The opening-up of the formal legal subject by acknowledging the real-life existence of global supply chains as legally relevant is one good example of the latter.

III. FROM ABSTRACT LEGAL CONCEPTS TOWARDS REAL LIFE – ALSO OF THE LEGAL SUBJECT?

The question to what extent private law, as opposed to for example social security law, can and should remain in its predominantly abstract approach to the legal subject has perhaps become more topical because of general pressures to bring private law language closer to real life. Personalisation of the subject could appear as a part of the much-discussed general tendency (both welcomed and deplored) of fragmentation of private law. General real-life oriented fragmentation of private law structures may have lowered the hurdle for Elon, Alice and John to enter the legal scene.

[18] C Riefa, 'Protecting Vulnerable Consumers in the Digital Single Market' (2022) 33 *European Business Law Review* 607, 611.

[19] See eg F Ippolito and S Iglesias Sánchez, *Protecting Vulnerable Groups: The European Human Rights Framework* (Oxford, Hart Publishing, 2015).

This is not the place to dive deeper into the issue of fragmentation as such. It relates both to the growing complexity of the late modern society and the simultaneous decline of a joint ethical authority. Both require the law to become more able to learn, to adapt flexibly to various societal challenges. For example in tort law, both in concrete assessments of negligence and in discussions on the development of stricter forms of liability,[20] such learning processes are obvious. As Gert Brüggemeier has noted, a highly differentiated society is incompatible with a generalised and formalised tort law.[21] Christian von Bar, based on his impressive analysis of European tort law, claims that 'modern tort law's specific instances are … defined not by legal categories but in terms of real-life circumstances which form the bases of the causes of action'.[22]

Obviously, Europeanisation also adds to the fragmentation and focus on real life. The pragmatic nature of much EU law, aiming at regulating real commercial situations, like distance-selling and time-sharing, and consciously avoiding or minimising the use of such national legal concepts that have roots in strong national traditions, pushes categories of real life into the discourse.[23] More generally, the internationalisation of law, including the growth of transnational law, also pushes legal reasoning in the direction of real life. This is of course commonplace for comparative lawyers applying the functional method.[24] The increasing cross-border movement of legal sources – in the EU one could speak of a free movement of legal sources – also focuses attention on how concrete real-life problems may be legally solved rather than on the conceptual legal structures that one could build around them.[25]

In private law circles the fragmentation of law, and the related opportunities to expand the relevance of details from real life, has often been deplored – the emerging legal culture has been characterised for example as a 'hamburger-, nasigoreng- and pommes-legal culture'.[26] Of course, there is room for critique, in particular if

[20] My examples on tort law are taken from my paper 'Strict Liability for Dangerous Activities in Nordic Tort Law – an Adequate Answer to Late Modern Uncertainty?' (2019) 16 *Otago Law Review* 219.

[21] G Brüggemeier, *Prinzipien des Haftungsrechts: Eine systematische Darstellung auf rechtsvergleichender Grundlage* (Baden-Baden, Nomos, 1999) 24.

[22] C von Bar, *A Common European Law of Torts,* Saggi, conferenze e seminari 19 (Roma, Centro di studi e ricerche di diritto comparato e straniero, 1996) 13.

[23] A good recent example is the Digital Content Directive (Directive (EU) 2019/770 of the European Parliament and of the Council of 20 May 2019 on certain aspects concerning contracts for the supply of digital content and digital services [2019] OJ L136/1), that is constructed around the notion of digital content instead of formal contract types, causing implementation problems in such Member States that systematise remedies related to contract types; see eg K Sein and G Spindler, 'The new Directive on Contracts for Supply of Digital Content and Digital Services – Conformity Criteria, Remedies and Modifications – Part 2' (2019) 15 *European Review of Contract Law* 365, 391.

[24] In relation to Europeanisation the so called Trento Project illustrates this well, searching for the 'common core' of European private law by discussing and comparing factual questions (real-life situations): see common-core.org.

[25] See eg the reasoning in the landmark case *White v Jones* [1995] 1 All ER 691, in which the English court discussed a concrete issue in comparative light, seeking advice in particular from German law, even though the legal conceptual structures related to the issue were different.

[26] UH Schneider, 'Europäische und internationale Harmonisierung des Bankvertragsrechts. Zugleich ein Beitrag zur Angleichung des Privatrechts in der Europäischen Gemeinschaft' (1991) 44 *Neue Juristische Wochenschrift* 1985, 1993.

fragmentation is just a result of intellectual laziness and poor drafting. One may also look, however, at the turn towards putting more weight on the pragmatic solution of real-life challenges in a positive light. It can be advantageous, as it offers new opportunities for legal development.

In general, the language of the real world and the language of the legal world should not be too far away from each other. If the distance grows too wide, there is a greater risk for translation errors. When legal reasoning takes place in an abstract legal sphere, a rule that seems sensible for parts of the situations covered by a concept from within this sphere may lead to unfortunate results with regard to other parts. The choice of rule within the legal sphere may even be made more or less randomly, based on what example the decision-maker has in mind – what concrete issue first reaches the courts. More generally, it might be easier to reach a well-functioning solution of a societal problem if one describes the real problem instead of distorting it by the use of abstract legal categories.[27]

A focus on real life does not only facilitate the search for pragmatic solutions; it also opens new opportunities for societally geared critique. In critical, counter-hegemonic discourse the nature of the legal language as a language of lawyer domination has been stressed. As Adam Gearey notes in his analysis of poverty law, even radical legal thinking may reproduce forms of domination through the legal language. Therefore a radical lawyer should not hide behind technical languages,[28] but rather focus on problem-solving in a way that resembles how 'ordinary folks' approach challenges.[29] The increasing use of law as an instrument of micro-politics, for example in tobacco cases and climate change litigation, also pushes the language in a real-life direction, as the causes of action often are real-life issues that cannot be easily subsumed under traditional legal categories.

Real-life reasoning also has the advantage of increasing the strength of democratic understanding and control of legal decision-making. It facilitates the understanding of legal processes and cases by others than professional legal experts. In other words, it increases transparency. A transparent legal order attempts to address societal problems in a language that the media and the public can sufficiently understand.

[27] To give just one very illustrative example on the need of pragmatism one may refer to the critique by C Wendehorst, 'The Draft Principles of European Unjustified Enrichment Law Prepared by the Study Group on a European Civil Code: A Comment' (2006) 7 *ERA Forum* 244, 245–58, of the rules on unjust enrichment in the Draft Common Frame of Reference. She shows how the fairly abstract and formal approach of the DCFR could be replaced by a discussion under eight practical headings, which would help developing the rules in connection with situations of real life. Her headings are: 'The unwinding of contracts', 'Expectations not realised', 'Undue performance to the creditor', 'Performance to a third party', 'Improvements and similar expenses incurred by a debtor', 'Expenses incurred by a non-debtor', 'Infringement by the enriched person alone' and 'Infringement by an intervener'. The concepts are still relatively abstract, but more concrete than the approach of the DCFR. According to Wendehorst the rules of the DCFR are 'extremely technical rules with a very high level of abstraction, many cross-references and a strange habit of not addressing the crucial points directly but rather in a very convoluted manner' (259). A pragmatic response to the challenges requires a sufficient focus on the real-life circumstances involved. For a defence of the choice of approach in the DCFR, see eg C von Bar, 'The Principles of European Law (PEL) on Benevolent Intervention in Another's Affairs and on Unjustified Enrichment' (2006) 7 *ERA Forum* 204.

[28] A Gearey, *Poverty Law and Legal Activism: Lives that Slide Out of View* (Abingdon-New York, Routledge 2018) 116.

[29] ibid 124ff.

In other words, the increasing real-life-oriented fragmentation of private law has several advantages (balancing the obvious and much-debated disadvantages): an improved ability to adopt targeted and pragmatic solutions; better opportunities to formulate a societally oriented critique of legal decision-making; and a democratically important growing transparency of legal reasoning. The examples that one can present on the increased weight of real-life reasoning, however, are mostly related to what could be called 'situational concretisation'. A general tort law rule on liability for dangerous activities may for example be scattered into case law and detailed legislation on various situations like blasting work, car racing, vaccinations, energy production and various modes of transportation. A general principle on unjust enrichment can be replaced by a discussion under several more practical situational headings. The question is whether one can treat person-related features of real life, like the poor financial situation of a party, in the same way as such situational references to real life. Is the introduction of Elon, Alice and John on the scene just an expression of the well-founded tendency towards putting more emphasis on real-life circumstances in private law decision-making, or does it require different treatment?

The three advantages of real-life orientation mentioned above – pragmatism, critique and transparency – at the outset seem to apply to personal concretisation as well. A new perspective of critique is perhaps the most apparent advantage with regard to financial personalisation. Self-evidently the introduction of Elon, Alice and John in roles that were previously performed by an abstract legal subject opens the field for new societally geared critique of the law and can inspire critically founded new kinds of decisions. Transparency also seems to grow. It increases the democratic understanding of the legal order if there is an open legal discussion on how differently or similarly law treats parties with different financial backgrounds. Understanding that the right to sleep under bridges has very different meaning for persons with different financial needs can push the reasoning in new directions.

Finally, as to pragmatism, the usefulness of reasoning related to the financial position of the parties is to some extent dependent on what goals society aspires to achieve with the rules of private law. Some may argue that there should be a division of labour between private law and public law, and place issues of solidarity (that would make the characteristics of the parties relevant) into the public law box alone.[30] In an era of fragmentation of law, however, this kind of clear-cut general definition of the task of private law does not seem very convincing. If welfarism in private law is an option – which I for various reasons think it should be – the pragmatic relevance of real-life data on the financial situation of the parties cannot be denied. One might at least ask: should the poor really pay more[31] – or should they even pay less?

At the outset the advantages of focusing to a greater extent on real-life issues seem to also apply to personalised data on the financial situation of the party.

[30] A Ripstein, 'Private Order and Public Justice: Kant and Rawls' (2006) 92 *Virginia Law Review* 1391. Another example is of course EJ Weinrib, *The idea of private law* (Cambridge MA, Harvard University Press, 1995).

[31] *cf* D Caplovitz, *The Poor Pay More* (New York-London, Free Press-Collier Macmillan, 1968).

There seems to be good arguments for an opening of the door, at least to some extent, for person-related, real-life-oriented descriptions of the legal subjects in a private law relationship. Perhaps Elon, Alice and John really should be given a chance? As the next section will show, not only societal needs, but also technological development seems to offer new instruments for accepting them in the cast.

IV. TOWARDS A PERSONALISED LEGAL SUBJECT?

The discussion concerning the legal relevance of personal properties in private law is not new. Today, however, digitalisation has added a feature to the picture that makes it particularly important to continue the discourse. Big data has broadened the practical opportunities to include personal elements in private law decision-making.

The discussion concerning the use of big data as a vehicle to personalise law has been quite intense and is well known. In the same way as medical science develops a personalised medicine adapted to the personal properties of each individual, lawyers are expected to shape a 'personalised law' to cater for the personal demands and needs of the parties. According to the adherents of personalisation, both the efficiency of private law and its accommodation to the preferences of the parties support the replacement of abstract private law (to some extent) by a more 'granular' collection of norms based on big data related to the situation and the parties at hand.

The examples used in this discussion are manifold. Some focus on preferences: the contractual default rules applicable to issues on which the contract is silent could be tied in a more detailed way to the preference structures of the parties.[32] Others relate to personal abilities: the relationship between the negligence standard and the level of care demanded of each individual could be more closely related to various ability-related properties of the party.[33] Consumer law information duties could be tailored to the information needs of the individual consumer.[34] These are of course not the only available examples; one could add many more.

In this context it is important to note that even information on the financial situation of the parties is regarded as something that could be included in the Big Data that would produce the granular norms.[35] For example, it has been suggested that financial health warnings by banks should be given more easily to 'extraverted customers with low incomes'.[36] Here reference to economic status is combined with the idea of personalising private law rules on the basis of personality types.[37] Personalised law

[32] See eg (critical) PM Bender, 'Limits of Personalization of Default Rules. Towards a Normative Theory' (2020) 16 *European Review of Contract Law* 366.

[33] See eg O Ben-Shahar and A Porat, 'Personalizing Negligence Law' (2016) 91 *New York University Law Review* 627.

[34] C Busch, 'Implementing Personalized Law: Personalized Disclosures in Consumer Law and Privacy Law' (2019) 86 *The University of Chicago Law Review* 309.

[35] P Hacker, 'Personalizing EU Private Law: From Disclosures to Nudges and Mandates' (2017) 25 *European Review of Private Law* 651, 661.

[36] Busch (n 34) 319.

[37] A Porat and LJ Strahilevitz, 'Personalizing Default Rules and Disclosure with Big Data' (2014) 112 *Michigan Law Review* 1417.

clearly includes need-oriented concepts referring to the financial position and needs of the party in its toolkit.

With the help of Big Data, artificial intelligence (AI) can learn to do the necessary assessments and develop granular norms based on past experience. The flexible assessments that the use of need-oriented concepts often require can be done more consistently by using such technology. This would make the application of the rules not only more consistent than they would be when applied by human courts alone, but also more efficient, as they could more easily be applied in mass litigation and not only in general-clause-based individual assessments. This might be true at least for those types of private law cases that produce a massive amount of data, like consumer law matters. There are, however, also areas of private law in which the cases are so individual that a sufficient learning base would not be as easy to achieve.

Personalised law means more technical possibilities to expressly take into account the poor financial situation of a party in private law decision-making, in particular in areas like consumer law. Should a welfarist private law not embrace this increased opportunity to strengthen such a person-related conceptuality, in order to promote the societal advantages of pragmatism, critique and transparency related to this move?

To state the advantages and the technological possibilities, however, does not yet suffice to answer the question of how far one should go in acknowledging the different financial needs of Elon, Alice and John. One also has to look for possible reasons for rejecting such a personalised conceptuality. The opportunities of large-scale application offered by digital technology might even enhance the possible worries related to this move. What seemed like an interesting option in particular cases in which real life seemed to challenge the justice embodied in traditional conceptuality might be less attractive when moved to a multiplied AI-driven granular legal context.

When discussing the reasons not to accept person-related descriptions of the private law subject, one candidate is obvious: the principle of equality. One could also add, more generally: what about rule of law?

V. THE PROBLEM OF EQUALITY

Equality is a basic principle in any society based on the rule of law. Law should treat similar cases in a similar fashion and different cases differently, with due regard to the nature of the differences.

As the principle of equality relates to the similarity of cases, the application of it requires a comparison. What cases are so similar that they should be treated equally? The meaning of the requirement of similarity is a key issue with regard to the application of the principle. The decisive question is what keys one should use when making the comparison. In the words of Gustav Radbruch, similarity is always an abstraction made from a chosen point of view.[38] It is not self-evident

[38] G Radbruch, *Rechtsphilosophie*, 6th edn (Stuttgart, Koehler, 1963) 126.

that the keys should lie in the conceptual structures of traditional private law. One could equally well found the equality demands on a conceptuality of real-life situations. Sometimes it would even be recommendable to base the equality assessment on similarity in practical experience rather than in conceptual structures.[39] The increasing focus on situations of real life rather than conceptual structures is not as such incompatible with the principle of equality. Some have even claimed that personalised law increases equality rather than decreases it, as one should include in the comparison the different outcomes that legal rules produce for different actors:

> If certain disclosures only work for certain actors, it would seem to violate equality to knowingly apply them to those actors who do not benefit from them. If a certain default rule produces an equitable outcome for some actors, but not for others who are clearly distinguishable with the help of Big Data, equality again demands to only apply the rule to the former. By making such differences legally relevant, personalization may further equality before the law.[40]

Above I have noted that many of the examples of the law orienting itself towards real life relate to situational fragmentation. Broader concepts and rules are replaced by a variety of rules concerning particular situations. This does not seem to give rise to problems of equality (at least when the situational focus does not have indirect discriminatory effects). In identical situations the treatment is equal, but there is no real equality problem if, for example, the liability rules for different forms of transportation are not the same. The problem of equality is more urgent in cases of personalised fragmentation, when discussing for example the legal relevance of the financial situation and other personal features of the parties. How far can one go in the direction of taking into account the financial situation of the parties, without running into obvious conflict with the principle of equality? To what extent is it acceptable to apply different private law rules to Elon, Alice and John? Does it suffice that in real life their financial needs obviously are different?

To be clear, in a society that cherishes the rule of law, generality is an important feature of law.[41] Completely individualised norms, applicable to Elon, Alice or John alone, are not acceptable. I mention this self-evident fact because the principle of generality seems to be by-passed in the odd cases of named Russian oligarchs and people on the lists of terrorists. One should obviously not expand the extreme individualisation used in these cases, naming particular individuals, to other areas of law. Therefore, when I refer to Elon, Alice and John I only use them as indications of persons with certain financial properties, not as names of individual persons.

Extremely person-related granular rules in effect come close to completely individual norms, and may run into the difficulty of not fulfilling the generality

[39] For an example, see A-L Sibony, 'Data and Arguments: Empirical Research in Consumer Law' in H-W Micklitz, A-L Sibony and F Esposito (eds), *Research Methods in Consumer Law: A Handbook*, Handbook of Research Methods Series (Cheltenham-Northampton, Edward Elgar, 2018) 165, 182.

[40] Hacker (n 35) 660.

[41] In his well-known analysis of rule of law, LL Fuller, *The Morality of Law*, rev edn (New Haven, Yale University Press, 1969) ch 2 lists generality as one of its important elements.

requirement.[42] Even somewhat less granular but personalised rules are questionable from the point of view of the principle of equality. This is obvious in cases when different rules would be applicable because of particularly sensitive features, such as ethnic origin,[43] but also in other cases equality concerns seem relevant. The more granular the rules are, the less they fulfil the requirement of generality. Outside of the sensitive sector one should at least be able to produce acceptable rational reasons for the personalised differences.[44]

The equality concern seems most obvious in cases where the variations of the rules are dependent on one personal feature alone, for example on the financial position of the party. This is not to say that it is unthinkable, as the Goddesses of social security justice and tax justice regularly make such distinctions. In private law, however, it has traditionally been more difficult to accept that a clearly designated group is treated differently than other groups. In particular in the border zones between the groups, the challenge of equality is difficult. Even though one in a certain situation could give reasons for treating a less affluent party more generously than a wealthy one, a party earning €21,000 a year would feel the rules to be unequal and unjust if she received less protection than another party with the yearly income of €19,000 (supposing that the borderline between the different rules would be set at an income of €20,000). Also when speaking about ability-oriented argumentation similar doubts may occur: a party who has a master's degree would certainly feel offended if her or his ability would be assessed more severely than the ability of one with a bachelor's degree only.

The application of such detailed rules would also require the parties to refer to and present evidence on the existence of relevant personal features. The court seldom has knowledge about the details of such features.

The fact that the use of detailed personal classifications as such can be debatable[45] does not mean that one should rule out the use of such elements in legal decision-making. In the examples mentioned in section I, personalised features are relied on as a part of a broader assessment in which other factors are also included. In the Finnish tort case, the adjustment of the amount of damages because of the tortfeasor's low income and lack of property was done in a setting where the court could take into account the total damage, the concrete behaviour of the party and the financial position of the other party (an insurance company). A similar discretion is entrusted to the court with regard to the opportunity to adjust interest on delayed payments. The same in fact also goes for much traditionally ability-oriented reasoning: when concrete arguments related to the personal ability of a tortfeasor are referred to, this happens in the context of multi-faceted assessment of negligence in

[42] *cf* O Ben-Shahar and A Porat, *Personalized Law: Different Rules for Different People* (New York, Oxford University Press, 2021) 163, who argue against challenges concerning equal treatment by describing personalised law as extremely individual-centered: 'People are never put into group "bins" under personalized law; each person is a bin of one.'

[43] Bender (n 32) 400–04. Ben-Shahar and Porat (ibid) ch 8, discuss these issues in in the light of the US Constitution (the Fourteenth Amendment Equal Protection Clause).

[44] So on personalisation in general Bender (n 32) 404–05.

[45] With the exception of some more or less traditional or established exceptions, such as the rules on guardianship and the regulation of gender equality.

the concrete case. The personal factors are in both the need-oriented and the ability-oriented cases referred to as parts of a general assessment for example of fairness or negligence.[46]

In such a general assessment the scale of the personalised features is sliding. There are no clearly delimited groups to which different rules apply. The particular financial need of a party is related to other facts of the case that contribute to the determination of the relevance of the need. Such an approach seems less objectionable from the point of view of the principle of equality.

In particular, when the reasoning does not focus directly on more or less lasting financial conditions of the parties, but rather on unforeseen changes in such features, it seems even less controversial to accept the relevance of arguments related to the personal financial status of a party. Rules on social *force majeure*, supporting the debtor who cannot pay a debt in time because of unemployment, illness or similar reasons, have been discussed not only in the Nordic setting.[47] One of the core aims of a welfare state is to reduce the effects of the uncertainty of life by supporting citizens hit by unemployment, illness or similar occurrences.[48] It is not surprising that this aim can have also implications for private law. It is perhaps telling that one of the examples of possible adjustment of unfair contract terms, in Finnish law drafting work as far back as the 1950s, was that a tenant who became blind during the tenancy should be able to claim adjustment of a contract term according to which he could not have a dog in the apartment.[49]

The sliding scale and the use of the facts on the financial situation of the party in an overall assessment neutralise the equality problem by avoiding a clear delimitation of a poor group that should be treated differently. This goes for decision-making (and legal dogmatics) by humans. The proponents of an AI-based far-reaching personalisation of private law, however, might claim that all the factors that a court might take into account in a general assessment of the relevance of the financial situation of Elon, Alice and John could be clearly defined through the material processed by the AI. Be that as it may, however, there is an important drawback for such AI-based application of the general assessments: the lack of transparency. Rule of law requires open and transparent (understandable) reasoning. This may be difficult to achieve in a situation in which several elements are included in complicated algorithms that even the lawyers using them cannot properly understand. I will finish with a few words on transparency and the rule of law.

[46] In more general terms one could speak about a contradiction between formality and solidarity which, according to RM Unger, *Law in Modern Society* (New York, The Free Press, 1976) 206ff, prevents the use of formal general rules in cases such as those discussed here: 'Everything will depend on issues like the degree to which the other person has acted wrongly in the particular relationship and his ability to bear the loss that would result from the exercise of power. These are not factors that can be made the basis of rules …'.

[47] France: *délai de grâce*; Germany: already U Reifner, *Alternatives Wirtschaftsrecht am Beispiel der Verbraucherverschuldung: Realitätsverleugnung oder soziale Auslegung im Zivilrecht* (Neuwied-Darmstadt, Luchterhand, 1979).

[48] R Eräsaari, *Sosiaalivaltio ja sosiaalipolitiikan itseymmärrys* (The Social State and the Self-understanding of Social Policy), Sosiaalipoliittisen yhdistyksen tutkimuksia 43 (Helsinki, Sosiaalipoliittinen Yhdistys, 1984) 113.

[49] *Komiteanmietintö* 1957:8, 25 (the *travaux préparatoires* to the Act on Tenancy, containing a fairness clause).

VI. CONCLUSION – RULE OF LAW?

In this chapter I have looked at the tendency to endue the abstract private law subject with more flesh and blood, by including references to personal features of the parties (in particular their financial situation) in legal reasoning. One might see this tendency as an expression of a general sliding towards the use of more real-life-oriented concepts in an increasingly fragmented law, making actors of private law better equipped to adopt targeted and pragmatic solutions, to formulate a societally oriented critique and to become more transparent in legal reasoning.[50] I have therefore tried to look at the fragmentation of descriptions of legal subjects not only as a problem, but also as a challenge and opportunity. At the same time, however, one should acknowledge that a straightforward use of personalised arguments has more or less obvious drawbacks as well.

It is problematic, at least from the point of view of the principle of equality. A detailed set of granular rules that would be different for clearly defined groups of parties – such as has been suggested by some proponents of personalised law – seems difficult to accept as such. On the other hand, it seems less objectionable to use arguments related to the financial position of a party as just one relevant fact in more general legal assessments. As far as a court is in a position to assess the fairness of a transaction or of a claim for compensation, it seems more natural to include person-related arguments in the assessment. Furthermore, in cases of changed personal circumstances the resort to personalised arguments seems more easily digestible.

This moderate approach is based on the acknowledgement of the weight of the principle of equality in the present context. A moderate acceptance of arguments related to the differences between Elon, Alice and John may also be challenged, like all real-life oriented flexible solutions, by other elements of the rule of law. The examples of subject variations raise the question how the legal order can and should cope with flexible personalisation, without losing the advantages of a rule of law-abiding and predictable Goddess of Justice.

This is not the place to dive into deep theoretical questions concerning the meaning of the rule of law, but I will mention one way that can, at least somewhat, help diminish the challenge that relates to the greater emphasis on flexible real-life concepts in legal reasoning: the transparency of legal reasoning. I have found it worthwhile to note it here, as it has a direct bearing on the discussion on AI-based personalisation.

Among other things, the rule of law requires a legal decision-making that both lawyers and citizens feel not to be arbitrary.[51] One way of reducing arbitrariness is to focus on the quality of the reasoning in which a decision-maker uses personalised arguments. In an uncertain epistemological and ethical environment in which new needs and challenges constantly arise and law becomes increasingly flexible, one is forced to seek the needed legal certainty in the predictability of arguments

[50] I have based my discussion of these issues on my book *Free Movement of Legal Ideas: Towards a Dynamic Europeanisation of Private Law* (Oxford, Hart Publishing, 2024).

[51] So eg J Raz, 'The Law's Own Virtue' (2019) 39 *Oxford Journal of Legal Studies* 1.

and ways of reasoning. A responsibility to provide sufficient and transparent legal reasons would offer at least some protection against arbitrary decision-making. Many scholars, in various contexts, have indeed commented on the need to connect legal certainty to quality of reasoning rather than predictability of results. Sufficient and open reasoning is seen as an important pillar of the rule of law in contemporary private law.[52]

In other words, a radically increased openness and transparency of reasoning can be understood as one of the keys to preserving the value of rule of law in a more flexible and real-life-oriented private law. If Elon, Alice and John are treated differently in a general assessment of the fairness of a certain outcome, the reason for this should be clearly explained. Only in this way may one ensure that the Goddess of Justice does not go too far in her observation of real life. As mentioned above, this is also a reason why AI-driven personalisation of complex decision-making may be difficult to accept, as not even the lawyers directly involved in the decision-making may sufficiently understand the algorithms to make the decision-making transparent. In addition, moral-psychological research indicates that people find it easier to accept assessments made by other humans than by robots.[53]

One may support the openness of reasoning by the creation of concepts that attract proper attention to the opportunity of personalised argumentation. Such conceptualisation would probably make the use of personalised arguments more acceptable, but also more transparent as part of the standardised legal language. As I alluded to above, however, one should not necessarily attempt to define such personalised concepts in some exact detailed way. Concepts relating to the poor financial situation of a party could function as triggers and headings when personalised issues are discussed as elements of more general assessments. In this vein one could use, for example, the above-mentioned concepts 'debtor with limited means', 'debtor in need of housing', 'low income debtor', 'unemployed debtor', 'ill debtor' and a 'debtor burdened with considerable maintenance liabilities'. The acceptance of such concepts as legal concepts would mean a step towards a closer connection of the language of private law to the challenges of real life, of the legal roles to the roles of real life.

[52] See eg HP Graver, 'Fornuft og følelser – om klassisk retorikk som modell for moderne juridisk metode' (2007) 120 *Tidsskrift for Rettsvitenskap* 527, 558, who in his analysis of legal rhetoric claims that an open account of possible arguments that seem credible in the legal context makes it easier to foresee in what direction legal decision-makers may be convinced to move in the future; E Paunio, *Legal Certainty in Multilingual EU Law: Language, Discourse and Reasoning at the European Court of Justice* (Farnham, Ashgate, 2013) 136, who, discussing legal certainty and multilingualism, speaks about a 'discursive legal certainty' that understands legal decision-making and legal reasoning as a communicative process in which for example a court communicates a message to its addressees; and J Smits, 'Plurality of Sources in European Private Law, or: How to Live With Legal Diversity?' in R Brownsword, H-W Micklitz, L Niglia and S Weatherill (eds), *The Foundations of European Private Law* (Oxford-Portland, Hart Publishing, 2011) 323, 334, who stresses that in European law one should 'move away from a focus on rules, principles and concepts (all key elements of a legal system) towards an identification of *arguments* for and against certain solutions'.

[53] See eg the interesting study by M Laakasuo et al, 'Moral psychology of nursing robots, Exploring the role of robots in dilemmas of patient autonomy' (2022) 54 *European Journal of Social Psychology* 108, doi.org/10.1002/ejsp 2890 (on decisions on forced medication). A feeling of being treated with respect and dignity may require the acceptance of a certain amount of individualised discretion: D Kahneman, O Sibony and CR Sunstein, *Noise: A Flaw in Human Judgment* (London, HarperCollins, 2021) 327.

Part III

Technology

11

Treating AI as a Legal Person: Simply a Means to a Regulatory End?

ROGER BROWNSWORD*

I. INTRODUCTION

According to Stuart Russell, if we were to recognise an artificial intelligence (AI)-enabled device as *itself* legally responsible for whatever damage has been caused, this would be a 'needless and even absurd elevation of the status of robots'.[1] Moreover, Russell claims, there is 'a danger that the increased use of machines in decisions affecting people will degrade the status and dignity of humans'.[2]

In this chapter, my focal question is whether we should recognise AI, or decentralised autonomous organisations (DAOs),[3] or indeed any smart technology as legal persons. However, I will reduce the sting of Russell's first point by narrowing the question so that we exclude both criminal law and public law. Hence, our question can be phrased as follows: *with reference to private law rules and private law relationships*, should we treat AI as a legal person?

If we follow the Hohfeldian mapping of private law relationships, 'legal person' is a place-holder for those who are parties to four basic legal relationships: right-duty; privilege (liberty)-no right; power-liability; and immunity-disability.[4] So, if we treat AI as a legal person, it can be placed on either side of all these relationships. For example, AI, as a legal person, might be treated as having claim rights or, correlatively, as having duties; or, it might be treated as having a power or, correlatively, as having a liability. Moreover, once we treat AI as a legal person, we might find that AI is: (i) the party on both sides of the particular legal relationship; (ii) the party on

* King's College London and Bournemouth University.

[1] S Russell, *Human Compatible: Artificial Intelligence and The Problem of Control* (London, Penguin Books, 2020) 126.

[2] ibid 126–27.

[3] The Law Commission is seeking to clarify the status of DAOs. See, Law Commission, 'Decentralised autonomous organisations (DAOs): Call for evidence' (November 2022), s3-eu-west-2.amazonaws.com/lawcom-prod-storage-11jsxou24uy7q/uploads/2022/11/DAOs-Call-for-Evidence-LC.pdf.

[4] WN Hohfeld, *Fundamental Legal Conceptions as Applied in Judicial Reasoning, and Other Legal Essays* (New Haven, Yale University Press, 1920).

just one side of the legal relationship (the other party being, for example, a human or a corporation); or (iii) not a party on either side of the relationship.

To propose that AI should be recognised as a legal person in these private law relationships goes beyond more limited proposals to recognise AI as a legal person only in some particular private law relationships – for example, only as a duty bearer where the rights holder is a human who is a claimant in an action for breach of contract or for negligence, or only as a right-holder for the purposes of copyright or patents[5] – or only in some particular context (such as insurance, where AI might feature in a progressively automated process of both making and dealing with applications, claims and complaints).[6] Nevertheless, in this chapter, I will assume that the proposal is for a more radical general recognition of AI as a legal person in private law relationships in the way that I have already outlined.

Given this proposal, how should we respond to it? In section II, I sketch two kinds of response.[7] One response, reflecting a human-centric coherentist view will resist treating AI as a legal person; the other response, reflecting a regulatory view, will be guided by whether such treatment of AI would be instrumental in serving specified policies. So, for example, while human-centric coherentism will push back against AI being treated as an IP rights-holder, regulatory thinking might lead to a different view if such treatment of AI would serve the policy objectives of patent and copyright law (such as supporting beneficial invention and innovation, nurturing new creative industries, and so on).[8] Or, again, if policy favours expedition in the settlement of insurance claims, regulators might see some advantage in treating claims-settling AI as a legal person.

In section III, I raise the question of whether what seems like a progressive regulatory instrumentalism might prove to be a hostage to fortune. Here, my argument aligns with Russell's caution that we need to be careful about handing over decisions to machines because this might degrade the status and dignity of humans. One way of articulating this concern is that a regulatory readiness to transpose concepts from human-centric contexts to technological contexts – such as the transposition not only of the concept of a legal person but also the concepts of autonomy, trust, justice, and respect, and so on – might be corrosive of human values. A second expression of concern is that the instrumental reason that is characteristic of the regulatory view might come to dominate and crowd out the human-centric principle that we should treat fellow humans with equal concern and respect, never simply as a means, but always as an end.

In both cases, the reservation about governance that is centred on regulatory-instrumentalist thinking is that it might have the effect of decentring not just humans

[5] For discussion of the latter, see, eg, S Chesterman, *We the Robots? Regulating Artificial Intelligence and the Limits of the Law* (Cambridge, Cambridge University Press, 2021).

[6] For a vision of the future, see R Balasubramanian, A Libarikian and D McElhaney, 'Insurance 2030 – The impact of AI on the future of insurance' (12 March 2021), www.mckinsey.com/industries/financial-services/our-insights/insurance-2030-the-impact-of-ai-on-the-future-of-insurance.

[7] *cf* B Bennett and A Daly, 'Recognising rights for robots: Can we? Will we? Should we?' (2020) 12 *Law, Innovation and Technology* 60.

[8] *cf* R Abbott, *The Reasonable Robot: Artificial Intelligence and The Law* (Cambridge, Cambridge University Press, 2020) ch 4.

but humans who have moral aspirations for themselves and their community, as well as governance that is orientated towards fairness and justice. Of course, it is not suggested that regulatory-instrumentalist legal thinking will *necessarily* have this effect or that it will be *sufficient* to have this effect; and, nor is it suggested that the recognition of AI as a legal person will have this effect. Nevertheless, given what we know about the disruptive effect of new technologies, the development and adoption of which can be facilitated by regulatory thinking, we need to address the proposal in question with our eyes wide open.[9]

There are two take-home messages in the chapter. The first is that there is more to the insistence that AI should be applied only in human-centric ways than that AI should never be applied in ways that are harmful to, or that present significant risks to, human interests. We might also want to insist that our thinking about the concept of a legal person and, concomitantly, our response to the proposal, does not lose sight of the centrality of humans (and of basic human values) to our understanding of legal relations. The second take-home is that, while the decision to treat AI as a legal person – even where a distinction is already accepted between legal persons who are 'natural' (humans) and those that are 'artificial' – would surely be a significant one, and while it might have consequences that we do not anticipate or welcome, it is the underlying regulatory thinking that drives the decision that presents the deeper challenge to human-centric governance and ethical applications of AI.

II. TWO RESPONSES

Our question is: *with reference to private law rules and private law relationships*, should we treat AI as a legal person? I suggest that lawyers will respond in two rather different ways. One response, by legal coherentists, is that legal doctrine is largely predicated on legal persons being human, from which it follows that AI should not be treated as a legal person – at any rate, not unless some ad hoc correction is required for the sake of fairness, justice or reasonableness.[10] By contrast, the other response is that the answer to the question depends purely and simply on whether treating AI as a legal person (at least as the default position) would be instrumentally rational relative

[9] There are many ways in which law might be 'disrupted'. It might be that the application of traditional legal doctrines, concepts, templates, classifications, and the like, to novel phenomena or circumstances associated with a new technology is problematic. Or, it might be that the disruption impacts on legal practice, on what we do and how we do it; or, that the disruptive impact is on our conceptual thinking, our values, or our attitudes, and so on. For discussion, see, eg, R Brownsword, 'Law and Technology: Two Modes of Disruption, Three Legal Mind-Sets, and the Big Picture of Regulatory Responsibilities' (2018) 14 *Indian Journal of Law and Technology* 1; 'Law Disrupted, Law Re-imagined, Law Re-invented' (2019) 1 *Technology and Regulation* 10; 'Political Disruption, Technological Disruption, and the Future of EU Private Law' in M Durovic and T Tridimas (eds), *New Directions in EU Private Law* (Oxford, Hart, 2021) 7, and 'Law, authority, and respect: three waves of technological disruption' (2022) 14 *Law, Innovation and Technology* 5. Moreover, rather like the process of coastal erosion, we should not conceive of disruption as a discrete event that happens at a particular point at a particular time: *cf* HY Liu, MM Maas, J Danaher, L Scarcella, M Lexer and L Van Rompey, 'Artificial Intelligence and Legal Disruption: A New Model for Analysis' (2020) 12 *Law, Innovation and Technology* 205.

[10] SD Warren and L Brandeis, 'The Right to Privacy' (1890) 4 *Harvard Law Review* 193.

to specified regulatory policies and objectives.[11] Whilst, for legal coherentists, the question is to be decided as a matter of principle, for regulatory lawyers, it is simply a matter of what serves policy.

Although I have sketched the contrast between coherentist and regulatory thinking in several other places,[12] I have not done so specifically with our current question in the spotlight. So, some words of elaboration are in order, first for coherentist and then for regulatory thinking.

A. The Coherentist Response

We can elaborate the coherentist response in three respects: by recalling the salient characteristics of the coherentist way of legal thinking; by reflecting on its implicitly human-centric understanding of law; and by spelling out what this means for its take on legal persons other than humans.

i. Coherentism: Salient Characteristics

For present purposes, we can identify six salient characteristics of coherentist legal thinking as follows.

First, for coherentists, what matters above all is the integrity and internal consistency of legal doctrine. Doctrinal coherence is viewed as desirable in and of itself. Secondly, coherentists believe that legal reasoning should be anchored to guiding general principles of law. As Ronald Dworkin famously put it 'judicial decisions in civil cases, even in hard cases …, characteristically are and should be generated by principle not policy'.[13] Thirdly, coherentists are not concerned with the fitness of the law for its regulatory purpose. To be sure, coherentists will recognise that there has to be some scope for doctrinal 'correction' or adjustment where the application of the general principles leads to outcomes that are manifestly 'unacceptable' (relative to community standards of fairness, justice and reasonableness). Nevertheless, this is distinguishable from initiating policy or making decisions about the priorities between competing policy objectives.[14] Fourthly, coherentists approach new technologies by asking how they fit within existing legal categories

[11] *cf* Abbott (n 8), who advocates 'a principle of *AI legal neutrality* asserting that the law should not discriminate between AI and human behavior' (3). While legal neutrality would not serve as a 'dispositive policymaking principle', it should be regarded as 'an appropriate default that may be departed from where there are good reasons for doing so' (4). According to Abbott, 'application of AI legal neutrality will help the law better achieve its underlying goals – whether promoting competition, improving safety, incentivizing innovation, or reducing antisocial behaviour' (134). However, Abbott does not advocate that AI should have 'rights or legal personhood' (4). In the present context, the neutrality principle would provide that, where AI is undertaking functions which either have been or could be undertaken by humans, and where those functions and their performance by humans is significant relative to the code of private law, then the AI should be treated in precisely the same way that a human would be.

[12] Brownsword (2018) (n 9) 1; *Law, Technology and Society: Re-imagining the Regulatory Environment* (Abingdon, Routledge, 2019); and *Law 3.0: Rules, Regulation and Technology* (Abingdon, Routledge, 2020).

[13] RM Dworkin, *Taking Rights Seriously*, rev edn (London, Duckworth, 1978) 84.

[14] *cf Thaler v Comptroller General of Patents Trade Marks and Designs* [2021] EWCA Civ 1374, where the members of the Court of Appeal were clear that, given both the history and the scheme of the Patents

(and then try hard to fit them in) – for example, developments in biotechnology, in information technology and in cryptotechnology, have raised (coherentist) questions about the way in which fundamental concepts and distinctions in property law map onto a range of 'things', such as cell lines, gametes, personal data and cryptoassets. Fifthly, coherentists assume that the function of private law, together with its guiding principles, is largely concerned with ex post correction and compensation. Sixthly, for coherentists, legal doctrine and the legitimacy of law are self-contained. Some legal principles and doctrines (such as 'good faith' in contract law) invite ethical elaboration; however, ethical and moral evaluation of the law is 'externalised'. The legitimacy of the law does not turn on Kantian criteria of duty, or Rawlsian criteria of right, or a Benthamite view of the good; these are external standards formulated beyond the boundaries of legal doctrine.

For coherentists, the focus is on the recognised legal concepts, categories and classifications; and this is accompanied by a certain reluctance to abandon these concepts, categories and classifications with a view to contemplating a bespoke response.[15] For example, rather than recognise new types of intellectual property, coherentists will prefer to tweak existing laws of patents and copyright. Similarly, in transactions, coherentists (guided by existing law) will want to classify emails as either instantaneous or non-instantaneous forms of communication (or transmission); they will want to apply the standard contracts template to online shopping sites; they will want to draw on traditional notions of agency in order to engage electronic agents and smart machines; and they will want to classify individual 'prosumers' and 'hobbyists' who buy and sell on new platforms (such as platforms that support trade in 3D printed goods) as either business sellers or consumers. As the infrastructure for transactions and interactions becomes ever more technological, the tension between this strand of common law coherentism and regulatory thinking becomes all the more apparent.

In sum, while coherentism exemplifies many of the virtues of what we understand by 'legalism' – and, for this reason, many will see no reason to apologise for it – it presupposes a world of, at most, leisurely change. It belongs to the age of the horse, not to the age of the autonomous vehicle or of algorithmic trading or of other AI applications.

ii. Human-centricity

In the above list of salient characteristics, I have not suggested that coherentism explicitly presupposes that law is a human-centric enterprise or, indeed, favours a particular conception of human-centric governance. Nevertheless, coherentism implicitly presupposes that law is the enterprise of subjecting human conduct to the governance of rules and principles. It goes without saying that the legal persons whose conduct is to be subjected to governance (including those who have governance responsibilities) are, paradigmatically, humans.

Act 1977, it was only a person who could be treated as the inventor, the Court reaching its conclusion 'without any need to examine the policy arguments raised by both parties' ([55] Birss LJ). Following the Court of Appeal's decision, there was an unsuccessful appeal to the UK Supreme Court; see [2023] UKSC 49.

[15] *cf* B Latour, *The Making of Law: An Ethnography of the Conseil d'Etat* (Cambridge, Polity Press, 2010) ch 4.

This, however, is not the end of it. Coherentism, I suggest, also assumes that legal rules reflect (or cohere with) some very basic (non-controversial) principles of social ordering in human communities. These principles, which include taking reasonable care, being truthful, keeping one's promises, and so on, shape the reasonable expectations that humans have in their dealings with one another. In this way, coherentist thinking presupposes a degree of alignment between the formal legal order and informal traditional rules.

iii. Legal Persons

In the light of the above, how will coherentists respond to the proposal to treat AI as a legal person? Quite simply, they will resist such a proposal unless they believe that it would be contradictory for them to resist such an extension or that, by failing to extend the classes of legal persons, the law is complicit in endorsing manifestly unacceptable results.

Given the human-centricity of legal coherentism, the argument from doctrinal contradiction is unlikely to have any traction: AI simply does not relate to humans in the way that humans relate to one another. Granted, AI can be trained to predict how humans will act, but there is more to human reasonable expectation than prediction; even if the prediction proves wrong, the expectation might still be judged to be reasonable (not as a prediction that has some basis but as a justified view about how another legal person *ought* to act).

If the argument is that the failure to recognise AI as a legal person is having unacceptable results – for example, if the use of AI is causing harm to the interests that human have in their person, property or personality, and if there is no human who can be identified as being in breach of a legal duty – then coherentists might be persuaded that AI should be treated as being subject to an appropriate duty of care so that those humans who are harmed can identify a relevant legal person to hold to account and from whom compensation can be sought. That said, the treatment of AI as having this particular legal duty would not yet amount to a general recognition of AI as a legal person; and, even in the particular case, there might need to be some regulatory intervention to set the framework for compensation so that the corelative legal rights of humans are effective.

B. The Regulatory Response

We can elaborate the regulatory response in three respects: by recalling the salient characteristics of the regulatory way of legal thinking; by considering whether and in what sense its understanding of law is human-centric; and by spelling out what this means for its take on legal persons other than humans.

i. The Regulatory View: Salient Characteristics

In contrast with coherentism, we can treat the following seven features as salient characteristics of regulatory thinking.

First, regulatory thinking is not concerned with the internal consistency of legal doctrine. When those who take a regulatory view raise questions about consistency, they are typically making sure that particular regulatory interventions will complement others in serving specified regulatory objectives.[16] Secondly, this view is entirely focused on whether the law is instrumentally effective in serving specified regulatory purposes. In regulatory circles, no one asks whether the law is 'coherent' – other than in the sense of asking whether a group of related interventions pushes in the required regulatory direction;[17] rather, the central question is whether the legal rules work. Thirdly, regulatory thinking has no reservation about creating new classificatory schemes or categories, or enacting new bespoke laws if this is an effective and efficient response to a question raised by new technologies.[18] Fourthly, the anchoring points for the regulatory approach are not the general principles that are established in the jurisprudence but current policy purposes and objectives. Fifthly, alongside its policy focus, the regulatory approach in relation to new technologies tends to be orientated towards striking an acceptable balance between benefits and risks.[19] Sixthly, the tilt of the risk-management mindset that goes with regulatory thinking is towards *ex ante* prevention rather than ex post correction. Seventhly, although regulatory thinking does not externalise ethics and morality, it tends to subordinate the legitimacy of regulatory positions to their effectiveness in achieving specified policy objectives. What regulatees might think about the legitimacy of regulatory processes and positions is relevant only to the extent that it bears on the effectiveness of the law.

The regulatory view is, thus, the (democratically) mandated language of legislators, policy-makers, and regulatory agencies. Conversely, while judges might have some responsibility for applying the spirit of policy-driven legislation, it is precisely the initiation and setting of regulatory policy that we think falls beyond the mandate of unaccountable judges.

The regulatory approach is not only policy-focused, but also relentlessly instrumentally rational. The question is: what works; what will serve certain specified purposes? When a regulatory intervention does not work, it is not enough to restore the status quo; rather, further regulatory measures should be taken, learning from previous experience, with a view to realising the regulatory purposes more effectively. Hence, the purpose of the criminal law is not simply to respond to wrongdoing (as corrective justice demands), but to reduce crime by adopting whatever measures of deterrence promise to work. Similarly, in a safety-conscious community, the purpose

[16] See, eg, the European Commission's proposal for an AI Liability Directive ('Proposal for a Directive of the European Parliament and of the Council on adapting non-contractual civil liability rules to artificial intelligence (AI Liability Directive)') COM(2022) 496 final, 2–3 (Consistency with existing policy provisions in the policy area).

[17] Again, see the proposal for an AI Liability Directive (ibid) 3–4 (Consistency with other Union policies).

[18] *cf* the Law Commission's Consultation Paper on 'Digital assets' (Law Com No 256, 28 July 2022) in which it is provisionally proposed that, the resilience and flexibility of English common law notwithstanding, a new 'third category' of 'data objects' should be recognised, this being distinct from the categories of personal property as either things in possession or things in action: available at s3-eu-west-2.amazonaws.com/lawcom-prod-storage-11jsxou24uy7q/uploads/2022/07/Digital-Assets-Consultation-Paper-Law-Commission-1.pdf.

[19] Again, see the proposal for an AI Liability Directive (n 16) 6 (Proportionality) and 7–8 (Stakeholder consultations).

of tort law is not simply to provide a compensatory response to wrongdoing, but to deter practices and acts where agents could easily avoid creating risks of injury and damage. For those lawyers who are regulatory-instrumentalists, the path of the law should be progressive: we should be getting better at regulating crime and improving levels of safety.

According to Edward Rubin, in the modern administrative state, the 'standard for judging the value of law is not whether it is coherent but rather whether it is effective, that is, effective in establishing and implementing the policy goals of the modern state'.[20] Certainly, one of the striking features of the EU has been the regulatory spirit that has informed the single market project and that continues now in the digital Europe project. As the Commission puts it:

> The pace of commercial and technological change due to digitalisation is very fast, not only in the EU, but worldwide. The EU needs to act now to ensure that business standards and consumer rights will be set according to common EU rules respecting a high-level of consumer protection and providing for a modern business friendly environment. It is of utmost necessity to create the framework allowing the benefits of digitalisation to materialise, so that EU businesses can become more competitive and consumers can have trust in high-level EU consumer protection standards. By acting now, the EU will set the policy trend and the standards according to which this important part of digitalisation will happen.[21]

Post-Brexit, regulators in the UK will pursue similar objectives in their own way but, in both the EU and the UK, we can expect the coherence of the law with traditional legal principles to be very much a secondary concern.

Last but not least, it is characteristic of the regulatory approach that the thinking becomes much more risk-focused – as, of course, is the case with the EU's Regulation on AI.[22] In the criminal law and in torts, the risks that need to be assessed and managed relate primarily to physical and psychological injury and to damage to property and reputation; in contract law, it is economic risks that are relevant. So, for example, we see in the development of product liability a scheme of acceptable risk management that responds to the circulation of products (such as cars or new drugs) that are beneficial but also potentially dangerous. However, this response is still in the form of a revised *rule* (it is not yet technocratic); and it is still in the nature of an ex post correction (it is not yet *ex ante* preventive). Nevertheless, it is only a short step from here to a greater investment in *ex ante* regulatory checks (for food and drugs, chemicals, and so on) and to the use of new technologies as preventive regulatory instruments.

[20] EL Rubin, 'From Coherence to Effectiveness' in R van Gestel, HW Micklitz, and EL Rubin (eds), *Rethinking Legal Scholarship* (New York, Cambridge University Press, 2017) 310–50, 328.

[21] European Commission, 'Digital contracts for Europe – Unleashing the potential of e-commerce' (Communication from the Commission to the European Parliament, the Council and the European Economic and Social Committee) COM(2015) 633 final, 7.

[22] OJ L 2024/1689, 12.7.2024. See, too, European Commission (2021) Explanatory Memorandum to the proposed Regulation on AI COM(2021) 206 final 2021/0106(COD), eur-lex.europa.eu/legal-content/EN/TXT/HTML/?uri=CELEX:52021PC0206&from=EN; and R Brownsword, 'AI and Fundamental Rights: the People, the Conversations, and the Governance Challenges' in D Moura Vicente, S de Vasconcelos Casimiro and C Chen (eds), *The Legal Challenges of the Fourth Industrial Revolution: The European Union's Digital Strategy*, Law, Governance and Technology Series 57 (Cham, Springer, 2023) 335.

In other words, it is only a short step from risk-managing regulatory-instrumentalist thinking to a more technocratic mind-set – a mind-set that seeks technological solutions to regulatory puzzles.

ii. Human-centricity

Regulatory thinking is certainly human-centric to the extent that it is orientated towards serving the purposes and policies of human communities. When the conditions for human communities are fairly static, the order established by legal rules will need little attention. However, as the conditions change – particularly where new technologies prompt disruption – so order needs to be more dynamic and legal rules need to be more responsive; and this means that legal thinking needs to become more regulatory. In such conditions, lawmakers need to ask, in a regulatory way, whether the legal rules of an earlier order are fit for purpose, especially whether they properly incentivise and support beneficial innovation while also safeguarding members of the community against unacceptable risks.[23]

In this spirit, the development of the limited liability company and the recognition of corporations as legal persons can be seen as regulatory initiatives designed, inter alia, to manage personal financial risk, and to encourage innovation and enterprise in increasingly technological societies – not so much a matter of coherentist logic as one of practical politics and economic efficiency.[24]

Taking this a step further, regulatory thinking can evolve in ways that, quite conspicuously, depart from the idea that the legal person is paradigmatically a human agent or that legal relations are paradigmatically between humans. Thus, we are now in a technology-sensitised period when consideration is being given to the use of AI as a tool for governance purposes, and to undertake legal and regulatory functions.[25] Legal officials and decision-makers give way to AI. Whether we associate LegalTech or RegTech with an extension of the category of legal persons, they are certainly harbingers of humans being less centrally involved in governance (and in those whose actions are subject to governance).

iii. Legal Persons

In a world in which governance is dominated by smart, connected machines, a world driven by regulatory policy, it would seem anachronistic to insist that only humans

[23] *cf* R Brownsword, 'Legal Regulation of Technology: Supporting Innovation, Managing Risk and Respecting Values' in T Pittinsky (ed), *Science, Technology and Society: New Perspectives and Directions* (New York, Cambridge University Press, 2019) 109–37, 109.

[24] *cf* Abbott (n 8), who remarks that the legal rights of corporations in relation to contracts and property 'exist only to improve the efficiency of human activities such as commerce and entrepreneurship' (4). The regulatory *raison d'être* for corporate legal personality, together with its distinctive separation of the company and its owners as well as its limited liability, merits an article in its own right; but, for further reflection, see *Salomon v A. Salomon and Co* [1897] AC 22; J Dewey, 'The Historic Background of Corporate Legal Personality' (1926) 35 *Yale Law Journal* 655; J Freedman, 'Small Businesses and the Corporate Form: Burden or Privilege?' (1994) 57 *MLR* 555; P Ireland, 'Limited Liability, Shareholder Rights, and the Problem of Corporate Irresponsibility' (2010) 34 *Cambridge Journal of Economics* 837.

[25] In other words, we are in the period of Law 3.0, see Brownsword (2020) (n 12).

can be legal persons. However, the regulatory view is not so much a refusal to be anachronistic as an insistence on treating the law as a tool to serve regulatory policy. Law is a means not an end in itself. It follows that concepts like that of a legal person are also means and the ends to be served are set by regulatory policies.

Of course, it does not follow from this that AI should be recognised as a legal person across the whole sweep of private law. Rather, it might well depend on the particular regulatory policy and the facts. For example, regulators might favour recognising AI as an inventor for the purposes of patent law but not as an author for the purposes of copyright law. So, although the regulatory view is likely to be more receptive than the coherentist view to our proposal for legal persons in private law, it might be quite selective and nuanced in treating AI as a legal person. And, it might also be quite selective in recognising AI as legal person with particular attributes in legal relationships. For example, it might recognise that AI can have duties as a legal person, but not rights.[26] However, none of this indicates any hesitation about accepting the general idea that we might recognise AI as a legal person; rather, the hesitation is merely about so recognising AI in a particular case.

III. TWO TROUBLING FUTURES

Let me start this section with a caveat about law and politics. While my instinct is that the regulatory approach asks the right questions as we attempt to govern AI or other new technologies, it does not follow that the political branch, reasoning in a regulatory way, is a better bet than the judicial branch and others reasoning in a coherentist way. Regulatory reasoning might pose the right questions, it might invite consideration of all governance options, and it might have the agility and responsiveness that coherentism lacks, but politics is politics. Even with better resourcing than the judicial branch, the political branch might not bring the same level of rigour and acuity to its reasoning as the judicial branch, and it certainly does not have the same independence or insulation against lobbying and other pressures. Moreover, regulators might overreach in trying to micro-manage matters that are better left to private agreement. Still, at least a regulatory approach has the scope to ask the right questions: namely, whether the law is fit for purpose, whether governance is broadly acceptable, and whether proposed applications of new technologies are compatible with the fundamental values of the community. So, my preference for *regulatory* thinking is a qualified one.

Nevertheless, looking ahead and echoing Russell, the rise of regulatory thinking might provoke concern about two troubling futures: one future, already here, is that we uncritically (and for instrumental reasons) project our human-centred moral concepts (such as autonomy, trust, justification, respect, etc) onto new technologies, including AI devices and systems, losing – or at least diluting – the meaning of such concepts in this translation; and the other future is one in which humans, having

[26] See, further, Abbott and neutrality (n 11).

narrowed their thinking to the regulatory approach lose sight of the importance of human values, of moral and ethical reason, and compromise their dignity.[27] Humans who reason predominantly (or, in future, perhaps, only) in a regulatory way might find that they are instrumentalised by both fellow humans and AI; but, long before that, if moral reason has been marginalised, the damage has already been done – to decentre human dignity is to decentre humans.

At this stage of the argument, it looks like we face a fork – one pathway is coherentist, the other is regulatory – and we have reservations about whichever path we choose. I will return to this fork, but the next step is to elaborate our dual concerns about the implications for humans if we allow regulatory reasoning to drive the argument for recognising AI or other technologies as legal persons.

A. Conceptual Transposition

Our human-centric notion of law envisages a certain mode of governance that serves the basic needs of groups of humans for order, stability, security and predictability. Moreover, the rules that structure the order are made by humans for humans and they bind both those who govern and those who are governed.

So, we start with the idea that law is a human enterprise; that those who govern will do so by reference to rules (there will be a code of conduct); and that humans as agents have the capacity to make choices about how they relate to others (whether to respect them, to trust them, to treat them fairly) and, concomitantly, about their compliance with the rules. Moreover, it is implicit in this concept of the legal enterprise that humans can be called to account for their choices (including for non-compliance with the rules) and that they should justify their conduct.

In line with this starting point, Amnon Reichman and Giovanni Sartor insist that

> central to the notion of law in a liberal democracy is its human nature: it is a product of human agency, its values and goals should reflect care for human agency, and its application should ultimately be at the hands of humans exercising agency … [To be sure, as some jurists suggest,] the question of legal validity, scope, and operative meaning of a particular rule as considered for application in a given set of facts cannot be fully separated from the underlying values embedded in the rule (as part of a set of rules and principles, governing a given field of human interaction). If this is indeed the case, discretion is a feature, not a bug. It is not clear that we can fully separate the question of 'what is the operative meaning of the rule with respect to a particular set of facts' from the question 'should we enforce that meaning in the given set of facts'. In that respect, would we rather have bureaucrats fully automated, without seeing the unique circumstances before them – the human being (not only the case number), applying for the exercise of state power (or its withdrawal) in a particular case? Certainly, there is a risk that relaxing the technical commitment to the

[27] *cf* R Brownsword, 'Human Dignity, Human Rights, and Simply Trying to Do the Right Thing' in C McCrudden (ed), *Understanding Human Dignity* (Proceedings of the British Academy 192) (Oxford, The British Academy and Oxford University Press, 2013) 345.

> conventional meaning of rules will result in biases or favouritisms, as may be the case when human judgment is exercised. But the alternative, namely removing all ambiguity from the system, may result in detaching law from its human nature, by removing agency and by supposing that codes can adequately cover all circumstances, and that human language is capable of capturing 'the reality' in a transparent, technical manner. The latter assumption is difficult to support.[28]

However, in our technological time, the human-centric view of law is challenged by a view of governance that relies far more heavily on technologies. In our modern communities, humans have at their disposal not only a range of technologies that can be deployed for regulatory purposes but also a perception that such tools might be more effective than rules.[29]

If a community is to smooth the passage from governance by humans and governance by rules to governance by technologies such as AI, it might suggest some continuity by transposing key concepts that inform our thinking about law as a human enterprise. We can see this happening with the concepts of trust and trustworthiness, with the idea of respect for the law, with autonomy, and with justice.

i. Trustworthy Technologies

Introducing what was then the proposed Regulation on AI, the European Commission explained that its purpose was to deliver

> an ecosystem of trust by proposing a legal framework for trustworthy AI. The proposal is based on EU values and fundamental rights and aims to give people and other users the confidence to embrace AI-based solutions, while encouraging businesses to develop them. AI should be a tool for people and be a force for good in society with the ultimate aim of increasing human well-being.[30]

At much the same time, in a press release, the Commission quoted Margrethe Vestager, Executive Vice-President for a Europe fit for the Digital Age, as saying: 'On Artificial Intelligence, trust is a must, not a nice to have. With these landmark rules, the EU is spearheading the development of new global norms to make sure AI can be trusted'.[31] Despite this commitment to trustworthy AI, the draft Regulation did not explicitly elaborate this *desideratum* (although, implicitly, the conspicuous focus on managing risks suggests that AI is trustworthy when it would be reasonable to judge that the risks it presents are acceptable). Moreover, when the focus shifts to trustworthy *humans* (in the provisions on the social scoring of humans), there is again no definition or elaboration.[32] Should we assume that the criteria for judging a human to be

[28] A Reichman and G Sartor, 'Algorithms and Regulation' in HW Micklitz, O Pollicino, A Reichman, A Simoncini, G Sartor and G De Gregorio (eds), *Constitutional Challenges in the Algorithmic Society* (Cambridge, Cambridge University Press, 2021) 131, 158.

[29] As developed in Brownsword (2020) (n 12).

[30] European Commission 'Explanatory Memorandum' (n 22).

[31] European Commission 'Europe fit for the Digital Age: Commission proposes new rules and actions for excellence and trust in Artificial Intelligence' Press release (21 April 2021), ec.europa.eu/commission/presscorner/detail/en/ip_21_1682. Similarly, see the proposal for an AI Liability Directive (n 16) *passim*.

[32] *cf* M Veale and FZ. Borgesius, 'Demystifying the Draft EU Artificial Intelligence Act' (2021) 22 *Computer Law Review International* 97, 100.

trustworthy are identical to those that are relevant to judging that AI is trustworthy? Or, is this trying to compare, so to speak, apples with oranges?

In another context, following the global financial crisis in 2008, one response to the loss of trust and confidence in banks and other financial intermediaries was to devise decentralised systems that would take out human intermediaries and their institutions, and place our trust in technologies for transfer of digital assets (instead of fiat currency) and registration that would make use of the best cryptography. Such was the promise of blockchain.[33]

However, trust in technology is not equivalent to trust in fellow humans.[34] To trust a person to do the right thing (or indeed to do anything) is to rely on them without any security or insurance even though one has reservations about doing so, and even though one is aware that there is a risk in doing so. In a context where humans are out of the loop, to trust a technology is to rely on it without any security or insurance because one has no reservations about doing so and because one treats such reliance as risk-free (or subject only to acceptable risks). Whereas, in the context of law's human-centric governance, to judge that a person is 'trustworthy' is to judge that a person will do the right thing even when they are disposed to (and have the opportunity to) do otherwise, in the context of governance by machines, it is a proxy for reliability. In an insightful analysis, Christoph Kletzer hits this nail on the head when he says:

> There are entirely different stakes at play in reliance and trust. Whilst reliance is a mundane and technical issue, trust is a morally laden issue that potentially concerns our very human essence. This makes it crucial to keep these two concepts neatly separated. Failing to do so leads to a host of misunderstandings not only about trust and reliance itself but also about the relationship of technology and law.[35]

So, on this analysis, parties who make use of AI or who commit their transaction to a blockchain, do not place their 'trust' in the technology, they merely rely on it; and, although we should not jump too quickly to this conclusion, we might infer that, by relying on the technology rather than their fellow human, they do not trust the latter (or regard the latter as trustworthy). Moreover, contrary to much of the conventional wisdom, it is not so much the difference between trust and trustworthiness that is critical as the difference between reliance based on trust (or trustworthiness) (which involves a judgement as to the moral character of a human) and mere reliance on technology (which signifies only the use of a tool or, at most, a prudential judgement – a judgement that might be more or less reflective, more or less informed as to the technology's fitness for purpose and its quality, more or less a matter of choice, but never morally judgmental).

[33] See, eg. P De Filippi and A Wright, *Blockchain and the Law: The Rule of Code* (Cambridge MA, Harvard University Press, 2018).

[34] See, eg, A Kerasidou and CX Kerasidou, 'AI in Medicine' in D Edmonds (ed), *Future Morality* (Oxford, Oxford University Press, 2021) 83, 86–88.

[35] C Kletzer, 'Law, Disintermediation and the Future of Trust' in LA DiMatteo, A Janssen, P Ortolani, F de Elizalde, M Cannarsa and M Durovic (eds), *The Cambridge Handbook of Lawyering in the Digital Age* (Cambridge, Cambridge University Press, 2021) 312, 322.

ii. AI and Respect

Similarly, where AI-enabled machines displace humans who previously were responsible for governance, how does the respect that is traditionally claimed for law's governance translate in a context where it is respect for governance by technologies that is demanded? Does this make any kind of sense?

Where governance is by machines, we wonder whether it is meaningful to continue to ask questions about the authority of law or respect for the law.[36] We sense that we need to have accountable humans in control of the governance to bottom-out these questions. However, if a community reaches a point where governance has been left to the machines, and where humans no longer doubt the direction given by the machines or think about compliance or non-compliance in technologically managed environments, then if respect means anything it connotes that humans have given up on having their own ideas about the governance of their communities – in every sense, governance is left to the technologies. Governance is no longer a human enterprise.

What this reveals is that the ambivalence that many humans have about reliance on technologies to do work otherwise done by humans runs deep into our conceptual thinking. As Kletzer says of the need to separate reliance (on machines) from trust (in humans), we also need to separate mere reliance on governance by machines from respect for governance by humans.

iii. Technologies and Human Autonomy

Whereas trustworthy technology is seen by its promoters as a good thing, it is not so clear what we should make of autonomous technologies. It is not so clear whether a technology that is fully autonomous should be welcomed as being super-efficient or should be feared (especially in the case of weapons systems) as being out of human control and dangerous. Moreover, it is not clear how the autonomy of a technology relates to the autonomy of a human (in any of its several contested conceptions). So, we should be careful not to assume that reference to 'autonomous technological systems' are synonymous with references to autonomous humans.

This point has been emphatically underlined by the European Group on Ethics in Science and New Technologies:

> It is therefore somewhat of a misnomer to apply the term 'autonomy' to mere artefacts, albeit very advanced complex adaptive or even 'intelligent' systems. The terminology of 'autonomous' systems has however widely gained currency in the scientific literature and public debate to refer to the highest degree of automation and the highest degree of independence from human beings in terms of operational and decisional 'autonomy'. But autonomy in its original sense is an important aspect of human dignity that ought not to be relativised.
>
> Since no smart artefact or system – however advanced and sophisticated – can in and by itself be called 'autonomous' in the original ethical sense, they cannot be accorded the moral standing of the human person and inherit human dignity. Human dignity as the

[36] See, at length, R Brownsword, *Technology, Governance and Respect for the Law: Pictures at an Exhibition* (Abingdon, Routledge, 2022).

> foundation of human rights implies that meaningful human intervention and participation must be possible in matters that concern human beings and their environment. Therefore, in contrast to the automation of production, it is not appropriate to manage and decide about humans in the way we manage and decide about objects or data, even if this is technically conceivable. Such an 'autonomous' management of human beings would be unethical, and it would undermine the deeply entrenched European core values. Human beings ought to be able to determine which values are served by technology, what is morally relevant and which final goals and conceptions of the good are worthy to be pursued. This cannot be left to machines, no matter how powerful they are.[37]

Clearly, if we treat the autonomy of humans as a virtue (as an attitude of always trying to do the right thing), then this is likely to lose a good deal in its translation to technology. On the other hand, if we treat human autonomy as simply meaning that the actions of a human are not controlled by another human, then the translation to a technology is more straightforward, but less ethically rich.

iv. Justice

Much modern law reflects a tension between rules and practices that rest on utilitarian calculations, and rules and practices that rest on considerations of fairness, rights and justice. Such, for example, is the tension between a criminal justice system designed for crime control and one that invests heavily in due process constraints.

Surveying a rapidly changing landscape of dispute resolution and analysing the insinuation of technologies into this aspect of governance, both in courts and out of courts, Ethan Katsh and Orna Rabinovich-Einy detect three key shifts as follows.[38] First, there is a shift from physical to virtual, or semi-virtual, settings: with this shift, individuals 'can access courts, evaluate their legal stance, communicate with the other party, and have a third party decide their dispute, all without having to physically attend the court or be restricted to court operating hours'. The second shift is 'from human intervention and decision making to automated processes'; and the third shift is 'from dispute resolution models that value confidentiality to models focused on collecting, using, and reusing data in order to prevent disputes'.[39]

That said, attachments to traditional ideas of fairness and justice persist and, as Katsh and Rabinovick-Einy ask, as we go through the shifts we might wonder:

> Will parties who participate in these processes feel that they have received their 'day in court' and have been 'heard'? Will users perceive these processes as fair? Will judges sustain their neutrality and authority, and will courts, relying on algorithms, maintain their legitimacy? …
>
> Adopting technology in the courtroom opens up new opportunities not only for making our existing processes less expensive and cumbersome and more accessible at all hours.

[37] European Commission, Directorate-General for Research and Innovation, European Group on Ethics in Science and New Technologies, 'Statement on artificial intelligence, robotics and "autonomous" systems (Publications Office, 9 March 2018), data.europa.eu/doi/10.2777/531856.

[38] E Katsh and O Rabinovich-Einy, *Digital Justice: Technology and the Internet of Disputes* (Oxford, Oxford University Press, 2017).

[39] See ibid 162–63.

> It could also change the very nature of court processes, with software playing an increasingly significant role in streamlining, resolving, and preventing claims. Indeed, there is promise for transforming our very understanding of the meaning of *justice*.[40]

While our ideas about what is convenient and what is efficient might remain fairly constant, there is no guarantee that citizens will judge that the gains in convenience and efficiency offset their questions about 'trust' in automated processes; and, the idea that our understanding of 'justice' might be transformed by these technology-driven forms of dispute-handling might seem less a promise than an unwelcome threat. If automated processes and technological dispute-handling are thought to be more about getting disputes *settled* rather than getting them settled *justly*, there might be resistance to rethinking the meaning of justice and, concomitantly, to the decentring of courts, rules and humans.[41]

In other words, if in human-centric law justice stands in opposition to utilitarian considerations, we should be very careful with a translation that aligns justice with utilitarian calculations in a technological context.

B. Crowding Out Human Values

Suppose that a community opens a debate about the use of AI in delivering healthcare. How might the regulatory conversation go?

It might start with questions about what can and cannot be done. Where things cannot be done, there might be a discussion about whether the community should invest in research and development that tries to find ways of overcoming the current technological limitations. However, for the time being, if the thing in question cannot be done, then that is the end of that part of the regulatory conversation, and the conversation now focuses on those deployments of AI that are possible – on what can be done.

The next question will be about the performance of AI; about how effective it is, how well it works relative to human comparators (for example, how well AI performs in reading MRI scans compared with a human radiologist), or how well it works when operating in conjunction with humans, or sequentially with humans, and so on. If the AI has not been tested and evaluated, this will be the next step.

[40] ibid 164–65.

[41] Famously, see OM Fiss, 'Against Settlement' (1984) 93 *Yale Law Journal* 1073. Fiss argues that the case for settlement is dubious. Thus, at 1075, Fiss says: 'I do not believe that settlement as a generic practice is preferable to judgment or should be institutionalised on a wholesale and indiscriminate basis. It should be treated instead as a highly problematic technique for streamlining dockets. Settlement is for me the civil analogue of plea bargaining: Consent is often coerced; the bargain may be struck by someone without authority; the absence of a trial and judgment renders subsequent judicial involvement troublesome; and although dockets are trimmed, justice may not be done. Like plea bargaining, settlement is a capitulation to the conditions of mass society and should be neither encouraged nor praised.' When Fiss treats settlement as analogous to plea bargaining, he sees a system that defects from its public commitments. Adjudication is not about simply putting an end to the dispute or restoring the peace, there is more to it than that. According to Fiss (1085), the role of adjudicators 'is not to maximise the ends of private parties, nor simply to secure the peace, but to explicate and give force to the values embodied in authoritative texts such as the Constitution and statutes: to interpret those values and to bring reality into accord with them. This duty is not discharged when the parties settle'.

Assuming that the AI's performance meets the required level of effectiveness, the next question might concern the preferences of the members of the community. Some might prefer AI; others might prefer the human touch. If the balance of preferences clearly favours use of the AI, then there is at least a prima facie regulatory case for permitting the proposed use of AI.

Against the proposal, a question might be asked about whether the use of AI would be prudent for the community as a whole. Granted, there might be efficiencies and economies with AI but, in the longer run, might this diminish the quality of care and might there be a risk that essential human skills would be lost? Such a question, however, does not threaten to block the proposal. Even regulators who are persuaded that there is something in such prudential concerns would see them as no more than a case for caution and monitoring of the roll-out of AI.

If the proposal is to be turned back, it will be for moral or ethical reasons. Even if the AI can be used, even if it can be deployed effectively, even if the majority prefer healthcare with AI than without it, and even if there are no prudential reservations, it might be argued that it simply would not be right to proceed.[42] This argument might focus on various ethical concerns – such as concerns about the loss of jobs, or possibly about human dignity or privacy – but, for our purposes, the details of the moral or ethical argument really do not matter. The point is that, in the regulatory conversation, this is not only the final consideration, it is also now the last stand against the use of AI. The burden of resistance, so to speak, is entirely on the moral argument.

If the moral argument were robust this might not be a problem; and, given the interest in classic moral puzzles of the kind presented by AI when confronted by trolley problems,[43] and the like, we might think that moral debate is alive and well. However, our moral discourse is problematic in two important respects. One is that, in many cases (including the trolley problem), we find that the protagonists espouse different approaches which lead to conflicting views; in other words, we find that we have a plurality of views. The other problem is that, even where there is consensus or convergence, and even where there is confidence in a moral judgement, sceptics will insist that, in the final analysis, no compelling argument can be given to ground the judgement – which is not to say that, for those who hold the views, morality does not matter but that the views rest purely and simply on the person in question being committed to that particular view (or 'opinion' as sceptics might term it).

For legal coherentists, where the thinking is circumscribed by doctrine and is inward-looking, moral and ethical debate is externalised; and, whether it is robust or not, it is irrelevant to coherentist reasoning and judgement. By contrast, regulatory thinking has to confront ethics because views about the legitimacy of governance can impact on what works. However, if moral philosophers and ethicists cannot resolve

[42] *cf* M Warnock, 'Philosophy and Ethics' in C Cookson, G Nowak, and D Thierbach (eds), *Eposium 1992: Genetic Engineering – The New Challenge: Conference Proceedings and Essay Competition* (Munich, European Patent Office, 1993) 67, 67; on genetic engineering, she said that we should always ask whether 'even if the benefits of the practice seem to outweigh the dangers, it nevertheless so outrages our sense of justice or of rights or of human decency that it should be prohibited whatever the advantages'.

[43] See JJ Thomson, 'The Trolley Problem' (1985) 94 *Yale Law Journal* 1395. Similarly, see the so-called 'tunnel' problem: J Millar, 'You should have a say in your robot car's code of ethics' *Wired* (9 February 2014), www.wired.com/2014/09/set-the-ethics-robot-car.

moral debates, regulators have no easy way of tapping into the pool of ethical expertise to settle on a position. In any case, what regulators really want is not the best view according to the experts so much as whatever view, if followed, will clear the way for effective law. Furthermore, on some matters, regulators might be able to legitimate their position by saying that they have simply followed the science but not so where the questions are ethical.

Accordingly, many would argue that legitimate governance has to rely on the integrity of process – the process of public engagement and deliberation – coupled with settling on positions that are 'acceptable'. However, while the notion of 'acceptability' might be a convenient shorthand for a number of elements of regulatory fitness that we might wish to see satisfied, in this usage it covers and compresses everything from personal preference to moral principle. The full range of considerations (whether matters of preference, prudence or morality) are taken into consideration but they are flattened and then reduced to a currency of positive and negative attitudes, to so many thumbs up and so many thumbs down, to so many likes and so many dislikes, before being subjected to 'balancing'. In this thicket of regulatory process, ethical and moral reason, and distinctively human values, lose their identity.

In this regulatory approach, three features are striking: questions of possibility and effectiveness dominate questions of legitimacy; propositions that are susceptible to testing along with evidence-based reasoning are regarded as superior to propositions that do not have these characteristics; and moral and ethical reason loses its identity in a hotch-potch of 'acceptability'.

Now, returning to the proposal to treat AI as a legal person, the concern might be that, if AI is treated as a legal person, this might lower the respect that humans have for one another – and, indeed, that AI, elevated to legal personhood might instrumentalise humans. However, these are not the concerns that I want to flag up. Rather, my concern is that the regulatory approach that eases the way to recognising AI as a legal person presents a threat to a human-centric view that treats the dignity of humans – in the sense of the human capacity and determination to do the right thing even when they have the opportunity to do the wrong thing[44] – as being their distinctive characteristic. Of course, if this view of humans is just wishful thinking, 'serious people' will argue that it should not be taken seriously. However, as the social and cultural psychologist Jonathan Haidt remarks, humans exhibit a 'strange mix of selfishness and selflessness'.[45] Human nature might be 'mostly selfish', but humans are capable of acts of altruism and, in many cases, 'they are willing to cooperate and work for the good of the group, even when they could do better by slacking, cheating, or leaving the group'.[46] Humans are complex and, despite the efforts of regulatory thinking, they are not one-dimensional, and they do not always act as short-term self-interested maximisers.

If we are concerned about the ways in which regulatory thinking might marginalise moral and ethical reason, a return to coherentism is not the answer. Rather,

[44] Brownsword (n 27).

[45] J Haidt, *The Righteous Mind: Why Good People Are Divided by Politics and Religion* (New York, Vintage Books, 2012) 222.

[46] ibid.

regulatory reasoning needs to reverse its prioritisation of effectiveness over legitimacy and, at the same time, disentangle moral from other kinds of practical reason.

IV. CONCLUSION

In this chapter, I have indicated how two contrasting legal paradigms – principles-guided legal coherentism and policy-orientated regulatory-instrumentalism – might respond to the proposal that, for the purposes of private law, AI should be treated as a legal person. While the former would resist the proposal, the latter would be open-minded and, indeed, might accept the proposal as the default rule for private law matters.

Without assuming that we should treat AI as a legal person, I have suggested that the coherentist approach is inadequate. This is because it not only fails to ask the right questions about the fitness of governance, but also because it externalises general ethical and moral debate. By contrast, regulatory thinking has the scope to ask the right questions but it, too, is deeply problematic so long as it subordinates questions of legitimacy to questions of effectiveness.

If we want our governance of AI to be human-centric, we need to reflect on what we understand by human-centricity and in what ways the context for human-centric governance might be compromised. While a decision to treat AI as a legal person would surely be a significant moment, so I have suggested, we should focus on the regulatory thinking that might drive such a decision. It is the prevalence of unreconstructed regulatory thinking that presents the underlying challenge to human dignity and, with that, human-centric governance.

Finally, let me add a few words about the fork (between a coherentist and a regulatory path) that I mentioned earlier. The question is: do we need to make a choice between these paths, ie to be either coherentist *or* regulatory in our thinking? The short answer is that we do not because there might be some governance exercises in which coherentist and regulatory lines of inquiry can complement one another. However, in the bigger picture, the point is that so long as coherentism and regulatory thinking remain 'unreconstructed', we will not achieve good governance by taking either path or by combining them. In the bigger picture, whether we think in a traditional legal way, focusing on the internal coherence of the body of doctrine, or in a policy-guided and instrumental regulatory way, or even if we combine both kinds of thinking, we must reconstruct our approach to governance so that it compatible with the conditions on which viable and flourishing human communities are predicated – that is, the basic conditions for human existence on Earth, together with peaceful co-existence within and between communities (such that humans can form and inhabit their own communities), and a context that allows individuals to exercise their capacity for free and informed self-direction and moral agency.[47]

[47] See, further, Brownsword (2019) (n 12); (2020) (n 12); n 36; *Rethinking Law, Regulation and Technology* (Cheltenham, Elgar, 2022); 'Informational Wrongs and Our Deepest Interests' in M Borghi and R Brownsword (eds), *Law, Regulation and Governance: Informational Rights and Informational Wrongs* (Abingdon, Routledge, 2023), and, for application in a non-technological context, 'Migrants, State Responsibilities, and Human Dignity' (2021) 34 *Ratio Juris* 6.

Whether we take the coherentist or the regulatory path in engaging with new technologies, we should do nothing that will compromise these preconditions. To the sceptics, we should say that if any human were to reject the imperative that these preconditions should be respected – for example, if they were to propose that it should be permissible to deplete the global planetary resource at will and to undermine the possibility of communities forming around their own projects and developing in their own way, then this should be rejected as being so unreasonable that no reasonable human could hold such a view. And, to those who propose that we should extend legal personality to AI or other smart technologies, the first question that we should ask is neither whether this would be doctrinally coherent nor whether it would serve our regulatory policies but whether this would be compatible with maintaining the preconditions for human social existence. Unless we can confidently answer that it would be so compatible, we should not proceed.

12

*The Self and the Commodified Self: Biotechnologies before the Bare Life**

VALENTINA CALDERAI

I. THE HUMAN BODY AND THE BUILDING OF THE IMPERSONAL

EVERY LAW STUDENT knows that persons and things are mutually exclusive categories. Persons are subjects of rights, whereas things are objects that can be bought, sold or freely given, used, modified, and even destroyed by the persons who own them. Yet through history these seemingly inflexible and irreconcilable categories have been proved so malleable and amenable to hybridisations and trade-offs that their purpose, one may assume, is not so much that of drawing an impassable line as to control the processes through which 'things' are treated as persons and 'persons' as things.[1]

That Roman law did not consider human beings *as such* as persons, following this insight, is less contingent on the institution of slavery than on the irrelevance of ontological distinctions to a concept set up for the expediency of circulation of wealth.[2] By contrast, the injunction *de homine libero exhibendo* that marked the nullity of stipulations through which a citizen was sold or agreed to be sold as a slave – *quia nec dari oportere intendi, nec aestimatio eius praestari potest*[3] – suggests that 'citizenship' in that culture transferred at least some of the ideas that in our culture are transferred by 'personhood', first and foremost its subtraction to relationships based on exchange value.

* The research for this article was funded by the European Commission under the programme Erasmus+ Action – Jean Monnet Chair – Call for Proposals 2022 – 101127426 – HeLDEn – ERASMUS-JMO-2023-HEI-TCH-RSCH.

[1] See R Esposito, *Third Person: Politics of Life and Philosophy of the Impersonal* (Oxford, Polity Press, 2018).

[2] Y Thomas, 'Le sujet de droit, la personne et la nature. Sur la critique contemporaine du sujet de droit' (1998) *Le Débat*, 85ff; Y Thomas, 'La valeur des choses. Le droit romain hors de la religion' (2002) 57 *Annales. Histoire, Sciences sociales*, 1431; Y Thomas, 'Fictio legis. L'empire de la fiction romaine et ses limites médiévales' (1995) *Droits* 17.

[3] D 45.1.103 (Modestinus). Adde: Pomp. 9 ad Sab. D. 18, 1, 6 pr.: 'Sed Celsus filius ait hominem liberum scientem te emere non posse nec cuiuscumque rei si scias <prohibitam> alienationem esse: ut sacra et religiosa loca aut quorum commercium non sit, ut publica, quae non in pecunia populi, sed in publico usu habeantur'.

Unlike modern law, Roman law carefully distinguished freedom according to the *ius civile* from freedom according to the *ius naturale*.[4] This abstraction from (the idea of) nature allowed Roman jurists to liken the status of free men to that of the *res nullius in bonis*, unseizable by reason of their religious or civic destination, thereby unifying the concepts of *res* and *persona* from a purely functional and remedial perspective.[5]

Medieval jurists, imbued with scholastic theology, first proposed that every man is a *persona*, laying the ground for the 'imperious' antithesis[6] of persons and things known by modern legal systems. The meaning of *res* shifted accordingly through the winding and perilous tracks connecting law, theology and politics in the early modern age.[7] A reverse function can be detected: as the concept of 'thing' becomes ever more abstract, that of 'person' seems to lean towards human nature. To the commentators, the notions of *res corporalis* still provided the foundations on which all owners' *dominia*, *directa* or *utilia*, must rest; to the humanist lawyers, it stretched beyond property rights to encompass the indirect object of claim rights on other people; to Jean Domat, well acquainted with Port-Royal Logic, the name '*chose*' is the correlative of '*droit*', understood as a general predicate about the subject of a legal clause, or 'personne', seen in the capacity of rightsholder: 'de sorte qu'on peut dire que l'état des personnes consiste dans cette capacité ou cette incapacité'.[8]

By the end of the eighteenth century, the idea of personhood as an abstract capacity, acknowledged in principle with respect to every human being as such, had crystallised in solemn declarations, beautifully exemplified by the first sentence of §16 ABGB: 'Jeder Mensch hat angeborne, schon durch die Vernunft einleuchtende Rechte, und ist daher als eine Person zu betrachten'. Here, the human body comes to the fore as the embodied person, *la personne en son corps*:[9] 'Sclaverey oder Leibeigenschaft, und die Ausübung einer darauf sich beziehenden Macht, wird in diesen Ländern nicht gestattet', §16 goes on, in perhaps the earliest apprehension of 'bare life' into a Civil Code.[10]

[4] D 50. 17. 32: 'Quod attinet ad ius civile, servi pro nullis habentur. Non tamen et iure naturali, quia quod ad ius naturale attinet, omnes homines aequales sunt'. See Y Thomas, 'Imago naturae. Note sur l'institutionnalité de la nature à Rome', in 'Théologie et droit dans la science politique de l'État moderne. Actes de la table ronde de Rome (12–14 novembre 1987)' (Rome, Publications de l'École française de Rome, 1991) 201, 202: 'Les juristes pensent nettement ces deux droits comme deux genres successifs et contradictoires: entre esclavage et liberté, statuts et égalité, propriété et jouissance commune, il y a toute la distance qui sépare l'histoire de ce qui n'est pas encore elle'.

[5] Y Thomas, 'Res, chose et patrimoine. Note sur le rapport sujet-objet en droit romain' (1980) 25 *Archives de philosophie du Droit* 413.

[6] S Pugliatti, 'Cosa in senso giuridico (Teoria generale)' in *Enciclopedia del diritto* XI (1962) 28.

[7] See R Tuck, *Natural Rights Theories. Their Origin and Development* (Cambridge, Cambridge University Press 1987); Y Thomas, 'Le sujet concret et sa personne. Essai d'histoire juridique rétrospective' in O Cayla and Y Thomas, *Du droit de ne pas naître. À propos de l'affaire Perruche* (Paris, Gallimard 2002) 89.

[8] J Domat, *Les loix civiles dans leur ordre naturel, Livre Préliminaire, Titre II* (Paris, Coignard, 1689–1694) 4, gallica.bnf.fr/ark:/12148/bpt6k3103451?rk=42918.

[9] X Dijon, *Le sujet de droit en son corps, une mise à l'épreuve du droit subjectif* (Bruxelles, Larcier, 1982).

[10] On 'bare life' as life exposed to (legal) violence, see G Agamben, *Homo sacer. Il potere sovrano e la nuda vita* (Torino, Einaudi, 1995) 74ff, developing a theme from W Benjamin, 'Zur Kritik der Gewalt' in R Tiedemann and H Schweppenhäuser (eds), *Gesammelte Schriften*, Band II-1 (Frankfurt aM, Suhrkamp, 1999) 179.

Through several shifts and turns, this representation endures. Personhood in our legal cultures applies to all living humans, considered as individuals and members of humankind: *Gattungswesen*.[11] This duplicity mirrors the legal regimes attached to physical persons – personality rights and fundamental rights – and the ambivalent status of the human body, at once an object to the exercise of individual choices and a barrier against seizure by public and private powers.

But the ancient notion of personhood as a pure enabling fiction[12] did not disappear. Besides juridical persons and a few remnants in inheritance law,[13] the notion can be seen at work whenever social and technological innovation 'nibbles away' at the special consideration given to the human body vis-à-vis the world of 'things'.[14] Through the Industrial Revolution, the fiction of an abstract subject mastering their body stood behind the separation of labour-power from personhood and ascription of an exchange value to the former in the early contractual infrastructures of mass production.[15] Today, the same fiction enables the race to recognise property interests in the human body, prompted by sweeping advances in the sciences and technologies of life.[16]

Long prepared by the steady enmeshing of bare life into creation of capital value,[17] the theological-political metaphor of body duplication is making a strange comeback

[11] J Habermas, *Die Zukunft der menschlichen Natur. Auf dem Weg einer liberalen Eugenik?* (Frankfurt aM, Suhrkamp, 2001) 76.

[12] P Vinogradoff, 'Juridical Persons' (1924) 24 *Columbia Law Review* 594, 602.

[13] See, eg, Art 119 Fr cc and Arts 462.3 and 784 It cc, concerning the capacity of conceptures – the child who has not yet been conceived – to succeed and receive as donee.

[14] BM Knoppers and HT Greely, 'Biotechnologies nibbling at the legal human' (2019) 366 *Science* 1455.

[15] See L Mengoni, 'La tutela giuridica della vita materiale nelle varie età dell'uomo' (1982) *Rivista trimestrale di diritto e procedura civile* 1117.

[16] MA Hermitte, 'Le corps humain hors du commerce, hors du marché' (1988) 33 *Archives de Philosophie du Droit* 323; JP Baude, *L'affaire de la main volée. Une histoire juridique du corps* (Paris, Éditions du Seuil, 1993); MJ Radin, *Contested Commodities: The Trouble with Trade in Sex, Children, Body Parts and Other Things* (Cambridge Mass, Harvard University Press, 1996); R Rao 'Property Privacy and the Human Body' (2000) 80 *Boston University Law Review* 359; FS Kieff (ed), *Perspectives on Properties of the Human Genome Project* (Amsterdam, Elsevier, 2003); D Dickenson, *Body Shopping: Converting Body Parts to Profit* (Oxford, Oneworld, 2009); N Hoppe, *Bioequity. Property and the Human Body* (Ashgate, Farnham, 2009); C Roth, *Eigentum an Körperteilen: Rechtsfragen der Kommerzialisierung des menschlichen Körpers* (Berlin, Springer, 2009); H Widdows and C Mullen, *The Governance of Genetic Information. Who Decides?* (Cambridge, Cambridge University Press, 2009); C Lenk, N Hoppe, K Beier and C Wiesemann (eds), *Human Tissue Research: A European perspective on the ethical and legal challenges* (Oxford, Oxford University Press, 2011); I Goold, K Greasley, J Herring et al (eds), *Persons, Parts and Property: How Should We Regulate Human Tissue in the 21st Century?* (Oxford, Hart, 2014); C Lafontaine, *Le corps-marché: La marchandisation de la vie humaine a l'ère de la bioéconomie* (Paris, Editions du Seuil, 2014; J Wall, *Being and Owning: The Body, Bodily Material, and the Law* (Oxford, Oxford University Press, 2015); JD Rainhorn and S El Boudamoussi (eds), *New Cannibal Markets. Globalization and Commodification of the Human Body* (Paris, Éditions de la Maison des sciences de l'homme 2015); M Cooper and C Waldby, *Clinical Labor: Tissue Donors and Research Subjects in the Global Bioeconomy* (Durham, Duke University Press, 2014); D Dickenson, *Property in the Body: Feminist Perspectives* (Cambridge, Cambridge University Press, 2017); KJ Strandburg, BM Frischmann, MJ Madison and (eds), *Governing Medical Knowledge Commons* (Cambridge, Cambridge University Press, 2017); M Quigley, *Self-Ownership, Property Rights, and the Human Body. A Legal and Philosophical Analysis* (Cambridge, Cambridge University Press, 2018); J Pila, 'Property in Human Body Parts: An Old Legal Question for a New Technological Age' in D Orentlicher and TK Hervey (eds), *Oxford Handbook of Comparative Health Law* (New York, Oxford University Press, 2020) 808.

[17] KS Rajan, *Biocapital. The Constitution of Post-genomic Life* (Durham, Duke University Press, 2006); Cooper and Waldby (n 16) 18ff.; A Fumagalli 'Twenty Theses on Contemporary Capitalism

amidst the secularised ideological fabric of the contemporary knowledge economy.[18] Whereas the 'mystic fiction' of the king's two bodies symbolised the permanence of sovereign power, the distinction between the body as a 'raw material or means of production'[19] and the body as an attribute of personhood testifies to the ongoing struggle to keep rights-bearing persons out of the market at the moment in which their bodies are traded.[20] Interestingly, both metaphors reference 'dignity' as representation.[21] As the king's body 'became the *instrumentum dignitatis* and the incarnation of his immortal office',[22] by the operation of human dignity the body of every single human stands as the body of humanity itself: *homo instrumentum humanitatis*. Finally, both concepts exhibit a characteristic vagueness. Just as the idea of sovereign dignity has historically worked both to strengthen and undermine the charismatic power of kings, the 'elusive' concept of dignity as representation can work either to 'constrain' or to 'empower' individual agency.[23]

Nowhere is the tension between the sacralisation of the embodied person and the remorseless commodification of 'bare life' more apparent than in medical research. In private law scholarship, hostility to the commodification of human body parts is sometimes grounded on personal identity.[24] Instead, a cross-referenced reading of the scattered regulations relevant to the supply chain of innovative medical therapies suggests that limits on property rights are less a tribute to personal identity and sovereign power of human beings over 'their' bodies than a reflex of the impersonal – as such, open to sharing – character of scientific enterprise as 'knowledge without a knower, … knowledge without a knowing subject'.[25] The epistemology of a great liberal thinker unmasks the anti-scientific strain in the neoliberal agenda of fully fledged processing of human bodies into ultimate 'fictitious commodities'.[26] Yet there is more to the debate on commodification than a cautionary tale on the tragedies of anti-commons[27] as the knowledge of life itself ultimately rests on the ambivalent

(Cognitive Biocapitalism)' (2011) 16 *Angelaki. Journal of the Theoretical Humanities* 7; N Rose, *The Politics of Life Itself: Biomedicine, Power and Subjectivity in the Twenty-First Century* (Princeton, Princeton University Press, 2007) 11ff.

[18] See EH Kantorowicz, *The King's Two Bodies. A Study in Medieval Political Theology* (Princeton, Princeton University Press 2016).

[19] Hermitte (n 16) 323.

[20] Pila (n 16) 823ff.

[21] See J Waldron, 'Dignity and Rank: In memory of Gregory Vlastos (1907–1991)' (2007) *European Journal of Sociology/Archives Européennes de Sociologie* 201, 235.

[22] Kantorowicz (n 18) 502.

[23] R Brownsword, 'Bioethics Today, Bioethics Tomorrow: Stem Cell Research and the Dignitarian Alliance' (2003) *Notre Dame Journal of Law, Ethics and Public Policy* 15, 20ff.

[24] H Schünemann, *Die Rechte am menschlichen Körper* (Frankfurt aM, Lang 1985) 58; C Halàsz, *Das Recht auf bio-materielle Selbstbestimmung. Grenzen und Möglichkeiten der Weiterverwendung von Körpersubstanzen* (Berlin, Springer, 2004) 20ff, 69ff; P Zatti, 'Il corpo e la nebulosa dell'appartenenza' (2007) *Nuova giurisprudenza civile commentata* 1.

[25] KR Popper, *Objective Knowledge: An Evolutionary Approach* (Oxford, Oxford University Press, 1979) 109.

[26] K Polanyi, *The Great Transformation. The Political and Economic Origins of Our Time*, 2nd edn (Boston, Beacon, 2001) 71ff; K Polanyi, 'Our Obsolete Market Mentality. Civilization Must Find a New Pattern' (1947) 3 *Commentary* 109.

[27] See MA Heller, 'The Tragedy of the Anticommons: Property in the Transition from Marx to Markets' (1998) 111 *Harvard Law Review* 621; MA Heller, *The Gridlock Economy: How Too Much Ownership Wrecks Markets, Stops Innovation and Costs Lives* (New York, Basic Books, 2008); MA Heller and

ontology of the human body, at once what makes each of us oneself and what we share with all human beings. Inextricably personal and impersonal, the body stands at the intersection between self-recognition and mutual recognition, individual and collective identities.[28]

II. THE OWNERSHIP DILEMMA

Because of its unique relation to donors, research on human tissues has the potential to trigger a paradigm shift in developmental biology and personalised healthcare.[29] However, along with expectations it also stirs concerns for the broad or open consent procedures required by research institutions to meet the interests of tissue donors and comply with the European framework on data protection.[30] Proposals have been advanced towards a change of paradigm based on dynamic consent and self-ownership.[31]

The standard approach to liabilities and rights over human tissues leads from the primacy of individual autonomy to the freedom to dispose of one's body within limits set by public policy. These limits can be sorted out into: (i) inalienability rules addressed to the rightholder, a somewhat unsettled category that nonetheless includes, for our purposes, commercialisation of the human body and its parts 'as such';[32] and (ii) prohibitions on unauthorised appropriation of the human body,

RS Eisenberg, 'Can Patents Deter Innovation? The Anticommons in Biomedical Research' (1998) 280 *Science* 698; J Buchanan and YJ Yoon, 'Symmetric Tragedies: Commons and Anticommons' (2000) 43 *Journal of Law and Economics* 1; S Levmore, 'Two Stories about the Evolution of Property Rights' (2003) 31 *Journal of Legal Studies* 421; MA Hall, 'Property, Privacy, and the Pursuit of Interconnected Electronic Medical Records' (2010) 95 *Iowa Law Review* 631; J Boyle, *The Public Domain. Enclosing the Commons of the Mind* (New Haven-London, Yale University Press, 2008) 160ff; G Resta, 'The Case against the Privatization of Knowledge: Some Thoughts on the Myriad Genetics Controversy' in R Bin, S Lorenzon and N Lucchi (eds), *Biotech Innovations and Fundamental Rights* (Milano, Springer, 2012) 11; JL Contreras, 'Genetic Property' (2016) 105 *Georgetown Law Journal* 1; JL Contreras, 'The False Promise of Health Data Ownership' (2019) 94 *NYU Law Review* 624; K Liddell et al, 'Patient data ownership: who owns your health?' (2021) 8 *Journal of Law and Biosciences* 1; L Determann, 'No One Owns Data' (2019) 70 *Hastings Law Journal* 1.

[28] P Ricoeur, *Soi-même comme un autre* (Paris, Éditions du Seuil, 1996) 369ff; P Ricoeur, *Le Juste* 1 (Paris, Esprit, 1995) 29ff.

[29] See the report of the Expert Group: European Commission, Directorate-General for Research and Innovation, 'Biobanks for Europe. A Challenge for Governance' (Brussels, Publication Office of the European Union, 2012); J Kinkorová, 'Biobanks in the era of personalised medicine: Objectives, challenges, and innovation' (2016) 7 *EPMA Journal* 2016; M Huch et al, 'The hope and the hype of organoid research' (2017) 144 *Development* 938; G Schneider, *Health Data Pools Under European Data Protection and Competition Law. Health as a Digital Business* (Cham, Springer, 2022).

[30] D Hallinan, 'Broad consent under the GDPR: an optimistic perspective on a bright future' (2020) 16 *Life Sciences, Society and Policy* 1.

[31] SN Boers, JJ Van Delden and AL Bredenoord, 'Broad consent is consent for governance' (2015) 15 *American Journal of Bioethics* 53; LM Beskow and KP Weinfurt, 'Exploring understanding of "understanding": The paradigm case of biobank consent comprehension' (2019) 19 *American Journal of Bioethics* 6; MA Lensink et al, 'Understanding (in) Consent for Governance' (2019) 19 *American Journal of Bioethics* 43.

[32] See Art 21 European Convention on Human Rights and Biomedicine (Oviedo, 1 December 1999) (ECHRB). This formula is almost literally repeated by Art 3.2 European Charter of Fundamental Rights (Nice, 18 December 2020, OJ 2000/C 326/391) and the European Directives on the Collection and Processing of Biological Materials and Experiments – respectively, Directive 2004/23/EC of the European

also in the form of intellectual property, protected by civil, administrative and criminal sanctions.[33]

Bolstered by a landmark decision of the California Supreme Court,[34] soon imitated by the European Convention on Human Rights in Biomedicine and the European Union,[35] the standard model entails two distinct allocation systems: raw materials circulate subject to market inalienability, whereas products obtained from the body are put on the market. In theory, each system can function independently from the other by combining specification and intellectual property: Taney gives her blood for free out of a commitment to human solidarity; Marshall, having discovered unique features in Taney's blood, develops a new product, for example a cell line, and obtains a patent, generating colossal profits. By contrast, in the standard model donor consent works as a switch point between market and non-market allocation: before consent is given, bodily materials are inalienable, and any act of disposal in return for payment would be null and void; after consent is legitimately obtained, they are a raw material like any other but unauthorised tampering is forbidden

Parliament and of the Council of 31 March 2004 on setting standards of quality and safety for the donation, procurement, testing, processing, preservation, storage and distribution of human tissues and cells [2004] OJ L 102/48, Art 12; Directive 2002/98/EC of the European Parliament and of the Council of 27 January 2003 setting standards of quality and safety for the collection, testing, processing, storage and distribution of human blood and blood components and amending Directive 2001/83/EC [2003] OJ L 33/30; Directive 2001/20/EC of the European Parliament and of the Council of 4 April 2001 on the approximation of the laws, regulations and administrative provisions of the Member States relating to the implementation of good clinical practice in the conduct of clinical trials on medicinal products for human use [2001] OJ L121/34 Art 4.

[33] See Art 22 ECHRB (making the right of medical personnel to store and use biological material taken during an operation for purposes unrelated to the operation subject to the patient's informed consent) and Arts 21–22 of the Additional Protocol to the Convention on Human Rights and Biomedicine concerning Transplantation of Organs and Tissues of Human Origin (Strasbourg, 24 January 2002) (2002 ECHRB Protocol), Art 13, vii of the Additional Protocol to the Convention on Human Rights and Biomedicine, concerning Biomedical Research (Strasbourg, 25 January 2005) (2005 ECHRB Protocol), imposing an obligation on researchers to obtain consent in relation to any 'foreseen potential further uses, including commercial uses, of the research results, data, or biological materials'). Following Art 5 of Directive 44/98/EC of the European Parliament and of the Council of 6 July 1998 on the legal protection of biotechnological inventions [1998] OJ L213/13: 'The human body, at the various stages of its formation and development, and at the simple discovery of one of its elements, including the sequence or partial sequence of a gene, cannot constitute patentable inventions'.

[34] *Moore v Regents of the University of California*, 51 Cal 3d 120 (1990). John Moore, *aka* 'l'homme aux cellules d'or' – B Edelman, *La personne en danger* (Paris, Presses Universitaires de France, 1999) 289ff – on the pretext of therapy a leukaemia patient, unwitting holder of a treasure *sub specie* of a rare blood protein, had endured overlong clinical trials, after which the researchers of the world-class university clinic that had treated him obtained a cell line (Mo Cell-Line), patented it and sold it to a pharmaceutical company, which in turn obtained nine patents, for a total value estimated at several billion dollars. Moore's action was based on the tort of conversion. This remedy grants the dispossessed owner of movable property damages, in this case, quantified based on the profits extracted from the commercial exploitation of the patent. The claim was dismissed by the district court (no property in the human body), affirmed by the Court of Appeal (recognition of a property right on one's own body), and finally rejected by the California Supreme Court, which nevertheless found the researchers liable for breaching the fiduciary patient–doctor relationship. See J Boyle, 'A Theory of Law and Information: Copyright, Spleens, Blackmail, and Insider Trading' (1992) 80 *California Law Review* 1416, 1516: 'As far as the majority is concerned, Mr. Moore is the author of his own destiny, but not of his spleen'. R Epstein, 'Steady the Course: Property Rights in Genetic Materials' in Kieff (n 16) 153, 158: 'The better view is conversion because it creates cleaner property rights in those cases in which individuals do enter into various kinds of business transactions'.

[35] See nn 32 and 33.

('car il n'est pas forcément satisfaisant pour l'individu de s'achever en cosmétiques'[36]). The dissociation of the power of disposal in return for payment from the right to consent to treatments testifies to the decoupling, in the representation of the human *soma*, between person (inestimable and unexploitable 'as such') and artefact (technically reproducible, indefinitely malleable, and subject to economic exploitation).

The question who can claim rights of access and control over human tissues and the products obtained from them is deemed pivotal within the scientific community.[37] Indeed, several important issues ultimately depend on whether we accept or deny the assumption that human tissues and cells extracted from the body are subjected to standards identical or akin to ownership. In the first case, donor consent transferred property rights over 'their' tissues, and research participants could freely choose whether to maintain or relinquish at least some rights over them, including a right over secondary uses, and eventually share in the proceeds of patents obtained by researchers.[38] By the same token, consent addressees – biobanks, researchers and research funders – would be the owners of tissues legitimately obtained.[39] In the second case,[40] donor consent would seem more like an act of authorisation and destination to research, while consent addressees would be regarded as custodians (biobanks) and users (researchers) of research infrastructures.[41] Likewise, different conclusions would follow regarding the rights and liabilities of researchers and research funders, the processing and sharing of samples and data, intellectual property rights over intermediate products instrumental to further research, and openness to commercialisation of final products.

III. WHAT PRICE CONSENT?

The tension between the no-property rule on the human body 'as such' and allocation to researchers and funding organisations of exclusionary rights over human

[36] Hermitte (n 16) 339.

[37] H Langhof et al, 'Access policies in biobank research: what criteria do they include and how publicly available are they? A cross-sectional study' (2017) 25 *European Journal of Human Genetics* 293; H Langhof et al 'Current practices for access, compensation, and prioritization in biobanks. Results from an interview study' (2018) 26 *European Journal of Human Genetics* 1572; L Coppola et al 'Biobanking in health care: evolution and future directions' (2019) 17 *Journal of Translational Medicine* 172; I Goold, 'Why Does It Matter How We Regulate the Use of Human Body Parts?' (2014) 40 *Journal of Medical Ethics* 3.

[38] A straightforward case for (intellectual) property rights is made by Epstein (n 34) 159. See also: L Bennett Moses, 'The Problem with Alternatives: The Importance of Property Law in Regulating Excised Human Tissue and In Vitro Human Embryos' in Goold et al (n 16) 197; I Goold and M Quigley, 'Human Biomaterials: The Case for a Property Approach' in Goold et al (n 16)231; S Douglas and I Goold, 'Property in Human Biomaterials: A new Methodology' (2016) 75 *Cambridge Law Journal* 478.

[39] HC Howard, Y Joli, et al, 'Informed consent in the context of pharmacogenomic research: ethical considerations' (2011) 11 *Pharmacogenomics Journal* 155.

[40] R Rao, 'Genes and Spleens: Property, Contract, or Privacy Rights in the Human Body?' (2007) 35 *Journal of Law, Medicine and Ethics* 2; K Greasley, '2; K Gre Rights in the Human Body: Commodification and Objectification' in Goold et al (n 16) 67ff; Pila (n 16) 833ff.

[41] R Brownsword, 'Rights, responsibility and stewardship: Beyond consent' (2009) in Widdows and Mullen (n 16) 99; NC Manson, 'The medium and the message: tissue samples, genetic information and data protection legislation' in Widdows and Mullen (n 16) 15; V Calderai, 'Consenso informato' in *Annali dell'Enciclopedia del Diritto* VIII (2015) 225.

specimens and products obtained from them has prompted the claim for acknowledgement of donor interests against the 'second enclosure movement' led by the pharmaceutical-industrial complex.[42] The analogy with movement at the roots of capital accumulation vividly depicts the reason behind patients' claim to ownership rights over 'their' tissues. The Lockean ideal of property as the foundation of freedom is summoned against colonisation of the world of life. In the distinct but intersected legal framework for the collection and treatment of information obtained from human tissues, 'uncertainty and uneasiness' persist as to the legitimacy of 'broad' or 'open' consent procedures based on requirements for permission limited to extraction, storage and future use of collected biological samples and associated data for unspecified research purposes.[43]

The flip side of the coin is repression of the social dimension of fundamental rights that creeps in when individual self-government is codified into property as an absolute subjective right over a 'thing'. Indeed, acknowledging a general property right on human tissues comes at the cost of cancelling the contexts, ripe with legal qualifications, which steer the ascription of liabilities and rights, with potentially dire implications for medical research. A lock of hair snipped in a barber's shop is a *res derelicta* that can be freely disposed of; a hospital has 'special waste' destined for destruction; in a laboratory is a biological sample, subject to an array of regulations aimed at ensuring safe procurement, storage, and transfer, privacy protection and data safety, legitimate access.[44] The same 'object' corresponds to different legal 'things', depending on their purpose: diagnosis, treatment, research, and so on.

Property rights offer incentives to internalise the costs of economic activities by forcing producers to pay for use of resources.[45] According to mainstream economic analysis of law, there is no limit to what can be owned, provided that it is 'scarce as well as desired'.[46] Much of the contemporary law of biotechnologies leads precisely from the assumption that 'biological constructs extracted from living nature can be patented by anyone ingenious enough to detach them from their physical surroundings and make them useful in commerce or industry'.[47] At the same time, all legal systems limit the extent of what can be deemed an object of individual property rights in the public interest. As a result, the incentive structures in human tissue research vary wildly,[48] depending on whether ownership categories are involved and of what

[42] See J Boyle, 'The Second Enclosure Movement and the Construction of the Public Domain' (2003) 66 *Law and Contemporary Problems* 33.

[43] Hallinan (n 30) 2ff.

[44] K Beier, 'Beyond the dichotomy of individualism and solidarity: Participation in biobank research in Sweden and Norway' in C Lenk et al (n 16) 65; Gottweis and Kaye (n 29).

[45] H Demsetz, 'Toward A Theory of Property Rights' (1967) 57 *American Economic Review* 347; H Demsetz 'Toward a Theory of Property Rights II: The Competition between Private and Collective Ownership' (2002) 31 *Journal of Legal Studies* 653.

[46] R Posner, *Economic Analyses of Law* (Aspen, Wolters Kluwer, 2014) 32ff.

[47] S Jasanoff, 'Taking Life. Private Rights in Public Nature' in KS Rajan (ed), *Lively Capital. Biotechnologies, Ethics and Governance in Global Markets* (Durham, Duke University Press, 2012) 155, 181.

[48] SR Munzer 'Common, Anticommons and Community in Biotechnological Assets' (2009) 10 *Theoretical Inquiries in Law* 271.

kind (private, public, or commons), with far-reaching implications for innovation, fundamental rights and public health.

The argument proposed here reverses the path that leads from the 'thingness' of detached body parts to consent as an act of ownership transfer. Instead of deriving legal rules from an unchecked ontological taxonomy, rights, liabilities and remedies are based on context-laden qualifications grounded on the applicable legal framework and functional analysis. This methodological approach elicits an inquiry into consent specifications in different contexts (A) and its relation to trust (B).

A. Different Contexts

Informed consent procedures mark the transition from raw materials to biological samples, prompting questions on the legal status of human tissues and donor rights, the feasibility of a common framework for data and samples, and the legitimacy of secondary uses. Across a broad spectrum of applications, the *leitbild* of self-ownership turns an issue of prevention and management of the negative externalities associated with genetic information processing into a veto power over any use of tissues and data not expressly authorised *ex ante* by the donor, unless anonymised, including uses unforeseeable at the time of collection and up to destruction of samples following withdrawal of consent.[49] Quite apart from the epistemic limits of information disclosure,[50] such a broad reading overlooks that: (i) total anonymisation is impossible;[51] (ii) its administrative costs are prohibitive, for much research on secondary data runs through years and decades; (iii) anonymity is undesirable whenever the value of secondary information is a function of first-level information traceability and processing, such as in epidemiological studies on the incidence of diseases across time and space. The idea of self-ownership casts a factitious uniformity over context-sensitive questions, the answers to which depend on the type of specimen collections or biobanks (general hospital biobanks; biobanks intended for research on specific diseases and conditions; population biobanks), data (*stricto sensu* personal and sensitive data, aggregated data, non-sensitive data), and research (epidemiological research, epigenetic studies, research on rare diseases).[52]

Research on rare genetic diseases presents a prima facie compelling case for ascribing quasi-proprietary rights of control to donors personally involved as patients or

[49] Italian Data Protection Authority, Aut 12.12.2013 (www.garanteprivacy.it/web/guest/home/docweb/-/docweb-display/docweb/2818993), following the Council of Europe Recommendation (2006) 4 (Art 15). The right to choose between anonymisation and destruction has been reasserted by the new Recommendation, CM/Rec(2016)6, Art 13.1. See M Macilotti, 'Reshaping Informed Consent in the Biobanking Context' (2012) 19 *European Journal of Health Law* 271.

[50] NC Manson and O O'Neill, *Rethinking Informed Consent* (Cambridge, Cambridge University Press, 2007) 15ff.

[51] JE Lunshof, R Chadwick, DB Vorhaus and GM Church, 'From Genetic Privacy to Open Consent' (2008) 9 *Nature Review Genetics* 406; Macilotti (n 49) 283.

[52] N Black, 'Secondary use of personal data for health and health services research: why identifiable data are essential' (2003) 8 *Journal of Health Services Research and Policy* 36; A Brand et al, 'Biobanking for Public Health' in J Taupitz et al, *Trust in Biobanking. Dealing with Ethical, Legal and Social Issues in an Emerging Field of Biotechnology* (Berlin, Springer, 2012) 3.

parents. Still, property rules may work against their expectations. In the aftermath of *Moore*, attempts by research participants to claim some rights of control and exert some 'voice' option for dissemination of research-generated technologies in the public interest have been dismissed based on an aggressive reading of 'consent' as an act of transfer of property right:[53] 'the property right in blood and tissue samples evaporates once the sample is voluntarily given to a third party'.[54]

These doctrines have encouraged the search for contract-based solutions, where researchers are granted a licence to use the materials in return for donor recognition of the power to share patent decisions and participation in royalties. The agreement between PXE Int, Inc, a non-profit organisation owning a biobank of biological samples and a group of researchers, made it possible to isolate the gene responsible for *Pseudoxanthoma elasticum*, a rare disorder causing degeneration of connective tissue, neglected by the pharmaceutical industry due to its extremely low incidence. New treatments were born.[55] In terms of transaction cost economics, this is a paradigmatic example of a hybrid response (unified contracting) to the inefficient outcome of pure outsourcing systems.[56] On the other hand, contract-based governance is vulnerable to transaction costs and power asymmetries. Conditions of bilateral dependence in research on rare genetic diseases, along with the possibility of organising a disease-defined community into a legal entity owning a biobank, can effectively curb failures of the market for medical treatments[57] and see that donors maintain a robust voice in

[53] See: *Greenberg v Miami Children's Hospital Research Institute Inc* 264 F Supp 2d 1064 (SD Fla 2003) and *Washington University v Catalona* 437 Fed Supp 2d 986 (ED Missouri 2006). In *Greenberg*, the families of children suffering from a rare congenital disease gave tissues, information, and funds to a researcher, with the informal understanding 'that any carrier and prenatal testing developed in connection with the research … would be provided on an affordable and accessible basis, and that … research would remain in the public domain to promote the discovery of more effective prevention techniques and treatments and, eventually, to effectuate a cure'. Following the researcher's decision to transfer the data and samples to another institution and patent the genetic test obtained, the donors assumed the defendant's wrongful interference with the plaintiff's property right in the tissue, as in *Moore* (n 34 and accompanying text). Unlike Moore, however, the *Greenberg* court found that research participants enjoy some limited property rights over their tissues, which should qualify as 'donations to research without any contemporaneous expectations of return'. The *Catalona* court went a step further, by narrowly constructing the meaning of consent as a 'gift' of bodily materials by research participants to research institutions. For critical analyses, see Rao (n 40) 3–5; HA Washington, *Deadly monopolies* (New York, Random House, 2011) 234. Of course, the exit/voice alternative provides a critical analysis framework: see AO Hirschmann, *Exit, Voice, and Loyalty: Responses to Decline in Firms, Organizations, and States* (Cambridge Mass, Harvard University Press, 1970).

[54] *Greenberg v Miami Children's Hospital* (n 53) 1075.

[55] DE Winickoff, 'Partnership in UK Biobank: A Third Way for Genomic Governance?' (2007) 35 *Journal of Law, Medicine and Ethics*, 450: 'PXE International has become a well-known model for the way it has leveraged its control of the biobank qua biocapital in order to achieve collective goals'.

[56] OE Williamson, 'The Theory of the Firm as a Governance Structure: From Choice to Contract' (2002) 16 *Journal of Economic Perspectives* 171.

[57] They can but need not. The capacity of private ordering to correct failures of the market for advanced therapies depends on the construction of consent as an act of transferral of the rights of control over human tissues, whose success in turn depends on the characteristics of the transaction. See EW Williams and R Coase, 'The Regulated Industries: Discussion' (1964) 54 *The American Economic Review* 192, 195: 'Contemplation of an optimal system … has directed economists' attention away from the main question, which is how alternative arrangements will actually work in practice. … It is no accident that in the literature … we find a category market failure but no category government failure. Until we realize that we are choosing between social arrangements which are all more or less failures, we are not likely to make much headway'.

managerial choices. Conversely, unilateral dependence and high organisational costs in research on high-incidence diseases highlight the limits of property and contract as techniques to promote and protect access to knowledge.[58]

B. Trust

Of the conditions for pursuit of knowledge, trust is possibly the most valuable, likely the most vulnerable,[59] most of all if the conditions for choosing *ex ante* are weak.[60] A privacy-obsessed approach to the government of biomedical research sees trust in the light of procedures for processing and circulating anonymised or pseudo-anonymised data and biological samples, unconcerned by the fact that anonymity, to the extent that it can[61] and must be safeguarded, is irrelevant to donor interest *qua* citizen to participate actively in scientific research.[62] Indeed, the 'rhetoric of anonymity'[63] obscures the circumstance that consent may safeguard interests other than privacy, such as the aspiration to bring values and convictions into public space, including the right to 'share in scientific advancement and its benefits'.[64]

The measure to which these aspirations can be realised depends on the idea of self-determination: as either a value with roots in the right to privacy or as an instrument for exercising civil, political and economic rights. Adhesion to the first model implies that donor values must be binding on researchers. This seemingly obvious conclusion is problematic whenever donor wishes are dictated by prejudice or superstition. Donors may oppose specific uses of their tissues based on scientifically inconsistent beliefs, such as the harmfulness of vaccines or hostility toward minorities or social

[58] Munzer (n 48) 282.

[59] O O'Neill, *Autonomy and Trust in Bioethics* (Cambridge, Cambridge University Press, 2002). S Lo Iacono and B Sonmez, 'The Effect of Trusting and Trustworthy Environments on the Provision of Public Goods' (2021) *European Sociological Review* 155.

[60] For an empirical analysis of different models of consent in different types of research see S Wallace, S Lazor and BM Knoppers, 'What is in a Clause? A Comparison of Clauses from Population Biobank and Disease Biobank Consent Materials' in Dabrock, Taupitz and Ried (n 52) 119.

[61] HT Greely, 'The uneasy ethical and legal underpinnings of large-scale genomic biobanks' (2007) 8 *Annual Review of Genomics and Human Genetics* 343; MC Tallacchini, 'Rhetoric of Anonymity and Property Rights in Human Biological Materials (HBMs)' (2005) 7 *Law and the Human Genome Review* 153, 164ff; JE Lunshof et al (n 51) 410: 'No promises of anonymity, privacy or confidentiality are made. The leading moral principle is veracity – telling the truth – which should precede autonomy'.

[62] S Rodotà, *Tecnologie e diritti* (Bologna, Il Mulino 1995) 29; MC Tallacchini, 'A Participatory Space Beyond the 'Autonomy Versus Property' Dichotomy' in D Mascalzoni et al, *The Ethics, Law and Governance of Biobanking* (Dordrecht, Springer, 2015) 21, 22: 'In many ways, privacy has become more a constructed 'myth' than a perceived need, a screen to protect the interests of the market more than those of the individual. Privacy can, in fact, be transformed into an obstacle, an undesired and paternalistic protective barrier, while showing one's face and name can, in some circumstances, be important for individuals'; B Prainsack and A Buyx, 'A Solidarity-Based Approach to the Governance of Research Biobanks' (2013) 21 *Medical Law Review* 71.

[63] Tallacchini (n 61) 163: 'As a legal standard, anonymisation of data is not simply the recognition that an effective procedure of encryption has been performed, but much more a legal fiction: it aims at hiding all remaining interest of the subject-of the-data with regard to biological materials.'

[64] Art 27.1 Universal Declaration on Human Rights. The 'right to science' is emphasised by E Vayena and J Tasioulas, 'The dynamics of big data and human rights: the case of scientific research' (2016) 374 *Philosophical Transactions of the Royal Society* A 374:20160129.

groups. Deference for individual choices cannot go so far as to warrant discriminatory biases and irrational beliefs without encroaching upon fundamental scientific and constitutional values. Bar the freedom to refuse or withdraw consent, donor control over the nature and purposes of research should be limited to general criteria linked to broad ethical, political and religious directives, with scant concession to idiosyncratic motivations.

From yet another perspective, uncertainty as to future uses of biological samples, the limits of anonymisation procedures, and the need for traceability can be effectively addressed by complementing open consent procedures with objective measures of protection (for instance, independent evaluation, supervisory bodies representing donors and publicity of results). What is often depicted as a quintessentially personal expression of individual sovereignty seems more like a process of multi-party communication grounded in the impersonal nature of knowledge and aimed at managing the crises of cooperation that stem from uncertainties, cognitive biases, organisational dysfunctions and professionals' habits.[65] The scientific and normative bases of cooperation between researchers and donors should not be left to the consideration, goodwill and civil commitment of individuals and civil society organisations. Rather, it is a question of citizenship that touches upon 'revision of the contract between science and society'[66] and, as such, must be addressed, *de jure condendo*, with institutional change.

IV. PROPERTY IN THE BODY. AN EVOLUTIONARY APPROACH

This section sketches out a theory of donor consent within the framework of an anti-naturalistic understanding of the objects of property rights – in a nutshell: from an act of disposal of property interests over a 'thing' existing *in rerum natura* to a stage within the process of mutual construction of rights and things.[67]

The tendency to identify what is perceived by the senses and can be recalled to the mind by 'the operation of reflection' as an 'object' is an epistemic obstacle to acknowledgement of the historical nature of legal qualifications,[68] with ripple effects on the idea of distributive justice. In the general legal meaning of the word, a 'good' or an 'asset' is a (tangible or intangible) 'thing', subject to estimation *à prix d'argent* (*cf* Article 2284 French Civil Code and Article 2740 Italian Civil Code). As the items included in the general class of goods change across space and time, the proportion between what is due to each person and what is left to the distribution of wealth and talents varies accordingly. This means that analysis of the determinants of distributive

[65] M Graziadei, 'Il consenso informato e i suoi limiti' in S Rodotà and P Zatti (eds), *Trattato di biodiritto* IV *I diritti in medicina* (Milano, Giuffrè, 2011) 191, 219ff.

[66] MC Tallacchini, 'Democrazia come terapia: la governance tra medicina e società' (2006) 22 *Notizie di Politeia* 15.

[67] See P Femia, 'Il campione biologico come oggetto di diritti. Bene giuridico e processi di valorizzazione' in D Farace (ed) *Lo statuto etico-giuridico dei campioni biologici umani* (Roma, Nuova Editrice Universitaria, 2016) 149.

[68] I Kant, *Critique of Judgment* (trans JH Bernard) (New York, Hafner, 1951) §40. The notion of *obstacle épistemologique* was developed by G Bachelard, *La formation de l'esprit scientifique: contribution à une psychanalyse de la connaissance objective* (Paris, Librairie philosophique J Vrin, 1938).

choices goes up a notch: from selection and ascription of entitlements over an asset to institution of the asset and limits to its exploitation. In other words, the problem of distributive justice (and the core of dissent) does not concern primarily the conditions for markets to produce fair, as well as efficient, results, but the choice between: (i) things open to (more or less regulated forms of) market allocation; (ii) things excluded from the market, but still open to non-market allocation systems; (iii) things subject to a regime of market-inalienability.

Since the 1970s, these choices have been driven by the convergence of supply-side economic policies and technological innovation, radiating worldwide from its US epicentre.[69] The result is an incessant flow of new, efficient proprietary assets,[70] obtained from 'enclosure' of the public domain and the commodification of things formerly excluded from appropriation,[71] including human and non-human genome,[72] reproductive capacities,[73] information extracted from any (social or natural) phenomenon or (public or private) activity observable through sensors or realized through networked terminals.[74]

Production of biotechnological assets then 'sees' the body as a natural resource. As the millennial history of trades in corpses and relics for medical and devotional markets suggests, the human body has never been entirely *extra commercium*.[75] Nevertheless, these transactions occurred in a grey area, verging on impiety and proscription, whilst the contemporary demand for biological tissues is set within the secularised framework of the knowledge economy.[76] The association established by continental Civil Codes between property rights and *res corporalis* (*cf* §90 BGB; Article 810 Italian Civil Code Article 544 French Civil Code) fits this *gestalt*,[77] with minimal adjustments required by relation of the thing to the donor.[78] By contrast, in

[69] U Mattei, 'Circolazione dei modelli giuridici', in *Annali dell'Enciclopedia del diritto*, I (Milano, Giuffrè, 2008) 173.

[70] Demsetz (n 45).

[71] Boyle (nn 28 and 42); BM Frischmann, 'Evaluating the Demsetzian Trend in Copyright Law' (2007) 3 *Review of Law and Economics* 649; A Gambaro, 'Dai beni immobili ai beni virtuali' (2009) in *XXI Secoloi*, www.treccani.it/enciclopedia/dai-beni-immobili-ai-beni-virtuali_%28XXI-Secolo%29.

[72] Kieff (n 16); Hoppe (n 16); JL Roberts, 'Progressive Genetic Ownership' (2018) 93 *Notre Dame Law Review* 1105; GS Alexander, EM Peñalver, JW Singer and LS Underkuffler, 'A Statement of Progressive Property' (2009) *Cornell Law Faculty Publications* 11.

[73] V Calderai, 'Breaking out of the Regulatory Delusion. The Ban to Surrogacy and the Foundations of European Constitutionalism' (2020) 20 *Global Jurist* 1.

[74] S Zuboff, 'Big other: Surveillance Capitalism and the Prospects of an Information Civilization' (2015) 30 *Journal of Information Technology* 75; S Zuboff, 'Surveillance Capitalism and the Challenge of Collective Action' (2019) 28 *New Labor Forum* 10.

[75] R Richardson, *Death, Dissection and the Destitute* (Chicago, University of Chicago Press, 1987) 54ff and PJ Geary, *Furta Sacra. Thefts of Relics in the Central Middle Ages* (Princeton, Princeton University Press 1990) 44ff (with an interesting reference to the trafficking of works of art).

[76] Rajan (n 17).

[77] Schünemann (n 24) 58. A sophisticated version of this insight is embedded in Art 5 It cc, whose 'atti di disposizione del corpo umano' slavishly draws out the ownership paradigm, as the 'external projection of a right' through which 'the subjection of the res to this power of the subject is expressed'. The German category of *Verfügungsgeschäfte* thus lends legal clothing to a metaphysics of the body as a portion of geometric space, identified in relation to its physical properties (*res extensa*), somewhat mysteriously linked with a spiritual subject (*res cogitans*). See C Castronovo, 'Il negozio giuridico dal patrimonio alla persona' (2009) 12 *Europa e diritto privato* 87.

[78] Halàsz (n 24).

common law jurisdictions, the centuries-old barrier against property interests in the human body cracked from the end of the twentieth century to the benefit of researchers and research funders.[79]

In both Civil Law and Common Law traditions, individuation by detachment provides the hook to attach human tissues to the world of natural 'things'. The time-honoured rules on fruits (*cf* Articles 820–21 Italian Civil Code, §953 BGB) and occupancy (*cf* Article 923 Italian Civil Code, §§958–58 BGB) have thus been bent to suit ascription of property rights to donors[80] and researchers[81] (in the latter case upon interpolation of voluntary relinquishment via donor consent).[82] Yet, at the same time, to be perceived as a resource the human body must go through a procedure of naturalisation or dehumanisation; it must be thought of as a 'thing' to qualify as an 'asset', an object of property interests.

In a seminal study, Yan Thomas has shown the role of procedure in the institution of things in Roman law.[83] A thing 'existed' for the law insofar as it was ritually or procedurally apprehended to be valued. Contemporary consent requirements work just the same: not so much as an act of disposal (*verfügungsakt*) but as a rite of passage, a performative act that imparts a positive qualification – a value – to something that otherwise would be only negatively qualified as 'hazardous waste' and destroyed.[84]

[79] *Moore v Regents of the University of California* (n 34). In a much-criticised decision, the Court of Appeal of England and Wales ordered the hospital where some patients had deposited their semen before undergoing treatment that could have led to infertility to pay damages, following the destruction of the sample, finding an infringement of a property right: *Yearworth and Others v North Bristol NHS Trust* [2009] 2 All ER 986 (CA). Interestingly, the plaintiffs had cited a well-known decision by the *Bundesgerichtshof*, based on identical facts, in support of a claim for damages for personal injuries (BGH, 9.11.1993, (1994) *Neue Juristische Wochenschrift* (NJW), 127, annotated by A Laufs and E Reiling 'Schmerzensgeld wegen schuldhafter Verletzung tiefgefrorenen Spermas? (1994) *Neue Juristische Wochenschrift (NJW)* 775ff). In that case, the Bundesgerichtshof upheld a claim for compensation for non-pecuniary damages (§253, former §847) for injury to physical integrity (§823) based on the functional unity between the semen and the body. SHE Harmon and G Laurie, 'Yearworth v. North Bristol NHS Trust: Property, Principles, Precedents and Paradigms' (2010) 69 *CLJ* 476, 491: 'The rather uninspired and uninspiring advancement of the property paradigm in Yearworth suggests that property was only used as a convenient vehicle through which to achieve a certain outcome. But the property model could lead to numerous harms, including exploitation and the dehumanisation of patients and people more generally'.

[80] Roth (n 16) 58ff. Italian scholars mainly reject this solution: CM Bianca, *Diritto Civile, 1, La norma giuridica. I soggetti* (Milano, Giuffrè 1978) 163.

[81] *Moore v Regents of the University of California* (n 34) 144; *Washington University v Catalona* (n 54) 999ff.

[82] *Washington v Catalona* (n 54).

[83] Thomas (n 2) 1431.

[84] The European regulatory framework is currently defined by Directive 2008/98/EC of the European Parliament and of the Council of 19 November 2008 on waste and repealing certain Directives OJ L312/3 (as amended by the Commission Regulation (EU) 1357/2014 of 18 December 2014 replacing Annex III to Directive 2008/98/EC of the European Parliament and of the Council on waste and repealing certain Directives OJ L369/89) and by Commission decision 2000/532/EC of 3 May 2000 replacing Decision 94/3/EC establishing a list of wastes pursuant to Article 1(a) of Council Directive 75/442/EEC on waste and Council Decision 94/904/EC establishing a list of hazardous waste pursuant to Article 1(4) of Council Directive 91/689/EEC on hazardous waste (notified under document number C(2000) 1147) (Text with EEA relevance) OJ L 226/3 (European List of Waste). Human tissues are identified (under Commission decision 2000/532/EC) by codes 180102 and 180103 (respectively body parts and organs including blood bags and blood preserves' and 'waste whose collection and disposal is subject to special requirements in view of the prevention of infection') of the List. See also Human Tissue Act 2004, s 44: material taken during

The lens of metaphysical dualism and sovereignty of the will conceals contexts that channel the meaning of consent. A sample of gametes stored in a fertility centre can be different 'things', depending on whether the sample comes from an anonymous donor or a patient before treatment that could lead to sterility.[85] The same 'object' – say an umbilical cord – is not the same 'thing' depending (a) on whether its collection was authorised, and (b) its destination (stem cell transplant, research or autologous implantation). These examples can be generalised. Legal 'things' are logical mediums, inhabitants of Popper's World 3:[86] qualifications and nexus of qualifications functional to identification and ascription of rights, liabilities and remedies. The autonomy of law from ontology is such that the same piece of matter originates different 'things', with different legal statuses, depending on their functions.

This insight is backed up by the observation that in all jurisdictions human tissues do not qualify as ownership by the simple fact of detachment, independently from ascription of rights, obligations and remedies ordinarily associated with property rights. Following this rule of recognition, human raw materials obtained in medical settings have neither exchange value (they cannot be sold) nor use value (except for diagnosis and therapy). By this double exclusion from the market and from direct exploitation, no public or private entities – not even donors – qualify strictly speaking as owners: no one can claim *uti dominus* possession; exercise the faculties of use, management, economic exploitation, disposition, exclusion; bring actions inherent in the *ius sequelae*, be expropriated, and so on, until precious little is left in the 'bundle'.[87] By the same token, consent cannot work as a transfer of property rights that *ex hypothesi* do not yet exist. Instead, we can observe that the general function of consent, authorising otherwise unlawful conduct,[88] is complemented by the destination of human tissues to research within the frame of 'appropriate consent procedures' (Article 22 ECHB) to bring into legal 'existence' certain things 'd'origine et à finalité humaine'.[89]

By contrast, human tissues stored in research facilities following donor consent do qualify as 'things', 'objects' of property interests. To understand what kind of 'things' researchers are dealing with, it is worth pausing a moment: are they the same things extracted from the body? Important clues come from language. The word 'specimen', commonly used by researchers, designates an artefact: selected, classified, stored to be used as a source of information, along with other specimens.[90]

the course of medical treatment is surplus tissue and can be treated as waste; Code de la santé publique, Art R1135-11: 'Les pièces anatomiques d'origine humaine destinées à l'abandon doivent être incinérées'; Decr Pres Repubblica n 254-2003, Art 10.

[85] See n 79.

[86] The world of abstract intellectual creations: Popper (n 25) 106ff.

[87] W Hohfeld, 'Fundamental Legal Conceptions as Applied in Judicial Reasoning' in WA Cook (ed), *Fundamental Legal Conceptions as Applied in Judicial Reasoning and Other Legal Essays by Wesley Newcomb Hohfeld* (New Haven, Yale University Press, 1920); A Honoré, 'Ownership' in AG Guest (ed), *Oxford Essays in Jurisprudence: A Collaborative Work* (Oxford, Oxford University Press, 1961) 107; ST Munzer, 'A Bundle Theorist Holds On to His Collection of Sticks' (2011) *Economics Journal Watch* 265; JL Contreras, 'The False Promise of Data Ownership' (2019) 94 *NYU Law Review* 624.

[88] Calderai (n 41).

[89] Hermitte (n 16).

[90] Manson (n 41) 15.

Depending on whether the emphasis is on the material or the informational dimension, human specimens are classified as non-excludable and non-rival goods, their normative status constantly teetering between the poles of (public or private) ownership and commons. Yet, as the time and work required for development of knowledge enter the picture, the assimilation of human specimens to the material support of genetic data is wanting in its implication that the information is somewhere in the sample, just like the apologue on justice in 'The Merchant of Venice' in the play.[91] Semiotically, the difference is the same that occurs between knowledge from symbolic communication (*signum artificiale*) and knowledge from experience (*signum naturale*). Whereas the former applies a code shared within a community, the latter proceeds inductively from observations. Unlike information communicated through conventional language and intentionally reproduced in a medium, genetic information requires scientific knowledge, technical skills, and a great deal of analysis, classification, and association with other information in order to be realised.[92] To say that the data are in the samples is like saying that the statue is in a block of marble.

Some corollaries follow from here: (i) unlike data, samples not (yet) analysed are potential information: 'produced and stored for epistemic purposes';[93] (ii) therefore, the regime of personal data protection should apply only to data; (iii) normative classifications based on data 'sources' are epistemically baseless: there is no such thing as inherently personal and sensitive data, but all data can be personal and sensitive in relation to the purposes for which they are collected and the uses to which they are put; (iv) since the uses that can be obtained from individual specimens are limited, potential knowledge is expressed by collections of specimens and data, along with sharing and connecting different collections.[94]

The latter feature supports the choice of biobanks as the basic unit of analysis. Biobanks are *universitates iuris*: pools of different items considered as a whole based on their purpose or destination. To an extent, the relevance of destination downplays the ownership issue. Public or private, non-profit or for-profit, management powers and exclusionary rights are framed in the public interest, so that a biobank can fulfil its purpose and operate as a medical research infrastructure, with powers and responsibilities instrumental to exercise of the functions of 'stewards' and 'trusted mediators' among different stakeholders.[95] The description of biobanks as research infrastructures is supported by the gradual convergence of European national legislation

[91] Manson and O'Neill (n 51).

[92] Manson (n 41) 31.

[93] Munzer (n 48) 271.

[94] G Laurie et al, 'Genetic databases. Assessing the benefits and the impact on human and patient rights. A World Health Organisation Report' (2004) 11 *European Journal of Health Law* 87, 92.

[95] This implies, as a minimum, adoption of measures aimed at granting access to researchers on a non-discriminatory basis while ensuring safe and efficient use of samples and information: see A Boggio, 'Population Biobanks' Governance: a Case Study of Knowledge Commons, in KJ Strandburg et al (n 16) 102, 106; The Deutscher Ethikrat, *Humanbiobanken für die Forschung* (Berlin, Deutscher Ethikrat, 2010); M Macilotti, *Le biobanche di ricerca. Studio comparato sulla "zona grigia" tra privacy e proprietà* (Trento, Università di Trento, 2013) 14.

towards integration in national healthcare and research systems.[96] The destination to the public interest is stronger if biobanks are entrusted to (public or private) entities operating as 'service units'[97] on a non-profit basis within national health systems, whereas it thins out if biobanks are owned by private bodies offering products and services on the market. However, even in this case obligations of registration and accreditation, control by administrative agencies, protocols for managing samples and data, and auditing procedures realise a substantive adjustment of property rights in the public interest.

The merit of sharing knowledge justifies management of biobanks as medical knowledge commons,[98] regardless of their allocation to public or private entities. The commons-based approach to biobanking does not imply nationalisation of genetic resources extracted from citizens' bodies,[99] as in the unfortunate Icelandic Medical Database Act and Biobank Act (1998), any more than it subscribes to expropriation of private biobanks. Separating the problem of destination from the problem of allocation cuts across the division between public and private ownership, highlighting the regulatory significance of management strategies. If a resource is an infrastructure whose purpose is the sharing of knowledge as a catalyst of innovation, that strategy must be built on non-discriminatory access.[100] As biological specimens are rival and excludable assets, trade-offs are required between openness and the need to limit resource depletion through overuse and misuse. This goal is fulfilled by legal regimes based on the principle of the broadest possible qualified access to samples and data. The backbone of such regimes, as far as concerns the legal status of human tissues, consists of legal and administrative procedures of independent research evaluation and compliance with (objective and subjective) individual rights and measures to protect societal interests.[101]

At the end of the supply chain, biotechnological products obtained from human tissues can be divided into intermediate and final products. In the wake of the doctrine pinned down by the US Supreme Court since the 1980s, the transition from 'things' subject to a regime of market-inalienability to 'things' subject to full-blown market regimes is controlled by §101 Patent Act, based on the principle of the novelty of the invention compared to substances existing in nature.[102] Accordingly, discoveries

[96] Gottweis and Kaye (n 29) 40ff.

[97] See the definition of the Italian National Committee for Biosafety and Biotechnology, 'Guidelines for the certification of Biobanks': 'service units, without direct profit, organised in technical units with quality, order and destination criteria, aimed at collecting and preserving human biological material and data related to it, for the purpose of medical research' (my translation).

[98] Boggio (n 95).

[99] Rao (n 40) 6ff.

[100] BM Frischmann, *Infrastructure. The Social Value of Shared Resources* (New York, Oxford University Press, 2012) 7ff.

[101] In this perspective, the proposal to substitute the equivocal denomination 'biobanks' with 'bioarchives: collections of public knowledge sources on the non-pecuniary value of life' is thus justified. See Femia (n 67) 190.

[102] *Diamond v Chakrabarty* 447 US 303 (1980); *Association for Molecular Pathology et al v Myriad Genetics, Inc, et al*, 569 US 12-398 (2013); *Mayo Collaborative Services v Prometheus Laboratories, Inc*, 566 US 10-1150 (2012).

that do not involve bio-engineering intervention,[103] including non-manipulated gene sequences,[104] are not eligible for patents.

This outcome was but a foregone conclusion. The patentability of isolated and purified DNA sequences had been a pillar of the 'global government of knowledge' established by the US Patent and Trademark Office and the European Patent Office,[105] echoed by Directive 98/44/EC on biotechnological inventions (Articles 3.2 and 5.2). By emphasising the functional dimension of innovation, the European Court of Justice assuaged the harsher effects of intellectual property, with the result of exempting scientific discoveries from patent rights.[106]

Criticisms of the expansion of intellectual property rights in this sector address the 'tragic scarcity' effects[107] of a mechanism that makes investment conditional upon the price system and collective action problems generated by the fragmentation of property rights at an early stage of research (anticommons).[108] Against this backdrop, the requirement of informed donor consent for filing a patent application if the invention involves human biological materials (Recital 26 Directive 44/98/EC) is the perfect *notion à consensus*: uplifting and useless,[109] it adds a new veto right without limiting the unfair distributive effects of intellectual property rights.[110]

[103] *Diamond v Chakrabarty* (n 102) 310 (distinguishing from *Funk Bro Seeds Co v Kalo Inoculant Co*, 333 US 127, 1948). Granting a patent in these cases would upset the balance between 'incentives that lead to creation, invention, and discovery' and 'imped[ing] the flow of information that might permit, indeed spur, invention'.

[104] *Association for Molecular Pathology et al v Myriad Genetics* (n 102): 'Myriad did not create or alter either the genetic information encoded in the BCRA1 and BCRA2 genes or the genetic structure of the DNA. It found an important and useful gene, but groundbreaking, innovative, or even brilliant discovery does not by itself satisfy the §101 inquiry'.

[105] Acting on an aggressive interpretation of international trade agreements. See P Drahos, *The Global Governance of Knowledge: Patent Offices and their Clients* (Cambridge, Cambridge University Press, 2010); G van Overwalle, 'Biotechnological Patents: Global Standards, European Approaches and National Accents' in D Wüger and T Cottier (eds), *Genetic Engineering and the World Trade System* (Cambridge, Cambridge University Press, 2008) 77ff.

[106] Case C-428/08, *Monsanto Technology LLC v Cefetra BV and others* ECLI:EU:C:2010:402. In a case that pitted Monsanto against two companies importing food products obtained from genetically modified organisms in breach of the patent, the Court made the application of Art 9 of the Directive (patent protection extends to all material 'in which the product is incorporated and in which the genetic information is contained and performs its function') conditional on the circumstance that the genetic information 'at the time of the alleged infringement, performs the function described in the patent application'. Importation of the product from a country that does not apply patent protection was then deemed lawful because the genetic sequence was inert and no longer performed the function described in the patent application.

[107] G Calabresi and P Bobbit, *Tragic Choices* (New York, Norton, 1978) 129ff.

[108] Above, section III.A and nn 57 and 58. See Heller and Eisenberg (n 27). Rebecca Eisenberg later partially corrected her thesis in light of empirical analyses: R Eisenberg, 'Noncompliance, Nonenforcement, Nonproblem? Rethinking the Anticommons in Biomedical Research' (2008) 45 *Houston Law Review* 1059, 1062; R Eisenberg, 'Patent Costs and Unlicensed Use of Patented Inventions' 2011) 78 *University of Chicago Law Review* 53 (the 'tragedy of the anticommons' depends not only on the excessive number of upstream patents but also on the restrictions introduced by the licensing system).

[109] At least in the general terms in which it has been transposed by Italian legislation: see Art 170-bis Cod Proprietà Industriale.

[110] Quite apart from enforcement and compliance difficulties originating from bilateral information costs: see JA Bovenberg, 'Moore's Law and the Taxman: Some Thesis on the Regulation of Property in Human Tissue' in M Steinmann, P Sýkora and U Wiesing (eds), *Altruism reconsidered: exploring new approaches to property in human tissue* (Farnham, Ashgate, 2009) 164. The examples of private biobanks born from disease-defined communities suggest that the success of such initiatives crucially hinges on an institutional design tailored to the transactions: above, section III.A and nn 55, 56.

Similarities across the Atlantic should not keep us from considering the impact of institutional alternatives on biotechnological innovation. Whereas US law looks at the raw material/specimens/product sequence through the lens of contract and property rights, European legal systems use the lens of public policy. The difference lies in the burden required to overcome the presumption of availability of a resource in the public domain or, conversely, to trigger patent protection in the face of an alleged infringement, particularly in the light of today's complex networked models of genetic and epigenetic interaction.[111] Under conditions of uncertainty, the general interest in sharing knowledge and including natural resources in the public domain provides quite different assumptions. In terms of information, exclusive control is evil unless it can be proven to be good.

V. CONCLUDING REMARKS

This chapter has critically examined the *Leitbild* of donor consent to medical research based on human tissues as an act of transfer of rights akin to property or possession, established on the asymmetric dualism between persons and things. The capture of the human body into that old dichotomy fits well with neoliberal intuitions of moral agency and the relentless extraction of capital value from 'bare life' in the knowledge economy. However, this stands at variance with understanding the body as an integral dimension of personhood and personal freedom in modern constitutions and declarations of rights.

The argument advanced through these pages represents donor consent as a performative act, whereby the law institutes human biological materials. The almost paradoxical double qualification attached to human tissues – medical waste and valuable resource – suggests that their assimilation to raw matter and means of production entails a threshold of indeterminacy between *persona* and *res* structurally similar to the 'sovereign ban' that in a well-known interpretation of biopolitics marks the law primaeval relationship to natural life.[112] No longer living matter but still not *res*, human tissues are abandoned to destruction unless they can be turned into exchangeable commodities and internalised into the value chain of the biomedical industry. Yet, in liberal societies the power to redeem matter from destruction is entrusted to donor consent to preserve our commitment to human dignity and the inviolability of embodied personhood.

Some implications of this insight align with reframing human specimens collected for research as communal or collective property. However, the categorisation here proposed does away with the need to justify the transition of human tissues from private to communal ownership, as tissues collected for research are *ab imis* attracted to the public dimension in consideration of the general interest in development of knowledge, regardless of the private or public nature of the legal entities who bear the responsibilities for their management. In this light, communal ownership or

[111] Munzer (n 48) 286ff.

[112] G Agamben, *Homo Sacer. Il potere sovrano e la nuda vita* (Torino, Einaudi, 1995) 34ff.

Commons means no more and no less than an approach to resource management 'by which a resource is shared within a community'.[113]

From a reconsideration of the time-honoured category of detached body parts, three corollaries follow: (i) Informed consent should be re-examined to limit donor control over research activities and outputs to broad ethical, political and religious considerations; (ii) secondary uses of samples and data for research purposes not expressly authorised *ex ante* by donors should be allowed without the necessity for a new consent procedure, nor should withdrawal of consent to data processing imply destruction of biological samples (bar previous *inter partes* commitments to that effect) or compensation (bar remuneration for any inconvenience suffered); (iii) legal research in this field should focus on risk management and protection against exploitation of clinical labour,[114] rather than ever elusive strategies to control 'bare life'.

[113] Frischmann (n 100) ix.
[114] Cooper and Waldby (n 16).

13

Rights for those who Unwillingly, Unknowingly and Unidentifiably Compute!

MICHAEL VEALE*

I. INTRODUCTION: COMPUT*ED* PERSONS, COMPUT*ING* PERSONS

FOR CENTURIES, STATISTICAL claims have been made about groups and applied to the individuals constituting them.[1] Mass profiling centring on individuals is somewhat newer, made possible with the ubiquity we see today by the scalability of sensing and computation.[2] Troves of scholarly papers and policy-related PDF files have been produced on the ways that profiling challenges fundamental rights.[3] Profiling is not a solely European legal phenomenon, featuring in laws on at least five continents.[4] Thinking about profiling typically draws attention to the persons and communities it directly affects, highlighting the risks that powerful actors use

* Associate Professor, Faculty of Laws, University College London.

[1] K de Vries, 'Identity, Profiling Algorithms and a World of Ambient Intelligence' (2010) 12 *Ethics and Information Technology* 71.

[2] M Hildebrandt, *Smart Technologies and the End(s) of Law: Novel Entanglements of Law and Technology* (Cheltenham-Northampton MA, Edward Elgar Publishing, 2015).

[3] Including OH Gandy, *The Panoptic Sort: A Political Economy of Personal Information* (Boulder, Westview Press, 1993); M Hildebrandt and S Gutwirth (eds), *Profiling the European Citizen: Cross-Disciplinary Perspectives* (Dordrecht, Springer, 2008); De Wetenschappelijke Raad voor het Regeringsbeleid (WRR), *Big Data in Een Vrije En Veilige Samenleving* (Amsterdam, Amsterdam University Press, 2016); Information Commissioner's Office, 'Big Data, Artificial Intelligence, Machine Learning and Data Protection' (2017), ico.org.uk/media/for-organisations/documents/2013559/big-data-ai-ml-and-data-protection.pdf; K Yeung, 'A Study of the Implications of Advanced Digital Technologies (Including AI Systems) for the Concept of Responsibility within a Human Rights Framework (MSI-AUT(2018)05)', rm.coe.int/a-study-of-the-implications-of-advanced-digital-technologies-including/168096bdab (Council of Europe 2018). This list goes on *ad infinitum*.

[4] See eg Regulation (EU) 2016/679 of the European Parliament and of the Council of 27 April 2016 on the protection of natural persons with regard to the processing of personal data and on the free movement of such data, and repealing Directive 95/46/EC (General Data Protection Regulation) [2016] OJ L119/1 (GDPR), Art 4(4); California Civil Code §1798.140 subd (z) (California Consumer Privacy Act of 2018, as amended by the California Privacy Rights Act of 2020); Data Protection Act 2019, s 2 (Kenya); Personal Data Protection Act 2000, s 20 (Argentina); Personal Information Protection Law 2021, Art 73 (China) (profiling here is described as 'automated decision-making', but defined similarly).

informationally derived insights to the detriment of individual and collective interests. It highlights the digital 'alter ego' present in informationalised systems, along with issues such as its accuracy, availability for scrutiny or contestation, and potential negative uses.[5]

This chapter argues that concerns around profiling must be complemented by a focus on the rights and interests of those that, often unwittingly and perhaps unwillingly, themselves contribute to computing that impacts individuals, groups and environments. The focus is not on how these individuals have their characteristics comput*ed*, but instead how they contribute to and support the comput*ing* of other people and their environments. In the worst case, these are individuals who are facilitating computing *unwillingly, unknowingly* and even *unidentifiably*.

Let's start with some background. Legally, the most salient regulatory regime governing profiling internationally is data protection.[6] Its material scope is the concept of 'personal data'.[7] This scope turns on whether an individual is either identified, or their potential identifiability.[8] It began with the societal concerns around databanks and inferences that could be made from this data, and grew in prominence throughout the second half of the twentieth century as society became increasingly informationalised,[9] reaching new heights in the 2010s during the 'Big Data' hype.[10] In recent years, data protection in Europe has been complemented by a range of other regimes with a variety of connected aims such as competition, fairness in the presence of powerful intermediaries, data for research, data reuse, cybersecurity, etc.[11]

Legal instruments in this area often confidently and explicitly assume that to build systems for profiling, inference and similar, one needs *access* to data, and that in order to build functionality or analysis, it is important to ensure that it flows.[12] This seems

[5] N Helberger et al, 'EU Consumer Protection 2.0: Structural Asymmetries in Digital Consumer Markets' (BEUC, March 2021), www.beuc.eu/sites/default/files/publications/beuc-x-2021-018_eu_consumer_protection_2.0.pdf.

[6] It is not the only relevant regime. Non-discrimination law, consumer law, privacy and surveillance law, all cover issues of profiling explicitly or implicitly. See generally J Adams-Prassl et al, 'Directly Discriminatory Algorithms' (2023) 86 *MLR* 144; N Helberger et al, 'The Perfect Match? A Closer Look at the Relationship Between EU Consumer Law and Data Protection Law' (2017) 54 *Common Market Law Review* 1427; E Kosta, 'Algorithmic State Surveillance: Challenging the Notion of Agency in Human Rights' (2022) 16 *Regulation and Governance* 212.

[7] GDPR, Art 4(1) ('any information relating to an identified or identifiable natural person').

[8] See generally N Purtova, 'From Knowing by Name to Targeting: The Meaning of Identification under the GDPR' (2022) 12 *International Data Privacy Law* 163.

[9] S Rodotà, *Elaboratori elettronici e controllo sociale* (Bologna, Il Mulino, 1973) 15; AF Westin and MA Baker, *Databanks in a Free and Fair Society* (New York, Quadrangle Books, 1972).

[10] See eg De Wetenschappelijke Raad voor het Regeringsbeleid (WRR) (n 3).

[11] These regimes are surveyed in more detail later in this chapter.

[12] See eg Regulation (EU) 2018/1807 of the European Parliament and of the Council of 14 November 2018 on a framework for the free flow of non-personal data in the European Union [2018] OJ L 303/59 (Free Flow of Non-Personal Data Regulation), Recital 1; Regulation (EU) 2022/1925 of the European Parliament and of the Council of 14 September 2022 on contestable and fair markets in the digital sector and amending Directives (EU) 2019/1937 and (EU) 2020/1828 (Digital Markets Act) [2022] OJ L265/1, Recital 3; European Commission, 'Proposal for a Regulation of the European Parliament and of the Council on harmonised rules on fair access to and use of data (Data Act)', COM(2022) 68 final (2022), Recital 4; European Commission, 'Proposal for a Regulation of the European Parliament and the Council on the European Health Data Space', COM(2022) 197 final (2022), Recital 37 ('Health Data Space Regulation'). The Data Governance Act is metaphorically premised on data access, although interestingly seeks to

so obvious that few are likely to stop and even realise it is an assumption. By this logic, amassing and accessing data is something that the state should facilitate if it wishes more data-intensive technologies to exist, and that placing obligations on the entity or location where this data is amassed is a regulatory access point to achieve policy objectives.

This assumption is flawed. In particular, it is not technologically neutral, as data protection law notably purports to be.[13]

Below, I will illustrate how a mindset centred on mediating access does little to protect people from individualised profiling in the context of fast-emerging privacy-enhancing technologies. I will then go on to look at how confidentially affecting individuals and communities using profiling and computation is possible for actors who can co-opt and/or orchestrate many individuals' devices to do the necessary computing. This raises the question of what rights persons unwittingly facilitating such computing do, might or should have, particularly when they object to the ends to which this computing aims at.

II. COMPUTING WITH CONFIDENTIALITY

Where law has intended to avoid misuse of communications infrastructure, it has often safeguarded these communications' confidentiality. In Europe, to ensure that a sender and recipient could communicate without being pried upon or intercepted and potentially damaging economic interests, constitutionally-grounded rights to confidentiality of communications emerged from the 1700s onward to ensure trust in trade, particularly in the presence of government postal monopolies capable of interception.[14] Today, where European states engage in interception, human rights law requires them to legislate to lift this confidentiality, and to provide frameworks of safeguards.[15] Firms providing electronic communications services in the EU are also forbidden from using the content or traffic data of messages or calls for their own further purposes without an authorising law or specific, explicit consent.[16] These

define access 'without necessarily implying the transmission or downloading of data'. See Regulation (EU) 2022/868 of the European Parliament and of the Council of 30 May 2022 on European data governance and amending Regulation (EU) 2018/1724 (Data Governance Act) [2022] OJ L 151/1, Art 7(13).

[13] GDPR, Recital 15; see generally BJ Koops, 'Should ICT Regulation Be Technology-Neutral?' in BJ Koops et al (eds), *Starting Points for ICT Regulation: Deconstructing Prevalent Policy One-liners*, Information Technology and Law Series (The Hague, TMC Asser Press, 2006).

[14] FJ Zuiderveen Borgesius and W Steenbruggen, 'The Right to Communications Confidentiality in Europe: Protecting Privacy, Freedom of Expression, and Trust' (2019) 20 *Theoretical Inquiries in Law* 291, 293–95.

[15] Directive 2002/58/EC of the European Parliament and of the Council of 12 July 2002 concerning the processing of personal data and the protection of privacy in the electronic communications sector (Directive on privacy and electronic communications) [2002] OJ L 201/37, Arts 5(1), 15(1) (hereafter 'e-Privacy Directive'); Joined Cases C-203/15 and C-698/15 *Tele2/Watson* ECLI:EU:C:2016:970, [89], [104]; see generally *Big Brother Watch and Others v UK*, App nos 58170/13, 62322/14 and 24960/15 (ECtHR, 25 May 2021) ECLI:CE:ECHR:2021:0525JUD005817013 (identifying 'end-to-end safeguards' for interfering with confidentiality using bulk interception powers).

[16] e-Privacy Directive (n 15), Art 5(1) (establishing confidentiality duties applicable to electronic communications service providers).

obligations were originally limited only to the inheritors of state telecommunications monopolies, but now expanded in scope to include providers of 'over-the-top' interpersonal communications services that piggyback on traditional networks, such as Meta's WhatsApp or Apple's iMessage or FaceTime.[17]

Legal confidentiality of communications is complemented by confidentiality secured through technological architecture.[18] Obfuscation practices such as steganography or early encryption achieving a similar result, or substituting for untrusted law, date back thousands of years.[19] Legal and policy efforts to resist them have a similarly lengthy history.[20] Following the Snowden revelations and increasingly diverse legal demands on Internet platforms from jurisdictions across the world, many messaging services became 'end-to-end' encrypted, encrypting content between recipients, rather than just between a recipient and an intermediary (who could be served a warrant).[21]

Encryption often frustrates state surveillance authorities, which are often intrinsically interested in accumulating the characteristics of people or the content of their communications in order to pass intelligence reports to other authorities.[22] When it comes to commercial firms' own incentives, the story becomes a little more complex. Platforms' interests around confidentiality can both align and diverge from states'.[23] They are likely to consider reputational reasons for encryption, as well as how encrypting specific content or functionality changes the balance of opportunities and liabilities for the firm.

For example, as we noted above, firms are not easily allowed to analyse data from interpersonal messaging services like WhatsApp or iMessage in the EU for their own ends.[24] Consequently, they have less to commercially gain from keeping this data in a form visible to them. They may have much to lose: reputation where privacy is a selling point;[25] costs from diverse international governmental orders to

[17] Directive (EU) 2018/1972 of the European Parliament and of the Council of 11 December 2018 establishing the European Electronic Communications Code [2018] OJ L 321/36, art 2(4–5) (hereafter 'EEEC') (extending the definition of electronic communications service providers upon which the e-Privacy Directive draws to include 'over-the-top' services). Some jurisdictional and other issues in this area await resolution in the potential e-Privacy Regulation, if it ever passes: see generally M Rojszczak, 'OTT Regulation Framework in the Context of CJEU Skype Case and European Electronic Communications Code' (2020) 38 *Computer Law & Security Review* 105439.

[18] See generally on the interplay of law and technological architecture, JR Reidenberg, 'Lex Informatica: The Formulation of Information Policy Rules through Technology' (1998) 76 *Texas Law Review* 553.

[19] See generally D Kahn, *The Codebreakers: The Story of Secret Writing* (New York, Macmillan, 1967); C Jarvis, *Crypto Wars: The Fight for Privacy in the Digital Age: A Political History of Digital Encryption* (Boca Raton-Abingdon, CRC Press, 2020) 16.

[20] See T Standage, *The Victorian Internet: the Remarkable Story of the Telegraph and the Nineteenth Century's Online Pioneers* (London, Phoenix Books, 1999) 110–11 (on attempts to regulate consumer encryption over the telegraph).

[21] Jarvis (n 19) 336–40.

[22] Jarvis (n 19); M Olsen et al, 'Don't Panic: Making Progress on the "Going Dark" Debate' (Berkman Center for Internet and Society at Harvard University, 1 February 2016), perma.cc/5T87-K7NV.

[23] S Gürses and C Diaz, 'Two Tales of Privacy in Online Social Networks' (2013) 11 *IEEE Security & Privacy Magazine* 29.

[24] See above, n 15.

[25] *cf* S Dechand et al, 'In Encryption We Don't Trust: The Effect of End-to-End Encryption to the Masses on User Perception' (2019) 2019 *IEEE European Symposium on Security and Privacy (EuroS&P)* 401.

retain or provide data;[26] and costs of content moderation that may be impossible where content is invisible.[27]

A. Encryption Beyond Interpersonal Messaging

Encryption is not just about sealing a message between two individuals. Encryption technologies have expanded and continue to expand into new areas of functionality.

To understand this, it helps to understand the practice of privacy engineering. Privacy engineers seek to characterise functionality of an existing system, and design a working replacement without privacy-invasive properties, such as by ensuring data never leaves a space of user control or trust.[28] New technologies have expanded the type of functionality that privacy engineers can reproduce, in particular technologies that allow one or more devices to undertake computation over data that is encrypted or otherwise unable to be accessed. They effectively seek to *decouple data access from data analysis*.

Such technologies include homomorphic encryption (which allows a party to operate over encrypted data and decrypt the result); secure multi-party computation (which allows multiple parties to collectively compute a result requiring data from all of them, without revealing anything to each other beyond what the result shows); and functional encryption (which allows certain questions to be asked of encrypted data). These building blocks can be combined to enable desired functionality while minimising information leakage – the aim of a field often called 'privacy engineering'.

We can use the term 'confidential computing' to describe such technologies. Confidential computing can be thought of as a subset of privacy-enhancing technologies (PETs). Using the term 'confidential computing' emphasises that confidentiality is just one, technocentric lens on privacy,[29] and leaves PETs as an overarching term for technologies that can be used to support privacy *beyond* confidentiality as well as through it. For example, PETs might go beyond confidentiality to help users separate out different online personas and signal how they wish themselves and their information to be treated in different contexts,[30] enable them to access data that relates to them,[31] to manage the profiles and inferences that apply

[26] eg Investigatory Powers Act 2016, Pt 4 (UK).

[27] See generally ST Roberts, *Behind the Screen: Content Moderation in the Shadows of Social Media* (New Haven-London, Yale University Press, 2019).

[28] S Gürses et al, 'Engineering Privacy by Design Reloaded' (Amsterdam Privacy Conference, 2015), perma.cc/C77G-5EP9.

[29] Note that some industry players have used confidential computing to refer mainly to the need for specific hardware, namely trusted execution environments (TEE). I understand computing broadly and do not introduce that restriction. See eg Confidential Computing Consortium, 'A Technical Analysis of Confidential Computing, v1.2' (October 2021) 2, perma.cc/H8L4-U55U.

[30] D Boyd, 'Faceted Id/Entity: Managing Representation in a Digital World' (PhD dissertation, Massachusetts Institute of Technology, 2002); H Nissenbaum, *Privacy in Context: Technology, Policy, and the Integrity of Social Life* (Stanford, Stanford University Press, 2010); AE Marwick and D Boyd, 'I Tweet Honestly, I Tweet Passionately: Twitter Users, Context Collapse, and the Imagined Audience' (2011) 13 *New Media & Society* 114.

[31] C Norris et al (eds), *The Unaccountable State of Surveillance: Exercising Access Rights in Europe* (Cham, Springer International Publishing, 2016).

to groups of people rather than individuals,[32] help limit coercive power in intimate relationships,[33] enable them to create credible false information in order to protect certain aspects of their identity,[34] or even use information as a tool for protest to confuse and break systems they consider privacy-invasive.[35] All of the above could or have been discussed as privacy, and all are either distinct from confidentiality or not fully encompassed by it.

Confidential computing has been applauded for opening up the typical space of trade-offs and possibilities to new applications and public benefit, such as measuring gender pay gaps where employers wish to keep salary data confidential,[36] or allowing agricultural markets to reach a clearing price where farmers wish to withhold information disclosing their productivity to avoid being extorted.[37] In general, it is a powerful and uncontroversial tool when all parties holding data wish to achieve some common aim, or are perhaps mandated by law to do so, but do not wish to share the disaggregated information with each other; and where all parties relating to the data agree with the ends of the computation.

It is standard practice in cryptographic research to explicitly describe the motivation of a new protocol in terms of a 'real-world' application of the scheme. These terse justificatory narratives have been described as a 'unique genre in the mathematical literature'.[38] While the research literature on such technologies often paints a rosy picture, sometimes the envisaged applications for these technologies stray into adversarial settings, where the individuals whose data is being processed may not wish this processing to occur. For example, Archer et al propose applications of homomorphic encryption for where 'Border control may wish to collect information from multiple sources to assess the risk of allowing someone to enter the country',[39] and to predict the risk of high school dropouts by 'integrating data across different institutions, in this case, schools, hospitals, welfare systems, police departments, and more'.[40] The

[32] A Vedder, 'KDD: The Challenge to Individualism' (1999) 1 *Ethics and Information Technology* 275; L Taylor et al (eds), *Group Privacy: New Challenges of Data Technologies* Philosophical Studies Series (Cham, Springer International Publishing, 2017).

[33] K Levy and B Schneier, 'Privacy Threats in Intimate Relationships' (2020) 6 *Journal of Cyber Security* 1.

[34] AL Allen, 'Lying to Protect Privacy' (1999) 44 *Villanova Law Review* 161; M Van Kleek et al, 'Computationally Mediated Pro-Social Deception' in *Proceedings of the 2016 CHI Conference on Human Factors in Computing Systems* (New York, Association for Computing Machinery, 2016) 552.

[35] B Kulynych et al, 'POTs: Protective Optimization Technologies' in *Proceedings of the 2020 Conference on Fairness, Accountability, and Transparency* (ACM, 2020), dl.acm.org/doi/10.1145/3351095.3372853; F Brunton and HF Nissenbaum, *Obfuscation: A User's Guide for Privacy and Protest* (Cambridge MA, The MIT Press, 2015).

[36] A Bestavros et al, 'User-Centric Distributed Solutions for Privacy-Preserving Analytics' (2017) 60 *Communications of the ACM* 37.

[37] P Bogetoft et al, 'Secure Multiparty Computation Goes Live' in R Dingledine and P Golle (eds), *Financial Cryptography and Data Security*, Lecture Notes in Computer Science 5628 (Berlin-Heidelberg, Springer, 2009).

[38] JF Blanchette, *Burdens of Proof: Cryptographic Culture and Evidence Law in the Age of Electronic Documents* (Cambridge MA, The MIT Press, 2012) 82.

[39] D Archer et al, 'Applications of Homomorphic Encryption' (Homomorphic Encryption Standardization 2017) 8–9, homomorphicencryption.org/white_papers/applications_homomorphic_encryption_white_paper.pdf.

[40] ibid 7.

UK–US 'Privacy Enhancing Technologies Challenge' typifies some of these dynamics in practice, with the respective governments awarding prize funding for systems that could scan and detect criminal financial transactions – a profiling task.[41]

Beyond the motivations, research literature into PETs typically makes several assumptions as to how the protocol works under different conditions. Does it stay secure even if some of the participants do not act honestly, instead choosing to compute something in a different way? However, from my reading of this literature, one assumption is rarely made explicit. Individuals participating in a protocol to achieve particular functionality are generally assumed to be doing so freely. If the protocol functionality does something they disapprove of, they do not have to participate. But the vast majority of devices in the modern informational economy are not able to be scrutinised to see what is running, with some, like Apple's iOS ecosystem, incredibly difficult for researchers to effectively examine.[42] Even were they to gain awareness, individuals also have little practical agency over what code runs on devices, particularly when this code is buried inside the operating system, or even on cryptographic hardware on device, as manufacturers provide few deep controls that alter the functioning of these systems. In practice, this unspoken assumption is routinely violated.

This draws attention to the role of the orchestrating entity, and their associated orchestration power. If individuals cannot easily scrutinise what is happening on their devices, then the organisation that in practice coordinates the protocol assumes a powerful role. In recent Internet standards work on confidentiality-preserving aggregation, these entities are referred to as 'leaders'.[43] Given the constraints in the modern informational economy, leaders have more power than such standards give them on paper.

B. Confidential Microtargeting

Confidentiality is no guarantee of desirable functionality, nor a guarantee of individuals' agency in participating in such functionality. This situation highlights the difference between privacy and confidentiality. In computing, scholars typically conflate the two, seeing privacy as a state of no undesired information leakage.[44] But broader theories of privacy highlight that this would be inappropriate. Nissenbaum's theory of contextual integrity highlights the appropriateness of information flows, without a focus on the identifiability of these flows.[45] Information can thus flow to others inappropriately even where it is in an encrypted form. Cohen's approach to privacy sees its role as to '[shelter] dynamic, emergent subjectivity from the efforts

[41] S Wellard and M Hardalupas, 'Privacy Enhancing Technologies (PETs) Prize Challenges Winners' (UKRI, 31 March 2023), www.ukri.org/blog/privacy-enhancing-technologies-pets-prize-challenges-winners.

[42] K Kollnig et al, 'Are iPhones Really Better for Privacy? A Comparative Study of iOS and Android Apps' (2022) 2 *Proceedings on Privacy Enhancing Technologies* 6.

[43] T Geoghegan et al, 'Distributed Aggregation Protocol for Privacy Preserving Measurement' (Internet-draft, IETF Datatracker, 13 March 2023), datatracker.ietf.org/doc/draft-ietf-ppm-dap/04.

[44] S Gürses, 'Can You Engineer Privacy?' (2014) 57 *Communications of the ACM* 20.

[45] Nissenbaum (n 30).

of commercial and government actors to render individuals and communities fixed, transparent, and predictable', seeking to protect 'situated practices of boundary management'.[46] Similarly, Hildebrandt draws attention to privacy's role in the development and maintenance of a person's fundamentally indeterminate identity.[47] The impact data can have upon somebody does not, given the nature of privacy engineering, depend on it being externally visible to any other person.

This becomes particularly clear when we see privacy technologies being used in optimisation and advertising systems. Google's highly publicised announcement in January 2020 that they would drop third-party cookies, a technology at the heart of their surveillance-based display advertising business since their acquisition of DoubleClick,[48] exemplifies this. Its *Privacy Sandbox* initiative proposed technologies such as FLoC (Federated Learning of Cohorts), where profiling through behavioural models and scores happens on your device. Most recently, it has started to roll out a related system, Topics, in its Chrome browser. This system analyses individuals' data on a device and places them into categories through which advertisers could target them. Other firms, like Meta and Mozilla, have proposed related systems, differing mostly in preferring advertising functionality to be carried out confidentially on cloud servers (which they might control) rather than on devices (which, except at the shallow level of the apps, they do not).[49] Already, Google, in partnership with MasterCard uses a form of confidential computing called private set aggregation to analyse which advertising campaigns brought in the most money by matching credit card data to online tracking data and returning aggregate, non-personal results, such as the total amount spent in a certain retailer by individuals who viewed a particular advert.[50] Apple meanwhile has filed a patent for generating user models for recommender systems, timeline generation and more based on federated learning, using individuals' devices to collaboratively train a shared model, which could be then deployed to predict how users in general would behave when shown certain content.[51]

Critics of systems such as Google's Privacy Sandbox have often focused on the fact that it is *not quite confidential enough*.[52] This is a shallow line of critique. Given that technologies like multiparty computation can, in theory, replicate any function, there is no theoretical reason why precisely the same, or indeed more invasive or detailed, analytic practices cannot be replicated using confidential computing techniques.

[46] JE Cohen, 'What Privacy is For' (2013) 126 *Harvard Law Review* 1904, 1905.

[47] M Hildebrandt, 'Privacy as Protection of the Incomputable Self: From Agnostic to Agonistic Machine Learning' (2019) 20 *Theoretical Inquiries in Law* 83.

[48] M Crain, 'A Criticial Political Economy of Web Advertising History' in N Brügger and I Milligan (eds), *The SAGE Handbook of Web History* (London, SAGE, 2019) 337.

[49] M Veale, 'Future of online advertising: Adtech's new clothes might redefine privacy more than they reform profiling' (netzpolitik.org, 25 February 2022), netzpolitik.org/2022/future-of-online-advertising-adtechs-new-clothes-might-redefine-privacy-more-than-they-reform-profiling-cookies-meta-mozilla-apple-google.

[50] M Ion et al, 'Private Intersection-Sum Protocol with Applications to Attributing Aggregate Ad Conversions' (2017) *Cryptology ePrint Archive*, Paper 2017/738, 14, eprint.iacr.org/2017/738.

[51] S Cosman et al, 'User Behavior Model Development with Private Federated Learning' (24 June 2021),. google.com/patent/US20210192078A1/en.

[52] See eg B Cyphers, 'Don't Play in Google's Privacy Sandbox' (Electronic Frontier Foundation, 30 August 2019), www.eff.org/deeplinks/2019/08/dont-play-googles-privacy-sandbox-1.

C. Confidential Analytics

Advertising still typically has direct individual impact, as targeting systems come back to affect users through the content they are exposed to. This is not the case for all systems that we can envisage being carried out using confidential computing techniques.

Contemporary personal devices have significant potential to learn about both users and their surroundings from sensors and other gathered records. For example, Apple phones constantly send geotagged information about the locations of nearby WiFi hotspots to update the firm's WiFi positioning system (WPS) database.[53] The firm also uses GPS sensors on its network of firms to establish aggregated current levels of congestion, and to estimate how busy venues or attractions are.[54] Apple and Google both use confidential computing technologies to improve their predictive keyboard systems by learning how users type,[55] and developed a protocol to collect aggregated data on individuals exposed to COVID-19, building further on the Exposure Notification system deployed in 2020.[56] Google has long used forms of distributed analytics throughout its products, such as RAPPOR, which could collect over 200 metrics from users of Google Chrome, informed by billions of daily reports.[57] It has been actively developing further technologies in this vein, including PROCHLO (named after a combination of the word 'privacy' with the Greek word for 'crowd', ókhlos, and Cobalt, an analytics tool for the firm's new Internet-of-Things operating system, Fuchscia.[58] Apple has similarly built scalable systems for constructing aggregate information, analytics and models about the world, recently through its Samplable Anonymous Aggregation primitive, a building block which would allow many types of aggregation to be computed.[59] Google also uses confidential computing techniques to build proprietary global datasets of how busy different businesses are at different times of day, and how popular particular dishes or services are at these businesses, based on review, location and search data.[60] Just because these

[53] Apple, 'Location Services & Privacy' (Apple Legal, 12 September 2022), perma.cc/T3T4-WCL2.

[54] ibid.

[55] A Hard et al, 'Federated Learning for Mobile Keyboard Prediction' (arXiv, 28 February 2019), arxiv.org/abs/1811.03604; Differential Privacy Team, 'Learning with Privacy at Scale' (2017) 1 *Apple Machine Learning Journal*, machinelearning.apple.com/research/learning-with-privacy-at-scale.

[56] Apple and Google, 'Exposure Notification Privacy-Preserving Analytics (ENPA) White Paper' (April 2021), covid19-static.cdn-apple.com/applications/covid19/current/static/contact-tracing/pdf/ENPA_White_Paper.pdf.

[57] A Bittau et al, 'Prochlo: Strong Privacy for Analytics in the Crowd' in *SOSP' 17. Proceedings of the 26th Symposium on Operating Systems Principles* (New York, Association for Computing Machinery, 2017) 441; I Mironov, 'Differential Privacy in the Industry: Challenges and Successes' (Formal privacy: Making an impact at large organizations: A session at the 2019 Joint Statistical Meetings, sponsored by the ASA Committee on Privacy and Confidentiality, 2019), perma.cc/R4U9-YD7R.

[58] Google Fuchsia, 'Cobalt: Telemetry with Built-in Privacy' (Google Git, 2023), fuchsia.googlesource.com/cobalt; Bittau et al (n 57).

[59] K Talwar et al, 'Samplable Anonymous Aggregation for Private Federated Data Analysis' (arXiv, 27 July 2023), arxiv.org/abs/2307.15017.

[60] M Guevara, 'Enabling Developers and Organizations to Use Differential Privacy' (Google for Developers, 5 September 2019), developers.googleblog.com/2019/09/enabling-developers-and-organizations.html.

systems claim to use confidential computing tools does not mean they provide sufficiently rigorous guarantees.[61] However, here it is useful to discuss these systems *as if* their guarantees were sufficient, to understand what the debate looks like in the cases where that is or could be true.

Considering only the use of rigorous confidential computing cleanses this set of practices of many of the concerns around personal data in the outputs, and draws our attention to the nature of the questions being asked. Some of the above seem innocuous, such as the most commonly used emoji for better user interfaces.

It is not difficult however to envisage controversial uses of such technologies. Let us consider a country that uses digital tactics to digitally target LGBT individuals, such as Egypt, Iraq, Jordan, Lebanon or Tunisia.[62] Imagine a smartphone provider, either of its own volition, or after a detailed warrant, uses its technology stack to produce information on where hidden LGBT venues are in a capital city. They could analyse browsing and app usage data to profile individuals on-device based on their sexuality, such as through web-browsing history, or looking for app installations such as Grindr or HER. They could look at historic location data for such individuals, again stored on device, and identify using confidential computing technologies such as private set intersection the times when multiple individuals flagged as LGBT coincided in space and time. Where significant numbers of these individuals coincided, as perhaps not to reveal anything about any one individual, this data could be compiled into a report. The resulting data, the location of meeting points, does not seem immediately personal. A company could convince themselves they are even just supporting good urban planning policy – similarly to how consulting firm McKinsey considered it was just supporting democratic participation when it provided a list of social media critics to the Government of Saudi Arabia, an act that was followed shortly after by the murder of an associate and funder of one of the critics, the journalist Jamal Khashoggi.[63]

Information asymmetries that relate to non-personal data can be reasons for concern. At times, they may, as the above hypothetical example, provide information that can betray the trust of, or can be weaponised against, a group or community.[64] At other times, they may lead to privately managed 'data doubles' of countries and national data collection efforts, creating a default where policy-relevant information about the world is created without the input of states, and, particularly for Majority World countries, may not by default be available to them.[65]

[61] See eg A Gadotti et al, 'Pool Inference Attacks on Local Differential Privacy: Quantifying the Privacy Guarantees of Apple's Count Mean Sketch in Practice' (31st USENIX Security Symposium (USENIX Security 22), 2022), www.usenix.org/conference/usenixsecurity22/presentation/gadotti.

[62] R Younes, '"All This Terror Because of a Photo": Digital Targeting and Its Offline Consequences for LGBT People in the Middle East and North Africa' (Human Rights Watch, 21 February 2023), hrw.org/report/2023/02/21/all-terror-because-photo/digital-targeting-and-its-offline-consequences-lgbt.

[63] W Bogdanich and M Forsythe, *When McKinsey Comes to Town: The Hidden Influence of the World's Most Powerful Consulting Firm* (New York, Doubleday, 2022) ch 13.

[64] See relatedly Taylor et al (n 32).

[65] L Taylor and D Broeders, 'In the Name of Development: Power, Profit and the Datafication of the Global South' (2015) 64 *Geoforum* 229.

D. Research Ethics Despite Confidentiality

Confidential computing forces us to consider the ethics of asking certain questions of human subjects or their environments, regardless of the identifiability of any individuals during the process. Research ethicists have noted that such research might be objectionable on the grounds that it is not *true*, it is not *fair*, or most difficult of all, it is not *wise*.[66] Let us consider these in turn.

We might object on epistemic terms to collective computations if the output may not be true, in the sense of methodological soundness. This could be due to concerns around sampling and representativeness,[67] scepticism around the assumptions underpinning behaviourist, biometric or psychometric predictive systems,[68] or doubt that certain social phenomena are rigorously captured by quantification.[69]

We might object on a wide array of fairness – effectively procedural – grounds around how the research was carried out. Was the research explained to participants? Were they given choices about their devices being used in this manner? Are participants being experimented upon, and under what conditions? Are there deceptive elements to the research?

Lastly, we may object to the *ends* of the research – to its wisdom. Is the knowledge being generated by this research good for society? This question is undoubtedly value-laden, but far from new, with fields and practices including technology assessment,[70] responsible research and innovation,[71] and the broader field of science and technology studies. When it comes to broad scientific endeavours, this can be difficult to reach consensus upon. Research ethics frameworks vary when considering the impact of research, with some opting for a medical practice-linked 'beneficence' criterion – do no harm – with others considering social value more broadly and less individually.[72] However, platform firms rarely claim to be disinterested knowledge-seekers, but to apply the information they receive, in particular to render individuals

[66] Compared to whether research is *true* or *fair*, whether it is *wise* is already one of the trickiest domains within research ethics. See generally KD Pimple, 'Six Domains of Research Ethics' (2002) 8 *Science and Engineering Ethics* 191.

[67] JJ Faraway and NH Augustin, 'When Small Data Beats Big Data' (2018) 136 *Statistics & Probability Letters* 142.

[68] LF Barrett et al, 'Emotional Expressions Reconsidered: Challenges to Inferring Emotion From Human Facial Movements' (2019) 20 *Psychological Science in the Public Interest* 1; Hildebrandt (n 47); see generally, F Kaltheuner (ed), *Fake AI* (Manchester, Meatspace Press, 2021).

[69] JC Scott, *Seeing like a State: How Certain Schemes to Improve the Human Condition Have Failed* (New Haven, Yale University Press, 1998); SE Merry, *The Seductions of Quantification: Measuring Human Rights, Gender Violence, and Sex Trafficking* (Chicago, University of Chicago Press, 2016); GC Bowker and SL Star, *Sorting Things Out: Classification and Its Consequences* (Cambridge MA, The MIT Press, 1999); HE Brady and D Collier (eds), *Rethinking Social Inquiry: Diverse Tools, Shared Standards* 2nd edn (Lanham, Rowman & Littlefield Publishers, 2010).

[70] J Schot and A Rip, 'The Past and Future of Constructive Technology Assessment' (1997) 54 *Technological Forecasting and Social Change* 251; DH Guston and D Sarewitz, 'Real-Time Technology Assessment' (2002) 24 *Technology in Society* 93.

[71] See generally DH Guston and J Stilgoe, 'Responsible Research and Innovation' in U Felt et al (eds), *The Handbook of Science and Technology Studies*, 4th edn (Cambridge MA, The MIT Press 2017) 853.

[72] R Rhodes, 'Rethinking Research Ethics' (2010) 10 *The American Journal of Bioethics* 19; FG Miller and H Brody, 'What Makes Placebo-Controlled Trials Unethical?' (2002) 2 *The American Journal of Bioethics* 3.

and groups more legible to computers for the purposes of intermediating valuable access to them, such as through microtargeting.[73] Informational applications and business practices are in general easier to reason about the desirability of than broad, open-ended or more foundational discovery. Considerations of the ends are important to distinguish participation in collective computing from other research aims – while some scholars argue participation in biomedical research might be an ethical duty, they generally exclude situations where the knowledge produced is privatised or IP-protected.[74]

E. Those who Unwillingly, Unidentifiably Compute

Just because individuals may be unidentifiable in collective, confidential computations, does not mean they cannot have a stake in them. Materially, they maintain, charge, repair, replace the devices that these computations are occurring upon. Even where the removal of a single person may not affect an aggregate result, as is the case with robust implementations of some techniques such as differential privacy, this should not distract us from how it is still the devices of these individuals, communities and populations that enable these computations, carried within, and often indistinguishable from, their private spheres. Individuals have a right to strike even though a single individual on strike will rarely be a meaningful form of protest. These rights are important because they bridge the individual and the collective.

Given the potential for confidential computing to be put to unethical ends, and a lack of clear current governance mechanisms for its direction, it is important to consider what legal rights individuals do, could or should have to frustrate or protest such unwanted computation. These rights can be seen as the legal parallels to protective optimisation technologies (POTs), a theoretical category of techniques to provide means for individuals to address the externalities of computing systems in the environment and expand avenues for their political contestation.[75] These include Web browser advocacy techniques such as AdNauseum, a plug-in to silently click all ads on a website to frustrate online tracking and targeting networks,[76] or creating fake location signals and fake locations on Google Maps through either network 'Sybil' attacks or the more visually striking dragging of an artist dragging

[73] JE Cohen, *Between Truth and Power: The Legal Constructions of Informational Capitalism* (New York, Oxford University Press, 2019).

[74] J Harris, 'Scientific Research is a Moral Duty' (2005) 31 *Journal of Medical Ethics* 242; GO Schaefer et al, 'The Obligation to Participate in Biomedical Research' (2009) 302 *Journal of the American Medical Association* 67.

[75] B Kulynych et al, 'POTs: Protective Optimization Technologies' in *FAT* 2020. Proceedings of the 2020 Conference on Fairness, Accountability, and Transparency* (New York, Association for Computing Machinery, 2020) 177; S Gürses et al, 'Stirring the POTs: Protective Optimization Technologies' in E Bayamlıoğlu et al (eds), *Being Profiled:Cogitas Ergo Sum* (Amsterdam, Amsterdam University Press, 2018) 24.

[76] Brunton and Nissenbaum (n 35); on protest through web extensions more generally, see KL Smith and E Guzik, 'Developing Privacy Extensions: Is It Advocacy through the Web Browser?' (2022) 20 *Surveillance & Society* 64.

a cart of active smartphones through the street.[77] Yet POTs are limited by the lack of control of users over their terminal devices, which can be co-opted for such computation. Platforms can also frustrate POTs by attempting to prohibit them, as Google has done with the AdNauseum extension in Chrome.[78] Such prohibitions on the kind of programmes that can run on top of another technology has been referred to as 'treacherous computing', often associated in the past with intellectual property rights, and placed in contrast to the 'free software' movement.[79] Google, for example, is pushing a new 'Web Environment Integrity' standard, effectively a standard whereby websites could check that individuals are running code as the website intended it to be run, rather than with any modifications, including those that may consist of individuals expressing ethical preferences.[80] This sits in stark contrast to researchers who seek to make plugins to give individuals more agency over how their software looks and functions, beyond what platforms and developers provide.[81]

To complement POTs, we can look to the law. Indeed, the law is not silent when it comes to rights for those who unwillingly, unidentifiably compute – although it is also far from coherent, enforced or complete.

III. LEGAL CONSIDERATIONS

Turning to European law, a range of regimes are relevant to individuals that facilitate computation, rather than those that are subject to it.

A. Data Protection Law

There are a range of roles individuals processing data on their devices could take under data protection law.[82]

[77] G Wang et al, 'Ghost Riders: Sybil Attacks on Crowdsourced Mobile Mapping Services' (2018) 26 *IEEE/ACM Transactions on Networking* 1123; S Weckert and M Ahlert, 'Hacking Google Maps' (Remote Chaos Experience (rC3), 2 January 2021), media.ccc.de/v/rc3-197911-hacking_google_maps.

[78] DC Howe and H Nissenbaum, 'Engineering Privacy and Protest: A Case Study of *AdNauseam*' in JM del Álamo, SF Gürses and A Datta (eds), *IWPE 2017 – International Workshop on Privacy Engineering: Proceedings of the 3rd International Workshop on Privacy Engineering, co-located with 38th IEEE Symposium on Security and Privacy* (S&P, 2017) 57.

[79] RM Stallman, *Free Software, Free Society, Selected essays of Richard M. Stallman*, 3rd edn (Boston MA, Free Software Foundation, 2015).

[80] T Claburn, 'Google Web Environment Integrity Draft Draws Developer Rage' (The Register, 25 July 2023), www.theregister.com/2023/07/25/google_web_environment_integrity.

[81] See eg K Kollnig et al, 'I Want My App That Way: Reclaiming Sovereignty Over Personal Devices' in *CHI EA' 21. Extended Abstracts of the 2021 CHI Conference on Human Factors in Computing Systems* (New York, Association for Computing Machinery, 2021); K Kollnig et al, '"We Are Adults and Deserve Control of Our Phones": Examining the Risks and Opportunities of a Right to Repair for Mobile Apps' in *FAccT' 23. Proceedings of the 2023 ACM Conference on Fairness, Accountability, and Transparency* (New York, Association for Computing Machinery, 2023) 22.

[82] See generally M Veale, 'Denied by Design? Data Access Rights in Encrypted Infrastructures' in J Ausloos and S P de Souza (eds), *Researcher Access to Digital Infrastructures* (Cambridge, Cambridge University Press forthcoming), osf.io/preprints/socarxiv/94y6r.

In a conventional understanding of data protection, those who compute are either controllers or processors, and those who are themselves comput*ed* are typically data subjects. Controllers determine the means and purposes of processing, while processors are supposed to be agents of controllers, acting on their instructions.

Individuals can fall into both categories, and may find themselves as data controllers, even in unexpected situations or in connection to their homes.[83] Yet as data protection law is founded on concerns of information asymmetry between data controllers and data subjects, it provides scant rights for controllers themselves beyond procedural rights in relation to actions in courts or by data protection authorities (DPAs). This has created some issues in complex informational environments. The Court of Justice of the European Union (CJEU), in an attempt to ensure *complete and effective protection*, has expanded the notion of joint controllership in a way which often gives actors nominal shared responsibility in settings vast power differentials where relationships are characterised by non-negotiable, 'clickwrap' contracts.[84] To this end, the CJEU has found joint controllership between Meta and both its plug-in users and its fan-page administrators.[85] There is little benefit to be derived by an individual coerced into computing from the category of joint controller.

An unwilling individual could also be a 'processor', which includes 'a natural or legal person … which processes personal data on behalf of the controller'.[86] The purpose of this concept is protect the processor from liability that should justly accrue to a controller, as long as such processors truly are simply acting upon instruction and not towards their own ends. Processors do not (co-)determine the means and purposes of processing, although this distinction has itself been difficult to maintain as cloud firms, which typically claim processor status, bring their own ways of applying computers to human challenges, which controllers may thoughtlessly adopt. Processors should be bound by contracts designed to allow the controller to maintain control, and be capable of effectively securing personal data. In heavily managed and technically controlled environments, such as the smartphone ecosystem, it may be possible for controllers to argue individual device-owners are processors, although this would likely require individuals to be compensated or coerced into quite invasive contractual terms, such as the auditing of their devices. Such an argument would similarly hinge on many of the factors found by the CJEU in its joint controllership decisions.[87] However, as with controllers, processors' right to refuse to compute

[83] Ji Chen et al, 'Who is Responsible for Data Processing in Smart Homes? Reconsidering Joint Controllership and the Household Exemption' (2021) 10 *International Data Privacy Law* 279. See also *Fairhurst v Woodard* [2021] 10 WLUK 151 (12 October 2021) (for an example of an individual with an Amazon Ring device being classed as a data controller).

[84] C Millard, 'At this Rate, Everyone Will Be a [Joint] Controller of Personal Data!' (2019) 9 *International Data Privacy Law* 217, 219; see generally D Kamarinou et al, 'Responsibilities of Controllers and Processors of Personal Data in Clouds' in C Millard (ed), *Cloud Computing Law* (Oxford, Oxford University Press, 2021) 294.

[85] Case C-210/16 *Wirtschaftsakademie Schleswig-Holstein* ECLI:EU:C:2018:388; Case C-40/17 *Fashion ID* ECLI:EU:C:2019:629. See generally R Mahieu et al, 'Responsibility for Data Protection in a Networked World: On the Question of the Controller, "Effective and Complete Protection" and Its Application to Data Access Rights in Europe' (2019) 10 *Journal of Intellectual Property, Information Technology and Electronic Commerce Law* 84.

[86] GDPR (n 4), Art 4(8).

[87] Chen et al (n 83).

is implicitly grounded in their freedom to contract, which in practice in the digital economy is limited by take-it-or-leave it *clickwrap* agreements which users have little practical agency over.[88]

The device owner may additionally or independently have rights as a data subject, with regard to the personal data stored on their own device.[89] Rights such as the right of access become important in this regard as personal data is not always surfaced within apps or operating systems, even where it is present and able to be computed over by the actors with practical control of that code.[90] Refusal to compute hinges on the ability to invalidate a legal basis of processing. The feasibility of this differs on both the legal basis, as well as the interaction of the legal basis with the broader technical and economic situation of the data subject – can they truly say 'no' without detriment?[91] However, these rights emerge because it is the individual's personal data itself that is being processed, rather than because a user of a device is contributing to data collection and computation. The overlap between such issues relies on the wide scope of personal data. It may not apply for some or all of the data captured by environmental sensors. Data collected by sensors on doorbells, cars, or even pets, may not always relate to the owner, however the owner's interests may still be implicated in the aims of these systems for the reasons given further above. The applicability of data subject rights would therefore need a case-by-case analysis, which in turn would require something to be known about the putative personal data and its characteristics. Convincing firms to reveal data that they do not believe to be personal will inevitably prove an uphill struggle.

Furthermore, rights hinging on personal data being processed typically end when such data no longer becomes personal, falling out of scope of the relevant law. Techniques such as local differential privacy seek to add noise to information *before* it leaves a device for the collective computation. Firms such as Apple argue that this leaves the data unable to be identified, although researchers are constantly challenging such claims.[92] This creates a further conceptual confusion as to what stages of processing data subject rights would apply to. For example, would transparency provisions even shed light on the later purposes for this data processing, or

[88] JA Obar and A Oeldorf-Hirsch, 'The Biggest Lie on the Internet: Ignoring the Privacy Policies and Terms of Service Policies of Social Networking Services' (2020) 23 *Information, Communication & Society* 128.

[89] It may be possible to hold the status of controller and subject simultaneously, see eg L Edwards et al, 'Data subjects as data controllers: a Fashion(able) concept?' (Internet Policy Review, 13 June 2019), policyreview.info/articles/news/data-subjects-data-controllers-fashionable-concept/1400.

[90] M Veale et al, 'When data protection by design and data subject rights clash' (2018) 8 *International Data Privacy Law* 105; C Norval et al, 'RECLAIMING Data: Overcoming App Identification Barriers for Exercising Data Protection Rights' in *UbiComp' 18. Proceedings of the 2018 ACM International Joint Conference and 2018 International Symposium on Pervasive and Ubiquitous Computing and Wearable Computers* (New York, Association for Computing Machinery, 2018) 921; Veale (n 82).

[91] Where they are a data subject, personal data processing requires a legal basis. If this basis is consent, the ability to refuse is guaranteed; for other legal bases, the ability to refuse differs. It can exist subject to a balancing test following an objection request, which only applies to 'legitimate interest' and 'public task' bases. For other bases, refusal is much harder. If processing is validly justified by necessity of contract, then refusal depends on the practicalities of contractual negotiation. If the legal basis justified by national or Union law, then it depends on any rights present in such law.

[92] Gadotti et al (n 61).

can controllers get away with anonymising and then doing unaccountably as they please? This is another instantiation of the issue scholars have raised with the 'phase-oriented' approach to data protection presented by the CJEU in *Fashion ID*, where considering data processing in conceptual stages limits the ability to see the purposes and political economy of the system as a whole.[93]

B. e-Privacy Law

According to the recitals of the e-Privacy Directive, 'Terminal equipment of users of electronic communications networks and any information stored on such equipment are part of the private sphere of the users requiring protection under the [ECHR]'.[94] This acknowledgement of the importance of what happens on devices such as smartphones in terms of human rights places e-privacy in an interesting position as a framework which may empower those who unwillingly and unidentifiably compute.

The e-Privacy Directive in effect provides that individuals must authorise data storage or access from their terminal devices for reasons that are strictly necessary for a service requested by that individual.[95] The data being stored or access need not be personal; and thus this regime usefully avoids some of the pitfalls that confidential computing presents data protection law. Its scope, the terminal device, is something that sits at the edge of a publicly available network such as the Internet, and thus includes smartphones, their web browsers, pedometers or smart home devices.[96] e-privacy law is the foundational reason that a server laying or accessing a web cookie must obtain consent, leading to its 'cookie law' moniker.[97] However, the law was designed with much more than cookies in mind, as it was also shaped to prevent companies running unnecessary *code* on users' devices without permission, in particular in response to malware installed by Sony BMG to attempt to limit users' ability to copy music CDs.[98]

Although its scope is broad, enforcement or regulatory guidance around the installation of code under e-privacy law is practically non-existent. Regulators have produced reams of documentation on cookies, which are typically analysed on a purpose-by-purpose basis, with guidance on which purposes are necessary and which not. In contrast, software installation is generally a take-it-or-leave-it affair. While a firm cannot secretly install software that is entirely unnecessary on your device, such

[93] R Mahieu and J van Hoboken, 'Fashion-ID: Introducing a Phase-Oriented Approach to Data Protection?' (European Law Blog, 30 September 2019), europeanlawblog.eu/2019/09/30/fashion-id-introducing-a-phase-oriented-approach-to-data-protection.

[94] e-Privacy Directive (n 15), Recital 24.

[95] e-Privacy Directive (n 15), Art 5(3).

[96] L Edwards, 'Privacy, Security and Data Protection in Smart Cities: A Critical EU Law Perspective' (2016) 2 *European Data Protection Law Review* 28.

[97] It is not the only reason, however; see M Veale and F Zuiderveen Borgesius, 'Adtech and Real-Time Bidding under European Data Protection Law' (2022) 23 *German Law Journal* 226; FJ Zuiderveen Borgesius, 'Personal data processing for behavioural targeting: which legal basis?' (2015) 5 *International Data Privacy Law* 163.

[98] E Kosta, 'Peeking into the cookie jar: the European approach towards the regulation of cookies' (2013) 21 *International Journal of Law and Information Technology* 380, 384–85.

as a rootkit, it is unclear at what point they have to start asking consent for code within a software package that may not be considered 'necessary'. It seems unlikely that regulators and courts will want to dissect computer programmes into necessary and unnecessary parts, especially given the wide array of software engineering strategies that exist and the fact much networked functionality resists simple decomposability, particularly when woven into complex algorithmic supply chains.[99]

Nevertheless, e-privacy law does go some way to providing rights to persons who unwillingly compute, although obtaining clarity and enforcement on complex issues like confidential computing may take a great deal of time and effort.

C. Digital Markets Act

The Digital Markets Act (DMA) focuses on *gatekeeper* entities, which include large operating systems, prohibiting certain practices which they have used to consolidate market power. Individuals are obviously not going to fall into the gatekeeper categories themselves, but the entities orchestrating the computing on their devices might. Parts of the DMA implicate freedoms around computing, and in doing so, may provide some further control.

Insofar as confidential computing may combine data, on device, from two different core services run by a gatekeeper, this may require the specific consent of the end-user, whether or not this data is personal data under data protection law.[100] For example, Apple runs an operating system (iOS), a number-independent interpersonal communications service (iMessage), a web browser (Safari), provides online advertising services (Attribution API), cloud computing services (iCloud) and a virtual assistant (Siri), all of which are in principle core platform services in the DMA if certain scale criteria are met. The DMA would require consent before combining data across these services.

The DMA also requires gatekeepers to allow and enable end-users to 'easily un-install any software applications on the operating system'. Whether this includes confidential computing processes depends on the granularity of the term 'application'. Modern operating systems run many different software processes in the background, while applications are typically a user facing combination of those which does not necessarily map to what is happening underneath the hood. At the moment, users cannot see these processes on a platform like iOS, and even if they could, there is no easily understood way to navigate these. Furthermore, platforms are unlikely to design them in ways where they can each be turned off with no additional impacts, instead tangling them up to claim necessity to run them. Relatedly, the DMA also requires gatekeepers to allow users to 'switch between, and subscribe to, different

[99] J Cobbe et al, 'Understanding Accountability in Algorithmic Supply Chains' in *FAccT'23: Proceedings of the 2023 Conference on Fairness, Accountability, and Transparency in Algorithmic Systems* (New York, Association for Computing Machinery, 2023) 1186.

[100] Regulation (EU) 2022/1925 of the European Parliament and of the Council of 14 September 2022 on contestable and fair markets in the digital sector and amending Directives (EU) 2019/1937 and (EU) 2020/1828 (Digital Markets Act) (DMA) [2022] OJ L265/1, Art 5(2).

software applications and services that are accessed using the core platform services of the gatekeeper'. This might look towards a day where there are a range of different protocols that users could choose to run, but again will depend on how low-level this is interpreted and enforced. While both provisions look promising, there will be a long way to go before it gives individuals real agency over code running on their devices.

D. Open Internet Regulation

It is worth giving the provisions in the Open Internet Regulation a short mention. This regulation, which is generally known as the EU's net neutrality law, provides that 'End-users shall have the right to … use and provide applications and services, and use terminal equipment of their choice … via their internet access service'. While this does not provide an ability for individuals to stop their devices being used in certain ways, it does remove restrictions that may be placed on individuals' computation freedom over networks they have access to.[101]

E. Other Largely Unhelpful Acts

Several recent pieces of European law are worth highlighting for being unhelpful in assisting individuals unwillingly computing. The Data Governance Act does not give mechanisms which support collective computing, or to steer its aim or purposes, but instead focuses on establishing intermediaries that 'obtain data from data holders'.[102] This act of obtaining data is, as mentioned previously, not technologically neutral. The draft Data Act, in trialogue at the time of writing, appears to use a test of either 'accessibility' (Parliament version) or being 'readily available' (Council version) to determine whether data should be provided, which as mentioned is likely to hit a conceptual challenge in light of confidential computing, as systems are designed precisely to make such data not readily available to either users or data controllers.[103] The Parliament version contains a further provision around granular consent to processing purposes, but it is unclear what this adds beyond data protection law.[104]

[101] Regulation (EU) 2015/2120 of the European Parliament and of the Council of 25 November 2015 laying down measures concerning open internet access and amending Directive 2002/22/EC on universal service and users' rights relating to electronic communications networks and services and Regulation (EU) No 531/2012 on roaming on public mobile communications networks within the Union (Open Internet Regulation) [2015] OJ L310/1, Art 3(1).

[102] Data Governance Act (n 12), Art 2(11)(a).

[103] European Parliament, 'Data Act: Amendments Adopted by the European Parliament on 14 March 2023 on the Proposal for a Regulation of the European Parliament and of the Council on Harmonised Rules on Fair Access to and Use of Data (Draft Data Act) (COM(2022)0068 – C9-0051/2022 – 2022/0047(COD))' (P9_TA(2023)0069, 14 March 2023); Council of the European Union, 'Proposal for a Regulation of the European Parliament and of the Council on Harmonised Rules on Fair Access to and Use of Data (Data Act) – Mandate for Negotiations with the European Parliament' (2022/047/(COD), 7543/23, 17 March 2023).

[104] Draft Data Act, European Parliament Position (n 103), Art 3(2b)(c).

This provision does not appear to have made it to the trialogue text.[105] These acts all seem to broadly place top-down obligations while hoping that bottom-up actions from affected persons will follow, without grappling with the underlying power dynamics in the computational infrastructures surrounding us today.[106]

IV. WHAT IS NEEDED?

The provisions above suffer from three, interlinked main issues, which in turn have associated directions of travel to remedy them.

A. Lessen the Focus on Accessibility of Data, and Make Devices Accountable to their Users

Where the above regimes do provide for autonomy and oversight of covert computing procedures, their provisions are typically scoped inappropriately around accessibility of data. We have seen how this scope functions poorly in confidential computing. This tension stems from a fundamental misunderstanding of the technically possible connections between the means and ends of computing. It links further to the challenges that law has faced in understanding the political economy of the digital world, and dealing with complex algorithmic supply chains and the varying, overlapping and tangled roles of the actors within it, and the power that they manage to wield.[107]

One direction would be to alter the law so that there is more active decision-making about the whole lifecycle of design, from conception to ongoing management, in relation to the responsibilities and obligations it brings. Should device and operating system manufacturing firms have to consider more principles in design than they do already, such as user agency and scrutiny of code? What would this look like in practice? How would such obligations compare considering a firm like Apple, which has significant control over its iOS ecosystem, compared to firms like Google, Samsung and Huawei, which all play varying and overlapping roles within a more complex, multi-actor Android ecosystem. Such debates seem likely to blend with other discussions, such as the form and extent of a *right to repair* in the digital world.

In the meantime, to deal with this legal tension under existing law, it may be necessary to see devices and operating systems as agents of a company, effectively extending the area they are responsible for by, for example, extending (joint) controllership under data protection law. Because companies have differing levels of control over devices, and devices 'access' data all the time (particularly when that data is stored on that device), this seems like it will be a hazardous, highly technical path for courts and regulators to navigate, and one doused in the type of legal uncertainty that will create advantageous delays for technology giants.[108] In particular, it will

[105] Draft Data Act, Trialogue Agreed Position (July 2023) (unpublished, on file with author).

[106] P Terzis, 'Building Programmable Commons' (2023) 15 *Law, Innovation, and Technology* 583.

[107] Cobbe et al (n 99).

[108] See generally JE Cohen, 'Law for the Platform Economy' (2017) 51 *University of California, Davis, Law Review* 133.

be difficult to draw a line between the day-to-day practices of a firm, such as data processing, and the conditions within which a firm undertakes such processing (eg over the operating systems and toolkits they have deployed). Given significant vertical integration, both of these are somewhat under firms' control – they both design the processing and the surrounding conditions – but with different levels of friction and cost involved in changing them. Such friction may impact upon proportionality tests for regulatory interventions, as well as higher friction changes (such as redesign) being more difficult for regulators and courts to deal with, as they will find it harder to understand possible and impossible changes, given how much this will be tied to internal practices and processes of firms and their networked systems. Datasets and their risks, in comparison, can be more easily understood in isolation.

Furthermore, some firms act in more strategic and indirect ways to control the technologies and conditions of their data processing and computation. An example is Google's more hands-off approach to steering software like Android through their influence over projects they claim to be open-source, or through influence in standards bodies. It will be hard, if not impossible, for regulators to direct or injunct firms to use their indirect forms of power. Yet to not acknowledge this potential is to pretend there is no orchestrating actor that can be subject to legal interventions when in practice, several exist.

B. Strengthen Capacities to Understand which Code is Necessary, and for What

A second flaw is identifiable, particularly from the analysis of the e-Privacy directive: the breakdown of necessity tests in code. Drawing a distinction between code that should be running on a device, potentially without user involvement or knowledge, and that which should not, initially might seem like a plausible task. However, contemporary software engineering is networked, modular, constantly changing and often poorly documented. Necessity implies that there be a task that necessity can be judged against; however, functionality in the modern digital economy is not static, but being constantly defined and redefined. Smartphones that were purchased for communication can later become public health tools. Web browsers became methods for distributed copyrighted content over streaming; cameras became methods of accessing links through QR codes, Bluetooth moved from connecting headphones to contact tracing. In this context, what is a computation strictly necessary for a service requested by the end-user, as the e-Privacy Directive requires to be identified as part of its test for whether or not consent is needed? What is the granularity of the service that an end-user has requested in a constantly morphing digital landscape?

Even if these questions can be answered, they will not be cheap to do so, and regulators will both be shy and will technically struggle to get deep into business models on exploratory grounds. Active capacity needs to be built to map and understand them. As it stands, regulators and legislators do not have a good idea of what key computational infrastructures in society do, how they work, and how they are changing. In practice, there is a reliance on the ad hoc reports of a few regulators, particularly competition regulators, to map out this space using their significant information gathering powers. Yet these regulators do not act with the broader motivations, such as ethics, informational power and human rights directly. This leaves a mismatch of capacity. This information gathering infrastructure is one that is an international no-brainer, given how globally similar these systems are. Only with such a live informational capacity for infrastructures of public importance can we hope to answer questions such as necessity of code in relation to any regime at all in a timely fashion.

C. Bound Unnecessary Functionality, and Create Institutions to Represent Preferences and Negotiate Software for Putatively Acceptable Computations

Devices should have accountability to their users in relation to computations which are not necessary to functionality that users have requested or that would reasonably expect and agree to. Outside of these acceptable bounds, there should be further authorising processes. Berjon describes the kind of hardware and software stacks we are talking about here as 'user agents'; systems which 'through a consensual arrangement, acts on behalf of the user, subject, to some degree, to the user's control, to represent the user in their dealings with other parties'.[109] He in effect argues that the necessary reliance on these agents to navigate the entirety of our digital environments means that they should have fiduciary duties placed upon them, such that they must not betray the individuals relying on them. Understanding what betrayal means is difficult, but will be the result of navigation using the informational capacities described above in the previous section.

Frameworks such as contextual integrity may further help us realise that delineating some of these boundaries need not be an impossible task.[110] Functionality required for a legitimate and legal business model is necessary. Unsurprising computation that is desirable for the security and good functioning of this is likely to be legitimate, such as to improve the way keyboard or speech recognition models work, or to analyse the quality and quantity of security risks. While such computation might give some firms a market advantage over others, relevant regulators can deal with that separately. Computation that seems to be associated with a different context, such as using smartphone sensors to compute for health research, planning policy, targeted advertising, or the operation of logistics businesses, sits outside the expected. This does not mean it is forbidden. It simply means we need to govern it based on its subject matter, rather than using hooks such as the identifiability of individuals within these datasets.

In existing law surveyed above, the closest we come to governing this is through take-it-or-leave-it consent. A right to refuse – that is, if you have the energy and awareness. This is a useful stop-gap, but comes too late in the process of working out which computation is legitimate, and which is not. Individuals cannot be expected to scrutinise all current and potential collective computations occurring on their device and come to ethical or political decisions on each one, just so that they can know whether or not to exercise a (probably quite hidden) veto right. While that may be

[109] R Berjon, 'The Fiduciary Duties of User Agents' (2021) SSRN Electronic Journal, papers.ssrn.com/sol3/papers.cfm?abstract_id=3827421.

[110] Nissenbaum (n 30).

useful in the most heinous, well-publicised cases, we have also seen in areas such as ad-tech how consent-based regimes start battles over what effective or ineffective consent looks like.[111]

This right to refuse has been built on by calls for prosumer law in a digital world, which take a step beyond saying no to considering where users go after that expression.[112] Such regimes recognise individuals not just as passive consumers of content and takers of rules, but active agents in networking and computation. Brown and Marsden, who use this term, focus on the ability to exit a network, with practical opportunities for interoperability within an interconnected world. But the issues highlighted in this piece indicate that a regime will have to steer existing networks rather than just promote exit entirely. It will have to disaggregate and unbundle necessary from unnecessary functions, and it will have to allow individuals to make political choices about what is necessary and unnecessary. This is partly because we are talking about the lowest level of services; not so much free-at-point-of-service, ad-supported apps or websites, but operating systems, low-level software and hardware upon which these potentially switchable services run. It is not easy for people, even for those with substantial technical expertise, to exit these. It is not typically free, and rarely cheap. Yet preferences are also distinct; we cannot rely on a homogenous global body or regulatory consensus to decide what research people are involved in, and what they are not. Preferences legitimately vary and should be allowed to, although representation can reduce decision fatigue.

This means we have to consider other methods of steering and preference aggregation. Consider the narrative around bottom-up data trusts, where individuals entrust certain decisions about computation for the public good to collectives.[113] Although this is centred still on the collation of data rather than the control of computation, alternative governance mechanisms are possible to imagine, where trusted intermediaries bring a constituency of potential computing individuals to the table, negotiate on the terms of the collective analytics or learning being sought, such as the distribution of knowledge at the end of the process, and if happy, recommend a certain default decision to their subscribed userbase. This contributes to the ideals of negotiating software, where we understand what information technologies are important in society, and create fora to mediate conflicts over its form and function.[114] More broadly, it connects to technology assessment methods considered by science and technology studies,[115] although these tend to operate at a higher conceptual level than the granular, rapid and constantly changing systems discussed here.[116]

Lastly, we should be wary of leaving this to the public sector to govern, at least in its current form. This is primarily because the governance of computation on

[111] See eg M Nouwens et al, 'Dark Patterns after the GDPR: Scraping Consent Pop-Ups and Demonstrating Their Influence' in *CHI 2020. Proceedings of the ACM Conference on Human Factors in Computing Systems* (New York, Association for Computing Machinery, 2020) 1.

[112] I Brown and CT Marsden, *Regulating Code: Good Governance and Better Regulation in the Information Age* (Cambridge MA, The MIT Press, 2013).

[113] S Delacroix and ND Lawrence, 'Bottom-up Data Trusts: Disturbing the "One Size Fits All" Approach to Data Governance' (2019) 9 *International Data Privacy Law* 236.

[114] M Nouwens, 'Negotiating Software: Redistributing Control at Work and on the Web' (PhD dissertation, Aarhus University, 2021).

[115] Guston and Sarewitz (n 70).

[116] S Gürses and J van Hoboken, 'Privacy after the Agile Turn' in E Selinger et al (eds), *The Cambridge Handbook of Consumer Privacy* (Cambridge, Cambridge University Press, 2018).

infrastructures like this in the public sector is currently highly securitised, and led by signals intelligence (SIGNIT) capabilities. These agencies often lack legitimacy, particularly when considered across the full range of countries affected by the international infrastructures, and are rarely responsive to democratic signals nor accountable to them due to the secrecy of their actions, forms and operational routines. Neither are they particularly experienced or adept in the kind of open and inclusive international cooperation needed to incorporate views from around the world. This is unfortunate, and it is a priority for future work to consider some of these structural problems in-depth as information technologies move from being communication tools to underpinning much of the way we know about and understand the world and our environments across sectors, interests and contexts.

V. CONCLUSION

Scrutiny has now long been placed on computation that may compromise individuals' fundamental rights. In a world of more distributed computing, our sensors and devices all are playing a role in turning the world into information. This act is not neutral but political, yet individuals are being coopted into these infrastructures without awareness, without an ability to steer them, and increasingly, under the excuse that their data is confidential and unidentifiable. But this is not all about personal data. Information does not have to be personal to be political; to confer power; or to influence the world.

We do not say that someone's vote at an election was unimportant because it was not pivotal. It has value in political and symbolic ways. As a mobilised block, it is not just important but pivotal. The same thing can apply with data. Individual data matters because it can be identified and create a security risk, but this is not the only reason. Individuals contributing data from the devices they purchase, charge, maintain, connect and direct should say something about the ends to which they wish information to be put. As it stands, it does not, because neither they, nor any entities representing them, co-determine these ends. All they do is maintain the means, typically without remuneration or acknowledgement.

Recognising the role of all of us in informationalising the world is crucial. The law has a role to play. A focus on comput*ed* persons should be complemented by rights for comput*ing* persons, recognising that enabling and facilitating computing is not something that individuals have to passively do, without voice or choice. There will be challenges – salience, importance – this is a subtle area and not one that everyone will have energy to engage in. Representative actors, avoiding the fallacy of individual responsibility, will be crucial in governance. This is because the link to the individual and their benefits is even more indirect than it can be for personal data and privacy concerns. Nevertheless, this chapter has identified several directions, assumptions and tensions. There remains more to do. As firms roll our more confidential computing technologies, civil society, academia, policymakers and the media should all ask *who benefits* – and *who decides*? Who is gaining and defining understanding, and through what process? We should test the promising areas of existing laws supporting comput*ing* individuals with regulators and in courts, and propose and develop them if and where they are found lacking.

Part IV

Society, Economy and Nature

14

The Remains of the Corporation: A Future of Fragmented Corporate Personhood

ANNA BECKERS*

I. INTRODUCTION: CREATING AND FRAGMENTING PERSONS

PERSONIFICATION IS CENTRAL to the law; it establishes the actors in legal processes to whom responsibility and obligations are addressed and rights are given. If we look into the history of personhood in law, we see a variety of actors that have, at some point, received the status of a person.[1] Similarly, we see a vanishing of person status for specific groups, processes or organisations, not unusually coming with violent implications of disappearance and invisibility.[2] This experience with rising and falling persons in law may provide us with some guiding direction on where to search for the future discussion of personhood. Quite comparable to historical experience, the current debate equally witnesses an ever-increasing body of literature on new subject status for different types of non-human entities, with robots or nature being the most viable candidate,[3] as well as discussions that

* Professor of Private Law and Social Theory, Faculty of Law, Maastricht University, The Netherlands.
This chapter is produced within the European Research Council Project *CHAINLAW: Responsive Law for Global Value Chains* [Grant Agreement No 101076292].

[1] For a historical perspective on the creation and typification of *personae*, N Van Dijk, 'In the Hall of Masks: Contrasting Modes of Personification' in M Hildebrandt and K O'hara (eds), *Life and the Law in the Era of Data-Driven Agency* (Cheltenham, Edward Elgar, 2020).

[2] For depersonification processes, J-C Suntrup, 'The Legal Person and Its Other: A Comparative View on Drawing and Effacing Boundaries in Various Cultural Contexts' (2017) 3 *On_Culture: The Open Journal for the Study of Culture*.

[3] *cf*, eg, for legal personhood of artificial intelligence: LB Solum, 'Legal Personhood for Artificial Intelligences', (1992) 70 *North Carolina Law Review* 1231; more recently SM Solaiman, 'Legal Personality of Robots, Corporations, Idols and Chimpanzees: A Quest for Legitimacy' (2017) 25 *Artificial Intelligence and Law* 155; J Turner, *Robot Rules: Regulating Artificial Intelligence* (Heidelberg/New York, Springer, 2018) ch 5; For nature, the classic: C Stone, 'Should Trees have standing? Towards Legal Rights for Natural Objects' (1972) 45 *Southern California Law Review* 450; from the more recent literature, eg, A Hutchison, 'The Whanganui River as a Legal Person' (2014) 39 *Alternative Law Journal* 179; A Fischer-Lescano, 'Nature as a Legal Person: Proxy Constellations in Law' (2020) 32 *Law & Literature* 237. For the combined analysis of robots and nature to develop a general thrust on personification, G Teubner, 'Rights

may push us to deconstruct our generalisable understanding of the person. Debates on identity and gender suggest that our generalisable category of the person becomes increasingly fragmented, as do current reconsiderations of the average consumer as an ideal legally protected person.[4] Hence, as much as history has shown a rise and fall of persons, current debates also surround status ascriptions, status changes and vanishing legal persons.

In this chapter, I examine these processes of making and fragmenting legal persons. My core example and area of application will be the personification of economic processes in the form of corporate personhood. In section II, I turn to the making of corporate persons. This implies an analysis of the history and theory of legal personification of economic entities as juridical persons. This, I suggest, has become one of the most successful examples of personifying non-human entities in law in which modes of social and legal personification have interacted. As a result, the corporate legal person has turned into a blueprint, an 'institutional repository', in the law regarding the justification for and the conditions of personifying non-human entities. Debates on the social and legal personification of other social processes show how corporate personhood serves as a powerful argumentative justification for imagining and institutionalising legal personhood for 'artificial' non-human entities. Hence, the creation of corporate legal personhood is not only a successful example of how the legal system personifies; it has been a process of personification that has arguably created a path dependency for justifying modes of personification in the law more generally. This leads to the conclusion that one future of corporate personhood lies in serving as the shape for our future discourses about who may qualify as a legal person.

Section III then turns to the opposite development, the fragmentation of persons, their disappearance and 'liquidation'. This analysis starts with an abstract discussion on the boundaries of personhood, its opposition to the character of things and the recent considerations about hybridisation of personhood in-between persons and things and, relatedly, a gradualisation of the person. As I then argue, such gradualisation may fit well with the actual future of the corporate person. Instead of a clear delineation and attribution to the person, we now encounter a situation in which various policy fields and societal expectations delineate different boundaries of the corporate person and its responsibility. More concretely, companies' increasing reliance on legal personhood to avoid rather than embrace responsibility has triggered, in the law, efforts to broaden responsibility concepts that extend beyond the corporate person. This has been accompanied with a process of institutionalising different collective units depending on different social expectations. This is most clearly visible in the regulation of corporations as lead firms in global value chains. The future of corporate personhood is thus a fragmented institutionalisation.

of Non-Humans? Electronic Agents and Animals as New Actors in Politics and Law' (2006) 33 *Journal of Law and Society* 497.

[4] See Vanessa Mak in this volume and V Mak, 'How can consumer interests be protected when consumer identities are increasingly diffuse?' in H-W Micklitz and C Twigg-Flesner (ed), *The Transformation of Consumer Law and Policy in Europe* (Oxford, Hart Publishing, 2023) 43.

As a general conclusion, this contribution proposes that the future for corporate legal personhood holds a somewhat ironic turn. It remains a stable image that underpins future debates on legal personhood and, with this, will arguably shape significantly many of the future discourses on the personification of non-humans. At the same time, it is not improbable that the corporate personification will be fragmented, and the unitary image of the corporate legal person will be replaced by a gradualised institutionalisation of other forms of economic organisation in the law with the related evolution of different forms of collective organisation. Such development could lead to a paradox in the legal system whereby the further evolution of the personhood of non-human entities will rely on a repository in the legal rules that have become an artefact without the existence of such image in reality.

II. THE MAKING OF CORPORATE PERSON

How can we conceive of the process of personifying mere economic processes as corporate legal persons? To answer that question, we will have to focus on the theoretical background of personification from a social (A) and legal (B) perspective. This theoretical framework can be applied to corporate personification to explain the development of corporate personhood of becoming a prime example about how law embraces social personification processes while still keeping its autonomy. This can provide the basis for relating corporate personhood to current debates about the personification of robots and nature (C), and conclude that the corporate process of becoming a legal person from mere social and economic activity is inherent in the arguments of granting personhood status to non-human entities.

A. Social Processes of Personification

Why are processes of personification prevalent and essential for society? Why does society rely on the mode of personification and assigning action capacity to make sense of organisational processes? Many motives are cited to explain the process historically and in today's society.[5] Depending on the disciplinary perspective taken, these range from the economists' ideal of reducing transaction costs to the sociologists' argument of coordination advantages and pooling of resources. Lawyers typically refer to the 'legal immortality' of legal persons – the church, the state, the company.[6] Social theory can thicken these arguments: systems theory points to the crucial advantages of personification for social systems in contact with their environment,[7]

[5] For motives of personification in 'traditional societies', W Ewald, 'Comparative Jurisprudence (I): What Was It Like to Try a Rat' (1995) 143 *American Journal of Comparative Law* 1889.

[6] For transaction costs, O Williamson, *The Economic Institutions of Capitalism: Firms, Markets, Relational Contracting* (New York, Free Press MacMillan Publishers, 1985) 110; for resource pooling, JS Coleman, *Foundations of Social Theory* (Cambridge MA, Harvard University Press, 1990) 325ff; for continuity *locus classicus* W Blackstone, *Commentaries on the Laws of England: In Four Books* (Philadelphia, Robert Bell, 1771) 467ff.

[7] N Luhmann, *Social Systems* (Stanford, Stanford University Press, 1995) ch 5 VI.

and Latour emphasises access and participation in the political ecology.[8] Teubner has added another important argument for non-human personification: this turns out to be a successful strategy for coping with uncertainty, especially the unpredictability of an entity's behaviour.[9] Personification transforms the relationship between humans and non-human entities from a person's relationship with an object into an alter-ego person-person relationship. This enables Ego to influence Alter's behaviour communicatively and to choose his own action in response to Alter's communication. The sociologist Armin Nassehi has refined this pointedly and applied it to the counterintuitive personification of algorithms:

> The computer or algorithm is then no longer a technical artefact with attribution potential, but a counterpart that appears either as an anthropomorphic actor in the case of natural language or as a corporate actor in the case of decision-making algorithms.[10]

Against this background, personification allows the system to 'see' an actor to whom a communicative response can be addressed instead of a thing that can be objectified, controlled, regulated or dominated. The personification then creates, as Niels van Dijk has stated pointedly for the law, 'a "point of imputation" for legal relations, a foothold in the legal system for attributing rights and obligations to someone'.[11]

This also means that personification does not mean to 'create' a human being, living organisation, mindful consciousness, or a social substrate in the encounter with non-human persons. Instead – it is an attribution based on 'talk incorporated'! As defined by Parsons, Luhmann and others, the collective actor is not a group of individuals. Instead, it is a social system, which is nothing but a chain of messages. Human minds and bodies are not parts of social systems, but parts of their environment. Their influence on the systems' internal operations is, of course, massive, but only an indirect one. Organisations are neither buildings, groups of people nor resource pools, but decision chains. The social reality of a non-human actor, the person's social substrate, arises from two premises: first, such a communication creates its identity as a self-description; second, actions are no longer ascribed to the actors that partake in the collective but to this self-description.[12]

Applied to the personification of corporations, this suggests that the corporate person does not arise with the discovery of a 'real entity'[13] or a 'nexus of contracts'[14] bundled together into an organisation. It also does not come out of the mere existence of economic processes. Instead, processes of personifying economic processes

[8] B Latour, *Politics of Nature: How to Bring the Sciences into Democracy* (Cambridge MA, Harvard University Press, 2004) 53ff.

[9] For this thesis, see Teubner (n 3) 503ff. Additional refinements on the personification of algorithms, A Nassehi, *Muster. Theorie der digitalen Gesellschaft* (CH Beck, Munich, 2019) 221ff.

[10] Nassehi (n 9) 224; similarly A Hepp, *Deep Mediatization*, Key Ideas in Media & Cultural Studies (London, Routledge, 2020).

[11] Van Dijk (n 1) 234.

[12] G Teubner, 'Enterprise Corporatism: New Industrial Policy and the "Essence" of the Legal Person' (1988) 36 *American Journal of Comparative Law* 130, 133.

[13] On real entity theory, O Gierke, *Associations and Law: The Classical and Early Christian Stages* (trans George Heiman) (Toronto, University of Toronto Press, 1977).

[14] MC Jensen and WH Meckling, 'Theory of the Firm: Managerial Behaviour, Agency Costs and Ownership Structure' (1976) 3 *Journal of Financial Economics* 305.

as corporations entered the stage at the critical point when industrial organisation became centred around the self-identification of a corporate organisation. It is no surprise that the fundamental decisions on the legal personhood of corporations[15] appeared at a time when, in industrial organisation, the discourse surrounding the underlying 'nature' of corporations became detached from the underlying state decision to grant personality (concession theories) and the aggregation of financial interest into understanding corporations as a dominant and real existing form of corporate organisation and self-standing decision-making.[16]

B. Legal Personification

This directly leads to how personification processes occur in the interaction between societal processes and legal rules. Is it the law that personifies autonomously, or does the law follow such social processes of personification, or do social processes follow legal rules? In the history of corporate personhood, one may find both positions; the initial theories of concession and fiction theories insisted on the autonomy of the law to grant the person status at will. As a result, the existence of companies as persons was perceived as dependent on the state's mercy and its law. In contrast, real entity theory treated legal personality as a consequence of recognising the social group as an existing real entity and relating legal processes to that. Similarly, contractarian theories understood the company merely as a nexus of existing relations that the law would transform into a corporate legal entity. However, both of these theories may not fully grasp the complexity of the issue of how legal and social processes of personification interact.

The 'anything goes' approach is far too superficial in understanding the interactions between law and societal changes in processes of personification. The understanding of entirely autonomous legal personification of companies as fictional entities existing at the mercy of the law does not consider the complex interactions between social and legal agency. Insisting on the freedom of personification of positive law ignores the normative requirements that the social context and the related expectations explicitly or implicitly place on law due to their own rationality and normativity. The personification of corporations has followed social transformations in which industrial organisation has begun to centre around the corporate form. As Teubner has it, the 'great innovation of the 19th century, the organisation and liberation of the corporation as a legal person, was initially nothing but the legal form for newly emerging industrial action centres'.[17]

Nevertheless, it is also too simple to assume that personification in law follows and uncritically adopts the societal status ascription. This perspective ignores that social systems personify autonomously and based on different criteria. The fact

[15] Trustees of Dartmouth College v Woodward 17 US (4 Wheat) 518 (1819); Salomon v A Salomon & Co Ltd [1896] UKHL 1.

[16] MJ Horwitz, 'Santa Clara Revisited: The Development of Corporate Theory' (1986) 88 *West Virginia Law Review* 173, 179ff.

[17] G Teubner, 'Unitas Multiplex: Corporate Governance in Group Enterprises' in G Teubner and D Sugarman (eds), *Regulating Corporate Groups in Europe* (Baden-Baden, Nomos, 1990) 68.

that some persons appear in the economic or political system but have no agency in law may provide manifold evidence for that. Legal personification maintains autonomy and recognises persons based on their own criteria. Against this background, lawyers have rightly insisted on the difference between social substrate and legal personhood for corporations, very prominently in the emphasis on the difference between the economic firm and the legal corporation[18] and the different characteristics of modern corporations in the various social systems and their disciplinary perspectives.[19] Law is specific in how it accepts corporate personhood compared to economic and social processes. What freedoms can legal personification then enjoy compared to personification in various areas of society? All and every freedom – that would be the answer in a good positivist manner. Even if various social processes of institutionalisation provide hints for legal personhood, there remains a fundamental difference between social and legal personification. Legal constructs are not 'derived' from pre-legal structures. Legal positivity is to be taken seriously, and a considerable degree of variability between the persons of law and those acting in other systems is expected.[20] This is precisely what systems theory suggests: the closure of the legal system to other social systems and the closure of legal doctrine to social theories are responsible for this variability.[21] Accordingly, nothing prevents the legal system from conferring legal personality on numerous objects – deities, saints, temples, land, rivers, works of art.

However, despite this high degree of freedom, considerable structural affinities exist between social and legal personification. They do not level out the is–ought distinction, but rather make visible open and latent interrelations between 'facts' and 'norms'. The processes of social and legal personification already run in parallel, namely as a selective ascription of agency to social communicative processes. Moreover, the law makes little use of its supposedly unlimited positivist freedom in practice. It tends to confer legal personality almost exclusively on entities already given actor status in social practice. This close correspondence of attribution processes certainly does not originate from natural law, legal logic, or the binding of law to social reality. Instead, it is based on a complex legal argument: What role should the law play when new social actors are constituted? This is not primarily about the stability of social processes, as is often mistakenly assumed, but about transformation.[22]

[18] J-P Robé, 'The Legal Structure of the Firm' (2011) 1 *Accounting, Economics, and Law* 1; S Deakin, 'The Juridical Nature of the Firm' in T Clarke and DM Branson (eds), *The Sage Handbook of Corporate Governance* (London, Sage Publications, 2012) 113.

[19] Insightful on this different treatment of the modern corporation from the different perspectives of law, economics, management, politics, the various Modern Corporation Statements developed by the Modern Corporation Project; see themoderncorporation.wordpress.com.

[20] For this argument in relation to personification of algorithms, G Wagner, 'Robot, Inc: Personhood for Autonomous Systems?' (2019) 88 *Fordham Law Review* 591, 597ff; G Wagner, 'Robot Liability' in R Schulze, S Lohsse and D Staudenmayer (ed), *Liability for Robotics and in the Internet of Things* (Baden-Baden/Oxford, Nomos/Hart, 2019) 27, 54.

[21] Extensively G Teubner, 'Law and Social Theory: Three Problems' (2014) *Ancilla Juris* 183.

[22] For responsiveness of law towards institution-generation and -transformation, D Wielsch, 'Contract Interpretation Regimes' (2018) 81 *Modern Law Review* 958, 961ff. Generally on the social adequacy of law understood as the potential of increasing irritation possibilities, N Luhmann, *Law as a Social System* (Oxford, Oxford University Press, 2004) 219ff.

For the evolution of corporate personification, Simon Deakin has put it pointedly:

> The law is part of social reality as well as shaping it. Thus to say that the corporation is, at one and the same time, a legal and an economic entity, is to understand it in terms of a multi-layered ontology. The legal or juridical form of the company reflects features of organisational or financial practice but, since it is not reducible to them, can also, over time, influence them. To use the language of systems theory, legal and economic conceptions of the firm are operatively closed, that is, distinct from each other in their modes of operation and self-reproduction, but cognitively open, that is, susceptible to mutual influence and coevolution.[23]

In this regard, corporate personhood has relied on and evolved from the social and, specifically, economic process of personification. Simultaneously, this creation of legal personhood for corporations has transformed into a stable normative idea in the law, an *idée directrice*,[24] about its capacity to assign social practices the legal action capacity through the concept of personhood. And these forms of personification have bounced back into the 'real' societal world; by creating rights and obligations to companies, companies have continuously adjusted their own communicative processes in other societal processes to appear as the person that they are assigned in law. To again point to Niels van Dijk:

> Legal fictions … are constructions always intended to shift attention back to the real world. There, they become reattached and reassigned to the acts of individuals who are represented in the legal narrative … This reattachment always entails concrete consequences, such as being attributed rights and obligations. A masked performance with performative effects.[25]

With these recursive feedback loops, personhood became stabilised over time, refining the status ascriptions following the social consequences of attribution of rights and obligations to then lead to changes in the social reality.

C. Corporate Personhood as a Blueprint?

Corporate personhood is one of the longstanding forms of personification of non-human – juristic – persons. It can be seen as one of the most successful and stable ideas in the law of personhood. As Naffine has it: 'the literature on the legal person is to a large extent preoccupied with the meaning of corporate personality'.[26] And the argument can be taken one step further. Establishing corporate persons in law has not only meant an ever-increasing debate on the nature and purpose of the corporate person; recent debates on personhood for other non-human entities also suggest

[23] S Deakin, 'The Corporation in Legal Studies' in G Baars and A Spicer (eds), *The Corporation: A Critical, Multi-Disciplinary Handbook* (Cambridge, Cambridge University Press, 2017) 47, 55.

[24] The concept of the *idée directrice* follows from M Hauriou, 'La Théorie de l'institution et de la fondation: Essai de vitalisme social' in M Hauriou, *Aux sources du droit* (Caen, Bloud & Gay, 1986 [1933]) 89.

[25] Van Dijk (n 1) 234ff.

[26] N Naffine, 'Who are the Law's Persons? From Cheshire Cats to Responsible Subjects' (2003) 66 *Modern Law Review* 346, 348.

that the construction of corporate legal personhood has turned out to be a normative anchor in the law about how the legal system can personify autonomously. This has shaped and steered broader discussions about the personification of non-human entities.

This is particularly true for the debate on robots and artificial intelligence, where the legal perspective on corporate personhood is regularly invoked as a parallel and justification for legal personification without needing to accept intelligence, consciousness or mind.[27] Corporate personhood and its evolution have become an intrinsic part of the debate on whether or not to assign personhood.[28] For artificial intelligence and autonomous technological systems, corporate personhood seems to be invoked not only as a metaphor or as a general justification for conceiving of personhood; some authors even recur the rules on company law as appropriate rules, directly or analogously, for e-persons.[29] Corporate personhood appears equally in the debate on the personification of nature,[30] although it is here not so much the specific rules of company law and corporate personality that are used but the overall normative idea that non-human processes, including nature, can be assigned personhood.[31] This is already visible in the early discussions on the legal personality, in Christopher Stone's ground-breaking text, 'Should Trees Have Standing?', where corporate personality is used as an argument to render nature rights imaginable and thinkable.[32]

Although other arguments are invoked in favour of the legal personality of nature and robots, it is striking that there is a regular reference to the corporate personality argument running through the debate. Corporate personality has become a robust guiding idea for debates on non-human personality, even if not directly transferable. In systems theory terms, this suggests that successfully integrating the corporate person into the programming structure provides a strong internal reception in the law for accommodating new forms of personhood. The *idée directrice* of corporate personification provides a guiding tool to connect new social expectations. Applying this to the question of the future of the corporate person, this suggests that corporate personality has a future as a continuing and discourse-steering idea about how to conceive of non-human personhood. Even if the corporate person is itself in a process of transformation – more on that below – the directing idea of corporate legal personality continues to exist. The future of corporate personhood may then lie in its history and construction that has made possible a discourse about legal autonomy and social dependence in future discourses of personhood.[33]

[27] Wagner (n 20) 598ff; Solaiman (n 3) 161; S Wojtczak, 'Endowing Artificial Intelligence with Legal Subjectivity' (2022) 37 *AI & Society* 205, 206ff; J Chen and P Burgess, 'The Boundaries of Legal Personhood: How Spontaneous Intelligence Can Problematize Differences Between Humans Artificial Intelligence, Companies and Animals' (2019) 27 *Artificial Intelligence and Law* 73, 79ff.

[28] *cf* Brownsword in this volume, section II.B.ii.

[29] Turner (n 3) 177ff; D Linardatos, Autonome und vernetzte Aktanten im Zivilrecht: Grundlinien zivilrechtlicher Zurechnung und Strukturmerkmale einer elektronischen Person (Tübingen, Mohr Siebeck, 2021) ch 13.

[30] Most explicitly, M Worthington and P Spender, 'Constructing Legal Personhood: Corporate Law's Legacy' (2021) 30 *Griffith Law Review* 348.

[31] For a description of this argument with subsequent critique, VAJ Kurki, 'Can Nature Hold Rights? It's Not as Easy as You Think' (2022) 11 *Transnational Environmental Law* 525, 527, 538ff.

[32] Stone (n 3) 452ff.

[33] Whether this is to be welcomed or criticised is a different question. To use the guiding idea of corporate personhood to make legal sense of other entities may limit very strongly how such new persons may

III. FRAGMENTING CORPORATE PERSONS

The idea of the corporate person persists, it seems. However, does this persistence also apply to the social and legal existence of the corporate person as such? As the corporation has been personified and is accepted as a corporate actor *par excellence*, the contribution could be ended with a positive note emphasising how powerful the idea of corporate personhood has been and still is. However, the corporate actor's current social and legal reality seems to suggest otherwise, as with the advent of large and globally operating companies, there has been an ironic move in the discussion on personhood. With globalisation, it has not only become possible for companies to operate globally. Companies as legal actors were also able to rely on the legal form and limited liability to disperse their action capacity while minimising risks. Limited liability has been a very old rule connected to corporate personhood, its use as a risk minimising strategy with a simultaneous expansion of action capacity beyond national frontiers seems a rather new phenomenon.[34]

As company lawyers have continuously highlighted, corporate legal personhood – and with it the concepts of separate legal personality, limited liability and asset lock-in – has served not only the goal of ascribing responsibility to a corporate subject with related underlying financial capacity; it has also led to the opposite, namely responsibility avoidance, by those very actors by creating separate legal persons.[35] While regularly acting as interlinked economic units, ie as persons in the economy, the legal personification has become a vehicle to avoid attribution of responsibility to the entity in question. In many areas, eg company, tax, tort and competition law, one can observe countering developments by which the law extends its notion of corporate responsibility. For instance, EU competition law contains prima facie assumptions to assign competition law infringements of a legally separated subsidiary to the group in case of 100 per cent shareholding.[36] In tax law, transfer-pricing rules and the arm's length principle assess legal relations between associated enterprises against the background of whether they should be considered within a group structure or market relations.[37] In tort law, several court rulings suggest that there may be an expanding responsibility ascription for wrongful conduct attributed to a corporate group.[38] Company law itself, in particular in the form of accounting rules,

be seen in the law. They may be associated with organisational and collective structures despite not being characterised as such. This normative analysis of whether continuity in personhood debates should be embraced needs to be reserved for a separate analysis.

[34] For the relation between limited liability, separate legal personality, globalisation and corporate group, see R Mares, 'Liability Within Corporate Groups: Parent Companies Accountability for Subsidiary Human Rights Abuses' in S Deva and D Birchall (eds), *Research Handbook on Human Rights and Business* (Cheltenham, Edward Elgar, 2020) 446ff.

[35] Most prominently for this argument, K Pistor, *The Code of Capital: How the Law Creates Wealth and Inequality* (Princeton, Princeton University Press, 2019) ch 3.

[36] Case C-97/08 P *Akzo Nobel and Others v European Commission*, ECLI:EU:C:2009:536 [2009] ECR I-8237; Case C-90/09 P *General Química SA and Others v European Commission*, ECLI:EU:C:2011:21 [2011]. On the evolution of corporate group responsibility under EU competition law, including reference to the most relevant literature, *cf* Ulfbeck in this volume, section III.D.

[37] OECD, 'Transfer Pricing Guidelines for Multinational Enterprises and Tax Administrations 2022' (OECD Publishing, 2022).

[38] Here, the developments are the strongest in relation to human rights and climate change and relate to the ground-breaking jurisprudence of English and Dutch courts: *Lungowe* v *Vedanta Resources* [2019]

has already expanded to consider consolidated accounts a long time ago.[39] To these trends in corporate groups, one may add the more recent legislative and jurisprudential debates on attributing companies the responsibility for their global supply chain that I will discuss below.[40] Such tendencies can, in the first place, be understood as an expansion of corporate personhood that remains below the formal legal personification. Collective units, such as undertakings in market competition, group pricing rules in taxation, or supply-chain structures, gradually expand the notion of the corporate person beyond its legal limits without, however, translating this into a fully fledged legal person. However, the recent stronger relation to the law and the various areas affected raise the question of whether the law would keep up with such development to also expand the notion of the legal personhood?

A. Two Debated Futures: Continuance or Expansion of Personhood?

In the legal debate, these developments have, indeed, led to several conceivable futures about the corporate legal person, two of which characterise the debate quite strongly: first, it may be possible that corporate personification in law persists and, as such ignores the move towards fragmentation in other areas. As stated above, the law is, in principle, free to assign legal personhood in complete autonomy. This is, admittedly, an unlikely scenario, but it is a position with strong advocates within the legal debate: concerning corporate human rights violations, there are scholars criticising tendencies of broader responsibility attribution due to intertwined global operations with the continuous insistence that this would lead to a (dangerous) 'erosion' of the principle of legal personhood and separate legal personality.[41] It also seems to underlie the position of scholars that may be sympathetic to the liability of companies for related entities in the group but insist on justifying such liability in their own responsibility attribution, such as fault, control or fraud.[42] However, seeing the legal and social developments in intertwining legally separated entities, this position may end up in the economic and social reality becoming detached from the legal conception. Given that the law needs to adapt to social processes,[43] such a scenario seems not only not too likely but also dangerous in making the law lose contact with social reality.

UKSC 20; *Okpabi and others* v *Royal Dutch Shell Plc and another* [2021] UKSC 3; *Vereniging Milieudefensie and others* v *Royal Dutch Shell Plc*, Rechtbank Den Haag (26 May 2021) ECLI:NL:RBDHA:2021:5337.

[39] Fourth Council Directive 78/660/EEC of 25 July 1978 based on Article 54(3)(g) of the Treaty on the annual accounts of certain types of companies, OJ L 222, 11–31; Seventh Council Directive 83/349/EEC of 13 June 1983 based on the Article 54(3)(g) of the Treaty on consolidated accounts, OJ L 193, 1–17.

[40] See section III.B.iii.

[41] This argument is particularly prevalent in the debate on responsibility for human rights violations in corporate groups: G Wagner, 'Haftung für Menschenrechtsverletzungen' (2016) 80 *Rabels Zeitschrift für ausländisches und internationales Privatrecht* 717, 761; M Habersack and M Ehrl, 'Verantwortlichkeit inländischer Unternehmen für Menschenrechtsverletzungen durch ausländische Zulieferer – de lege lata und de lege ferenda' (2019) 219 *Archiv für die civilistische Praxis* 155, 197.

[42] Extensively on this debate, the legal strategies and their components, the contribution by Ulfbeck, in this volume, 336ff and, specifically concerning the English cases *Vedanta* and *Okpabi* (n 38), section 343ff.

[43] Cross-reference above.

A second conceivable future is the discussion on expanding the notion of corporate legal personhood and identifying new responsibility subjects. Currently, this seems to be a dominant position among corporate law scholars. Enterprise or entity theory of the company are examples of this position.[44] The debates on networks as legal concepts seems to be moving in a quite similar direction. While not assigning the network the status as a formal legal person, there is recognition of the emergent collective properties of networks that need to be reflected in the legal rules.[45] From this perspective, we may see neither perseverance nor the vanishing of corporate personhood, but a transformation and significant expansion by which the emergent collective properties visible in economic and social operations are reflected in the law.[46]

Both positions, preserving corporate personality and expansion, have in common their shared interest in maintaining personification as an instrument for economic processes of interlinked enterprises for the sake of accommodating these new collective units and related responsibility ascription. Hence, in the continuance or expansion of corporate personhood, we may see one conceivable future of the corporate person, one that would indicate the rise of a new entity that could qualify for the legal person status.

B. A Third Future: Fragmented and Gradual Corporate Personhood

Against both approaches, I suggest that one may also need to inquire – and possibly embrace – a third, quite different future of corporate personhood. Rather than maintaining or transforming corporate personhood, we may also face a future of fragmentation of personhood in which gradualisation of collectivity is key. To understand this phenomenon, we need to dive deeper into the theoretical discussion surrounding depersonification and the problematising of the person/thing divide to then relate this to the developments on corporate personhood.

i. The Person–Thing Divide and its In-between(s)

Quite surprisingly, in debates on legal personhood, the process of 'unmaking' legal persons as well as problematising the distinction between person and non-person has not been very prominent. While an abundance of literature analyses the processes of making persons in law, the process of disappearing persons and the phenomenon of the in-between of person and non-person has received little attention. The strongest approximation to these processes can be traced back to critical voices in the debate

[44] See, for enterprise theory, the classic AA Berle, 'The Theory of Enterprise Entity' (1947) 47 *Columbia Law Review* 343; further, PI Blumberg, 'The Transformation of Modern Corporation Law: The Law of Corporate Groups' (2005) 37 *Connecticut Law Review* 605.

[45] See, specifically, G Teubner and H Collins, *Networks as Connected Contracts. With an Introduction by Hugh Collins* (trans Michelle Everson) (Oxford-Portland, Hart Publishing, 2011); M Amstutz and G Teubner (eds), *Networks. Legal Issues of Multilateral Co-operation* (Oxford-Portland, Hart Publishing, 2009); PM Baquero, *Networks of Collaborative Contracts for Innocation* (Oxford, Hart Publishing, 2022).

[46] This is also the normative conclusion put forward by Vibe Ulfbeck in her contribution.

on new legal subjectivity – nature, algorithms, animals – that discuss problems with personification and insist on its exclusionary tendencies.[47] In corporate personhood, the term is hardly known.[48] The fragmentation of established subjects still seems to be a development beyond imagination.

Likely reasons for this lack of attention are the negative imaginary associations that come with the process of depersonification. The term alludes to the terrible movements in which humans have been degraded from the status of personhood, examples being many but very prominently at different times: slaves, African Americans, Jews and women.[49] It is understandable that with this imaginative connotation, processes of depersonification are viewed with scepticism, and they certainly need to be treated with a good portion of care and reflection. However, as the political theorist Roberto Esposito argues pointedly, there are equally violent implications in the existence of the category of person and its clear distinction to non-persons. By assigning personhood, we simultaneously exclude. In fact, assigning of personhood engages in invisible depersonification processes, because of the assigning of everything that is not a person into the category of things.[50] Hence, when discussions concern the lack of recognising a concept as a person, the person–thing distinction requires it to enter the category of things, and, as Esposito would argue, consequently, be related to processes of commodification, use and exploitation. The distinction between persons and things has a long-standing intellectual heritage and characterises much of our day-to-day thinking as well as legal categories. Hence, questioning the distinction means to embark upon the difficult task to identify a place for ambiguous instances that are in-between. Esposito analyses this based on the concept of the body, but also biologists have shown how nature can occupy such place in-between and how indigenous knowledge may lead the way to this.[51]

Esposito suggests questioning the distinction between persons and things, and allowing a third possibility, like Latour's hybrids.[52] The suggestion may then be to open up our categories, not to broaden the concept of the person to allow it to accommodate ever more social processes but to conceive of new categories in-between persons and non-persons that have a fragmented status and are neither a complete person nor a non-person. Instead, they are in-betweens on a gradual differentiation between persons and things. The debate on artificial intelligence may provide a helpful example to make the point: in place of an *ex ante*-established normative understanding of how artificial intelligence operates, an exciting repository of proposals has now emerged, ranging from granting limited legal personhood[53] to conceiving them as

[47] On algorithms: M Petersmann and D Van Den Meerssche, 'On Phantom Publics, Clusters, and Collectives: Be(com)ing Subject in Algorithmic Times' (2023) *AI & Society* 107; on nature: M Petersmann, 'In the Break (of Rights and Representation): Sociality Beyond the Non/Human Subject' (2023) *The International Journal of Human Rights*.

[48] The only reference to depersonification concerning corporate personhood can be found in P Ireland, 'Company Law and the Myth of Shareholder Ownership' (1999) 62 *Modern Law Review* 32, 41, 48ff.

[49] Suntrup (n 2) 11.

[50] R Esposito, 'Persons and Things' (2016) 39 *Paragraph* 26, 31ff.

[51] See, for instance, the beautiful book of RW Kimmerer, *Braiding Sweetgrass: Indigenous Wisdom, Scientific Knowledge and the Teaching of Plants* (Minneapolis, Milkweed Editions, 2015).

[52] Esposito (n 50) 34ff with a view to the in-between status argument of Latour (n 8) 70ff.

[53] G Teubner, 'Digital Personhood? The Status of Autonomous Software Agents in Private Law' (2018) *Ancilla Juris* 107; J-E Schirmer, 'Artificial Intelligence and Legal Personality: Introducing "Teilrechtsfähigkeit":

hybrids[54] or attributing another status in-between.[55] Such in-between understandings may account for the fact that artificial intelligence is not assigned a full person status, but still operates in society beyond the status of a mere object that is employed.

However, for corporations, such a perspective of inquiring an evolving status in-between has not yet been fully explored, even though newer developments exist that suggest a strong tendency towards fragmentation of the corporate entity. Therefore, my aim in this last section is to explore precisely how such recent regulatory developments in relation to corporate groups and supply chains may point to a future status in-between person, object or structure: a status in which different laws, policies and societal expectations will each result in different forms of institutionalisation and, as a consequence, status ascriptions. This may have the result that the corporation appears, in the future, as a fragmented entity in which the degree of personhood may differ in relation to how the social expectations become institutionalised.

In light of what has been described above on the process of making persons, such movement towards fragmentation is initiated when the corporate actor no longer communicates about itself as an actor. Corporations as persons may become fragmented when their communicative self-ascriptions do not result in a self-identity. This may explain why proponents of expanding corporate personhood for corporate groups invoke many arguments that are related to such communicative processes. Recognising the corporate group is justified with the reference to the communicative 'essence' of the corporate person in the form of consolidated accounts,[56] common management,[57] policies, group interests[58] and decision-making processes: expansion of corporate personhood is to be found in the fact that the corporate group now may be able to 'speak about itself' and have agents speaking on its behalf. However, my argument below is to show we see in the newer rules on corporate groups and supply chains how specifically such communicative 'essence' disappears. I will separate the argument first to discuss the situation with corporate groups and then turn to supply chains.

A Partial Legal Status Made in Germany' in T Wischmeyer and T Rademacher (eds), *Regulating Artificial Intelligence* (Cham, Springer, 2019).

[54] M-C Gruber, 'Legal Subjects and Partial Legal Subjects in Electronic Commerce' in T Pietrzykowski and B Stancioli (eds), *New Approaches to Personhood in Law: Essays in Legal Philosophy* (Frankfurt aM, Lang, 2016); I would qualify our work on social-digital institutionalisation of artificial intelligence and related actor-status to fall within this category A Beckers and G Teubner, *Three Liability Regimes for Artificial Intelligence: Algorithmic Actants, Hybrids, Crowds* (Oxford, Hart Publishing, 2021).

[55] R Calo, 'Robotics and the Lessons of Cyberlaw (2015) 103 *California Law Review* 513, 549: 'we may be on the cusp of creating a new category of legal subject, halfway between person and object'. For a detailed treatment of different current proposals for status in-between ranging from Kurki's bundle theory of rights to Pietrzykowski's non-personal subjects of law proposal, to a gradient theory of personhood; *cf* the analysis by DJ Gunkel, *Person, Thing, Robot: A Moral and Legal Ontology for the 21st Century and Beyond* (Cambridge MA, The MIT Press, 2023) 151ff. The authors also provide another noteworthy proposal to establish a relational category of 'Things'.

[56] In this direction of reading the rules on consolidated accounts, H Fleischer, 'Europäisches Konzernrecht: Eine akteurzentrierte Annäherung' (2017) 46 *Zeitschrift für Unternehmens- und Gesellschaftsrecht* 1, 18ff.

[57] C Teichmann, 'Towards a European Framework for Cross-Border Group Management' (2016) 13 *European Company Law* 150.

[58] P-H Conac, 'Director's Duties in Groups of Companies – Legalizing the Interest of the Group at the European Level' (2013) 10 *European Company and Financial Market Review* 194.

ii. The Corporate Group: Fragmentation in Disguise

With the advent of large-scale enterprises operating in different jurisdictions and using the legal form to avoid risks, discussions have taken place on the relationship between economically and managerially intertwined but legally separated entities. As already anticipated above, in this process, discussions led to countering the advantages of legal separation with an expansion of responsibility attributions towards the corporate group. This would entail a future of expanding personhood to the group. This movement in the law is supported by other disciplinary perspectives: media studies has been analysing the corporate group as an actor by showing how it has been communicatively and artistically established as an actor,[59] and political sciences work increasingly with the multinational enterprise as an autonomous actor in international relations.[60] Moreover, legal theory grapples with the idea of multinational corporations as having their own legal orders with their own inside/outside distinctions in delineating functional territories of corporations.[61]

And yet, the rules on corporate groups do not necessarily suggest that we see a uniform expansion of corporate group personality now to include the conglomerate of financially or managerially dependent subsidiaries. One may also understand the various legislative and case law analyses to move into a fragmentation in disguise. While the tone of legislative initiatives and recent case law is directed towards expanding responsibility to cover new corporate group arrangements, the legislative interventions draw the boundaries of responsibility differently. For instance, analysing a variety of EU instruments related to corporate groups, Fleischer has been pointing to systematic tensions between the various rules on company groups. Different rules applying to corporate groups cover them differently and use various techniques to achieve this purpose.[62]

This suggests that it is not the corporate group as such that turns out to become a hybrid in-between an organisational person and a conglomerate of mere market transactions.[63] Instead, legal rules and related societal expectations constitute the corporate group differently depending on regulatory and policy objectives, societal expectations and path dependency. In corporate groups, one may see the different legal-institutional embedding in the contrasting models between tort law and competition law, as presented by Ulfbeck.[64] One may also see it in the different legal treatment between internal and external corporate group rules, ie the rules focussing on the relation within the corporate group between its various entities and the

[59] D Daniel, Konzern und Moderne: Die verbundene juristische Person in der visuellen Kultur 1880–1980 (Frankfurt am Main, Klostermann, 2016).

[60] JG Ruggie, 'Multinationals as global institution: Power, authority and relative autonomy' (2018) 12 *Regulation & Governance* 317; for the relation between these political processes and the subjects of international law, F Johns, 'Theorizing the Corporation in International Law' in A Orford and F Hoffmann (ed), *The Oxford Handbook of the Theory of International Law* (Oxford, Oxford University Press, 2016) 635.

[61] H Lindahl, 'A-Legality: Postnationalism and the Question of Legal Boundaries' (2010) 73 *Modern Law Review* 30.

[62] Fleischer (n 56) 31ff.

[63] On which, early on Teubner (n 17) 82ff.

[64] See, Ulfbeck, in this volume.

external rules that relate the group as an entity with responsibility to externally affected parties.

In chapter nineteen, Ulfbeck concludes sceptically on the reading of current legislative and case law development as an evolving 'group thinking'. At the same time, she carefully raises the argument in favour of argumentative parallels between the different conceptions of groups that may, if considered, allow treating corporate groups as persons.[65] It is in this conclusion that our contributions may take other directions. My argument is to understand the increasing fragmentation of corporate group rulings as precisely an invitation to 'hybridise' the corporate group and identify its social status as fragmented in dependence on specific fields. In corporate groups, this fragmented thinking may be obscure because corporate groups still oscillate between a common self-ascription through policies, marketing, management and the move towards decentralisation. When considering the related rules on corporate supply chains, we may see that the future rules on corporate responsibility for various interests are complicated to bring under the umbrella of personality.

iii. Value Chain Legislation and Case Law: Fragmentation in Full Swing

By rules on corporate supply-chain responsibility, I mean the increasing number of legislative initiatives by which companies are now expected to include, into their core operations, considerations about their supply chains or value chains. The earliest of these laws were the rules on non-financial, now sustainability, reporting by which companies are expected to consider the impacts of their supply chains in their annual reports.[66] Such rules have recently been adopted to include corporate supply-chain responsibility in the companies' risk management systems.[67] In the policy area of supply-chain security, the EU has also been adopting new rules regarding critical entities that need to oversee and test their resilience in crises.[68] Moreover, in case law, we also see a move towards ascribing companies responsibility for their contractually affiliated supply chains and the effects that this may have.[69]

[65] Ulfbeck, 350.

[66] Directive 2014/95/EU of the European Parliament and of the Council of 22 October 2014 amending Directive 2013/34/EU as regards disclosure of non-financial and diversity information by certain large undertakings and groups, OJ L330/1: as of 2023, the Directive will be gradually replaced by Directive (EU) 2022/2464 of the European Parliament and of the Council of 14 December 2022 amending Regulation (EU) No 537/2014, Directive 2004/109/EC, Directive 2006/43/EC and Directive 2013/34/EU, as regards corporate sustainability reporting, OJ L322, 16 December 2022; in the US: Dodd-Franck Wall Street Reform and Consumer Protection Act 2010, s 1502, see, for the UK: Modern Slavery Act 2015, s 54.

[67] See, for instance, the German Lieferkettengesetz and the French Devoir de Vigilance and the recent Directive (EU) 2024/1760 of the European Parliament and of the Council of 13 June 2024 on corporate sustainability due diligence and amending Directive (EU) 2019/1937 and Regulation (EU) 2023/2859, OJ L2024/1760.

[68] Directive (EU) 2022/2557 of the European Parliament and of the Council of 14 December 2022 on the resilience of critical entities and repealing Council Directive 2008/114/EC, OJ L333.

[69] See, in the UK, *Hamida Begum* v *Maran Ltd* [2021] EWCA Civ 326; and in the Netherlands under tort law for climate change duties, Rechtbank Den Haag, *Milieudefensie* v *Shell* (n 38) and, under contract law for labour law violations Rechtbank Amsterdam, *Vert Asia Ltd and Vert Fashion Company Ltd v G-Star Raw CV and others*, 22 November 2023, ECLI:NL:RBAMS:2023:7299.

With these novel developments towards what we may call corporate supply-chain responsibility, we encounter a further argumentative move into interpreting such rules as an expansion of corporate responsibility and, ultimately, personhood. Whereas previously, the question was about the extension of the corporate person to the collective corporate group, we now see the parallel development with an integration of contractually affiliated entities and other forms of economic networks (such as platforms). In tort law, a burgeoning literature focuses on expanding corporate group responsibility to supply chains regarding human rights and environmental protection.[70] Similarly, anthropologically informed legal scholarship emphasises tendencies to integrate the supply chain within the images, documents and practices of corporations. This results in increasingly questioning the separation between the corporate entity and its supply and distribution network.[71]

However, with the advent of these supply chain laws, it becomes increasingly difficult to bring these under the umbrella of a unified legal understanding. In that vein, others have already argued that the evolution of value chains suggests a strong fragmentation of entities due to a lack of a common interest structure in such networks.[72] Value chains indicate a change in the responsibility ascriptions to individual actors that were the corporation.[73] In this context, new responsibility concepts in legislation and case law fragment the supply chain by delineating responsibility through different categories, thus drawing the boundaries differently. While it is a common denominator of the rules to include engagement with business partners and identifying the impacts of other entities in the chain, the techniques for delineating the boundaries of responsibility are very different. Regarding the most explicit corporate supply chain legislation, namely reporting and due diligence obligations, corporations are exposed to different ways of integrating the supply chain into their communicative activities. Within reporting laws, the delineation of corporate responsibility, the boundary is drawn by the concept of materiality, and, since the newest sustainability reporting rules, double materiality. This criterion gives the company loose guidance to define and communicate about the space and actors it is responsible for. The company should decidedly not look to the inside (what interests and impacts are material for the corporate performance), but to the outside (what is material for sustainability) to define where it needs to cast its net in drawing the boundaries of its responsibility. Such a perspective already shows fragmentation. The boundaries are drawn differently when looking into newly evolving due diligence obligations. In due diligence, the delineation of responsibility takes place via the concept of 'tiers' of responsibility and through the concept of risks. Corporations cannot turn to their interests; they need to translate societal risks related to their suppliers into manageable risk categories and distinguish based on tiers (how far away is the risk?) and severity (what is the

[70] C Bright, A Marx, N Pineau and J Wouters, 'Toward a Corporate Duty for Lead Companies to Respect Human Rights in Their Global Value Chains?' (2020) 22 *Business and Politics* 667; H Collins, 'Fat Cats, Production Networks, and the Right to Fair Pay' (2021) 85 *Modern Law Review* 1.

[71] KB Sobel-Read, 'Reimagining the Unimaginable: Law and the Ongoing Transformation of Global Value Chains into Integrated Legal Entities' (2020) 16 *European Review of Contract Law* 160.

[72] KH Eller, 'Is "Global Value Chain" a Legal Concept?' (2020) 16 *European Review of Contract Law* 3.

[73] A Tsing, 'Supply Chains and the Human Condition' (2009) 21 *Rethinking Marxism: A Journal of Economics, Culture and Society* 148, 151.

societal impact of the risk?).[74] What needs to be integrated as part of the company's risk management and what needs to be communicated about what belongs to the corporate responsibility sphere is no longer an internal question but a translation of societal factors into a corporate risk management strategy.

In addition, the corporate actor is defined differently in the policy fields that regulate supply chains. As I have argued elsewhere, the value chain is related to the corporation very differently depending on the policy field that we are discussing. Integration of the value chain into corporate personhood may still be a conceivable perspective when discussing sustainability policies and due diligence. In this case, we, indeed, see the value chain as becoming institutionalised as an extension of the corporate person, as a 'dangerous object' to be controlled,[75] a vicarious agent[76] or even as part of the corporate entity itself. However, in other areas of supply chain regulation, the corporate entity is subrogated to the state and its geopolitical decisions, becoming itself an agent to execute decisions.[77] In consumer law, the corporation becomes a communicative mediator between consumers and producers and a node in the network of related actors responsible to the consumer.[78] In the field of digitalisation, the companies involved in the production and operation of digital devices equally become a network of actors with a related fragmentation of responsibilities.[79] This suggests that what we see is not one new evolving category of an actor, but a differentiated allocation of responsibility and related recognition of emergent properties depending on a legal field and the different social expectations.

iv. What is Left? Persons, Hybrids, Fragmentation

The question then is whether this result is more akin to what Esposito refers to with Latour – a new hybrid category between persons and things – or, indeed, a depersonification. As I propose in this contribution, we may encounter a fragmentation

[74] On this comparison between sustainability reporting and due diligence, A Beckers, 'Global Value Chains in EU Law' (2023) 42 *Yearbook of European Law* 322, 331ff.

[75] M-P Weller and L Nasse, 'Menschenrechtsarbitrage als Gefahrenquelle' (2020) 22 *Zeitschrift für Unternehmens- und Gesellschaftsrecht (ZGR) Sonderheft* 107; J Salminen, 'From Product Liability to Production Liability: Modelling a Response to the Liability Deficit of Global Value Chains on Historical Transformations of Production' (2019) 23 *Competition & Change* 420.

[76] V Ulfbeck and A Ehlers, 'Tort Law, Corporate Groups and Supply Chain Liability for Workers' Injuries: The Concept of Vicarious Liability' (2016) 13 *European Company Law* 164.

[77] See, in particular the package on supply-chain resilience, ie the adopted Directive on critical entities: Directive (EU) 2022/2557 of 14 December 2022 on the resilience of critical entities and repealing Council Directive 2008/114/EC, L133 OJ 27 December 2022, 164–98 and the provisional political agreements between European Parliament and Council on the Critical Raw Materials Act of 13 November 2023 (based on European Commission, 'Proposal for a Regulation of the European Parliament and of the Council establishing a framework for ensuring a secure and sustainable supply of critical raw materials and amending Regulations (EU) 168/2013, (EU) 2018/858, 2018/1724 and (EU) 2019/1020' COM (2023) 160 final) and the Internal Market Emergency and Resilience Act on 2 February 2024 (based on European Commission, 'Proposal for a Regulation of the European Parliament and of the Council establishing a Single Market Emergency Instrument and repealing Council Regulation No 2679/98' COM(2022) 459 final).

[78] For this argument, R Ravalli, *Externalities of Production in GVCs: An EU Consumer Perspective* (PhD thesis, European University Institute, 2022) ch 3.

[79] See, extensively, on this development concerning the AI Act, H-W Micklitz and G Sartor, Compliance and Enforcement of the AI Act (2024) 42 *Yearbook of European Law*, forthcoming.

of personhood and thus rely on the concept of status ascriptions in between. One could understand the economic processes underlying supply chains and group formations as, in fact, a form of structured process that is not yet personified. Systems theory has been coining the concept of the un-person for such processes.[80] It has also been increasingly used to explain our relation to the sphere of digital operations that does not communicate in the strict sense.[81] Furthermore, this notion may fit with the developments we see with the economic processes we then categorise into companies, corporate groups and supply chains. The legal rules that stabilise these depersonified economic processes through the personification of single entities, groups or supply chains with various boundaries influence whether the entity we see is a person, a group, a network or a fragmented entity. Corporate responsibility and personality can no longer be determined in a clear-cut manner but may have shifting boundaries, which may suggest that the future of the corporate person may lie in a fragmented institutionalisation depending on different legal fields and policy objectives.

IV. CONCLUSION

This chapter has attempted to search for the future of the corporate person in light of current broader debates on legal personhood and the increasing regulatory initiatives that attempt to bring other actors into the scope of responsibility of the corporate person. To that end, two futures of corporate personhood were explored: first, corporate personification remains a normative idea in the law about processes of personification that, in the future, may serve as a blueprint and imaginary lens through which other processes of personification are looked at in the law. Second, the future of the corporate person remains highly uncertain, and predictions may vary. Ulfbeck concludes her chapter with a future that may lie in the expansion of personhood, ie 'corporate groups beginning to look like legal persons'.[82] However, the alternative proposed here is that we may see a gradualisation of personhood and related fragmentation of the corporate person. This would mean that in relation to different issues, legal fields and social expectations, the corporate person evolves differently and with different boundaries, leading ultimately to an undoing of the uniformity of the corporate person and a differentiated institutionalisation.

[80] AC Braun, Latours Existenzweisen und Luhmanns Funktionssysteme: Ein soziologischer Theorienvergleich (Wiesbaden, Springer VS, 2017) 102ff.

[81] For this concept for the social understanding of interconnected digital technology we have relied on Beckers and Teubner (n 54) 116ff.

[82] Ulfbeck, in this volume, 35.

15

The Contractualisation of the Consumer Worker

VANESSA MAK*

I. INTRODUCTION

ONE OF THE defining societal developments of the past decades is the 'contractualisation' of work and consumer relations. By this I mean that legal relations between workers and employees, and between businesses and consumers, which since the last century have been governed by an increasingly regulated contract law, are being supplanted by more flexible legal relationships as a result of the alternative forms of work and consumption that have emerged. This can be illustrated by the rise of flex-workers on online platforms such as Uber, Deliveroo and Amazon Mechanical Turk. In consumer markets the classic model of business-to-consumer (B2C) relations has been challenged by the emergence of 'prosumers', ie consumers offering products and services for purchase on online platforms such as Amazon, Vinted and Marktplaats.nl.[1] The new forms of flex-work and prosumption are in most cases not subject to specific rules for worker or consumer protection, but are governed by the general rules of contract law.

This development can be seen as a reversion to the situation that applied before the industrial revolution led to a major leap in the regulation of work and consumption. General rules of contract law provide the default framework within which parties are free to determine the terms and conditions of their individual agreements. Seeing that contract laws in Europe are sophisticated systems of rules, principles and practices, one would expect them to be able to provide a balanced framework that does justice to the interests of all parties involved.

In this chapter, however, I will argue that this hypothesis is incorrect. General contract laws cannot provide sufficient basis for the regulation of new types of worker and consumer contracts, and the need remains to develop specific rules for the protection of weaker parties. What is open to question, however, is who counts as a

* Vanessa Mak is a professor of Civil Law at Leiden University.

[1] In the literal sense of the word the 'prosumer' is a consumer who himself produces goods or services. *cf* A Toffler, *The Third Wave* (New York, Bantam Books, 1980) 280. I use the term in a broader sense, including also consumers who sell goods that they have not produced themselves on online platforms.

weaker party in today's worker and consumer markets. Also, the question is whether a reconceptualization or recategorisation of weaker parties requires amendments to the ways in which rights and duties in private law are allocated.

The chapter will develop its argument in three parts. First, an overview will be presented of legal issues that have arisen in European legal systems concerning prosumer contracts (section II.A) and flex-work through online platforms (section II.B). This overview is not meant to be exhaustive. It should illustrate which legal issues arise that general contract laws cannot provide suitable solutions for. Second, the chapter will examine how the problems identified in section II could be resolved. To that end, section III compares ways in which contract laws could be amended to deal with the new vulnerabilities and opportunities that affect workers and consumers in today's markets. It will also consider whether alternative instruments, such as private regulation in the form of standards or codes of conduct, could contribute to developing suitable rules. Finally, section IVs consider the interplay between worker and prosumer protection. Existing laws have developed into silos in which specific aspects – eg, labour law and consumer law – are regulated. The rules developed in these sectors, however, in their application affect the same person. The worker is also a consumer, and vice versa. The chapter examines whether, and if so which, meaningful connections can be made between contract laws' approaches to worker and prosumer protection.

One preliminary note concerning the scope of the enquiry. The focus will primarily be on legislative instruments of the European Union, such as EU consumer law directives and the recently adopted Digital Services Act (DSA).[2] Where the analysis requires it, reference will also be made to the contract laws of selected EU Member States. If broader conclusions are to be drawn for future directions in EU legislation or beyond, the comparison of legal systems would have to be more comprehensive in scope.

II. THE PROBLEMS OF CONTRACTUALISATION: DECONSTRUCTING THE 'CONSUMER' AND THE 'WORKER'

The rise of online platforms has created new opportunities for consumers and workers, but sometimes at the cost of rights applicable in offline markets. This section presents a brief overview, illustrating which gaps have come to the fore in the protection of weaker parties in contract and tort law.

A. Deconstructing the 'Consumer'

I have examined the changing image(s) of the consumer elsewhere.[3] Briefly summarised, the notion of the consumer is changing under the influence of

[2] Regulation (EU) 2022/2065 of the European Parliament and of the Council of 19 October 2022 on a Single Market For Digital Services and amending Directive 2000/31/EC (Digital Services Act) [2022] OJ L277/1.

[3] V Mak, 'How Can Consumer Interests be Protected When Consumer Identities are Increasingly Diffuse?' in H-W Micklitz and C Twigg-Flesner (eds), *The Transformation of Consumer Law and Policy in Europe* (Oxford, Hart, 2023) 43.

developments in digital markets, platform markets and the pursuit of sustainability.[4] First, consumers in digital markets are subject to new vulnerabilities. They are vulnerable to exploitation as they are subjected to sophisticated and opaque techniques seeking to manipulate their purchasing decisions.[5] In this context, the existing information-oriented approach of consumer laws may no longer suffice.[6] Second, consumers in platform markets can move to the supply side of the market and become so-called 'prosumers' (conflating the concept of 'consumer' and 'producer').[7] The question is whether they should be subject to the responsibilities of traders, and which balance should be struck between their responsibilities and those of the platform. Under current regulation the platform often escapes liability, as it is not privy to the contract between the prosumer and the buyer, but that outcome requires a reassessment in the light of the market power vested with platforms. Third, consumers are part of the strategy adopted by governments and policy-makers to achieve more sustainable approaches to consumption. For consumer law, this demands a re-evaluation of the consumer protection-oriented approach adopted in B2C relationships. Should consumers not share the responsibility to make sustainable choices, as consumer-citizens, and how can that be achieved?[8]

Comparing these three trends, the problems of contractualisation arise mostly in relation to the 'prosumer' concept. The protection of the digital consumer is primarily one of regulation, or regulatory private law. It demands a reassessment of the rules applicable to B2C relationships. The reassessment of consumer responsibilities in light of sustainability also focuses on the regulation of the business–consumer relationship. In both cases, the aim is to establish how private law can contribute to the pursuit of external goals, namely market regulation in digital markets and sustainability as a societal goal. Whilst these reassessments may lead to new regulation, based on refined consumer concepts, they do not turn to contract law as such as the primary framework for solutions.

The examination of the prosumer category, however, does turn to contract law as a framework for determining which solutions can be found, and which outcomes can be justified. It starts from the premise that existing 'consumer' and 'trader' categories in private law are not sufficiently able to balance the interests of consumers, prosumers and platforms. Several shortcomings have already been identified in the literature. They will be discussed below in section III.A.

[4] These themes are central also to the EU's consumer agenda 2020–2025; see Communication from the Commission to the European Parliament and the Council, 'New Consumer Agenda strengthening consumer resilience for sustainable recovery' COM(2020) 696 final.

[5] For example, algorithmic manipulation through targeted advertising; *cf* G Wagner and H Eidenmüller, 'Down by Algorithms? Siphoning Rents, Exploiting Biases, and Shaping Preferences: Regulating The Dark Side of Personalized Transactions' (2019) 86 *The University of Chicago Law Review* 581.

[6] N Helberger, O Lynskey, H-W Micklitz, P Rott, M Sax and J Strycharz, 'EU Consumer Protection 2.0. Structural Asymmetries in Digital Consumer Markets' (BEUC Report, March 2021), beuc.eu/publications/beuc-x-2021-018_eu_consumer_protection.0_0.pdf.

[7] *cf* Toffler (n 1).

[8] See eg E Terryn, 'A Right to Repair? Towards Sustainable Remedies in Consumer Law' (2019) 27 *European Review of Private Law* 851.

B. Deconstructing the 'Worker'

The question of regulating the protection of flex-workers has centred primarily on whether they fit into existing categories of 'workers' or 'employees', with associated rights concerning payment, working hours, pensions and insurance. Notably, the term 'worker' and 'employee' are not always synonyms. In UK law, for example, they denote different categories with specific rights attached to them. An employee is someone with an employment contract, with all associated benefits, such as pension rights, insurance, annual leave, and the cover of anti-discrimination law and unfair dismissal protection. On the other side of the spectrum are the self-employed, or independent contractors, who have none of these rights and have to fend for themselves. The UK recognises an in-between third category, the worker, who has a basic floor of rights, including the national minimum wage and paid annual leave.[9] Other jurisdictions within the EU also recognise a third category in between employees and the self-employed.[10]

By comparison, EU law has used the term 'worker' in different ways in labour law regulation. The case law of the CJEU has provided some guidance by identifying at least three relevant aspects of employment relationships: (i) the performance of effective and genuine economic activities; (ii) remuneration; and (iii) subordination.[11] The implementation of the Directive on Transparent and Predictable Working Conditions (TPWC Directive), however, is likely to raise new questions. Its 'worker' definition is broad, but it does not fit neatly into the diverse categories of employment relations used in various EU Member States.[12] Another proposal for an EU Directive on Platform Work intends to provide a more clearly defined benchmark.[13] Recognising that the determination of employment status takes place at the national level, the proposed Directive includes an obligation for the Member States to have appropriate procedures in place to verify and ensure the correct determination of that status (Article 3(1) of the proposal). It also includes a legal presumption in Article 4(1), holding that 'the contractual relationship between a digital labour platform that … controls the performance of work and a person performing platform work through that platform shall be legally presumed to be an employment relationship'. The requirement of 'control' is substantiated in Article 4(2) of the proposal. It requires that at least two out of five conditions are fulfilled, relating to remuneration, performance of the

[9] A Adams-Prassl, J Adams-Prassl and D Coyle, 'Uber and Beyond: Policy Implications for the UK', The Productivity Institute, Productivity Insight Paper No 1 (March 2021), bennettinstitute.cam.ac.uk/wp-content/uploads/2020/12/PIP001_Uber_and_Beyond_FINAL_.pdf.

[10] eg Italy, Germany and Spain. D Georgiou, 'The New EU Directive on Transparent and Predictable Working Conditions in the Context of New Forms of Employment' (2022) 28 *European Journal of Industrial Relations* 193, 201.

[11] Case C-66/85 *Lawrie-Blum* ECLI:EU:C:1986:284, [1986] ECR 2121. See Georgiou (n 10) 197.

[12] Directive (EU) 2019/1152 of the European Parliament and of the Council of 20 June 2019 on transparent and predictable working conditions in the European Union [2019] OJ L186/105 (TPWC Directive). Georgiou (n 10) 197; B Bednarowicz, 'Delivering on the European Pillar of Social Rights: The New Directive on Transparent and Predictable Working Conditions in the European Union' (2019) 48 *Industrial Law Journal* 604, 612.

[13] European Commission, 'Proposal for a Directive of the European Parliament and of the Council on improving working conditions in platform work' COM(2021) 762 final.

work, supervision, freedom to organise one's work and restrictions on the possibility to build a client base or to perform work for another third party. While this presumption would provide greater legal certainty and protection for platform workers, the consequences of being given employment status depend on national law, which means that diversity will continue to exist for platform workers within the EU.[14]

Much of labour law regulation therefore remains an issue of national law. It is important to take note of the discourses that have taken place in various EU Member States, as they provide indications as to how legal systems regard the position of workers vis-à-vis the self-employed. As in consumer law, there is a question of determining who may benefit from the categorical protection designated to a 'weaker party' (in this case the worker or employee) and who falls outside that category and is therefore considered to have the capacity to look after his or her own interests.

III. CONTRACT LAW SOLUTIONS: RECONSTRUCTING THE 'CONSUMER' AND THE 'WORKER'

While the challenges to the 'consumer' and 'worker' categories in private law are by now well known, straightforward solutions have not yet presented themselves. This section will examine along which lines contract law may be redesigned in order to provide more tailored rules for the new types of relationships that have emerged in the platform economy. The discussion starts with an analysis of consumer and prosumer protection and then moves to the worker. It takes EU law as a main point of reference, but diverges to national laws where the analysis requires so.

A. Protecting Consumers and Prosumers

Existing private laws provide a framework for the rights and obligations of traders and consumers. If a trader acts professionally, the relationship will be classified as a B2C relationship and consumer protection rules apply. In other cases, there is a consumer-to-consumer (C2C) relationship, which is governed by the general rules of contract law. Rules relating to specific contracts may also apply, such as for purchase, exchange, rent or assignment. This set of rules, principles and practices provides a framework within which the interests of the parties can be balanced. The main rule here is that an online platform, as a third party, is in principle outside the legal relationship between users. Exceptions to that rule are possible if the law so provides, for instance the platform's duty to inform consumers whether a trader is acting professionally or privately,[15] or on grounds of extra-contractual liability.

[14] For an analysis, see M Kullmann, '"Platformisation" of Work: An EU Perspective on Introducing a Legal Presumption' (2022) 13 *European Labour Law Journal* 66.

[15] Directive (EU) 2019/2161 of the European Parliament and of the Council of 27 November 2019 amending Council Directive 93/13/EEC and Directives 98/6/EC, 2005/29/EC and 2011/83/EU of the European Parliament and of the Council as regards the better enforcement and modernization of Union consumer protection rules [2019] OJ L328/7, Art 4.

Arguably, this framework is not well tailored to situations in which the trader on an online platform is a non-professional trader, ie a prosumer. The following subsections examine which legal problems arise in the contractual relationships between consumer, prosumer and online platform (section i) and under what conditions the addition of a 'prosumer' category to contract law could be considered, as well as how it might improve the legal framework (section ii).

i. Allocation of Rights and Duties in Prosumer–Consumer–Platform Relations

Several problems can be identified in the ways in which contractual duties and liability in tort are allocated. What connects them is that prosumers tend to bear most of the risks and responsibilities towards consumers with whom they contract, while online platforms as third parties to the contract between prosumer and consumer escape liability. The question is whether that allocation of rights and duties is justifiable. The following specific examples can illustrate the problem.

First, prosumers may be exposed to liability towards consumer-buyers contracting with them, for example if goods are defective and cause harm to the consumer, or if information concerning the product characteristics is misleading. Under existing regulation, the prosumer will often be solely liable. Platform operators cannot be held liable, in most cases, because they are not party to the contract between prosumer and consumer-buyer and therefore not responsible for unsatisfactory performance. Product liability under the EU's Product Liability Directive cannot be directed to platforms if they are not the producer, importer or distributor of the goods.[16] Further, most platforms benefit from the 'host exemption' of the E-commerce Directive,[17] holding that hosts are not liable for illegal information posted by users unless they were alerted to it and failed to remove it. The DSA, adopted in 2022 and applicable from February 2024, maintains that exemption.[18] In consequence, prosumers, whether professional traders or not, will often bear the burden of liability. As the weaker party in relation to the platform, plus the one less sizeable and less likely to provide an adequate remedy to the consumer, one may wonder whether this outcome is justifiable.[19]

[16] Council Directive 1985/374/EEC of 25 July 1985 on the approximation of the laws, regulations and administrative provisions of the Member States concerning liability for defective products [1985] OJ L210/29. This Directive is under review; see for updates eg ec.europa.eu/growth/single-market/goods/free-movement-sectors/liability-defective-products_en. Also under review is Directive 2001/95/EC of the European Parliament and of the Council of 3 December 2001 on general product safety [2001] OJ L11/4. The European Commission published a proposal for a new general product safety regulation in 2021, see 'Proposal for a Regulation of the European Parliament and of the Council on general product safety, amending Regulation (EU) No 1025/2012 of the European Parliament and of the Council, and repealing Council Directive 87/357/EEC and Directive 2001/95/EC of the European Parliament and of the Council' COM (2021) 346 final. For updates, see further europarl.europa.eu/legislative-train/theme-a-new-push-for-european-democracy/file-revision-of-the-general-product-safety-directive.

[17] Directive 2000/31/EC of the European Parliament and of the Council of 8 June 2000 on certain legal aspects of information society services, in particular electronic commerce, in the Internal Market (Directive on electronic commerce) [2000] OJ L178/1.

[18] Digital Services Act (n 2), Art 6(1).

[19] C Busch, 'Rethinking Product Liability Rules for Online Marketplaces: A Comparative Perspective', European Legal Studies Institute Osnabrück, Research Paper Series No 21-01, dx.doi.org/10.2139/ssrn.3897602.

Second, platform operators often bind external traders to strict performance targets through contractual standard terms. Non-compliance leads to warnings and eventually denial of access to the platform. Regulation (EU) 2019/1150 on fairness in platform-to-business relationships goes some way towards protecting small traders.[20] However, this Regulation applies only to professional traders on online platforms, not to non-professional prosumers.

The DSA and the recently published proposal for a revised Product Liability Directive go some way towards addressing these issues. However, the steps that they take (or propose) to ensure a safer digital market are relatively minor improvements for rebalancing the relationships between platforms and prosumers. The DSA contains a rule, laid down in Article 6(2) and Recital 23, stating that the host exemption for online platforms does not apply where the trader is acting under the authority or the control of the platform. Recital 23 mentions one example, namely 'where the provider of an online platform that allows consumers to conclude distance contracts with traders determines the price of the goods or services offered by the trader'. In response to this provision, online platforms are likely to take care of designing their activities in such a way that they do not exercise authority or control over third-party traders.

A provision laid down in Article 6(3) of the DSA, concerning the liability of platforms in cases of apparent authority or control goes one step further. According to this provision, the host exemption does not apply where the platform presents information or enables a transaction in a way 'that would lead an average consumer to believe that the information, or the product or service that is the object of the transaction, is provided either by the online platform itself or by a recipient of the service who is acting under its authority or control' (Article 6(3) and Recital 24 of the DSA). The proposed new Product Liability Directive follows the rule in Article 6(3) and adds that an online platform can be held liable for product liability in the circumstances set out in that provision, unless it promptly identifies a relevant economic operator based in the EU (to whom liability would be directed under the new Directive).[21] Unfortunately, Article 6(3) does not clarify in what circumstances the presumption arises that a recipient of the hosting service (ie a trader on an online platform) is acting 'under the authority or control' of the platform. The viewpoint of the 'average consumer' of EU law, itself a debated concept in EU consumer law, does not offer a particularly helpful benchmark for clarification. Recital 24 only provides a few aspects by way of illustration:

> Examples of such behaviour could be where an online platform fails to display clearly the identity of the trader, as required by this Regulation, where an online platform withholds the identity or contact details of the trader until after the conclusion of the contract concluded between the trader and the consumer, or where an online platform markets the product or service in its own name rather than in the name of the trader who will supply that product or service.

[20] Regulation (EU) 2019/1150 of the European Parliament and of the Council of 20 June 2019 on promoting fairness and transparency for business users of online intermediation services [2019] OJ L186/57.

[21] European Commission, 'Proposal for a Directive of the European Parliament and of the Council on liability for defective products' COM (2022) 495 final, Art 7(6) and Recital 28.

Otherwise, as also stated in Recital 24,

> it should be determined objectively, on the basis of all relevant circumstances, whether the presentation could lead an average consumer to believe that the information in question was provided by the online platform itself or by traders acting under its authority or control.

One may wonder whether it would have been helpful to include a more elaborate list of indicative criteria.[22]

ii. Integrating the 'Prosumer' into Contract Law

In the absence of more specific rules delineating the responsibilities of platforms and non-professional traders, one hypothesis to follow through with further research could be that the regulation of private law relationships in the platform economy requires the introduction of a 'prosumer' category and rules tailored to it. If that route were to be taken in regulation, the consequence could be that rules will be designed which in certain circumstances hold platform operators jointly and severally liable for harm caused by prosumers to consumers. What will need to be examined is in what circumstances this should be the case. In that respect, it is helpful to take account of existing legal frameworks for third-party liability in contract law, and by extension in tort.

The starting point for such an analysis requires an understanding of the way in which contract law deals with third parties, meaning parties that are in some way affected by the contractual agreement between others, even though they themselves are not party to the contract. In the triangle between consumer, prosumer and platform each of the parties is a third party to the others' agreement. The consumer is a third party to the contract between platform and prosumer; the prosumer is a third party to the contract between platform and consumer; and perhaps most important, the platform is a third party to the contract between consumer and prosumer. We have seen in the previous section to which legal problems this leads. Nonetheless, regarded from the perspective of contract laws' framework for third-party rights and duties, it makes perfect sense to not hold an online platform liable for defective performance by a prosumer of his obligations under the prosumer–consumer contract. That is in line with the principle of privity of contract, which most European legal systems maintain as a general rule.

However, this does not mean that contract law precludes the liability of online platforms alongside, or perhaps even independently from, prosumers. Many national contract laws recognise exceptions to the general rule of privity. Such exceptions could exist in the form of giving legal effect to contract clauses benefiting third parties,[23] or in awarding damages in tort if a breach of contract affects a third party whose interests the contracting parties should have taken into account.[24] The ratio behind such

[22] *cf* C Busch and V Mak, 'Putting the Digital Service Act in Context' (2021) 10 *Journal of European Consumer and Market Law* 109.

[23] For examples, see Art 6:253 of the Dutch Civil Code and UK Contracts (Rights of Third Parties) Act 1999, s 1.

[24] See in the Netherlands the leading case of the Dutch Supreme Court, 24 September 2004, NJ 2008, 587, ECLI:NL:HR:2004:AO9069 (*Vleesmeesters/Alog*). In certain circumstances damages may be awarded even

exceptions is that the autonomy of parties to determine to whom and on what terms they wish to be legally bound – which underlies the doctrine of privity – works in two directions. Parties are not only entitled to pursue their own self-realisation, enabled by a contract law framework that enables them to make autonomous choices; they also have to allow others to achieve theirs. That means that the autonomy of parties is bounded by the autonomy of others, even if those others as third parties are external to the contractual agreement.[25]

This is of course a simplification and further nuances can be discerned in a comparative analysis of national private laws. Still, as a general description of the rules and principles at play in European private laws, it can provide a basis for a reassessment of the position of the prosumer in relation to online platforms. More specifically, the following aspects could be examined.

First, the definition of a 'trader' in EU consumer could be refined. The European Court of Justice (CJEU) provided some guidance in *Kamenova*, concerning the definition of the 'trader' in the Unfair Commercial Practices Directive.[26] The list of characteristics provided by the Court sets out when a natural person selling products through an online platform should be considered a trader. It takes into account, inter alia, whether the sale takes place in an organised manner, whether the seller has specific expertise with regard to the products offered, whether the seller has a legal status allowing her to engage in commercial activities (eg registration with a chamber of commerce), whether the seller is subject to VAT, and whether the seller regularly purchases new or second-hand goods in order to resell them.[27] This list, however, is not exhaustive and Member States may maintain their own assessment criteria alongside the guidance given by the CJEU.

It would help if the European legislator took a step further and identified objective criteria, applicable across the entire field of EU consumer law directives, as to when a trader shifts from a non-professional to a professional trader. This could potentially result in the introduction of a separate 'prosumer' category. Elements that would be of specific relevance in this regard are the amount and frequency of sales or service provision, the expertise of the prosumer with regard to the transactions concluded, whether the sales are intended to generate profit, and whether the sales are conducted in an organised manner. Seeing that the variety of platforms is great, the list of objective factors could also contain variations.[28] A comparative analysis of national legal systems could provide inspiration for determining lists of objective criteria.

Second, also at the European level, rules could be introduced that are tailored to this new prosumer category. The DSA does not contain a rule to this effect.[29]

if the non-performance of the contract does not constitute a breach; see Dutch Supreme Court, 14 July 2017, ECLI:NL:HR:2017:1355 (*Vissers/Compaen*).

[25] *cf* A de Dijn, *Freedom: An Unruly Story* (Cambridge MA, Harvard University Press, 2020); A Keirse and T Bouwman, 'Nudging Financial Decisions: Protecting Weaker Parties while Promoting Autonomy' (2019) 54 *Texas International Law Journal* 201, 202.

[26] Case C-105/17 *Kamenova* ECLI:EU:C:2018:808, [2018]. See also C Twigg-Flesner, 'Bad Hand? The "New Deal" for EU Consumers' (2018) 15 *Zeitschrift für das Privatrecht der Europäischen Union* 166.

[27] Case C-105/17 *Kamenova* (n 26) [38].

[28] *cf* B Devolder, *Gebruikersbescherming in de deeleconomie. Een nieuw evenwicht in de contractuele driehoek* (dissertation KU Leuven 2021) 221–24.

[29] See the discussion of Art 6(3) DSA above, para III.A.i.

Inspiration could however be found in another set of rules, namely the Model Rules on Online Platforms, drafted under the aegis of the European Law Institute (ELI).[30] Article 20 of the ELI Model Rules states:

> If the customer can reasonably rely on the platform operator having a predominant influence over the supplier, the customer can exercise the rights and remedies for the non-performance available against the supplier under the supplier-customer contract also against the platform operator.

This rule is inspired by the US case *Oberdorf v Amazon*, in which Amazon was held to be liable as a seller, even though the actual sale and delivery of goods was done by third-party sellers on the platform.[31] That rule does not distinguish between third-party sellers acting in a professional or a non-professional capacity. The rule laid down in Article 20 of the ELI Model Rules likewise does not distinguish between professional and non-professional suppliers.[32]

Article 20 proposes that the supplier is not solely liable, but that the platform operator can be held liable too if it exercises a 'predominant influence' over the supplier. It also gives an indicative list of factors that may help determine whether the platform had such a predominant influence, including: a) the supplier–customer contract is concluded exclusively through facilities provided on the platform; b) the platform operator withholds the identity of the supplier or contact details until after the conclusion of the supplier–customer contract; c) the platform operator exclusively uses payment systems which enable the platform operator to withhold payments made by the customer to the supplier; d) the terms of the supplier–customer contract are essentially determined by the platform operator; e) the price to be paid by the customer is set by the platform operator; f) the marketing is focused on the platform operator and not on suppliers; or g) the platform operator promises to monitor the conduct of suppliers and to enforce compliance with its standards beyond what is required by law. The specification of such criteria makes the rule more predictable in its application than DSA, Article 6(3).[33] The rule could serve as inspiration for prosumer-tailored legislation or regulation.

Further, existing rules of EU consumer law could be reassessed and potentially amended in light of rebalancing the interests of prosumers and online platforms. Directives that would merit such a reassessment include the Unfair Contract Terms Directive (UCTD),[34] the Unfair Commercial Practices Directive (UCPD),[35] the

[30] The text of the model rules is available at www.europeanlawinstitute.eu/fileadmin/user_upload/p_eli/Publications/ELI_Model_Rules_on_Online_Platforms.pdf.

[31] *Oberdorf v Amazon.com*, 930 F3d 136 (3d Cir 2019), and see the comments to Art 20 of the ELI Model Rules.

[32] Incidentally, the Model Rules use the term 'supplier' rather than 'trader' when referring to the user of platform services (*cf* the DSA's 'recipient of the service'). The term 'supplier' is defined as 'any natural or legal person who uses a platform for marketing goods, services or digital content to customers, or who has been suggested to customers by a platform' (Art 2(d) of the ELI Model Rules).

[33] See above para III.A.i.

[34] Council Directive 93/13/EEC on unfair terms in consumer contracts [1993] OJ L95/29.

[35] Directive 2005/29/EC of the European Parliament and of the Council of 11 May 2005 concerning unfair business-to-consumer commercial practices in the internal market and amending Council Directive 84/450/EEC, Directives 97/7/EC, 98/27/EC and 2002/65/EC of the European Parliament and of the Council and Regulation (EC) No 2006/2004 of the European Parliament and of the Council ('Unfair Commercial Practices Directive') [2005] OJ L149/22.

Consumer Rights Directive (CRD),[36] the Consumer Sales Directive (CSD)[37] and the Digital Content Directive (DCD).[38]

Notably, other forms of regulation or policy making should also be considered. The revision of EU legislation is a lengthy exercise and it seems unlikely that law reforms will be introduced in the near future, seeing that the DSA has just reached its final stage of adoption. The Product Liability Directive is currently going through a process of revision and perhaps some gains can be made there still.[39] However, that Directive only covers product liability, leaving aside other instances in which prosumers and/or platforms may be held liable by consumers. Misleading information or loss resulting from the faulty performance of services are not covered. That means that other avenues will have to be explored. One particularly promising route is offered by private regulation, which can take the form of standardisation or the creation of model rules. Standardisation bodies, such as CEN, CENELEC or ISO, tend to have a swifter decision-making process than legislators at the EU or the national level. For example, ISO standards for the design and reliability of recommender systems appeared in 2018, well before the EU legislator made a first attempt at regulation in the 2020 DSA proposal. Moreover, even if standards are of a voluntary nature and therefore not binding, they tend to have a high adoption ratio in practice.[40] Another alternative could be provided by model rules. These are also non-binding rules and can provide inspiration to legislators or have more direct practical effects if contracting parties choose to incorporate them into their contract. The ELI Model Rules already provide an example for the rules that could apply to contracts concluded with online platforms. Article 20 of the Model Rules moreover covers one important issue concerning the liability of platform operators besides professional traders. These provisions could be elaborated, adding rules more specifically tailored to prosumers.

B. Protecting 'Workers'

Another category of weaker parties concerns workers in the platform economy. How can contract law provide solutions for their protection? I will briefly discuss the case law on this issue, comparing the Netherlands and England as legal systems in which the highest courts have been asked to rule on the classification of flex-workers on online platforms. Based on the analysis of the case law, some observations will be made on the ways in which contract law could provide solutions. As a caveat,

[36] Directive 2011/83/EU of the European Parliament and of the Council of 25 October 2011 on consumer rights [2011] OJ L304/64.

[37] Directive (EU) 2019/771 of the European Parliament and of the Council of 20 May 2019 on certain aspects concerning contracts for the sale of goods, amending Regulation (EU) 2017/2394 and Directive 2009/22/EC, and repealing Directive 1999/44 [2019] OJ L136/28.

[38] Directive (EU) 2019/770 of the European Parliament and of the Council of 20 May 2019 on certain aspects concerning contracts for the supply of digital content and digital services [2019] OJ L136/1.

[39] See G Veldt, 'The New Product Liability Proposal – Fit for the Digital Age or in Need of Shaping Up? An Analysis of the Draft Product Liability Directive' (2023) 12 *Journal of European Consumer and Market Law* 24.

[40] ISO 20488:2018, Online consumer reviews – Principles and requirements for their collection, moderation and publication.

it should be noted that the possibilities for contractual solutions are more limited in this context than in the case of consumer law for at least two reasons. First, the position of workers is embedded in regulation going beyond their characterisation as economic actors. Regulation also concerns pension rights, benefits and welfare rights, parental leave, as well as the right to form a union and the right to strike. Second, the broader regulatory context within which labour relations are embedded also entails that most competences for regulation are situated at the national level, and that the EU in comparison to consumer markets has less space to regulate.[41]

A brief analysis of the case law concerning flex-workers on online platforms can serve as an illustration for the ways in which a movement towards contractualisation has started to erode the protection of workers built up in labour laws (section III.B.i). In England and the Netherlands, two legal systems in which case law has emerged on the status of platform workers, courts can be seen to struggle with the qualification of flex-workers. In terms of outcome, they tend to lean towards the application of worker or employment protection. However, it could be that they choose this route because the other one – holding that flex-workers are self-employed – is even less attractive. Still, the classification as 'workers' or 'employees' does not fully address the vulnerability of flex-workers. Labour relations in the platform economy may need an altogether different approach, for which contract law could provide inspiration (section III.B.ii).

i. 'Worker', 'Employee' or Self-employed

Looking at the case law, and starting with England, it can be seen that the question put to the courts was whether work relations moderated through online platforms should fall under the same regulation as other types of employment. In a sense, drivers offering taxi services through a platform like Uber were conducting the same work as taxi drivers operating as part of existing organisations. However, Uber took the position that these drivers were self-employed. The drivers were, according to Uber, performing services solely for and under contracts made with passengers, albeit that these contracts were concluded through the agency of Uber.[42] Being self-employed they would not qualify for the national minimum wage, paid annual leave and other workers' rights.

The UK Supreme Court, following the judgment of the Court of Appeal, held that taxi drivers offering their services through Uber's platform should be considered workers, not self-employed. It based that decision on an analysis of the way in which Uber's relationship with its drivers was structured through contractual terms and codes of conduct, with the platform exercising an extensive degree of control over the drivers. In the words of Lord Leggatt:[43]

> Taking these factors together, it can be seen that the transportation service performed by drivers and offered to passengers through the Uber app is very tightly defined and controlled

[41] *cf* H-W Micklitz, *The Politics of Justice in European Private Law. Social Justice, Access Justice, Societal Justice* (Cambridge-New York, Cambridge University Press 2018) 356–57.

[42] *Uber BV and others (Appellants) v Aslam and others (Respondents)* [2021] UKSC 5 [42].

[43] *Uber v Aslam* (n 42) [101].

> by Uber. Furthermore, it is designed and organised in such a way as to provide a standardised service to passengers in which drivers are perceived as substantially interchangeable and from which Uber, rather than individual drivers, obtains the benefit of customer loyalty and goodwill. From the drivers' point of view, the same factors – in particular, the inability to offer a distinctive service or to set their own prices and Uber's control over all aspects of their interaction with passengers – mean that they have little or no ability to improve their economic position through professional or entrepreneurial skill. In practice the only way in which they can increase their earnings is by working longer hours while constantly meeting Uber's measures of performance.

In those circumstances, the Supreme Court held that the platform's drivers are not genuinely self-employed, and thus are entitled to the full set of rights and protections associated with their status as workers. In this regard, it should be noted that the UK recognises a separate category of 'workers', who benefit from some rights but not the full extent of employees hired under an employment contract.[44]

Somewhat along similar lines is the outcome a case that was decided by the Dutch Supreme Court in March 2023, concerning Deliveroo.[45] Like Uber, Deliveroo provides a platform through which service contracts can be concluded between users. In the case of Deliveroo the services offered are meal deliveries from restaurants to customers using a Deliveroo cyclist. The question here, similar to the UK Uber case, is whether such couriers should be regarded as employees or self-employed. It should be noted that the Netherland does not recognise other categories, such as the UK's intermediate 'worker' category. Furthermore, Deliveroo decided to discontinue its operations in the Netherlands by the end of 2022. That does not mean that the question concerning the classification of its couriers as 'employees' is no longer relevant: the company will still be subject to claims for payment of unpaid salary, pension payments and tax claims.[46]

The Advocate-General, who in the Dutch court system advises the Supreme Court, held earlier that Deliveroo couriers should be regarded as employees. She based her opinion primarily on the control criterion laid down in Article 7:610 of the Dutch Civil Code, which for an employment agreement requires that work is carried out 'in service of' the other party. According to the Advocate-General, work is carried out in service of the other party if it is embedded within the business structure of the employer. Whether that is the case has to be determined on the basis of the factual arrangements made for carrying out the work. The classifications that the parties give to the contract is not relevant.[47] Besides that, the Advocate-General points out that the Supreme Court would be in a position to give guidance on the application of the control criterion in *Deliveroo* with a view to providing greater legal certainty for flex-workers.

[44] For example, they miss out on pension rights, parental leave, and rights associated with employment such as the right to strike. See Adams-Prassl et al (n 9).

[45] Dutch Supreme Court, 24 March 2023, ECLI:NL:HR:2023:443 (*Deliveroo*). For an in-depth analysis of the societal context and legislative developments, see the opinion of Advocate-General De Bock on this case of 17 June 2022, ECLI:NL:PHR:2022:578.

[46] For an analysis in Dutch, see www.zipconomy.nl/2022/08/deliveroo-vertrekt-uit-nederland-een-analyse.

[47] Opinion of Advocate-General De Bock in *Deliveroo* (n 45) [7.2] and [8.1]–[8.25].

Notably, the Advocate-General in the Deliveroo case finds that the flexibility associated with platform work does not stand in the way of qualifying workers' contracts as employment contracts. She considers in particular the freedom of Deliveroo couriers to arrange a replacement if they happen to be unavailable for a ride; and the contractual freedom of the courier to log onto the system at any time of their choosing.[48] In the UK Supreme Court's decision in *Uber v Aslam* it was held in a similar vein that the qualification of worker extended to the times that drivers were logged into the Uber app and ready to accept trips, and should not be restricted to the times that drivers were driving passengers to their destination. According to Lord Leggatt: 'the existence and exercise of a right to refuse work is not critical, provided there is at least an obligation to do some amount of work'.[49]

The Dutch Supreme Court in its judgment of 24 March 2023 followed the Advocate-General's opinion in many respects, though not all. The Supreme Court confirmed that the contract must be classified based on the actual rights and obligations arising from it, and that it is irrelevant whether the parties intended the contract to be classified as an employment contract or not.[50] However, the Supreme Court was unwilling to provide a general guideline for distinguishing flex-work from employee status. It stated that it is up to the national and European legislators to determine which conditions should apply.[51] The Court's reluctance in this respect could be explained by the fact that a general guideline on classification would apply to all types of flex-work, not just platform work, and would therefore have far-reaching ramifications also for other sectors such as education and health care. The Court regarded that as a choice for the legislator, who has the democratic legitimacy to make such decisions. Nevertheless, notwithstanding that no general guideline is provided, the Court held that the circumstances of the case would justify the classification of Deliveroo-couriers as 'employees' under the Dutch Civil Code.[52] The circumstance that couriers are able to choose their own working hours and even have the freedom to have their work carried out by another were not considered, in the given circumstances, to stand in the way of this classification.[53]

What these cases show is that courts are willing to qualify services contracts between platforms and flex-workers as workers' or employment contracts, regardless of the flexibility in terms of the amount of work or working hours associated with them. In the UK the protection offered is somewhat less than for employees hired under an employment contract, as the system recognises an intermediary 'worker' category. Still, in both jurisdictions flex-workers can, depending on the conditions of their work and the control exercised by the platform, be given the protection of workers or employees and are not by definition regarded as self-employed.

Is this approach tenable in the long run? Responses in the literature to the litigation faced by Uber and Deliveroo point out the risks of placing too much confidence

[48] Opinion of Advocate-General De Bock in *Deliveroo* (n 45) [9.11] and [10.4].
[49] *Uber v Aslam* (n 42) [126].
[50] *Deliveroo* (n 45) [3.2.3]–[3.2.4].
[51] *Deliveroo* (n 45) [3.2.6].
[52] *Deliveroo* (n 45) [3.2.5]ff.
[53] *Deliveroo* (n 45) [3.3.4]–[3.3.5].

in worker protection through the classification as 'worker' or 'employee'. That might be the better solution for the short term, but it does not address structural problems associated with flex-work through online platforms. Amongst these are that in jurisdictions such as the UK workers may get a minimum level of protection, but not the full protection of workers hired under an employment contract. Flex-workers are in many ways no better off than workers on zero-hours contracts, who are often also in the lower income ranges and who are vulnerable to exploitation. It is a general policy question whether governments should do more to protect these groups, in particular in light of the large increase of flexible, and therefore precarious, working arrangements.[54] The Dutch legislator is considering introducing specific regulation for the protection of flex-workers, which would be applicable to platform workers and would complement legislation adopted at the EU level.[55]

ii. Contract Law Mechanisms

In the meantime, mechanisms exist in contract law that can indirectly contribute to greater protection of workers. Examples are: (i) the monitoring of non-competition clauses (to safeguard the freedom of choice of profession and indirectly the ability to earn an income);[56] (ii) information rights for workers to help them make informed choices about the labour relation that they enter into (TPWC Directive); and (iii) collective labour agreements. These mechanisms, however, generally go less far in protecting the weaker party than EU rules of consumer protection, which in part can be explained by the EU's more limited competence in the field of labour law.[57] Furthermore, the EU has not introduced rules specifically tailored to flex-workers on online platforms, although the proposed Directive on Platform Work may change that. In the meantime, even the TWPC Directive, which was seen as a step towards regulating work in the platform economy, does not explicitly deal with these categories. Furthermore, employers or platforms can potentially escape application of the Directive by tailoring working hours so that contracts fall outside the scope of the Directive.[58]

[54] Adams-Prassl et al (n 9) 13.

[55] See eg *Kamerstukken II* 2020/21, 29 544, nr 1028; SER Advisory Report, 'How does the platform economy work?' (Social and Economic Council of the Netherlands (SER) 2021), www.ser.nl/en/Publications/platform-economy.

[56] The fundamental right of freedom of profession is relied on by courts as a ground on which to invalidate non-competition clauses; see C Perfumi and C Mak, 'The Impact of Fundamental Rights on the Content of Contracts: Determining Limits to Freedom of Contract in Family and Employment Relations' in G Brüggemeier, A Colombi Ciacchi and G Comandé (eds), *Fundamental Rights and Private Law in the European Union. II. Comparative Analyses of Selected Case Patterns* (Cambridge, Cambridge University Press, 2010) 33, 61–64.

[57] For an exploration of the rationalities of protection in employment relations see C Leone, *The Missing Stone in the Cathedral. Of Unfair Terms in Employment Contracts and Coexisting Rationalities in European Contract Law* (dissertation University of Amsterdam, 12 June 2020).

[58] The Member States 'may decide not to apply the obligations in this Directive to workers who have an employment relationship with predetermined and actual working time is equal to or less than an average of three hours per week in a reference period of four consecutive weeks. Time worked with all employers forming or belonging to the same enterprise, group or entity shall count towards that three-hour average' (Art 1(3) TPWC Directive, n 12).

Beyond specific provisions in labour law, contract law can give rise to obligations of an employer or contractor towards workers, potentially giving them some protection. Contractual rules for services contracts, in particular, can have a broad scope of application and they can apply to many contracts in which one party has agreed to complete a job on behalf of another party. Although services law is to a large extent non-harmonised by EU legislation, most European legal systems recognise services as a category to which specific contractual rules apply and there is some similarity as to their content. In relation to workers, depending on the classification of contractual relations between the parties involved, duties of care may arise. I will illustrate this by briefly setting out the applicable rules in English and in Dutch law. Similar rules apply in French, German and Polish law as well as in other European jurisdictions.[59]

In English law, a rule that a service should be performed 'with reasonable care and skill' applies to suppliers for all services contracts, albeit with variation. Business-to-business (B2B) and C2C services contracts are covered by section 13 of the Sale and Supply of Goods and Services Act 1982 (SSGA), which prescribes an implied term concerning the supplier's duty of care. The Act does not, however, prescribe statutory remedies for breach of that duty. With the introduction of the Consumer Rights Act 2015 (CRA), the duty of care of service suppliers in consumer contracts (ie B2C) was elaborated. The CRA had the specific aim to better integrate consumer contracts in the framework of the SSGA as well as the Sale of Goods Act 1979.[60] Part 1 of the CRA, moreover, gives consumers statutory remedies for non-compliance by suppliers, thereby making it clear which remedies will in any case be available. These remedies are a right to enforce terms about services, a right to repeat performance, and a right to price reduction (sections 54–46 CRA).

In Dutch law, similar duties to take reasonable care apply to services contracts, following from the rules on specific contracts. In terms of scope, specific rules apply to services contracts

> under which one of the parties ('the service provider') has engaged himself towards the other party ('the client') to perform work on another basis than an employment agreement, which work consists of something else than the making of a tangible construction, the safekeeping of property, the publication of a work or the transportation of persons or goods' (Article 7:400(1) DCC).

It should be noted that this provision excludes employment agreements from the scope of the Code's section on services agreements. However, the rules may still apply to workers, seeing that many modern types of work relations do not qualify as employment contracts, in particular in the gig economy. When applicable, the Dutch rules concerning services agreements impose duties of care on both parties to the contract. The service provider – ie the worker – must observe the care of a prudent service provider (Article 7:401 DCC). Conversely, the client – which could be a contractor but potentially also a platform like Uber – should make sure that directions given to the service provider are 'responsible' and given in time (Article 7:402 DCC).

[59] *cf* the PELSC, in particular the comments to Art 1:107. See Barendrecht et al *Principles of European Law on Service Contracts (PELSC)* (Berne-BrusselsMunich, Sellier, 2005).

[60] P Giliker, 'The Consumer Rights Act 2015. A Bastion of European Consumer Rights?' (2017) 37 *Legal Studies* 78, 83.

Arguably, in all legal systems the existing rules do not go far enough for safeguarding the economic position of the service provider (ie the worker). In that context, a plea could be made for a reassessment of the duty of care of a client towards a service provider. As a starting point, one would need a clear definition as to which new forms of work exist, to whom labour law should apply, which aspects of labour law should apply, and what additional rules would be required to protect new categories of workers.[61]

C. Some Conclusions

In sum, a reconstruction of contract law rules applicable to new types of consumers and workers could result in more tailored rules, balancing the interests of prosumers and workers in relation to online platforms. This could lead, for example, to joint and several liability towards consumers of online platforms with a 'dominant influence' over prosumers. In worker relationships, duties of care could be used as a mechanism in contract law through which to develop more specific rules on the rights and duties of workers.

The development of new contractual rules and frameworks can occur through legislation or regulation, but also through private rulemaking, for example in the form of standards. The latter route could be the most promising in the short term, as rulemaking processes for standardisation tend to be shorter than legislative procedures. Also, the legislative framework has for some issues – such as the relationship between prosumers and online platforms – reached a temporary conclusion, as the DSA has now been adopted and is unlikely to be amended in the short term. The revision of the Product Liability Directive could still add some new rules on liability of online platforms. However, those rules will not cover all aspects relevant to the contractual relationships between prosumer, consumer and online platform. For example, misleading information[62] or loss resulting from the faulty performance of services are not covered.

IV. THE CHALLENGE: A HOLISTIC APPROACH TO THE 'CONSUMER WORKER'

The processes of contractualisation of consumer and worker relations have been discussed individually above. That seems fitting, as consumer law and labour law are shaped by different forces. Although the consumer and the worker share characteristics as 'weaker parties' in contractual relations, the ways in which contract law and

[61] For an exploration of some of these questions, see F Hendrickx, 'Regulating new ways of working: From the New "Wow" to the New "How" (2018) 9 *European Labour Law Journal* 195.

[62] Beyond the rules on liability for unfair commercial practices if a platform omits information on the (non-) professional status of a trader; Art 6(a) CRD and Art 7(4)(f) UCPD, as added by the Modernisation Directive (Directive (EU) 2019/2161 of the European Parliament and of the Council of 27 November 2019 amending Council Directive 93/13/EEC and Directive 98/6/EC, 2005/29/EC of the European Parliament and of the Council as regards the better enforcement and modernization of Union consumer protection rules [2019] OJ L328/7).

public law have regulated their legal protection differ significantly. That is apparent also at the level of EU law, where consumer protection has been developed through extensive harmonising legislation in the field of consumer contract and (to a lesser extent) tort law, whilst labour law has mostly been influenced by case law giving effect to EU law principles, such as the principle of non-discrimination.[63]

Could the reconstruction of the 'consumer' and the 'worker' concepts nonetheless not have further-going implications? Seeing that these concepts will generally apply to the same individual – who is a consumer in one context and a worker in another, buying goods on an online platform one day whilst earning money as a flex-worker the next day – can a more holistic approach be developed? Would that entail a contractualisation of all legal relations, or something different? It is too soon to draw broad conclusions. On the basis of the foregoing analysis, the following observations can be made.

A. The Contractualisation of the Consumer Worker: New Autonomies, New Vulnerabilities

Generally speaking, the contractualisation of consumer and worker relationships creates possibilities for individuals – or in private law terms, natural persons – to have a greater say in how they give shape to the ways in which they take part in markets and to how they work. In that sense, the autonomy of consumers and workers is enhanced. They are not by definition the weaker party in relation to a professional contracting party. However, since these new opportunities come into being through the mediation of online platforms, other vulnerabilities arise.

Looking first at the position of consumers, it can be said that prosumerism on online platforms provides low-threshold access to online marketplaces for consumers who see opportunities to become active on the supply side. This can start as a hobby and remain a hobby, or become a more extensive and organised activity. For some prosumers, these activities can even generate an income. In that sense, their contractual autonomy is enhanced. At the same time, as discussed in the preceding sections, prosumers are vulnerable to liability towards consumer-buyers with whom they contract, whilst the online platforms through which they operate often escape liability. In some cases, they may also be bound to burdensome terms and conditions imposed by the platform, such as customer satisfaction targets.[64]

For flex-workers on online platforms, the narrative is broadly similar, at least at the general level of autonomy and vulnerabilities. They have the flexibility to work without having to comply with job qualifications that would apply in many other places. For example, taxi and delivery services only require access to a car or bicycle, and time. It is the business model on which companies like Uber, hailed initially as

[63] *cf* Micklitz (n 41) 201ff.

[64] eg Amazon's conditions for sellers; see V Mak, *Legal Pluralism in European Contract Law* (Oxford, Oxford University Press, 2020) 181–83. These terms and conditions can apply to non-professional traders too, as Amazon gives access to sellers regardless of whether they act in a professional or non-professional capacity.

a prototype for the 'sharing economy',[65] built their success. However, in the meantime that success story has been modified by reports of exploitation of flex-workers and a lack of employment protection (eg in setting working hours). Furthermore, from a socio-economic perspective this type of work can be criticised for trapping lower-income groups in work that offers them little financial security and even a lower income than they might earn in a more traditional job.[66] It should be noted that at the time of writing regulatory responses to address these new vulnerabilities are gaining momentum. The case law discussed above shows that national courts are inclined to grant platform workers the protection of 'employees' or, as a third category in the UK, 'workers'.[67] At the same time, the European legislator as well as national legislators are considering regulation that would provide guidelines on determining employment status. These developments could lead to greater legal certainty for flex-workers on online platforms. Still, as the determination of their employment status depends on national law, differences will continue to exist throughout the EU. Also, platforms would under the proposed EU Directive on Platform Work have the possibility to disprove the presumption of employment status.[68]

B. Solutions in Contract Law

As examined above, mechanisms in contract law can provide a basis for developing solutions that are better tailored to the position of consumers and prosumers, as well as workers on online platforms than current rules are. Such solutions could take the form of a reassessment of tripartite relationships, examining whether online platforms can be held liable alongside or instead of non-professional traders by consumers contracting through the platform. Such a reassessment could even lead to the introduction of a third 'prosumer' category in contract law, besides the existing categories of traders and consumers.

In relation to work, contract law also contains mechanisms that could support a better protection of flex-workers. Seeing that many contracts of flex-workers can under national laws be classified as contracts of assignment, employers are bound by duties of care obliging them to act in a 'responsible' manner. This provides a basis for developing more specific agreements that protect flex-workers, for example with regard to timely notice concerning working hours or transparency with regard to performance targets. It would be of interest to examine whether real-life contracts already contain clauses specifying the ways in which duties of care affect labour relations. Further, guidelines or regulation could be developed to fortify duties of care in contract law. Besides such efforts, the proposed regulation of flex-work and, more

[65] The sharing economy was initially seen as an alternative to the traditional corporate-centred model, enabling a 'crowd-based capitalism' by facilitating peer-to-peer exchange. See A Sundararajan, *The Sharing Economy. The End of Employment and the Rise of Crowd-Based Capitalism* (Cambridge MA, MIT Press, 2016).

[66] I Ness (ed), *The Routledge Handbook of the Gig Economy* (Abingdon-New York, Routledge, 2022).

[67] See section III.B.

[68] Proposal for an EU Directive on Platform Work (n 13), Art 5.

specifically, platform work could lead to greater certainty as to when a worker would acquire employment status, with the associated rights and benefits.

C. Concluding Remarks

Taking account of the gaps in the protection of weaker parties that the contractualisation of consumer and worker relationships has created, it has been argued that contract law itself could provide a starting point for developing new solutions. Contract laws, in particular at the national level of the EU Member States, contain well-developed rules, principles and doctrines that can provide a framework within which assessments can be made as to how far protection can and should go. For example, in relation to prosumers, the doctrine of privity is important. It sets limitations to the liabilities of parties that are not bound by contract; but it also gives guidance for determining in which circumstances non-contractual liability may arise.

In order to take the analysis beyond this initial exploration, further research will be needed. In particular, fundamental questions concerning the scope of autonomy in contract law will require a reassessment. It is well-established in most theories underlying European contract law that the law should enable contracting parties to make choices that enable them to effectively pursue goals of self-realisation. At the same time, this underlying supposition entails that parties should sometimes be curtailed in exercising their rights, as they have to respect the autonomy of others. How to strike the balance between the autonomies' of parties, in particular in contractual relations where one party is considered weaker, requires renewed attention in light of the contractualisation of consumer and worker relations.

16

The Legal Personalisation of Nature: A Problem of Method

MURIEL FABRE-MAGNAN

THE ENVIRONMENTAL ISSUE is on the national and international political agendas. In the age of what is now known as the Anthropocene, there finally seems to be agreement on the urgent need to change the way we look at our environment.[1]

The innovative legal initiatives taken by certain countries are often cited as examples. In India in 2017, for example, the High Court of Uttarakhand granted the Ganges and the Yamuna, its main tributary, as well as glaciers and lakes, 'legal personality' (although these decisions were overturned by the Supreme Court). The New Zealand Parliament, for its part, recognised one of the country's rivers, the Te Awa Tupua, as a living entity with legal personality: according to its declaration, the river is an indivisible and living whole, 'extending from the mountains to the sea, including all its physical and metaphysical elements'.

A finger is then pointed at the cultures of continental law, which remain stuck on the distinction between persons and things inherited from Roman law. Anything that is not a person is in principle classified as a thing, and is subject, barring exceptions, to the system of ownership. Things that are not appropriated (air, space, the high seas or wild species) are more difficult to protect, and are subject to a great deal of looting and pillaging.

The question of the legal status of nature is not just a theoretical one. It carries with it an ethic that alone gives us a chance of avoiding 'collapse'[2] predicted by many observers.

The binary division of persons and things certainly appears today to be a dead end (section I), but reformulating the debate presupposes resolving certain epistemological and methodological difficulties specific to law (section II).

[1] See the precursory appeal of H Jonas in *The Imperative of Responsibility. In Search of an Ethics for the Technological Age* (Chicago, Chicago University Press, 1984) 6–7: 'An object of an entirely new order – no less than the whole biosphere of the planet – has been added to what we must be responsible for because we now have power over it.'

[2] J Diamond, *Collapse: How Societies Choose to Fail or Succeed* (New York, Viking Press, 2005).

I. THE IMPASSES OF THE BINARY DIVISION OF PERSONS AND THINGS

The two qualifications of 'thing' (section A) and 'person' (section B) are in fact insufficient to give nature an appropriate legal status.

A. Inadequacy of the Classification of a Thing

Everyone agrees that the term 'environment' is a bad start. It evokes what surrounds human beings, and accentuates both anthropocentrism and the rupture between the human subject and its environment.

As the Japanese philosopher Watsuji Tetsurô has explained,

> what is generally understood by the natural environment is a thing that, in order to become an object, has been freed from its concrete ground, human mediation. When we think of the relationship between this thing and human life, the latter is itself already objectified.[3]

In the western Cartesian tradition, human beings are still described as 'masters and possessors of nature'. It does not do justice to the vital dependence of human beings on these 'things' and to the interdependence of all living beings, human and non-human alike. Nor does it protect and enhance qualitative concepts such as biodiversity.

Even the most modern analyses, such as the reappraisal of the notions of the commons or the common heritage, which are giving rise to a resurgence of work, and which are supposed to be figures of the inappropriable, remain in reality based on the same paradigm. It is still a question of thinking about the use of things by people, even if this use is common rather than individual. However, it is an illusion to think that it would be enough to change the holder of the right when it is necessary to change the normative structure itself. The legal relationship with nature must not be limited to its use and exploitation, even if this is extended to a greater number of people. Moreover, it is not enough to avoid ownership in order to resolve all the difficulties (see the classic example of the Franciscan quarrel over ownership, which led to the invention of trusts[4]).

B. The Unsuitability of the Concept of a Person

However, the term 'person' is also inappropriate and illusory.

The law certainly makes use of fictions, and legislators or judges could technically extend to animals or to nature qualifications made for human beings.[5]

[3] W Tetsurô [1889–1960], *Fûdo, le milieu humain* (commentary and translation by A Berque) (Paris CNRS éditions, 2011) Preamble, 35.

[4] See L Parisoli, 'L'involontaire contribution franciscaine aux outils du capitalisme' in A Supiot (ed), *Tisser le lien social* (Paris, Éditions de la Maison des sciences de l'homme, 2004) 229.

[5] In France, there was a famous debate between supporters of the 'theory of fiction', arguing that only the legislator could create new legal persons, and supporters of the 'theory of reality', arguing that legal personality could be conferred on groups of persons acting autonomously, even if the legislator had not expressly granted them this status. In a decision of 28 January 1954, the Court of Cassation ruled in

To produce its effects, however, a fiction must retain a certain anchorage in reality and, above all, a certain functionality. The notion of legal personality is a technique whose very purpose is to establish an entity at which rights and duties can be imputed, and above all to organise the relationship between human liberty and responsibility. Legal personality is indeed a fiction that makes it possible to act in the legal arena, for example to enter into contracts, or even to go to court, with in return the duty to account for one's actions and the way in which one's liberty has been used.

The example of juridical persons has also shown the abuses inherent in the extensive attribution of legal personality. The screen of legal personality allows a great deal of fraud to take place, when it makes it impossible to identify the real persons responsible, who are hidden behind the juridical person. The fictitious empowerment of 'persons' who do not have the means to exercise it can also lead, paradoxically, to their being left even more to their own devices, with the main perverse effect of the corresponding irresponsibility of human beings (which we are also seeing emerging in relation to the legal status of robots).[6]

The inadequacy of the notion of rights, or even human rights, for legal entities was demonstrated, for example, in the *Citizens United* decision in 2010, in which the US Supreme Court accepted that commercial companies could, through the First Amendment protecting freedom of expression, invest freely, ie without any limit on the amount, in election campaigns (President Obama said that he could not 'think of anything more devastating to the public interest').

Far from being neutral, the anthropomorphism from which they have benefited[7] has in fact gone hand in hand with the extension of the domain of the market. Georges Ripert once said that the 'great skill' of modern capitalism 'consisted in considering the personality of juridical persons to be exactly the same as that of human beings'. He added that 'liberal capitalism cannot conceive of any desire to stifle the personality of societies'[8] and noted: 'Isn't the best way to conceal their power to confuse them in the crowd?'[9]

The much-vaunted objective of personalising nature also needs to be clarified from a technical point of view. In reality, many associations (ie juridical persons under private law) already aim to defend certain aspects of the environment. What's more, in France, for example, public administrative bodies (again, juridical persons under public law) have been set up specifically to manage certain sites, such as national parks or rivers, for example the 'Conservatoire de l'espace littoral et des rivages lacustres'

favour of the 'reality' of legal persons by recognising the legal personality of works councils in companies. According to the highest court, legal personality is not a creation of the law; it belongs, in principle, to any grouping that is able to express itself collectively in defence of lawful interests that are therefore worthy of legal recognition and protection'.

[6] See M Fabre-Magnan, 'Du bon usage de la personnalité juridique en matière de responsabilité écologique' (2021) *Germinal. La République écologique* 155.

[7] See V Wester-Ouisse, 'Dérives anthropomorphiques de la personnalité morale: ascendances et influences' (2009) *JurisClasseur Édition Générale* 137; V Wester-Ouisse, 'La jurisprudence et les personnes morales. Du propre de l'homme aux droits de l'homme' (2009) *JurisClasseur Édition Générale* 121.

[8] G Ripert, *Aspects juridiques du capitalisme moderne*, 2nd edn (Paris, Libraire Générale du Droit de Jurisprudence, 1951) 74.

[9] ibid.

(Conservatory for coastal areas and lakeshores), set up in 1975 to acquire parcels of coastline to prevent them from being built on or artificialised.

On the other hand, it is inappropriate to assert that these juridical persons 'are' the natural entities whose interests they represent, for example that it is a river or a forest that 'is' the juridical person. It is obvious that it is not the river or the mountain that will enter into contracts or take direct legal action, but their representatives.[10] It is therefore essential that the juridical persons created (and above all the individuals who operate them) can be held liable for their actions, particularly if they perform their obligations badly, or even fraudulently. Identifying absolutely the natural entity (the site) and the juridical entity whose purpose is to manage and safeguard it would then have the perverse effect of making this type of liability action impossible: one does not act in liability against oneself.

The only real question, therefore, is not whether a legal entity can be set up to safeguard certain sites – there is no legal doubt that this is the case, since such legal entities already exist – but whether or not the state should agree to delegate their creation or operation to private individuals or, at the very least, to organise citizen participation around these projects. This is an avenue worth exploring, even if we all know the risks involved, and the precautions that need to be taken to avoid the power grabs that sometimes hide behind altruistic claims.[11]

The metaphors used are undoubtedly striking for the general public, and we can even admit that they are effective from a militant point of view, but the jurist must warn against this enthusiasm which has counterproductive effects.

Using freedom of expression to make the voice of animals or nature heard is a metaphor that again risks confusing the messages and not advancing their cause, while risking weakening the voice of human beings. Doesn't speaking of slavery in relation to orcas held in captivity also euphemise the human suffering for which the term was previously reserved?[12]

Proposals to describe animals and nature as 'persons' or to attribute 'rights' to them may help to ease our consciences, and they obviously offer some people a narcissistically rewarding posture, but they are not enough to discharge our debt or to account for our dependence on our environment. Augustin Berque has made some astute observations about our tendency 'to fetishise the environment as compensation for the massacre we make of it elsewhere'.[13]

Under a subversive guise, it is simply a question of tipping nature or animals over to the side of people, and thus of renewing the subject/object dichotomy that we need, on the contrary, to try to overcome. The human being is only one being among

[10] It is clear that 'we will always be the ones to make nature speak' (F Ost, *La nature hors la loi. L'écologie à l'épreuve du droit* (Paris, La Découverte, 1995) 14).

[11] See P Brunet et J Rochfeld, 'De l'animisme juridique à base scientifique: une voie pour la nature?' in N Baya Lafitte et al (eds), *Le droit à l'épreuve de la société des sciences et des techniques. 'Liber amicorum' en l'honneur de Marie-Angèle Hermitte*, Diálogos' Incontri con la cultura giuridica latino-americana (Torino, Accademia University Press, 2021) 340.

[12] In February 2012, a California federal court had to examine a case in which it was argued that paragraph 1 of the 13th Amendment to the US Constitution prohibiting slavery should apply to five orcas held in captivity in two amusement parks in San Diego and Orlando (*Tilikum et al v Sea World Parks & Entertainment Inc and Sea World, LLC* 842 F Supp 2d 1259 (SD Cal 2012)).

[13] A Berque, *Écoumène. Introduction à l'étude des milieux humains* (Paris, Belin, 2000) 29.

others, and like all living beings he depends on a vital environment and evolves in a world of his own that he has created.[14]

How, moreover, can we seriously argue that the qualification of person would enable us to move away from our anthropocentrism, when in reality it is a matter of imposing even more on other living beings categories made by and for human beings? By its very definition, law is a discourse and, as such, it necessarily addresses beings of language.[15]

Lastly, the proposal is impossible to put into practice except for a few emblematic places. For animals too, it is impossible to give them all legal personality or rights. So which animals should we choose? The great apes? What about small chicks crushed by the thousands or bees exterminated? Shouldn't they also be protected as a matter of urgency? Or insects, whose disappearance is highly problematic? These qualifications also show that we continue to think in terms of individuals when we should be thinking in terms of species and even ecosystems.

In short, although the ecological issue is now the focus of a great deal of attention and research, the legal responses to it are still very inadequate, because they are locked into the old paradigms, even those that are presented in new guises.

The importance of the issues at stake calls for a radical conceptual and theoretical change, a scientific revolution in the sense of Thomas Kuhn. The law in fact operates very largely on the epistemological model described by this author, with undoubtedly even greater inertia, due to the fact that it is not an experimental science. Its statements cannot be falsified, and confronting them with reality rarely produces irrefutable proof. Interpretation is also more flexible. All these particularities make it possible to maintain for longer a semblance of coherence to a whole that in reality is cracking. However, the fractures are now all too visible. As we have seen in other eras, new institutions need to be devised.

II. REFORMULATING THE QUESTION. EPISTEMOLOGICAL AND METHODOLOGICAL DIFFICULTIES SPECIFIC TO LAW

The legal translation of these observations and objectives is much more complex than it seems, and public debates on the subject often ignore the epistemological status of the law.

Changing the legal classification of animals and nature is pointless if it is not accompanied by a status requiring all human beings to respect other living beings. Thus, recognising that 'animals are living beings endowed with sentience', as

[14] See the valuable phenomenological work of R Barbaras, in particular *L'appartenance. Vers une cosmologie phénoménologique* (Peeters, Bibliothèque Philosophique de Louvain, 2019), which shows that if every being (living or non-living, for that matter) belongs to the world and inhabits the world, it also brings the world into existence by this very engagement; every being, human or non-human, and even living or non-living, thus unfolds the ground to which it belongs.

[15] See G Aïdan, 'L'intériorité comme question. Contribution à une théorie du sujet de droit non-humain' in G Aïdan and D Bourcie, *Humain Non-humain. Repenser l'intériorité du sujet de droit*, Droit et société 60 (Paris, Libraire Générale du Droit de Jurisprudence, 2020) 95, who shows that the imputation of norms presupposes the recognition of minimal psychological and cognitive aptitudes, without which it would not be possible to consider that a subject is the recipient of legal norms.

Article 515-14 of the French Civil Code resulting from the law of 16 February 2015 does, is undoubtedly a necessary awareness; it is not enough, however, if the same article continues, without drawing any consequences from its premises, that 'ruled by the laws that protect them, animals are subject to the regime of property'. The assertion that animals are sentient living beings is in itself highly inadequate because, taken literally, it implies only a duty not to cause them suffering, which admittedly would not be so bad, but is still highly inadequate given the scale of the issues at stake.

In fact, this debate involves tackling one of the most classic but also the most controversial and persistent[16] question in legal theory, namely the 'is–ought problem', ie the relationship between 'to be' and 'ought-to-be'.

To simplify, two opposing answers are most often given. The majority supports what is known as 'Hume's law', ie that we cannot deduce what ought to be solely from statements about what is.[17] Conversely, what we call 'jusnaturalists' claim to read or discover, if not in the word of God, at least in the examination of nature or the nature of things, the rule to be applied.

The truth undoubtedly lies between the two. Admittedly, the rule of law is the result of arbitration and choices of a political nature about what ought to be. However, the rule is not unrelated to the factual issue it is intended to regulate. The philosopher Jean-Louis Gardies has expressed this idea best. In response to what he saw as 'Hume's error',[18] he insisted on the fundamental ambiguity of the gap between facts and institutions. There is certainly, he said, a rupture between the two, which is 'the least debatable aspect of a certain positivism', but, at the same time, 'the structure of the institution itself depends closely on the conditions of nature'. In other words, 'you can either take up a challenge or not' and, he adds,

> if you take it up, there are several ways of doing so; however, we can only take up a challenge because that challenge is brought to us, and the way in which it is brought to us conditions to a certain extent the various ways in which we can take it up.

In short, if what ought to be cannot be deduced mechanically from what is, it cannot be said to be totally foreign to it, because what is at least gives the terms in which the question is posed.[19] So it is these two terms that need to be examined more precisely, but the question of what is, and that of its distinction from what ought to be, are not so simple in their turn.

[16] "See L Kolakowski, 'The persistence of the sein-sollen dilemma' (1977) 10 *Man and World* 194.

[17] See D Hume, *A Treatise of Human Nature*, Book III 'Morals' (1739) part 1, section 1: 'I can't forbear adding an observation that may be found of some importance. In every system of morality I have met with I have noticed that the author proceeds for some time reasoning in the ordinary way to establish the existence of a God, or making points about human affairs, and then he suddenly surprises me by moving from propositions with the usual copula 'is' (or 'is not') to ones that are connected by 'ought' (or 'ought not'). This change is imperceptible, but it is highly important. For as this 'ought' (or 'ought not') expresses some *new* relation or affirmation, it needs to be pointed out and explained; and a reason should be given for how this new relation can be – inconceivably! – a deduction from others that are entirely different from it. Authors don't ordinarily take the trouble to do this, so I recommend it to you; and I'm convinced that paying attention to this one small matter will subvert all the vulgar systems of morality and let us see that the distinction between vice and virtue is not based merely on the relations of objects, and is not perceived by reason.'

[18] JL Gardies, *L'erreur de Hume* (Paris, Presses Universitaires de France, 1987) 118–19.

[19] For more details, see our book *L'institution de la liberté*, 2nd edn (Paris, Presses Universitaires de France, 2023).

A. 'Is'

What is, or the challenge to which we must respond legally, is not simply a matter of observing the facts or the nature of things. Like any concept, it also involves a way of looking at and talking about the world.

In other words, what is, or appears to us, is already structured by our representations and by language. We then cannot hope to achieve the Copernican revolution needed to give ecology its rightful place without a radical change in our representations.[20] In the same way, it is because the dignity of the human being signifies first and foremost his infinite value, priceless as Kant says, that we have been able to deduce from it a principle of dignity requiring that the human being be treated with the corresponding respect.[21]

With this in mind, it is necessary to enhance the perception and representation we have of our vital environment, and the various types of discourse that contribute to this help to raise the awareness necessary for a change in behaviour. Among all these discourses, the legal discourse (its words and its rules) can also contribute in return to consolidating the importance of safeguarding our natural environment. Indeed, while the law must keep pace with changes in society and customs, it does more than that. It also has an active role, in the sense that it has a feedback effect on our representations and on the state of the society in which we live.

Being aware of other ways of seeing the world, in particular through other major cultures, is obviously invaluable in this respect. It allows us to put our certainties into perspective and to shake our most solidly anchored categories. In return, this step aside gives us a chance to better perceive the strangeness of our own constructions. In the past, for example, we judged and condemned animals or the dead, and we still accept today that a commercial company can be criminally responsible or the holder of human rights. Our representations are also imbued with beliefs and ideologies: one author has for instance rightly pointed out that the discourses in our cultures that try to convince us of the need to personalise nature or animals are imbued with the idea that these non-human legal subjects are endowed with an interiority.[22]

Comparative law also enables us to distinguish between the universal and the relative. In reality, legal answers are very rarely universal. On the other hand, questions often are: all the world's great cultures are faced with the question of how to treat beings, whether human or non-human, living or non-living, and they give rise to an impressive variety of representations and cosmogonies.

This does not mean, however, that we can import foreign solutions without restraint. The law is deeply rooted in a culture.[23] All comparatists know that rules

[20] See B Latour, N Schultz, *Mémo sur la nouvelle classe écologique. Comment faire émerger une classe écologique consciente et fière d'elle-même* (Paris, Éditions La Découverte, 2022), which call for 'a change of cosmology' (66).

[21] See M Fabre-Magnan, 'Le statut juridique de la dignité' (2014) 58 *Droits* 167.

[22] See G Aïdan, 'L'intériorité comme question. Contribution à une théorie du sujet de droit non-humain' in G Aïdan and D Bourcier (eds), *Humain Non-humain. Repenser l'intériorité du sujet de droit*, Droit et société 60 (Paris Cedex, Librairie générale de droit et de jurisprudence, 2020) ch 8, who shows how the project of attributing legal personality to non-human beings increasingly finds its justification in the discovery of an interiority of these beings.

[23] See P Legrand, notably *Fragments of Law as Culture* (Deventer, WEJ Tjeenk Willink, 1999).

and institutions are like transplants which, without precautions, risk being rejected or leading to new divergences.[24] Moreover, law and language are inseparable: each law, like each language, carries with it a vision of the world. Even when the word has an equivalent in the other language, the thing meant is often radically different.[25]

This discrepancy is particularly apparent in the subject we are dealing with, and a quick 'tour of the world of concepts' shows that the very word 'nature' is in fact largely untranslatable, and reveals highly variable relationships to our 'environment'.[26] The same applies to the concept of 'person'.

The methodology of comparison thus conceals profound ethical issues. Our own categories of thinking are not universal, as is sometimes claimed, out of ignorance or imperialism. We need to be careful not to impose our own concepts and representations on other visions of the world,[27] which would ruin all efforts at mutual understanding.

But neither can we pretend to appropriate the ways of thinking of other cultures without losing along the way the context that gives them their power and meaning.

How can we seriously maintain that indigenous, Indian or sub-Saharan cultures would recognise the 'legal personality' and 'rights' of rivers or mountains, when the anthropologists have long been saying that the notion of law as we know it is typically Western?

How can we believe that this is exactly our legal notion of the person, when Marcel Mauss, in his famous essay on the person, masterfully showed that 'Our notion of the human person is still fundamentally the Christian notion'?[28]

So when the Maori tribes wanted Te Awa Tupua to be given legal personality, it was to recognise that she was a living person who could now 'own herself'.[29] On the contrary, the personality of our Western legal cultures, for example the legal personality of companies, does not prevent appropriation by others. In our legal cultures, other techniques are used to exclude private property, for example by recognising the public nature of property, even though this qualification has proved to have certain shortcomings, particularly in cases where states fail to act.

Taking the categories of other cultures at face value sometimes leads, under the guise of decentring and de-Westernising the viewpoint, to caricaturing and making a mockery of those cultures. We overlook the fact that these cultures, like ourselves,[30] have recourse to metaphors, which we should not deprive them of by taking their statements literally.

[24] See Gunther Teubner's famous article, 'Legal Irritants: Good Faith in British Law or How Unifying Law Ends up in New Divergences' (1998) 61 *MLR* 11.

[25] See B Cassin, *Vocabulaire européen des philosophies. Le dictionnaire des intraduisibles* (Paris, Le Robert-Le Seuil, 2004).

[26] See P Legendre (ed), *Tour du monde des concepts* (Paris, Fayard, 2014), preface JN Robert, afterword S Sharma.

[27] For an illuminating example of the ravages of the concept of property in certain African cultures, see D Liberski-Bagnoud, *La Souveraineté de la Terre. Une leçon africaine sur l'habiter* (Paris, Éditions du Seuil, 2023).

[28] M Mauss, 'Une catégorie de l'esprit humain: la notion de personne celle de "moi"' (1938) 68 *The Journal of the Royal Anthropological Institute of Great Britain and Ireland* 263.

[29] See the scrupulous and rigorous analyses of S Bourgeois-Gironde, *Être la rivière. Comment le fleuve Whanganui est devenu une personne vivante selon la loi* (Paris, Presses Universitaires de France, 2020).

[30] Richard 1st was called Richard the Lionheart and Bossuet was nicknamed the Eagle of Meaux.

In short, representations cannot be decreed, prescribed or exported; they are slowly forged within cultures.[31]

Certain questions underlying legal qualifications must also remain largely outside the law. For example, it is not the role of legislators or judges to pronounce on the essence of nature or animals. The attempt to legalise and impose a particular way of seeing the world or nature can quickly undermine freedom of thought and freedom of conscience, and even religious freedom. The aim of the law is simply to agree, *hic et nunc*, on how nature or animals should be treated and not mistreated.

Nor is the legal question, as it might be in moral philosophy, to know why nature should be protected, in other words whether it should be protected 'for its own sake' or in the interests of human beings. A great deal of progress has already been made in asserting the need and the right (which admittedly still needs to be legally strengthened and guaranteed) of human beings to live in a healthy environment, where animal and plant biodiversity is assured, where animals are not mistreated and where nature is not ransacked. It is not insignificant to argue that, on all these points, the humanity of human beings is at stake. Echoes of this idea can be found in the decision of the Colombian Supreme Court, which on 5 April 2018 upheld the claim of young plaintiffs (aged between seven and 26) complaining about environmental degradation. According to the Supreme Court, measures must be taken to preserve the Amazon rainforest, because it is 'the existence of human beings' that is at stake.

Of course, more needs to be done. The law is not just about knowledge, it is also about action. No common policy or international regulation will be possible without the development of a common legal vocabulary, and a shared minimum that can make sense in all cultures.

B. 'Ought-to'

However, we must not lose sight of the fact that the real legal issue lies in the 'ought to be', ie in the way in which the law prescribes how natural elements and ecosystems should be treated at a given time in a given society, and in the sanctions it attaches to these obligations, which are an indication of the importance attached to these rules.

In this respect, one of the main advances has been the realisation (which has taken a long time in our cultures …) that environmental harm is a damage. It is clear that what is at stake here are our representations, ie, the way we see and value our planet. On 9 February 2000, the European Commission adopted a 'White Paper on Environmental Liability', which led to a directive of 21 April 2004 'on environmental liability with regard to the prevention and remedying of environmental damage', recognising the concept of ecological damage,[32] even though this was not really a

[31] Portalis said the same thing about the law in a famous sentence in the Preliminary Discourse on the French Civil Code of 1804 (JEM Portalis, *Discours préliminaire du premier projet de Code civil* (1804), classiques.uqac.ca/collection_documents/portalis/discours_1er_code_civil/discours_1er_code_civil.pdf: 'People's codes are made over time; but, strictly speaking, they are not made' (translation by the author).

[32] Directive 2004/35/CE of the European Parliament and of the Council of 21 April 2004 on environmental liability with regard to the prevention and remedying of environmental damage [2004] OJ L 143/56.

liability regime but rather an administrative police regime.[33] The aim is to recognise not only damage to appropriate property, but also what French law calls 'pure' or 'objective' ecological damage, ie, damage to common things: to elements of nature that are not appropriate or even not appropriable, or to qualitative elements such as biodiversity.[34]

As evidence of the essential importance we now attach to the environment, at least in theory, there has also been a movement towards the 'constitutionalisation' or 'fundamentalisation' of environmental law, which opens up certain prospects.[35] Article 37 of the Charter of Fundamental Rights of the European Union is devoted to 'Protection of the environment' and states that 'A high level of environmental protection and the improvement of the quality of the environment must be integrated into the policies of the Union and ensured in accordance with the principle of sustainable development'. In France, a constitutional law of 1 March 2005 gave constitutional status to a Charter of the Environment adopted in 2004, which contains, in addition to the right of everyone to live in a balanced environment that respects health, the duty of everyone to preserve and improve the environment, to prevent the damage that they are likely to cause to it, and to contribute to make reparation for the damage that they have caused. It also states that 'public policies must promote sustainable development'.[36]

The real legal issues, however, lie elsewhere, and the personalisation of nature or the attribution of rights to other living beings seems like a form of entertainment and indeed a way of concealing the real problems.

Admittedly, the question of who can take legal action is crucial, particularly when the damage caused does not involve damage to appropriate property for which the owner can claim compensation. It is mainly in this context that the question of the legal personalisation of nature takes on its full meaning. As we have seen, however, legal entities already exist to represent the interests of high symbolic places, rivers, parks, mountains or coastlines. The central question is whether these actions should

[33] See GJ Martin, 'De quelques évolutions du droit contemporain à la lumière de la réparation du préjudice écologique par le droit de la responsabilité civile' (2020) *La Revue des juristes de Sciences Po* 71.

[34] Some of the first steps towards ecological liability were taken by the Law of 8 August 2016 for the Reconquest of Biodiversity, Nature and Landscapes, www.ecologie.gouv.fr/sites/default/files/Title_V_Law_on_biodiversity_8_th_of_August_2016_French%20_ABS_legislation.pdf, which introduced important provisions on compensation for ecological damage into the French Civil Code. The driving force had been an important decision by the French Court of Cassation handed down on 25 September 2012 (Bulletin criminal 2012, n° 198) in the case of the sinking of the Erika (Bulletin criminal 2012, n° 198). See the pioneering work of GJ Martin and L Neyret, *Nomenclature des préjudices environnementaux* (Paris, LexisNexis, 2012), which argued for the need to distinguish between, 'on the one hand, the constituent elements of ecosystems (water, air, soil, fauna, flora), the functions that these elements perform and that enable ecosystems to function and perpetuate and, finally, the services that these same ecosystems render to man'. The new Article 1247 of the French Civil Code now defines ecological damage as 'non-negligible harm to the elements or functions of ecosystems or to the collective benefits derived by man from the environment' (translation by the author).

[35] See C Perruso, *Le droit à un environnement sain en droit international* (PhD dissertation, Université Paris 1 and University of São Paulo, Paris, 2019).

[36] In an important decision on 31 January 2020 (Décision n° 2019-823 QPC), the French Constitutional Council concluded that 'the protection of the environment, the common heritage of human beings, constitutes an objective of constitutional value'.

remain public actions, undertaken by states, when the latter have demonstrated their inaction in this area. In many countries, individuals have taken legal action on the grounds that states have failed to act and to fulfil their obligations. We can hope that if environmental issues become an electoral issue, leaders will find an incentive to act, even if the difficulty is that in these areas, the scale of a state is notoriously insufficient. On the other hand, we also know what the risks are of privatising these actions, in particular that anyone could set themselves up as a prosecutor, with the added difficulty of complicating the issue of the allocation of any sums obtained in court.

In reality, it is not so much the determination of creditors that poses a problem as that of debtors, those who must be held responsible and firmly dissuaded from causing ecological damage.

There is indeed no real shortage of techniques and legal tools to achieve this, the effectiveness of which could be formidable: for example, a simple ban on polluting rivers or seas, sanctioned by strict liability requiring all the damage caused to be made good, with this civil obligation also being backed up by substantial criminal penalties.

Admittedly, it is often difficult to pinpoint who is responsible when damage is caused by the addition of micro-decisions and micro-damages. It is therefore difficult to know who is to blame for climate change. In many cases, however, the origin of land or water pollution can be traced, and its effects attributed to those responsible. The famous Roman law adage 'Ubi emolumentum, ibi onus' would already prevent polluters from externalising the harmful effects caused to the environment while pocketing the profits correlative to the damaging activity.

Penalties could also be reviewed to improve their effectiveness, for example by largely recognising punitive damages as a means of combating lucrative misconduct, or by allowing the judge to allocate the sums awarded to the actual repair of the environment. The confiscation of sources of pollution could also be considered.

Over and above civil and criminal liability, the law as a whole needs to be rethought to take account of ecological issues,[37] and in particular the fundamental categories that structure our law: the notion of property and its corollary, that of ownership, which must no longer be seen as the power to use or even destroy one's property, or as the right to exclude all others;[38] the notion of contract, which must incorporate the sustainability dimension;[39] the notion of responsibility, which has always been crucial to understanding social change (its role in the emergence of the welfare state is well known,[40] and which is now showing its limitations in the face of

[37] See. eg, U Mattei and A Quarta, *The Turning Point in Private Law. Ecology, Technology and the Commons*, Elgar Studies in Legal Theory (Cheltenham, Edward Elgar, 2019) 171.

[38] See G Giraud, *Composer un Monde en commun. Une 'théologie politique' de l'Anthropocène* (Paris, Éditions du Seuil, 2022).

[39] See Y Queinnec, 'Le contrat durable. Contours du concept et pistes d'exploration' in I Daugareilh (ed), *Responsabilité sociale de l'entreprise transnationale et globalisation de l'économie* (Brussels, Bruylant, 2010); and M Fabre-Magnan, 'What is a Modern Law of Contract. Elements for a New Manifesto for Social Justice in European Contract Law' (2017) 13 *European Review of Contract Law* 376.

[40] See F Ewald's work, notably *L'État providence* (Paris, Grasset, 1986).

ecological challenges.[41] There are many other legal disciplines that could be revised accordingly, such as company law and procedural law.

All these technical legal issues are far more difficult and incomparably more effective when it comes to trying to repair what can be repaired and treating nature with due respect and, above all, trying to prevent rather than cure.

[41] See M Fabre-Magnan, 'Postface – Pour une responsabilité écologique' in GJ Martin et L Neyret (n 34) 387.

17

Public Policy and Dignity of the Individual

GIOVANNI PASSAGNOLI

I. THE DIGNITY OF INDIVIDUALS BETWEEN PUBLIC POLICY AND MORALITY: THE CONCEPTUAL ISSUE

THE RELATIONSHIP BETWEEN public policy and morality has been debated for a long time in the Italian system. It is characterised by the tendency to progressively draw the latter into the former due to the acknowledged difficulty of attributing a shared foundation to morality, and to the enduring force of the rule of non-repetition of services in execution of an immoral transaction.

Currently the central protection of the dignity of individuals[1] is combined both with a deterioration in the practice of morality and with the correlated expansion of the scope of relevance of public policy.

[1] The distinction between 'individual' and 'person' is in a certain sense mediated precisely by 'dignity' and, it can be said, its clarity is diluted hand in hand with attenuation of the distinction between public law and private law. The idea of 'the person' expresses a relational concept: it identifies an individual capable of being in a relationship with other individuals, at the same time as it distinguishes them from each other. The concept of the individual is generic, while that of the person refers to a specific and determined individual in all their concrete existential traits, since it is in the person that freedom and the other fundamental values that characterise it are developed. In particular, it is the influence of Christianity that identifies dignity as the fundamental value which characterises the human person more than any other. See G Maritain, *La persona e il bene commune*, 5th edn (Brescia, Morcelliana, 1978); S Cotta, 'Persona (filos.)'in *Enciclopedia del diritto* XXXIII (1983) 159; E Berti, 'Genesi e sviluppo del concetto di persona nella storia del pensiero occidentale' in D Castellano (ed), *Persona e diritto: atti del convegno interdisciplinare internazionale* (Udine, Missio, 1990) 17; G Basti, *Il rapporto mente-corpo nella filosofia e nella scienza* (Bologna, Edizioni Studio Domenicano, 1991) 334ff: 'Definendo l'uomo come persona si intende designare il singolo uomo nella sua interezza, concretezza e unità psicofisica di soggetto metafisico (sostanza) capace di pensiero e libertà e per questo capace di relazionarsi come tale nei confronti di Dio, degli altri uomini e del resto degli enti che compongono l'universo.' ['By defining man as a person, one intends to designate the individual man in his entirety, concreteness and psychophysical unity as a metaphysical subject (substance) capable of thought and freedom, and for this reason capable of relating as such to God, to other men and to the rest of the entities that make up the universe.']; F Viola, 'Lo statuto giuridico della persona in prospettiva storica' in G Pansini (ed), *Studi in memoria di Italo Mancini* (Napoli, Edizioni Scientifiche Italiane, 1999) 621ff; G Limone, *Persona e memoria. Oltre la maschera: il compito del pensare come diritto alla filosofia* (Rubbettino, Soveria Mannelli, 2017); N Galasso, Sulla distinzione tra individuo e persona' (2018) *La Cultura* 267.

It is well-known that the principle of dignity is a core principle of modern legal systems, as documented in many international, supranational and constitutional legal sources.[2] More debated, however, is the issue of correct classification of the consequences if a contract contflicts with the principle of dignity. Identifying the applicable contractual remedy is particularly complex. In fact, two different aspects need to be taken into consideration: protection of the person; and the exercise of economic freedom. In other words, the need to protect negotiating autonomy would require reducing any form of external interference on its exercise as much as possible, while issues connected to protection of the person and their dignity would require effective control over the content of the contract. The tension existing between these opposing needs explains why the problem of the consequences deriving from the conclusion of a contract contrary to the principle of dignity arises primarily at the level of the criteria for the validity of the act.

As will be explained below, the growing importance attributed to human dignity in the contractual sphere is shown above all in those sectors where the exercise of negotiating autonomy is more closely linked to personality rights. Here dignity takes the form of a general clause that acts as a limit to the exercise of economic freedoms,

[2] The concept of dignity found its first normative acknowledgment in the Weimar Constitution in Art 151(1), which provided that the order of economic life should be compliant with the principles of justice so as to guarantee a 'dignified existence for all'. After the Second World War, this value found strong recognition at the international level with the: Universal Declaration of Human Rights of 1948; the European Convention for the Protection of Human Rights and Fundamental Freedoms (ECHR) of 1950; the Convention on the Rights of the Child of 1989; and then the Charter of Fundamental Rights of the European Union (the Nice Charter) of 1989. Dignity is a central value in the ECHR, which dedicates the preamble and no less than five articles in Title I to it, from which emerges an image of dignity as the very basis of all fundamental rights. The Nice Charter also opens with Chapter I, entitled 'Human Dignity', and affirms its inviolability, declaring that it must not only be 'respected' but also 'protected', thus enunciating a clear promotional indication. The Italian Constitution, as will be said later, does not provide a specific rule on dignity, but explicitly refers to it in various provisions, such as in Art 3 ('equal social dignity'), Art 36 ('dignified existence') and Art 41 ('human dignity'). Some of the main national and international studies on human dignity are the following: O Schachter, 'Human Dignity as a Normative Concept' (1983) 77 *American Journal of International Law* 848; G Alpa, 'Dignità. Usi giurisprudenziali e confini concettuali' (1997) *Nuova giurisprudenza civile commentata* 415. P Grossi, 'Dignità umana e libertà nella Carta dei diritti fondamentali dell'Unione europea' in M Siclari (ed), *Contributi allo studio della Carta dei diritti fondamentali dell'Unione europea* (Torino, Giappichelli, 2003) 41; P Grossi, 'La dignità nella costituzione italiana' (2008) *Diritto e società* 31; F Viola, 'Dignità umana' in *Enciclopedia filosofica* (2006) 2863; F Sacco, 'Note sulla dignità umana nel "diritto costituzionale europeo"' in S Panunzio (ed), *I diritti fondamentali e le Corti in Europa* (Napoli, Jovene, 2005) 600; D Schefold, 'La dignità umana' in S Panunzio (ed), *I costituzionalisti e la tutela dei diritti nelle Corti europee* (Padova, CEDAM, 2007) 55; A Pirozzoli, *Il valore costituzionale della dignità. Un' introduzione* (Roma, Aracne, 2007); G Piepoli, 'Tutela della dignità e ordinamento della società secolare in Italia' in *Studi in onore di Nicolò Lipari* (Milano, Giuffrè, 2008); P Becchi, *Il principio dignità umana* (Brescia, Morcelliana, 2009); S Hennette Vauchez, 'Une dignitas humaine: vieilles outres, vin nouveau' (2009) *Droits. Revue française de théorie juridique* 59; G Resta, *Dignità, persona e mercati* (Torino, Giappichelli, 2014); L Vincenti, *Diritti e dignità umana* (Roma-Bari, Laterza, 2009); G Azzoni, 'Dignità umana e diritto privato' (2012) *Ragion pratica* 75; G Terlizzi, *Dal buon costume alla dignità della persona. Percorsi di una clausola generale* (Napoli, Edizioni Scientifiche Italiane, 2013); C McCrudden (ed), *Understanding Human Dignity* (Oxford, Oxford University Press, 2013) 393ff; A Barak, *Human Dignity. The Constitutional Value and the Constitutional Right* (Cambridge, Cambridge University Press, 2015); G Repetto, 'La dignità umana e la sua dimensione nel diritto costituzionale europeo' (2016) *Diritto pubblico* 247; P De Sena, 'Dignità umana in senso oggettivo e diritto internazionale' (2017) *Diritti umani e diritto internazionale* 573; L Ferrajoli, 'Dignità e libertà' (2019) *Rivista di filosofia del diritto* 23.

the content of which is likely to change gradually over time with the evolution of customs and with social sensitivity filtered, as is inevitable, by judicial evaluation.

These brief considerations are already sufficient to highlight the importance of reflecting upon the issue of the role and evolution of the concept of human dignity in the Euro-unitarian dimension.

II. THE DEBATED RELATIONSHIP BETWEEN PUBLIC POLICY AND MORALITY IN THE ITALIAN LEGAL SYSTEM

The irruption of fundamental principles into the exercise of economic freedoms in general, and negotiating autonomy in particular, means that the new delineation of public policy comes to include the reasons and the scope of relevance of protection of human dignity. As will be demonstrated through analysis of an interesting jurisprudential case study, today a strong link exists between public order and human dignity. Indeed, the concept of public order no longer refers only to the abstract and generalised individual as a component of society, but has gradually opened up to include within it the more dynamic and complex concept of the person with their set of fundamental values, starting with human dignity.[3]

To understand the results of this evolution, it is worth looking first the law data.

Evidently, even if we stop at considering mere constitutional data, which – as is known – refers back to international and supranational principles, coordination between Articles 2 and 41(2) of the Italian Constitution requires a rethink of the institutions of contract law in a key of necessary consistency with the foundations of personalism. Dignity in this way – as has been perspicaciously observed for years – takes on the function of an 'internal limit that configures every subjective situation', founding the 'construction of a European model of society and market'.[4]

From this perspective, it is necessary, first and foremost, to highlight the debated relationship between the concepts of public policy and morality in the Italian legal system.

Despite the fact that in the Italian legal system the concept of morality continues to be officially a rule of contract invalidity, recently it has tended to fade and lose its autonomous role, being progressively confused with the concept of public policy.

[3] The affirmation of constitutional principles and values of a personal nature determines the assumption of a commitment by the public authorities to intervene not only to protect the individual rights of individuals, but also and above all to promote the rights of the person and of their dignity as a guarantee of their full manifestation. The Constitution therefore expresses 'a vision that places at the center not so much the individual understood as a being in his/her own right, isolated from the social context of reference, but the human person in his/her social relationships, the centre of attribution of rights and duties; and a guarantee not only of "security from" potential intrusions into individual spheres of freedom, but also of the "security of" being able to fully express one's personality, through the constitutional patrimony of rights and within the context of (and not regardless of) the social context of reference' (these words belong to TF Giupponi, 'La sicurezza e le sue "dimensioni" costituzionali' in S Vida (ed), *Diritti umani. Trasformazioni e reazioni* (Bologna, Bononia University Press, 2009) 275).

[4] See G Vettori, 'La disciplina generale del contratto nel tempo presente' (2004) *Rivista di diritto privato* 313.

It is therefore interesting to recall the two main factors that contribute to the tendency described.

First and foremost, it is a long-established and shared observation that the prevailing secular and pluralist connotation of today's society, together with the crisis of cognitivism, make it very difficult to hypothesise – and all the more difficult to make objective in rational argumentative paths – a unitary collective conscience, which would not then be an arbitrary generalisation of moral axiology or customs practised by particular groups or classes.

Nor has it been helpful in this sense to link morality to the fundamental canons of public and private honesty, since in this way it is superimposed on good faith and correctness, which, despite some uncertainties, operate on a different level with respect to the criteria of validity. Moreover, they are in many ways incompatible even with the different, controversial and increasingly uncertain *rationes* that, from time to time, are adduced to justify the traditional discipline of non-repetition of immoral transactions under Article 2035 of the Italian Civil Code.

This has led to the idea that morality, far from being an expression of extra-legal values – transcendent or sociologically grounded – is a concept that, in the axiological context outlined by constitutional and European Union principles, has now undergone a process of substantial legalisation: in other words, it has taken on the features of a criterion firmly enshrined in those principles.

On this point, in my opinion, negative judgements with respect to this process – almost as if it were a neo-positivistic drift or, worse, a manifestation of legal absolutism, albeit authoritatively expressed[5] – cannot be shared. Quite the contrary is the case. The latitude and pervasiveness of purely constitutional principles – if understood, as seems necessary, in their material meaning – emphasise their aptitude to support changes in the legal system induced by the factual dimension of socio-economic and cultural contexts. At the same time, this makes them suitable for incorporating the contents of international and supranational legal sources. After all, in the complex network of super-ordination and equi-ordination between principles, it is precisely the balancing characterising their implementation that partakes of the characteristics of hermeneutics: with the consequence that they too are inevitably imbued with the factuality that the latter presupposes.[6]

As already mentioned, the second and concurrent factor is given by the parallel evolution of the notion of public policy.[7] This takes place along two complementary lines.

[5] Above all, see R Sacco 'I buoni costumi (la nozione)' in R Sacco and G De Nova, *Il contratto*, 4th edn (Torino, UTET, 2016) 1003ff.

[6] Unrivalled, in the reflection on Paolo Grossi's pages, is the analysis of hermeneutic factuality and effectiveness carried out by G Benedetti, '"Ritorno al diritto" ed ermeneutica dell'effettività' in G Benedetti, *Oltre l'incertezza. Un cammino di ermeneutica giuridica* (Bologna, Il Mulino, 2020) 109, 126ff; and, more generally, G Benedetti, *Oggettività esistenziale dell'interpretazione* (Torino, Giappichelli, 2014).

[7] On the concept of public policy see *ex multis*: L Paladin, 'Ordine pubblico' in *Nuovissimo Digesto italiano XII* (1965) 130; A Guarnieri, *L'ordine pubblico e il sistema delle fonti del diritto civile* (Padova, CEDAM, 1974); A Guarnieri, 'Ordine pubblico' in *Digesto delle Discipline Privatistiche*, 4th edn (1995) 155; U Allegretti, 'Ordine pubblico e libertà costituzionali' (1976) *Rivista trimestrale di diritto pubblico* 486; GB Ferri, 'Ordine pubblico (dir. priv.)' in *Enciclopedia del Diritto*, XXX (1980) 1040; GB Ferri, 'L'ordine pubblico economico (a proposito di una recente pubblicazione)' now in GB Ferri, *Saggi di diritto civile* (Rimini, Maggioli, 1983) 341; G Panza, 'Ordine pubblico – I) Teoria generale' in *Enciclopedia Giuridica*

First of all, it appeared freed from the original traces of statism and is now identified with the founding principles of the legal system. However, on this point, clarification is of fundamental importance.

Principles assume an extraordinary latitude and a natural dynamism if understood in their twofold sense, which seems to me to be correct: that is, on the one hand as hierarchically superordinate principles, because they are of constitutional relevance in the broad sense; and on the other, as principles derivable from the *rationes* of the total aggregation of positive choices of the ordinary legislator.

Thus, while the former grounds the content of public policy by deduction, the latter feeds it inductively through generalisation of the foundations of legislative policies that follow one another over time.

The process of disarticulation of public policy – net of the obvious relativity of any schematism – is now articulated into economic and non-economic public policy, of direction or protection, and knows sector specifications in every sphere of the relevance of autonomy. So it is also relevant in the sense of favouring its attractiveness.

In this context, it becomes plausible to sustain, on the one hand, the decay – if not yet the abrogation, as has happened elsewhere – of morality as a criterion of validity; and on the other, absorption of the spheres of application of morality into that of non-economic public policy, otherwise known as moral or philanthropic.[8]

The consequent convergence of the rules concretely operating towards a bipartite criterion of validity – imperative norms and public policy – is then increasingly similar, beyond the nominalistic *trompe l'oeil* and the many peculiarities of each system, to the system proper to the German *gute Sitten*[9] or the public policy of common law.[10]

Ultimately, as far as is relevant here, it can be said that abandonment of the notion of morality in no way implies the complete overcoming of the logic underlying this clause, but rather its evolution into a different criterion, more compatible with today's secular and pluralistic societies.[11] A criterion in which, on a symbolic level,

Treccani XXII (1995) 5ff; L Lonardo, *Ordine pubblico e illiceità del contratto* (Napoli, Edizioni Scientifiche Italiane, 1993); G D'Amico, 'Ordine pubblico e illiceità contrattuale' in F Di Marzio (ed), *Illiceità, immeritevolezza, nullità* (Napoli, Edizioni Scientifiche Italiane, 2004) 34; F Caroccia, *Ordine pubblico. La gestione dei conflitti culturali nel diritto privato* (Jovene, Napoli, 2018); G Perlingieri and G Zarra, *Ordine pubblico interno e internazionale tra caso concreto e sistema ordinamentale* (Napoli, Edizioni Scientifiche Italiane, 2019).

[8] D Carusi, 'Prestazione (immoralità della)' in *Enciclopedia giuridica Treccani* (2003) 3ff.

[9] The concept of *gute Sitten*, as elaborated by German jurisprudence, is by no means limited to the perspective of morality, but includes the perspective of the constitutional principles of the system. Indeed, it is well known that the German legal system, unlike the French and Italian legal systems, does not use tripartition of the criteria for the validity of a contract, but, in continuity with Roman law, distinguishes only between illegal and immoral agreements. *cf* K Simitis, *Gute Sitten und ordre public* (Marburg, NG Elwert, 1960); W Flume, *Allgemeiner Teil des bürgerlichen Rechts. Band 2. Das Rechtsgeschäft* (Berlin, Springer, 1965) 365ff; F Wieacker, *Storia del diritto privato moderno: con particolare riguardo alla Germania*, II (Milano, Giuffrè, 1980) 31ff; Terlizzi (n 2) 71ff; A Guarneri, 'La scomparsa delle *bonnes moeurs* dal diritto contrattuale francese' (2017) *Nuova giurisprudenza civile commentata* 404ff.

[10] On this point see again Guarneri (n 9) 5ff. With specific reference to the concept of public policy in the common law system see: GH Treitel, *The Law of Contract*, 4th edn (London, Stevens and Sons, 1975) 278; D Lloyd, *Public Policy – A Comparative Study in English and French Law* (London, University of London Press, 1953); J Chitty, *Chitty on Contracts, I, General Principles*, 24th edn (London, Sweet and Maxwell, 1977) 954.

[11] The evolution of the concept of morality towards protection of human dignity, as a principle that nourishes the content of public order, is cross-sectional to many subjects, moving away from the narrow

substitution of the 'values of the individual' for customs, which, even if good, are evidently the 'product of society',[12] is not in doubt. However, it is a different matter, which nevertheless has relevant implications, whether these values of the individual are to be understood in a subjective or objective key.[13] I will shortly return to this point, including through case law.

III. EXERCISE OF ECONOMIC FREEDOMS AND THE DIGNITY LIMIT

In the light of the above considerations, it is necessary to reflect upon the relationship between individual contract autonomy and the principle of dignity. As the case law shows, European judges usually evoke the principle of dignity as a limit to the exercise of economic freedom with the specific purpose of strengthening protection of the human person. So analysis of the most significant decisions of the courts of some

sphere of sexuality and matrimonial and religious choices and ending up including the matter of the end of life, of decisions in the health sphere, of those connected with making one's body available. With special regard to the latter, they flow into the contractual matter that is the subject of this contribution, to the extent that such choices form, as it happens, the subject of a contractual agreement. The subject has been delved into, among others, by: U Breccia, *Il contratto in generale* (Torino, Giappichelli, 1999) 178; G Resta, 'Contratto e persona' in V Roppo (ed), *Trattato del contratto VI. Interferenze* (Milano, Giuffrè, 2006) 15, who observes: 'Oggi anche a seguito della crescente valorizzazione dei principi di dignità e di autodeterminazione, i quali hanno trasformato l'ordine pubblico di protezione in un ordine pubblico "filantropico", tale postulato non ha più un significato univoco, ma si atteggia in maniera differente a seconda della particolare tipologia dei beni e degli interessi coinvolti' ['Today, also as a result of the increasing valorisation of the principles of dignity and self-determination, which have transformed the public order of protection into a "philanthropic" public order, this postulate no longer has a univocal meaning, but takes on a different guise depending on the particular type of goods and interests involved']; M Robles, 'La rilevanza del buon costume nel diritto privato attuale' (2010) *Rivista di diritto privato* 83, 110ff; A Nicolussi, 'Autonomia privata e diritti della persona' in *Enciclopedia del diritto* (2011) 133. See, for Italian case law: Corte Cass, 1 August 1986 n 4927 (1987) *Il Foro italiano* I 494ff; Corte Cass, 8 June 1993 n 6381 (1994) *Nuova giurisprudenza civile commentata* 339; Corte Cass, 15 February 2001 n 7523 (2001) *Diritto fallimentare* 1190; Corte Cass, 21 December 2012 n 13713 (2013) *I Contratti* 223.

[12] See Terlizzi (n 2) 145: 'Decency recalls the tradition and values of a community; and it is this that helps us understand the symbolic value of its elimination. The appeal to the dignity of the individual is the answer to the difficulty of recognising, in the face of social pluralism, the customs of a community with a homogeneous basis' (translated by the author); Nicolussi (n 11) 146ff.

[13] The concept of human dignity can be interpreted in two different ways. In the subjective sense, dignity coincides with the self-determination of each subject and responds to the fundamental protection of the person with respect to the hetero-determination of their choices. However, there is an obvious risk of relativism and, in some ways, difficulty in applying such an approach, which ends up legitimising as many definitions of dignity as there are points of view, emptying it of operational significance. On the other hand, in its objective meaning, although necessarily free from metaphysical or simply natural law interpretations, dignity appears to be freed from the will of the individual, and to be identified rather with the axiological recognition shared by the members of a given community, the expression of legally relevant collective values, and also the source – in a clear though not always conscious Kantian derivation – of the duties of individuals towards the communities to which they belong. On that point, which goes beyond the scope of this reflection, although it constitutes a fundamental juncture of the matter, see, among many others: J Waldron, 'Dignity Rank and Rights: The 2009 Tanner Lectures at UC Berkeley' (2009) New York University Public Law and Legal Theory Working Papers, 151, tannerlectures.utah.edu/_resources/documents/a-to-z/w/Waldron_09.pdf; S Hennette-Vauchez, 'A human *dignitas*? Remnants of the ancient legal concept in contemporary dignity jurisprudence' (2011) 9 *International Journal of Constitutional Law* 32; M Di Ciommo, *Dignità umana e Stato costituzionale. La dignità umana nel costituzionalismo europeo* (Firenze, Passigli, 2010); G Monaco, 'La tutela della dignità umana: sviluppi giurisprudenziali e difficoltà applicative' (2011) *Politica del diritto* 45; C Le Bris, *L'humanité saisie par le droit international public* (Paris, Librairie générale de droit et de jurisprudence, 2012); De Sena (n 2) 573ff; Ferrajoli (n 2) 23ff.

Member States is a fundamental step towards understanding under what conditions they use the principle of dignity.

First of all, aside from the well-known 1981 case of the German Federal Administrative Court on peep-shows,[14] it is crucial to bring to mind significant French decisions on prohibition of the full veil (*burqa*) in public places. In particular, this case law expresses the contrast between two superior courts: on the one side, the Council of State,[15] which opposes the ban because it conflicts with the principle of dignity, subjectively interpreted, and, more specifically, with the dignity of the woman who individually chooses to wear the *burqa*; and on the other side, the Constitutional Council, for its part, affirms the necessity of the ban in a democratic society, precisely to protect the dignity of women, this time interpreted according to the objective dimension, in coherence with republican values of freedom and equality.[16]

The same conflict also emerges in a well-known case that is even more relevant with reference to analysis of the relationship between dignity and economic freedom: this case decided by the French Council of State in 1995 concerned the so-called 'launching of the dwarf'.[17] This case expresses exactly the dignity/freedoms antithesis from the perspective of the inalienability of dignity once again interpreted in an objectified sense. According to the decision under examination, dignity, conceived as an objective value, is not alienable and thus is liable to prevail over other fundamental freedoms. Consequently, it is represented as a standard that is not based on an individual subject, but on humanity as a whole, in order to protect the entire collectivity;[18] hence, it ends up representing a synthesis between freedom and equality.[19]

[14] See BVerwG, 15 December 1981 (1982) *Neue Juristische Wochenschrift (NJW)* 664. See further BVerwG, 30 January 1990 (1990) *Juristen Zeitung (JZ)* 382. In these pronouncements, the German courts affirm the primacy of the dignity of the person over a woman's expression of consent, this being an 'objective and inalienable value' that cannot be validly renounced. On this issue see T Discher, 'Die Peep-Show-Urteile des BverwG' (1991) *Juristische Schulung* 642.

[15] See Conseil d'État, 'Étude relative aux possibilités juridiques d'interdiction du port du voile intégral' (report to the Prime Minister on 20 March 2010), www.conseil-etat.fr/publications-colloques/etudes/etude-relative-aux-possibilites-juridiques-d-interdiction-du-port-du-voile-integral.

[16] See Conseil Constitutionnel, decision n 2010-613, 7 October 2010, *Journal Officiel*, 12 October 2010, 18345 n 2 ECLI:FR:CC:2010:2010.613.DC. With reference to this issue see: M Verpeaux, 'Dissimulation du visage, la délicate conciliation entre la liberté et un nouvel ordre public' (2010) *L'Actualité Juridique Droit Administratif* 2373; A Gaillet, 'La loi interdisant la dissimulation du visage dans l'espace public et les limites du contrôle pratiqué par le Conseil constitutionnel' (2012) 2 *Société, Droit et Religion* 47; MC Amorosi, 'L'ordine pubblico nell'esperienza francese' (2018) *Politica del Diritto* 22, who notes that, according to some scholars, this approach of French constitutional jurisprudence leads to a return to a moral conception of public order.

[17] See Conseil d'État, Ass, 27 October 1995 (1996) *Recueil Dalloz* 177: 'Considérant qu'il appartient à l'autorité investie du pouvoir de police municipale de prendre toute mesure pour prévenir une atteinte à l'ordre public; que le respect de la dignité de la personne humaine est une des composantes de l'ordre public; que l'autorité investie du pouvoir de police municipale peut, même en l'absence de circonstances locales particulières, interdire une attraction qui porte atteinte au respect de la dignité de la personne humaine.' ['Whereas it is up to the municipal police authority to take any measure to prevent a breach of public order; whereas respect for the dignity of the human person is one of the components of public order; whereas the municipal police authority may, even in the absence of particular local circumstances, prohibit an attraction that undermines respect for the dignity of the human person.'].

[18] With the same opinion, G Resta, 'La disponibilità dei diritti fondamentali e i limiti della dignità. Note a margine della Carta dei Diritti' (2002) *Rivista di diritto civile* 801.

[19] See S Rodotà, *Il diritto di avere diritti* (Roma, Laterza, 2012) 184–85. The enunciation of the principle of dignity within the Charter of Rights bears witness to what Rodotà calls 'the true legacy of post-war constitutionalism': 'If the "revolution of equality" had been the hallmark of modernity, the "revolution of

The question whether dignity can be balanced is therefore of crucial importance.

The more restrictive interpretative approach seems today to be receding with respect to the consideration that the content and amplitude of dignity, if removed from any metaphysics, can only be determined in relational terms, as European case law itself provides.[20] It is precisely the Court of Justice – before[21] and after the Lisbon Treaty – that is definitely in favour of the admissibility of balancing.

Just a few examples can be useful.

With reference to the *Schmidberger* case of 2003, a fundamental right prevails over economic freedom.[22] Schmidberger is a German transport company that brought an action before the court complaining about having been hampered from the exercise of its business by a demonstration of an environmental association on a section of the Brenner motorway as granted by authorisation of the Republic of Austria. The company claimed compensation from the Republic of Austria for damages deriving from infringement of the freedom of movement of goods set by Article 34 TFEU. Although infringement of the principle of free movement seems to be realised from a theoretical point of view, that infringement, according to the Court of Justice, is to be regarded as fully justified due to 'measures incompatible with respect for human rights' recognised by the constitutional traditions of each of the Member States and by international treaties, starting with the ECHR.

Similarly, in the *Omega* case of 2004, respect for human dignity prevails over the free movement of services and goods, operating as a limit to self-determination.[23] In this case, the Court of Justice was asked to verify whether the decision, taken by the *Bundesverwaltungsgericht*, to prohibit a murder simulation game, albeit in accordance with German law, was contrary to the following principles: freedom to provide services and free circulation of goods provided for respectively by Articles 28 and 49 of the EEC Treaty (now Articles 34 and 56 TFEU). The Court of Justice

dignity" marks a new time, it is the child of the tragic twentieth century, it opens the era of the relationship between the person, science and technology' (translated by the author). Dignity is thus conceived as a 'synthesis of freedom and equality', or rather, as a concept aimed at integrating the fundamental principles of freedom, equality and solidarity.

[20] See G Resta, 'La Dignità' in K Seelman and P Becchi (ed), *Dalla bioetica al biodiritto* (Napoli, Bibliopolis, 2007) 283.

[21] In this connection, one is reminded of the judgment in the *Wachauf* case in which the Court of Justice stated that 'the fundamental rights recognised by the Court are not, however, absolute, but must be considered in relation to their social function. Consequently, restrictions may be imposed on the exercise of those rights, in particular in the context of a common organisation of a market, provided that those restrictions in fact correspond to objectives of general interest pursued by the Community and do not constitute, with regard to the aim pursued, in a disproportionate and intolerable interference, impairing the very substance of those rights' (Case C-5/88 *Wachauf v Bundesamt für Ernährung und Forstwirtschaft* ECLI:EU:C:1989:321 [18]). The Court ruled on the compatibility between the prohibition on disseminating information on the possibility of terminating a pregnancy in Art 40 of the Irish Constitution and the freedom to provide services guaranteed by Art 59 of the Treaty of Rome, which would include the freedom to provide termination of pregnancy. The Court held that the activity of termination of pregnancy constitutes a 'service' that cannot be impeded by national legislation.

[22] Case C-112/2000 *Eugen Schmidberger, Internationale Transporte und Planzüge v Republik Österreich* ECLI:EU:C:2003:333.

[23] Case C-36/02 *Omega Spielhallen- und Automatenaufstellungs-GmbH v Oberbürgermeisterin der Bundesstadt Bonn* ECLI:EU:C:2004:614. For a comment see ME Gennusa, 'La dignità umana vista da Lussemburgo' (2005) *Quaderni costituzionali* 174.

confirmed the decision, respecting the need to protect the principle of human dignity as provided by Article 1 of the *Grundgesetz* and, at the same time, complying with the core principles of the European system, according to which respect for fundamental rights is also capable of restraining lawfully fundamental economic freedoms. In particular, according to the Court of Justice, 'Community law does not preclude an economic activity consisting in the commercial exploitation of games simulating murder from being prohibited by a national measure adopted on grounds of the protection of public order because that activity violates human dignity'.[24]

In other cases, European case law balances both dignity and the needs of the market in a different way, letting economic freedoms prevail over the right to strike. In particular, according to the Court of Justice in the *Viking* case, freedom of establishment prevails over the right to strike, even though the latter represents a fundamental right forming part of the general principles of European law.[25] On the basis of the reasoning of the judgment, such a right, from the European perspective, would be relevant only as a restriction on freedom of establishment guaranteed by European law; at the same time, even if it appears justified in the abstract, it must be subjected to the conditions deriving from the principle of proportionality. Consequently, with reference to this case, collective action by the trade unions cannot be considered proportionate. In sum, recognition of freedom of establishment or of freedom to provide services restricts the possibility of exercise of a right recognised by national constitutions.

However, human dignity once again becomes an insurmountable limit in the field of biotechnological inventions. This offers proof of the consideration that dignity, far from having a sole meaning, is 'enacted upon in different ways depending on the particular type of goods and interests involved'.[26] Meaningful, in this regard, is the 2011 case *Oliver Brüstle v Greenpeace eV*.[27]

[24] Case C-36/02 (ibid) [41].

[25] See Case C-438/05 *International Transport Workers Federation and Finnish Seamen's Union v Viking Line ABP and OÜ Viking Line Eesti* ECLI:EU:C:2007:772. See also, in an even more restrictive sense, Case C-341/05 *Laval un Partneri* ECLI:EU:C:2007:809, in which the Court ruled that exercise of the right to strike in the present case (concerning the posting of workers in the context of transnational provision of services) could not even be regarded as pursuing ends worthy of protection. On this subject see: MV Ballestrero, 'Le sentenze Viking e Laval: la Corte di Giustizia "bilancia" il diritto di sciopero' in (2008) *Lavoro e diritto* 389; R Zahn, 'The Viking and Laval Cases in the Context of the European Enlargement' (2008) *Web Journal of Current Legal Issues*.

[26] See Resta (n 11) 15ff.

[27] Case C-34/10 *Oliver Brüstle v Greenpeace eV* ECLI:EU:C:2011:669. The Court notes that, according to its preamble, Directive 98/44/EC (Directive 98/44/EC of the European Parliament and of the Council of 6 July 1998 on the legal protection of biotechnological inventions [1998] OJ L213/13) aims to encourage investments in the field of biotechnology; however, exploitation of biological material of human origin must be carried out with respect for fundamental rights and, in particular, human dignity. According to Recital 16, patent law must be exercised with respect for fundamental principles that guarantee human dignity and integrity. Thus, it is relevant that in the light of the fundamental value of dignity, 'any human ovum from fertilisation, any unfertilised human ovum into which the nucleus of a mature human cell has been implanted and any unfertilised human ovum which, by parthenogenesis, has been induced to divide and develop' is to be regarded as a human embryo; that the prohibition on patenting 'uses of human embryos for industrial or commercial purposes' (Art 6(2)(c) of the Directive on the legal protection of biotechnological inventions) is to be interpreted as prohibiting the use of human embryos for industrial or commercial purposes. Art 2(c) of the Directive on the legal protection on biotechnological inventions includes uses for research purposes since 'the fact of granting a patent to an invention implies, in principle,

Even in Italy, despite the lack of an explicit constitutional provision on human dignity, the case law of the Constitutional Court has long developed an interpretative approach aimed at enhancing the implicit or explicit references present in the constitutional text, starting from Articles 2, 3, 41, 36 and 32(2) of the Constitution. According to this approach, human dignity and the value of human individuals are supreme principles of the constitutional order. Sometimes, dignity is not absolutely part of the balancing with other principles, but in other cases it tends to be relativised to the extent that the unconditional prevalence of the 'essential core' of fundamental rights is upheld.

Despite the restriction of the visual angle only to rulings concerning limits on economic freedoms, the Court has on several occasions affirmed that any restrictions on freedom of economic initiative must be justified by interests of constitutional rank.[28] However, identification of those interests should not appear arbitrary and they should not be pursued by clearly incongruous measures.[29] The balancing rule is embedded in what has been described, and precisely with reference to the principle of proportionality. Therefore, constitutional judges express the tendency to admit a necessary balancing between constitutionally recognised interests, while at the same time affirming the existence of an essential and inalienable core of fundamental rights that cannot be compressed. According to this approach, fundamental rights may well be balanced against other values, but only if this sacrifice answers needs which are particularly deserving of protection – that is, by the need to reconcile these rights with others, such as those expressed by the market – provided that the inalienable core is never harmed.

In the same direction stands the idea that the Constitutional Court has the task of ensuring maintenance of respect for the essential core of fundamental rights.

the industrial and commercial exploitation of that invention' and, therefore, in the present case, of the embryos used; that it is therefore contrary to the value of dignity (and therefore cannot be the subject of a patent) for a process to use biological starting material obtainable only by the prior destruction of human embryos. For a comment on the *Olivier Brüstle* decision: V Altamore, *La tutela dell'embrione tra interpretazione giudiziale e sviluppi della ricerca scientifica, in una recente sentenza della Corte di Giustizia europea (C-34/10 Olivier Brüstle v Greenpeace eV)* (2011) Forum di Quaderni costituzionali (2 December 2011), www.forumcostituzionale.it/wordpress/?p=3266; R Conti and R Foglia, 'Protezione giuridica delle invenzioni biotecnologiche e nozione di embrione umano' (2011) *Corriere giuridico* 1733 (case note to *Olivier Brüstle*, above). For a partially different opinion see: Case C-377/98 *Netherlands v Parliament and Council* ECLI:EU:C:2001:523. On this issue see: S Gobbato, 'Direttiva sulle invenzioni biotecnologiche ed obblighi internazionali degli Stati membri nella sentenza della Corte di Giustizia' (2002) *Il Diritto dell'Unione Europea* 519.

[28] See Corte Cost, decision of 20 July 2012 n 199 ECLI:IT:COST:2012:199, www.federalismi.it. With this decision, the Constitutional Court intended to dictate certain principles in economic matters oriented towards development of competition. Having reaffirmed the principle that in the economic sphere 'everything that is not expressly forbidden by law is permitted', it states that the task of the (state and regional) legislature is to 'maintain forms of regulation of economic activity aimed at guaranteeing, among others – in addition to compliance with international and EU obligations and full observance of the constitutional principles linked to the protection of health, the environment, cultural heritage and public finance – in particular the protection of safety, freedom, human dignity, to safeguard the social utility of every economic activity, as Art 41 Const. requires'. The Court clarifies that the general principle of liberalisation of economic activities requires that 'any restrictions and limitations on free economic initiative must find precise justification in interests of constitutional rank or in the further interests that the State legislature has listed in Article 3(1)' (translated by the author).

[29] See Corte Cost, decision of 10 March 2015 n 56 ECLI:IT:COST:2015:56, www.federalismi.it.

Consequently, for example, budget needs can compress the fundamental right to welfare under Article 38 of the Constitution and even the right to health under Article 32 of the Constitution, but not their essential core, the 'hard core' of fundamental rights.[30]

Not surprisingly, the Constitutional Court has applied the balancing rule in several decisions concerning Article 41 of the Constitution, with reference to protection of workers' dignity. This means that employer autonomy is subject to the limit of protection of dignity, but only within the borders of intangibility of the inalienable core of fundamental rights; beyond the latter, evidently, there can be space for balancing the values of dignity and economic freedom, which are opposed in this context.[31]

IV. FINAL REMARKS

The considerations in this chapter show that protection of human dignity in contract matters is bound to play a specific role with reference to the European perspective.

According to the preceptive meaning of Article 1 of the Nice Charter, human dignity is an inviolable principle which fulfils the function of an interior limit for each subjective situation. Violation of this limit may imply nullity of contract, as well as contract non-performance or compensation for damages.

In any case, even if no longer included in the concept of morality because it is related to public policy, the principle of dignity plays a crucial role for 'the edification of an European model of society and market'.[32] Consequently, it is clear that a new concept of public policy is emerging, mainly directed towards promoting and protecting human dignity. The more dignity assumes relevance within specific cases, the more it is possible to restrict the exercise of economic – and thus contract – freedom any time the latter is not lawful. Even if, as previously noted, the concept of dignity is difficult to define, undoubtedly it involves a wider field of application than the concept of morality. This latter concerns usages and habits of a society in a specific historical period, while dignity concerns the fundamental values of human beings.

[30] See Corte Cost, decision of 10 May 2012 n 119, ECLI:IT:COST:2012:119, www.federalismi.it: 'the demands of public finance cannot assume, in the legislature's balancing act, such a preponderant weight as to compress the irreducible core of the right to health protected by the Constitution as an inviolable sphere of human dignity' (translated by the author).

[31] See Corte Cost 11 February 1988 n 159 (1988) *Giurisprudenza costituzionale* 553; Corte Cost 15 May 1990 n 241 ECLI:IT:COST:1990:241 (1991) *Rassegna di diritto civile* 613; Corte Cost 30 June 1994 n 268, ECLI:IT:COST:1994:268 (1995) *Giurisprudenza italiana* 588. A remarkable judgment, albeit in the different and controversial field of biomedicine issues, is Corte Cost 9 March 2021 n 33 ECLI:IT:COST:2021:33 (2021) *Giurisprudenza Costituzionale* 357, with case note by F Astone, *Procreazione di coppie same sex e status dei figli: un problema di discrezionalità legislativa?* (ibid 357); F Rimoli, 'Diritto all'omogenitorialità, best interest of the child e famiglia "naturale": un problema ancora irrisolto' (2021) *Giurisprudenza Costituzionale* 339; G Ferrando, 'La Corte costituzioanle riconosce il diritto dei figli di due mamme o di due papà ad avere due genitori' (2021) *Famiglia e diritto* 704; MC Venuti, 'Diritti dei figli vs. genitorialità same-sex: antitesi o composizione? Il dialogo (muto?) tra la Corte costituzionale e il legislatore italiano' (2021) *Nuova giurisprudenza civile commentata* 949. This judgment, in the matter of surrogacy, starting from the relationship of mutual integration between all fundamental rights, assumes the necessary balance between protection of the dignity of the woman and the child's interest.

[32] See G Vettori, *Diritto dei contratti e 'Costituzione' europea. Regole e principi ordinanti* (Milano, Giuffrè, 2005) 29ff.

Ultimately, the tendency to include human dignity within the concept of public order realises the goal of increasing the commitment undertaken by States to promote the human person, so as to guarantee the building of a (European) society whose development is truly inspired by the binomial 'person and market'. The latter is to be understood in the sense that legitimate expression of freedom of private economic initiative cannot be separated from respect for the fundamental rights of the person; with consequent rebounds of this on the validity criteria of contracts, as indeed is well illustrated by the jurisprudential cases cited.

It is clear that, in this perspective, judges play a crucial role in defining the meanings and the field of application of the principle of dignity which in turn allows constant evolution of its contents and constant adaptation to changes within society.

18

The Human Person and Data: Beyond the Individualistic Approach

GIORGIO RESTA

I. THE PERSON, DATA AND DIGITAL TRANSITION

THE RELATIONSHIP BETWEEN a human person and their data is among the most important questions of the law of personality rights. Generally, this question has been approached starting from two main assumptions, which sometimes remain unexpressed. The first is the idea that data are an immaterial extension of the personality and that they relate to one specific individual. The second is the concern that free flow data could be dangerous to the interests of the person; so the main objective of any data law should be to reduce the volume of data available and strictly control the conditions of data processing. These assumptions were widely shared at the time of the first data protection schemes, but they are facing serious challenges in the context of digital transition. Data are to a large extent relational data, as the example of the social network clearly highlights; above all, data-sharing in modern democracies has become an imperative no less important than data protection. The EU is an interesting laboratory in which to try to perceive the future shape of relationships between the person and their data. A new paradigm of data governance is on the rise, but so far sufficient clarity is lacking on how to coordinate the previous framework with the current tendencies of data law. Looking at the literature on the topic might single out three main alternative approaches to the problems of data control:[1] a) public ownership; b) individual data control; and c) commons or collective ownership with fiduciary connotations.

This chapter is not intended to present arguments for or against a particular approach, but rather to investigate recent transformations in European data law that have this debate in mind. The aim is to show that no holistic model is possible or

[1] M Micheli et al, 'Emerging models of data governance in the age of datafication' (2020) 7 *Big Data and Society* 1; S Ranchordás and A Klop, 'Data-driven regulation and governance in smart cities' in A Berlee et al, *Research Handbook in Data Science and Law* (Cheltenham-Northampton, Edward Elgar, 2018) 245ff; T Scassa, 'Designing Data Governance for Data Sharing: Lessons from Sidewalk Toronto' (2020) *Technology and Regulation* 44ff.

desirable because in most digital relations the three different nodes of public, private and collective are deeply intertwined. Any modern data law is therefore called upon to balance such dimensions, finding a proper regulatory space for state agencies, individuals and collective actors. The evolution of European data law seems to confirm these assumptions.

II. TRANSFORMATIONS OF EUROPEAN DATA LAW: FROM DATA PROTECTION TO DATA-SHARING

The European data governance system has traditionally paid more attention to concerns framed in terms of data protection over those of data-sharing. The regulatory framework related to the processing of personal data has gained a culturally and axiologically superordinate position, while a comparatively minor role has been played by other segments of data law, such as that concerning access to data, reuse of public sector information, or intellectual property itself (with the specific offshoots of disciplines on protection of databases and industrial secrecy).[2] One could speak, with some simplification, of a unipolar model. The reasons are easy to understand and lie largely in the historical background of legislation on data protection, which has been developed since the 1970s, first within national legal systems and then gradually penetrated by the system of the Council of Europe (Convention 108 of 1981) and the European Union (starting with Directive 95/46/EC).[3] Fifty years of applying the legislation in question have given it a systematic, organic and complete character that cannot be found in any other statutory scheme on control of information.

In addition, on the level of principles, data protection law undoubtedly stands at the top of the system, in line with a public discourse that has always emphasised the link between these guarantees and post-war constitutionalism, which arose from the rubble of twentieth-century totalitarian experiences. The choice made by the EU Charter of Fundamental Rights to introduce a specific provision on the right to protection of personal data (Article 8) in addition to the right to respect for private life now offers clear testimony to this. All this has resulted in a position of primacy, both in terms of hierarchy of sources, and in terms of completeness of scientific elaboration, of data protection law with respect to other fields of law designed to regulate circulation of information.

It is perhaps not hazardous to foresee that this primacy is gradually destined to break down and give way – for the reasons explained below – to a multipolar model in which concerns in terms of data protection will coexist and enjoy a similar weight to those concerning data access and data reuse. As one author put it, the relevant shift will be from *Datenschutzrecht* to *Datenwirtschaftsrecht*.[4]

[2] T Streinz, 'The Evolution of European Data Law' in P Craig and G de Búrca (eds), *The Evolution of EU Law*, 3rd edn (Oxford, Oxford University Press, 2021) 902, 915; PC Johannes, 'Europäisches Datenrecht – ein Spickzettel' (2022) *Newsdienst der Zeitschrift für Datenschutz – Aktuell* 1166.

[3] S Rodotà, *Tecnologie e diritti*, 2nd edn (Bologna, Il Mulino, 2021).

[4] B Steinrötter, 'Das "Datenwirtschaftsrecht" als neues Teilrechtsgebiet im Recht der Daten. Einführende Bemerkungen zur neuen ZD-Beitragsreihe' (2021) *Newsdienst der Zeitschrift für Datenschutz* 543;

The EU Commission Communication on the 'European strategy for data'[5] seems to embrace just such an evolution. The choices made by the Data Governance Act (DGA), destined to be further integrated and systematised with the Data Act (still at the stage of a Commission proposal), represent a first step in this direction. So it is no coincidence that the DGA is opting for an autonomous definition of 'data'[6] as: 'any digital representation of acts, facts or information and any compilation of such acts, facts or information, including in the form of sound, visual or audiovisual recording' (Article 2(1)).

This formula marks a clear departure from the previous approach, on the one hand because it delineates an *Oberbegriff* capable of encompassing both personal and non-personal data, and on the other because it emphasises the syntactic dimension of data.[7] In other words, while the notion of personal data is centred on the character of the referability of a specific piece of information to a specific individual – the emphasis being on the semantic dimension of data as the bearer of information – the formula accepted by the DGA disregards this aspect and accentuates the idea of the 'encoding' of states of the world through digital representation.[8] In this move a subtle shift is detectable in the logic underlying the discipline in question: it is no longer aimed at pre-establishing a mechanism for safeguarding certain incorporeal goods by reason of the knowledge potential they can release in relation to a person.

What prevails, instead, is the intention to prefigure a system of rules concerning the circulation and use of data in relation to their formal structure (and namely their readability by an automatic system), regardless of the type of meanings they are capable of conveying.[9] On a teleological level, this change in structure is reflected in the shift from an essentially restrictive regulation to one of a promotional nature concerning the use of data.

In short, the new 'data strategy' marks a strong discontinuity in the system of data governance. The pre-existing approach, confronted with the new technological reality of big data and artificial intelligence, has been shown to be deficient from many points of view, but especially from the two perspectives of the absence of incentives to share data (personal and non-personal) and the ineffectiveness of the protection apparatus with respect to the reality of informational capitalism.

As observed by Viktor Mayer Schönberger, statistical findings show that around 85 per cent of the data collected in Europe is not reused.[10] This is common to both the

D Staudenmayer, 'Der Verordnungsvorschlag der Europäischen Kommission zum Datengesetz. Auf dem Weg zum Privatrecht der Datenwirtschaft' (2022) *Europäische Zeitschrift für Wirtschaftsrecht)* 596.

[5] European Commission, 'A European Strategy for Data' (Communication) COM(2020) 66 final.

[6] Before the DGA, EU law only defined 'personal data' (G Resta, 'Towards a unified regime of data-rights? Rapport de synthèse' in T Pertot (ed), *Rechte an Daten* (Tübingen, Mohr Siebeck, 2020) 231, 236).

[7] H Zech, 'Besitz an Daten?' in Pertot (n 6) 21, 91; J Drexl, 'Designing Competitive Markets for Industrial Data. Between Propertisation and Access' (2017) 8 *Journal of Intellectual Property, Information Technology* 257.

[8] See M Martini, 'Datenhoheit. Annäherung an einen offenen Leitbegriff' (2021) *MultiMedia und Recht-Beilage* 3, 4.

[9] B Steinrötter, 'Gegenstand und Bausteine eines EU-Datenwirtschaftsrechts' (2021) *Recht Digital* 480, 481; F Rosenkranz and M Scheufen, 'Die Lizenzierung von nicht-personenbezogenen Daten. Eine rechtliche und rechtsökonomische Analyse' (2022) 2 *Zeitschrift für Digitalisierung und Recht* 159, 168.

[10] T Ramge and V Mayer Schönberger, *Fuori i dati! Rompere i monopoli delle informazioni per rilanciare il progresso* (Milano, Egea, 2021) 39.

personal data sector, which, as the pandemic experience has shown, could be reused more effectively for public interest purposes, such as promoting scientific research and supporting health policies; and *the non-personal data sector*, such as industrial data and data held by public administrations. This represents a de facto restraining factor in terms of innovation, given that this – and the reference is not limited to the industrial sector – is today largely data-driven.

On the other hand, even in the regulatory framework in which the preponderant demand is that of control rather than that of sharing, and in particular of personal data, the regulatory mechanism developed by the European legislator has in some respects proved ineffective in the face of the organisational and market practices that have emerged in the context of the digital economy. In particular, the emphasis placed since Directive 95/46/EC on the mechanism of informed consent as the main legal basis for lawful data processing – alongside other legal bases, listed in Articles 6 and 9 of Regulation 2016/679 – has triggered a process of bureaucratisation of consent in relations with both private and public entities.[11] Above all, in the context of online relations, consent has been translated into that famous 'fig-leaf' that Guido Calabresi and Stefano Rodotà mentioned many years ago, aimed at hiding a highly asymmetrical reality in which the idea of the data subject's self-determination has turned out to be little more than a label with no operational feedback.[12]

Many empirical studies show how so-called privacy policies (information in the language of the legislator) are drafted in such a complex and articulated manner that in the majority of cases (some surveys indicate 75 per cent of cases) they are not even read.[13] Moreover, this is a rational choice, given that the chances of negotiating the terms of data processing are extremely low, allowing for the inclusion of consent in unilaterally predetermined forms (often aimed at regulating other aspects of the contractual relationship, such as a social network service or the management of an email box) and not susceptible to modification except for marginal aspects.[14] Moreover, it has been pointed out that even if the subject is able to express a conscious determination of will in the relationship with the first data controller (primary markets), maximum opacity reigns over the rest of the value chain and hence over subsequent ruse of data (secondary markets).[15] On the other hand, it is clear for all to see that the large digital oligopolies have acquired their boundless market shares precisely thanks to their strategies of extracting value from people's data, regarded as freely appropriable resources.[16] Therefore, one of the most frequent criticisms levelled at the European data protection model is that, while the legislation in question has in

[11] C Wendehorst, S Schwamberger and J Grinzinger, 'Datentreuhand – Wie hilfreich sind sachenrechtliche Konzepte?' in Pertot (n 6) 103ff.

[12] S Rodotà, *Elaboratori elettronici e controllo sociale* (Bologna, Il Mulino, 1973) 47ff, 133; S Rodotà, 'Protezione dei dati e circolazione delle informazioni' now in Rodotà (n 3) 79ff.

[13] TJ Gerpott, 'Datenschutzerklärungen – Materiell fundierte Einwilligungen nach der DS-GVO. Empirischer Forschungsstand und Verbesserungsfelder' (2020) *MultiMedia und Recht* 739.

[14] M Kamp and M Rost, 'Kritik an der Einwilligung. Ein Zwischenruf zu einer fiktiven Rechtsgrundlage in asymmetrischen Machtverhältnissen' (2013) 37 *Datenschutz und Datensicherheit* 80.

[15] Wendehorst, Schwamberger and Grinzinger (n 11) 103ff; V Zeno-Zencovich, 'Do "Data Markets" Exist?' (2019) *MediaLaws* 22.

[16] JE Cohen, *Between Truth and Power: The Legal Construction of Informational Capitalism* (New York, Oxford University Press, 2019).

some cases made reuse of data for public interest purposes more complicated (think only of the biomedical research sector, which suffers both from a lack of coordination at European level concerning the regime of secondary use of clinical data[17] and from insufficient guarantees at domestic level[18]), at the same time it has not succeeded in putting up a strong barrier against commercial parasitism carried out on the basis of resources that are consubstantial to the sphere of personal identity.

III. THE DGA AND THE THREE DIMENSIONS OF DATA GOVERNANCE

So it is understandable that the Communication 'European Data Strategy'[19] highlights the need for a change with respect to each of the above-mentioned aspects, with the overall aim of not dispersing the opportunities created by AI and promoting – at all levels – greater circulation and sharing of data.[20] The DGA takes up this challenge by operating on three main fronts: a) reuse of data in public hands; b) intermediation services for data exchange; and c) data altruism.

IV. PUBLIC AND PRIVATE

The provisions operating on the first point move in a line of continuity with the pre-existing body of law, broadening the scope of the principles established by the directives on open data and reuse of public sector information,[21] based on the premise that 'data that has been generated or collected by public sector bodies or other entities at the expense of public budgets should benefit society' (Recital 6 DGA). The DGA extends the scope of these principles to certain categories of data, namely those protected on grounds of commercial confidentiality, statistical confidentiality, protection of intellectual property rights or protection of personal data (Article 3(1)). The main limitation of this model is that no specific obligations or enforceable rights are laid down with regard to access to public data for reuse purposes, but the modalities under which reuse can be granted are regulated in Articles 4–8 (prohibition of exclusive arrangements, data format and availability requirements, limitation of extra-EU transfer, licence fees, one-stop shop).[22]

[17] C Wiese Svanberg, 'Article 89 Safeguards and derogations relating to processing for archiving purposes in the public interest, scientific or historical research purposes or statistical purposes' in C Kuner et al (eds), *The EU General Data Protection Regulation (GDPR): A Commentary* (Oxford, Oxford University Press, 2020) 1240.

[18] G Comandè, 'Ricerca in sanità e data protection, un puzzle … risolvibile' (2019) *Rivista italiana di medicina legale e del diritto in campo sanitario* 187.

[19] EU Commission (n 5).

[20] Steinrötter (n 9) 483ff.

[21] EU Directive 2019/1024 of the European Parliament and of the Council of 20 June 2019 on open data and the re-use of public sector information (recast) OJ L 172/56; R Schildbach, 'Zugang zu Daten der öffentlichen Hand und Datenaltruismus nach dem Entwurf des Daten-Governance-Gesetzes. Datenwirtschaftsrecht IV: Mehrwert für das Teilen von Daten oder leere Hülle?' (2022) *Newsdienst der Zeitschrift für Datenschutz* 148.

[22] D Tolks, 'Die finale Fassung des Data Governance Act. Erste Schritte in Richtung einer europäischen Datenwirtschaft', (2022) *MultiMedia und Recht* 444, 445–46.

The underlying policy is consistent with the pre-existing framework,[23] but probably not as innovative as the policy pursued by the Data Act Proposal, which rather than insisting on the flow of data from 'government to business', shifts the axis of regulation to the opposite register: 'business to government'.[24] Starting from an operational reality that is often characterised by significant asymmetry between the information assets enjoyed by certain private entities, which are granular and continually updated, and public information assets, which are frequently dispersed in non-communicating silos, the Proposal brings together a gamut of solutions already emerged in domestic law (particularly in France),[25] as well as at the EU level.[26] It therefore codifies the model known in the literature as 'reverse PSI'[27] by outlining a general mechanism of compulsory data transfer – both non-personal and personal after pseudonymisation (Article 17(2)(d); Article 18(5)) – from the private sector to the public sector.[28] This is a rather strong innovation, considering that until now the preference had always been given to voluntary models of data transfer.[29]

Should the Proposal be approved 'as is', then public administrations will be able, in the hypotheses of 'exceptional necessity' (Article 15 DGA), to have recourse to an authoritative mechanism of access to private datasets, subject to payment of an indemnity – not due only in cases of public emergency – inclusive of the costs of duplication and transfer, as well as a 'reasonable margin'. It is worth underscoring that the hypotheses of exceptional necessity include not only cases of prevention or management of a public emergency, but also the circumstance where:

> [T]he lack of available data prevents the public sector body or Union institution, agency or body from fulfilling a specific task in the public interest that has been explicitly provided by law; and (1) the public sector body or Union institution, agency or body has been unable to obtain such data by alternative means, including by purchasing the data on the market at market rates or by relying on existing obligations to make data available, and the adoption of new legislative measures cannot ensure the timely availability of the data.

It is evident that in this way the premises are in fact laid for a sort of compulsory transfer of data in the public interest, which could represent the equivalent of the eminent domain in the digital society. It is no coincidence that this provision has been one of the most controversial of the entire Proposal.[30]

[23] A Hartl and A Ludin, 'Recht der Datenzugänge. Was die Datenstrategie der EU sowie der Bundesregierung für die Gesetzgebung erwarten lassen' (2021) *MultiMedia und Recht* 534.

[24] Tolks (n 22) 449.

[25] Loi n° 2016-1321 of 7 Octobre 2016, 'Loi pour une république numérique', Art 17ff.

[26] A Vigorito, 'Government Access to Privately Held Data: Business-to-Government Data Sharing. Voluntary and Mandatory Models' (2022) 20 *European Journal of Comparative Law and Governance* 1; H Richter, 'Zugang des Staates zu Daten der Privatwirtschaft' (2020) 53 *Zeitschrift für Rechtspoliti* 245; H Richter, 'The Law and Policy of Government Access to Private Sector Data (B2G Data Sharing)' in Bundesministerium der Justiz und für Verbraucherschutz, Max-Planck-Institut für Innovation und Wettbewerb (ed), *Data Access, Consumer Interests and Public Welfare* (Nomos, Baden-Baden, 2021) 529.

[27] Y Poullet, 'From *open data* to *reverse PSI* – A new European policy facing GDPR' (2020) *European Public Mosaic* 42.

[28] R Podszun and C Pfeifer, 'Datenzugang nach dem EU Data Act: Der Entwurf der Europäischen Kommission' (2022) *Gewerblicher Rechtsschutz und Urheberrecht* 953, 958.

[29] Vigorito (n 26) 14.

[30] Podszun and Pfeifer (n 28) 958.

V. THE COLLECTIVE DIMENSION

The second profile is addressed in Chapter III of the DGA. This sets out the requirements for data intermediation services, prescribing procedural notification requirements (Article 11), substantive conditions for provision of the service (Article 12), and public supervision mechanisms (Articles 13–14). It is important to note that, according to the new definition proposed in Article 2(11), a data intermediation service is defined as:

> [A] service which aims to establish commercial relationships for the purposes of data sharing between an undetermined number of data subjects and data holders on the one hand and data users on the other, through technical, legal or other means, including for the purpose of exercising the rights of data subjects in relation to personal data.

Significantly, services such as Google or Facebook, which collect data from users by offering services that are formally free of charge and then make extra profits by licensing aggregated, analysed and organised data in machine-readable format to third parties, are expressly excluded from the parameters of the notion.[31] According to Article 2(11)(a), services that 'obtain data from data holders and aggregate, enrich or transform the data for the purpose of adding substantial value to it and license the use of the resulting data to data users, without establishing a commercial relationship between data holders and data users' do not fall under data intermediation services.

By establishing a certain and transparent legal framework, the DGA is intended to stimulate greater data-sharing, also in continuity with a policy aimed at creating new specific 'European data spaces', each with its own functional and regulatory features.[32] One of the fundamental prerequisites for achieving these objectives is to increase the confidence of 'data holders' in the neutrality and reliability of the brokerage service (Recitals 5 and 32). So it is understandable that services based on the model of industrial exploitation of data have already been excluded in terms of definition; and that the principle of neutrality has been formulated as the first of the substantive requirements to be observed for provision of the service.[33]

Indeed, Article 12(a) requires that a data intermediation services provider 'shall not use the data for which it provides data intermediation services for purposes other than to put them at the disposal of data users and shall provide data intermediation services through a separate legal person'.

Similarly, Article 12(m) establishes a fiduciary obligation for the hypothesis that the intermediation service concerns personal data, with a view to further enhancing the transparency and reliability of the service:

> [T]he data intermediation services provider offering services to data subjects shall act in the data subjects' best interest where it facilitates the exercise of their rights, in particular by informing and, where appropriate, advising data subjects in a concise, transparent, intelligible and easily accessible manner about intended data uses by data users and standard terms and conditions attached to such uses before data subjects give consent.

[31] M Hennemann and L von Ditfurth, 'Datenintermediäre und Data Governance Act' (2022) *Neue Juristische Wochenschrift* 1905, 1908.

[32] Tolks (n 22) 446.

[33] As regards the neutrality principle, Hennemann and von Ditfurth (n 31) 1906.

This last remark leads one to dwell on the taxonomy of intermediary services proposed by the DGA and the meaning it takes on in practice. Article 10(1) contemplates three very different types of intermediation services.

A. Exchange or Data Pools

The first type focuses on sharing of data between market players by means of exchange or by establishing data pools. This refers to intermediation services between 'data owners' and 'potential users' of data, which 'may include bilateral or multilateral exchanges of data or the creation of platforms or databases enabling the exchange or joint use of data'. In the Commission's assessment, B2B exchange is still at an unsatisfactory level but, if properly supported, could generate positive effects in terms of innovation and value-added services. The fundamental problem is that, in the absence of exclusive rights on exploitation of industrial data – so far persuasively rejected by the EU law-maker[34] – the only instrument of protection is represented by material availability, and therefore by de facto control over such resources. Consequently, an understandable reluctance exists on the part of economic operators to exchange or directly share the most relevant datasets unless appropriate guarantees are ensured in terms of security of storage, limits to data use, absence of conflicts of interest, and so on. The conditions laid down in Article 12 (in particular paragraphs (b), (f)–(h) and (l)) are aimed precisely at creating a favourable ground for the pooling of data by reducing transaction costs resulting from information asymmetries.[35] Qualified intermediaries endowed with adequate reputational capital – even beyond existing experiences of global marketplaces and industrial data platforms[36] – could facilitate the matching of supply and demand, contributing to development of interoperable formats and at least indirectly ensuring a form of supervision over the use of data.[37]

B. Data Trusts

The second type, according to Article 10(b), consists of:

> [I]ntermediation services between data subjects that seek to make their personal data available or natural persons that seek to make non-personal data available, and potential data users, including making available the technical or other means to enable such services, and in particular enabling the exercise of the data subjects' rights provided in Regulation (EU) 2016/679.[38]

[34] Rosenkranz and Scheufen (n 9) 168; Steinrötter (n 9) 482; Resta (n 6) 242.

[35] H Richter, 'Europäisches Datenprivatrecht: Lehren aus dem Kommissionsvorschlag für eine "Verordnung über europäische Daten-Governance"' (2021) 29 *Zeitschrift für europäisches Privatrecht* 634.

[36] Hennemann and von Ditfurth (n 33) 1906.

[37] ibid 1910.

[38] F Bravo, 'Intermediazione di dati personali e servizi di *data sharing* dal GDPR al *Data Governance Act*' (2021) *Contratto e impresa Europa* 199.

If in the previous hypothesis the main concern is to stimulate data-sharing, in this case the need is to strengthen conscious exercise of the right to informational self-determination (*informationelle Selbstbestimmungsrecht*). As noted above, contemporary data markets amplify the power gap between individual and professional counterparts, making the manifestation of consent little more than a formal act with no actual decision-making value.[39] Similarly, rights under the GDPR Article 15ff are not always effective, either because the necessary incentives to overcome the costs of inertia involved in exercising the right are lacking or because of limited chances of achieving effective supervision over how data are used. Hence the idea, long advanced, that the involvement of associations and other entities such as civil liberties associations and trade unions in the function of assistance and support of the individual concerned may help to strengthen the effectiveness of remedies related to data processing.[40] The DGA seems to move along this line, foreshadowing some forms of support to individuals both in the phase preceding expression of consent (Article 12(1)(m); Recital 30) and in the phase of exercise of the data subject's rights and of exercise of the relevant remedies (Article 2(1)(11); Article 10(1)(b)). If the model is clear in general terms, it remains to be seen how these rules fit in with the organisational forms found in practice.

In this regard it is appropriate to distinguish at least two hypotheses, characterised by starkly different functional features.

The first is related to 'personal information management services',[41] which consist of the offer to the public, for commercial purposes, of professional data management services (an example, recently brought to the attention of the Italian Data Protection Authority, is Weople).[42] These may include technical tools for customising declarations of consent with regard to specific sectors or processing operations, activities aimed at collective negotiation of rights with a view to monetising personal data, and assistance in the exercise of the data subject's rights (one typically thinks of the exercise of the right to portability, as referred to in Article 20 GDPR). In its most advanced forms, this organisational form could resemble copyright collecting societies.[43]

The second is that of not-for-profit data management, for instance in the fields of scientific research and healthcare. In this regard, very widespread is the formula of 'data trust' (or in its German transposition, *Datentreuhand*), which in turn can be broken down into different operational typologies, all characterised by the fiduciary

[39] See above, section II.

[40] European Data Protection Supervisor, 'EDPS Opinion 9/2016. Opinion on Personal Information Management Systems. Towards more user empowerment in managing and processing personal data' (20 October 2016), edps.europa.eu/sites/edp/files/publication/16-10-20_pims_opinion_en.pdf; Wendehorst, Schwamberger and Grinzinger (n 11).

[41] B Falkhofen, 'Infrastrukturrecht des digitalen Raums. Data Governance Act, Data Act, und Gaia-X' (2021) *Europäische Zeitschrift für Wirtschaftsrecht)* 787, 790.

[42] weople.space. See Bravo (n 38) 216.

[43] L Specht-Riemenschneider et al, 'Die Datentreuhand. Ein Beitrag zur Modellbildung und rechtlichen Strukturierung zwecks Identifizierung der Regulierungserfordernisse für Datentreuhandmodelle (2021) *MultiMedia und Recht-Beilage* 25, 27.

nature of the powers ascribed to the manager and by segregation of the information assets subject to the trust.[44]

C. Data Cooperatives

The third category is represented by data cooperatives.[45] These are defined by Article 2(15) as:

> intermediation services offered by an organisational structure constituted by data subjects, one-person undertakings or SMEs who are members of that structure, having as its main objectives to support its members in the exercise of their rights with respect to certain data, including with regard to making informed choices before they consent to data processing, to exchange views on data processing purposes and conditions that would best represent the interests of its members in relation to their data, and to negotiate terms and conditions for data processing on behalf of its members before giving permission to the processing of non-personal data or before they consent to the processing of personal data.

Prevalent in this case is a mutualistic purpose, based on the assumption that by creating a collective structure aimed at socialising the value of data, its individual members would gain not only in monetary terms, but also and above all in terms of control over how data are processed and used on a secondary basis. Some examples that have emerged in practice, such as data cooperatives created by taxi drivers (Driver's seat), by patients (salus.coop), or by fishers (PescaData), show how data cooperatives can represent – especially on a local scale – an interesting system of data management with an entrepreneurial character but alternative to the patterns of extractive capitalism.[46] It is no coincidence that, within the debate on smart cities, reference has often been made to the cooperative model, together with the data trust, as a preferable organisational alternative to the profit-making enterprise.[47]

D. Data Altruism

Article 15 exempts 'recognised data altruism organisations' as well as 'other not-for-profit entities insofar as their activities consist of seeking to collect data for objectives of general interest, made available by natural or legal persons on the basis of data altruism' from the procedural and substantive regulation of intermediation services.

[44] Specht-Riemenschneider et al (n 43) 25ff; Wendehorst, Schwamberger and Grinzinger (n 6) 103ff.

[45] H Baars et al, 'Cooperative Approaches to Data Sharing and Analysis for Industrial Internet of Things Ecosystems' (2021) 11 *Applied Sciences* 7547; M Micheli et al, 'Emerging models of data governance in the age of datafication' (2020) 7 *Big Data & Society* 7; S Delacroix and ND Lawrence, 'Bottom-up data trusts: Disturbing the "one size fits all" approach to data governance' (2019) 9 *International Data Privacy Law* 236.

[46] E Bietti et al, *Data Cooperatives in Europe: A Legal and Empirical Investigation*, White Paper created as part of The New School's Platform Cooperativism Consortium and Harvard University's Berkman Klein Center for Internet & Society Research Sprint (2021), cyber.harvard.edu/sites/default/files/2022-02/Data_Cooperatives_Europe-group2.pdf.

[47] M Petras, 'Demokratischer Datenschutz. Kooperative Privatheit in der "Smart City"' (2021) *MultiMedia und Recht* 862, 864.

The intention is to carve out a set of favourable rules for collective entities that, operating on a non-profit basis, seek to stimulate collection of personal and non-personal data and their use for purposes of general interest.[48] This is where the third pivot on which the DGA framework hinges.

Data altruism is defined by Article2(16) as:

> [T]he voluntary sharing of data on the basis of the consent of data subjects to process personal data pertaining to them, or permissions of data holders to allow the use of their non-personal data without seeking or receiving a reward that goes beyond compensation related to the costs that they incur where they make their data available for objectives of general interest as provided for in national law, where applicable, such as healthcare, combating climate change, improving mobility, facilitating the development, production and dissemination of official statistics, improving the provision of public services, public policy making or scientific research purposes in the general interest.[49]

We are evidently distant from the logic of market intermediation designed to establish coordinated exploitation models (as in data pools) or systems of monetisation of data linked to their reuse for commercial purposes. However, we are not far from the hypothesis of the data trust, and indeed data altruism organisations represent a clear example of its application.[50] The experience of the COVID-19 pandemic was of central importance from this point of view because it brought out the importance of data-sharing, while also showing some of the limitations of the EU data protection regulation.[51] It should be noted, for instance, that in Germany – where the consent of the data subject has been considered an adequate legal basis for data processing through tracing apps, in contrast to Italy[52] – the Robert Koch Institut has promoted an application (Corona-Datenspende) aimed at enabling donation by citizens of personal data collected by smart devices, such as smart watches, for epidemiological and pandemic response purposes.[53] Similarly, several organisations, such as Google or Facebook, have made aggregated population mobility data available to governments to identify clusters and track the spread of the virus. Generalising this approach, the DGA assigns a specific role to non-profit organisations engaged in collection and subsequent allocation of data for purposes of general interest, providing a detailed regulatory framework to ensure the transparency and independence of these organisations, avoiding creation of misaligned incentives.

[48] P von Hagen and L Völzmann, 'Datenaltruismus aus datenschutzrechtlicher Perspektive. Wechselwirkung zwischen DGA und DS-GVO' (2022) *Multimedia und Recht* 176.

[49] As regards data altruism, see M Taddeo, 'Data Philanthropy and Individual Rights' (2017) 27 *Minds and Machines* 1; B Prainsack, 'Data Donation: How to Resist the iLeviathan' in J Krutzinna and L Floridi (eds), *The Ethics of Medical Data Donation* (Cham, Springer, 2019) 9.

[50] S Kempny, H Krüger and M Spindler, 'Rechtliche Gestaltung von Datentreuhändern. Ein interdisziplinärer Blick auf "Data Trusts"' (2022) *Neue Juristische Wochenschrift* 1646, 1648.

[51] K Kuner, 'Data Crossing Borders: Data Sharing and Protection in Times of Coronavirus' Verfassungsblog.de (15 April 2020), verfassungsblog.de/data-crossing-borders.

[52] D Samardzic and T Becker, 'Die Grenzen des Datenschutzes – Der beschränkte Schutz durch Freiwilligkeit und Einwilligung bei Corona-Apps' (2020) *Europäische Zeitschrift für Wirtschaftsrecht* 646.

[53] J Kühling and R Schildbach, 'Corona-Apps. Daten- und Grundrechtsschutz in Krisenzeiten' (2020) *Neue Juristische Wochenschrift* 1545, 1546; Robert Koch Institut, 'Die Corona-Datenspende', corona-datenspende.de.

So the first requirement is to register with the public register of altruistic data organisations established by Article 19 DGA. This is subject to fulfilment of a series of requirements specified in Article 18 (including the profit-making purpose, the functionally separate structure for the activities in question, and compliance with the code set out in Article 22). Secondly, Article 20 requires maintenance of up-to-date registers, while Article 21 sets out a series of obligations and principles to protect data controllers, including the obligation to provide information (mainly relating to objectives of general interest), a prohibition on using data for objectives other than those of general interest for which the data subject or data holder allows processing, technical assistance in the phase of providing or withdrawing consent, and security in data storage. The underlying intention, consistent with what has already been observed with regard to data brokering services, is to bolster public confidence in the trustworthiness of such organisations (Recital 46), thus enabling other forms of nudging that support altruistic motivations (for instance, public awareness campaigns) to find a viable routing system. Also worth noting is the provision of a European altruism data form aimed at enabling collection of consent in a uniform format in all the Member States (Article 25);[54] an issue that raises the big question – widely debated especially in the context of scientific research and unfortunately left unresolved by the DGA (see Recital 50) – of the limits of admissibility of 'broad consent'.[55]

This is where the scope of European intervention comes to a halt, both because no precise provisions are envisaged either on relations between the 'donor' of data and altruistic organisations, or on those between such organisations and third parties who are the final recipients of data;[56] and because Article 16 is unequivocal in referring the Member States to adoption of targeted policies to support data altruism, including through adoption of specific organisational or technical measures.

VI. THE *CHIAROSCURO* OF THE EUROPEAN MODEL

A closer look shows that the DGA reveals both light and shadow.

As for the positive aspects, the underlying policy aimed at fostering data sharing deserves appreciation. As illustrated above, this legislation is no longer marked by a defensive attitude, but is intended to open up information silos and to foster a more systematic exploitation of the value of data – both personal and non-personal – through constitution of common data spaces. This is crucial both in terms of industrial policy – since in the medium term it could contribute to reducing the strategic dependence of European actors on large transnational data platforms[57] – and in terms of social policies, since any innovation process aimed at exploiting the opportunities unleashed by artificial intelligence techniques inevitably requires availability of structured data parks in machine-readable and interoperable format. Clearly,

[54] von Hagen and Völzmann (n 48) 177.
[55] Schildbach (n 21) 151.
[56] ibid.
[57] M Denga, 'Digitale Souveränität durch Datenprivatrecht?' (2022) *Gewerblicher Rechtsschutz und Urheberrecht* 1113.

such functional orientation of the new European data governance system cannot lead to erasure of those guarantees – in particular with reference to the processing of personal data – that have been painstakingly built up during a long process of interaction between domestic and supranational law.[58] However, it requires a delicate operation of adapting the pre-existing legal framework to the new reality defined by the digital transition.

It is precisely in relation to this aspect that some shadows of the European regulatory framework emerge. A first criticism concerns the excessive bureaucratic burden and the idea that provision of an adequate institutional framework can in itself lead to the results desired. Due to the limitation of the Union's competences, it cannot be ignored that mere definition of a new legal form for intermediation services or for data altruism organisations is not in itself a guarantee of the economic attractiveness of these activities and thus of effectively undertaking them.[59] In the absence of adequate incentive policies, first and foremost of a fiscal nature, and in the presence of a dense network of procedural and substantive obligations that generate not insignificant compliance burdens, the risk is that the real impact of such discipline will be less satisfactory than hoped for,[60] not least because in order to contest the supremacy of transnational platforms the new subjects would have to scale up and reach high dimensional and organisational levels.

A second order of considerations relates to the system's difficulty in coordinating with the pre-existing regulatory framework and the still too limited scope of its adjustments.[61] From this point of view, one of the key problems is the inherent tension between the GDPR and legislation designed to encourage data-sharing. The legislator's choice was to reaffirm the prevalence of the GDPR in case of conflict and to exclude that the DGA could constitute a valid legal basis for processing and affect rights and obligations under data protection law (Article 1(3)). The foreseeable effect of such a model of interaction is a weakening of the tools deployed by the DGA to promote greater data flow.

It will suffice to consider just three examples. The first concerns so-called data altruism. The idea of 'donation' of data for certain purposes of general interest is in itself appealing, as it seems capable of bridging the gap between the regulatory model concerning the human body, its parts and products (which is centred on the idea of a solidarity gift as the only tool available by the parties) and that of data.[62] However, in the absence of binding provisions amending the requirement of specificity of consent, established by Articles 2 and 7 GDPR, and therefore allowing data subjects to authorise the processing of personal data for certain areas or lines of research or other social policies, data altruism risks turning into a mere cosmetic formula, a regulatory marketing device with no significant operational impact.[63]

[58] A Roßnagel, 'Grundrechtsschutz in der Datenwirtschaft. Vorsorgepflichten in der Data-Governance' (2021) 54 *Zeitschrift für Rechtspolitik* 173.

[59] Richter (n 35) 646ff.

[60] In this sense, Hennemann and von Ditfurth (n 33) 1910.

[61] Falkhofen (n 41) 790.

[62] G Resta, 'Contratto e diritti fondamentali' in *Enciclopedia del Diritto – I tematici*, I, *Contratto* (2021) 291ff, 302, 306.

[63] Schildbach (n 21) 152ff.

The second example concerns the relationship between data intermediaries and the exercise of the data subject's rights (the same theme emerges in relation to the authorisation of data processing, and will be dealt with below). In order for the trustees to be able to effectively perform the tasks assigned to them, it would appear necessary to grant them the power to take the place of the data subject in the exercise of their rights under Article 15ff GDPR.[64] However, it is doubtful whether such a solution is practicable in the light of existing law. On the one hand, the DGA uses ambiguous expressions, reflecting an ill-concealed uncertainty as to the nature of the powers claimed by the trustees. Article 2(1)(11), in defining data brokering services, refers to a function instrumental to establishment of business relationships between data subjects and data users 'including for the purpose of exercising the rights of data subjects in relation to personal data'. Recital 30, after stating that the use of intermediary services could make it possible to 'enhance the agency of data subjects, and in particular individuals' control over data relating to them', envisages a mere assistance role. Indeed, it is stated that intermediaries

> would assist individuals in exercising their rights under Regulation (EU) 2016/679, in particular giving and withdrawing their consent to data processing, the right of access to their own data, the right to the rectification of inaccurate personal data, the right of erasure or right 'to be forgotten', the right to restrict processing and the right to data portability, which allows data subjects to move their personal data from one data controller to the other.

The expressions used in this provision seem to suggest that the function assigned to data intermediaries is merely that of technical management of a data subject's consent (as happens with 'personal information management services'), thus confirming the idea of the absence of autonomous decision-making power in the hands of the trustee. On the other hand, according to a literal understanding of Article 80(1) GDPR, the possibility of granting a mandate to collective bodies and organisations is restricted only to the lodging of complaints before the administrative authority and to judicial actions under Article 77ff GDPR.[65] By contrast, the exercise of the data subject's rights under Article 15ff GDPR seems to be outside the possible scope of a mandate. Although a more liberal interpretation of Article 80 GDPR would appear not to be precluded,[66] undeniably a more courageous wording of the GDPR would have helped to remove this uncertainty and legitimise a solution more functional to the purposes pursued.

The last example concerns data cooperatives. It must first be noted that, as regards the exercise of the data subject's rights under Article 15ff GDPR, the final version of the DGA marks significant progress compared to the original Proposal. Indeed, Recital 24 of the Proposal, specifically concerning cooperatives, stated: 'in this context it is important to acknowledge that the rights under Regulation (EU) 2016/679 can

[64] C Beise, 'Datensouveränität und Datentreuhand' (2021) *Recht Digital* 597

[65] See also European Data Protection Board, 'Guidelines 01/2022 on data subject rights – Right of access' (18 January 2022) 27, edpb.europa.eu/our-work-tools/our-documents/guidelines/guidelines-012022-data-subject-rights-right-access_en.

[66] For a different and more convincing reading of Art 80, see Specht-Riemenschneider et al (n 43) 43.

only be exercised by each individual and cannot be conferred or delegated to a data cooperative'.[67] Any references to the terms 'conferring' and 'delegating' have disappeared from the final text of the Regulation. Instead, the corresponding Recital 31 now states that 'it is important to acknowledge that the rights under Regulation (EU) 2016/679 are personal rights of the data subject and that data subjects cannot waive such rights'. Although EU law provisions should not be interpreted on the basis of concepts and categories of domestic law, it is reasonable to assume that while the prohibition of renunciation, as a typical abdicative act, implies the impossibility of conferral on a company (an act with effect *in rem*), it does not preclude conclusion of a contract of mandate, as an act with effect *in personam*. It would thus seem to open up a wider operational space at least for the external protection of data subjects' rights by a data cooperative acting as a representative of its members.[68]

That said, a second problem arises, which does not concern the 'negative' dimension of protection against third parties, but rather the 'positive' dimension of contractual exploitation. The very logic of a company with a mutual purpose would suggest the appropriateness of recognising a conferral of data, with correlative dispositive powers entrusted to the company. However, the legislative formulas seem to exclude such a possibility, both because featuring among the obligations imposed on intermediation services is that of neutrality (Article 12(a)), so as to exclude any data analytics that is preordained to a negotiation with third parties (this, for instance, is the organisational logic of Drivers' seat and of other cooperatives in the mobility sector);[69] and because the DGA on several points seems to expressly limit the role of cooperatives – and all the more so of other data intermediaries – to consultancy prior to manifestation of consent, or at most to that of transmitting to third parties the documentation of the data subject's will.

In other words, consent is considered by the DGA as a personal act that cannot be delegated to third parties.[70] Recital 31 makes clear that one of the main objectives of data cooperatives is:

> [T]o strengthen the position of individuals in making informed choices before consenting to data use, influencing the terms and conditions of data user organisations attached to data use in a manner that gives better choices to the individual members of the group or potentially finding solutions to conflicting positions of individual members of a group on how data can be used where such data relates to several data subjects within that group.

Article 12(m), in outlining the fiduciary character of the obligations incumbent on personal data intermediaries (which include cooperatives), contemplates specific advisory duties, so as to provide data subjects with adequate information on the third party's business proposals 'before data subjects give consent'.

[67] Similarly, the European Data Protection Board and the European Data Protection Supervisor, 'EDPB-EDPS Joint Opinion 03/2021 on the Proposal for a regulation of the European Parliament and of the Council on European data governance (Data Governance Act)' 35, edpb.europa.eu/system/files/2021-03/edpb-edps_joint_opinion_dga_en.pdf.

[68] Specht-Riemenschneider et al (n 43) 41ff.

[69] Bietti et al (n 46) 17–18.

[70] Denga (n 57) 1118.

On the other hand, even at the level of the general theory of consent to data processing, the prevailing opinion excludes the possibility of representation (but this is not uncontroversial).[71] Consent is regarded as an act of a personal nature, not capable of being delegated to a third party. It is therefore not surprising that the legislator of the DGA has been deeply cautious and has not departed from these assumptions. However, it must frankly be recognised that the instrument of the data cooperative – in order to effectively achieve its social purposes and to challenge the primacy of the profit-making business model – requires a wider scope of action and an enabling legal framework.[72] For this reason, the totem of the personal nature of consent, which constitutes a bulwark of self-determination in the sphere of market relations, transposed to the sphere of fiduciary relations and cooperative businesses would perhaps deserve to be overcome. Furthermore, one could incidentally note that long experience of the interaction between contract law and personality rights has revealed, in the folds of doctrinal declamations, unexpected spaces for the exercise of private autonomy.[73] This could teach us that it is only a matter of time until the possibility of representation in the expression of consent to the processing of data will be recognised.[74] Incidentally, Article 8 GDPR expressly provides that those exercising parental authority may validly express consent for a minor, and mere silence as to the hypothesis of voluntary representation cannot in itself be understood as a prohibition.[75]

VII. BEYOND DATA INDIVIDUALISM

In conclusion, the itinerary undertaken at the European level on the whole deserves appreciation. However, one must hope for a further effort in terms of enhancing the relational and collective dimension of data processing,[76] including by opening up more decisively to contractual autonomy, beyond the straits imposed by an excessively individualistic reading of the system outlined by the GDPR. If a more decisive step is not taken in this direction, it is hard to see how to resolve the basic contradiction arising from the fact that the GDPR and the Data Act intend to create a data market, while data protection legislation is aimed at removing data from the market.

[71] S Ernst, 'Die Einwilligung nach der Datenschutzgrundverordnung. Anmerkungen zur Definition nach Art. 4 Nr. 11 DS-GVO' (2017) *Newsdienst der Zeitschrift für Datenschutz* 110, 111.
[72] Bietti et al (n 46) 18.
[73] G Resta, *Autonomia privata e diritti della personalità*, (Napoli, Jovene, 2005) 320ff; V Zeno-Zencovich, 'Profili negoziali degli attributi della personalità' (1993) *Il Diritto dell'informazione e dell'informatica* 545.
[74] Specht-Riemenschneider et al (n 43) 41–42.
[75] ibid.
[76] S Viljoen, 'A Relational Theory of Data Governance' (2021) 131 *Yale Law Journal* 573.

19

Collective Units as Subjects of Liability in Collective Interest Cases

VIBE ULFBECK

I. INTRODUCTION

ONE OF THE characteristics of a legal person is that liability attaches to it. However, the question of how to attach liability to a legal person who is not a natural person has posed itself as a fundamental challenge. One of the reasons is that fault-based liability is the universal liability rule in tort law.[1] The rule imposes liability for infringement of behavioural standards in society but in its classic version also contains, as something central, a subjective element, placing emphasis on psychological aspects, that is, the state of mind of the wrongdoer. Thus, a classic liability assessment involves assessing whether the wrongdoer committed the tort intentionally or negligently. The subjective element becomes a challenge when the wrongdoer is not an individual but a collective unit, such as a company, which does not have a mind of its own.

An early common law case, *Lennard's Carrying Co Ltd v Asiatic Petroleum Co Ltd*[2] expresses the problem and a possible solution:

> [A] corporation is an abstraction. It has no mind of its own any more than it has a body of its own; its active and directing will must consequently be sought in the person of somebody who for some purposes may be called an agent, but who is really the directing mind and will of the corporation.

The idea expressed here is to identify the company with its management and impose liability on the company for fault committed by management. This rationale for imposing liability on the company is broadly recognised and sometimes applied under the concept of 'organ liability'.[3]

[1] See, eg, PETL Art 4.101, and European Group of Tort Law, *Principles of European Tort Law, Text and Commentary* (Wien-New York, Springer, 2005) 64.

[2] (1915) AC 705 at 713.

[3] See, eg, BGB §31: Haftung des Vereins für Organe: 'Der Verein ist für den Schaden verantwortlich, den der Vorstand, ein Mitglied des Vorstands oder ein anderer verfassungsmäßig berufener Vertreter durch eine in Ausführung der ihm zustehenden Verrichtungen begangene, zum Schadensersatz verpflichtende

However, liability for the company goes much further than this. Notably, companies may become liable for the acts of their employees and simply for the acts of 'the company itself' acting as a legal person.

In the following, techniques for establishing this kind of liability for companies are described and grouped in models (section II). Subsequently, it is tested whether these models can also be traced in terms of dealing with liability related to groups of companies in certain areas of the law. In other words, it is examined whether groups of companies, although not recognised as legal persons, may look that way from a liability perspective (section III). Section IV concludes.

II. TECHNIQUES FOR IMPOSING LIABILITY ON A COLLECTIVE UNIT

A. Model I: Actual Control Liability

Originally, liability for employees was framed as fault-based employer's liability for negligence in the choice of workers for employment or negligence in the instruction of workers to carry out their tasks. This was in line with the basic notion of corrective justice: loss must be transferred from the victim to the wrongdoer in order to achieve justice. The most classic version of this type of liability recognises only liability of the employer for actions it has specifically and expressly commanded and/or consented to.[4] In other words, it is liability for actual control or liability for 'taking control'. In the following, this will be called the actual control liability model, or Model I.

B. Model II: Potential Control Liability – Hidden Vicarious Liability

Fault-based liability thinking was heavily involved in the establishment of vicarious liability, which can be seen as the next step. An example is Article 1384 of the original French Civil Code from 1804. According to the preparatory works 'those on whom it is imposed can blame themselves, at the very least, for weakness, others for bad choices, all for negligence'.[5] In other words, vicarious liability was based on a presumption of fault.

The idea of fault-based liability as underlying vicarious liability is also reflected in the German solution, which under BGB Article 831 allows for the employer to be exempted from vicarious liability if it can show to have exercised reasonable care in selecting the person deployed.

Even in versions of vicarious liability that now allow for exemption of liability through proof of fault, strict liability of the employer for the negligence of employees

Handlung einem Dritten zufügt'. See in general, P Giliker, *Vicarious Liability in Tort: A Comparative Perspective* (Cambridge, Cambridge University Press, 2010) 46; RB Thompson, 'Unpacking Limited Liability: Direct and Vicarious Liability of Corporate Participants for Torts of the Enterprise' (1994) 47 *Vanderbuilt Law Review* 1, 8.

[4] Early English law was in line with this; see A Gray, *Vicarious Liability, Critique and Reform* (Oxford, Hart Publishing, 2018) 209. Later on, implied consent was assumed: Gray (ibid) 209.

[5] Giliker (n 3) 8–9.

is also legitimised by a reasoning that links to notions of fault-based liability at a more abstract level. Thus, inherent in classic vicarious liability thinking is the idea that the employer is vicariously liable for employees because it has the right to instruct them. This can also be described as liability based on 'potential control'. Translating this into the language of fault-based liability, it can be seen as liability for not actually taking control over something that should have been controlled. In the following this will be called the potential control liability model, or Model II. Potential control liability has also been used to justify vicarious liability for independent contractors, where potential control is in fact retained.[6]

C. Model III: Pure Vicarious Liability

Today, the principle of vicarious liability for employees, understood as strict liability of the employer for the negligence of its employees, is established across jurisdictions.[7]

This is widely legitimised on the basis that the employer is the better risk-bearer since:

(1) it is the employer that benefits economically from the acts of employees;
(2) the employer can distribute the risk over a large group of people;
(3) by establishing and running an enterprise, the employer creates a risk which should justly be borne by the enterprise; and
(4) placing the risk on the employer encourages risk reduction in the future (deterrence).

By relying on these criteria, vicarious liability became a forerunner for what in US law came to be termed 'enterprise liability'[8] (see further below). Pure vicarious liability cuts the link to fault-based liability of the employer but retains the requirement of fault on the part of employees. In the following this will be called the 'pure vicarious liability' model, or Model III. The pure vicarious liability model has also been used to justify liability for independent contractors carrying out inherently dangerous activities.[9]

D. Model IV: The Anonymous and Cumulative Liability Model

With companies and enterprises in general growing in size, both vicarious and direct liability models developed further. With many employees in the same organisation,

[6] V Ulfbeck and A Ehlers, 'Direct and Vicarious Liability in Supply Chains' in V Ulfbeck, A Andhov and K Mitkidis (eds), *Law and Responsible Supply Chain Management: Contract and Tort, Interplay and Overlap* (Abingdon-New York, Routledge 2019) 102 with further references.

[7] Reflected in PETL, Art 6.102; Giliker (n 3) 1. See also P Giliker, *Vicarious Liability in the Common Law World* (Oxford, Hart Publishing, 2022).

[8] On vicarious liability as the forerunner to enterprise liability, see GC Keating, 'The Theory of Enterprise Liability and Common Law Strict Liability' (2001) 54 *Vanderbuilt Law Review* 1285, 1310.

[9] D Brodie, *Enterprise Liability and the Common Law* (Cambridge, Cambridge University Press, 2014) 152; E Hendersen, 'Liability to employees of Independent Contractors Engaged in Inherently Dangerous Work: A workable Workers' Compensation Proposal' (1980) 48 *Fordham Law Review* 1165, Ulfbeck and Ehlers (n 6) 105–07 with references.

it may not always be possible to pinpoint who in fact committed a tortious act. Sometimes, it may also be the case that there is no act of a single employee that can in itself be regarded as tortious, but the cumulative effect of several small mistakes committed by different employees in sum constitutes a tortious act that causes damage. These situations have been handled differently in different legal systems. Many European legal systems recognise vicarious liability for what could be called 'anonymous errors' and 'cumulative errors'.[10] They allow for imposition of vicarious liability in the situations just described.

German law solves the same problem in a different way. Thus, under the concept of 'organisational tort' German law has established the possibility to impose fault-based liability for poor company organisation on the basis of BGB Article 823.[11] The concept basically supplements the widely criticised and narrowly framed Article 831 on vicarious liability.[12] It thereby also covers situations in which there may not be anything for which to blame a specific employee but had things been better organised, damage would have been avoided.

With the introduction of the concepts of liability (whether direct or vicarious) for anonymous and cumulative errors, the link to the idea of liability as connected to the individual fault of a specific person in the organisation becomes weaker. In the following this will be called the anonymous and cumulative liability model, or Model IV.

E. Model V: The Unit as Wrongdoer: Enterprise Liability

The concepts of liability for anonymous and cumulative errors blur the picture of company liability as vicarious liability for others and pave the way for thinking of liability as simply attached to the activities 'of the company', that is, the collective unit as whole. This also aligns with the way the matter often appears to the outer world: it is the company that has caused the damage. The general tendency to objectify assessments of whether someone has acted negligently[13] facilitates this development and speaking about 'negligence of the company'.

PETL Article 4.202 uses the concept of 'enterprise liability' to capture the development described above. The provision actually goes one step further in that it imposes fault-based liability with a reversed burden of proof on the enterprise.[14] One of the

[10] See in general the country reports in J Spier, *Unification of Tort Law: Liability for Damage Caused by Others* (Aalphen aan den Rhin, Kluwer Law International, 2003), eg on the UK, France, Israel, Poland, Spain and Switzerland. Also Scandinavian law recognises the concept; see eg Vibe Ulfbeck, *Erstatningsretlige Grænseområder*, 2nd edn (Copenhagen, DJØF, 2010) 2050.

[11] G Spindler, *Unternehmensorganisationspflichten. Zivilrechtliche und öffentlich-rechtliche Regelungskonzepte* (Cologne, Heymann, 2001); G Bruggemeier, *Common Principles of Tort Law* (London, British Institute of International and Comparative Law, 2004) 126. See also P Rott and V Ulfbeck, 'Supply Chain Liability of Multinational Corporations?' (2015) 23 *European Review of Private Law* 415, 425–26.

[12] Giliker (n 3) 11 with reference to Zimmermann labelling the provision 'a major source of embarrassment'.

[13] See eg. PETL Commentary (n 1) 69.

[14] On enterprise liability thinking within negligence law, see Keating (n 8) 1329.

ideas behind the rule is to address the problem of cumulative and anonymous errors and the impossible position of the victim, having to otherwise prove what went wrong in the company and who is to blame.[15]

Ultimately, the problem of attaching liability to a collective unit can be resolved by applying a liability concept that does not rely on subjective, fault-based assessments, namely strict liability. This has been done in such areas as injuries at work, product liability law, and certain types of environmental liability, where liability is attached to the company as a collective unit and legal person.[16] In the US, strict liability in these areas was developed on the basis of 'enterprise liability' thinking, the core of which is said to be:

(1) activities should bear their characteristic accident costs; and
(2) accident costs should be distributed among the members of the enterprise so that the costs of an injury are shared by those who profit from the activity.[17]

Thus, the focus has moved from liability for 'acts' to liability for 'activities', thereby also from a focus on liability of individuals to a focus on liability of the enterprise, justified by distributive justice thinking. In the following this will be called the enterprise liability model, or Model V.

F. Summing Up

The development of techniques for attaching liability to a company as a legal person took its starting point in proving fault on the part of the employer. The concept of control was central. The development has been one from liability for 'taking control' with employees (actual control liability, Model I) to liability for 'not taking control' (potential control liability, Model II). The connection with fault-based liability is clearest in Model I, but still remains in the background as a justification in relation to the potential control liability model, which can also be seen as a form of 'hidden vicarious liability'. This also means that in reality there can be a thin line between fault-based liability and control-based vicarious liability. In contrast, vicarious liability in its pure model cuts the link to fault-based liability of the employer by placing emphasis on distributive justice arguments as a justification for vicarious liability but maintains the requirement of fault on the part of an employee (pure vicarious liability

[15] PETL commentary (n 1) 116. For US law, see likewise, Thompson (n 3), with further references.

[16] Under the product liability law, liability is strict and the subject of liability is 'the producer', ie most often a company; see eg Council Directive 85/374/EEC of 25 July 1985 on the approximation of the laws, regulations and administrative provisions of the Member States concerning liability for defective products [1985] OJ L 210/29 Art 3. Under workers' compensation acts, liability is often strict and liability rests on 'the employer', often a company; see, eg, K Oliphant and G Wagner, *Employers' Liability and Workers' Compensation (Tort and Insurance Law)* (Berlin, De Gruyter, 2012). Under Directive 2004/35/CE of the European Parliament and of the Council of 21 April 2004 on environmental liability with regard to the prevention and remedying of environmental damage [2004] OJ L143/56, Art 8, liability is strict and rests on the 'operator', often a company.

[17] Keating (n 8) 1286.

model, Model III). Later on, the ties to fault committed by an individual employee were loosened through recognition of the concepts of anonymous and cumulative errors (cumulative and anonymous liability model, Model IV) and lastly by recognising liability for fault committed by 'the unit itself', detached from individual fault or simply as strict liability of the unit (enterprise liability, Model V).

In short, overall development can be traced from focusing on fault of individuals and notions of corrective justice towards a focus on the unit as the wrongdoer under enterprise liability thinking embedding notions of distributive justice, sometimes also called 'collective justice'.[18] Put even more briefly: 'a move from a framework in which interpersonal justice is paramount to one in which notions of what is best for society are dominant'.[19]

III. EXPLORING THE APPLICABILITY OF THE MODELS IN CORPORATE GROUPS

A. The Relationship between Company Law and Tort Law

The fact that companies as collective units can, through various legal techniques, attract liability begs the question whether the same goes for groups of companies as collective units.

However, when asking whether the techniques for imposing liability on the company for the acts of its employees can be transferred 'one level up' to the setting of corporate groups, the role of company law as a possibly 'complicating factor' must be addressed.

In company law, it is a basic principle that companies in corporate groups are separate legal entities that are responsible for their own acts. Company law operates few exceptions to this general rule, allowing for a parent company to be held liable for the acts of the subsidiary. One such exception is that the parent company is not protected against liability if the parent company and the subsidiary are in fact not kept apart as separate entities.[20] Another is that the parent company may also incur liability for the acts of the subsidiary if corporate constructions have been used for circumvention purposes to evade liability.[21] In the following, 'veil piercing' will be used as a shorthand expression for these doctrines developed in company law.[22] The question is whether veil piercing principles exhaustively regulate the extent to which parent companies can be held liable for the acts of their subsidiaries and thereby block the application of tort law, or whether ordinary tort law rules, including the five liability models described above, can apply as an alternative basis for liability of the parent company for acts of the subsidiary.

[18] R Rabin, 'Some Thoughts on the Ideology of Enterprise Liability' (1996) 55 *Maryland Law Review* 1190, 1193.

[19] ibid 1193 fn 22.

[20] SS Svendsen, *Vicarious Liability for Group Torts* (Copenhagen, ExTuto, 2023) 84.

[21] ibid 84.

[22] On unclear terminology, see eg ibid 86.

Today, it seems broadly recognised that veil piercing doctrines at least do not rule out the application of direct, fault-based liability in a corporate group setting.[23] This means that a parent company may incur liability for damage caused by the acts of a subsidiary if the parent company has itself acted negligently *and* this can be seen as a cause of the damage (Model I). A closely connected liability model is the idea of parent company liability based on actual control through 'de facto directorship' of the subsidiary.[24]

With acceptance of the application of direct tort liability as an alternative to veil piercing doctrines developed in company law, one might think that the way were paved for also applying other tort law concepts as alternatives.[25] However, it is less clear how the law stands with regard to the relationship between other tort law concepts and company law. National law may also display differences.

For example, in German legal theory it has been argued that there is no reason why the German version of the vicarious liability rule found in BGB §831 should not apply to parent companies for the acts of their subsidiaries[26] (Model II).

However, other scholars have questioned whether there is 'room' for pure vicarious liability (Model III) in the context of groups of companies seen in the light of existing company law principles.[27] In US law, it has been held that imposing vicarious liability on a parent company for the negligent acts of its subsidiary would only be possible if traditional veil piercing requirements were fulfilled.[28] This exemplifies the approach that the veil piercing rules in company law exhaustively regulate vicarious liability models.

[23] For a broad comparative study, see L Enneking, *Foreign Direct Liability and Beyond* (The Hague, Eleven International Publishing, 2012); Svendsen (n 20). For German Law, C König, 'Deliktshaftung von Konzernmuttergesellschaften' (2017) *Archiv für die civilistische Praxis* 611, 629: 'Eine deliktische Haftung der Konzernmutter ergibt sich zunächst unproblematisch dann, wenn sie selbst bzw. ihre verfassungsgemäß berufenen Vertreter gemäß § 31 BGB alle Tatbestandsmerkmale des jeweiligen Deliktstatbestands erfüllen'. With reference to BGB §830, König also points out that liability of the parent company can be in the shape of contributory acts, aiding and abetting: König (n 23) 638. The observation has also been made in US law that a parent company can incur direct liability based on its own tortious acts connected to the acts of the subsidiary, see PI Blumberg, 'Accountability of Multinational Corporations: The Barriers Presented by Concepts of the Corporate Juridical Entity' (2001) 24 *Hastings International and Comparative Law Review* 297, 311 with reference eg to *Doe I v Unocal Corp plc,* 110 F Supp 2d 1294 (CD Cal 2000), 395 F 3d 932 (9th Cir 2002). In UK law, early cases in this direction include *Connelly v RTZ Corp* [1997] 3 WLR 373 (HL); *Sithole v Thor Chemicals Holdings Ltd*, No JC 98 647, 779, 798 (QBD 31 July 1998), [2000] WLR 14211830; Thompson (n 3) 39–40.

[24] Under this concept, the parent would be held liable to the subsidiary for its negligent acts if it has actual control of the subsidiary to such an extent that this can be seen as de facto directorship of the subsidiary. In these situations, the parent company is treated *qua* the formal directors of the subsidiary, and can be held liable for infringement of fiduciary duty towards the subsidiary. However, it does not establish a right for third parties to claim damages. See K Hofstetter, 'Parent Responsibility for Subsidiary Corporations. Evaluating European trends' 39 (1990) *The International and Comparative Law Quarterly* 576 on French and Swiss law and the proposal for the Ninth EU directive on company groups form 1985 on the notion of 'de facto directorship'.

[25] Concurrency principles applied in many jurisdictions pull in this direction. Concurrency principles allow for claimants to choose the cause of action which is more favourable to them in case of overlap between two or more legal doctrines, eg contract and tort.

[26] König (n 23) 657.

[27] See, eg, M Petrin 'Assumption of Responsibility in Corporate Groups: *Chandler v Cape plc*' (2013) 76 *MLR* 589, 613. In his 1990 article, Hofstetter mentions that using vicarious liability in this context is something that has not yet been tested by the courts: Hofstetter (n 24) 591.

[28] *United States v Bestfoods* 524 US 51 (1998); Blumberg (n 23) 310.

Likewise, in German law it is regarded as uncertain whether the principle of organisational liability (Model IV) can apply to groups of companies. Thus, it has been argued that the extent to which the parent company has a duty to organise a corporate group is exhaustively regulated by the law on corporate groups (*Konzern recht*).[29]

The ultimate question is whether the concept of enterprise liability can be transferred to the area of corporate groups, namely the idea that liability should be placed with the better risk-bearer and should be distributed in such way that those who benefit from an activity also bear the cost of it. At the corporate group level, the rationale would be that some corporate groups can be regarded economically as a single unit. Moreover, it has been argued that since subsidiaries at least theoretically act for the benefit of the group as a whole, it should be possible to hold various corporate actors in the group liable for the acts of other actors.[30] Put differently, under enterprise liability theory, since everyone in the group profits from the acts of everyone else, everyone in the group should also bear the costs of the negligent acts of everyone else in the group. In this way, each corporate member of the group comes to represent the group and the group appears as a whole and as the subject of liability to the outer world (Model V). In UK law, this approach was expressed in the case *Newton-Sealy v Armor Group Services Ltd*:[31]

> This case raises the issue of liability within a corporate group. It is sometimes described as an issue of enterprise liability. Persons deal with a business, as in this case an international business, and do not necessarily distinguish between its different corporate members. From their point of view they are dealing with the enterprise as a whole. Something goes wrong and they seek to hold the group liable through its most convenient member or members.[32]

As will be explained below, recent English case law seems to support the approach that general tort law principles are also applicable in the context of groups of companies.

On the basis of the above, it can at least not be taken for granted that company law in general rules out applying the liability models identified above in the context of groups of companies. The following section examines whether traces of these liability models appear in areas of the law where tort – as put by Dearborn – is typically 'at its sharpest'.[33] These are areas that can be described as 'collective interest' areas, that is, areas of the law that raise questions of general interest or concern protection of common goods, or both. One might expect these areas of the law to be the first to reflect changes in the direction of expansion of liability. In line with this, it has been argued in US legal theory that enterprise liability should be accepted with regard to mass torts, human rights, and environmental harms.[34]

[29] König (n 23) 667, with reference at 670 to Spindler. König (n 23) argues at 670 that there is no exhaustive regulation of liability towards third parties (but maybe towards the subsidiary).

[30] M Dearborn 'Enterprise Liability: Reviewing and Revitalizing Liability for Corporate Groups' (2009) 97 *California Law Review* 195, 210–11.

[31] *Newton–Sealy v Armor Group Services Ltd & Ors* [2008] EWHC 233 (QB).

[32] *Newton* (n 31) Legal ground 1.

[33] Dearborn (n 30) 207.

[34] ibid 260. See also Blumberg (n 23) 308 on the influence of public policy concerns on notions of piercing and vicarious liability. AA Berle Jr, 'The Theory of Enterprise Entity' (1947) 47 *Columbia Law Review* 343, 354, finding that case law as it stood actually reflected prioritising public interest over corporate structure.

On that basis, three areas of the law which have seen recent significant developments in European law, have been chosen:

(1) the environment and human rights;
(2) climate change litigation; and
(3) market and competition law infringements.

B. The Environment and Human Rights

i. The Environment and Human Rights as Collective Interests

The environment is generally considered a common good and protection of the environment a collective interest. In contrast, the purpose of human rights is to protect the individual. However, protection of human rights also serves the much broader purpose of underpinning democracy and securing minimum rights that mitigate extreme inequality and social unrest. At the global level, the developed world has a collective interest in not sustaining pollution and abuse of workers in the developed world because it leads to excessive and unsustainable consumption in the developed world. In this way, environmental and human rights issues are often linked as is also reflected in the following analysis of recent case law and regulatory initiatives.

ii. Case Law

In a series of recent cases, the British courts have been faced with issues concerning the possible liability of parent companies for the activities of their subsidiaries. The first was *Chandler v Cape*[35] concerning the liability of a UK parent company for work injuries in a subsidiary which was also based in the UK. The court held the parent liable on the basis that it had assumed responsibility for the employees of the subsidiary. Subsequent cases – *Unilever*,[36] *Vedanta*[37] and *Okpabi*[38] – have concerned parallel questions of parental liability for subsidiaries based in the developing world for environmental damage and damage to human health. All three cases were concerned with procedural matters, raising the question whether the cases gave rise to 'real issues to be tried' or 'arguable cases'. In these cases, the liability standard has been clarified.

Unilever concerned the possible liability of the UK-based parent company for personal injury caused to employees of the subsidiary based in Kenya when violence broke out following an election. The appellate court did not find this to be an arguable case, but clarified the liability standard in the following way:

> There is no special doctrine in the law of tort of legal responsibility on the part of a parent company in relation to the activities of its subsidiary. Parent and subsidiary are separate legal persons, each with responsibility for their own separate activities. A parent company

[35] *David Brian Chandler v Cape plc* [2012] EWCA Civ 525. For an analysis see Root and Ulfbeck (n 11) with further references.
[36] *AAA & Others v Unilever PLC and Unilever Tea Kenya Limited* [2018] EWCA Civ 1532.
[37] *Vedanta Resources PLC and another (Appellants) v Lungowe and others* [2019] UKSC 20.
[38] *Okpabi and others (Appellants) v Royal Dutch Shell Plc and another (Respondents)* [2021] UKSC 3.

> will only be found to be subject to a duty of care in relation to an activity of its subsidiary if ordinary, general principles of law of tort regarding the imposition of a duty of care on the part of the parent in favour of a claimant are satisfied in the particular case.[39]

The *Vedanta* case builds on this. It concerned the possible liability of a UK-based parent company for the acts of their subsidiary based in Zambia. The subsidiary had operated a mine in the area and in doing so it had polluted the areas with toxics, affecting the environment and the health of people in the vicinity. In the case, 1826 Zambian citizens sued the parent company claiming damages. While the case was only decided with regard to procedural issues, it includes clear considerations on what would be the rationale for imposing liability.

Firstly, it is made clear that following *Unilever*, no special liability rule applies to the liability of a parent company for the acts of its subsidiary. Ordinary principles of tort law apply.[40] Based upon this, the court stated at [49] (Lord Briggs):

> [D]irect or indirect ownership by one company of all or a majority of the shares of another company … may enable the parent to take control of the management of the operations of the business or of the land owned by the subsidiary, but it does not impose a duty upon the parent to do so … Everything depends on the extent to which, and the way in which, the parent availed itself of the opportunity to take over, intervene in, control, supervise or advise the management of the relevant operations (including land use) of the subsidiary.

Thus, the court specifically emphasises that there is no duty on the part of a parent company to take control of the activities of a subsidiary. Consequently, liability depends on whether the parent company has actually taken control. It is also pointed out that control must have been taken with regard to relevant activities (not just control of the company in general).

In the concrete case, the court found that a sufficient amount of control might have been taken. Thus, [61] reads:

> But I regard the published materials in which Vedanta may fairly be said to have asserted its own assumption of responsibility for the maintenance of proper standards of environmental control over the activities of its subsidiaries, and in particular the operations of the Mine, and not merely to have laid down but also implemented those standards by training, monitoring and enforcement, as sufficient on their own to show that it is well arguable that a sufficient level of intervention by Vedanta in the conduct of the operations of the mine may be demonstrable at trial.

In emphasising the actual taking of control, and control being exercised not just at the general level but in relation to the activity which caused the harm, the liability standard resembles the early, fault-based liability standard for employers taking actual control of their employees with regard to the activities causing the harm (Model I).

[39] *Unilever* (n 36) [36]. Hereby, the court made clear how the Chandler ruling should be interpreted.

[40] *Vedanta* (n 37) [54]. This was also held in *Unilever* (n 36) [136]. On the general 'breakthrough' for the application of direct tort liability in this context, see eg M Petrin and B Choudbury, 'Group Company Liability' (2018) 19 *European Business Organisation Law Review* 771, 778; P Morgan, 'Vicarious Liability for Group Companies: The Final Frontier of Vicarious Liability' (2015) 31 *Journal of Professional Negligence* 276, 279 and 285.

In deciding the more recent case of *Okpabi*, the UK Supreme Court relied on the *Vedenta* reasoning. Additionally, the *Okpabi* case concerned the procedural question whether there was 'a real issue' to be tried with regard to the possible liability of the Shell parent company for an oil spill caused by the activities of a Nigerian subsidiary. The Supreme Court found this to be the case and referred to the formulation by Lord Briggs in the *Vedanta* ruling cited above. Furthermore, Lord Hamblen elaborated:

> [C]ontrol is just the starting point. The issue is the extent to which the parent did take over or share with the subsidiary the management of the relevant activity (here the pipeline). That may or may not be demonstrated by the parent controlling the subsidiary. In a sense, all parents control their subsidiaries. That control gives the parent the opportunity to get involved in management. But control of a company and de facto management of part of its activities are two different things.[41]

Here, too, it is made clear that if liability is to be based on 'control', then it is necessary to show that the parent company has taken actual control of the specific activities that caused the injury. Control at a more general level is insufficient. So the *Okpabi* reasoning can also be categorised as Model I reasoning.

iii. The Corporate Sustainability Due Diligence Directive

The directive on corporate sustainability due diligence (CSDDD)[42] introduces a new model for imposition of liability on parent companies. The overarching goal of the CSDDD is to create accountability for human rights infringements and damage to the environment. The tool used for achieving this goal is to impose 'due diligence' obligations on parent companies with regard to activities carried out, not only by themselves but also by their subsidiaries, whether based inside or outside of the EU, and by their business partners. The obligations are specified in Articles 7–16. They include inter alia a duty to adopt a code of conduct for subsidiaries and business partners.[43] Moreover, not living up to the central obligations is sanctioned by liability. Thus, according to Article 29, the parent company may incur liability if it has failed to live up to obligations under Article 10, which concerns prevention of infringements, and Article 11, which concerns the obligation to bring adverse impacts to an end. Thus, the CSDDD forces a certain amount of control with subsidiaries and business partners. It is a condition for imposition of liability that the damage or injury caused is protected by one of the instruments in the Annex to the CSDDD. This limits the applicability of the CSDDD. Furthermore, it is a condition that the company has acted intentionally or negligently in not living up to its obligations under Articles 10 and 11. Since these obligations are themselves 'due diligence' obligations, it is not entirely clear what the explicit mention of 'intent and negligence' adds to the liability standard. It can be seen as emphasiing that liability is fault-based.

[41] *Okpabi* (n 36) [147].

[42] DIRECTIVE (EU) 2024/1760 OF THE EUROPEAN PARLIAMENT AND OF THE COUNCIL of 13 June 2024 on corporate sustainability due diligence and amending Directive (EU) 2019/1937 and Regulation (EU) 2023/285.

[43] Art 7(2)(b).

Overall, the CSDDD forces some amount of control on the part of the parent company with its subsidiaries and establishes liability of the parent company for injury or damage caused by subsidiaries which the parent is obliged to control. Moreover, it is failure to take this control that can lead to liability under the CSDDD. This could also be regarded as liability for 'potential control'. In this way, parental liability under the CSDDD could be seen as resembling what has been described above as Model II.

C. Climate Change Litigation

Climate change is a fundamental challenge that affects everyone. Managing the climate crisis is a crystal-clear collective interest.

The climate crisis is currently being addressed not only through regulatory initiatives but also through litigation. Suits have targeted states for not having sufficiently ambitious policies in place to fight climate change,[44] and similar suits have recently been brought against corporations. One such suit was brought by the Dutch NGO Milieudefensie (MD) against Royal Dutch Shell (RDS), a case decided by the Hague District Court in 2021.[45]

RDS is a holding company of the Shell Group. It is the direct or indirect shareholder of over 1,100 companies in the Shell Group established worldwide. The Shell Group produces and trades oil, gas and other energy sources. MD argued that the Shell Group is a major contributor to carbon emissions and thereby climate change, and that RDS was not doing enough to reduce emissions. It asked the Court to rule that RDS should be obliged to introduce a climate change policy by 2030 that would reduce the Group's aggregate emissions by 45 per cent compared to 2019 levels, thereby living up to the goals in the Paris Agreement.[46]

The Court found for the claimants and ruled that the duty to reduce emissions followed from the unwritten standard of care under Book 6, Section 162 in the Dutch Civil Code.[47] In interpreting the duty of care, the Court referred to ECHR Articles 2 and 8, noting that these obligations are not directly binding on corporations but can be factored in when the duty of care standard is interpreted.[48] It also referred to the UNGPs.[49] Finally, it referred to 'the consensus that in order to limit global warming to

[44] Most notably the *Urgenda* ruling: *The State of the Netherlands (Ministry of Economic Affairs and Climate Policy) v Stichting Urgenda* ECLI:NL:HR:2019:2007.

[45] *Milieudefensie and others v Royal Dutch Shell PLC*, ECLI:NL:RBDHA:21:5339. The decision immediately generated several case comments: see eg C Macchi and J van Zeben, 'Business and human rights implications of climate-change litigation: Milieudefensie et al v Royal Dutch Shell' (2021) 30 *Review of European, Comparative and International Environmental Law* 409; O Spijkers, 'Friends of the Earth Netherlands (Milieudefensie) v Royal Dutch Shell' (2021) 5 *Chinese Journal of Environmental Law* 237. See also V Ulfbeck, 'Climate Change in Tort Law? The New Regulatory and External Effect of Suits against Private Actors' in A Beckers, H-W Micklitz, R Vallejo and P Letto-Vanamo (eds), *The Foundations of European Transnational Private Law* (Hart, 2024).

[46] Legal ground 3.1.

[47] Legal ground 4.4.1. Today, a similar duty has been introduced in the CSDDD article 22.

[48] Legal ground 4.4.9.

[49] Legal grounds 4.4.17 and 4.4.18.

1.5 degrees Celsius, reduction pathways that reduce emissions by a net 45% in 2030, relative to 2010 levels, and by a net 100% in 2050, should be chosen'.[50]

With regard to the question for whom should RDS be regarded as responsible, the Court refers to the GHG Protocol[51] and distinguishes between:

- Scope 1 emissions, which are direct emissions from sources owned or controlled in full or in part by the organisation itself;
- Scope 2 emissions, which are indirect emissions from third-party sources from which the organisation has purchased or acquired electricity, steam or heating for its operations; and
- Scope 3 emissions, which are all other indirect emissions from activities of the organisation but occurring from greenhouse gas sources owned or controlled by third parties, such as other organisations or consumers, including emissions from the use of third-party-purchased crude oil and gas.[52]

With regard to the companies in the Shell Group and business relations, the Court reasoned as follows:

> Due to the policy-setting influence RDS has over the companies in the Shell group, it bears the same responsibility for these business relations as for its own emissions. The far-reaching control and influence of RDS over the Shell Group means that RDS' reduction obligation must be an obligation of result for omissions connected to own activities of the Shell group. This concerns RDS's Scope 1 emissions and the part of RDS's Scope 2 emissions that can be ascribed to the Shell companies. From the perspective of the Shell group as a whole this constitutes the Scope 1 emissions of the Shell Group.[53]

The court concludes that 'the RDS is obliged to reduce the CO2 emissions of the Shell group's activities by a net 45 % at the end of 2030, relative to 2019, through the Shell group's corporate policy'[54] and that 'this reduction obligation relates to the Shell Groups entire energy portfolio and to the aggregate volume of all emissions (Scope 1 through 3)'.[55]

The emphasis on the 'policy-setting' influence of RDS over the companies in the Shell group resembles the reasoning embedded in the concept of the 'organisational tort', described above under Model IV.[56] In addition, lack of interest in identifying which particular companies in the group may have acted negligently in favour of focusing on the cumulative (aggregate) emissions of the entire group can be seen as a parallel to the reasoning behind the concepts of anonymous and cumulative errors,

[50] Legal ground 4.4.29.

[51] Internationally recognised standards for calculating emissions: see www.wri.org/initiatives/greenhouse-gas-protocol.

[52] Legal ground 2.5.4.

[53] Legal ground 4.4.23.

[54] Legal ground 4.4.55.

[55] ibid.

[56] The focus on the policy-setting ability of RDS is now also reflected in a new suit by the NGO Client Earth against management members of Shell RDS for breach of company law duties: see www.clientearth.org/latest/press-office/press/clientearth-files-climate-risk-lawsuit-against-shell-s-board-with-support-from-institutional-investors.

also described above under Model IV. Moreover, the 'group thinking' in the decision is underlined by the focus on Scope 2 emissions of RDS equalling Scope 1 emissions of the group as such. This can be seen as pulling in the direction of enterprise liability thinking (model V); see further below.

D. Market and Competition Law Infringements

The third example is the area of competition law. Competition law has been the primary tool for creation of the EU common market, based on the philosophy that a well-functioning market will serve the collective interest of all citizens in the EU by hindering excessive product prices that must be paid by all consumers. The past decade has seen increased focus on the role played by private enforcement of competition law through liability suits. This was clearly reflected in adoption of Directive 2014/104 EU on damages for competition law infringements (the Damages Directive).[57] The development raises the question: which legal entity can be held liable for infringements? According to the Damages Directive, Article 1(1), anyone who has suffered damage can claim compensation from 'the undertaking' that has caused the damage. The Directive does not define the concept of 'undertaking'. In contrast, the concept has been defined with regard to public law enforcement of the rules through a long development in CJEU case law, now codified in the ECN+ Directive.[58] Thus, according to Article 2(10) of the ECN+ Directive, an 'undertaking' is defined as 'any entity engaged in an economic activity, regardless of its legal status and the way in which it is financed'. In other words, focus is on the 'economic unit', which may be a legal entity as a company or a group of legal entities as a group of companies.[59] According to Article 15(3), Member States must ensure that 'for the purpose of imposing fines on parent companies and legal and economic successors of undertakings, the notion of undertaking applies'. It is not explained how the notion of the undertaking should apply for imposing fines if the undertaking is not a legal person. A fine cannot be imposed on a unit that is not a legal person. However, the preamble, para 46, explains that:

> Accordingly, NCAs [National Competition Authorities] should be able to apply the notion of undertaking to find a parent company liable, and impose fines on it, for the conduct of one of its subsidiaries, where the parent company and its subsidiary form a single economic unit. To prevent undertakings escaping liability for fines for infringements of Articles 101 and 102 TFEU through legal or organisational changes, NCAs should be able to find legal or economic successors of the undertaking liable, and to impose fines on them, for infringements of Articles 101 and 102 TFEU, in accordance with the case law of the Court of Justice of the European Union.

[57] Directive 2014/104/EU of the European Parliament and of the Council of 26 November 2014 on certain rules governing actions for damages under national law for infringements of the competition law provisions of the Member States and of the European Union [2014] OJ L349/1.

[58] Directive (EU) 2019/1 of the European Parliament and of the Council of 11 December 2018 to empower the competition authorities of the Member States to be more effective enforcers and to ensure the proper functioning of the internal market [2018] OJ L 11/3.

[59] On the concept of the economic unit in competition law, see, eg, D Baily and LE Johns (ed), *Bellamy & Child, European Union Law of Competition*, 8th edn (Oxford, Oxford University Press, 2018) 91.

Thus, with regard to public law enforcement, the 'undertaking' has for long been identified as 'the economic unit'. In practice this means that if the undertaking is not a legal person then separate legal entities in the unit can be held liable for infringements committed by others.

A series of recent decisions from the CJEU confirms that the same principles apply in terms of private enforcement. Most clearly, this was expressed in in the *Skanska* decision from 2019,[60] where the CJEU stated:

> [T]he concept of 'undertaking', within the meaning of Article 101 TFEU, which constitutes an autonomous concept of EU law, cannot have a different scope with regard to the imposition of fines as compared with actions for damages for infringement of EU competition rules.

The Court found that in a liquidation situation, claims for damages could be brought against a 'successor company' forming part of the economic unit. However, given the broad formulation of the legal grounds for the decision, there can be no doubt that a parent company can now also be held liable for competition law infringements committed by a subsidiary which forms part of the same economic unit.[61] Thus, with regard to public enforcement this has been clearly established in case law from the CJEU. For example, in *Imperial Chemical Industries*,[62] it was held that the parent company can become liable for infringements committed by a subsidiary if the parent company exercises a decisive influence on the subsidiary, as they then form an 'economic unit'. The parent company exercises a decisive influence if the subsidiary – despite its status as an independent legal entity – does not freely decide on its behaviour on the market, but largely follows instructions from the parent company.[63] Furthermore, following the *Akzo* ruling, the presumption is that a parent company exercises a decisive influence if it owns all or the majority of the shares in the subsidiary[64] or has all the voting rights related to shares in the subsidiary.[65] This rule of presumption must also be applicable in private enforcement cases as the concept of the economic unit is the same in both public enforcement and private enforcement cases. Under the presumption rule, it is not necessary to show involvement of the parent company in a concrete infringement committed by the subsidiary. Control exercised at the general level is sufficient.[66]

In this way, the legal reasoning resembles Model II reasoning above. It has also been suggested in legal literature that parent company liability for acts of a subsidiary,

[60] Case C-724/17 *Vantaan Kaupunki v Skanska Industrial Solutions Oy and others* ECLI:EU:C:2019:204.

[61] V Ulfbeck, 'Vicarious liability in Groups of Companies and in Supply Chain – Is Competition Law Leading the Way?' (2019) 3 *Market and Competition Law Review* 117ff; W Wurmnest, 'Liability of "undertakings" in damages actions for breach of Articles 101, 102 TFEU: Skanska' (2020) 57 *Common Market Law Review* 915, 925. For an overview of case law leading up to *Skanska* decision (n 60), see eg KE Sørensen, 'Groups of Companies in the case law of the Court of Justice of the European Union' (2016) 27 *European Business Law Review* 393.

[62] Case C-48/69 *Imperial Chemical Industries Ltd v Commission* ECLI:EU:C:1972:70.

[63] ibid, Legal grounds 132–36.

[64] Case C-516/15 *Akzo Nobel NV and others v EU Commission* ECLI:EU:C:2017:314, legal grounds 54–55.

[65] Case C-595/18 *The Goldman Sachs Group Inc v Commission* ECLI:EU:C:2021:73, legal ground 35.

[66] Case C-90/09 *General Quimica SA and Others v Commission* ECLI:EU:C:2011:21, legal ground 38.

based on *Skanska*, should be regarded as a type of vicarious liability.[67] However, subsequent case law shows that liability is farther reaching than that. Thus, in the *Sumal* decision of 2021,[68] it was held that a subsidiary could be held liable for the acts of a parent company. Since the subsidiary does not control the parent company, the reasoning for imposing liability on the subsidiary is disconnected from the concept of vicarious liability. Instead, the Court explains that the subsidiary is held liable on the basis that it constitutes a part of the economic unit which committed the infringement. The subsidiary is thereby regarded as having (partly) committed the infringement itself. The court puts it this way:

> When such an economic unit infringes Article 101(1) TFEU, it is for that unit, in accordance with the principle of personal responsibility, to answer for that infringement. In that regard, in order to hold any entity within an economic unit liable, it is necessary to prove that at least one entity belonging to that economic unit has committed an infringement of Article 101(1) TFEU, such that the undertaking constituted by that economic unit is to be treated as having infringed that provision.

It is unclear whether liability is strict in the decision and under the Damages Directive,[69] but the formulation clearly shows that the Court regards a group of companies forming an economic unit as a proper subject of liability. Moreover, in accordance with enterprise liability theory, liability attaches to the individual legal persons that constitute the economic unit, profit from being part of it and represent the unit to the outer world (Model V).

The policy reasons underlying the concept of enterprise liability – what is best for society – is also clearly reflected in the emphasis by the CJEU on the needed deterrent effect of imposition of liability in order to make the market work.[70]

IV. DISCUSSION AND CONCLUSION

While groups of companies are not formally recognised as legal persons, one might ask whether there are signs that liability patterns are changing in a direction that reflects thinking about certain groups of companies as collective units.

The cases described above and recent regulatory initiatives concerning liability in corporate groups can be seen to reflect a certain openness towards the idea of 'group thinking'. Thus, the analysis shows that almost all of the tort liability models identified for attaching liability to a company for the acts of employees have been used in the context of corporate groups in the collective interest areas examined. Indeed, the move from liability for taking control to liability for not taking control pulls in this direction. The same goes for applying notions of 'aggregate' damage caused by

[67] Ulfbeck (n 61).
[68] Case C-882/19 *Sumal, SL v. Mercedes Benz Trucks España SL* ECLI:EU:C:2021:800.
[69] Compare the Damages Directive (n 57), Art 3.
[70] See eg *Skanska* (n 60), legal grounds, 45 and 46. According to Dearborn, enterprise liability has also been established in the field of antitrust law in US law; Dearborn (n 30) 231 with reference to *Copperweld Corp v Independent Tube Corp*, 467 US 752 (1984).

different legal entities taken together and for the use of the enterprise liability concept in the area of competition law.

However, on a closer look, the development towards 'group thinking' must be described as hesitant. In general, liability models that allow for construing liability as direct fault-based liability for one member of the group seem to be preferred. Even the area of climate change litigation – which in many ways might be seen as characterised by novel legal thinking – liability is still based on the idea of fault in the shape of poor organisation by the parent company. Thus fault-based liability still seems to be the safest way of establishing liability. In addition, recent English case law explicitly rejects basing parent liability of notions of potential control (hidden vicarious liability) and there are no examples of the use of pure vicarious liability (Model III).

It might be assumed that the reluctance towards applying vicarious liability models stems from the view that principles of veil piercing should be regarded as the company law version of vicarious liability that exhaustively deals with the extent to which a company can be held liable for the acts of another. This line of thinking appears inconsistent given that other tort law principles are applied as alternatives to piercing models. As with the other liability models, whether or not to apply vicarious liability in the corporate group setting should be determined by policy considerations, not by 'mechanical' reference to company law piercing principles as the exhaustive regulation.[71]

The farthest reaching liability model, enterprise liability (Model V) is only used in the area of competition law. Here it seems to be the overriding objective of securing a well-functioning market which has driven development, now codified in the Damages Directive that specifies the 'undertaking' as the subject of liability. The fact that there is a regulatory framework whose objective is clearly indicated to be protection of the market through this concept may perhaps explain why enterprise liability has come to be established in this collective interest area.

More generally, however, one may wonder why it is only collective interest in the market that carries enterprise liability but not other collective interests. It can hardly be argued that securing the market is more important than securing human rights, the environment and the climate. Time will show if the small signs of development we are witnessing in case law and new regulatory frameworks are indicators of a movement towards more collective justice thinking in more collective interest areas. The result would be corporate groups beginning to look like legal persons.

[71] Some policy considerations are found here and there in legal theory, see, eg, Thompson (n 3) 32–33 arguing that 'extended' shareholder liability will complicate the standardised pricing of shares and generate excessive monitoring costs.

Index

Introductory Note

References such as '178–79' indicate (not necessarily continuous) discussion of a topic across a range of pages. Wherever possible in the case of topics with many references, these have either been divided into sub-topics or only the most significant discussions of the topic are listed. Because the entire work is about the 'future of the person', the use of this term (and certain others which occur constantly throughout the book) as an entry point has been restricted. Information will be found under the corresponding detailed topics. Cross-references in a form such as '*see also individual countries*' direct the reader to headings in a particular class (eg in this case 'Germany') rather than a specific '*individual countries*' entry.

www.ingramcontent.com/pod-product-compliance
Ingram Content Group UK Ltd.
Pitfield, Milton Keynes, MK11 3LW, UK
UKHW020845290926
15470UKWH00004B/1572

9 781509 982721